Breaking Through
COLLEGE READING

Breaking Through
COLLEGE READING

ELEVENTH EDITION

Brenda D. Smith
Professor Emerita, Georgia State University

LeeAnn Morris
Professor Emerita, San Jacinto College

PEARSON

Boston Columbus Hoboken Indianapolis New York San Francisco
Amsterdam Cape Town Dubai London Madrid Milan Munich Paris Montreal Toronto
Delhi Mexico City São Paulo Sydney Hong Kong Seoul Singapore Taipei Tokyo

In memory of my Mother and my Father
                              —B.D.S.

To the students whose dreams rest on college success
                              —L.M.

Editorial Director: Eric Stano
Program Manager: Anne Shure
Development Editor: Janice Wiggins
Product Marketing Manager: Allison Arnold
Field Marketing Manager: John Meyers
Executive Digital Producer: Stefanie A. Snajder
Digital Editor: Tracy Cunningham
Content Specialist: Julia Pomann
Project Manager: Ellen MacElree

Project Coordination, Text Design, and Electronic
    Page Makeup: Cenveo® Publisher Services
Cover Design Lead: Beth Pacquin
Cover Designer: Carie Keller, Cenveo® Publisher
    Services
Cover Images: Getty Images / Inmacor
Senior Manufacturing Buyer: Roy L. Pickering, Jr.
Printer/Binder: Courier Kendallville
Cover Printer: Courier Kendallville

Acknowledgments of third-party content appear on pages 557–558, which constitute an extension of this copyright page.

10 9 8 7 6 5 4 3 2__V011__17 16 15

Student Edition ISBN 10: 0-321-99419-1
Student Edition ISBN 13: 978-0-321-99419-6

A la Carte ISBN: 0-13-387568-7
A la Carte ISBN: 978-0-13-387568-3

www.pearsonhighered.com

CONTENTS

Preface xv

Chapter 4 Vocabulary 141

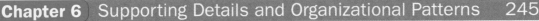

Chapter 8   Analytical Reasoning   369

Chapter 9 Critical Reading   419

PREFACE

The eleventh edition of *Breaking Through* upholds the philosophy and purpose that undergirded previous editions—to guide students to be independent readers who can understand, digest, and retain the material in college level texts. Like its predecessors, the eleventh edition aims to motivate and equip students to achieve their academic and career goals while building background knowledge. The instructional methods emphasize strategic learning in individual and collaborative contexts. The eleventh edition teaches effective reading techniques; provides extensive practice (within the text and online); provides independent, partner, and group activities; and engages students with reading selections on a variety of topics that are pertinent to the college community.

NEW AND SPECIAL FEATURES IN THE ELEVENTH EDITION

- **Fifteen new reading selections** complement the previous edition's favorites. Together, the 30 featured readings provide interesting insights into academic disciplines and examples of literary forms. New articles in the areas of business, communication, criminal justice, history, psychology, and science engage readers in the work of these fields. Textbook excerpts, essays, narratives, and newspaper feature articles represent the various types of writing that college students encounter.

- This edition features a thorough **reorganization of topics** to address the critical skills and strategies that students need early in the course and which they can apply immediately in all of their classes: To that end, student success, test taking, and reading efficiency appear in Chapter 1; stages of reading and textbook learning appear in Chapters 2 and 3.

- This edition debuts a **capstone chapter** (Chapter 10) for students to apply the strategies developed as they work through the text. A collection of real-life survivor stories challenges readers to analyze and draw conclusions about traits that enable humans to triumph over difficult situations. The chapter offers a variety of ways for students to synthesize and present their discoveries. This new chapter expands the Casebook of previous editions and integrates it with the rest of the book.

- Brief, enticing **video clips** available through MyReadingLab, which accompanies this book, now give students glimpses into the topics of 12 of the featured readings. Carefully selected to capture students' interest, they provide background knowledge and concrete links to the selections.

- A **new, complete Academic Textbook Chapter** opens a set of practical appendixes to provide authentic practice for managing college level textbooks. References to this chapter appear in the Textbook Learning chapter (Chapter 3) and encourage students to apply "read to learn" strategies in an actual college text. Taken from a communications textbook, this "Interpersonal Relationships" chapter is inherently interesting and relevant.

- Clear **Learning Objectives**, **Collaborative Problem Solving and Extended Writing** activities, **Vocabulary Lessons**, **Vocabulary Enrichment**, **Reader's Tips**, and **Everyday Reading Skills** remain as popular features in this edition.

- The longer selections in this chapter—and the activities and apparatus that bookend them—can now all be found in **MyReadingLab**. This gives students the opportunity to engage with the readings and submit their work to their instructors online. This integration with MyReadingLab also provides instructors with an easier way of grading and tracking their students' performance.

- **QR codes** also accompany each of the longer selections, giving students the opportunity to hear an audio recording of the reading. We have found this to be a feature that helps ESL students and native English speakers alike.

New locations for **MyReadingLab** icons in each chapter direct students to relevant electronic material at the precise times they need it. Repeating a feature that is particularly helpful for ESL students, **QR codes** lead to links where they can hear audio versions of the readings. In the Annotated Instructor's Edition, **Lexile levels** replace the grade-level equivalencies in the previous edition. Lexiles appear next to longer readings and in the Contents to help instructors guide students appropriately. Like grade-level equivalents, Lexiles reflect mechanical elements, such as word and sentence length but not necessarily concept difficulty. Other factors like the reader's interest, background knowledge, and depth of the concepts should contribute to the instructor's judgment in assigning readings.

ORGANIZATION OF THE TEXT

The eleventh edition of *Breaking Through* features a significant reorganization of chapters and topics to better reflect students' pressing needs at the beginning of their college experience. **Chapter 1**, "Successful Reading," contains three critical areas that are fundamental to successful college reading: student success topics, comprehension test-taking strategies, and tips for improved reading efficiency. Because many colleges now offer student success courses, the material on this topic is streamlined in this edition. The coverage of test-taking and reading efficiency in Chapter 1 includes fewer exercises, but additional practice appears in **Appendix 5**, "Test Taking Preparation and Practice," and **Appendix 6**, "Practice for Reading Efficiency." Foundational material continues in **Chapter 2**, "Stages of Reading," and **Chapter 3**, "Textbook Learning." In **Chapter 3**, students are referred to Appendix 1, Sample Textbook Chapter, for expanded practice in a complete college textbook chapter. **Chapter 4**, "Vocabulary," focuses on vocabulary strategies, such as context clues and word structure. The chapter also includes practice on dictionary, thesaurus, and glossary use, exercises on analogies, and spelling often confused words.

Chapter 5, "Topic, Main Idea, and Supporting Details," develops recognition of these key text elements through textbook excerpts. Because these aspects of prose are inherently intertwined, **Chapter 6**, "Supporting Details and Organizational Patterns," extends the work in Chapter 5 and emphasizes supporting details and their relationship to the organization pattern.

Chapter 7, "Inference," progresses to the next level of reading and thinking with a concentration on inferences and the importance of considering clues, such as the details provided, the language used, and the reader's schemata. **Chapter 8**, "Analytical Reasoning," brings students to the analysis level with attention focused on problem solving, analytical reasoning, and interpreting graphic illustrations. **Chapter 9**, "Critical Reading," challenges students to read critically by recognizing the author's purpose, point of view, tone, use of facts and opinions, and recognizing logical fallacies.

Chapter 10, "Survivor Casebook: Apply Your Reading Skills," is designed as a capstone experience in which students put all of their reading skills to work with a themed collection of readings. They will explore the characteristics that gird and support people in extreme situations. Stories of real-life survivors of sex trafficking, cancer, serious debt, homelessness, and personal tragedy engage and inspire. Students are challenged to analyze these stories—and perhaps their own experiences—and to synthesize their conclusions in a final assignment. The chapter includes a variety of suggested works that will reflect students' thinking.

Six useful **Appendixes** provide extension, specific support, and additional practice, and include a full communications textbook chapter, spelling rules, help with figurative language especially directed to ESL students, and extra practice on test taking and reading efficiency.

BOOK-SPECIFIC ANCILLARY MATERIALS

MyReadingLab™ MyReadingLab, a complete online learning program, provides additional resources and effective practice exercises for developing readers. MyReadingLab accelerates learning through layered assessment and a personalized learning path utilizing the Knewton Adaptive Learning Platform™, which customizes standardized educational content to piece together the perfect personalized bundle of content for each student. With over four thousand exercises and immediate feedback to answers, the integrated learning side of MyReadingLab reinforces learning throughout the semester.

Annotated Instructor's Edition (AIE) (0-13-385539-2)
An exact replica of the student text, with answers provided on the write-in lines in the text.

Instructor's Manual (ISBN 0-13-408187-0)
The instructor's manual features lecture hints, in-class activities, and handouts to accompany each chapter, as well as sample course outlines and other helpful resources for structuring and managing a developmental reading course. Available both in print and for download from the Instructor Resource Center.

Test Bank (ISBN 0-13-387569-5)
The test bank includes two tests per chapter, with a variety of questions in the multiple-choice, true-false, essay, and short answer formats.

MyTest Test Bank (ISBN 0-13-408186-2)
Pearson MyTest is a powerful assessment generation program that helps instructors easily create and print quizzes, study guides, and exams. Select questions from the test bank to accompany *Breaking Through* or from other developmental reading test banks; supplement them with your own questions. Save the finished test as a Word document or PDF or export it to WebCT or Blackboard. Available at www.pearsonmytest.com.

PowerPoint Presentation (ISBN 0-13-01247-X)
PowerPoint presentations to accompany each chapter consist of classroom-ready lecture outline slides, lecture tips and classroom activities, and review questions. Available for download from the Instructor Resource Center.

Answer Key (ISBN 0-13-401246-1)
The Answer Key contains the solutions to the exercises in the student edition of the text. Available for download from the Instructor Resource Center.

ACKNOWLEDGMENTS

We want to thank Eric Stano, Editorial Director, for overseeing this eleventh edition of *Breaking Through*. We especially appreciate his understanding of this field and his insights from conversations and observations during innumerable college visits throughout the country. He guided and supported us from beginning to end. Likewise, the professional expertise yet personal touch of our Development

Editor, Janice Wiggins, was invaluable. As always, her ability to shape our ideas and the contributions of our reviewers into a workable plan was the backbone that strengthened and improved each revision. For the many experts "behind the scenes" whose contributions were essential to producing this book, many thanks! Finally, we would like to recognize the reviewers of the tenth edition whose practical suggestions were vital to this revision:

Almarie Jones, Gloucester County College; Andrew McCarthy, William Patterson University; Clint Stevens, Kaskaskia College; Karen Becker, Youngstown State University; Kim Thomas, Polk State College; Lisa Parra, Johnson County Community College; Raymond Elliott, St. Philip's College; Stacy Corbin, Estrella Mountain Community College; Valerie Ann Schantz, Delaware County Community College; and Patricia Whitney, Eastern New Mexico University.

Brenda D. Smith

LeeAnn Morris

Breaking Through
COLLEGE READING

1 Successful Reading

Learning Objectives

From this chapter, readers will learn:

1 To prepare mentally for reading success
2 To adopt successful reading behaviors
3 To plan for success on reading tests
4 To recognize types of comprehension questions
5 To increase reading efficiency

Everyday Reading Skills: Using Mnemonics

THINK SUCCESS

Learning Objective 1

Prepare mentally for reading success

Are you ready to work on your reading skills? What does it take to become a successful reader? All readers, no matter how good they are at reading, can improve in one way or another. Some readers focus on better comprehension, while others want to expand their vocabulary. Many college students want to finish reading assignments more quickly and effectively. Some just want to pass their school's required reading test. Whether you aim to improve in one or several of these areas, you can be sure your work will pay off because effective reading is an essential, fundamental, and rewarding lifelong skill.

This book focuses on strategies for managing the materials that you will read in college: textbooks, novels, research articles, short stories, news reports, essays, biographies, and how-to manuals. Whether you read them on a page or on an electronic screen, you will need good skills. You can accomplish a lot if you start with a goal, a positive attitude, and a determination to succeed!

Set Goals

Start by thinking big. What are your life and career goals? A written reminder placed on your desk, over your bed, or on your class notebooks can be an inspiring reminder. How will college help you achieve your dreams?

Next, narrow your focus to reading. How will effective reading help you do well in college? Think about the reading you do now. What do you read? Do you enjoy it? Do you dislike reading? Why? What kind of reading do you expect to do in your college courses? In your dream job? In what area do you most want to improve?

Complete "Personal Feedback 1" on the next page. Share your answers with your classmates and instructor. Then, most importantly, commit yourself to action!

Create a Positive Attitude

Keeping your big dreams in mind, remember that reaching them requires taking thousands of small steps every day. Your attitude as you take each step will color the results, so why not do so with a positive spirit? Learning is rewarding and fun. It is one of the most satisfying human activities. Although it is sometimes frustrating and challenging, the payoff is worth the struggle. You control your attitude. Remember your dreams, and enjoy the journey!

Persevere

Have you heard the expression "Ninety percent of success is just showing up"? In college, in a job, or in a relationship, sometimes truly "showing up" is the key to success. This is easy when things are going well, but it takes determination when things are tough. A college professor once described the results of a student's research study on the difference between students who finished their degrees and those who did not. Do you think it was money? Time? Family support? Intelligence? No! The only difference between the completers and noncompleters was perseverance—sticking with it. Determination to stick with it, even when it was hard, was the most important factor in success. The good news is that perseverance is something each of us controls. Just "showing up" and making a good effort at every step will get us to our goals.

In what ways does Reading 1, "Bouncing Back from Failure," show the importance of having a goal, a positive attitude, and perseverance?

PERSONAL FEEDBACK) 1   Name _____

1. In five years, what do you hope to be doing professionally and personally?

   (a) Professionally: _____

   (b) Personally: _____

2. What is your college degree or certificate goal or major? _____

3. What kinds of materials do you read?_____

4. What do you most enjoy reading? _____

   (Examples: Biographies, science fiction, romance or action novels, poetry, how-to books, history, newspapers, magazines, textbooks, etc.)

5. List three ways in which good reading skills will help in your professional, college, and personal life.

   (a) _____

   (b) _____

   (c) _____

6. In which area (s) of reading would you most like to improve?_____

   (Examples: Comprehension, efficiency, vocabulary, test taking, etc.)

Share your responses as directed by your instructor.

Reading 1

BOUNCING BACK FROM FAILURE

It is a very rare person who achieves a dream without meeting problems and disappointments along the way. Even the people we consider the most successful have made mistakes, suffered setbacks, and felt discouraged. What makes some people keep going after a failure? In this article you will find five good suggestions and the inspirational story of a person who overcame many obstacles on the way to success. What suggestions can you use in your life?

There's an old Japanese proverb that counsels: "Fall seven times, stand up eight." But how do you get back up when you've fallen flat on your face? Below you'll find five tips to help you gather the pieces and pull yourself back together after you've failed.

1. Always expect success. However, you need to get rid of the notion of the "overnight success" or the "get-rich-quick-scheme." People who appear to be overnight successes have actually spent a lot of time beforehand honing their skills. Success requires a lot of preparation and a prolonged effort. Unfortunately, there are a lot of people who feel like failures when something doesn't work immediately, and they just give up. If you don't succeed right away, this doesn't mean that you've failed. Recognize that setbacks are simply part of the process and that hard work and perseverance are two of the most important ingredients of success. If you've failed in the short run, it simply means you need to take a longer term view of success.

2. Do not identify yourself with your failures. You are not your actions. To say that you have failed many times is not the same thing as saying that you are a failure. Whatever happens, keep referring to yourself, in your conversations with others and in your self-talk, as someone who has the full capacity to succeed.

3. Create a "fame wall." Hang your diplomas or certificates on this wall. You can also add framed photographs of yourself with your friends and family having fun or sharing a close moment. Anything that gives you a sense of accomplishment can go up on the wall. In times of failure, refer to your wall. It will serve as a reminder that you have succeeded in the past and that you will succeed again in the future.

4. Collect stories about people who have failed and then gone on to become successful so that you can use them as inspiration when you're down. For example, consider the following life story.

This person:

At age 22—Failed in business;
At age 23—Was defeated for the State Legislature;
At age 24—Again failed in business;
At age 25—Was elected to the State Legislature;
At age 26—His sweetheart died;
At age 27—He suffered a nervous breakdown;
At age 29—Was defeated for the office of speaker;
At age 31—Was defeated for elector;
At age 34—Was defeated for Congress;
At age 37—Was elected to Congress;
At age 39—Was defeated for Congress;
At age 46—Was defeated for the Senate;
At age 47—Was defeated for Vice-President;
At age 49—Was defeated for the Senate;
At age 51—Was elected President of the United States.
This person was Abraham Lincoln.

5. Keep things in perspective; do not overgeneralize. The fact that you've failed at something does not mean that your life is over. It does not mean that your reputation is forever ruined and that you'll never get another chance. Don't make the situation bigger or more pervasive than it really is. Instead, remember the famous line:

"And this too shall pass . . ."

—5 Tips for Overcoming Failure, by Marelisa Fábrega

EXERCISE 1

Think and Write. Answer the following questions.

1. How have you responded to past failures and disappointments?

   _____

   _____

2. Select two of the tips in this article and explain how you might apply them

   to your life. _____

   _____

   _____

3. What does the quote below mean to you?

   "No matter how you feel, get up, dress up, and show up for life."

   —Regina Brett, columnist and blogger

   _____

   _____

   _____

ACT SUCCESSFUL

Learning Objective 2

Adopt successful reading behaviors

If 90% of success is showing up, what is the remaining 10%? One could make a good case that effort—doing something—is the rest of the equation. What actions contribute to success in a reading course? The answer is many of the same efforts that good students make in every course. Adopting the following habits is an excellent start in achieving success in college.

Manage Your Time

Time management is one of the biggest challenges for many college students. In addition to class readings, writing, test preparation, labs, and other course assignments, students must find time for jobs, family responsibilities, relationships, exercise, a fulfilling social life, and sleep. If this seems difficult to you, take comfort in knowing you are not alone. However, you can also feel confident that you can do it just as millions of other students have done. Here are some time management strategies:

1. **Make a schedule and follow it.** Use the Weekly Time Chart on page 7 or create your own electronic version. Making a few blank copies first will be helpful.

   - Enter all of the activities whose times are repeated each week, like classes, work, and so forth.

- Calculate the number of hours you are in class each week. Multiply that number by 2 to find the number of hours you should plan for study each week. (Some experts recommend three hours of study for every hour in class. The number will vary depending on how hard the class is for you and the timing of major assignments.)
- Plug in your study hours—all of them. Look for time before, after, and between classes and other scheduled activities. Write "Study reading" or "Study math" in the slots.
- Add your other activities.
- Adjust the plan as needed from week to week, but stick to the basic framework.

2. Use a to-do list.

- Each day, jot a list of the things you want to accomplish.
- Put them in priority order, with the most important first. Include tasks that can be done in a few minutes along with those that will take more time.
- Cross out or check items as you finish them. This will give you a sense of accomplishment.

3. Use a monthly calendar.

- Enter major assignments, tests, and events for the semester.
- Use this calendar as a reminder for your to-do list. Allow plenty of time in advance to do the big things.

Reader's TIP   Time Savers

Make a habit of using time wisely. Analyze your current activities according to the following principles of time management to gain greater control of yourself and your environment.

1. Plan. Keep an appointment book by the day and hour. Write a daily to-do list. Use a notepad or an electronic device.
2. Start with the most critical activity of the day and work your way down to the least important one.
3. Ask yourself, "What is the best use of my time right now?"
4. Don't do what doesn't need doing.
5. Concentrate completely on one thing at a time.
6. Block out big chunks of time for large projects.
7. Make use of 5-, 10-, and 15-minute segments of time.
8. Keep phone calls and texts short or avoid them.
9. Listen well for clear instructions.
10. Learn to say No! to yourself and others.
11. Limit your online, television, video game, and text messaging time.
12. Strive for excellence but realize that perfection may not be worth the cost.

Study the Course Syllabus

The syllabus should be the first reading task in your reading class and in every course you are taking. It might be posted on the college or course Web site or handed out in class, probably on the first day. The syllabus is a document that explains the purpose and contents of the course and how grades are determined.

WEEKLY TIME CHART

Time	Sunday	Monday	Tuesday	Wednesday	Thursday	Friday	Saturday
8–9							
9–10							
10–11							
11–12							
12–1							
1–2							
2–3							
3–4							
4–5							
5–6							
6–7							
7–8							
8–9							
9–10							
10–11							
11–12							

Tear out and submit to your instructor.

Total hours in class each week   _____

_____ X3 (Number of study hours per class each week)

Total number of study hours to include
in the weekly schedule.   = _____

It contains important information about support services and college rules. Usually, the syllabus also explains your professor's class policies. Just as you are expected to know motor vehicle laws, you are expected to know the rules of your college course.

If your instructor has provided a term calendar of due dates, take time in the first week of class to add them to your monthly calendar. Plan ahead so you have plenty of time to do your best work.

EXERCISE 2   Carefully read the syllabus for your reading course and then refer to it to answer the following questions:

1. The rubric, number, and title of this course are _____
_____ .

2. The professor's name is _____. When can you visit the professor's office? _____

3. What is the stated purpose of the course? _____
_____

4. What materials are required for this course? _____
_____

5. How will your grade be determined? _____
_____

6. What is the policy on attendance? _____

7. Is there a penalty for late work? _____

8. Does the syllabus describe any student support services? _____ If so, what are they? _____
_____

9. What questions do you have about the syllabus or the course? _____
_____

10. If your professor included a calendar of due dates, what is the first assignment and when is it due? _____
_____

Preview Your Textbooks

Understand How Your Textbook Is Organized so You Can Use It to Your Best Advantage.   Quickly flip through the book to absorb some of its features. Do you see pictures, graphs, text boxes, exercises or other special features? Now glance at the title page. Who is the author, and what are the author's credentials? Examine the table of contents. Do you see any features that are repeated in most or all chapters? Get an idea of the topics that are covered. Look at the end of the table of contents. Are there special sections that may be of use to you? Is there an answer key? An index? A glossary? Do this with every textbook you have.

EXERCISE 3 Read the table of contents of this text and glance through the chapters. Notice the format of the chapters and selectively scan the subheadings. Preview the text to answer the following questions:

1. How many chapters are in this book? _____

2. Other than the obvious differences of topics covered, how does the organizational format of Chapter 3 differ from the format of Chapter 4?

   _____

   _____

   _____

3. What is MyReadingLab? _____

   _____

4. What is the purpose of Summary Points? _____

   _____

5. In which chapter will you find information on making inferences?

   _____

6. In Chapter 5, Main Idea, what other words are sometimes used to mean the same as *main idea*? _____

   _____

7. Name five college subjects represented in the longer selections at the end of the chapters. _____

   _____

8. In which chapter will you learn more about patterns of organization?

   _____

9. What is the purpose of Appendix 1? _____

   _____

10. In which chapter will you find hints on time management? _____

Mark Your Textbooks

Get the Most From Your Books and Use Them as Learning Tools. Read your textbooks with a pen or highlighter in hand and mark information that you will most likely need to know later. A well-marked textbook is a treasure that you may want to keep as a reference for later courses.

 Don't miss an opportunity to learn by being reluctant to mark in your text. Marking your text actively involves you in reading and studying. The small amount of money that you receive in a textbook resale may not be worth what you have lost in active involvement. Some books, such as this one, are workbooks. Use this book to practice, to give and get feedback, and to keep a record of your progress.

TEST SMART ON READING COMPREHENSION

At this point in your life, you have probably taken many reading comprehension tests. These tests are designed to assess your skill in understanding written passages. They differ from **content tests** that measure your knowledge of a subject you have studied. Some comprehension tests are **standardized tests** that are given to thousands of students and are used for college admission or placement. Others are tests given in a reading class to measure progress.

Awareness of test-taking strategies can help you achieve your highest potential. Although some of the following suggestions are obvious, you might be surprised at how often students overlook them. Whether a comprehension test determines placement in college courses or assesses your progress in a reading class, it is important to your future. Give yourself the best chance to do well by following the test-taking tips below.

As you read the next three sections, highlight or underline the key test-taking tips.

Before the Test: Prepare Mentally and Physically

Learn as much as you can about the test ahead of time. For example, what form will it take? Reading comprehension tests almost always have a number of reading selections that you have not already seen. Each passage is followed by a set of questions. Also, learn how the test will be given. Will you read and answer questions on a computer or use pencil and paper? Some comprehension tests have a time limit. Find out how much time you will have to finish. Placement tests and other standardized tests often have practice versions. Use them. This will sharpen your skills and show you how to best manage your time. Know how the results will be used. If the test is given for placement in college classes, the score determines the classes you can take. If the test is part of the work in a reading class, your performance will influence your course grade.

When you have learned about the test and have practiced, you're ready to prepare for the physical challenges. Get a good night's sleep the night before and eat healthy, protein-rich meals. These foods will provide your brain with the staying power to focus throughout the test. Avoid foods and drinks that are heavy in sugar, refined carbohydrates, and caffeine. Arrive a little early so that you have time to settle and calm yourself. Avoid comparing test preparation notes with other students. Relax and stay confident in your own preparation.

During the Test: Relax and Focus

Breathe deeply and slowly, and remind yourself that you are ready. Test anxiety is manageable with good preparation, measured breathing, and visualizing methods. Quickly look over the test to plan your timing and then begin reading the first selection. Most experts advise students to read the selection carefully first. Trying to answer questions before or without reading at all doesn't work. If you have prepared well before test day, you have already predicted the kinds of questions that will appear on the test. Read the selection first and then tackle the questions.

Work steadily while staying alert and focused. Approach each reading as a chance to learn something new or to enjoy the author's style. When you're finished, check to see that you have answered every question. Do not overthink but do change answers that you are fairly sure are wrong. If other students finish before you, ignore them. What matters is giving your best effort, not racing to the finish.

After the Test: Assess Your Preparation and Learn From Test Results

Many students ignore this phase of test taking, but they are missing an opportunity to improve. Take a moment to assess your preparation. Was it enough? Will you do anything differently next time? Be sure you are present and alert when the test results are given back. Analyze them carefully. In what areas did you do well? Are there certain kinds of questions you missed more often than others? Did you make careless errors? Write notes to yourself about what worked well and what you will do differently next time.

Reader's TIP — Test Preparation Checklist

As a reminder to use effective preparation strategies on reading comprehension tests, refer to the checklist in Appendix 5. Making several blank copies will allow you to use the checklist every time you take a test.

Your instructor may ask you to turn in the completed checklist.

- Review the list as you begin preparing.
- After the test, honestly complete the checklist.
  Mark the strategies you used.
  Write the strategies that worked best.
  List the strategies you will use next time.

RECOGNIZE COMMON TYPES OF COMPREHENSION QUESTIONS

Learning Objective 4

Recognize types of comprehension questions

Reading comprehension test questions follow certain predictable patterns. For example, almost all passages have one question about the main idea. Learn to recognize the types of questions and how to answer them. Put yourself in the place of the test writer. What methods did he or she use when creating correct answers and incorrect distractors? Well-written distractors are tempting incorrect answers that force the test taker to use knowledge and logic. The following section gives you practice and guidance on taking reading comprehension tests.

The passage below is a typical comprehension test selection. Approach it as you would a test passage by focusing your attention and marking important points. When you have finished reading it, think about the main point its author is making. Continue by studying the tips on recognizing and answering the six major question types: main idea, detail, inference, author's purpose, vocabulary, and essay questions. All the questions refer to Reading 2. The marginal notes reflect a reader's possible thought processes.

Reading 2

SALTWATER SLAVES

What is this about? Time frame?

5 stages

Stage 2?

Stage 3

Very descriptive. All senses involved

Luck and personal strength

Inhuman

The grim transatlantic voyage was different for every person. Still, the long nightmare of deportation contained similar elements for all. The entire journey, from normal village life in Africa to slavery beyond the ocean, could last a year or two. It unfolded in at least five stages, beginning with capture and deportation to the African coast. The initial loss of freedom—the first experience of bound hands, harsh treatment, and forced marches—was made worse by the strange landscapes and unfamiliar languages. Hunger, fatigue, and anxiety took a steady toll as young and old were marched slowly toward the coast through a network of traders.

The next phase, sale and imprisonment, began when a group reached the sea and African traders transferred "ownership" of the captives. European buyers put them in iron chains alongside hundreds of other captives. After several months, canoes transported the captives through the surf to a waiting vessel. (Their hands were bound, so if a canoe capsized, it meant certain drowning.) Once aboard, the captives might have suffered in the sweltering hold for weeks while the captain cruised the coast in search of additional human cargo. Crew members sometimes raised nets surrounding the deck to prevent attempts at escape or suicide.

The ship's captain decided when to begin crossing the Atlantic Ocean, the frightening third phase that was the middle passage. The Africans below deck were trapped in the dark, crowded, and stinking hold. The rolling of the ship on ocean swells brought seasickness and painful chafing from lying on the bare planks. Alexander Falconbridge, who sailed as a surgeon on several slave ships, recorded that "those who are emaciated frequently have their skin and even their flesh entirely rubbed off, by the motion of the ship, from the . . . shoulders, elbows and hips so as to render the bones quite bare."

Historians have documented more than 27,000 slave voyages from Africa to the Americas, and in each one, many factors came into play to shape the Atlantic crossing. These included the route, the season, the adequacy of supplies, the crew's skills, and the ship's condition. The resolve of the prisoners, the possibility of piracy and ocean warfare, and the ravages of disease also became factors. A change in weather conditions or in the captain's mood could mean the difference between life and death.

While the grim details varied, the overall pattern remained the same. The constant rolling of the vessel; the sharp changes in temperature; the crowded, filthy conditions; and the constant physical pain and mental anguish took a heavy toll. Pregnant mothers gave birth or miscarried; women were subjected to abuse and rape by the crew. Sailors threw the dead to the sharks and even used corpses as bait, catching sharks that they then fed to the captives.

Stage 4

For the starving survivors of the Atlantic ordeal, two further stages remained in their descent into slavery: the selling process and the time called "seasoning." The selling process on American soil could drag on for weeks or months, as prospective owners examined and prodded the newcomers in dockside holding pens. Those purchased were wrenched away from their shipmates with whom they had formed strong links during their miseries at sea. Slaves often were auctioned in groups, or parcels, to ensure sale of the weak along with the strong. A final journey brought them to the particular plantation where many would work until they died.

Stage 5 Kindness or practicality?

Like soldiers today?

How would a slave trader tell the story?
What is the main point?

Most Africans did not begin their forced labor immediately. Instead, they entered a final stage, known as "seasoning," which lasted several months or longer. The newcomers were known as "saltwater slaves," in contrast to "country-born slaves" who had grown up in America from birth. Seasoning gave newcomers time to mend physically and begin absorbing a new language. Inevitably, many suffered from what we call "posttraumatic stress disorder," or PTSD.

As adults and children recovered from the trauma of the middle passage, they faced a series of additional shocks: foreign landscapes, strange foods, unfamiliar tasks, and even new names. Worst of all, fresh arrivals met a master or overseer who was determined to turn them into obedient servants. Repeatedly, the powerful stranger used force to demand the slaves' obedience, destroy their hope, and crush any thoughts of resistance.

—*Created Equal: A History of the United States,*
Fourth Edition, by Jacqueline Jones, et al.

Main Idea Questions

Main idea questions ask you to identify the author's main point. These questions are often stated in one of the following forms:

The best statement of the main idea is . . .

The author's main point is . . .

The author is primarily concerned with . . .

The central theme of the passage is . . .

Incorrect responses to main idea items fall into two categories: (1) Some are too broad or general. They suggest that the passage includes much more than it actually does. For example, for a passage describing the hibernation of goldfish in a pond during the winter, the title "Fish" would be much too general to describe the specific topic. (2) Other incorrect answers are too narrow. They focus on details within the passage that support the main idea. The details may be attention getting and interesting, but they do not describe the central focus. They are tempting, however, because they are direct statements from the passage.

If you have difficulty understanding the main idea of a passage, reread the first and last sentences. Sometimes, but not always, one of these sentences will give you an overview or focus.

EXERCISE 4

Answer the following main idea items on the passage about "saltwater slaves." Then read the handwritten remarks describing the student's thinking about whether a response is correct.

_____ 1. The best statement of the main idea of this passage is

a. Slavery in America

(Too broad and general)

b. Slaves suffered seasickness, abuse, and horrible pain during the ocean crossing.

(Important detail, but the statement does not reflect the entire passage)

c. Historians have documented more than 27,000 slave voyages from Africa to the Americas, and in each one, many factors came into play to shape the Atlantic crossing.

(Tempting, but only talks about the Atlantic crossing, not the other stages of the journey)

d. The traumatic journeys of captured Africans and their arrival in America as "saltwater slaves" happened in stages over a year or two.

(Forms an "umbrella" that covers all of the major parts of the passage)

For more help answering main idea questions, refer to "Answering Topic and Main Idea Test Questions" on page 189; for additional practice, refer to Appendix 5, page 544.

Detail Questions

Detail questions check your ability to understand material that is directly stated in the passage. To find or double-check an answer, note a key word in the question and then quickly glance at the passage for that key word or a synonym. When you locate the key word, reread the sentence for clarification. Detail questions fall in the following patterns:

The author states that . . .

According to the author . . .

According to the passage . . .

All of the following are true except . . .

A person, term, or place is . . .

Incorrect answers to detail questions tend to be false statements. Test writers like to use pompous or catchy phrases stated directly from the passage as distractors. Such phrases may sound authoritative but mean nothing.

EXERCISE 5

Answer the following detail question on the passage about "saltwater slaves." Then note the handwritten remarks reflecting the thinking about whether a response is correct.

_____ 1. According to the passage, "saltwater slaves" experienced all of the following stages *except*

(Note the use of "except"; look for the only false item to be the correct answer.)

a. a stage when they waited in America to be sold.

(This is the fourth stage described in the selection.)

b. the crossing of the Atlantic ocean in a slave ship.

(The passage describes the horrible details of this third stage.)

c. a forced march across land from their home villages.

(This is the first stage described in the passage.)

d. sailing immediately upon arrival at the sea from their villages.

(After the land journey, they were sold and sometimes waited weeks on the ship before sailing. This is the only false statement, so it has to be the answer.)

For additional practice answering detail questions, refer to Appendix 5, page 545.

Inference Questions

An inference is something that is suggested but not directly stated. Clues in the passage lead you to make assumptions and draw conclusions. Items testing implied meaning deal with the attitudes and feelings of the writer that emerge as if from behind or between words. Favorable and unfavorable descriptions suggest positive and negative opinions toward a subject. Sarcastic remarks indicate the motivation of characters. Look for clues that help you develop logical assumptions. Inference questions may be stated in one of the following forms:

The author believes (or feels or implies) . . .

It can be inferred (deduced from clues) from the passage . . .

The passage (or author) suggests . . .

It can be concluded from the passage that . . .

Base your conclusion on both what is known and what is suggested. Incorrect responses to implied meaning items tend to be false statements that lack logical support.

EXERCISE 6 Answer the following inference questions on the passage about "saltwater slaves." Then note the handwritten remarks reflecting the thinking about whether a response is correct.

_____ 1. The author believes that

a. the slave trade should have been stopped sooner.

(The details present a negative picture, but the passage says nothing to propose this.)

b. the slave trade flourished only because slavery was legal in the United States.

(Although this might be true, the passage does not discuss the reasons for the slave trade or describe other destinations for slave ships. The word "only" suggests a false statement.)

c. the slave trade was wrong.

(The very negative emotional language and details suggest the author feels strongly that the slave trade was immoral.)

d. some captives escaped from the slave traders.

(Some probably did escape, but the passage does not mention this.)

For additional practice answering inference questions, refer to Appendix 5, page 545.

Author's Purpose Questions

The purpose of a passage is not usually stated. Instead, it is implied and is related to the main idea. In responding to a purpose item, you are answering the question,

"What was the author's purpose in writing this material?" The tone of the passage and the type of publication (textbook, newspaper editorial, or novel, for example) are good clues.

EXERCISE 7   Reading comprehension tests tend to include three basic types of passages, each of which suggests a separate set of purposes. Study the outline of the three types shown in the Reader's Tip box and answer the question on the "saltwater slaves" passage. Then note the handwritten remarks reflecting the thinking about whether an answer is correct.

Reader's TIP   Types of Test Passages

Factual Passages

What? Science, sociology, psychology, or history articles

How to Read? Read for the main idea and do not get bogged down in details. Remember, you can look back.

Author's Purpose?

- To inform
- To explain
- To describe

Example: Textbooks

Opinion Passages

What? Articles with a particular point of view on a topic

How to Read? Read to determine the author's opinion on the subject. Then judge the value of the support included and decide whether you agree or disagree.

Author's Purpose?

- To argue
- To persuade
- To condemn
- To ridicule

Example: Newspaper editorials, advertisements

Fiction Passages

What? Articles that tell a story

How to Read? Read to understand what the characters are thinking and why they act as they do.

Author's Purpose?

- To entertain
- To narrate
- To describe
- To shock

Examples: Novels and short stories

_____ 1. The author's purpose in writing this passage is

a. to entertain the reader with an interesting account of the slave trade.

(The passage is interesting, but it seems to be from an American history textbook and is probably not meant for entertaining reading.)

b. to inform the reader of the conditions in the stages of Africans' journey to becoming slaves in America.

(The passage focuses on the stages of the journey and on the horrible conditions. It appears to be from a textbook, so the purpose is most likely to inform and explain.)

c. to persuade the reader to oppose slavery in any form.

(The descriptions are horrifying, but no position on slavery is stated.)

d. to condemn modern forms of slavery.

(The passage is about the Africa-to-America slave trade. It says nothing about slavery today.)

For additional practice answering author's purpose questions, refer to Appendix 5.

Vocabulary Questions

Vocabulary items test your general word knowledge as well as your ability to figure out meaning by using context clues. Vocabulary items are usually stated as follows:

As used in the passage, the best definition of _____ is. . . .

Both word knowledge and context are necessary for a correct response. Go back and reread the sentence before the word, the sentence with the word, and the sentence after the word to be sure that you understand the context and are not misled by unusual meanings. Be suspicious of common words such as *industry,* which seems simple on the surface but can have multiple meanings.

EXERCISE 8

Answer the following vocabulary question on the passage "saltwater slaves." Then note the handwritten remarks reflecting the thinking about whether an answer is correct.

_____ 1. As used in the third paragraph, the best definition of *chafing* is

a. splinters.

(This could happen from lying on wood planks, but Falconbridge's quote suggests something else.)

b. disease.

(This wouldn't necessarily happen from lying on bare planks, and it doesn't fit with the surgeon's comment.)

c. muscle soreness.

(Falconbridge's quote suggests damage to the skin, not the muscles.)

d. rubbing away of the skin.

(This would happen if a person lay on wood planks for a long time. It fits with the surgeon's comment.)

For additional practice answering vocabulary questions, refer to Appendix 5, page 546.

Essay Questions

Essay questions are not common in reading comprehension tests that are used for college admission or placement, such as SAT, ACT, COMPASS, and so on. However, your reading instructor is likely to ask for written responses to assigned readings and test passages. The following tips can help you respond well.

EXERCISE 9

Consider the following question about "saltwater slaves" as you respond to the items below. Reading the handwritten notes that explain some answer choices will help you think through the process of responding to an essay question.

List and describe the stages that slaves from Africa usually experienced as they traveled from their home to American plantations.

Read the Question Carefully.   Be sure you are clear about what you are expected to write.

_____ 1. Which of the following is the best focus for your answer to the essay question above?

a. The terrible conditions on the ship during the Atlantic crossing

   (This is just one of the stages in the journey.)

b. The five stages of the journey, in order

   (This responds directly to the question.)

c. The feelings of confusion, fear, and sadness that the African must have experienced

   (The question asks about the stages, not for a general description of feelings. They can be mentioned in the description of each stage or as a closing.)

d. The physical hardships of the journey

   (This can be mentioned in the descriptions, but the focus should be on what happened in each stage.)

Notice Key Words in the Question.   Essay questions commonly use certain key action words. The list below gives hints about how to respond to an essay question.

Compare: List the similarities.

Contrast: Note the differences.

Criticize: State your opinion and stress the weaknesses.

Define: State the meaning and use examples so the term is understood.

Describe: State the characteristics so the image is vivid.

Diagram: Make a drawing that demonstrates relationships.

Discuss: Define the issue and elaborate on the advantages and disadvantages.

Evaluate: State positive and negative views and make a judgment.

Explain: Show cause and effect and give reasons.

Illustrate: Provide examples.

Interpret: Explain your own understanding of and opinions on a topic.

Justify: Give proof or reasons to support an opinion.

List: Record a series of numbered items.

Outline: Sketch the main points with their significant supporting details.

Prove: Use facts to support an opinion.

Relate: Connect items and show how one influences another.

Review: Give an overview with a summary.

Summarize: Retell the main points.

Trace: Move sequentially from one event to another.

_____ 2. The key words in the essay question about "saltwater slaves" suggest which of the following plans?

    a. Explain your opinions on the topic of slavery.
    b. Show cause and effect and give reasons.
    c. Name the five stages of the journey and describe what happened in each one.
    d. Connect items and show how one influences another.

Reword the Question to Form the First Sentence of Your Essay Answer.
This method makes the main point clear and helps you stay on track as you write the rest of the answer.

_____ 3. Which of the following is the best opening sentence for your essay response?

    a. Slaves from Africa usually experienced five stages in the journey from their home to plantations in America.
    b. Slaves experienced terrible conditions on the way to America.
    c. The history of slavery in America included much human suffering.
    d. The first stage of the journey to slavery in America began with capture from home in African villages.

Organize Your Answer Before You Write. A brief informal outline will guide your writing and might even earn points if you are unable to finish the full written answer.

_____ 4. Which of the following best guides an answer to the essay question?

    a. Stage 1 Capture
       Stage 3 Middle passage
       Stage 4 Sale in America
       Stage 5 PTSD

       (Not enough information about each stage; Stage 2 missing)

    b. Stage 1
       Stage 2
       Stage 3
       Stage 4
       Stage 5

       (No description of the stages)

    c. Stage 1
        Stage 2
        Stage 3   Middle passage
                    Ocean crossing
                    Terrible conditions in the ship's hold
        Stage 4
        Stage 5   Seasoning
                    Physical recovery, adjustment, PTSD
                    Forced into obedience

(Good information on Stages 3 and 5 but not enough for the others)

    d. Stage 1   Capture and march to the sea
                    Bound hands, harsh treatment
        Stage 2   Sale and imprisonment
                    Dangerous transport from shore to ship
        Stage 3   Middle passage
                    Ocean crossing
                    Terrible conditions in the ship's hold
        Stage 4   Selling process in America
                    Could take weeks/months
        Stage 5   Seasoning
                    Physical recovery, adjustment, PTSD
                    Forced into obedience

(All stages and descriptions included)

Use Formal Language, Correct Spelling, and Correct Grammar. Expect this as the standard for every academic assignment. You are not texting or posting on social media. Use the paragraph form unless the question suggests something else (e.g., to draw a timeline of the slave journey.)

Write for Points. Essay test grades almost always depend on a **rubric**—a set of expectations with points attached. For this essay on "saltwater slaves," a rubric like this might be used:

    15 points total:

    10 points for the names and descriptions of the five stages (2 points each)

    3 points for an opening sentence that restates the question

    2 points for formal style, spelling, and grammar

5. Using the rubric above, assign a grade to each of the following answers to the question:

    List and describe the stages that slaves from Africa usually experienced as they traveled from their home to American plantations.

    Essay #1: Grade _____

_____ Name and description of each stage (0–10 points)

_____ Opening sentence (0–3 points)

_____ Formal style, spelling, grammar (0–2 points)

Whew! The life of a slave was really hard. First, they were taken from their homes. Next, they were moved to ships and travelled over the oshun to America. The jurney were very hard and many people got sick. Next, they arrived in America and got sold. At the plantation they had a chance to get better, but they had PTSD and tons of work to do the rest of their life.

Essay #2: Grade _____

_____ Name and description of each stage (0–10 points)

_____ Opening sentence (0–3 points)

_____ Formal style, spelling, grammar (0–2 points)

Slaves from Africa usually experienced five stages in the journey from home to plantations in America. First, they were captured from their home villages by slave traders, bound with ropes, and marched cruelly over land to the sea. On arrival they were sold to European buyers and transported to waiting ships. They often endured this second stage trapped for weeks in the heat until the captain set sail. The third stage, the middle passage, was the Atlantic ocean crossing. The conditions during this phase were especially horrible due to disease, illness, abuse, and physical injury, and many died. The fourth stage began when the ship docked in America. There buyers examined the slaves and settled on sale prices. Finally, when slaves arrived at their owner's plantation, the "seasoning" stage began. During this time slaves recovered their health, began to adjust to their new surroundings, and were forced into obedience. These "saltwater slaves," slaves born in Africa, suffered traumatic physical and emotional hardships during these five stages of their journey.

For additional practice answering essay questions, refer to Appendix 5.

READ EFFICIENTLY

Learning Objective 5

Increase reading efficiency

College students often wish that they could finish their reading assignments more quickly while still understanding the material. If you are not zipping through a book at 1,000 words per minute, does it mean you are a slow reader? No! If you don't score 100 % on comprehension questions, does it mean you did not understand what you read? No! Speed and comprehension depend on your reason for reading. Can you improve your reading speed and comprehension? Yes! It is possible to improve both. This textbook focuses mostly on improving comprehension, but the next section offers some good strategies for improving speed while maintaining comprehension goals.

Match Rate to Purpose

Efficient readers adjust their speed and reading technique to match the material and their purpose for reading it. Surely, you do not read everything the same way, do you? Do you approach a textbook reading assignment in the same way as an Internet page? Do you read a novel like you read a letter from your boss? A textbook assignment requires complete comprehension and recall, so an efficient reader takes time to read carefully and thoroughly. An Internet page, on the other hand, most likely holds passing interest and can be read very quickly. A novel that you are reading for pleasure does not demand remembering all the characters and plot details, but a letter from your boss deserves close attention.

The following chart illustrates the point of efficient reading.

EFFICIENT READING: ADJUSTING RATE AND TECHNIQUE TO MATERIAL AND PURPOSE			
Material	**Purpose for Reading**	**Technique**	**Rate**
Textbooks	Complete comprehension and long-term recall	Study reading (thorough, careful, note taking)	Slow
Novels	Pleasure—short-term recall	Standard (usual, personal method)	Medium (baseline rate)
News and magazine articles, Internet pages	General information, main ideas, and major details	Skimming (reading titles, headings, and first sentences only)	Fast
Television schedule, Internet surfing, Googling, dictionary, reference books, etc.	Specific information	Scanning (focusing only on needed information)	Fastest

Increase Reading Rate

Efficient readers know that the most important reading goal is achieving their desired level of understanding. That said, it is possible to increase reading speed and still accomplish your comprehension goal. Adopting certain reading habits will improve speed in every reading situation. Practice the tips in this section, and if you want to work harder on reading speed, refer to the extra practices in Appendix 6. Begin here by determining your baseline reading rate.

 **EXERCISE 10** Read the following selection at your normal reading speed and aim for four correct answers out of the five at the end of the reading. Time your reading so that you can calculate your words-per-minute rate. Use a stopwatch or a watch with a second hand. Record your starting time in minutes and seconds. When you have completed the selection, record your finishing time in minutes and seconds. Answer the questions that follow and use the chart to determine your rate.

Starting time: _____ minutes _____ seconds

Reading 3

CHILDREN MAY BE HAZARDOUS TO YOUR HAPPINESS

 It's the American dream—getting married, buying a home, and settling down to have children. Everyone knows that parenthood is one of the great joys of life and that it contributes greatly to one's happiness and sense of well-being. But in that regard, everyone may be wrong: Research shows that not only does having children not necessarily produce increased happiness, but also it may actually reduce it.

Sociologist Robin Simon, who studied thousands of American families, summarized her findings this way: "Parents experience lower levels of emotional well-being, less frequent positive emotions, and more frequent negative emotions than their childless peers. In fact, no group of parents—married, single, step or even empty nest—reported significantly greater emotional well-being than people who never had children."

Of course, parenthood is not without its rewards. Despite lower levels of happiness, parents also report more purpose, more meaning, and ultimately more satisfaction with life than nonparents. But research data do not show that children bring greater happiness to their parents.

Why, then, does the belief that children bring great happiness persist? One possible reason is that we learn beliefs from our parents. People who believe that parenting is a satisfying, life-enhancing experience are more likely to have children than are people who don't. The former group has more children to whom to pass on their beliefs, while the latter group's less rosy perspective is less likely to get transmitted to the subsequent generation.

Another reason for people's continued faith in the joys of parenting has to do with selective recall. When people conjure up memories of their parenting experiences, they are likely to focus on the relatively rare best of times: a baby's first words or first smile, a fun day at the park, or graduation day. The stresses of parenthood—nighttime feedings, dirty diapers, fighting siblings, piles of dirty laundry, and so forth—may be much more common but tend to recede into the background when parents reflect back on their experience.

So when parents are asked whether having children enriched their lives, they tend to respond in the affirmative. But when parents' current sense of well-being is actually measured at various points in time, the truth emerges: Parents are not actually happier than people who do not have children, and on some measures, the parents actually seem to do worse. Again, the culprit seems to be the day-to-day stresses that parenthood brings. On any given day, parents have fewer freedoms, more worries, and more domestic drudgery to deal with than do their childless peers.

Ultimately, of course, many worthwhile pursuits in life, such as marriage or a career (not to mention pursuing a college education), bring their fair share of daily hassles and headaches. The hope is that in the balance the occasional moments of joy and accomplishment make it all worthwhile.

(472 words)

—*Development Across the Life Span,* Sixth Edition,
by Robert S. Feldman

Finishing time: _____ *minutes* _____ *seconds*

Reading time in seconds = _____

Words per minute = _____ *(see Time Chart)*

TIME CHART

Time in Seconds and Minutes	Words per Minute
60 (1 min.)	472
80	354
90	315
100	283
110	257
120 (2 min.)	236
130	218
140	202
150	189
160	177
170	167
180 (3 min.)	157
190	149

Answer the following with *T* (true) or *F* (false).

_____ 1. The author assumes that most people think being a parent brings happiness.

_____ 2. Robin Simon's study showed that people with children are happier than childless people.

_____ 3. This article mentioned no benefits to having children.

_____ 4. According to the article, one reason for a belief in the greater joys of parenthood is that people tend to recall the pleasant experiences and forget the unpleasant ones.

_____ 5. The author is trying to convince readers not to have children.

Were you able to read normally and answer four out of the five questions correctly? Analyze your reading experience in this exercise. Did you maintain your focus on the reading? Did you find yourself going back to reread it at times? The following section offers good strategies that will increase your reading rate and thus increase your reading efficiency.

Be Aggressive—Attack!

Grab that book, sit up straight, and try to get some work done. Don't be a passive reader who watches the words go by but lacks understanding and involvement. Be active. Look for meaning with a strong intellectual curiosity and try to get something out of what you read. Drive for the main idea.

Faster reading does not mean poorer comprehension. Moderate gains in speed usually result in improved comprehension because you are concentrating and thinking more.

Concentrate

Our eyes cannot actually read. We read with our minds. Thus, getting information from the printed page comes down to concentration. The faster you read, the harder you must concentrate. It is like driving a car at 75 miles per hour as opposed to 35 miles per hour. You are covering more ground at 75 miles per hour, and it requires total concentration to keep the car on the road. Faster reading is direct, purposeful, and attentive. There is no time to think about anything except what you are reading.

Both external and internal distractions interfere with concentration. External distractions are the physical things around you. Are you in a quiet place? Is the television going? Can you hear people talking on the telephone? Are you being interrupted by someone asking you questions? You can control most external distractions by prior planning. Be careful in selecting your time and place to study. Choose a quiet place and start at a reasonable hour. Set yourself up for success.

Internal distractions, however, are much more difficult to control. They are the thoughts in your mind that keep you from concentrating. Again, prior planning will help. Keep a to-do list as described earlier in this chapter. Making a list and knowing that you will check back over it will help you stop worrying about your duties and responsibilities. Make an effort to spend more time *doing* something than *worrying* about something.

Visualizing can also help concentration. If you are reading about ostriches, visualize ostriches. As much as possible, try to see what you read as a movie. Use your imagination and all five of your senses to improve your comprehension.

EXERCISE 11   In the list below, the key word is in boldface. Among the words to the right, mark the one most similar in meaning to the key word. In this exercise, you are looking quickly for meaning. This will help you think fast and effectively.

1. **recall**	read	guide	remember	fail	forgive
2. **sanitary**	new	fine	equal	clean	straight
3. **physician**	health	doctor	coward	elder	teacher
4. **motor**	car	horse	wagon	shine	engine
5. **first**	primary	last	finally	only	hard
6 **look**	stick	serve	glance	open	wait
7. **usual**	common	neat	best	cruel	kindness
8. **quick**	noisy	near	fast	finish	give
9. **annoy**	logic	make	win	disturb	set
10. **shout**	cry	action	most	fear	force

Stop Regressions

A **regression** is going back and rereading what you have just finished. Does this ever happen to you? Certainly some textbook material is so complex that it requires a second reading, but most of us regress even when the material is not that complicated. The problem is simply "sleeping on the job." Your mind takes a nap or starts thinking about something else while your eyes keep moving across the page. Hence, halfway down the page, you wonder, "What am I reading?" and you plod back to reread and find out. Then, after an alert rereading, the meaning is clear, but you have lost valuable time.

Regression can be a habit. You know you can always go back and reread. Break yourself of the habit. The next time you catch yourself going back to reread because your mind has been wandering, say, "Halt, I'm going to keep on reading." This will put more pressure on you to pay attention the first time. Remember, reading the assignment twice takes double the time. Try to reread only when it is necessary for difficult material.

Avoid Vocalization

Vocalization means moving your lips as you read. It takes additional time and is generally a sign of an immature reader. A trick suggested by specialists to stop lip movement is to put a slip of paper in your mouth. If the paper moves, your lips are moving, and you are thus alerted to stop the habit.

Subvocalization refers to the little voice in your head that reads out loud for you. Even though you are not moving your lips or making any sounds, you hear the words in your mind as you read. Some experts say that subvocalization is necessary for difficult material, and others say that fast readers are totally visual and do not need to subvocalize. The truth lies probably somewhere between the two. You may find that in easy reading you can eliminate some of your subvocalization and only hear the key words, whereas on more difficult textbook material, subvocalization reinforces the words and gives you better reading comprehension. Because your work will be primarily with textbook reading, do not concern yourself with subvocalization at this time. In fact, sometimes you may need to read particularly difficult textbook passages aloud in order to understand them fully.

Expand Fixations

Your eyes must stop for you to read. These stops, which last for a fraction of a second, are called **fixations**. If you are reading a page that has twelve words to a line and you need to stop at each word, you have made twelve fixations, each of which takes a fraction of a second. If, however, you can read two words with each fixation, you will make only half the stops and thus increase your total reading speed.

You might say, "How can I do this?" and the answer has to do with peripheral vision. To illustrate, hold up your finger and try to look only at that finger. As you can see, such limited vision is impossible. Because of peripheral vision, you can see many other things in the room besides your finger. Research has shown that the average reader can see approximately 2.5 words per fixation.

Read the following phrase:

in the barn

Did you make three fixations, one on each word, or did you fixate once? Now read the following word:

entertainment

How many fixations did you make? Probably one, but as a beginning reader in elementary school, you most likely read the word with four fixations, one for each syllable. Your use of one fixation for *entertainment* dramatizes the progress you have already made as a reader and indicates the ability of the eyes to take in a number of letters at one time. The phrase *in the barn* has nine letters, whereas *entertainment* has thirteen. Does it make any sense to stop three times to read nine letters and once to read thirteen? Again, the reason we do so is habit. If you never expected or tried to read more than one word per fixation, that is all you are able to do.

The key to expanding your fixations is to read phrases or thought units. Some words seem to go together automatically and some don't. Words need to be grouped according to thought units. Your fixation point, as shown by the dot in the following example, will be under and between the words forming the thought unit, so your peripheral vision can pick up what is on either side of the point.

Read the following paragraph by fixating at each indicated point. Notice how the words have been divided into phrase units.

FASTER READING

A faster   reading speed   is developed   through practice
•   •   •   •
and concentration.   Your reading rate   also depends
•   •   •
on how much   you know   about a subject.
•   •   •

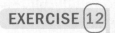

EXERCISE 12 In the following list, the key phrase is in boldface. Among the words on the line below, mark the phrase that is most similar in meaning to the key phrase. This exercise will help you increase your eye span and grasp meaning quickly from phrases.

1. **to have your own**
   wish for more   share with others   keep for yourself   be harmed by fire
2. **finish a task**
   lessen the impact   clean the attic   turn on the lights   complete a job
3. **sing a song**
   hum a tune   work for pleasure   leave for vacation   wish on a star
4. **manage a business**
   lose your job   lock the door   seek employment   run a company
5. **sit for a while**
   make ends meet   rest in a chair   learn new ways   fall into bed

Use a Pen as a Pacer

Using a pen to follow the words in a smooth, flowing line can help you set a rhythmical pace for your reading. In elementary school, you were probably taught never to point at words, so this advice may be contrary to what you have learned. However, it can be an effective speed-reading technique.

The technique of using a pen as a pacer is demonstrated in the following example. Use a pen to trace the lines shown so that it goes from one side of the column to the other and returns in a Z pattern. Because you are trying to read several words at a fixation, it is not necessary for your pen to go to the extreme end of either side of the column. After you have finished, answer the comprehension questions with *T* (true) or *F* (false).

EXAMPLE

BREAKING FOR MEMORY

Researchers have found that taking a series
of short breaks during a long
study period can enhance memory
and thus improve your recall
of the information. The breaks should be
a complete rest from the task
and should be no longer than
ten minutes. You may choose
to break every 40 or 50 minutes.
During your break, you will experience
what experts call memory consolidation
as the new information is linked
and organized into knowledge networks.
According to some experts, deep breathing
and relaxation exercises can also help
by improving the flow of oxygen to the brain.

(100 words)

Time in seconds = _____

_____ 1. Fifty-minute breaks are recommended during long study periods.

_____ 2. Memory consolidation means improving the flow of oxygen to the brain.

EXPLANATION The answers are (1) *false* and (2) *false*. Although it may seem awkward at first, practice using a pen to read in a Z pattern on light material such as newspaper or magazine articles to get accustomed to the technique. It will not only force you to move your eyes faster, but it will also improve your concentration and keep you alert and awake.

Try using your pen as a pacer for the first five or ten minutes of your reading to become familiar with the feeling of a faster, rhythmical pace. When you tire, stop the technique, but try to keep reading at the same pace. If, later in the reading, you feel yourself slowing down, resume the technique until you have regained the pace. This is a simple technique that does not involve expensive machines or complicated instruction, and *it works*! Pacing with the Z pattern *will* increase your reading speed.

EXERCISE 13 Read the following passage using your pen as a pacer in the Z pattern. Answer the comprehension questions with *T* (true) or *F* (false).

Passage 1

NETIQUETTE

The rules   and guidelines   for acceptable behavior   on the Net
are called netiquette.   Be careful   to say   what you mean
and to say it   with care.   You cannot   double-click   and take
it back.   Keep your   messages short   and to the point.   People who
receive hundreds   of e-mails   each day are more likely   to respond
to short ones.   Although you   are hidden   from view,   appearances
are important.   Proofread   your messages.   Other people   will judge
your intelligence   and education   by the spelling,   grammar,   punctuation,
and clarity   of your messages.   If you   want your messages   to be taken
seriously,   present your   best face.

(100 words)

—*Computer Confluence: Exploring Tomorrow's Technology,*
Third Edition, by George Beekman

Time in seconds = _____

_____ 1. According to the author, once a message is sent, you can double-click and retract it.

_____ 2. The author suggests that grammar and punctuation are not important in e-mail messages to close friends.

Passage 2

I HAVE A SENSE OF HUMOR

According to the journalist Norman Cousins, laughing is internal jogging, and when you laugh, you are exercising all your internal organs. Not only does laughter feel good, it is essential to good health and a sense of well-being. Cousins has good reason to believe this. Some years ago he was diagnosed with a terminal illness and given just two months to live. Instead of spending his precious time remaining in the hospital, he checked into a hotel and watched, read, or listened to every humorous movie, book, and audiotape he could get his hands on. He virtually laughed himself well. Many years later, still in excellent health, Cousins was convinced, as were his doctors, that laughter accounted for his recovery! In fact, the medical school at UCLA invited him to join its faculty to teach interns how to lighten up.

Cousins' amazing story holds a lesson for all of us. We can all stand to lighten up a little—to find the genuine humor in an embarrassing moment, in a mistake, in a situation that is so serious that we need to laugh to keep from crying. Humor at its best means being able to laugh at yourself. Look for opportunities to see the lighter side of life and to share the experience of being human with others who can laugh with you, not at you. Cultivate the habit of walking on the "light" side of life.

(237 words)

—*The Career Fitness Program: Exercising Your Options,*
Seventh Edition, by Diane Sukiennik et al.

Time in seconds = _____

_____ 1. Norman Cousins had humorous movies, books, and audiotapes brought to his hospital room to speed his recovery.

_____ 2. Cousins was invited to teach student interns about humor.

Preview Before Reading

Do not start reading without looking over the material and thinking about what you need to accomplish. Think about the title and glance over the material, looking for key words and phrases. Read the boldface and italic type. Decide what you think the selection is going to be about and what you want to know when you finish it. What is your prior knowledge on the subject? Prepare to add new information or change existing ideas. A few minutes spent on such an initial survey will help you read more purposefully and thus more quickly.

Set a Time Goal for an Assignment

Each time you sit down to do an assignment, count the number of pages you need to complete. Estimate the amount of time it will probably take you and then look at the clock and write down your projected finishing time. Make your goal realistic and pace yourself so that you can achieve it. Having an expectation will help you speed up your reading and improve your concentration. Do not become an all-night victim of Parkinson's law, which states that the job expands to fit the time available. Don't allow yourself all night or all weekend to read twenty-five pages. Set a goal and then try to meet it.

Practice

You cannot improve your running speed unless you get out and run. The same is true with reading. To learn to read faster, practice faster reading techniques every day.

SUMMARY POINTS

1 How can I prepare mentally for reading success? (page 2)
Think like a winner. Set long-term career and college goals and then work back to your reading class. Approach reading and learning with a positive attitude. Persevere—stick to your goals—especially when it is difficult.

2 What are some key behaviors for reading success? (page 5)
Learn to manage your time by creating a schedule for study and other activities and using it. Use a to-do list and a monthly calendar, too. Study the course syllabus carefully. Preview the textbook for every class and develop the habit of marking it as you read.

3 How can I plan for success on reading tests? (page 10)
Before the test, learn as much as you can about it. Use practice tests if they are available. During the test, relax and focus. Manage your time as you read the passages and then answer the questions. After the test, take time to analyze your preparation. Review the test when it is returned and analyze the results to avoid repeating mistakes on the next test.

4 How can I recognize and answer types of comprehension questions? (page 12)
Main idea: Ask what point the author's major details make about the topic. Incorrect answers are too broad or too narrow. The first and last sentences might be clues.
Detail: Look for key words in the question. Verify your answer by checking back in the passage.
Inference: Use logic and the clues in the passage that support your answer.
Author's purpose: The type of passage suggests the writer's purpose. Determine whether the passage type is factual, opinion, or fiction.
Vocabulary: Reread the sentences surrounding the word and use the context clues to determine its meaning.
Essay: Read the question carefully, looking for key action words. Reword the question to start the response. Organize your answer before writing. Use formal language and write for points.

5 How can I improve my reading efficiency? (page 21)
Match your reading rate to the material and your purpose for reading. Develop and practice efficient reading habits: Be aggressive, concentrate, stop regressions, avoid vocalization, expand fixations, use a pen as a pacer, preview before reading, and set a time goal.

COLLABORATIVE   PROBLEM SOLVING

Form a five-member group and select one of the following activities. After reading this chapter, brainstorm and then outline your major points. Create a poster or a brief skit to present your findings.

➤ Make a list of the top ten ways to fail a reading class.

➤ Make a list or demonstrate with a skit some common roadblocks that students face in a reading class and how to get around them.

➤ Model a conversation between a successful and an unsuccessful reading test taker about what went wrong and what went right.

➤ Make a chart or create a demonstration showing common distractions that students face when they are doing a reading assignment *and* how to combat them.

Using Mnemonics

Mnemonics is a technique that helps you organize and recall. It works by stimulating your senses through pictures, sounds, rhythms, and other mental "tricks" to create extrasensory "handles" or hooks that make it easier for your brain to arrange and retrieve information. Given a list of 12 nouns to remember, students who link them in a story remember more than students who just try to memorize them as unrelated items. Weaving such a story is called *narrative chaining*, because the technique links, organizes, and gives meaning to unrelated items. The following are suggested mnemonic techniques for college learning.

Reading Aloud

Although you may not think of reading aloud as a mnemonic, you use additional senses when you read out loud. Memory experts explain that your eyes *see* the material on the page and your ears *hear* the information. Your mouth, tongue, lips, and throat *feel* the sensation of speaking the words. This is particularly effective for studying lecture notes after class or before an exam.

Writing It Down

Writing works in a similar way to reading aloud, because you feel your hand transcribing the information. Thus, summarizing, annotating, note taking, outlining, and mapping add sensory steps to learning. Always take notes during a class lecture to reinforce the spoken information.

Creating Acronyms

Create **acronyms**—using the first letter of each word you want to remember. A well-known example of this technique is using HOMES to remember the great lakes: *H*uron, *O*ntario, *M*ichigan, *E*rie, *S*uperior.

Creating Acrostics

Form a sentence in which the first letter of each word corresponds to the first letter of each word in a list you want to remember. For example, *my very eager mother just served us nuts* is an **acrostic** for remembering the eight planets in our solar system: *V*enus, *E*arth, *M*ars, *J*upiter, *S*aturn, *U*ranous, *N*eptune in order of their distance from the Sun. Silly and unusual acrostics can be especially easy to remember.

Using Rhythms, Rhymes, and Jingles

Use rhythms, rhymes, and jingles to create additional handles for your brain to use to process and retrieve. Most students never forget the year Christopher Columbus came to America because they learned the rhythmic rhyme, "In fourteen-hundred-and-ninety-two/Columbus sailed the ocean blue."

Making Associations

Make a connection between seemingly unrelated ideas by using pictures, nonsense ideas, or connected bits of logic. For example, two easily confused words are *stationary,* which means standing still, and *stationery,* meaning letter-writing paper. To remember the difference, note that *station<u>a</u>ry* is spelled with an "a," which relates to the "a" in *st<u>a</u>nding still; stationery* is spelled with an "e," which relates to *l<u>ette</u>rs*.

Conjuring Mental Images

Create a picture, perhaps a funny picture, just as you would on a vocabulary concept card. Picture a *voracious* reader as a shark greedily eating a book.

Using Key Word Images

To learn foreign language vocabulary, use the sound of the new word to relate to an image of a known word. For example, the Spanish word for horse is *caballo,* which is pronounced *cab-eye-yo.* Associate *eye* as the key word and picture a horse with only one large eye looking into a taxi cab.

EXERCISE 1

1. Create an association to remember that *cereal* is a breakfast food and *serial* is a numerical order. _____

   _____

2. Create an acrostic to remember the elements that make up the vast majority of molecules in living things: carbon, hydrogen, nitrogen, oxygen, phosphorus, and sulfur. _____

   _____

3. Create a rhyme or jingle to remember that World War II ended in 1945.

   _____

Reader's TIP　　Remembering Information

- Hook information to mental signs that are easy to remember.
- Link information to other information that you already know.
- Sense information by touching, writing, or speaking.
- Rehearse information by writing and speaking to yourself.

2 Stages of Reading

Learning Objectives

From this chapter, readers will learn:

1 To use the three stages of good reading
2 To preview before reading
3 To understand the meaning and importance of a *schema*
4 To understand the meaning and importance of *metacognition*
5 To use six thinking strategies during reading to integrate existing and new knowledge
6 To apply active recall methods after reading

Everyday Reading Skills: Selecting a Book

WHAT IS THE READING PROCESS?

In the past, experts thought of reading comprehension as a *product*. They assumed that if you could pronounce the words fluently, you would automatically be able to comprehend them. Instruction focused on practicing and checking for the correct answers rather than on explaining comprehension skills. Newer approaches, by contrast, teach reading comprehension as a *process* in which you use your understanding of different skills and stages to achieve an understanding of the whole. Students are now taught how to predict upcoming ideas, activate existing knowledge, relate old information with new, form a main idea, and make inferences.

STAGES OF READING

Learning Objective 1

Use the three stages of good reading

Good reading is divided into three thinking stages:

1. **Before reading:** *Preview* to find out what the material is about, what you already know about the topic, and what you need to find out while reading.
2. **During reading:** *Integrate* old and new knowledge, anticipate upcoming information, visualize, mark the text, and assess your own understanding in order to make adjustments.
3. **After reading:** *Recall* and react to what you have learned.

Many experts have devised study skills strategies that break these three thinking stages into small steps. A historical example is SQ3R, which was devised by Francis P. Robinson at Ohio State University. The letters stand for *Survey*, *Question*, *Read*, *Recite*, and *Review*. Any such system can be successful, but all are designed to systematically engage the reader in thought *before*, *during*, and *after* reading.

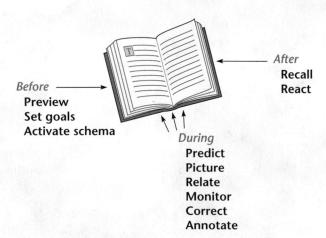

Before ⟶ Preview
Set goals
Activate schema

During — Predict
Picture
Relate
Monitor
Correct
Annotate

After — Recall
React

Stage One: Preview

Learning Objective 2

Preview before reading

Previewing is a method of assessing the material, your knowledge of the subject, and your goals for reading. Try to connect with the topic and get an overview of the assignment before starting on the first paragraph. At the beginning of each new course, preview the table of contents of your new textbook to get an overview of the scope of the material. Before reading a chapter, use the signposts, such as subheadings, boldface or italic type, and summaries, to anticipate what you will be learning.

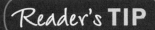

Reader's TIP — **Questions for Previewing**

Use the following questions as guides to energize your reading and help you become an active learner.

1. What is the topic of the material?
2. What do I already know about the subject?
3. What is my purpose for reading?
4. How is the material organized?
5. What will be my plan of attack?

Signposts for Previewing. Notice the following typical features of college textbooks when previewing. These are the parts to read when previewing a textbook chapter:

1. Introductory Material. A textbook chapter usually begins with an introduction. This section prepares the reader for the major ideas that will be covered. Pay close attention to it!

2. Learning Questions. Many textbook chapters start with questions designed to heighten your interest and stimulate your thinking. Such questions directly relate to what the material covers and thus help you set goals.

3. Title. The title of a book, chapter, or article is the first clue to its meaning. Some titles are designed to be clever to attract attention, but most try to communicate the important thought in the text. Identify the *who, what,* or *why* of the title to anticipate the content of the material and its importance to you.

4. Headings and Subheadings. These are the titles of the sections and subsections within chapters that, like the major titles, describe the content. Usually headings and subheadings appear in boldface or italic type and outline the author's message. Turn them into questions to anticipate what you will need to know from the reading. For example, the heading "Estimating Revenue Potential" in a marketing text could be changed to "How Do You Estimate Revenue Potential?"

5. Italics, Boldface, and Numbers. Italic and boldface type highlight words that merit special emphasis. These words are usually terms that you will need to define and remember. Numbers are also used to list important details that you may need to learn.

6. Visual Aids or Marginal Notations. A biology professor at a major university tells his students to at least look at the illustrations and read the captions in the assigned material before coming to class, even if they don't read the assignment. He wants his students to have a visual overview. Authors use photos, charts, and graphs to enhance meaning, heighten interest, and help readers visualize information. Additional notations and definitions may be added in the page margins to further simplify the material for the reader.

7. Concluding Summary or Review. Most textbook chapters end with a summary of the most important points, which may be several paragraphs or a list of the important ideas. Regardless of its form, the summary helps you recall the material and reflect on its importance.

EXERCISE 1

To get an overview of this chapter, look at the learning questions at the opening of the chapter on page 33. Read the Summary Points on page 48 and scan the headings, subheadings, and the boldfaced and italicized words. Spend a few moments reviewing the contents of the Reader's Tip boxes. Now, answer the following questions:

1. What are the three stages of reading? _____

2. What is the purpose of previewing? _____

3. List the six thinking strategies that good readers use during reading:

_____

4. What is meant by *recall*? _____

_____

_____

_____

5. How do good readers reflect? _____

_____

_____

Previewing Material Without the Signposts.

Some of the material that you will read in college does not have all of the typical features that guide readers through textbooks. Magazine and newspaper articles, essays, and short stories, for example, often lack headings and subheadings, and an obvious introduction and summary. Previewing is still an important step in absorbing the ideas in them, however.

Use the features that your reading materials do have—titles or visual aids, for example. In addition, get an overview of the selection by quickly reading the first paragraph, glancing at the first sentence of each paragraph, and reading the last paragraph. Previewing these parts will familiarize you with the topic, main point, and some of the details and prepare you to understand more fully in Stage 2.

The Power of Prior Knowledge.

Experts say that prior knowledge is the most important factor in reading comprehension. Thus, if you know very little about a subject, the initial reading in that area will be difficult. The good news, however, is that the more you know, the easier it is for you to read and learn. Every new idea added to your framework of knowledge about a subject makes the next reading assignment on the topic a little bit easier.

Students who already know a lot about history may think that American history assignments are easy. But students who perhaps excel in science and know little history might disagree. Because of prior knowledge, most students would probably agree that senior-level college courses are much easier than freshman survey courses.

Learning Objective 3

Understand the meaning and importance of a *schema*

Previewing to Activate Schemata.

Your prior knowledge on a subject is a schema. According to theory, a **schema** (plural, *schemata*) is the skeleton of knowledge in your mind on a particular subject. As you expand your knowledge, the skeleton grows. Here's another way to think about a schema: A schema is like a computer chip in your brain that holds everything you know on a particular subject. You pull it out when the need arises, add to it, and then return it to storage.

Your preview of the material will help you know which "computer chips" to activate. Call on what you already know and blend it with the new ideas. If you embellish the new thoughts with your past experience, your reading will become more meaningful.

Students tend to know more than they think they know. No matter how unfamiliar the topic may seem, you can probably provide some small link from your own experience. Pick up the signals from the written material and use them to retrieve prior knowledge and form a link of understanding with the next text.

PERSONAL FEEDBACK 1   Name _____

1. What was your favorite subject in high school, and why?_____

   _____

2. What magazines do you like to read? _____

   _____

3. What sections do you like to read in the newspaper? _____

   _____

4. What is the best book you have read? _____

   _____

5. What television programs do you watch regularly? _____

   _____

6. How does prior knowledge seem to relate to your areas of greatest interest?

   _____

Share your responses as directed by your instructor.

EXAMPLE   Read the following sentence and activate your schema. Identify a knowledge link. Briefly describe an idea or image that comes to mind.

> Cuba became an obsession of American policy makers in 1959, when Fidel Castro and rebels of his 26th of July Movement ousted America's longtime ally Fulgencio Batista.
>
> —*A People and a Nation* by Mary Beth Norton et al.

EXPLANATION   You may know little Cuban history, but you probably know that Miami, Florida, has a large and flourishing Hispanic population, begun by people who left Cuba. Do you know why they left Cuba? Link this knowledge of Cubans in Florida to the new information. What is the relationship of Cuba and the United States today?

Stage Two: Integrate Knowledge

If you watch two students reading silently, can you tell which student comprehends better? Probably not. The behaviors of good silent readers are thinking behaviors that cannot be observed or learned by watching others. These behaviors, however, need not be mysterious to college students.

Learning Objective 4

Understand the meaning and importance of *metacognition*

Knowing About Knowing.   A myth in reading is that good readers begin an assignment, race through it, and never stop until the last period. In fact, however, *good readers work hard* to assimilate the information they read. If they do not understand or if they get confused, they go back and reread to resolve the confusion. Good readers also understand the processes involved in reading and consciously control them. This awareness and control of the reading process is called **metacognition,** which experts define as "knowing about knowing."

Some students don't know when they don't know. They continue to read even though they are not comprehending. Poor readers tolerate such confusion because they either don't realize that it exists or don't know what to do about it. Poor readers focus on facts, whereas good readers try to assimilate details into a larger cognitive pattern. Good readers monitor their own comprehension. In other words, they supervise their own understanding of the material. They recognize inadequate comprehension and interrupt their reading to seek solutions.

Learning Objective 5

Use six thinking strategies during reading to integrate knowledge

Six Thinking Strategies of Effective Readers.   When they want full comprehension and recall, effective readers, both consciously and subconsciously, use the six thinking strategies below.

1. Predict: Make Educated Guesses.   Good readers make predictions about thoughts, events, outcomes, and conclusions. With the appearance of each new character in a James Patterson mystery novel, the reader makes a guess about who the culprit might be. Textbook predictions, although a little less dramatic, are equally important. While reading the facts in a science text, for example, you may be anticipating the concluding theory.

As you read, your predictions are confirmed or denied. If they prove invalid, you make new predictions. For example, in reading an economics text, you may predict that inflation hurts everyone. But after further reading, you discover that real estate investors make money by selling at inflated prices. Thus, your initial predictions have proved invalid, and you readjust your thinking on inflation. Your predictions involved you with the author's thinking and helped you learn.

EXAMPLE   What are your predictions for the rest of the section based on these beginning sentences?

> At least one bank recognized opportunity in this situation. Instead of classifying low-to-moderate-income Hispanics as credit risks to be avoided at all costs, Puerto Rico–based Banco Popular saw them as an untapped market for personal and business banking services. Having witnessed Banco Popular's success, mainstream banks such as Chase and Citibank are. . . .
>
> —*Business*, Sixth Edition, by Ricky W. Griffin and Ronald J. Ebert

EXPLANATION   The rest of this section explains how traditional banks are moving aggressively into the Hispanic market to offer banking services and win customers.

2. Picture: Form Images.   For good readers, the words and the ideas on the page trigger mental images that relate directly or indirectly to the material. Because these mental images depend on the reader's experience, visualization is a highly individualistic process. One learner might read about Maine and picture the countryside and the rockbound coast, whereas another, with no experience of the area, might visualize the shape and location of the state on a map. Images are like movies in your head. You form a visualization to enhance the message in the text. Fiction quickly moves you into a new world of enjoyment or terror through visualization. Expository or textbook writing may require more imagination than fiction, but the images created also strengthen the message.

EXAMPLE   Describe your visualizations for the following passage.

> A dress so loud it hurts my eyes. There are yellows and oranges enough to throw back the light of the sun. I feel my whole face warming from the heat waves it throws out. Earrings gold, too, and hanging down to her shoulders. Bracelets dangling and making noises when she moves her arm. . . .

> —*"Everyday Use"* from *In Love & Trouble: Stories of Black Women* by Alice Walker

EXPLANATION   Imagine a woman dressed in yellows and oranges that are perhaps too bright with long earrings and dangling bracelets. Depending on prior knowledge, you may visualize someone you know.

3. Relate: Draw Comparisons.   When you relate your existing knowledge to the new information in the text, you are embellishing the material and making it part of your framework of ideas. A phrase or a situation may remind you of a personal experience that relates to the text. For example, a description of ocean currents may remind you of a strong undertow you once fought while swimming. Such related experiences help you digest the new experience as part of something that you already know.

EXAMPLE   Are these methods of coping with stress helpful to you?

> A third effective buffer between stressors and illness is exercise. People who are physically fit have fewer health problems than people who are less fit even when they are under the same pressures. They also show lower physiological arousal to stressors. These activities, along with any others that calm your body and focus your mind—prayer, music, dancing, baking bread—are all good for health.

> —*Psychology*, Tenth Edition, by Carole Wade and Carol Tavris

EXPLANATION   What do you do to relieve stress? Which of the methods mentioned seem most useful? Name two other activities that "calm your body and focus your mind."

4. Monitor: Check Understanding.   Monitor your ongoing comprehension to test your understanding of the material. Keep an internal summary of the information as it is presented and how it relates to the overall message. Your summary will build with each new detail as long as the author's message is consistent. If, however, certain information seems confusing or erroneous, stop and seek a solution to the problem. Monitor and supervise your own comprehension. Remember that poor readers accept confusion, but good readers seek to resolve the difficulty. Good readers demand complete understanding and know whether it has been achieved.

EXAMPLE What is confusing about the following sentence?

> "Another such victory like that on July 1," wrote Richard Harding Davis, "and our troops must retreat."
>
> —*America and Its People*, Third Edition,
> by James Martin et al.

EXPLANATION The words *retreat* and *victory* refer to opposite ideas. Usually the defeated army retreats. Davis must mean that the victory was too costly and thus was hardly a victory at all. Davis must be speaking sarcastically, but a second reading might be necessary to figure this out.

5. Resolve Gaps in Understanding. Do not accept gaps in your reading comprehension. They may signal a failure to understand a word or a sentence. Stop and resolve the problem so that you can continue to synthesize and build your internal summary. Seek solutions to confusion. Usually, this means rereading a sentence or looking back at a previous page for clarification. If an unknown word is causing confusion, the definition may emerge through further reading. Changing predictions is also a corrective strategy. For example, while reading a geography textbook, you may be predicting that heavy rains saved a country from famine, but, as the conclusion emerges, it seems that fertilizers and irrigation were the saviors. If you cannot fill the gaps yourself, seek help from the instructor or another student.

EXAMPLE How could you seek to understand the scope of time mentioned in this textbook excerpt?

> . . . [T]hose who study Earth science must routinely deal with vast time periods— millions or billions (thousands of millions) of years. When viewed in the context of Earth's 4.6-billion-year history, an event that occurred 100 million years ago may be characterized as "recent" by a geologist, and a rock sample that has been dated at 10 million years may be called "young."
>
> —*Earth Science*, Thirteenth Edition, by Edward J. Tarbuck
> and Frederick K. Lutgens

EXPLANATION First, are there any words whose definitions are unclear to you? Do you know the meaning of *vast* or *context*, for instance? If not, using the clues in the paragraph or consulting a dictionary will help. If you're not sure what a geologist does, check the glossary in the back of the textbook. Next, is there a timeline or other visual aid on the nearby pages that will help to put the huge periods of time into perspective?

6. Annotate the Text as You Read. By circling, underlining, and writing brief notes in the margins, you will be reacting to the material and highlighting the important information. This is a critical thinking process that will help you understand and remember the material. Keeping your brain and your pen active while you read will help you stay focused and prevent your mind from wandering. An added bonus is that you will create a record of your thinking that you can return to when preparing for a test.

EXAMPLE   Notice how marking the text makes the major details stand out.

1990s rap

(2 common techniques)

In the 1990s one of the elements of rap music shifted toward the DJs or turntablists who created sounds by manipulating the turntables on which LPs were played. The most commonly used technique involves moving the record rapidly back and forth while it is being played. DJs battle each other in displays of virtuosity. They work with two turntables simultaneously, cutting in and out of the sound made by scratching, while the other LP is playing. . . .

Sampling involves the use of a short extract of a previous recording as a musical element in a new recording. The most commonly used samples are those of a recognizable riff or a catchy instrumental introduction from a song. Sung or spoken extracts can also be sampled. . . .

—*Understanding Music,* Fifth Edition,
by Jeremy Yudkin

EXPLANATION   As you read the text, did you notice that the passage describes a term, *turntablists,* and two characteristics of rap music? By circling the term and underlining its meaning, they are made visually clear. Similarly, circling the two characteristics and underlining the most important parts of their descriptions make the information stand out from the minor details. The marginal notes serve as labels for the marking. This process keeps the reader active and thinking. Plus, the annotations serve as a great aid to recall in the after-reading stage. Whether you circle, underline, make marginal notes, or use some combination of these methods depends on the material itself and your purpose for reading.

Applying All Six Thinking Strategies.   The following passage illustrates the use of the six thinking strategies. Some of the reader's thoughts appear as handwritten comments in the margins. Keep in mind that each person reacts differently. This example merely represents one reader's attempt to integrate knowledge.

EXAMPLE   Which of the six thinking strategies do the handwritten, marginal notes represent?

PREVENTING FLOODS: FOR BETTER OR WORSE?

Attempts to prevent floods might cause them? What is a levee? Like the flooding in New Orleans during Hurricane Katrina? I can see this in my mind.

Human interference with the stream system can worsen or even cause floods. A prime example is the failure of a dam or an artificial levee. These structures are built for flood protection. They are designed to contain floods of a certain magnitude. If a larger flood occurs, the dam or levee is overtopped. If the dam or levee fails or is washed out, the water behind it is released to become a flash flood. The bursting of a dam in 1889 on the Little Conemaugh River caused the devastating Johnstown, Pennsylvania, flood that took some 3,000 lives. A second dam failure occurred there again in 1977 and caused 77 fatalities.

—*Earth Science,* Thirteenth Edition, by Edward J. Tarbuck
and Frederick K. Lutgens

EXPLANATION   The handwritten comments demonstrate the reader's use of several thinking strategies: Predicting, monitoring and recognizing the need to correct, relating, and picturing. Using these strategies improves comprehension and demonstrates *metacognition*—awareness and control of the reading process.

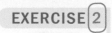 For the following passages, answer the questions and make a conscious effort to use the six strategies as you read:

1. Predict (develop hypotheses)
2. Picture (develop images)
3. Relate (link prior knowledge with new ideas)
4. Monitor (notice ongoing comprehension)
5. Use corrective strategies (fix comprehension problems)
6. Annotate (mark the text)

Passage 1

ONCE UPON A SEPTEMBER DAY

Another meeting! One after another without coming up with a proposal that would fly.

This one took place in early September and (not surprisingly) only a few people showed up—12, to be precise. And so they talked for some days and finally came up with a plan for still another meeting, eight months hence. It was hoped this would offer sufficient time to generate interest in the matter.

They also moved the location. It was not that the September site had been unpleasant—on the contrary, the facilities were quite good—but variety in meeting places might induce more individuals to attend.

They were a relatively young group; the average age was 42. The youngest was 30 and the oldest 82 and prone to nod during long meetings. Although some were lackluster in ability, most were able and would later move to high executive positions.

They were together for 116 days, taking off only Sundays and 12 other days. And you might have guessed it: During a very hot summer they were without air conditioning. In addition to the formal sessions of the entire group, much of their work was done in committee and after hours.

There was still criticism of the final proposal. It was much too short, some argued—only 4,000 words. Four months of work and only 4,000 words! It was scarcely enough to fill a few sheets of paper. But 39 of them felt it was the best they could come up with. It was good enough to sign, which they did on the 17th day of September, 1787.

And they called their proposal the Constitution of the United States.

—"Once Upon a September Day" by Thomas V. DiBacco,
The Los Angeles Times, September 28, 1983

1. What did you predict to be the purpose of the meeting? _____
2. Who did you picture as the attendees of the meeting? _____
3. The passage mentions that the site of the meeting place had been changed with the hope that more individuals would attend. Have you experienced this same problem (a meeting at which not too many people showed up)? What sort of incentives are used to induce people to attend meetings?

_____

_____

_____

4. Why do you suppose the meeting was continued so many times?

_____

_____

_____

5. Underline any part of the passage that you found confusing or that you needed to reread.

6. Did you annotate as you read? Now that you know the topic, go back and circle the clues.

Passage 2

REAL LIFE CRIME SCENE INVESTIGATION

The popular television show CSI (Crime Scene Investigation) has brought the role of the crime scene investigator to the public, creating considerable interest in forensic science. Of course, crime scene investigators require very specific training with regard to crime scene protection and the identification and preservation of evidence, and not every law enforcement agency is able to support a dedicated CSI unit. A description of the crime scene unit (CSU) is provided by Michael Weisberg:

> The CSU provides support services in the form of crime processing, fingerprint identification, and forensic photography. The CSU responds to major crime scenes to detect, preserve, document, impound and collect physical evidence. The unit assists in the identification of unknown subjects, witnesses and victims involved in criminal investigations. . . . The CSU will work closely in conjunction with the Detective Bureau in providing assistance in follow-up investigations, as well as subject apprehension and arrest. Members of the CSU may be either sworn or non-sworn.

—*Criminal Investigation: The Art and the Science,* Sixth Edition, by Michael D. Lyman

1. Have you seen television shows that feature crime scene investigation situations? Explain how your experience or lack of it affected you as you read this passage. _____

_____

_____

_____

_____

2. What is the meaning of *forensic*? _____

_____

In what way did knowing the definition affect your understanding of this passage? _____

3. Where do you think crime scene investigators receive training?

_____

_____

4. Does the crime scene unit help to catch offenders? _____

Underline anything in the passage that supports your answer.

5. Was there anything in the passage you did not understand? Write it here:

_____

6. Did you annotate to emphasize the important details?

_____

Stage Three: Recall

Learning Objective 6

Apply active recall methods after reading

Recall is your review of what you have read. Recall is self-testing and can be a silent, oral, or written recitation. When you recall, you take an additional few minutes to tell yourself what you have learned before you close the book. Poor readers tend to finish the last paragraph of an assignment, sigh with relief, and close the book without another thought. Study strategies developed by experts, however, stress the importance of a final recall or review stage. The experts emphasize that this final step improves both comprehension and memory.

As a part of monitoring your comprehension, maintain a running summary as you read. The end of an assignment is the time to give voice to this internal summary and review the material for gaps of knowledge. You can do the recall step in your head, aloud, or on paper. To recall, talk to yourself and test your understanding. Pull the material together under one central idea or generalization, and then review the relevant details and commit them to memory.

> ### Reader's Tip   React and Reflect
>
> After recalling what an author has said, evaluate its significance for you by answering the following questions:
>
> - Did I enjoy the reading? Why or why not?
> - Was the selection well written? Explain specifics.
> - Do I agree or disagree with the author? Why or why not?
> - How many of the author's ideas do I accept?

Do not neglect this last stage. From a metacognitive point of view, you are adding related ideas to existing schemata and creating new knowledge networks or "computer chips" for storage. Active recall makes a significant difference in what you retain from your reading.

How to Recall.   The recall stage of reading can be silent or voiced, organized conversation with yourself or others, or a written reorganization. What method you choose depends on the difficulty of the material or your purpose for learning. Keep in mind that the goal is self-testing. Rather than wait for the professor's inquiry, answer your own question, "What did I get from this material?"

Think About It.   What was the main point? What did you learn from each section? Do you have opinions or experiences related to this topic?

Talk About It.   Say out loud, to yourself or to someone else, what you learned from the selection. Voice your opinions, questions, and experiences.

Write About It.   If your purpose is to remember the information for the long term—for a test, perhaps—make notes on a separate sheet of paper. Use your text annotations as the basis for the notes. If your purpose is for the short term or general recall, so that you can join a discussion with friends, for example, write a one- or two-sentence summary. You might also write any questions you want to discuss about the topic.

Feel free to accept or reject ideas according to your prior knowledge and the logic of the presentation. Your response is subjective, but as a critical thinker, you should base it on what you already know and what you have just found out.

EXAMPLE   Read the following passage and decide what it is about and whether you agree or disagree with the author.   •

> What held Americans together as they set off into the 21st century was a common loyalty to a set of ideas about economic opportunities and individual liberties. Unlike such nations as Germany and Israel, where citizenship was extended automatically only to people of a certain ethnicity, the United States awarded citizenship to all those who were born within its borders, regardless of ethnicity or race. Those born elsewhere became citizens on the basis not of their past lineage but of their future commitments—of their newly sworn loyalty to the U.S. Constitution, with its guarantees of freedom and its responsibilities of citizenship.
>
> —*Created Equal: A History of the United States*,
> Fourth Edition, by Jacqueline Jones et al.
> Pearson Education, Inc.

EXPLANATION   Do you agree with the author's statement? Do Americans agree on the economic opportunities and freedoms offered by their country? Should immigrants receive these benefits? Immigration and the chance of citizenship are issues about which many people have strong feelings. Perhaps your opinions and experiences influence your response to this passage.

EXERCISE 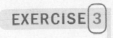 Read the following passages and decide whether you agree or disagree with their messages. You are giving your *reactions* to the ideas, so there are no right or wrong answers. Think and react.

Passage 1
GENDER DIFFERENCES

Men and women differ with respect to gossip, according to Deborah Tannen in *You Just Don't Understand: Women and Men in Conversation*. It isn't that one group gossips and the other does not. It is the subjects of their talks. "When most men talk to their friends or on the phone," Tannen says, "they may discuss what's happening in business, the stock market, the soccer match, or politics. For most women, getting together and talking about their feelings and what is happening in their lives is at the heart of friendship."

Men and women differ when it comes to lecturing and listening. Experimental studies support Tannen in finding that "men are more comfortable than women in giving information and opinions and speaking in an authoritative way to a group, whereas women are more comfortable than men in supporting others."

—*You Just Don't Understand: Women and Men in Conversation*
by Deborah Tannen

1. What is the message? _____

_____

2. Why do you agree or disagree with these assertions of gender differences on gossip, lecturing, and listening?
   (a) Gossip? _____
   (b) Lecturing? _____
   (c) Listening? _____

Passage 2
MY LIFE IS GONE: ONE CRANK USER'S STORY

Twenty-five-year-old Jennifer Smith hasn't a clue whether it is night or day. A regular user of "crank" or methamphetamine, Smith has been wide awake for five days.

On Monday night, she left her three-year-old daughter at a friend's house, promising to be back before long. Then the drug ride started. Crank produces a high that keeps the user madly active to the point of forgetting about time, ignoring food, and even neglecting children.

Now Jennifer sits on a barstool, gulping shots of bourbon in the hope that the drinks will calm her nerves. She looks around for her boyfriend, forgetting that he ditched her two days ago. She wonders, too, what happened to her purse, in which she had a child support check she hoped would pay for more drugs.

Smith strikes up a conversation with a man she has known for several years. "Crank makes you lose everything," she stammers, reaching for the rest of her bourbon.

What has she lost? The list begins with her purse and her boyfriend and includes her good looks, her job, her hopes for the future, and most important, the child she calls her "little angel."

"I'm not afraid, though," she says, shaking her head. "I've cranked for seven years. . . I'm getting pretty used to losing everything."

—*Social Problems*, Fifth Edition, by John J. Macionis
Pearson Education, Inc.

1. What is the message? _____

_____

2. Do you have any sympathy for Jennifer? Explain. _____

_____

3. Do you think of Jennifer's situation mainly as a personal problem or a social problem? Why? _____

_____

ASSESS YOUR PROGRESS AS A LEARNER

This textbook creates an artificial environment for you to learn about your own reading. Normally after reading, you do not answer ten comprehension questions and ten vocabulary questions. You read, reflect, and move on. In this book, however, the questions are provided to help you monitor your thinking. To improve your skills, reflect seriously on what you are getting right and what you are getting wrong. Making a good homework or classwork grade is part of the process, but it is not the real purpose. Understanding and improving are the goals, and they require your active participation as a learner. Assume responsibility for your own improvement.

Levels of Reading Comprehension

In order to give you more insight into your strengths and weaknesses, the comprehension questions at the end of each long reading selection in this text are labeled *main idea*, *detail*, and *inference*. These question types represent different levels of sophistication in reading that can be ranked and defined as follows.

    1. Literal—What did the author say? These are detail questions about the facts, and the answers are clearly stated within the material. This is the beginning level of reading comprehension, the least sophisticated level. You might be able to answer detail questions and still not understand the overall meaning of the passage.

    Example: Captain Thomas Hunt came to Plymouth Bay to capture Indians for the slave market. (True or False)

PERSONAL FEEDBACK) 2   Name _____

1. Why do you think students are reluctant to recall (Stage 3) what they have read?

_____

2. What have you learned in this chapter that is positive about your reading habits?

_____

_____

3. What three immediate changes would you suggest for your own reading improvement?

    a. _____

    b. _____

    c. _____

Share your responses as directed by your instructor.

2. Interpretive—What did the author mean by what was said? These are main idea and inference questions. In order to answer, you must interpret the facts along with the author's attitude, using implied meaning to make assumptions and draw conclusions. At this level, you are considering both what is stated and what is unstated in order to figure out what the author is trying to say.

Example: The author suggests that Squanto's Pawtuxet Indian tribe valued all of the following except (a) bravery, (b) endurance, (c) wealth, or (d) strength.

3. Applied—How does the author's message apply to other situations? These are questions that call for reaction, reflection, and critical thinking. This is the highest level of sophistication and involves analyzing, synthesizing, and evaluating. You are putting together what was said with what was meant and applying it to new situations and experiences. You are attempting to make wider use of what you have just learned.

Example: Explain how the cultural values, goals, and ethics of the Native Americans as illustrated by Squanto in his youth differed from those of the European settlers and thus caused conflict.

Use the questions in this book as diagnostic information. What do your responses tell you about yourself? What kinds of questions do you always answer correctly? What do your errors tell you about your reading? Learn from your mistakes and begin to categorize your own reading strengths and weaknesses. Throughout the course, refer back to previous work as a reference for your own development. Keeping records and reflecting on your own learning are essential parts of your improvement plan.

SUMMARY POINTS

1 What are the three stages of good reading? (page 34)
Stage 1: Before reading, preview to find out what the material is about.
Stage 2: During reading, integrate existing knowledge with the new information.
Stage 3: After reading, actively recall what you have learned.

2 What should I read during a preview? (page 34)
Read the introductory material, learning questions, title, headings and subheadings, special print, visual aids, and concluding summary or review. When these features are lacking, read the first paragraph, the first sentence of each major paragraph, and the last paragraph.

3 What is a schema, and why is it important? (page 36)
A schema is the skeleton of knowledge in your mind on a particular subject. Usually, readers have several schemata surrounding a topic. They are important because what we already know allows us to relate and link to the new material, thus understanding and remembering it better.

4 What is *metacognition*, and why is it important? (page 38)
Metacognition is the awareness and control of the reading and thinking process. It is important because of the control it provides. Awareness of comprehension problems enables the reader to do something about them, and awareness of good comprehension causes readers to repeat successful methods.

5 How can I integrate existing knowledge with the new information during Stage 2? (page 38)

Apply the six thinking strategies that good readers use: predict, picture, relate, monitor your understanding, correct gaps in understanding, and annotate the text.

6 What active recall methods will help me remember the material? (page 44)

Think about it. Talk about it. Write about it. Use your annotations to review.

COLLABORATIVE) PROBLEM SOLVING

Form a five-member group and select one of the following activities. Brainstorm and then outline your major points. Choose a member to present the group findings to the class.

➤ Make a list of five questions about your college at the literal level.

➤ Make a list of five questions about your college at the interpretive level.

➤ Make a list of five questions about your college at the applied level.

➤ Explain how recalling, connecting, and reacting help you remember what you have read.

SELECTION

1

SELECTION 1 Criminal Justice   MyReadingLab™

Visit Chapter 2: Stages of Reading in MyReadingLab to complete the Selection 1 activities.

"The good of the people is the chief law."

—Cicero (106–43 BCE)

Psychological theories of criminal behavior focus on personality traits and behavior. Crime-control methods based on psychological views center on treating individuals with appropriate therapy to overcome their criminal tendencies. These methods rely on some measure of "dangerousness," or how likely the person is to do harm. Several important issues surround such psychological views. Should a mentally ill person be treated by the courts in the same way that a sane person is treated? What determines whether or not a person is insane? Can a mentally ill person who commits a crime be "cured" so that he or she can function safely in normal society?

THINKING BEFORE READING

Preview the selection for clues to content. Activate your schema and anticipate what you will learn. Predict the author's ideas and determine your purpose for reading. Think!

Have you heard news stories about people who have committed crimes and claimed that they were insane at the time?

What is the definition of *insanity*?

Why might society hesitate to punish mentally ill offenders in the same way that it punishes sane individuals?

This selection will probably tell me _____.

VOCABULARY PREVIEW

Are you familiar with these words and figures of speech?

abruptly	incarceration	took a dive	schizophrenia	severity
competent	acquittal	alluded	surmised	psychosis

Is there a difference between *surmised* and *inferred*?

Do you see a familiar word part in *psychosis* that might hint at the meaning?

Your instructor may choose to give a brief vocabulary review before or after reading.

THINKING DURING READING

As you read, use the six thinking strategies of a good reader: predict, picture, relate, monitor, correct, and annotate. Mentally answer the questions in the margins as you read.

WAS ERIC CLARK INSANE OR JUST TROUBLED?

Have you had an experience so alarming that it seemed unreal?

The phone roused Terry Clark from sleep. She eyed the clock: 5 A.M. Who could be calling at this hour?

"Flagstaff Police Department," a voice announced abruptly. The next minutes and hours would pass like a slow-moving horror film where the evil emerges bit by bit.

> ## Reader's TIP — Reading and Studying Criminal Justice
>
> - Identify criminal acts in legal terms. Make lists to commit to memory.
> - Distinguish between the types of crimes and categories of criminals. Use charts to form groups.
> - Know the legal behaviors and responsibilities required for making an arrest and gathering evidence. Make timelines.
> - Understand the processes of the courts and the sequencing of legal actions. Create a flowchart for a visual display.
> - Relate possible legal decisions and police actions to the balance of police powers and democratic freedoms.

5   At first, investigators told her only that a policeman had been shot. She heard a name, Officer Jeff Moritz. He was called to the neighborhood after residents reported a pickup circling round and round, blaring loud music.

    Her son Gentry's pickup sat abandoned—driver's side door flung open, keys in the ignition, a Dr. Dre CD in the player—next to the sidewalk where the police officer had 10 died.

    Her son was the prime suspect. Not Gentry, though, who had been at home in bed, safe. Her other son, Eric. The one who had been a star football player and a good student with dreams.

    The one who just two months earlier had called his mother and father aliens.

SLAYING SHOCKED TOWN

Whose side would the town probably take?

15 What happened in those early morning hours of June 21, 2000, left an entire town in shock. The victim was the only police officer ever killed in the line of duty in this mountain community north of Phoenix.

    He was a caring cop who cut firewood for the handicapped and bought burgers for hungry transients he arrested. He was a husband and father with one young son and a 20 second on the way.

    The accused was a 17-year-old high school senior who had a history of marijuana use and had been arrested two months earlier for drunken driving and drug possession. Police had found two dozen hits of LSD in his car.

    A portrait quickly emerged of a drug-crazed teen with no regard for life. But as the 25 facts slowly surfaced so did a different picture of Eric Michael Clark—that of a decent boy from a stable family who had descended into schizophrenia.

    With this revelation came a question: How do you measure justice when a killer is a mentally ill kid?

What was the verdict?

    It took three years for Eric Clark to be found competent to stand trial. His lawyers 30 pushed for a verdict of "guilty except insane," meaning incarceration in a psychiatric facility. Instead, a judge found him guilty of first-degree, intentional murder and sentenced him to life in prison, where treatment isn't assured.

What were the legal issues in the U.S. Supreme Court case? 35

On Wednesday, the U.S. Supreme Court is scheduled to take up the case of *Clark v. Arizona* and the issue of just how difficult states can make it for criminal defendants to prove insanity.

It's the first time the court has dealt with a direct constitutional challenge to the insanity defense since lawmakers around the country imposed new restrictions following John Hinckley's acquittal by reason of insanity in the 1981 shooting of President Reagan.

40 "When is it just to punish, or not?" says Richard Bonnie, director of the Institute of Law, Psychiatry and Public Policy at the University of Virginia. "There are some cases where a person was so mentally disturbed at the time of the offense that it would be inhumane and morally objectionable to convict and punish them."

SIGNPOSTS OF MENTAL ILLNESS

Looking back now, Terry Clark remembers things, little things, and wonders when it all started.

What were the signs of mental illness? 45

Eric was a gifted athlete who played soccer, baseball, basketball, football. As a running back at Flagstaff High, he was one of the young stars selected to play varsity and dreamed of becoming a professional athlete. Then he lost interest in sports.

He had been popular—a homecoming court nominee—but his friends quit calling. His grades, usually As and Bs, took a dive.

50 On June 21, 1999, Terry and her husband, Dave, had their son admitted to Aspen Hill, a local mental health facility. He'd abandoned his car on a road.

At Aspen Hill, Eric tested positive for marijuana, and Terry wondered whether drugs had triggered his behavior. But doctors alluded to something else—the possibility of schizophrenia. With no mental illness on either side of the family. Terry pushed that idea aside.

55 Eric seemed to improve and she had him discharged after only three days. "He's getting better," Terry convinced herself. He got worse.

That fall, Eric quit school. He became obsessed with Y2K, took his dad's debit card and charged $1,700 worth of survival gear. He wore layers upon layers of clothing and carried his possessions in a garbage bag.

60 When January 1, 2000, came and went, Eric's mood improved. He went back to high school. "He's getting better," Terry thought again—until Eric started mentioning "them."

That April, Eric suddenly referred to her as an alien. Eric called his father an alien, too. "If you'd go get some tools," he told them matter-of-factly, "I'd show you."

Terry now believed the doctors were right about schizophrenia. She was relieved
65 when, that same month, Eric was arrested on drunken driving and drug charges; she thought that would lead to getting help. But authorities decided to postpone prosecution until Eric turned 18 later in the year.

She and Dave searched for counselors, but Eric refused to go. Terry left messages at treatment facilities that were never returned.

70 On June 19, 2000, Eric called his mother an alien again. "How would you like to be me," he said, "and never know who your real mother is?"

Terry contacted her lawyer and begged him to convince the county to pursue the drug charges. Prosecutors still wanted to wait until Eric was an adult, so he'd face longer prison time if convicted.

INTENT OR INSANITY?

75 Investigators surmise that sometime after 1:30 A.M. on June 21, 2000, Eric made his way home, sneaked into his brother Gentry's bedroom, took his keys and left in Gentry's truck.

What happened after that, and why, no one can know for certain; Eric never talked about the events of that morning.

At the 2003 trial, prosecutors and defense attorneys agreed that Eric suffered from
80 paranoid schizophrenia and was mentally ill. But legal insanity is another matter; Arizona law spells out its limited use as a defense.

What are the arguments for the prosecution?

"A person may be found guilty except insane if, at the time of the commission of the criminal act, the person was afflicted with a mental disease or defect of such severity that the person did not know the criminal act was wrong," the law states.

85 The Prosecutor, Assistant Attorney General David Powell, argued Eric did know. "Officer Moritz walked into . . . an ice-cold ambush," he said at trial.

What are the arguments for the defense?

Defense lawyers insisted Eric's psychosis was so severe he was incapable of hatching such a plan.

They noted that two months after the shooting, Eric called his parents from jail and
90 told them Flagstaff was a "platinum city" inhabited by 50,000 aliens. Before hanging up, he added: "The only thing that will stop aliens are bullets."

In his appeal to the U.S. Supreme Court, lawyer David Goldberg asserts that Arizona law is so restrictive that it violates a mentally ill defendant's right to a fair trial.

For one, he says, Arizona law prohibited the trial court from considering Eric's mental
95 illness in weighing whether he intentionally killed the police officer. Testimony about his mental illness was not permitted until the second phase of the two-part trial.

Goldberg also argues that Arizona's right-wrong test is too narrow in determining legal insanity. Eric might have known that killing was wrong in the abstract, Goldberg says, but if he believed Moritz was an alien, "he didn't understand the nature of what he was doing."

100 The Supreme Court's decision, expected later this year, could also mean a retrial for Eric Clark, something the Moritz family would see as unjust.

"An angry young man who sets out to kill a cop, or anybody else, ought to be locked up for the rest of his life," says the victim's father, Dan Moritz, a psychologist who questions whether Clark actually is a paranoid schizophrenic.

105 For the Clarks, a new trial would mean a chance for their son to receive psychiatric care.

"Lock him up for his crime," Terry Clark says, "but treat him for his mental illness, please. Eric didn't choose to be mentally ill. It chose him."

(1,361 words)

—Pauline Arrillaga, "Was Eric Clark Insane or Just Troubled?"
The Associated Press, April 15, 2006. Copyright © 2006 by The
Associated Press. All rights reserved. Reprinted with permission.

Author's note: Eric Clark's conviction was upheld by the U.S. Supreme Court.

THINKING AND WRITING AFTER READING

RECALL Self-test your understanding.

Your instructor may choose to give you a brief comprehension review.

REACT Do you agree more strongly with Eric Clark's mother or with Officer Moritz's family? Why? _____

_____

_____

REFLECT Have you seen a movie or a television show about people who have a mental illness? Do you know anyone with a mental illness? What kind of therapy or treatment did they receive? Was it successful? _____

_____

_____

THINK CRITICALLY If you had been on the jury in Eric Clark's trial, how do you think you would have decided? _____

_____

_____

THINK AND WRITE Imagine that you are either the lawyer defending Eric Clark or the one prosecuting him. Write the main arguments that you would present to support your case. _____

_____

_____

EXTENDED WRITING Develop the main arguments that you listed above into a persuasive essay. Your purpose is to convince a jury that Eric Clark is either guilty or not guilty of first-degree murder. Use the facts presented in the article as you make your case.

Interpret THE QUOTE

Now that you have finished reading the selection, "Was Eric Clark Insane or Just Troubled?" go back to the beginning of the selection and read the opening quote again. How is the "good of the people" best served? By giving harsh sentences that do not allow for treatment of mentally ill criminals or by giving sentences that do allow for treatment? Explain your answer on a separate sheet of paper.

Name ————————————————

Date ————————————————

COMPREHENSION QUESTIONS

Answer the following with *a, b, c,* or *d,* or fill in the blank. In order to help you analyze your strengths and weaknesses, the question types are indicated.

Main Idea ———— 1. The best statement of the main idea of this selection is

   a. Eric Clark's case involved Flagstaff's first death of a police officer in the line of duty.

   b. Eric Clark's case highlights the difficulty of determining how the law should be applied to a mentally ill person who commits a crime.

   c. Eric Clark stole a car and murdered a police officer.

   d. People who commit murder should be punished in the same way, whether or not they are insane.

Detail ———— 2. Which of the following statements describes Eric Clark before signs of mental illness appeared?

   a. He had a difficult childhood and was often in trouble at school.

   b. He was a quiet, sweet child who was shy in social situations.

   c. He was a poor student who struggled in school.

   d. He was a well-liked athlete.

Inference ———— 3. At about what age did Eric Clark begin to show signs of mental illness?

   a. as an infant

   b. age 5

   c. age 16

   d. age 18

Detail ———— 4. When Eric Clark was tried in Arizona, the court

   a. found him not guilty by reason of insanity.

   b. sentenced him to treatment in a mental health facility.

   c. pronounced him guilty and sentenced him to death.

   d. found him guilty and sentenced him to life in prison.

Inference ———— 5. The information in this selection suggests that

   a. the laws in Eric Clark's state are more harsh toward mentally ill offenders than in other states.

   b. the laws determining punishment for mentally ill offenders are the same throughout the United States.

   c. the laws defining insanity are the same in all states.

   d. the legal definition of insanity is very clear.

Detail _____ 6. The early signs of Eric Clark's mental illness included

a. a history of marijuana use.

b. seeing visions of people and things that were not there.

c. violent acts against his classmates.

d. loss of interest in athletics, friends, and school.

Inference _____ 7. The author suggests that the shooting of President Reagan by John Hinckley

a. raised questions about whether insanity is an acceptable defense.

b. had no bearing on Eric Clark's case.

c. resulted in an incorrect punishment for Hinckley.

d. made it clear that it is inhumane to convict and punish someone who is mentally ill.

Answer the following with *T* (true) or *F* (false).

Detail _____ 8. Eric and his brother Gentry were both involved in the murder.

Inference _____ 9. Eric had been arrested before the murder of Officer Moritz.

Detail _____ 10. The U.S. Supreme Court ruled in favor of Eric Clark.

VOCABULARY

Answer the following with *a*, *b*, *c*, or *d* for the word or phrase that best defines the boldface word used in the selection. The number in parentheses indicates the line of the passage in which the word appears. In addition to the context clues, use a dictionary to more precisely define the technical terms.

_____ 1. "a voice announced **abruptly**" (3)

a. quietly

b. bluntly

c. easily

d. prettily

_____ 2. "to be found **competent**" (29)

a. dead

b. sick

c. capable

d. unable

_____ 3. "meaning **incarceration**" (30)

a. freedom

b. therapy

c. imprisonment

d. hospitalization

_____ 4. "John Hinckley's **acquittal**" (38)

a. judgment of not guilty

b. terrible act

c. personality

d. youth

_____ 5. "As and Bs **took a dive**" (49)

a. improved

b. went swimming

c. were earned

d. got worse

_____ 6. "But doctors **alluded** to" (53)

a. referred

b. demanded

c. allowed

d. tried

_____ 7. "the possibility of
schizophrenia" (53–54)

    a. a kind of cancer
    b. a mental illness
    c. drug addiction
    d. heart disease

_____ 9. "defect of such
severity" (83)

    a. lightness
    b. evil
    c. seriousness
    d. unimportance

_____ 8. "Investigators
surmise" (75)

    a. are sure
    b. state
    c. testify
    d. infer

_____ 10. "Eric's **psychosis** was so
severe" (87)

    a. serious mental illness
    b. jail time
    c. punishment
    d. reaction

Your instructor may choose to give a brief vocabulary review.

ASSESS YOUR LEARNING

Review questions that you did not understand, found confusing, or answered incorrectly. Seek clarification. Indicate beside each item the source of your confusion and notice the question type. Make notes beside confusing vocabulary items to help you remember them. Use your textbook as a learning tool.

Visit Chapter 2: Stages of Reading in MyReadingLab to complete the Selection 2 activities.

"I have never had to face anything that could overwhelm the native optimism and stubborn perseverance I was blessed with."

—**Sonia Sotomayor, Justice of the U.S. Supreme Court**

Dr. Calvin Mackie is a motivational speaker, author, inventor, and former professor of mechanical engineering at Tulane University. He began college in developmental reading because of weak test scores and went on to earn two bachelor's degrees, a master's degree, and a doctorate in mechanical engineering.

THINKING BEFORE READING

Preview the selection for clues to its content. Because this essay does not have headings, your preview should include quickly reading the first paragraph, the first sentence of each paragraph, and the last paragraph. The title, background information on the author, and marginal notes will also help prepare you for a thorough reading. Predict the author's ideas and determine your purpose for reading. Think!

What does the title suggest about the author's message? What kind of race do you think he will discuss?

Anticipate the author's ideas and determine your purpose for reading. Think!

I'll read this to find out. _____.

VOCABULARY PREVIEW

Are you familiar with these words?

myopic	invincibility	perseverance	matriculation	marathon
emulate	tribulations	adversity	cherish	swiftest

Does *myopic* refer to a problem with vision?

What superpowers make Superman *invincible*?

When did you *matriculate* into college?

Your instructor may choose to give a brief vocabulary review before or after reading.

THINKING DURING READING

As you read, use the six thinking strategies of a good reader: predict, picture, relate, monitor, correct, and annotate. Mentally answer the questions in the margins as you read.

Reader's TIP — Reading and Studying an Essay

Ask yourself the following questions:

- What is the theme, thesis, or main idea?
- How do the details and examples develop the theme?
- How does the title aid in understanding the essay?
- What is the author's attitude toward the subject?
- What images contribute to the theme of the essay?
- What is the conclusion? How is it significant?

RUN THE RACE . . . IT'S YOURS TO RUN

While working on my doctoral degree, I learned many different aspects of fluid dynamics, material processing, and hydrodynamic stability, but more importantly I learned a lot about myself and about life. The myopic view which accompanies our youth presents us with a Superman-type attitude of invincibility that is assisting in our daily defeat academically, socially, and psychologically. Education is a lifelong process that does not end with the presentation of a sheepskin after a finite time of instruction and examinations. After 10 years of college and four technical degrees, I had the virtues of sacrifice and perseverance instilled in me. Matriculation at two institutions has taught me that life is a race; not a 100-yard dash, but a marathon with hills and hurdles that challenge you physically and mentally. To run and win a marathon, one must continue to train, because the course is never the same, and the challenges are forever increasing.

Real model not a role model? 15

In any race, inspiration, endurance and models are needed. I am not speaking of a role model but a real model, someone who has run the race and fought the battles and won! Presently, we live in an information age where corporate takeovers and downsizing are staples of Corporate America's culture. Advances in computers, communications, and transportation are transforming national markets into global markets, and the number of employees necessary to perform identical tasks of 10 years ago is continuously decreasing. At the end of the day, at the end of the race, who will be the last one standing? Real models of perseverance, strength, and character are needed not only to demonstrate how to run the race of life, but also to present us with functional, honest reasons why we should run this race.

Impressive accomplishment! 30

Who is my real model? 35

Today many of our youth are choosing not to run in any race. Many of us are questioning the necessity or validity of a college degree or post-baccalaureate studies. When I graduated from high school with an 800 Scholastic Aptitude Test (SAT) score and began Morehouse College in remedial reading, there were not too many people betting that four years later I would graduate number one in mathematics, number five in the graduating class, magna cum laude, and a member of Phi Beta Kappa National Honor Society. Well, as a little "happy-headed boy" growing up in the inner city of New Orleans, I spent end less hours searching for someone, a real model, that I could emulate, model myself after, and call my hero. After years of searching, I found a person whom I could hold responsible for the successful course that my life has taken. This man took me, unformed and shapeless, and molded me into a young man who is physically and psychologically prepared to take on the trials and tribulations that life has in store for me. This remarkable person, this remarkable man, is my father. Through his life experiences, he transformed my line of thinking, value system, and motivation.

40 The son of a sharecropper and one of 14 children, he could not attend school regularly because he had to pick cotton from sun up to sun down to help support his family in St. Francisville, Louisiana. Although he only completed junior high school, he is the co-owner of a successful business. He often tells me how each day on his way to the fields he would cry and pray that tomorrow he would be able to attend school. We often laugh together when he tells me that the only time he made an "A" or a "B" in school 45 was when he received an "A" for absent or a "B" for boy. Therefore, when I think of his accomplishments and all of the adversity he had to overcome, I realize that the seemingly impossible is actually possible. He has made me realize that an education is something that everyone does not have the opportunity to obtain. It is an opportunity that all of us should cherish! Over the years, people often wondered why I study so hard and so long. 50 The reason is that a long time ago I realized that I am not attending school just for Calvin Mackie; I am attending school for my mother, my father, and everyone else who did not have that opportunity.

Every Sunday, I anxiously wait for his call to inspire me to take on the world and all of its challenges. No, during our conversations his subjects and verbs do not always agree. 55 No, he does not have a M.D., Ph.D., J.D. or D.D.S., but he is the greatest man that I know and love. So, this is one man's story, proof that the race of life is not won by the swiftest or the strongest, the smartest or the slickest, but by those who endure to the end. So straight from the heart, brothers and sisters, run the race and shun not the struggle, for you have been the lucky ones chosen to run. Run the race of life—for it's yours to run!

(834 words)

—From *The Black Collegian* by Calvin Mackie, PhD

THINKING AND WRITING AFTER READING

RECALL Self-test your understanding.

Your instructor may choose to give you a brief comprehension review.

REACT Dr. Mackie's accomplishments are impressive. Does his story inspire you to achieve your goals? Why or why not? _____

REFLECT What qualities do you have that will help you achieve your goals? _____
_____

THINK CRITICALLY Dr. Mackie's father is his "real model." What qualities do you think an inspirational "real model" must have? _____
_____.

THINK AND WRITE In Chapter 1, you were challenged to name your career and college goals. Now consider the obstacles that might get in your way. What are they, and how will you handle them?

Obstacle	Solution
_____	_____
_____	_____
_____	_____

EXTENDED WRITING   Think of a time when you struggled with something and overcame the difficulty. Write a letter of advice and inspiration to a fictional person who is facing the same or a similar problem.

Interpret THE QUOTE

Go back to the beginning of the selection and read the opening quote again. Do you think that optimism—a belief that things will turn out well—and perseverance can overcome any problem that a person might face?

Name _____

Date _____

COMPREHENSION QUESTIONS

Answer the following with *a*, *b*, *c*, or *d*, or fill in the blank. In order to help you analyze your strengths and weaknesses, the question types are indicated.

Main Idea _____ 1. The best statement of the main idea of this selection is

    a. Dr. Mackie's father did not have a college education, but he became a successful businessman.

    b. With inspiration, endurance, and a "real model," you can succeed in the race of life.

    c. Every person faces difficulties in life.

    d. Dr. Mackie's father provided inspiration and confidence for his son.

Detail _____ 2. Dr. Mackie graduated college with what distinction?

    a. first in his graduating class

    b. fourth in his graduating class

    c. fifth in his graduating class

    d. last in his graduating class

Detail _____ 3. How long was Dr. Mackie in college and graduate school?

    a. four years

    b. five years

    c. eight years

    d. ten years

Inference _____ 4. Based on the selection, which of the following would Dr. Mackie consider to be the best "real model"?

    a. a person who struggled in school and graduated

    b. the owner of a company handed down through his or her family

    c. the smartest person in the high school class

    d. a good looking, successful teen idol

Main Idea _____ 5. The main point of the second paragraph is:

    a. Advances in technology are reducing the number of jobs available.

    b. Corporate takeovers and downsizing are part of corporate America.

    c. Models of strength and character are needed to show how and why to try our best.

    d. Be the last one standing at the end of the race.

Detail _____ 6. Dr. Mackie's father finished which level of schooling?

    a. fourth grade

    b. high school

    c. one year of college

    d. junior high school

Inference _____ 7. We can infer from the selection that

    a. Dr. Mackie found that high school was fairly easy.

    b. Dr. Mackie was not a strong student in high school.

    c. Dr. Mackie found that college was fairly easy.

    d. Dr. Mackie's greatest academic strength was reading.

Answer the following with *T* (true) or *F* (false).

Inference _____ 8. Dr. Mackie knew as a young child that his father was his best "real model."

Detail _____ 9. Dr. Mackie scored 800 on the SAT.

Detail _____ 10. Dr. Mackie was a member of Phi Beta Kappa.

VOCABULARY

Answer the following with *a, b, c,* or *d* for the word or phrase that best defines the boldface word used in the selection. The number in parentheses indicates the line of the passage in which the word appears. In addition to the context clues, use a dictionary to more precisely define the technical terms.

_____ 1. "the **myopic** view" (4)

    a. farsighted

    b. nearsighted

    c. optimistic

    d. immature

_____ 2. "attitude of **invincibility**" (5)

    a. unable to be defeated

    b. weakness

    c. uncertainty

    d. snobbery

_____ 3. "presentation of a **sheepskin**" (7)

    a. coat

    b. grade

    c. rug

    d. diploma

_____ 4. "sacrifice and **perseverance**" (9–10)

    a. loyalty

    b. kindness

    c. determination

    d. honesty

_____ 5. "**Matriculation** at two institutions" (10)

    a. failure

    b. admission

    c. success

    d. graduation

_____ 6. a **marathon** with hills (11)

    a. short run

    b. easy task

    c. 100-yard dash

    d. long-distance race

_____ 7. "model that I could **emulate**" (32)

    a. admire

    b. respect

    c. love

    d. follow

_____ 8. "**adversity** he had to overcome" (46)

    a. hatred

    b. hardships

    c. prejudice

    d. disabilities

_____ 9. "all of us should **cherish**" (49)

a. attack
b. fear
c. treasure
d. respect

_____ 10. "won by the **swiftest**" (56)

a. most determined
b. smartest
c. strongest
d. fastest

Your instructor may choose to give a brief vocabulary review.

ASSESS YOUR LEARNING

Review questions that you did not understand, found confusing, or answered incorrectly. Seek clarification. Indicate beside each item the source of your confusion and notice the question type. Make notes beside confusing vocabulary items to help you remember them. Use your textbook as a learning tool.

SELECTION 3 Environmental Science   MyReadingLab™

Visit Chapter 2: Stages of Reading in MyReadingLab to complete the Selection 3 activities and Building Background Knowledge video activity.

"I am only one, but still I am one. I cannot do everything, but still I can do something. I will not refuse to do something I can do."

—Helen Keller

According to the New York State Department of Environmental Conservation, nearly 2.5 billion bottles of water a year are sold in that state. That's enough to reach the moon if they were stacked end to end. The petroleum used to make these bottles equals enough gasoline to fuel 120,000 automobiles for a year. Nationally, only 10% of plastic water bottles are recycled. Of course, we use many other plastic products every day, too—car bodies, shoes, disposable cups, fast-food containers, grocery bags—to name just a few. What happens to these items when we're through with them? What might be done to reduce plastic waste?

THINKING BEFORE READING

Preview the selection for clues to content. What do you already know about recycling plastic items? Activate your prior knowledge. Anticipate the author's ideas and your purpose for reading. Think!

What plastic items do you use regularly?

Do you recycle any of the plastic materials you use? Why or why not?

What are the benefits of recycling plastic?

I'll read this to find out _____

BUILDING BACKGROUND KNOWLEDGE — VIDEO

Bottled Water, Wasted Energy?

To prepare for reading Selection 3, answer the questions below. Then, watch a video that examines the effects of bottled water on the environment.

How does your tap water compare in taste to bottled water?

Do you believe that bottled water is safer than tap water?

How would you feel about giving up bottled water to cut back on the amount of plastic waste in the environment?

This video helped me _____.

VOCABULARY PREVIEW

Are you familiar with these words?

memorable	disposable	recycling	identification	surrounded
voluntary	economical	density	manufacturers	consumers

Does *recycling* always mean melting and making something new?

Is something *economical* if it is inexpensive?

Are you a *consumer* of plastic?

Your instructor may choose to give a brief vocabulary review before or after reading.

THINKING DURING READING

As you read, use the six thinking strategies of a good reader: predict, picture, relate, monitor, correct, and annotate. Mentally answer the questions in the margins as you read.

Reader's TIP   Reading and Studying Science

- Master a concept by explaining it in your own words.
- Draw your own scientific models and diagram the processes to reinforce learning them.
- Use illustrations as a reading and review tool before exams.
- Use chapter summaries as study checklists to be sure you have reviewed all the chapter material.
- Think like a scientist at the textbook Web site by participating in virtual research activities.
- Use mnemonics to memorize. For example—**M**any **P**eople **F**ind **P**arachuting **A**larming—to remember the five kingdoms, which are Monera, Protista, Fungi, Plantae, and Animalia.
- Know the theories that you are applying in the lab and their significance.
- Blend lecture, lab, and textbook notes.

PLASTICS

Why would someone advise plastics as a future career in 1967?

The 1967 film *The Graduate* was filled with unforgettable lines. One of the most memorable was advice offered to a young Dustin Hoffman, whose character was trying to decide what to do with his life.

Adult offering advice: I just want to say one word to you—just one word—

5   Hoffman: Yes sir.

Adult offering advice: Are you listening?

Hoffman: Yes sir, I am.

Adult offering advice: Plastics.

Today we're surrounded by plastics. We couldn't live without them. And they're so
10   cheap we use them to make disposable products—water bottles, picnic cups, grocery bags, milk jugs—the list goes on and on. We throw away so much plastic that many cities have recycling programs. But recycling plastic isn't as simple as just melting it down and forming it into something new. There are many *types* of plastics. You can't simply mix one with another and expect to get something usable.

PLASTIC IDENTIFICATION CODES

15   That's why the Society of the Plastics Industry developed plastic identification codes. Most plastic containers fall into one of six categories. Each category has a name and a number. It's the number that shows up on containers, surrounded by three arrows forming a triangle. In most cases you'll find it near the bottom center of a container. Using identification codes was voluntary when they were first introduced. But today most states
20   require it. The codes make it *much* easier to sort plastics.

Does my state require it?

The seven different identification codes for plastics. Code seven is used when nothing else fits.

RECYCLING PLASTICS

But just because plastics are sorted properly doesn't mean they can be recycled. Some types are economical to recycle. Others aren't. Plastic number one—polyethylene terephthalate—is easy to recycle. Water and soda bottles are commonly made from it. Plastic number two—high density polyethylene—is also pretty good. It's found in milk
25   and laundry detergent jugs, and it's often recycled into plastic lumber and made into decks or park benches.

Plastic number five—polypropylene—isn't so easy to recycle. It's used for yogurt and margarine tubs because it handles grease and chemicals so well. Disposable dishes are made of plastic number six—polystyrene. It's also used to make Styrofoam products like
30   packing peanuts and insulated cups. Some cities recycle number one and two plastics, but they ask residents to sort out and throw away the other numbers because there's no recycler the city can sell them to. They go to the landfill with all the other waste. Plastic manufacturers and consumers are aware that some plastics are harder to recycle than

Which types can I recycle?

others, but solving the problem's not as easy as using only recyclable plastics. Different
35 plastics have different properties. The plastic used to make a soda bottle may not be good
for making forks and knives.

Is this a promising field for today's college graduates?

So engineers keep looking for improved plastics—plastics that do their job and aren't
bad for the environment. Today, we might want to give not one, but two words of advice
to the graduate: *better* plastics.

(480 words)

—"Plastics" from Houston Public Radio's *Engines of
Our Ingenuity* by E. Andrew Boyd. Reprinted
with the permission of E. Andrew Boyd.

WHAT DO THE CODES MEAN?

The Product Identification Code was introduced by the Society of the Plastics Industry,
Inc. which provides a uniform system for the identification of different polymer types
and helps recycling companies to separate different plastics for reprocessing. Manufacturers of plastic products are required to use PIC labels in some countries/regions and can
voluntarily mark their products with the PIC where there are no requirements. Consumers
can identify the plastic types based on the codes usually found at the base or at the side
of the plastic products, including food/chemical packaging and containers. The PIC is
usually not present on packaging films, as it is not practical to collect and recycle most of
this type of waste.

Plastic Identification Code	Type of Plastic Polymer	Properties	Common Packaging Applications
01 PET	Polyethylene terephthalate (PET, PETE)	Clarity, strength, toughness, barrier to gas and moisture	Soft drink, water, and salad dressing bottles; peanut butter and jam jars
02 PE-HD	High density polyethylene (HDPE)	Stiffness, strength, toughness, resistance to moisture, permeability to gas	Water pipes, hula hoop rings, five-gallon buckets, milk, juice, and water bottles; the occasional shampoo/toiletry bottle
03 PVC	Polyvinyl chloride (PVC)	Versatility, ease of blending, strength, toughness	Blister packaging for nonfood items; cling films for nonfood use. Not used for food packaging, as the plasticisers needed to make natively rigid PVC flexible are usually toxic. Nonpackaging uses are electrical cable insulation, rigid piping, vinyl records.
04 PE-LD	Low-density polyethylene (LDPE)	Ease of processing, strength, toughness, flexibility, ease of sealing, barrier to moisture	Frozen food bags; squeezable bottles, e.g., honey, mustard; cling films; flexible container lids
05 PP	Polypropylene (PP)	Strength; toughness; resistance to heat, chemicals, grease, and oil; versatile; barrier to moisture	Reusable microwaveable ware, kitchenware, yogurt containers, margarine tubs, microwaveable disposable take-away containers, disposable cups and plates
06 PS	Polystyrene (PS)	Versatility, clarity, easily formed	Egg cartons; packing peanuts; disposable cups, plates, trays, and cutlery; disposable take-away containers
07 O	Other (often polycarbonate or ABS)	Dependent on polymers or combination of polymers	Beverage bottles; baby milk bottles; nonpackaging uses for polycarbonate: compact discs; "unbreakable" glazing; electronic apparatus housings

Based on resin identification codes developed by the Society of the Plastics Industry, 1988.

THINKING AND WRITING AFTER READING

RECALL Self-test your understanding.

Your instructor may choose to give you a brief comprehension review.

REACT Does this article convince you that recycling plastic items is good practice? Why or why not? _____

_____

REFLECT How do your habits contribute to helping or harming the environment?

_____

THINK CRITICALLY There are costs involved in recycling efforts. Are you willing to pay extra for your city to recycle the plastic items that you discard? Why or why not?

_____

THINK AND WRITE Now that you have read the article and the chart, examine the list of plastic items that you made before reading and add to it any materials you regularly use that you missed. Next, list the items that you are willing to recycle or even do without. _____

_____

EXTENDED WRITING Using the lists that you made, write an article that could be published in your college newspaper. First, describe the kinds of materials that you and other students use frequently. Next, suggest ways in which recycling could be encouraged on your campus or in your city.

Interpret THE QUOTE

Go back to the beginning of the selection and read the opening quote again. What can individuals do to protect the environment? What can you do?

Name _____

Date _____

COMPREHENSION QUESTIONS

Answer the following with *a, b, c,* or *d,* or fill in the blank. In order to help you analyze your strengths and weaknesses, the question types are indicated.

Main Idea   _____ 1. The best statement of the main idea of this selection is

    a. A career in developing different plastics is a promising choice for a college graduate.
    b. People should recycle plastic waste to better protect the environment.
    c. There are seven identification codes for plastics.
    d. Plastic identification codes allow for more effective recycling efforts.

Detail   _____ 2. Soft drink bottles are made of this type of plastic.

    a. polyethylene terephthalate
    b. polyvinyl chloride
    c. low density polyethylene
    d. polystyrene

Detail   _____ 3. According to the article and chart, which of the following items is most difficult to recycle?

    a. milk jugs
    b. salad dressing bottles
    c. disposable dishes
    d. water pipes

Inference   _____ 4. We can infer from the article that there are fewer recyclers for some plastic items because _____.

    a. the cost of recycling them is too high to be economical
    b. not enough people are interested in recycling those items
    c. citizens have not requested that their cities begin recycling those items
    d. people do not use many of those items

Main Idea   _____ 5. Which of the following best describes the topic of this article?

    a. plastics
    b. plastic identification codes
    c. reasons to recycle plastic items
    d. plastic recycling programs

Detail   _____ 6. The chart explains that this plastic is toxic.

    a. HDPE
    b. LDPE
    c. PET
    d. PVC

SELECTION 3

Inference _____ 7. We can infer from the selection that _____.

    a. only major cities can afford to have recycling programs

    b. some cities sponsor recycling programs

    c. all cities in the United States are required to have recycling programs

    d. cities should sponsor recycling programs

Answer the following with *T* (true) or *F* (false).

Inference _____ 8. One should not store water in a container made of polyvinyl chloride.

Detail _____ 9. According to the article, most states now require the use of identification codes on plastic items.

Detail _____ 10. The plastic identification codes were developed by the U.S. government.

VOCABULARY

Answer the following with *a, b, c,* or *d* for the word or phrase that best defines the boldface word used in the selection. The number in parentheses indicates the line of the passage in which the word appears. In addition to the context clues, use a dictionary to more precisely define the technical terms.

_____ 1. "most **memorable** advice" (1–2)

    a. valuable

    b. unforgettable

    c. surprising

    d. often heard

_____ 2. "make **disposable** products" (10)

    a. throw-away

    b. unusable

    c. inexpensive

    d. practical

_____ 3. "**recycling** programs" (12)

    a. natural

    b. environmental

    c. cleaning

    d. treatment for further use

_____ 4. "**identification** codes" (15)

    a. legal

    b. pass

    c. labeling

    d. restricted

_____ 5. "**surrounded** by three arrows" (17)

    a. marked

    b. enclosed

    c. underlined

    d. defined

_____ 6. "using codes was **voluntary**" (19)

    a. permissible

    b. preferable

    c. impossible

    d. not required

_____ 7. "**economical** to recycle" (22)

    a. cost-effective

    b. expensive

    c. easy

    d. frivolous

_____ 8. "high **density** polyethylene" (24)

    a. toxicity

    b. compaction

    c. frequency

    d. power

_____ 9. "plastic **manufacturers**" (33)

    a. materials
    b. handlers
    c. makers
    d. engineers

_____ 10. "**consumers** are aware" (33)

    a. composers
    b. owners
    c. sellers
    d. users

Your instructor may choose to give a brief vocabulary review.

ASSESS YOUR LEARNING

Review questions that you did not understand, found confusing, or answered incorrectly. Seek clarification. Indicate beside each item the source of your confusion and notice the question type. Make notes beside confusing vocabulary items to help you remember them. Use your textbook as a learning tool.

ADDITIONAL VOCABULARY LESSONS

Use the vocabulary lessons in this textbook to expand your vocabulary. Each lesson follows a structural approach and links words through shared prefixes, roots, and suffixes. The words are organized into clusters or families to enhance memory, to organize your learning, and to emphasize that most new words are made up of familiar old parts. Strengthen your vocabulary by identifying your old friends in the new words. Then apply your knowledge of word parts to unlock and remember the meanings of the new words.

Your instructor may choose to introduce the words at the beginning of the week, assign review items for practice, and quiz your knowledge of the words at the end of the week. Learn over 200 words through this easy word-family approach.

SELECTION

3

VOCABULARY LESSON

Not, Not, and Not

Study the following prefixes, words, and sentences.

Prefixes   *in, im*: not   *dis*: not   *un*: not

Words with *in* or *im* = *not*

Can *invisible* fences restrain pets? Will the *inability* to type help you with the computer?

- inadequate: not enough

  Having *inadequate* health care causes many flu victims to go untreated.

- inaccessible: not able to be reached

  Some mountain areas are *inaccessible* except by foot.

- inclement: not mild

  Keep an umbrella handy for *inclement* weather.

- intolerable: not bearable

  Children learn by suffering consequences for their *intolerable* behaviors.

- inhospitable: not welcoming

  The *inhospitable* island was cold, windy, and barren.

- insatiable: cannot be satisfied

  Young readers have an *insatiable* desire for more Harry Potter.

- improbable: not likely to occur

  Because of overbooking, a doctor's appointment today is *improbable*.

- immoral: not conforming to accepted standards of right and wrong.

  The politician's *immoral* actions were scorned by the voters.

- impassable: blocked

  With the bridge washed out from the flood, the road was *impassable*.

- immortal: cannot die

  An *immortal* flame burns to honor the assassinated president.

- immobilized: rendered not able to move

  The zookeepers had to *immobilize* the lion before treating its infected foot.

Words with *dis* = *not*

Do the tabloids *dishonor* celebrities? Can you *disclaim* a relative?

- disarm: take weapons away

  The troops were *disarmed* after the surrender.

- disadvantage: handicap

  The major *disadvantage* of the sofa is that its light-colored fabric easily shows dirt.

- discredit: cause disbelief in

  To *discredit* his character, the opposition circulated a rumor about drugs.

- disgrace: shame

  With an indictment pending, the mayor resigned in *disgrace*.

- disloyal: unfaithful

  The *disloyal* employee revealed company secrets.

- distrust: doubt

  If you *distrust* the management, don't invest your money in the company.

- disconcerted: upset

  The workers were *disconcerted* and even angry about the computer virus.

- disregard: not pay attention to

  If you have already paid, please *disregard* this bill.

- dissolved: melted away

  The sugar *dissolved* into the hot espresso.

- disinherit: to deny an inheritance

  Few parents will *disinherit* a child.

Words with *un = not*

Is an *unsaid* rule clearly stated? Is an *uneducated* guess mostly luck?

- unable: not having the ability

  Because of a shortage, the company was *unable* to ship the software.

- unabridged: not shortened

  For the derivation of words, use an *unabridged* dictionary.

- unaffected: not touched

  Although we saw the funnel, our house was *unaffected* by the tornado.

- unaltered: not changed

  With no additional work, the original plans remain *unaltered*.

- untouchable: cannot be touched

  The children were told that the food was *untouchable* until the guests arrived.

Review

Part I

Answer the following with *T* (true) or *F* (false).

_____ 1. An abridged dictionary contains more than an unabridged dictionary.

_____ 2. Counties seek inaccessible voting locations for citizens.

_____ 3. A disinherited relative receives no gift from the deceased.

_____ 4. An invisible correction can be easily detected.

_____ 5. To discredit a source is to cast doubt on its worth.

_____ 6. Renters usually desire intolerant landlords.

_____ 7. An immobilized elephant is unlikely to charge.

_____ 8. An unaltered proposal remains in its original format.

_____ 9. Disloyal fans boost the morale of a team.

_____ 10. Powdered milk will dissolve in water.

Part II

Choose the best word from the list to complete each of the following sentences.

| inadequate | disregard | unaffected | immoral | disgrace |
| impassable | disarm | inclement | untouchable | disconcerting |

11. The three-foot snow left the roads _____.

12. Humor can _____ the anger of a complaining customer.

13. The _____ weather did not stop the snow skiers from skiing.

14. The _____ actions of the spouse were grounds for the divorce.

15. In a museum, signs indicate that the paintings are _____.

16. By not traveling, they were _____ by the hotel shortage.

17. The _____ protesters rudely interrupted the speaker.

18. Spenders who _____ money may soon be in debt.

19. To get good grades, do not take tests with _____ preparation.

20. When convicted of the crime, the defendant hung her head in _____.

Selecting a Book

The next time you are in the market for a good read, you might spend some time browsing the shelves of a bookstore or library, or perhaps you will do your browsing on the Web. Whichever method you use, your chances of success are greater if you exercise your critical thinking skills. Like clothing and groceries, books are products and the presentation matters. Book covers and quick descriptions are slick marketing tools designed by experts to entice you to make a purchase through pictures, testimonials, and exaggeration. Cut through the hype and decide if the book will be of interest to you.

Any one book might be sold with several different covers to appeal to a variety of audiences. The testimonials by other authors are carefully selected to present a positive image, and customer ratings should also be viewed with an analytical mind. Summary blurbs and excerpts are chosen to present the most appealing aspects of the book. Remember that exciting advertising can make even boring books look good.

Of course, you can buy new and used books at local bookstores or online. Remember, though, that you can also borrow books from the library. Many libraries lend electronic books for downloading to your electronic reader.

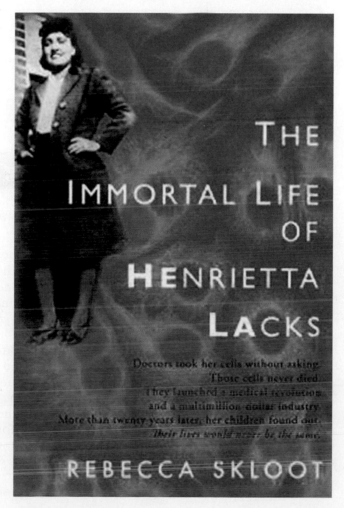

THE IMMORTAL LIFE OF HENRIETTA LACKS

Doctors took her cells without asking.
Those cells never died.
They launched a medical revolution
and a multimillion-dollar industry.
More than twenty years later, her children found out.
Their lives would never be the same.

REBECCA SKLOOT

New York Times Best Seller

Her name was Henrietta Lacks, but scientists know her as HeLa. She was a poor black tobacco farmer whose cells—taken without her knowledge in 1951—became one of the most important tools in medicine, vital for developing the polio vaccine, cloning, gene mapping, and more. Henrietta's cells have been bought and sold by the billions, yet she remains virtually unknown, and her family can't afford health insurance. This phenomenal *New York Times* best seller tells a riveting story of the collision between ethics, race, and medicine; of scientific discovery and faith healing; and of a daughter consumed with questions about the mother she never knew.

EXERCISE 1

Refer to the preceding figure to answer the following questions.

1. Is this book on the *New York Times* Best Sellers list? _____

_____

2. Who is the author? _____

3. What is the book's topic? _____

_____

4. Is this book fiction or nonfiction? (See the definitions that follow if you are not sure.) Justify your response. _____

_____

Reader's TIP   Selecting a Book

After locating a book that looks interesting, investigate further using these strategies.

- Read the blurbs introducing the book. Do they entice you? Is it the kind of book you have enjoyed in the past?
- Read the first page and at least one other page if possible. Most bookstore Web sites allow a peek inside the book. Do you like the writing style? Is it comfortable for you to read? Does the first page grab your attention?
- Read about the author. Have you enjoyed other books by the author? Have friends recommended the author? If the book is nonfiction, what are the author's credentials?
- If the book is nonfiction, review the table of contents and scan the index. Is this material that you want to learn more about? Look at the illustrations and read the captions. Are you intrigued?
- Glance at the testimonials or customer reviews? Are they consistent? Do the reasons given address your personal concerns?

Consult Best-Seller Lists

If you want to know what books other people are buying, consult a best-seller list. Your bookstore or your city newspaper may publish one. If not, the *New York Times* Best Sellers list is nationally respected. Such lists are sometimes divided into best-selling fiction and nonfiction, and then further divided into hardbound books—which are published first and cost more—and paperbacks. Similar to a listing of top-grossing movies, a ranking on a best-seller list indicates quantity, but not necessarily quality. Bookstores often post their own lists of local best-selling suggestions. Lists are easily available at online book sellers' Web sites.

Sample a Variety of Fiction and Nonfiction

Fiction is writing that has been invented by the imagination. The **novel,** the literary form for the imaginative and pleasurable stories of contemporary fiction, is longer than a short story but presents the same elements of **plot, character, theme, setting,** and **tone**.

Nonfiction is a piece of writing based on true events. The label of *nonfiction* includes biographies and books about travel, art, music, decorating, computers, cooking, and other special interests. Some are historical works in which dialogue may be invented based on known facts about the actual people and events of a given time period. Such books can be difficult to distinguish from fiction.

EXERCISE 2

Visit a local bookstore or log on to an online bookstore and pretend you have $100 to spend on books. Review both fiction and nonfiction books and make your choices. Record the title and author of each book you select, as well as a one- or two-sentence summary of what you think the book will be about and why you may want to read it.

3 Textbook Learning

Learning Objectives

From this chapter, readers will learn:

1 To use active methods that aid recall
2 To annotate texts during the reading stage
3 To use the Cornell method of note taking
4 To write a summary
5 To make outline notes
6 To make notes using mapping

Everyday Reading Skills: Reading News and Feature Stories in the Newspaper

EXPECT TO LEARN FROM READING

Learning Objective 1

Use active methods that aid recall

Expect to know something after you have read a textbook assignment. Don't just watch the words go by. Use learning strategies to select key elements and to prepare for remembering. In this chapter, you will learn to use annotating, summarizing, outlining, and mapping to aid concentration and prepare information for study.

The process of reading, marking, and organizing textbook information takes time. Many students ask, "How much do I need to do?" The answer to this question is, "Typically, the more you do, the more you learn." In other words, it is better to read the text than not to read the text. What's more, it is better to read and mark than only to read. Finally, it is better to read, mark, and take notes in some form (summary, Cornell notes, outline, or map) than just to read and mark. Your choices depend on the amount of time you can dedicate to learning and how important it is to understand and remember the material. "Time on task" is a critical element in college success.

ANNOTATE

Learning Objective 2

Annotate texts during reading

Annotating is a system of marking that includes underlining and notations. It is the first and most basic step for all of the other organizing strategies.

When to Annotate

Annotate during reading in the "Integrating Knowledge" stage, but after a complete thought is presented. Many students tend to mark too much, and over-marking wastes valuable review time. Wait until a complete thought has been presented to separate the most important ideas from the least important ones. A thought unit may be as short as one paragraph or as long as an entire section under a subheading. Marking the text is a key part of Stage Two—Integrating Knowledge. The annotations record what is important enough to include in your notes later, and the thinking involved helps keep your mind from wandering.

How to Annotate

The word *annotate* is used to suggest a notation system for selecting important ideas that goes beyond straight lines and includes numbers, circles, stars, and written comments, such as marginal notes, questions, and key words. Annotating includes marking the words *and* making notes in the margin. With practice, students tend to form their own notation systems, which may include a variation of the following examples.

⬯ Main idea (or write the topic in the margin beside the paragraph)	{} Section of material to reread for review
— Supporting material	①,②,③ Numbering of important details under a major issue, usually written in the margin
✬ Major trend or possible essay exam question	? Didn't understand and must seek advice
✓ Important smaller point to know for multiple-choice item	Topic, Def. or Ex. Notes in the margin
[ ] Word that you must be able to define	How does it operate? Questions in the margin
⬓ A key issue to remember	∿ Indicating relationships

Unless you are reading a library book, annotate for study reading. Students who are using borrowed books that must be kept clean often use sticky notes to record key information. Have you been annotating throughout this text as you have been reading? (The correct answer to this question should be yes!) If your instructor were to say at this moment, "Take fifteen minutes to review for a quiz on the last two chapters," could you quickly review your annotations? Remember, you can waste time reading for the purpose of learning if you do not annotate. Thoughtful annotating is one of your best learning tools.

EXAMPLE The following passage was taken from a college psychology textbook. Do you recognize the definition and example organizational pattern and that the details are presented in order of increasing importance? Notice how the passage is annotated and how the annotations become the basis for the note taking examples on the following pages.

HOW WE REMEMBER: REHEARSAL

Def.

3 Strategies

①

An important technique for keeping information in short-term memory and increasing the chances of long-term retention is rehearsal, the review or practice of material while you are learning it. Some strategies for rehearsing are more effective than others.

Maintenance rehearsal involves merely the rote repetition of the material. You are taking advantage of maintenance rehearsal when you look up a phone number and then

Ex.

repeat it over and over to keep it in short-term memory until you no longer need it. This kind of rehearsal is fine for keeping information in short-term memory, but it will not always lead to long-term retention.

②

A better strategy if you want to remember for the long haul is elaborative rehearsal. Elaboration involves associating new information with material that has already been stored or with other new facts. Suppose, for example, that you are studying the hypothalamus. Simply memorizing the definition of *hypothalamus* is unlikely to help much. But if you can elaborate on the concept of hypothalamus, you are more likely to remem-

Ex.

ber it. For example, knowing that *hypo* means "under" tells you its location, under the thalamus. Many students try to pare down what they are learning to the bare essentials, but in fact, knowing more details about something makes it more memorable; that is what elaboration means.

③

A related strategy for prolonging retention is deep processing or the processing of meaning. If you process only the physical or sensory features, such as how the word *hypothalamus* is spelled and how it sounds, your processing will be shallow even if it is elaborated. If you recognize patterns and assign labels to objects or events ("The hypothalamus is below the thalamus"), your processing will be somewhat deeper. If

Ex.

you fully analyze the meaning of what you are trying to remember (for example, by encoding the functions and importance of the hypothalamus), your processing will be deeper yet.

—Adapted from *Psychology*, Tenth Edition,
by Carole Wade and Carol Tavris

The learner's task is not just to read but also to earmark relevant ideas for future study. To be an efficient learner, do not waste time.

EXERCISE 1   Read the following passage and use the suggested annotations on page 82 to organize the material and mark key ideas for later study. Respond with *T* (true) or *F* (false) to the comprehension items.

SPATIAL DISTANCES

The way in which you treat space, a field of study called **proxemics**, communicates a wide variety of messages. Edward Hall distinguishes four distances that define the type of relationship between people and identifies the various messages that each distance communicates.

In **intimate distance**, ranging from actual touching to 18 inches, the presence of the other individual is unmistakable. Each person experiences the sound, smell, and feel of the other's breath. You use intimate distance for love-making and wrestling, for comforting and protecting. This distance is so short that most people do not consider it proper in public.

Personal distance refers to the protective "bubble" that defines your personal space, which measures from 18 inches to 4 feet. This imaginary bubble keeps you protected and untouched by others. You can still hold or grasp another person at this distance—but only by extending your arms—allowing you to take certain individuals such as loved ones into your protective bubble. At the outer limit of personal distance, you can touch another person only if both of you extend your arms.

At **social distance**, ranging from 4 to 12 feet, you lose the visual detail you have at personal distance. You conduct impersonal business and interact at a social gathering at this distance. The more distance you maintain in your interactions, the more formal they appear. Many people in executive and management positions place their desks so that they are assured of at least this distance from employees.

Public distance, measuring from 12 to more than 25 feet, protects you. At this distance, you can take defensive action if threatened. On a public bus or train, for example, you might keep at least this distance from a drunkard. Although you lose fine details of the face and eyes at this distance, you are close enough to see what is happening.

—*Essentials of Human Communication*, Fourth Edition,
by Joseph A. DeVito

Check your annotations with a study buddy. Could you study the essentials from the annotations without rereading the passage?

_____ 1. Intimate distance is appropriate for social gatherings.

_____ 2. The greater the social distance, the more formal the interaction appears.

TAKE NOTES

Note taking involves using your own words and separate paper to condense the key ideas that you have marked in your text while annotating. Simply jotting these ideas down on paper is note taking, but putting notes into an organized form makes them clearer and easier to use for study purposes. Four common forms of note taking are presented in the following pages.

When to Take Notes

Take notes from textbooks in the "Recall" stage, after reading and annotating. Take notes from lectures while the speaker talks, and revise them later. Record major topics and supporting details, but avoid trying to write everything.

Learning Objective 3

Use the Cornell method of note taking

The Cornell Method of Note Taking

The Cornell method, one of the most popular systems of note taking, includes the following steps:

1. Draw a line down your paper 2.5 inches from the left edge to create a wide margin for key words and a wider area on the right for explanatory details. (Some students prefer to follow the more formal guidelines for Cornell notes and write complete sentences in this column.)
2. After reading and annotating a selection, review your annotations and write the key details in the left-hand column. Use your marginal notes as a guide.
3. Write the explanatory details in the right-hand column. Use phrases or complete sentences, as in the more formal style. Align the details on the right with their labels on the left. Use your text markings as a guide.

You will probably notice that as you create your notes, you are also correcting your annotations. You may find that you failed to mark important information or that you annotated too much. To study Cornell-style notes, cover the details in the right-hand column and use the labels in the left-hand column to quiz yourself or a study partner.

Abbreviations.   Use shortcuts. Develop your own system of abbreviations for note taking for both textbook and lecture notes. Some students mix shorthand symbols with their regular writing.

EXAMPLE   The following is an example of how the Cornell method might be used to organize notes for future study of the passage about rehearsal strategies on pages 83–84.

How We Remember: Rehearsal	
Rehearsal Def.	Important for memory. Some strategies more effective than others Review of material while learning
3 Strategies Maintenance rehearsal Def. Ex.	Okay for short-term memory Rote repetition Repeating a phone number only as long as you need it
Elaborative rehearsal Def. Ex.	More effective; details aid memory Associating new information with existing information Hypothalamus: hypo- means below; the hypothalamus is below the thalamus
Deep processing Def. Ex.	Most effective method Processing the meaning; adding labels, recognizing patterns Associate the hypothalamus with its purpose and importance

When to Use Cornell-style Notes.   This method is useful for textbook study and class lectures. The marginal topic notes placed on the left are particularly helpful in organizing the study of a large body of material for a midterm or final exam.

EXERCISE 2   Read the following passage about population growth in poorer nations. Annotate it, and then use the Cornell method to take notes for future use. Write your notes in the box that follows the selection. Respond with *T* (true) or *F* (false) to the comprehension items.

POPULATION GROWTH

Why do people in the countries that can least afford it have so many children? We must take the role of the other so we can understand the world as *they* see it. As our culture does for us, their culture provides a perspective on life that guides their choices. Let's consider three reasons why bearing many children plays a central role in the lives of millions upon millions of poor people around the world.

First is the status of parenthood. In the least industrialized nations, motherhood is the most prized status a woman can achieve. The more children a woman bears, the more she is thought to have achieved the purpose for which she was born. Similarly, a man proves his manhood by fathering children. The more children he fathers, especially sons, the better—for through them his name lives on.

Second, the community supports this view; many people share values and closely identify with one another. Children are viewed as a sign of God's blessing. Accordingly, a couple should have many children. By producing children, people reflect the values of their community and achieve status. The barren woman, not the woman with a dozen children, is to be pitied.

These factors certainly provide strong motivations for bearing many children. Yet, there is a third incentive. For poor people in the least industrialized nations, children are economic assets. These people have no Social Security or medical and unemployment insurance. This motivates them to bear *more* children, not fewer, for when parents become sick or too old to work—or when no work is to be found—they rely on their children to take care of them. The more children they have, the broader their base of support. Moreover, children begin contributing to the family income at a young age.

To those of us who live in the most industrialized nations, it seems irrational to have many children. And *for us it would be*. Understanding life from the framework of people who are living it, however—the essence of the symbolic interactionist perspective—reveals how it makes perfect sense to have many children. For example, consider the following incident, reported by a government worker in India:

> Thaman Singh (a very poor man, a water carrier) … welcomed me inside his home, gave me a cup of tea (with milk and "market" sugar, as he proudly pointed out later), and said: "You were trying to convince me that I shouldn't have any more sons. Now, you see, I have six sons and two daughters and I sit at home in leisure. They are grown up and they bring me money. One even works outside the village as a laborer. *You told me I was a poor man and couldn't support a large family. Now, you see, because of my large family I am a rich man."*

Conflict theorists offer a different view of why women in the poor nations bear so many children. They would argue that these women have values that support male dominance. To father many children, especially sons, demonstrates virility, giving a man valued status in the community. From a conflict perspective, then, the reason poor people have so many children is that men control women's reproductive choices.

—From James M. Henslin, *Sociology: A Down-to-Earth Approach*, 7th ed. © 2007 (excerpt from pages 583–585). Reproduced by permission of Pearson Education, Inc.

_____ 1. In poor countries throughout the world, poverty tends to increase rather than decrease the desire for a large number of children.

_____ 2. A barren woman is a mother.

_____ 3. In the least industrialized nations, an inability to bear children results in lower status for a woman.

_____ 4. For poor people in the least industrialized countries, children are viewed as their social security for old age.

TOPIC: WHY PEOPLE IN POOR COUNTRIES HAVE LOTS OF CHILDREN	
1. Status	Motherhood is a woman's purpose
	Proves a man's manhood
2. Community supports this view of gender roles	Children are sign of God's blessing
	Shows support of community's values and achieves status
3. Children are economic assets	Rely on children to care for parents in old age
Conflict theory explanation	Different view
	Because men control women's reproductive choices

Summarizing

Learning Objective 4
Write summaries

A **summary** is a short, concise method of stating the main idea and significant supporting details of the material. Think of it as the key words and phrases linked by complete sentences and presented in paragraphs.

When to Summarize. Professors frequently ask students to take notes in the form of a summary on assigned readings. Such readings, which are usually in the library or on the Internet, might include chapters from related texts, short stories, research articles from online periodicals, or scholarly essays from books or periodicals. The preparation of a written summary can demonstrate to the professor that you have a clear understanding of the main points of the assignment. A summary can provide you with reference notes for later study, and it can be useful when you are organizing information from several sources for a long research paper.

Reader's TIP · How to Write a Summary

- Remember your purpose; be brief.
- In the text, underline the key ideas you want to include.
- Begin your summary with a general statement, the main idea, that unites the key ideas.
- Include the key ideas that support the general statement. Link these ideas in sentences and show their significance.
- Delete irrelevant or trivial information.
- Delete redundant information.
- Use your own words to show your understanding of the material. Don't try to camouflage a lack of comprehension by copying from the original.
- Do not include your opinions or anything that is not in the original.

How to Summarize. When you write a summary, put the ideas into your own words. If you need to quote an author directly, place quotation marks around the *exact* wording to avoid plagiarism. Keep in mind the purpose of your summary. The way you will use the information will influence the number of details you include. Generally, be brief but make your point. A summary is usually just one paragraph. A summary should never be as long as the piece it is summarizing!

EXAMPLE The following is a summary of the passage on rehearsal strategies (pp. 83–84). Notice that the first sentence states the main ideas and the others concisely state the major supporting details.

How We Remember: Rehearsal

> Rehearsal, repeated review of material while learning it, is important to establishing memory. Some rehearsal strategies are more effective than others. Maintenance rehearsal is simple, rote repetition like what one does when repeating a telephone number for only as long as the number is needed. This is adequate for short-term memory. The next strategy, elaborative rehearsal, is more effective. It involves associating the new information with existing knowledge. For example, recognizing that hypo– means "below" is helpful in remembering that the hypothalamus is below the thalamus. The most effective rehearsal method is deep processing. In this method, meaning is developed by adding labels and recognizing patterns. Connecting the hypothalamus with its function and importance provides a more lasting memory.

EXERCISE 3 Annotate the following passage and then write a summary of it. Include only the most important details in your summary and exclude the irrelevant ones. For example, this passage is dramatized by an anecdote, but does the information belong in the summary? Respond with *T* (true) or *F* (false) to the comprehension items.

RATTLESNAKE SURPRISE

David Chiszar, a professor in the psychology department at the University of Colorado, got a big surprise when he walked into his laboratory in 1995. His laboratory shelves are lined with dozens of glass cases; behind the glass, the subjects of Dr. Chiszar's research coil a safe distance from the professor and any visitors brave enough to enter. Although most are eerily silent, an occasional research subject emits a dry, rattling sound when the professor passes by. Dr. Chiszar is a herpetologist—in particular, he studies snakes. The day of the surprise, he went to the glass case that held a 14-year-old female timber rattlesnake. Timber rattlesnakes are poisonous but relatively unaggressive snakes that are found only in the eastern half of the United States. Severe declines in timber rattlesnake populations have led several states, including New York and Massachusetts, to list it as a threatened or endangered species, making it illegal to harass, kill, or collect timber rattlesnakes.

Dr. Chiszar had raised this timber rattlesnake since she was a two-day-old baby, not much bigger than an earthworm. Now, as he peered into her cage, he was astonished to see a tiny rattlesnake baby next to the 2½-foot-long female snake. Even though she had never been in contact with a male snake, she had given birth to a male timber rattlesnake. Like other pit vipers, timber rattlesnakes don't lay eggs, but bear their young alive. Genetic studies showed that the baby snake really was the offspring of the 14-year-old rattler and that he didn't have a "father" in the usual sense of the word.

Although it may surprise you, such events are not all that rare in the world of reptiles, some birds, and insects. In fact, some species of whiptail lizards and geckos lack males entirely. The females of these species routinely produce offspring without the requirement for fertilization.

—*Biology: Life on Earth,* Sixth Edition, by Teresa Audesirk,
Gerald Audesirk, and Bruce Byers

Written Summary

Timber rattlesnakes _____

_____

_____

_____

_____ 1. The female timber rattlesnake produced a male offspring without any contact with a male.

_____ 2. The 14-year-old mother rattlesnake had been isolated in captivity since it was two days old.

EXERCISE 4   Annotate the following passage and write a summary of it. Respond with *T* (true) or *F* (false) to the comprehension items.

BUSINESS ETIQUETTE

A major component of managing your impression is practicing good etiquette. **Business etiquette** is a special code of behavior required in work situations. *Manners* has an equivalent meaning. Both manners and etiquette generally refer to behaving in a refined and acceptable manner. Business etiquette is much more than knowing how to use the correct fork or how to dress in a given situation. Businesspeople today must know how to be at ease with strangers and with groups, be able to offer congratulations smoothly, know how to make introductions, and know how to conduct themselves at company social functions. Studying etiquette is important because knowing and using proper business etiquette contributes to individual and business success. People who are considerate of the feelings of others, and companies who are courteous toward customers, are more likely to succeed than their rude counterparts.

Business etiquette includes many aspects of interpersonal relations in organizations. What is considered proper etiquette and manners in the workplace changes over time and may vary with the situation. At one time, addressing one's superior by his or her first name was considered brash. Today it is commonplace behavior. A sampling of etiquette guidelines is nevertheless helpful. A general principle of being considerate of the feelings of work associates is more important than any one act of etiquette or courtesy.

ETIQUETTE FOR WORK BEHAVIOR AND CLOTHING

General work etiquette includes all aspects of performing in the work environment, such as completing work on time, punctuality, being a good team player, listening to others, and following through. For instance, having the courtesy to complete a project when it is due demonstrates good manners and respect for the work of others.

Clothing might be considered part of general work behavior. The casual standards in the information technology field, along with dress-down days, have created confusion about proper office attire. A general rule is that *casual* should not be interpreted as sloppy, such as torn jeans or a stained sweatshirt. Many companies have moved back toward emphasizing traditional business attire, such as suits for men and women. In many work situations, dressing more formally may constitute proper etiquette.

INTRODUCING PEOPLE

The basic rule for introductions is to present the lower-ranking person to the higher-ranking person regardless of age or sex. "Ms. Barker (the CEO), I would like you to meet my new coworker, Reggie Taylor." If the two people being introduced are of equal rank, mention the older one first. Providing a little information about the person being introduced is considered good manners. When introducing one person to the group, present the group to the individual. "Sid Foster, this is our information systems team." When being introduced to a person, concentrate on the name and repeat it soon, thus enhancing learning. A fundamental display of good manners is to remember people's names and to pronounce them correctly. When dealing with people senior to you or of higher rank, call them by their last name and title until told otherwise. (Maybe Ms. Barker, above, will tell you, "Please call me Kathy.")

It is good manners and good etiquette to remember the names of work associates to whom you are introduced, even if you see them only occasionally. If you forget the name of a person, it is better to admit this than to guess and come up with the wrong name. Just say, "I apologize, but I have forgotten your name. Tell me once more, and I will not forget your name again."

A major change in introducing people is that men and women are now both expected to extend their right hand when being introduced. Give a firm, but not overpowering, handshake, and establish eye contact with the person you are greeting.

—Human Relations: Interpersonal, Job-Oriented Skills, Eighth Edition, by Andrew J. DuBrin

Written Summary

Begin with a general statement about business etiquette. Link the key ideas and do not include irrelevant information.

_____

_____

_____

_____

_____

_____

_____

_____

_____ 1. The passage indicates that *etiquette* and *manners* have about the same meaning.

_____ 2. In introductions, present the higher ranking person to the lower ranking one.

Outlining

Learning Objective 5

Make outline notes

Outlining is a form of note taking that gives a quick display of key issues and essential supporting details. Outlining uses indentations, numbers, and letters to show levels of importance. The outline forces you to sort out significant details and decide on levels of importance. Being able to outline shows that you understand main ideas and can distinguish between major and minor supporting details.

When to Outline. Outlining can be used to take notes on a textbook chapter or a class lecture or for brainstorming the answer to an essay question.

How to Outline. Letters, numbers, and indentations are used in an outline to show levels of importance. In a standard outline, Roman numerals mark items of greatest importance and letters indicate supporting details. The greater the distance from the left margin an item is listed, the less significance it is afforded. Your outline need not be perfect, but it should use indentation and some form of enumeration. Always remember that you are outlining to save time for later study and review. Don't cram all your facts on half a sheet of paper when you need several sheets. Give yourself plenty of room to write. You

Reader's TIP   Creating an Outline

The following is the format for a model outline. Notice how the numbers, letters, and indentations show the importance of an idea.

Main Point or Topic

   I. Primary supporting idea

      A. Secondary supporting detail

      B. Secondary supporting detail

      C. Secondary supporting detail

  II. Primary supporting idea #2

      A. Secondary supporting detail

      B. Secondary supporting detail

         1. Minor supporting detail or example

         2. Minor supporting detail or example

 III. Primary supporting idea #3

      A. Secondary supporting detail

      B. Secondary supporting detail

want to be able to look back quickly to get a clear picture of what is important and what supports it.

When taking notes in outline form, be brief and to the point. Use phrases rather than sentences. Record the main points, including key explanatory words, but leave out the insignificant details or "fillers."

Remember, making a picture-perfect outline is not critical; the important thing is to distinguish between the primary supporting ideas and the secondary supporting details. In an informal study outline, you can show the same levels of importance with indentations and bullets.

EXAMPLE   The following example shows how the passage on rehearsal strategies (see pp. 83–84) might be outlined for future study. Again, notice how the annotations were used to create the outline.

How We Remember: Rehearsal

  I. Rehearsal

    A. Def: Review of material while learning

    B. Important for memory

    C. Some strategies more effective than others

 II. Maintenance rehearsal

    A. Def: Rote repetition

    B. Ex: Repeating a phone number only as long as it is needed

    C. Okay for short-term memory

III. Elaborative rehearsal

    A. Def: Associating new information with existing information

    B. Ex: Hypo– means "below," so the hypothalamus is below the thalamus

    C. Details make this strategy more effective

IV. Deep processing

    A. Def: Developing meaning by adding labels and recognizing patterns

    B. Ex: Associating the hypothalamus with its purpose and importance

    C. Most effective method

EXPLANATION Reviewing the outline provides all the information needed to study the material. For active review, try reproducing your outline notes from memory, or make a copy, cut it up, and reconstruct the parts in the appropriate order.

 Make a study outline for the following material. Annotate first and then organize your notes into an outline.

THE SIX TYPES OF LOVE

EROS: BEAUTY AND SENSUALITY

Erotic love focuses on beauty and physical attractiveness, sometimes to the exclusion of qualities you might consider more important and more lasting. The erotic lover has an idealized image of beauty that is unattainable in reality. Consequently, the erotic lover often feels unfulfilled. In defense of eros, however, it should be noted that both male and female eros lovers have the highest levels of reward and satisfaction when compared with all other types of lovers (Morrow, Clark, & Brock 1995).

LUDUS: ENTERTAINMENT AND EXCITEMENT

Ludus love is seen as fun, a game to be played. To the ludic lover, love is not to be taken too seriously; emotions are to be held in check lest they get out of hand and make trouble. Passions never rise to the point at which they get out of control. A ludic lover is self-controlled and consciously aware of the need to manage love rather than to allow it to control him or her. The ludic lover is manipulative, and the extent of one's ludic tendencies has been found to correlate with the use of verbal sexual coercion (Sarwer, Kalichman, Johnson, Early, et al. 1993). Ludic-oriented sexually coercive men also experience less happiness, friendship, and trust in their relationships than do noncoercive men (Kalichman, Sarwer, Johnson, & Ali 1993). Ludic lover tendencies in women are likewise related to a dissatisfaction with life (Yancey & Berglass 1991).

STORGE LOVE: PEACEFUL AND SLOW

Like ludus love, **storge love** lacks passion and intensity. Storgic lovers do not set out to find lovers but to establish a companion-like relationship with someone they know and with whom they can share interests and activities. Storgic love develops over a period of time rather than in one mad burst of passion. Sex in storgic relationships comes late, and when it comes it assumes no great importance. Storgic love is sometimes difficult to separate from friendship; it is often characterized by the same qualities that characterize friendship: mutual caring, compassion, respect, and concern for the other person.

PRAGMA: PRACTICAL AND TRADITIONAL

The **pragma lover** is practical and wants compatibility and a relationship in which important needs and desires will be satisfied. In its extreme, pragma may be seen in the person who writes down the qualities wanted in a mate and actively goes about seeking someone who matches up. The pragma lover is concerned with the social qualifications of a potential mate even more than personal qualities; family and background are extremely important to the pragma lover, who relies not so much on feelings as on logic. The pragma lover views love as a necessity—or as a useful relationship—that makes the rest of life easier. The pragma lover therefore asks such questions about a potential mate as, "Will this person earn a good living?" "Can this person cook?" and "Will this person help me advance in my career?"

MANIC LOVE: ELATION AND DEPRESSION

The quality of mania that separates it from other types of love is the extremes of its highs and lows, its ups and downs. The **manic lover** loves intensely and at the same time worries intensely about and fears the loss of the love. With little provocation, for example, the manic lover may experience extreme jealousy. Manic love is obsessive; the manic lover has to possess the beloved completely—in all ways, at all times. In return, the manic lover wishes to be possessed, to be loved intensely. It seems almost as if the manic lover is driven to these extremes by some outside force or perhaps by some inner obsession that cannot be controlled.

AGAPE: COMPASSIONATE AND SELFLESS

Agape is a compassionate, egoless, self-giving love. Agape is nonrational and nondiscriminative. Agape creates value and virtue through love rather than bestowing love only on that which is valuable and virtuous. The agapic lover loves even people with whom he or she has no close ties. This lover loves the stranger on the road, and the fact that they will probably never meet again has nothing to do with it. Jesus, Buddha, and Gandhi practiced and preached this unqualified love. Agape is a spiritual love, offered without concern for personal reward or gain. The agapic lover loves without expecting that the love will be returned or reciprocated. For women, agape is the only love style positively related to their own life satisfaction.

—*Human Communication*, Sixth Edition,
by Joseph A. DeVito

Six Types of Love

I. Eros: Beauty and Sensuality

  A. Focus: _____

  B. _____

  C. _____

  D. _____

II. Ludus: Entertainment and Excitement

  A. Focus: _____

  B. _____

  C. _____

  D. _____

III. Storge: Peaceful and Slow

  A. Focus: _____

  B. _____

  C. _____

  D. _____

IV. Pragma: Practical and Traditional

    A. Focus: _____

    B. _____

    C. _____

    D. _____

V. Manic: Elation and Depression

    A. Focus: _____

    B. _____

    C. _____

    D. _____

VI. Agape: Compassionate and Selfless

    A. Focus: _____

    B. _____

    C. _____

    D. _____

EXERCISE 6

Make a study outline for the following material. Annotate first and then organize your notes into an outline.

DRUG TESTS

Employers bear a crushing economic burden—estimates run as high as $100 billion—owing to drug and alcohol abuse by employees. These costs arise from high turnover, poor work performance, absenteeism, increased medical claims, low morale, theft, and other factors.

The drug-abusing employee is late three times as often as his coworkers, asks for time off twice as often, has two and one-half times as many absences of eight or more days, is five times more likely to file a workers' compensation claim, and is involved in accidents more than three times as often.

Typical on-the-job symptoms of drug abuse are inability to pay attention, difficulty with simple arithmetic, prolonged trips to the restroom, frequent absenteeism, poor personal hygiene, lapses in memory, and inattention to detail.

Given the social gravity and bottom-line expense of the drug problem, it is understandable that most American companies now screen for drug abuse during the pre-employment process. In most cases, this testing takes place as an ordinary and relatively inexpensive part of the pre-employment physical.

—Interviewing for Success,
by Arthur H. Bell and Dayle M. Smith

Drug Abuse by Employees

   I. Costs to Employers

       A. _____

       B. _____

       C. _____

       D. _____

       E. _____

       F. _____

       G. _____

  II. Symptoms of Drug-Abusing Employees

       A. _____

       B. _____

       C. _____

       D. _____

       E. _____

       F. _____

       G. _____

EXERCISE 7   Make a study outline for the following material. Annotate first and then organize your notes into an outline.

BUILDING SKILLS TO REDUCE STRESS

Dealing with stress involves assessing all aspects of a stressor, examining your response and how you can change it, and learning to cope. Often we cannot change the requirements at our college, assignments in class, or unexpected stressors. Inevitably, we will be stuck in classes that bore us and for which we find no application in real life. We feel powerless when a loved one dies. Although the facts cannot be changed, we can change our reactions to them.

ASSESSING YOUR STRESSORS

After recognizing a stressor evaluate it. Can you alter the circumstances to reduce the amount of distress you are experiencing, or must you change your behavior and reactions to reduce stress levels? For example, you may have five term papers due for five different courses during the semester, but your professors are unlikely to drop such requirements. However, you can change your behavior by beginning the papers early and spacing them over time to avoid last-minute panic.

CHANGING YOUR RESPONSES

Changing your responses requires practice and emotional control. If your roommate is habitually messy and this causes you stress, you can choose from among several responses. You can express your anger by yelling; you can pick up the mess and leave a nasty note; or you can defuse the situation with humor. The first reaction that comes to mind is not always the best. Stop before reacting to gain the time you need to find an appropriate response. Ask yourself, "What is to be gained from my response?"

LEARNING TO COPE

Everyone copes with stress in different ways. Some people drink or take drugs; others seek help from counselors; and still others try to forget about it or engage in positive activities, such as exercise. **Stress inoculation**, one of the newer techniques, helps people prepare for stressful events ahead of time. For example, suppose you are petrified about speaking in front of a class. Practicing in front of friends or in front of a video camera may inoculate you and prevent your freezing up on the day of the presentation. Some health experts compare stress inoculation to a vaccine given to protect against a disease. Regardless of how you cope with a situation, your conscious effort to deal with it is an important step in stress management.

DOWNSHIFTING

Today's lifestyles are hectic and pressure-packed, and stress often comes from trying to keep up. Many people are questioning whether "having it all" is worth it, and they are taking a step back and simplifying their lives. This trend is known as **downshifting**. Moving from a large urban area to a smaller town, exchanging the expensive SUV for a modest four-door sedan, and a host of other changes in lifestyle typify downshifting. Some dedicated downshifters have given up television, phones, and even computers.

Downshifting involves a fundamental alteration in values and honest introspection about what is important in life. When you consider any form of downshift or perhaps even start your career this way, it's important to move slowly and consider the following.

a. *Determine your ultimate goal.* What is most important to you, and what will you need to reach that goal? What can you do without? Where do you want to live?

b. *Make a short-term and a long-term plan for simplifying your life.* Set up your plan in doable steps, and work slowly toward each step. Begin saying no to requests for your time, and determine those people with whom it is important for you to spend time.

c. *Complete a financial inventory.* How much money will you need to do the things you want to do? Will you live alone or share costs with roommates? Do you need a car, or can you rely on public transportation? Pay off credit cards and eliminate existing debt, or consider debt consolidation. Get used to paying with cash.

—Health: The Basics, Sixth Edition, by Rebecca J. Donatelle

Building Skills to Reduce Stress

   I. Assessing Your Stressors

      A. _____

      B. _____

  II. Changing Your Responses

      A. _____

      B. _____

 III. Learning to Cope

      A. _____

      B. _____

      C. _____

 IV. Downshifting

      A. _____

      B. _____

Mapping

Learning Objective 6

Make notes using mapping

Mapping visually condenses material to show relationships. A map is a diagram that places important topics in a central location and connects major points and supporting details in a visual display that shows degrees of importance. The previous study methods are linear in nature, whereas mapping uses space in a free and graphic manner.

When to Map.   A map provides a quick reference for overviewing a chapter to stimulate prior knowledge, emphasize relationships, and aid recall. College students use maps or charts to reduce information for memorizing from lecture notes and textbooks.

How to Map.   To prepare a map, do the following:

1. Draw a circle or a box in the middle of a page and in it write the subject or topic of the material.
2. Determine the main ideas that support the subject and write them on lines radiating from the central circle or box.
3. Determine the significant details and write them on lines attached to each main idea. The number of details that you include will depend on the material and your purpose.

Maps are not restricted to any one pattern but can be formed in a variety of creative shapes, as the following diagrams illustrate.

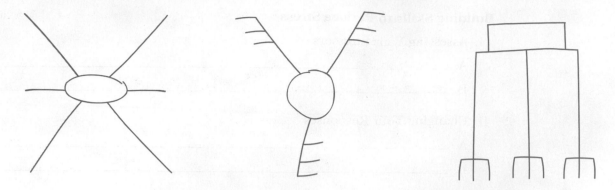

The following is an example of how the passage on rehearsal strategies might be mapped for future study. Many forms and shapes are acceptable as long as the connections represent the correct relationships among major and minor details.

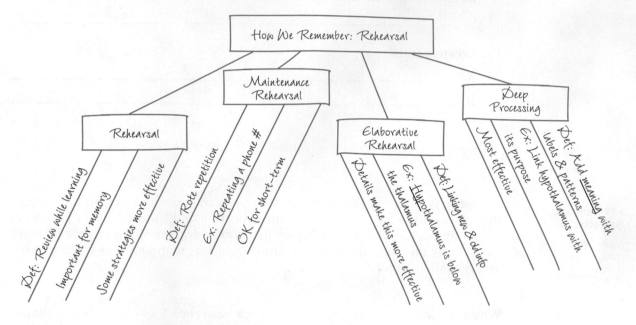

EXPLANATION   Mapping works best when only a few major details are displayed. The same active study methods suggested for outline notes work well for maps: Re-create the map from memory, or make a copy, cut it up, and reconstruct it like a jigsaw puzzle.

EXERCISE 8

Read and annotate the following passage and then map the key ideas. The structure of the map is provided. Insert the topic first. Next, arrange the supporting ideas to radiate appropriately.

RELIEF FOR INJURIES

For the past several hundred years many injuries were treated with heat—steaming baths where leisurely soaking was encouraged, hot water bottles, or electric heating pads or wraps. It was assumed that since heat speeded up metabolism, it would also speed the healing process. Today's researchers have proved that just the opposite is true. . . . Heat does speed up body processes but it also stimulates injured tissue and dilates blood vessels.

In turn, this causes swelling to increase and enlarges the pools of blood and fluid, actually slowing healing. Even if there is no injury, heat after exercising can cause aches and pains. A quick, cool shower is recommended after your jog rather than a hot tub.

Four basic first aid procedures are used in treating the majority of runners' injuries.

STOP ACTIVITY

The first and most critical is to stop jogging as soon as the symptom appears. About the only pain you can run through is a side stitch. Joggers who insist on running with pain or walking off an injury usually incur further harm. Even though the pain does not become more intense, continuing the activity may aggravate the injury and prolong healing.

APPLY COLD

Cold packs are now universally accepted as the best first aid for virtually any jogging injury and constitute the second step in treatment. Chilling numbs the pain and minimizes swelling and inflammation by constricting blood and lymph vessels. Apply cold packs at least twice a day until the swelling and tenderness disappear. The ice pack should not be left in place longer than 30 minutes at one time. Muscle cramps are one of the few conditions associated with jogging where heat instead of cold should be applied.

IMMOBILIZE AND ELEVATE

Injuries that would benefit from being immobilized and/or given additional support should be wrapped with an elastic Ace-type bandage. This wrapping should be snug, but not tight enough to inhibit blood circulation. This third step should be taken before the final step of elevating the injured body part. Elevation not only helps drain fluid from the area, but also prevents blood and fluid from rushing to the area, thereby causing further swelling.

— *Jogging Everyone,* by Charles Williams
and Clancy Moore

EXERCISE 9

Read and annotate the following passage and map the key ideas. The structure of the map is provided. Insert the topic first and then arrange the supporting ideas to radiate appropriately.

TYPES OF CRIME

In the United States, the Federal Bureau of Investigation gathers information on criminal offenses and regularly reports the results in a publication called *Crime in the United States*. Two major types of crime make up the FBI "crime index."

Crimes against the person are *crimes that direct violence or the threat of violence against others.* Such violent crimes include murder and manslaughter (legally defined as "the willful killing of one human being by another"), aggravated assault ("an unlawful attack by one person upon another for the purpose of inflicting severe or aggravated bodily injury"), forcible rape ("the carnal knowledge of a female forcibly and against her will"), and robbery ("taking or attempting to take anything of value from the care, custody, or control of a person or persons by force or threat of force or violence and/or putting the victim in fear").

Crimes against property encompass *crimes that involve theft of property belonging to others.* Property crimes include burglary ("the unlawful entry of a structure to commit a [serious crime] or a theft"), larceny-theft ("the unlawful taking, carrying, leading, or riding away of property from the possession of another"), auto theft ("the theft or attempted theft of a motor vehicle"), and arson ("any willful or malicious burning or attempt to burn the personal property of another").

A third category of offenses, not included in major crime indexes, is **victimless crimes**, *violations of law in which there are no readily apparent victims.* Also called "crimes without complaint," they include illegal drug use, prostitution, and gambling. The term "victimless crime" is misleading, however. How victimless is a crime when young people have to steal to support a drug habit? What about a young pregnant woman who smokes crack and permanently harms her baby? Perhaps it is more correct to say that people who commit such crimes are both offenders and victims.

—*Sociology*, Tenth Edition,
by John J. Macionis

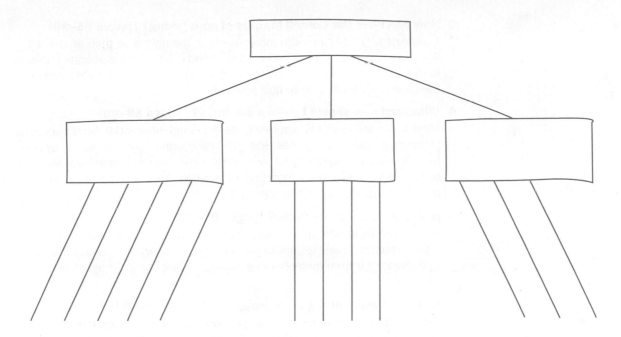

EXERCISE 10   On a separate sheet of paper, make a study map or chart to diagram the essential information in the passage titled *The Six Types of Love* (see Exercise 5).

TAKE ORGANIZED LECTURE NOTES

Develop an efficient system for organizing class lectures. Professors speak rapidly yet expect students to remember important information. The Cornell method uses marginal notes to emphasize main points, whereas the outline format shows importance through indentation. Maps are more difficult to construct during a lecture. Whichever system you use, allow yourself plenty of room to write. Considering your investment in college, paper is inexpensive. Use a pen, not a pencil, to avoid smudges. Try writing on only one side of the paper so you can backtrack later to add information when the professor summarizes. If you use a tablet or laptop computer in class, set up the form in advance. Compare your lecture notes with those of other students. Why would some professors say, "I can tell how much a student understood by looking at his or her lecture notes"?

EXERCISE 11   Choose a study buddy and divide the work in order to compare the two note taking systems: the Cornell method and the modified outline format. Ask permission and, if possible, both of you visit a history, psychology, sociology, or political science class. One of you should take notes using the Cornell method and the other using an informal version of the outline format. After class, compare notes and decide which method works better for you.

SUMMARY POINTS

1 What active methods can be used to assist recall? (page 82)
Annotating while reading and making notes after reading are very effective recall methods.

2 How can I effectively annotate my textbooks? (page 82)
Use a system of circling, underlining, consistent symbols, and marginal notes.

3 How can I use the Cornell Method of note taking? (pages 85–86)

Construct a "T" diagram with more space on the right side than on the left. Write major details and labels in the left-hand column and elaborating details in the right-hand column. Study the notes by covering the right side and using the ideas on the left side to quiz yourself.

4 When and how should I write a summary? (pages 88–89)

Summaries are useful for capturing the essential information from supplemental reading materials, such as research articles and short stories. They are usually one paragraph. In your own words, begin with the main idea and continue with the important supporting information. A summary should not include any ideas that are not in the original material.

5 How can I use outline notes? (pages 92–93)

Display the topic with primary and secondary supporting details, using indentations, numbers, and letters to show levels of importance. Study the outline by re-creating it from memory or by making a copy, cutting it apart, and reassembling it.

6 How can I make notes using mapping? (pages 99–100)

Mapping is a highly visual note taking form that uses interconnecting shapes and lines to illustrate the relationships among the topic, major details, and minor details. Maps work best with a limited amount of information. Study by drawing the map from memory or by making a copy, cutting it into parts, and putting it back together like a jigsaw puzzle.

For more practice on textbook learning, refer to the sample textbook chapter in Appendix 1, page 509.

COLLABORATIVE PROBLEM SOLVING

Form a five-member group and select one of the following activities. After reading this chapter, brainstorm and then outline your major points. Create a poster or a brief skit to present the group findings to the class.

➤ Go to Appendix 1, "Sample Textbook Chapter," on page 509. Have each group member select a section to annotate and make notes. Try for a variety of note taking forms. Share the notes within the group to assess their value in preparation for an imagined test.

➤ List ten tips for taking good lecture notes.

➤ List ten items that you can purchase that will help you get organized for successful study.

➤ Choose three students in your group to play the roles of lecturer, poor listener and note taker, and good listener and note taker.

PERSONAL FEEDBACK) 1

Name _____

1. What format do you prefer for note taking? Why? _____

_____

_____

2. What has been your experience with marking your texts (annotating)? How would you evaluate your annotating in light of what you have learned in this chapter?

_____

_____

_____

3. Why should you take notes on one side of a notebook page only? _____

_____

_____

4. What value do you see in making notes from your textbook reading? _____

_____

_____

5. What do you feel are the five major differences in academic expectations between

high school and college? _____

_____

_____

Share your responses as directed by your instructor.

SELECTION 1  **Business**   MyReadingLab ™

Visit Chapter 3: Textbook Learning in MyReadingLab to complete the Selection 1 activities.

"If you take a print magazine with a million person circulation, and a blog with a devout readership of 1 million, for the purpose of selling anything that can be sold online, the blog is infinitely more powerful, because it's only a click away."

—Timothy Ferriss, Author

Have you wondered why the advertisements that pop up on your computer screen sometimes tempt you with the things that you most want? Online shopping and social networking offer irresistible information to companies that are looking for buyers for their products. The tools to track our online behavior are becoming more and more sophisticated, and companies are using them to target potential buyers. Some people say this benefits shoppers by saving time, but others say it invades privacy.

THINKING BEFORE READING

Preview the selection for clues to its content. Activate your schema and anticipate what you will learn. Predict the author's ideas and determine your purpose for reading. Think!

What do you know about how your online activities are being tracked and how the information is used?

If you were in charge of marketing products for your company, would you use tracking information to target potential buyers?

I'll read this selection to find out _____

_____.

VOCABULARY PREVIEW

Are you familiar with these words?

unsolicited	unvarnished	scrutinize	savvy	trolling
legions	myriad	eavesdropping	adept	proponents

If a friend gives *unsolicited* advice, is it always welcome?

Is an *unvarnished* response a truly honest one?

Are *proponents* of an idea for or against it?

Your instructor may choose to give a brief vocabulary review before or after reading.

THINKING DURING READING

As you read, use the six thinking strategies of a good reader: predict, picture, relate, monitor, correct, and annotate. This selection includes marginal notes to help guide your comprehension. Add notes of your own as you mark the text.

CORNELL NOTES

Annotate the selection and then make Cornell notes as if to prepare for an exam.

Reader's **TIP** | **Reading and Studying Business**

- Activate your schema with the introductory profiles and boxed material that describe an actual company with a current business dilemma. These illustrate the chapter concepts.
- Connect business theories with a real company's problems or solutions to make learning easier. Use the business illustrations to visualize the concepts.
- Cross-reference your reading with the illustrative photographs, tables, flowcharts, figures, and copies of real advertisements. Sketch your own models of business and marketing processes and concepts. Use these visual learning tools to enhance your learning.
- Use the exercises to reinforce chapter topics, strengthen your research skills, and expand your knowledge. Instructional software may come with your text with practice quizzes and other instructional help.
- Use the tips that suggest how to market yourself by applying the chapter's concepts in your career search. For example, tips may offer advice on how to identify and access the major employment pipelines (*distribution channels*) for your product (you) in your career search.

MARKETING ONLINE: THE WEB KNOWS WHAT YOU WANT

Main point!

Like surveys & sales numbers?

①

Ex

Thanks to the growing world of blogs, social networks, and other Internet forums, marketers now have near-real-time access to a flood of online consumer information. It's all there for the digging—praise, criticism, recommendations, actions—revealed in what consumers are saying and doing as they surf the Internet. Forward-looking marketers are now
5   mining valuable customer insights from this rich new vein of unprompted, "bottom-up" information.

Whereas traditional marketing research provides insights into the "logical, structured aspect of our consumers," says Kristin Bush, senior manager of consumer and market knowledge at P&G (Proctor & Gamble), online listening "provides much more of the
10 intensity and more of the naturalness that consumers are truly giving you when they offer up their opinion unsolicited."

Listening online might involve something as simple as scanning customer reviews on the company's brand site or on popular shopping sites such as Amazon.com or BestBuy.com.

Such reviews are plentiful, address specific products, and provide unvarnished customer reac-
15 tions. Amazon.com alone features detailed customer reviews on everything it sells, and its customers rely heavily on these reviews when making purchases. If customers in the market for a
company's brands are reading and reacting to such reviews, so should the company's marketers. Many companies are now adding customer review sections to their own brand sites. Both
positive and negative feedback can help the company learn what it is doing well and where
20 improvement is needed.

+ & — comments help

Many sources of info

At a deeper level, marketers now employ sophisticated
Web-analysis tools to listen in
on and mine nuggets from the
25 churning mass of consumer
comments and conversations
in blogs, in news articles, in
online forums, and on social
networking sites such as Face-
30 book or Twitter. But beyond

monitoring what customers are *saying* about them online, companies are also watching
what customers are *doing* online. Marketers scrutinize consumer Web-browsing behavior
in precise detail and use the resulting insights to personalize shopping experiences. Consider this example:

Watch browsing habits too

35   A shopper at the retail site FigLeaves.com takes a close look at a silky pair of women's
slippers. Next, a recommendation appears for a man's bathrobe. This could seem terribly
wrong—unless, of course, it turns out to be precisely what she wanted. Why the bathrobe? Analysis of FigLeaves.com site behavior data—from mouse clicks to search queries—
shows that certain types of female shoppers at certain times of the week are likely to be
40 shopping for men.

Ex

What a given customer sees at the site might also depend on other behaviors. For
example, shoppers who seem pressed for time (say, shopping from work and clicking
rapidly from screen to screen) might see more simplified pages with a direct path to the
shopping cart and checkout. Alternatively, more leisurely shoppers (say, those shopping
45 from home or on weekends and browsing product reviews) might receive pages with
more features, video clips, and comparison information. The goal of such analysis is to
teach Web sites "something close to the savvy of a flesh-and-blood sales clerk," says a
Web-analytics expert. "In the first five minutes in a store, the sales guy is observing a customer's body language and tone of voice. We have to teach machines to pick up on those
50 same insights from movements online."

Ex

More broadly, information about what consumers do while trolling the vast expanse of the Internet—what searches they make, the sites they visit, what they buy, with whom they connect—is pure gold to marketers. And today's marketers are busy mining that gold.

On the Internet today, everybody knows who you are. In fact, legions of Internet com-
55 panies know your gender, your age, the neighborhood you live in, who your Facebook and Twitter friends are, that you like pickup trucks, and that you spent, say, three hours and 43 seconds on a Web site for pet lovers on a rainy day in January. All those data stream through myriad computer networks, where it's sorted, cataloged, analyzed, and then used to deliver ads aimed squarely at you, potentially anywhere you travel on the Internet. It's
60 called *behavioral targeting* —tracking consumers' online behavior and using it to target ads to them. So, for example, if you place a cell phone in your Amazon.com shopping cart but don't buy it, you might expect to see some ads for that very type of phone the next time you visit your favorite ESPN site to catch up on the latest sports scores.

That's amazing enough, but the newest wave of Web analytics and targeting takes
65 online eavesdropping even further—from *behavioral targeting* to *social targeting*. Whereas behavioral targeting tracks consumer movements across Web sites, social targeting also mines individual online social connections. Research shows that consumers shop a lot like their friends and are five times more likely to respond to ads from brands friends use. Social targeting links customer data to social interaction data from social networking sites.
70 So, instead of just having a Zappos.com ad for running shoes pop up because you've recently searched for running shoes (behavioral targeting), an ad for a specific pair of running shoes pops up because a friend that you're connected to via Twitter just bought those shoes from Zappos.com last week (social targeting).

Online listening. Behavioral targeting. Social targeting. All of these are great for mar-
75 keters as they work to mine customer insights from the massive amounts of consumer information swirling around the Web. The biggest question? You've probably already guessed it. As marketers get more adept at trolling blogs, social networks, and other Web domains, what happens to consumer privacy? Yup, that's the downside. At what point does sophisticated Web research cross the line into consumer stalking?

80 Proponents claim that behavioral and social targeting benefit more than abuse con-
sumers by feeding back ads and products that better match their interests. But to many consumers and public advocates, following consumers online and stalking them with ads feels more than just a little creepy. Behavioral targeting, for example, has already been the subject of congressional and regulatory hearings. The Federal Trade Commission has
85 recommended the creation of a "Do Not Track" system (the Internet equivalent to the "Do Not Call" registry), which would let people opt out of having their actions monitored online.

Good for marketers; not good for consumers?

② *Def*

Ex

③ *Def*

Ex

Watching my FB & Twitter too?

What do I think?

What gov't can do

*Business's view.
Would consumers
agree?*

Despite such concerns, however, online listening will continue to grow. And, with appropriate safeguards, it promises benefits for both companies and customers. Tap-
90 ping into online conversations and behavior lets companies "get the unprompted voice of the consumer, the real sentiments, the real values, and the real points of view that they have of our products and services," says P&G's Bush. "Companies that figure out how to listen and respond . . . in a meaningful, valuable way are going to win in the marketplace." After all, knowing what customers really want is an essential first step in creating customer value. And, as one online information expert puts it, "The Web knows what you want."

(1,137 words)

From *Marketing: An Introduction*, Eleventh Edition,
by Gary Armstrong and Philip Kotler

STUDY NOTES

Use your annotations to make Cornell-style notes of the selection.

THINKING AND WRITING AFTER READING

RECALL   Self-test your understanding.

Your instructor may choose to give you a brief comprehension review.

REACT   Do you object to the practice of personalizing advertisements by tracking your Internet behavior? Why or why not? How do you feel about advertisers using your social networking contacts to tailor advertisements? _____

_____

REFLECT   Describe an example of behavioral targeting or social targeting from your own experience. _____

_____

THINK CRITICALLY   Does the fact that tracking tools are available to advertisers make it almost necessary for them to use them to keep up with competitors? Explain your thoughts. _____

_____

_____

THINK AND WRITE   Is it ethical to use the marketing techniques described in this article? If so, explain your position. If not, what can be done to stop the practice? List your thoughts in outline form.

Position: _____

_____

I. Reason 1 _____

_____

    A. Example or further explanation _____

_____

    B. Example or further explanation _____

_____

II. Reason 2 _____

_____

    A. Example or further explanation _____

_____

    B. Example or further explanation _____

_____

EXTENDED WRITING Organize your thoughts from the outline above in the form of a blog post. Take a stand either supporting the use of tracking as a marketing method or opposing it. Explain your position clearly to convince readers.

Interpret THE QUOTE

Now that you've finished reading the selection, "Marketing Online: The Web Knows What You Want," go back to the beginning of the selection and read the opening quote again. Its author, Timothy Ferris, is a writer of best-selling nonfiction books on business and life, such as *The 4-Hour Work Week*. He gains exposure for his books and philosophies by blogging and interacting with other bloggers. How does his quote connect with the methods described in the reading selection?

Name —————————————————

Date —————————————————

COMPREHENSION QUESTIONS

Answer the following with *a*, *b*, *c*, or *d*, or fill in the blank. In order to help you analyze your strengths and weaknesses, the question types are indicated.

Main Idea ———— 1. The best statement of the main idea of this selection is

    a. Listening online includes scanning customer reviews.

    b. Too much personal information is available on the Internet.

    c. When companies use social targeting, they are watching what our friends say and do online and are using the information to send advertisements to us.

    d. Companies are using information from our online shopping comments and behavior and social network contacts to personalize targeting of online advertisements.

Detail ———— 2. Kristin Bush of Proctor & Gamble says that she likes online listening as a marketing tool mainly because ————————————.

    a. it gives logical information.

    b. it provides a natural look at consumers' opinions

    c. it provides good sales numbers.

    d. it is helpful for in-store sales associates.

Detail ———— 3. Which of the following is *not* included in online listening, according to the article?

    a. tracking consumers' Web searches

    b. monitoring customer comments on company Web sites

    c. monitoring customer reviews of products that customers have bought

    d. tracking both positive and negative comments from consumers

Inference ———— 4. When a company notices that you looked at a tablet computer on several shopping Web sites and then places an advertisement for their tablet on your next Internet destination, the company is using which marketing method?

    a. online listening

    b. traditional marketing

    c. behavioral targeting

    d. social targeting

Main Idea ———— 5. The main point of the last paragraph in the article is

    a. Web marketing methods benefit consumers.

    b. Companies that use Internet marketing techniques well will succeed.

    c. Many people are concerned that Web marketing invades privacy.

    d. Safeguards are necessary to protect privacy.

Detail _____ 6. Tracking consumers' online activities and using the information to personalize advertisements is called which of the following?

    a. social targeting
    b. online listening
    c. traditional marketing
    d. behavioral targeting

Inference _____ 7. We can infer from the selection that _____.

    a. Online marketing methods will stop due to privacy concerns.
    b. Online marketing methods are good for business and will continue.
    c. Companies will find new ways to market products, beyond online methods.
    d. Companies will stop social targeting but continue online listening and behavioral targeting.

Answer the following with *T* (true) or *F* (false).

Inference _____ 8. Some protections for online privacy are probably necessary.

Detail _____ 9. Some people feel that online marketing methods benefit consumers.

Detail _____ 10. Social targeting connects interactions on Facebook and Twitter to customer data and future advertisements.

VOCABULARY

Answer the following with *a, b, c,* or *d* for the word or phrase that best defines the boldface word used in the selection. The number in parentheses indicates the line of the passage in which the word appears. In addition to the context clues, use a dictionary to more precisely define the technical terms.

_____ 1. "offer their opinions **unsolicited**" (11)

    a. without being asked
    b. welcomed
    c. invited
    d. rudely

_____ 2. "**unvarnished** customer reactions" (14)

    a. unpainted
    b. emotional
    c. honest
    d. angry

_____ 3. "Marketers **scrutinize**" (32)

    a. glance at
    b. ignore
    c. talk about
    d. examine

_____ 4. "the **savvy** of a" (47)

    a. know-how
    b. kindness
    c. ignorance
    d. hiring

_____ 5. "**trolling** the vast expanse" (51)

    a. searching
    b. speeding
    c. writing
    d. reading

_____ 6. "**legions** of Internet companies" (54)

    a. some
    b. large numbers
    c. a few
    d. all

_____ 7. "**myriad** computer networks" (58)

a. specific
b. special
c. countless
d. several

_____ 8. "online **eavesdropping**" (65)

a. behavior
b. searching
c. listening in
d. shopping

_____ 9. "get more **adept** at" (77)

a. sneaky
b. careful
c. popular
d. skilled

_____ 10. "**Proponents** claim that" (80)

a. enemies
b. opponents
c. supporters
d. friends

Your instructor may choose to give a brief vocabulary review.

ASSESS YOUR LEARNING

Review questions that you did not understand, found confusing, or answered incorrectly. Seek clarification. Indicate beside each item the source of your confusion and notice the question type. Make notes beside confusing vocabulary items to help you remember them. Use your textbook as a learning tool.

SELECTION 2 Communication MyReadingLab™

Visit Chapter 3: Textbook Learning in MyReadingLab to complete the Selection 2 activities.

"An eye can threaten like a loaded and leveled gun, or it can insult like hissing or kicking; or, in its altered mood, by beams of kindness, it can make the heart dance for joy."

—Ralph Waldo Emerson

We draw conclusions about people through what their eyes communicate. A lifted eyebrow suggests surprise, and a narrowed gaze hints at skepticism. We say "Look me straight in the eye" to search for truth. On the other hand, a furtive glance arouses suspicion. To both lubricate and protect the eyes, we normally blink an average of fifteen times a minute, but excessive blinking can cause us to question sincerity. The eyes have been called the "mirrors of the soul." How accurate are we in reading the eyes?

THINKING BEFORE READING

Preview the selection for content and organizational clues. Activate your schema and anticipate what you will learn. Predict the author's ideas and determine your purpose for reading. Think!

Why does the expression "The couple locked eyes" suggest romance?

When speaking to a group, do you make eye contact with each member of the audience?

When do your pupils become dilated?

After reading this selection I will probably know _____.

VOCABULARY PREVIEW

Are you familiar with these words?

duration	gaze	perceive	compensate	avert
auditory	intuitive	dilated	constricted	profound

Why do you want to be *compensated* for your hard work?

How is *intuitive* related to *intuition*?

Is a *profound* statement worthy of remembering?

Your instructor may choose to give a brief vocabulary review before or after reading.

THINKING DURING READING

As you read, use the six thinking strategies of a good reader: predict, picture, relate, monitor, correct, and annotate.

MAPPING

Annotate the selection and then use mapping to create notes to prepare for an essay exam.

> ## Reader's TIP — Reading and Studying Communication
>
> Ask yourself the following questions as you read a communications text.
>
> - How can I improve as a communicator and a conversationalist?
> - How do I react to other people? Am I open to new ideas?
> - How can I become a more valuable group member or a more productive group leader?
> - Am I afraid to speak in public? How can I lessen that fear?
> - What actions and expressions should be avoided in opening and closing a speech?

EYE COMMUNICATION

The messages communicated by the eyes vary depending on the duration, direction, and quality of the eye behavior. For example, in every culture there are rather strict, though unstated, rules for the proper duration for eye contact. In much of England and the United States, for example, the average length of gaze is 2.95 seconds. The average length of

5   mutual gaze (two persons gazing at each other) is 1.18 seconds. When the duration of eye contact is shorter than 1.18 seconds, you may think the person is uninterested, shy, or preoccupied. When the appropriate amount of time is exceeded, you may perceive this as showing high interest.

In much of the United States, direct eye contact is considered an expression of honesty and forthrightness. But the Japanese often view eye contact as a lack of respect.
The Japanese will glance at the other person's face rarely and then only for a very short
period. In many Hispanic cultures, direct eye contact signifies certain equality and so
should be avoided by, say, children when speaking to a person in authority. Try visualizing the potential misunderstandings that **eye communication** alone could create when
people from Tokyo, San Francisco, and San Juan try to communicate.

The direction of the eye also communicates. Generally, in communicating with
another person, you will glance alternatively at the other person's face, then away, then
again at the face, and so on. When these directional rules are broken, different meanings are communicated—abnormally high or low interest, self-consciousness, nervousness
over the interaction, and so on. The quality of the gaze—how wide or how narrow your
eyes get during interaction—also communicates meaning, especially interest level and
such emotions as surprise, fear, and disgust.

EYE CONTACT

You use eye contact to serve several important functions.

- **To monitor feedback**. For example, when you talk with others, you look at them
  intently and try to understand their reactions to what you're saying. You try to read
  their feedback, and on this basis you adjust what you say. As you can imagine, successful readings of feedback will help considerably in your overall effectiveness.

- **To secure attention**. When you speak with two or three other people, you maintain
  eye contact to secure the attention and interest of your listeners. When someone fails
  to pay you the attention you want, you probably increase your eye contact, hoping
  that this will increase attention.

- **To regulate the conversation**. Eye contact helps you regulate, manage, and control
  the conversation. With eye movements you can inform the other person that she or
  he should speak. A clear example of this occurs in the college classroom, where the
  instructor asks a question and then locks eyes with a student. This type of eye contact
  tells the student to answer the question.

- **To signal the nature of the relationship**. Eye communication also can serve as a "tie
  sign" or signal of the nature of the relationship between two people—for example,
  to indicate positive or negative regard. Depending on the culture, eye contact may
  communicate your romantic interest in another person, or eye avoidance may indicate respect. Some researchers note that eye contact serves to enable gay men and
  lesbians to signal their homosexuality and perhaps their interest in someone—an
  ability referred to as "gaydar."

- **To signal status**. Eye contact is often used to signal status and aggression. Among
45 many younger people, prolonged eye contact from a stranger is taken to signify
aggressiveness and frequently prompts physical violence—merely because one person looked perhaps a little longer than was considered normal in that specific culture.

- **To compensate for physical distance**. Eye contact is often used to compensate for
increased physical distance. By making eye contact you overcome psychologically the
50 physical distance between yourself and another person. When you catch someone's
eye at a party, for example, you become psychologically closer even though you may
be separated by considerable physical distance.

EYE AVOIDANCE

The eyes, sociologist Erving Goffman observed in Interaction Ritual, are "great intruders."
When you avoid eye contact or avert your glance, you allow others to maintain their privacy.
55 You probably do this when you see a couple arguing in the street or on a bus. You turn
your eyes away, as if to say, "I don't mean to intrude; I respect your privacy." Goffman
refers to this behavior as **civil inattention**.

Eye avoidance also can signal lack of interest—in a person, a conversation, or some
visual stimulus. At times, like the ostrich, we hide our eyes to try to cut off unpleasant stimuli.
60 Notice, for example, how quickly people close their eyes in the face of some extreme unpleasantness. Interestingly enough, even if the unpleasantness is auditory, we tend to shut it out
by closing our eyes. At other times, we close our eyes to block out visual stimuli and thus to
heighten our other senses; for example, we often listen to music with our eyes closed. Lovers
often close their eyes while kissing, and many prefer to make love in a dark or dimly lit room.

PUPIL DILATION

65 In the fifteenth and sixteenth centuries, Italian women used to put drops of belladonna
(which literally means "beautiful woman") into their eyes to enlarge the pupils so that
they would look more attractive. Research in the field of **pupillometrics** supports the
intuitive logic of these women: Dilated pupils are in fact judged more attractive than
constricted ones.

70   In one study, for example, photographs of women were retouched. In one set of photographs the pupils were enlarged, and in the other they were made smaller. Men were then
asked to judge the women's personalities from the photographs. The photos of women
with small pupils drew responses such as cold, hard, and selfish; those with dilated pupils
drew responses such as feminine and soft. However, the male observers could not verbalize
75 the reasons for the different perceptions. Both pupil dilation itself and people's reactions to
changes in the pupil size of others seem to function below the level of conscious awareness.

Pupil size also reveals your interest and level of emotional arousal. Your pupils enlarge when you're interested in something or when you're emotionally aroused. When homosexuals and heterosexuals were shown pictures of nude bodies, the homo-
80 sexuals' pupils dilated more when viewing same-sex bodies, whereas the heterosexuals' pupils dilated more when viewing opposite-sex bodies. These pupillary responses are unconscious and are even observed in persons with profound mental retardation. Perhaps we find dilated pupils more attractive because we judge them as indicative of a person's interest in us. That may be why models, Beanie Babies, and Teletubbies have
85 exceptionally large pupils.

Although belladonna is no longer used, the cosmetics industry has made millions selling eye enhancers—eye shadow, eyeliner, false eyelashes, and tinted contact lenses that change eye color. These items function (ideally, at least) to draw attention to these most powerful communicators.

(1,114 words)

—From Joseph A. DeVito, *The Interpersonal Communication Book*, Thirteenth edition. Published by Pearson Education, Inc. Copyright ©2013. Adapted by permission of the publisher.

STUDY NOTES

Use your annotations to make a map of significant elements of eye communication.

THINKING AND WRITING AFTER READING

RECALL Self-test your understanding.

Your instructor may choose to give you a brief comprehension review.

REACT Why do you feel uncomfortable when eyes are locked in a mutual gaze for more than 1.18 seconds? _____

_____

REFLECT Try the suggested experiment of adjusting the percentage of interaction time for gazing. With another student, first let the speaker gaze for 62 to 75 percent of the time, and then have the speaker gaze for only 38 to 41 percent of the time. Next, try the same percentages for the listener. Describe the difficulties and your reactions. _____

_____

THINK CRITICALLY How do college instructors use eye contact to enhance instruction? Give examples of a variety of effective strategies that you have observed.

_____

_____

THINK AND WRITE   Why do you agree or disagree that the eyes are the "mirrors to the soul"? Give examples of when you feel you have been both correct and incorrect in "reading the eyes." _____

_____

_____

EXTENDED WRITING   College professors often ask essay questions on tests. They expect clear, concise answers that demonstrate knowledge of the topic and that directly answer the question. Successful students predict possible essay questions and practice answering them. If you have not done so already, create a map that illustrates the main points and key details of this selection. Use your map notes to write an answer to the following question that might be asked on an essay test:

In one paragraph, describe at least four of the six functions of eye contact that are explained in "Eye Communication." Include an example in your description of each function.

Interpret THE QUOTE

Now that you have finished reading the selection, "Eye Communication," go back to the beginning of the selection and read the opening quote again. On a separate sheet of paper, describe what Emerson means when he says that an eye can "threaten like a loaded and leveled gun." Also, describe two situations in which you used your eyes to communicate joy or anger.

Name —————————————

Date —————————————

COMPREHENSION QUESTIONS

Answer the following with *a, b, c,* or *d,* or fill in the blank. In order to help you analyze your strengths and weaknesses, the question types are indicated.

Main Idea ———— 1. The best statement of the main idea of the selection is

    a. Eye contact in different cultures varies according to duration, direction, and quality.

    b. Eye contact communicates several different messages that vary according to duration, direction, and quality.

    c. When the rules are broken for eye contact, the messages can range from self-consciousness to fear and disgust.

    d. The appropriateness of eye contact can be measured in the length of seconds of duration and the percentage of time gazing while listening.

Detail ———— 2. Direct eye contact is considered a sign of equality in

    a. Japan.

    b. England.

    c. the United States.

    d. Latin America.

Detail ———— 3. For a speaker to be considered within the "normal" range, an appropriate percentage of time spent gazing while talking is

    a. 39 percent.

    b. 45 percent.

    c. 62 percent.

    d. 75 percent.

Inference ———— 4. The author suggests that in the United States, a short duration of eye contact will most likely be interpreted as

    a. aggression.

    b. status for the speaker.

    c. love interest.

    d. inattention.

Inference 5. In what cases might civil inattention be inappropriate? ————

————————————————————

Detail ———— 6. Belladonna was all of the following *except*

    a. eye drops used by Italian women.

    b. a fifteenth- and sixteenth-century beauty enhancer.

    c. eye medication with beautifying side effects.

    d. an Italian word meaning "beautiful woman."

Detail _____ 7. According to research findings discussed in the passage, the general viewer's pupil dilation reactions when viewing pictures of nude bodies were all of the following *except*

    a. varying in emotional arousal for different groups.

    b. emotionally arousing for homosexuals viewing same-sex pictures.

    c. emotionally arousing for heterosexuals viewing same-sex pictures.

    d. made without conscious awareness.

Answer the following with *T* (true), *F* (false), or *CT* (can't tell).

Detail _____ 8. In referring to the quality of eye communication, the author is describing how wide or narrow the eyes are during interaction.

Detail _____ 9. The eyes can silently be used by a speaker to indicate the next person to speak.

Detail _____ 10. A high level of eye contact by the listener shows a lack of status for the speaker.

VOCABULARY

Answer the following with *a, b, c,* or *d* for the word or phrase that best defines the boldface word as used in the selection. The number in parentheses indicates the line of the passage in which the word appears. In addition to the context clues, use a dictionary to more precisely define the technical terms.

_____ 1. "depending on the **duration**" (1)

    a. strength

    b. length

    c. ability

    d. meaning

_____ 2. "length of **gaze**" (5)

    a. look

    b. clarity

    c. direction

    d. quality

_____ 3. "may **perceive** this" (7)

    a. deny

    b. dismiss

    c. object to

    d. recognize

_____ 4. "used to **compensate** for" (48)

    a. calculate

    b. make up

    c. detract

    d. vary

_____ 5. "**avert** your glance" (54)

    a. turn toward

    b. intensify

    c. extend

    d. turn away

_____ 6. unpleasantness is **auditory**" (61)

    a. seen

    b. imagined

    c. heard

    d. real'

_____ 7. "**intuitive** logic" (68)

    a. instinctive

    b. ancient

    c. stylish

    d. historic

_____ 8. "**dilated** pupils" (68)

    a. colored

    b. narrowed

    c. enlarged

    d. painted

_____ 9. "**constricted** ones" (69)

    a. narrowed
    b. enlarged
    c. closed
    d. unadorned

_____ 10. "**profound** mental retardation" (82)

    a. slight
    b. deep
    c. recent
    d. confusing

Your instructor may choose to give a brief vocabulary review.

ASSESS YOUR LEARNING

Review questions that you did not understand, found confusing, or answered incorrectly. Seek clarification. Indicate beside each item the source of your confusion and notice the question type. Make notes beside confusing vocabulary items to help you remember them. Use your textbook as a learning tool.

Visit Chapter 3: Textbook Learning in MyReadingLab to complete the Selection 3 activities and Building Background Knowledge video activity.

"You cannot propel yourself forward by patting yourself on the back."

—Chinese Proverb

Dr. Bernard Suran reports in the Florida Bar News *that when asked, "Would you like to become a better person?" most people surprisingly respond with a resounding "maybe" rather than an enthusiastic "of course." Why bother to change if life is not holding your feet to the fire in a reaction to circumstances? Genuine change is difficult, requiring a firm commitment and an organized plan. Dr. Suran says, "What motivates best is the realm of possibility, if we allow ourselves to consider the prospect of becoming even more awesome than we already are."*

THINKING BEFORE READING

Preview for content and organizational clues. Activate your schema and anticipate what you will learn. Predict the author's ideas and determine your purpose for reading. Think!

What circumstances can give people the impetus to change unwanted behaviors?

What is a positive reinforcement?

How do Olympic athletes use imagery and psychology to excel?

I think this selection will say that _____.

BUILDING BACKGROUND KNOWLEDGE — **VIDEO**

The Five "S"s of Conscious Eating

To prepare for reading Selection 3, answer the questions below. Then, watch this video about a method of forming healthy eating habits.

Do you have certain habits that you would like to change?

What methods have you or others used to change an unhealthy or irritating habit?

How might where you eat affect how much you eat?

This video helped me _____.

VOCABULARY PREVIEW

Are you familiar with these words?

coaxed	acknowledgment	languish	vigilance	commitment
scenario	inducement	premise	irrational	resort

How can someone be *coaxed* into a *commitment* they do not want to make?

What *scenario* might cause someone to resort to an extreme lifestyle change?

Your instructor may choose to give a brief vocabulary review before or after reading.

THINKING DURING READING

As you read, use the six thinking strategies of a good reader: predict, picture, relate, monitor, correct, and annotate.

ANNOTATING

Annotate the selection in order to make an outline of significant elements in behavior change.

Reader's TIP   Reading and Studying Health

- Use learning aids provided within the text. Such items might include running glossaries on pages, checklists, discussion and application questions, and summaries.
- Answer any marginal questions placed within a chapter.
- Review and understand procedures by following the graphics provided.
- Design your own concept cards (see Chapter 4) to help learn new vocabulary.
- Draw simple figures or symbols to aid your understanding and recall of concepts.

BEHAVIOR CHANGE

Mark Twain said that "habit is habit, and not to be flung out the window by anyone, but coaxed downstairs a step at a time." The chances of successfully changing negative behavior improve when you make gradual changes that give you time to unlearn negative patterns and to substitute positive ones.

STAGING FOR CHANGE

5 On any given day, countless numbers of us get out of bed and resolve to begin to change a given behavior "today." Whether it be losing weight, drinking less, exercising more, being nicer to others, managing time better, or some other change in a negative behavior, we start out with high expectations. In a short time, however, a vast majority of people fail and are soon doing whatever it was they thought they shouldn't be doing.

10   After considerable research, Dr. James Prochaska and Dr. Carlos DiClimente believe that behavior changes usually do not succeed if they start with the change itself. Instead, they believe that we must go through a series of "stages" to adequately prepare, or ready, ourselves for that eventual change.

Precontemplation. People in the precontemplation stage have no current intention
15 of changing. They may have tried to change a behavior before and may have all but given up, or they may just be in denial and unaware of any problem.

Contemplation. In the contemplation stage, the person recognizes that he or she has a problem and begins to think about the need to change. Despite this acknowledgment, people can languish in this stage for years, knowing that they have a problem but never
20 finding the time or energy to make the change.

Preparation. Most people in this stage are close to taking action. They've thought about several things they might do and may even have come up with a plan.

Action. In the action stage, the individual begins to follow the action plan he or she has put together. Unfortunately, too many people start behavior change here rather than
25 going through the first three stages. Without a plan, without enlisting the help of others, or without a realistic goal, failure is likely.

Maintenance. Maintenance requires vigilance, attention to detail, and long-term commitment. Many people reach their goals, only to relax and slip back into the undesired behavior.

30   **Termination.** In this stage, the behavior is so ingrained that the current level of vigilance may be unnecessary. The new behavior has become an essential part of daily living.

CHOOSING A BEHAVIOR-CHANGE STRATEGY

Once you have analyzed all the factors that influence what you do, you must decide which behavior-change technique will work best for you. These techniques include shaping, visualization, modeling, controlling the situation, reinforcement, and changing
35 self-talk.

Shaping.

Regardless of how motivated you are, some behaviors are almost impossible to change immediately. To reach your goal, you may need to take a number of individual steps, each designed to change one small piece of the larger behavior. This process is known as shaping.

40   For example, suppose that you have not exercised for a while. You decide that you want to get into shape, and your goal is to jog three to four miles every other day. So you start slowly and build up to your desired fitness level gradually.

Visualization.

Mental practice and rehearsal can help change unhealthy behaviors into healthy ones. Athletes and others use a technique known as imagined rehearsal to reach their goals. By
45 visualizing their planned action ahead of time, they are better prepared when they put themselves to the test.

For example, suppose you want to ask someone out on a date. Imagine the setting (walking together to class) for the action. Then practice exactly what you're going to say ("Minh, there's a great concert this Sunday and I was wondering if") in your mind and out
50 loud. Mentally anticipate different responses ("Oh, I'd love to, but I'm busy that evening") and what you will say in reaction ("How about if I call you sometime this week?"). Careful mental and verbal rehearsal—you could even try out your scenario on a friend—will greatly improve the likelihood of success.

Modeling.

Modeling, or learning behaviors through careful observation of other people, is one of
55 the most effective strategies for changing behavior. For example, suppose that you have trouble talking to people you don't know very well. One of the easiest ways to improve your communication skills is to select friends whose "gift of gab" you envy. Observe their social skills. Do they talk more or listen more? How do people respond to them? Why are they such good communicators?

Controlling the Situation.

60 Sometimes, the right setting or right group of people will positively influence your behaviors. Many situations and occasions trigger certain actions. The term **situational inducement** refers to an attempt to influence a behavior by using situations and occasions to control it.

For example, you may be more apt to stop smoking if you work in a smoke-free office,
65 a positive situational inducement. By carefully considering which settings will help and which will hurt your effort to change, you will improve your chances for change.

Reinforcement.

A **positive reinforcement** is a reward that is given to increase the likelihood that a behavior change will occur. Each of us is motivated by different reinforcers. Although a special T-shirt may be a positive reinforcer for young adults entering a race, it would not be for a
70 40-year-old runner who dislikes message-bearing T-shirts.

Changing Self-Talk

Self-talk, or the way you think and talk to yourself, can also play a role in modifying health-related behaviors. Here are some cognitive procedures for changing self-talk.

Rational-Emotive Therapy—This form of cognitive therapy or self-directed behavior change is based on the premise that there is a close connection between what people say to themselves and how they feel. According to psychologist Albert Ellis, most emotional problems and related behaviors stem from irrational statements that people make to themselves when events in their lives are different from what they would like them to be.

For example, suppose that after doing poorly on an exam, you say to yourself, "I can't believe I flunked that easy exam. I'm so stupid." By changing this irrational,"catastrophic" self-talk into rational, positive statements about what is really going on, you can increase the likelihood that positive behaviors will occur. Positive self-talk might be phrased as follows: "I really didn't study enough for that exam, and I'm not surprised I didn't do very well. I'm certainly not stupid. I just need to prepare better for the next test." Such self-talk will help you to recover quickly from disappointment and take positive steps to correct the situation.

85   **Meichenbaum's Self-Instructional Methods**—Behavioral psychologist Donald Meichenbaum is perhaps best known for a process known as stress inoculation, which subjects clients to extreme stressors in a laboratory environment. Before a stressful event (e.g., going to the doctor), clients practice individual coping skills (e.g., deep breath ing exercises) and self-instruction (e.g., "I'll feel better once I know what's causing my

90   pain"). Meichenbaum demonstrated that clients who practiced coping techniques and self-instruction were less likely to resort to negative behaviors in difficult situations. In Meichenbaum's behavioral therapies, clients are encouraged to give themselves "self-instructions" ("Slow down, don't rush") and "positive affirmations" ("My speech is going fine—I'm almost done!") instead of self-defeating thoughts ("I'm talking too fast—my

95   speech is terrible") whenever a situation seems to be getting out of control.

     Blocking/Thought Stopping—By purposefully blocking or stopping negative thoughts, a person can concentrate on taking positive steps toward behavior change. For example, suppose you are preoccupied with your ex-partner, who has recently deserted you for someone else. You consciously stop dwelling on the situation and force yourself to

100 think about something more pleasant (e.g., dinner tomorrow with your best friend). By refusing to dwell on negative images and forcing yourself to focus elsewhere, you can save wasted energy, time, and emotional resources and move on to positive change.

(1,294 words)

—From *Health: The Basics*, Fifth Edition,
by Rebecca J. Donatelle

STUDY OUTLINE

Use your annotations to make an outline of significant elements in behavior change.

THINKING AND WRITING AFTER READING

RECALL   Self-test your understanding.

Your instructor may choose to give you a brief comprehension review.

REACT   Why are positive role models important for success? How has your behavior been affected by negative role models? Who has been a positive role model for you? _____

_____

REFLECT   Why are people reluctant to initiate behavior change? How do past experiences lessen enthusiasm? _____

_____

THINK CRITICALLY   What behavior would you most like to change? Outline your plan for success.

THINK AND WRITE Why do we engage in negative self-talk? How can negative self-talk be self-defeating and positive self-talk be uplifting? What does self-talk say about the power of language? How would you like to change your own self-talk?

_____

_____

_____

EXTENDED WRITING Scholarly journal articles usually begin with an abstract. An abstract is a summary, usually one paragraph, that concisely presents the main point and supporting details. Researchers read the abstract to determine if the article contains information that fits their purpose. If so, they read the article carefully. If not, they move on to other articles. Use your outline of this selection to write a summary that could be used as an abstract for researchers.

Interpret THE QUOTE

Now that you have finished reading the selection, "Behavior Change," go back to the beginning of the selection and read the opening quote again. What is its message about changing behavior? Name one personal situation in which you can apply it.

Name ——————————————————

Date ——————————————————

COMPREHENSION QUESTIONS

Answer the following with *a, b, c,* or *d,* or fill in the blank. In order to help you analyze your strengths and weaknesses, the question types are indicated.

Main Idea ———— 1. The best statement of the main idea of the selection is

    a. Behavior change is the science of learning new, positive patterns to replace previous negative actions.

    b. Successful behavior change begins with precontemplation, and then other stages follow.

    c. Shaping, visualization, and modeling are the significant strategies for behavior change.

    d. Successful behavior change begins with adequate preparation and continues with a variety of strategies and techniques to gradually alter thoughts and actions.

Inference 2. What did Mark Twain mean by saying, "habit is habit, and not to be flung out the window by anyone, but coaxed downstairs a step at a time"? ————————————————————

——————————————————————————

——————————————————————————

Inference ———— 3. Establishing realistic goals, identifying rewards for milestones, and seeking support from friends is the stage of change labeled

    a. precontemplation.

    b. contemplation.

    c. preparation.

    d. termination.

Detail ———— 4. The strategy of learning behaviors through watching other people is called

    a. shaping.

    b. visualization.

    c. modeling.

    d. reinforcement.

Inference ———— 5. To achieve a weight loss goal, not making your usual weekly purchase of M & M's is an example of the behavior-changing strategy called

    a. shaping.

    b. modeling.

    c. controlling the situation

    d. reinforcement.

Detail ———— 6. Rational-emotive therapy is based on the premise that

    a. feelings are manipulated by what we tell ourselves.

    b. coping techniques such as deep breathing can reduce stress.

    c. forcing yourself to focus elsewhere removes the negative thought.

    d. language is more powerful than thought.

Inference _____ 7. For a weight loss goal, replacing thoughts of chocolate candy with thoughts of the Friday night basketball game is an example of
a. rational-emotive therapy.
b. self-instruction.
c. Meichenbaum's coping strategy.
d. blocking.

Answer the following with *T* (true), *F* (false), or *CT* (can't tell).

Detail _____ 8. Prochaska and DiClimente believe that failure occurs when people start with the change itself.

Detail _____ 9. In Meichenbaum's self-instructional method, clients pretend to experience the dreaded event in order to practice coping skills.

Detail _____ 10. Visualization is the observation and imitation of positive behaviors of others.

VOCABULARY

Answer the following with *a, b, c,* or *d* for the word or phrase that best defines the boldface word used in the selection. The number in parentheses indicates the line of the passage in which the word appears. In addition to the context clues, use a dictionary to more precisely define the technical terms.

_____ 1. "**coaxed** downstairs" (2)
a. forced
b. persuaded
c. thrown
d. scattered

_____ 2. "Despite this **acknowledgment**" (18)
a. denial
b. fulfillment
c. opportunity
d. admission

_____ 3. "people can **languish**" (19)
a. pine away
b. progress
c. contemplate
d. evolve

_____ 4. "requires **vigilance**" (27)
a. courage
b. watchfulness
c. intelligence
d. energy

_____ 5. "long-term **commitment**" (28)
a. confidence
b. frustration
c. management
d. obligation

_____ 6. "try out your **scenario**" (52)
a. enactment
b. dream
c. argument
d. sentences

_____ 7. "situational **inducement**" (61–62)
a. stop
b. error
c. enticement
d. replacement

_____ 8. "based on the **premise**" (74)
a. hope
b. feeling
c. idea
d. emotion

_____ 9. "**irrational** statements"
(76)

    a. illogical
    b. angry
    c. hateful
    d. threatening

_____ 10. "**resort to** negative
behaviors" (91)

    a. escape through
    b. go back to
    c. hide under
    d. yearn for

Your instructor may choose to give a brief vocabulary review.

VOCABULARY ENRICHMENT

A. **Context Clues:** Select the word from the list that best completes the
sentences.

coaxed	acknowledgment	languish	vigilance	commitment
scenario	inducement	premise	irrational	resort

1. Without becoming a "warrior against pleasure," you do not want to
   silently watch a friend _____ to undesired behaviors.

2. Money can be a strong and effective _____ to motivate behavior changes.

3. Denial can cause people to _____ in a state of indecision and
   fail to embrace change.

4. Entering the termination stage is an _____ that maintenance has been successful.

5. During the contemplation stage of change, a gentle nudge from a friend
   may have _____ the contemplator to get started.

6. Emotive therapy or self-talk can calm the nerves and help prevent
   _____ behavior.

7. Without proper _____, a dieter can slip back into old habits of
   snacking and not exercising.

8. Significant others can assist a loved one in making a _____ to
   lasting change.

9. If you accept the _____ that positive reinforcements promote
   change, seek to individualize incentives for maximum motivation.

10. Write a _____ in which you are tempted to revert to your old
    bad habits but, instead, skillfully conquer your demons.

SELECTION 3

SELECTION 3

B. **Thesaurus:** Use a thesaurus, either the computer or book version, to find four alternative words for each of the following:

1. indication _____

2. habit _____

3. beginning _____

4. agreement _____

5. respect _____

ASSESS YOUR LEARNING

Review questions that you did not understand, found confusing, or answered incorrectly. Seek clarification. Indicate beside each item the source of your confusion and notice the question type. Make notes beside confusing vocabulary items to help you remember them. Use your textbook as a learning tool.

VOCABULARY LESSON

For or Against?

Study the prefixes, words, and sentences.

Prefixes *pro*: for, forward, forth *anti, ant*: against *contra*: against

Words with *pro = for, forward, forth*

Do medical *procedures* require signed forms? Can you *proceed* inside with a ticket?

- Pro-choice: for abortion rights

  The *pro-choice* rally was held on the steps of the state capitol.

- Proponent: supporter

  Are you a *proponent* of building another oil pipeline in Alaska?

- Procure: to get or gain

  Campers need to *procure* supplies a week prior to departure.

- Profess: to openly admit

  I *profess* to enjoying double fudge chocolate brownie cake.

- Prolific: bringing forth young or fruit

  The *prolific* young couple had six small children.

- Proficient: showing skill

  To be *proficient* in Spanish requires a knowledge of grammar.

- Proliferate: to bring forth by rapid production

  Fast-food restaurants seem to *proliferate* near interstate highway exits.

Words with *anti* or *ant = against*

Do *antiabortionists* use signs? Will an *anticoagulant* stop bleeding?

- Antacid: a counteracting agent for acidity of the stomach

  Take an *antacid* tablet for a burning stomach.

- Antagonism: a strong feeling against a person or idea

  After they had shared several funny jokes, the *antagonism* between them evaporated.

- Antarctic: the opposite of the North Pole

  The *Antarctic* region is south of the Arctic.

- Anticlimax: a letdown from a greater event

  After the previous night's celebration, New Year's day was an *anticlimax*.

- Antipathy: a strong feeling of dislike

  The business partner's *antipathy* toward the accused swindler was evident.

- Antithesis: a contrast of ideas

  The son's liberal ideas are the *antithesis* of his father's conservative policies.

- Antibody: a substance in the body opposing diseases

  The scientists worked to create an *antibody* for the new flu strain.

- Antidote: a remedy for poison

  Jungle travelers carry an *antidote* for snake bites.

- Antifreeze: a substance to slow the freezing process

  Check your car for *antifreeze* before the first frost.

Words with *contra* = *against*

Does sex education stress *contraceptives*? Are *controversial* issues frequently argued?

- Contraband: illegal

  Contraband items can be seized by the police.

- Contradict: to speak against

  To *contradict* a speaker, you must be sure of your facts.

- Contrarian: person who takes contrary views

  Reasoning with a *contrarian* is not always possible.

Review

Part I

Answer the following with *T* (true) or *F* (false).

_____ 1. An antidote is an amusing story.

_____ 2. A prolific plant bears many fruits.

_____ 3. Supplies can be procured by illegal means.

_____ 4. A contrarian would be comfortable in a role involving questioning.

_____ 5. Pro-choice advocates demonstrate against abortion clinics.

_____ 6. If you contradict the evidence, you disagree with the facts.

_____ 7. An athlete must be proficient to play on a professional team.

_____ 8. A sick person usually welcomes an antibody.

_____ 9. A controversial news story seldom generates further discussion.

_____ 10. For a peaceful relationship, mutual antagonism should be resolved.

Part II

Choose the best word from the list as a synonym for the following.

profess	antacid	antithesis	proponent	antifreeze
procedure	controversy	anticlimax	contraband	antipathy

11. Liquid solution for machines _____

12. Feeling of dislike _____

13. Smuggled drugs _____

14. Admit _____

15. Medication _____

16. Plan _____

17. Opposite _____

18. Disagreement _____

19. Supporter _____

20. Disappointment _____

SELECTION 3

Reading News and Feature Stories in the Newspaper

Readership of daily newspapers is declining across the United States and elsewhere as more people rely on the Internet, television, and radio to learn the news. These media often provide a briefer, summary version of news events to satisfy a busy public and then produce special segments or links for people who want greater depth. The Everyday Reading Skills feature in Chapter 4 examines electronic news sources. Whether the news source is electronic or printed on paper, however, the formats are similar. Understanding how newspapers and news reports are organized will help you get the most from them. The following Everyday Reading Skills section explains the features you will encounter whether you read an online or print version of a newspaper.

What do you usually read first if you read a newspaper? You probably already have a pattern for reading your favorite parts. To help you locate different topics, newspapers are divided into *sections*: national and international news; local or regional news; sports; entertainment and the arts (including music, movies, and television); classified advertisements; plus any other categories that the editors believe are appropriate for the local community. The front page always carries the most important news stories from all the categories. Those articles are often continued on a later page where other articles related to the lead story appear. Some newspapers include an index on the front page to help you locate high-interest articles or regular sections.

Understand the Evolution of Newspaper Style

To appreciate the organization of newspaper stories, you must first understand that the journalistic style of newspaper writing developed as a response to the telegraph machine, a new technology that could break down at any time.

As protection against a communication breakdown or a deadline cutoff, as well as to ensure that readers received the most important parts of the news story, reporters got into the habit of including only the most important points in the first paragraphs. The major and minor details of the story were then placed in the following paragraphs in *descending* order of importance. Thus, the **inverted pyramid** format of news writing was invented. Although technology has improved dramatically, this format has continued.

Reader's TIP Reading a News Story

- Get an overview from the headline and photographs.
- Answer the 5 *W*'s and the *H*.

Who is the story about?
What happened?
When did it happen?
Where did the event or events take place?
Why did this event occur?
How did this happen?

- Continue to read according to the amount of detail desired.

News Stories

News stories are the front-page articles that objectively report facts in descending order of importance. The **lead** is the first paragraph, which catches the reader's attention, often summarizes the essential points of the story, and establishes a focus. Many leads contain the 5 *W*'s and the *H*: *Who, What, When, Where, Why,* and *How*? Think of the first paragraph as a condensed version of the event.

Subsequent paragraphs present details in a hierarchy of importance. A news story has no ending but rather tapers down from major to minor details. As you read further, more complete information is given about the six basic questions. Your level of interest will determine how far you read for more details. The following excerpt is an example of the inverted pyramid format in a news story.

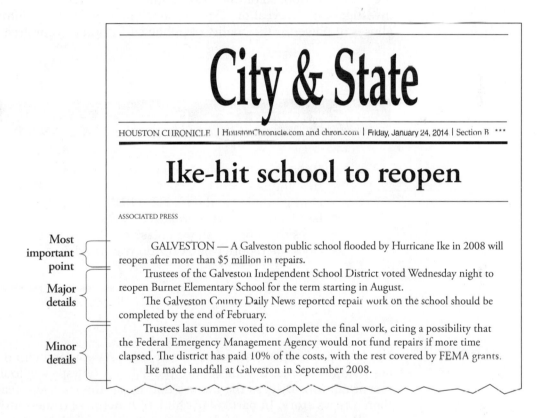

City & State

HOUSTON CHRONICLE | HoustonChronicle.com and chron.com | Friday, January 24, 2014 | Section B ***

Ike-hit school to reopen

ASSOCIATED PRESS

Most important point — GALVESTON — A Galveston public school flooded by Hurricane Ike in 2008 will reopen after more than $5 million in repairs.

Major details — Trustees of the Galveston Independent School District voted Wednesday night to reopen Burnet Elementary School for the term starting in August.

The Galveston County Daily News reported repair work on the school should be completed by the end of February.

Minor details — Trustees last summer voted to complete the final work, citing a possibility that the Federal Emergency Management Agency would not fund repairs if more time elapsed. The district has paid 10% of the costs, with the rest covered by FEMA grants.

Ike made landfall at Galveston in September 2008.

EXERCISE 1 Select a news story that you find interesting and clip it from a newspaper. Identify the Who, What, When, Where, Why, and How on a separate sheet of paper. On the news clipping itself, draw an inverted pyramid over the most important points.

Feature Stories

Feature stories differ from news stories in their timeliness, style, and length. Whereas news stories cover breaking news, a feature story might discuss less time-sensitive issues, such as a profile of an actor or an important local

139

businessperson, the reopening of a historical hotel, or a new lifestyle trend. In other words, stories such as these would have a similar impact if you read them today or five days from now. Unlike the inverted pyramid style of news stories, the style of feature stories is characterized by a beginning, a middle, and an end, as well as a thesis. The feature may take up one or two complete pages of the newspaper. Other shorter articles related to the same primary topic often accompany feature stories.

Feature stories are usually found in the section that is appropriate to their subject. In the previous examples, an actor's profile would be found in *arts/entertainment*, the profile of a local businessperson would be in the *business section*, the refurbishing of a landmark hotel would be in *local news*, and new trends would be in the *lifestyle* or *living section*. They add a fresh angle to recent news by including overlooked or undisclosed information. *Exposés* are based on in-depth investigation to reveal or "expose" shocking or surprising information, such as abuses of power or the quality of public education in your area.

Reader's TIP   Reading a Feature Story

- How does the angle or focus of a feature story differ from that of a straight news story?
- How credible are the sources cited?
- Is it factual or sensationalized?
- Does the reporter show a bias?
- Does the reporter judge, or do you decide?

EXERCISE 2

Locate a newspaper feature story that interests you and clip it or print it if you are reading online. If your college publishes a newspaper, look for a story in a recent edition. Discuss the factors that make this article a feature story rather than a news story. In particular, think of timeliness (time-sensitivity), style, and length. What is the angle of the story, and why is it being printed now? Circle any credible sources that are cited and underline sentences or phrases that show a positive or negative bias by the reporter.

4 Vocabulary

Learning Objectives

From this chapter, readers will learn:

1 To use strategies to attack and remember new words
2 To use context clues to unlock the meaning of unfamiliar words
3 To use common word parts to unlock meaning
4 To use a dictionary to find rich information about words
5 To find synonyms and antonyms in a thesaurus
6 To consult the glossary to define words used in the textbook
7 To refine word knowledge by solving analogies
8 To spell easily confused words

Everyday Reading Skills: Getting Information from News Web Sites and Online Communities

EXPANDING VOCABULARY

Learning Objective 1

Use strategies to attack and remember new words

Recognizing the meaning of words is essential to understanding what you read. If you have a weak vocabulary and stumble over unknown words when you read, you will lose your train of thought and end up concentrating on words rather than on meaning. A poor vocabulary severely limits your reading comprehension and speed.

Research tells us that you are already very successful at building vocabulary. On the average, you have learned 3,000 to 5,000 words each year from kindergarten through twelfth grade. Experts estimate that only 300 new words are taught each year by a teacher, so congratulate yourself that you have learned approximately 2,700 words every year on your own! Were you afraid of new words? Apparently not, because during each of those years, you met 15,000 to 30,000 unknown words and survived. That makes you a very efficient vocabulary builder. Continue to expand your vocabulary knowledge by using those skills that have already made you an expert.

To the college reader, being able to recognize a large number of words is more important than being able to use each one of them. Studies show that we use only about 20 percent of the words we know. The average high school graduate recognizes about 50,000 words and uses only 10,000, whereas the average college graduate recognizes around 70,000 words and uses approximately 15,000. This means that during your years in college, you probably will learn about 20,000 new words.

The English language contains about 1 million words. This number includes technical words in all disciplines, many of which the average person would never use. As a college student, however, you are becoming an expert in a particular field and a mini-expert in several areas. Each time you take a course in a new discipline, you face a vocabulary that is unique to that subject. It takes a little time and a lot of effort to master these new words. After overcoming the initial shock of vocabulary adjustment for each new course, you will find that reading becomes easier and comprehension improves.

PERSONAL FEEDBACK) 1   Name _____

1. What do you feel are the benefits of having a large vocabulary?

   _____

   _____

2. List ten adjectives that describe you. Stretch your vocabulary and go beyond simple one- and two-syllable words. _____

   _____

   Share your responses as directed by your instructor.

Unlocking Meaning While Reading

The best way to expand vocabulary is to read! Reading exposes you to many words that you do not use or hear in your everyday conversations. What do you do when you come to a word that you don't know while you are reading? Do not be afraid of unfamiliar words and do not ignore them. Instead, use the tools that you have at your disposal to unlock them. Remember that your first goal is to understand the material you are reading. The three strategies below are your best weapons in attacking unfamiliar words.

Use Context Clues.   To figure out the meaning of a new word, do not immediately charge off to the dictionary and record a definition as if it were one more addition to a giant list of words. Contrary to what you may have heard, the dictionary is a *last* resort when you aren't sure what a word means. Instead, first try to figure out the meaning from the **context clues** in the sentence or paragraph in which the word is used. What do the surrounding words—the context—tell you about the new word?

Use Knowledge of Word Parts   Another way to discover the meaning of a word is to examine its parts. Do you recognize any prefixes, suffixes, or roots, such as *pseudo* (meaning *false*) or *nym* (meaning *name*) in the word *pseudonym*? If you know these word parts, you can easily figure out that *pseudonym* means a false name rather than a real one. Samuel Clemens's use of the name Mark Twain is an example of a pseudonym.

Use the Glossary and the Dictionary.   If a word is specific to a subject area, such as the marketing term *promotional mix*, refer to the glossary in the back of the textbook for a definition that pertains specifically to that field. If all of these strategies fail to unlock the meaning of a new word and you can't understand what you are reading without a definition of the word, then go to the dictionary. But if the word is not essential to your general comprehension, skip it entirely or come back to it later. Your purpose for reading is to get meaning, not to collect vocabulary words. As you read more and encounter more new words, your vocabulary will naturally expand. Make a habit of noticing new words and try to remember them by association.

Remembering New Words

As you read this section on remembering new words, you might notice that memorizing words and definitions is not included. Memorizing is seldom effective for the long term. Instead, focus on understanding the meaning and recognizing the spelling and sound of the word. Think about how the word is used and repeat your exposure to it until it becomes part of your growing vocabulary.

Use Association.   Certain new words, especially college-level words, are hard to remember because you don't hear them every day and can't easily work them into casual conversation. To latch on to a new word, form an association with it. Try to remember the word in the context in which it was used. Visualize the word or a situation pertaining to the word. Always try to think of a new word in a phrase, rather than in isolation. For example, do you know the word *hovel*? A hovel is a small, miserable place to live that offers little or no comfort. The cartoon

HOVEL
(HUV ul)
a small, miserable dwelling;
an open, low shed
Link: **SHOVEL**

"The mice's HOVEL was an old, rusted SHOVEL."

EDIFICE
(ED uh fis)
a building, especially one of imposing
appearance or size
Link: **ATE A FACE**

HE ONLY EATS THE FINEST BUILDINGS!

"The Great Kong ATE the north FACE of the EDIFICE."

above on the left associates the word *hovel* with the word *shovel* and illustrates the word using the phrase: "The mice's HOVEL was an old, rusted SHOVEL." In the cartoon to the right, notice the association between the word EDIFICE and "ATE A FACE." These associations create a lasting picture in your mind.

Use Concept Cards. To speed up the process of expanding your vocabulary, you can also use **concept cards**. *Concept* means idea. On a concept card, you expand the definition of a single word into a fully developed idea. You are creating a kind of story for the new word by providing a sentence, a picture, and a source reference.

Keep a concept card file of new words. Include more than the usual "mystery word" on the front of the card and the definition on the back. Use the technique of association and on the front of the card write the word within a meaningful phrase or sentence, or both. Also on the front, note where you encountered the new word. On the back of the card, write the definition and, to add a further memory link, draw a picture that illustrates the way you are using the word in your phrase or sentence. See the examples of concept cards on pages 145, 146, and 148.

When making concept cards, your limits depend only on your creativity and talent. For example, in *Vocabulary Cartoons*, a book by Sam, Max, and Bryan Burchers, the authors link the sounds within words to exaggerated visual images. The resulting cartoons, as shown above, depict the links and suggest the definitions by using sound associations and visual images, along with humor, to improve memory.

Practice Your New Words. Review your concept cards regularly. Look at the word on the front and quiz yourself on the definition. When you feel that you

FRONT

surrogate mother

The baby monkey preferred
the terry cloth surrogate mother

Psychology textbook

BACK

Def: substitute, as in the wire
mothers in experiments with
monkeys

have a clear understanding of the meaning, use your new word in writing or in conversation.

Notice the words around you. As you begin to pay attention to unfamiliar terms in print and in conversation, you will more than likely discover that you encounter many interesting new words.

TYPES OF CONTEXT CLUES

Learning Objective 2

Use context clues to unlock the meaning of unfamiliar words

The first line of attack on a new word is to try to figure out the meaning from its *context*, or the way it is used in the sentence or paragraph. There are several types of context clues. The following examples show how each type can be used to figure out the meaning of a word.

Definition

The unknown word is defined within the sentence or paragraph. Sometimes commas or dashes signal the definition.

EXAMPLE   The explorers landed in an *alien* environment, a place both foreign and strange to their beloved homeland.

EXPLANATION   The definition is set off by a comma following the phrase in which the word appears. *Alien* means *strange* or *foreign*.

EXERCISE 1   For each of the context clue exercises in this section, underline the context clue and mark *a, b, c,* or *d* for the meaning closest to that of the boldface word. Do not use a dictionary.

_____ 1. The CIA was engaged in **covert** activities in South America that were not made public.
   a. foreign
   b. dishonest
   c. dangerous
   d. hidden

FRONT   BACK

covert operations

in South America

CIA activities

hidden or secret

_____ 2. The meeting was brief, and the message was **concise** and to the point.

    a. laborious
    b. lengthy
    c. short
    d. important

_____ 3. If we have to have a pet around the house, get one that is **docile** and easy to manage.

    a. gentle
    b. short
    c. sick
    d. young

_____ 4. The professor gave an **ultimatum** about tardiness, saying today would be the last time anyone would be allowed to enter class late.

    a. final demand
    b. new proposal
    c. lecture
    d. choice

_____ 5. Checking the references in the bibliography for errors was **tedious** and uninteresting.

    a. educational
    b. necessary
    c. exhausting
    d. boring

Elaborating Details

Descriptive details suggest the meaning of the unknown word.

EXAMPLE   The natives were *hostile* when the settlers approached their village. They lined up across the road and drew their weapons. The settlers were afraid to go farther.

EXPLANATION   As described in the sentences after the word, *hostile* must mean *unfriendly*.

EXERCISE 2

_____ 1. **Wearily**, the young woman climbed into bed after a long night shift for a well deserved nap.
   a. relieved
   b. bored
   c. tired
   d. sadly

_____ 2. The gaping wound bled **profusely,** needing several bandages to absorb its flow.
   a. lightly
   b. unnoticeably
   c. slowly
   d. greatly

_____ 3. The boy received a **superficial** cut, the cat's claw having barely grazed his skin.
   a. shallow
   b. visible
   c. deep
   d. lengthy

_____ 4. The instructions left for the babysitter were **delineated** in several sentences with great detail.
   a. ignored
   b. described
   c. discovered
   d. questioned

_____ 5. The politician went on and on with his **harangue** while his fellow senators were forced to keep listening.
   a. noisy laughter
   b. simple explanation
   c. prolonged speech
   d. short conversation

Elaborating Examples

An anecdote or example before or after the word suggests the meaning.

EXAMPLE   The bird's appetite is *voracious*. In one day he ate enough worms to equal three times his body weight.

EXPLANATION   Because the bird ate an extraordinary amount, *voracious* means extremely *hungry* or *greedy*.

EXERCISE 3

_____ 1. The dancer's movements were not rehearsed but were a **spontaneous** response to the music.

    a. planned
    b. simple
    c. unplanned
    d. smooth

_____ 2. The embargo will **restrict** previously flourishing trade with the country and stop the goods from entering the seaport.

    a. promote
    b. enlist
    c. renew
    d. confine

_____ 3. The **affluent** members of the community live in big homes with swimming pools.

    a. friendly
    b. wealthy
    c. athletic
    d. political

FRONT   BACK

affluent people

wealthy: having lots of money

_____ 4. Because the employer had never heard of the three companies listed as references, she was **dubious** about the applicant's previous work history.

    a. relaxed
    b. unconcerned
    c. doubtful
    d. hopeful

_____ 5. The ophthalmologist gave a favorable **prognosis**, saying that in two weeks her vision would be clear and she would no longer need the dark glasses.

    a. forecast
    b. prescription
    c. warning
    d. notification

Comparison

A similar situation suggests the meaning of the unknown word.

EXAMPLE   The smell of the flower was as *compelling* as a magnet's pull on a paper clip.

> **EXPLANATION** Because a magnet will pull a paper clip to it, the comparison suggests that the smell of the flower had a strong attraction. *Compelling* means *forceful*.

EXERCISE 4

_____ 1. I am as **skeptical** about its chances of success as I am about my chances of winning the lottery.
   a. doubtful
   b. confident
   c. remorseful
   d. hopeful

_____ 2. Confirming an appointment before leaving the office is as **prudent** as never letting your gas tank go lower than one-quarter full.
   a. annoying
   b. reckless
   c. rewarding
   d. wise

_____ 3. With a great deal of feeling, Ellen made an **impassioned** plea for her family to adopt the stray puppy.
   a. illogical
   b. soft-spoken
   c. emotional
   d. short-lived

_____ 4. Because there is always a first time for everything, each of us is a **novice** at some point in our lives.
   a. fool
   b. master
   c. manager
   d. beginner

_____ 5. If the climber is in fact a circus performer, it is **plausible** that he attempted such a dangerous feat on the tall building.
   a. doubtful
   b. impossible
   c. terrible
   d. believable

Contrast

An opposite situation suggests the meaning of the unknown word.

EXAMPLE In America she is an *eminent* journalist, even though she is virtually unknown in England.

EXPLANATION The phrase *even though* signals that an opposite is coming. Thus, *eminent* means the opposite of *unknown;* it means *well-known* or *famous.*

EXERCISE 5

_____ 1. Unlike **introverted** people, very talkative folks love crowds and conversation.
   a. quiet
   b. loud
   c. friendly
   d. hostile

_____ 2. His favorites were not the old stories of days gone by but the works of more **contemporary** authors.
   a. intelligent
   b. recent
   c. revolutionary
   d. meaningful

_____ 3. He did not mean to cause the problem. While looking for his hat, the young man **inadvertently** knocked over the lamp.
   a. purposely
   b. knowingly
   c. unintentionally
   d. suddenly

_____ 4. Now that she is an adult college student who is in control of her emotions, she no longer engages in the **infantile** outbursts that marked her behavior as a child.
   a. immature
   b. sudden
   c. angry
   d. short

_____ 5. Although she had had a crush on him all fall, Maria's interest in Michael began to **wane** when he asked two other girls to the holiday party.
   a. grow
   b. lessen
   c. accelerate
   d. intensify

WANE
(wain)
to decrease gradually
Link: **RAIN**

"Snowmen WANE in the RAIN."

EXERCISE 6   Use context clues to determine the meanings of the boldface words, which appear frequently in health textbooks.

1. A condition such as arthritis can limit a person's **range of motion** in the shoulders, hips, wrists, and other joints. _____

2. Low **carbohydrate** diets are difficult to follow for lovers of sweets, baked goods, pasta, and potatoes. _____

3. Racehorses are sometimes given a **diuretic** to reduce body fluids before racing. _____

4. Exercise physiologists suggest that people who exercise at the appropriate level of **intensity** ought to be able to carry on a conversation at the same time. _____

5. Final exams would be excellent examples of **stressors** for most students. _____

Multiple Meanings of a Word

Some words are confusing because they have several different meanings. For example, the dictionary lists more than 30 meanings for the word *run*. To determine the proper meaning, use the context of the sentence and paragraph in which the word occurs. Many of the **multiple-meaning words** are simple words that are used frequently. If you are puzzling over an unusual use of a common word, consider the context and be aware that the word may have another meaning.

EXERCISE 7 The boldface words in the following sentences have multiple meanings. For each word, write a second sentence in which the word is used differently.

1. The puppy snuggled in the **covers.** _____

    _____

2. The **pitch** was low and inside home plate. _____

    _____

    _____

3. Her neighbors objected to the dog **run** in her backyard. _____

    _____

    _____

4. I **suspect** it was your brother's mess. _____

    _____

    _____

5. Debbie had no **choice** in the matter, for it was already decided. ____

    _____

6. The orchestra members took a **bow** at the end of the performance. ____

    _____

7. Water spilled over the **stern** of the ship during the height of the storm.

    _____

8. Nicholas prefers four slices of cinnamon **toast** for breakfast. _____

    _____

9. The waves began to **break** along the beach. _____

    _____

10. You cannot **hide** from the truth. _____

    _____

WORD PARTS

Learning Objective 3

Use common word parts to unlock meaning

Many words that at first may seem totally foreign to you are actually made up of words that you already know. One authority claims that learning approximately 30 key word parts will help you unlock the meaning of about 14,000 words. Although this claim may be exaggerated, it emphasizes the importance of roots, prefixes, and suffixes. Word parts are clues to the meaning of new words.

Look at the following family of words. Some may be familiar, and some may be new to you. You probably know the meaning of the first two words and thus can deduce that *ped* means *foot*. Try to figure out the meaning of the other *ped* words by applying your knowledge of closely related words.

Pedal: lever pressed by the foot

Pedestrian: person walking on foot

What do the following words mean? Use the clues to write the definitions.

quadruped: _____ (Hint: quadruplets?)

centipede: _____ (Hint: turn of the century?)

pedometer: _____ (Hint: odometer?)

Roots

The **root** is the stem or basic part of the word. The roots that we use are derived primarily from Latin and Greek. For example, *port* is a root derived from Latin meaning *to carry,* as in the word *porter. Thermo* is a Greek word meaning *heat,* as in *thermometer.* In both cases, additional letters have been added to the word, but the meaning of the word has not changed. Knowing the definition of the root helps unlock the meaning of each word.

EXAMPLE   The root forms *duc, duct,* and *duce* mean *to lead.* This root branches out into a large word family. Use the root to supply appropriate words to complete the following three sentences.

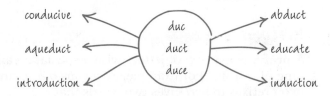

1. If the factory is ready, the new line of furniture will go into _____ in September.

2. The company is trying to cut down overhead in order to _____ expenses.

3. Legitimate business expenses can be _____ from your taxes if you keep the proper receipts.

EXPLANATION   The correct answers are *production, reduce,* and *deducted.*

EXERCISE 8   Complete the following sentences by using the given root to form an appropriate word.

grad, gred, gres: take steps, go, degree

1. The seniors will _____ from high school the first week in June.

2. The mountain trail began as a _____ climb and became steeper toward the top.

3. If we continue to work through lunch and all afternoon, we should make enough _____ on our project to finish by five o'clock.

port: carry

4. If we could _____ fewer goods into this country, our balance of payments would improve.

5. _____ toilets were set up along the streets during the festival.

6. Private contributions and volunteers _____ the efforts of the Salvation Army.

7. The organized _____ to and from the game will be by bus.

cred: believe

8. We could not believe what we saw; the feat was _____.

9. Some law schools in the country are not fully _____ by the state, and their courses do not transfer to other schools.

10. Derogatory remarks were made about his performance in an effort to _____ him.

Prefixes

A **prefix** is a group of letters with a special meaning that is added to the beginning of a word. For example, *ex* means *out of* and *im* means *into*. Adding these two prefixes to *port* gives two words that are opposite in meaning. *Export* means to send something out of the country, whereas *import* means to bring something in. Again, knowing the prefixes can help you identify the meaning.

EXAMPLE   The prefix *trans* means *across, over,* and *beyond.* Write a word beginning with *trans* to complete each of the following three sentences.

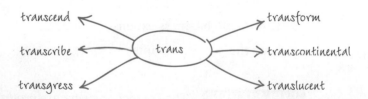

1. The radio station can now _____ programs to a wider audience.

2. Since she did not speak French, he acted as _____ while she conducted business in Paris.

3. When the business _____ was completed, the two executives shook hands.

EXPLANATION   The correct answers are *transmit, translator,* and *transaction.*

EXERCISE 9   Complete the following sentences by using the given prefix to form an appropriate word.

dis: take away, not, deprive of

1. When catching criminal suspects, the police carefully _____ them to remove any item that could be used as a weapon.

2. Because she missed the review in the last class before the final exam, the student was at a _____ in studying for the test.

3. Hospital employees are instructed to use special containers to _____ of used needles.

mis: wrong, bad

4. Because the child _____ in the restaurant, he was not allowed to go again.

5. The answer was not a lie, but it did _____ the truth.

6. Because of the lawyer's error, the judge declared a _____ and court was adjourned.

pre: before

7. Even a fortune-teller could not have _____ the fun we had scuba diving.

8. Police recommend alarm systems as a type of crime _____.

9. The student was so _____ with her mathematics assignment that she did not hear the doorbell ring.

10. If you order online, you will need a credit card to _____ for the concert tickets.

Suffixes

A **suffix** is a group of letters with a special meaning that is added to the end of a word. A suffix can alter the meaning of a word as well as the way the word is used in the sentence. For example, the *er* in *porter* means the *person who* and makes the word into the name of a person. But adding *able*, which means *capable of*, to *port* does not change the meaning as much as it changes the way the word can be used in the sentence. Some suffixes, therefore, have more meaning than others, but all alter the way the word can be used in a sentence.

EXAMPLE   The suffix *ist* means *one who* or *that which*. Write a word ending with *ist* to complete each of the following three sentences.

1. If you have a toothache, go to your _____ immediately.

2. The _____ struck the keys of the instrument with such force that the floorboards shook.

3. The picture was painted by a well-known American _____.

EXPLANATION The correct answers are *dentist*, *pianist*, and *artist*.

EXERCISE 10 Complete the following sentences by using the given suffix to form an appropriate word.

ion, sion, tion: act of, state of, result of

1. To honor his birthday, we invited his friends to a party and had a big

   _____.

2. If you don't clean out the wound and use a bandage, you are likely to get an

   _____.

3. The _____ bridge was held in the air by cables descending from two towers on either side of the river.

4. Use your _____ to visualize the festive atmosphere of music and outdoor dining.

ship: office, state, dignity, skill, quality, profession

5. After breaking her leg and missing two weeks of class, the student was advised to apply for a _____ withdrawal and make a fresh start the next semester.

6. The university also offered merit _____ that were not based on financial need.

7. The infantry soldier demonstrated excellent _____ by hitting the red mark with each shot.

less: without

8. Because the show was boring, I became _____ and could not sit still.

9. A baby lamb is _____ against fierce and determined predators.

10. Suffering from insomnia, she spent many _____ nights walking the halls.

DICTIONARIES

Learning Objective 4

Use a dictionary for rich information about words

Use a dictionary as a last resort for finding the definition of a word while you are reading, unless the word is crucial to your understanding. Stopping in the middle of a paragraph breaks your concentration and causes you to forget what you were reading. Even if you are reading on an electronic screen, resist the temptation to click immediately for the online dictionary. Use context and word part clues first so that you are more likely to remember the word and its meaning, and then check the online dictionary. Whether you are reading a printed page or a computer screen, mark words that you want to learn. When you have finished reading, make concept cards and add the words to your vocabulary.

Dictionaries contain more than just the definition of a word. They contain the pronunciation, the spelling, the derivation or history, the parts of speech, and the many different meanings that a word may have. An entry may also include an illustration or give context examples of the use of the word in a phrase. Consider the following entry.

Source: By permission. From *Merriam-Webster's Collegiate® Dictionary, 11th Edition.* © 2011 by Merriam-Webster Incorporated (www.Merriam-Webster.com).

Online dictionary entries always contain the basic information—definitions, pronunciation, spelling, and parts of speech. They also have the ability to include sound and video details. However, they might or might not provide information such as word origin and history. The electronic entry below contains an audio option, so you can hear the pronunciation. It is indicated by the three "horn" icons. This entry contains only the noun form of the word *ski*.

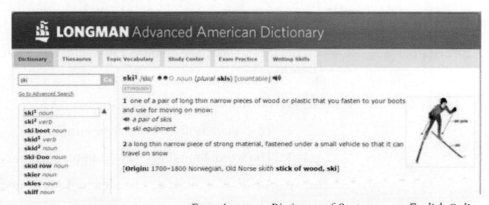

From *Longman Dictionary of Contemporary English Online* http://www.ldoceonline.com/dictionary/ski_1

Guide Words

The two words at the top of each printed dictionary page are called *guide words*. They represent the first and last words on the page. Because the words in the dictionary are in alphabetical order, you can use the guide words to quickly determine if the word you are looking for is on that particular page. The guide words for the sample entry are *skate* and *skid*.

In an online dictionary, of course, guide words are unnecessary. Entering or clicking on the word in question takes you straight to its dictionary entry.

Pronunciation

Each word is divided into sounds after the boldface main entry. Letters and symbols are used to indicate special sounds. A key to understanding the special sounds appears with a click or at the bottom of one of the two pages open to you in a printed dictionary.

Spelling

Spellings are given for the plural form of the word (if the spelling changes) and for any special endings. This is particularly helpful when letters are dropped or added to form the new word. In the sample entry, the plural of *ski* can be spelled correctly in two ways, either *skis* or *ski*. The first spelling is usually the preferred one.

Word Meaning

Frequently a word has many meanings. For example, *car* means automobile as well as the cargo part of an airship. In such a case, the dictionary uses a number to indicate each new meaning. In the sample entry, notice that a ski can be a narrow strip of wood or a piece of material that resembles a ski.

Parts of Speech

For each meaning of a word, the part of speech is given in abbreviated form. For example, *n* means *noun, adj* means *adjective, adv* means *adverb*, and *vi* or *vt* means *verb*. Other abbreviations are listed in the section in the front of your dictionary. In the example, *ski* is both a noun and a verb.

Word History

The language in which the word originally appeared is listed after the pronunciation or at the end of the entry. For example, *L* stands for Latin and *Gk* stands for Greek. Usually the original meaning is also listed. *Ski* is derived from the Norwegian (Norw) word *skith*, which means "stick of wood."

EXERCISE 11 Consult the dictionary page on page 159 to label the statements as either *T* (true) or *F* (false).

_____ 1. Garnish is a synonym for the word *adorn*.

_____ 2. To *adulate* is also to flatter or admire.

_____ 3. The word *Adonai* is taken from an ancient Greek myth.

_____ 4. An *admonition* is a severe form of punishment.

_____ 5. The word *adobe* can be used to refer to both a structure and a type of clay.

_____ 6. If a topic is discussed *ad nauseam,* most listeners are likely to be tired of hearing about it.

_____ 7. The word *Adonis* is used to refer to a young man of great intelligence.

_____ 8. To *admire* someone is to dislike them.

_____ 9. *Adolescent* is a term used for young people in high school.

_____ 10. Someone who dislikes raw vegetables would be unlikely to *adore* fresh salads.

ra·bil·i·ty \ˌad-m(ə-)rə-ˈbi-lə-tē\ *n* — **ad·mi·ra·ble·ness** \ˈad-m(ə-)rə-bəl-nəs\ *n* — **ad·mi·ra·bly** \-blē\ *adv*

ad·mi·ral \ˈad-m(ə-)rəl\ *n* [ME, fr. AF *amiral* commander & ML *admiralis* emir, *admirallus* admiral, fr. Ar *amīr-al-* commander of the (as in *amīr-al-baḥr* commander of the sea)] (15c) **1** *archaic* : the commander in chief of a navy **2 a** : FLAG OFFICER **b** : a commissioned officer in the navy or coast guard who ranks above a vice admiral and whose insignia is four stars — compare GENERAL **3** *archaic* : FLAGSHIP **4** : any of several brightly colored nymphalid butterflies — compare RED ADMIRAL

admiral of the fleet (1660) : the highest-ranking officer of the British navy

ad·mi·ral·ty \ˈad-m(ə-)rəl-tē\ *n* (15c) **1** *cap* : the executive department or officers formerly having general authority over British naval affairs **2** : the court having jurisdiction over questions of maritime law; *also* : the system of law administered by admiralty courts

ad·mi·ra·tion \ˌad-mə-ˈrā-shən\ *n* (15c) **1** *archaic* : WONDER **2** : an object of esteem **3** : delighted or astonished approbation

ad·mire \əd-ˈmī(-ə)r\ *vb* **ad·mired; ad·mir·ing** [MF *admirer,* to marvel at, fr. L *admirari,* fr. *ad-* + *mirari* to wonder, fr. *mirus* astonishing] *vt* (1560) **1** : to regard with admiration **2** *archaic* : to marvel at ~ *vi, dial* : to like very much ⟨I would ~ to know why not —A. H. Lewis⟩ ***syn*** see REGARD — **ad·mir·er** *n* — **ad·mir·ing·ly** \-ˈmī-riŋ-lē\ *adv*

ad·mis·si·ble \əd-ˈmi-sə-bəl, ad-\ *adj* [F, fr. ML *admissibilis,* fr. L *admissus,* pp. of *admittere*] (1611) **1** : capable of being allowed or conceded : PERMISSIBLE ⟨evidence legally ~ in court⟩ **2** : capable or worthy of being admitted ⟨~ to the university⟩ — **ad·mis·si·bil·i·ty** \-ˌmi-sə-ˈbi-lə-tē\ *n*

ad·mis·sion \əd-ˈmi-shən, ad-\ *n* (15c) **1 a** : the act or process of admitting **b** : the state or privilege of being admitted **c** : a fee paid at or for admission **2 a** : the granting of an argument or position not fully proved **b** : acknowledgment that a fact or statement is true — **ad·mis·sive** \-ˈmi-siv\ *adj*

ad·mit \əd-ˈmit, ad-\ *vb* **ad·mit·ted; ad·mit·ting** [ME *admitten,* fr. L *admittere,* fr. *ad-* + *mittere* to send] *vt* (15c) **1 a** : to allow scope for : PERMIT ⟨~*s* no possibility of misunderstanding⟩ **b** : to concede as true or valid ⟨*admitted* making a mistake⟩ **2 a** : to allow entry (as to a place, fellowship, or privilege) ⟨an open window had *admitted* rain⟩ ⟨*admitted* to the club⟩ **b** : to accept into a hospital as an inpatient ⟨he was *admitted* last night for chest pains⟩ ~ *vi* **1** : to give entrance or access **2 a** : ALLOW, PERMIT ⟨~*s* of two interpretations⟩ **b** : to make acknowledgment — used with *to* ***syn*** see ACKNOWLEDGE

ad·mit·tance \əd-ˈmi-tᵊn(t)s, ad-\ *n* (1536) **1 a** : the act or process of admitting **b** : permission to enter **2** : the reciprocal of the impedance of a circuit

ad·mit·ted·ly \əd-ˈmi-təd-lē, ad-\ *adv* (1804) **1** : as has been or must be admitted ⟨an ~ inadequate treatment⟩ **2** : it must be admitted ⟨~, we took a chance⟩

ad·mix \ad-ˈmiks\ *vt* [back-formation fr. obs. *admixt* mingled (with), fr. ME, fr. L *admixtus*] (1533) : to mix in

ad·mix·ture \ad-ˈmiks-chər\ *n* [L *admixtus,* pp. of *admiscēre* to mix with, fr. *ad-* + *miscēre* to mix — more at MIX] (1605) **1 a** : the action of mixing **b** : the fact of being mixed **2 a** : something added by mixing **b** : a product of mixing : MIXTURE

ad·mon·ish \ad-ˈmä-nish\ *vt* [ME *admonesten,* fr. AF *amonester,* fr. VL **admonestare,* alter. of L *admonēre* to warn, fr. *ad-* + *monēre* to warn — more at MIND] (14c) **1 a** : to indicate duties or obligations to **b** : to express warning or disapproval to esp. in a gentle, earnest, or solicitous manner **2** : to give friendly earnest advice or encouragement to ***syn*** see REPROVE — **ad·mon·ish·er** *n* — **ad·mon·ish·ing·ly** \-ni-shiŋ-lē\ *adv* — **ad·mon·ish·ment** \-mənt\ *n*

ad·mo·ni·tion \ˌad-mə-ˈni-shən\ *n* [ME *amonicioun,* fr. AF *amonicion,* fr. L *admonition-, admonitio,* fr. *admonēre*] (14c) **1** : gentle or friendly reproof **2** : counsel or warning against fault or oversight

ad·mon·i·to·ry \əd-ˈmä-nə-ˌtȯr-ē\ *adj* (1594) : expressing admonition : WARNING — **ad·mon·i·to·ri·ly** \-ˌmä-nə-ˈtȯr-ə-lē\ *adv*

ad·nate \ˈad-ˌnāt\ *adj* [L *adnatus, adgnatus,* pp. of *adgnasci* to be born in addition, grow later — more at AGNATE] (1661) : grown to a usu. unlike part esp. along a margin ⟨a calyx ~ to the ovary⟩ — **ad·na·tion** \ad-ˈnā-shən\ *n*

ad nau·se·am \ad-ˈnȯ-zē-əm *also* -ˌam\ *adv* [L] (1647) : to a sickening or excessive degree

ad·nexa \ad-ˈnek-sə\ *n pl* [NL, fr. L *annexa,* neut. pl. of *annexus,* pp. of *annectere* to bind to — more at ANNEX] (1899) : conjoined, subordinate, or associated anatomical parts — **ad·nex·al** \-səl\ *adj*

ado \ə-ˈdü\ *n* [ME, fr. *at do,* fr. *at* + *don, do* to do] (14c) **1** : heightened fuss or concern : TO-DO **2** : time-wasting bother over trivial details ⟨wrote the paper without further ~⟩ **3** : TROUBLE, DIFFICULTY

ado·be \ə-ˈdō-bē\ *n* [Sp, fr. Ar *al-ṭūb* the brick, fr. Copt *tōbe* brick, fr. Egypt *ḏbt*] (1748) **1** : a brick or building material of sun-dried earth and straw **2** : a structure made of adobe bricks **3** : a heavy clay used in making adobe bricks; *broadly* : alluvial or playa clay in desert or arid regions — **ado·be·like** \-ˌlīk\ *adj*

adobe 2

ado·bo \ə-ˈdō-bō, ä-ˈt͟hō-bō\ *n, pl* **-bos** [Sp] (ca. 1951) : a Philippine dish of fish or meat usu. marinated in a sauce containing vinegar and garlic, browned in fat, and simmered in the marinade

ad·o·les·cence \ˌa-də-ˈle-sᵊn(t)s\ *n* (15c) **1** : the state or process of growing up **2** : the period of life from puberty to maturity terminating legally at the age of majority **3** : a stage of development (as of a language or culture) prior to maturity

[1]**ad·o·les·cent** \-sᵊnt\ *n* [F, fr. L *adolescent-, adolescens,* prp. of *adolescere* to grow up — more at ADULT] (15c) : one that is in the state of adolescence

[2]**adolescent** *adj* (1785) **1** : of, relating to, or being in adolescence **2** : emotionally or intellectually immature — **ad·o·les·cent·ly** *adv*

Ado·nai \ˌä-də-ˈnȯi, -ˈnī\ *n* [Heb *ʼădhōnāy*] (bef. 12c) — used in place of *YHWH* as a name of the God of the Hebrews during prayer recitation

Ado·nis \ə-ˈdä-nəs, -ˈdō-\ *n* [L, fr. Gk *Adōnis*] (1565) **1** : a youth loved by Aphrodite who is killed at hunting by a wild boar and restored to Aphrodite from Hades for a part of each year **2** : a very handsome young man

adopt \ə-ˈdäpt\ *vb* [ME, fr. MF or L; MF *adopter,* fr. L *adoptare,* fr. *ad-* + *optare* to choose] *vt* (1500) **1** : to take by choice into a relationship; *esp* : to take voluntarily (a child of other parents) as one's own child **2** : to take up and practice or use ⟨~*ed* a moderate tone⟩ **3** : to accept formally and put into effect ⟨~ a constitutional amendment⟩ **4** : to choose (a textbook) for required study in a course ~ *vi* **1** : to adopt a child ⟨couples choosing to ~⟩ **2** : to sponsor the care and maintenance of ⟨~ a highway⟩ — **adopt·abil·i·ty** \-ˌdäp-tə-ˈbi-lə-tē\ *n* — **adopt·able** \-ˈdäp-tə-bəl\ *adj* — **adopt·er** *n*

syn ADOPT, EMBRACE, ESPOUSE mean to take an opinion, policy, or practice as one's own. ADOPT implies accepting something created by another or foreign to one's nature ⟨forced to *adopt* new policies⟩. EMBRACE implies a ready or happy acceptance ⟨*embraced* the customs of their new homeland⟩. ESPOUSE adds an implication of close attachment to a cause and a sharing of its fortunes ⟨*espoused* the cause of women's rights⟩.

adopt·ee \ə-ˌdäp-ˈtē\ *n* (1892) : one who is adopted

adop·tion \ə-ˈdäp-shən\ *n* (14c) : the act of adopting : the state of being adopted

adop·tion·ism *or* **adop·tian·ism** \-shə-ˌni-zəm\ *n, often cap* (1874) : the doctrine that Jesus of Nazareth became the Son of God by adoption — **adop·tion·ist** \-sh(ə-)nist\ *n, often cap*

adop·tive \ə-ˈdäp-tiv\ *adj* (15c) **1** : made or acquired by adoption ⟨the ~ father⟩ **2** : of or relating to adoption — **adop·tive·ly** *adv*

ador·able \ə-ˈdȯr-ə-bəl\ *adj* (1611) **1** : worthy of being adored **2** : extremely charming ⟨an ~ child⟩ — **ador·abil·i·ty** \-ˌdȯr-ə-ˈbi-lə-tē\ *n* — **ador·able·ness** \-ˈdȯr-ə-bəl-nəs\ *n* — **ador·ably** \-blē\ *adv*

ad·o·ra·tion \ˌa-də-ˈrā-shən\ *n* (15c) : the act of adoring : the state of being adored

adore \ə-ˈdȯr\ *vt* **adored; ador·ing** [ME *adouren,* fr. AF *aurer, adourer,* fr. L *adorare,* fr. *ad-* + *orare* to speak, pray — more at ORATION] (14c) **1** : to worship or honor as a deity or as divine **2** : to regard with loving admiration and devotion ⟨*adored* his wife⟩ **3** : to be very fond of ⟨~*s* pecan pie⟩ ***syn*** see REVERE — **ador·er** *n* — **ador·ing·ly** *adv*

adorn \ə-ˈdȯrn\ *vt* [ME, fr. L *adornare,* fr. *ad-* + *ornare* to furnish — more at ORNATE] (14c) **1** : to enhance the appearance of esp. with beautiful objects **2** : to enliven or decorate as if with ornaments ⟨people of fashion who ~*ed* the Court⟩

syn ADORN, DECORATE, ORNAMENT, EMBELLISH, BEAUTIFY, DECK, GARNISH mean to enhance the appearance of something by adding something unessential. ADORN implies an enhancing by something beautiful in itself ⟨a diamond necklace *adorned* her neck⟩. DECORATE suggests relieving plainness or monotony by adding beauty of color or design ⟨*decorate* a birthday cake⟩. ORNAMENT and EMBELLISH imply the adding of something extraneous, ORNAMENT stressing the heightening or setting off of the original ⟨a white house *ornamented* with green shutters⟩, EMBELLISH often stressing the adding of superfluous or adventitious ornament ⟨*embellish* a page with floral borders⟩. BEAUTIFY adds to EMBELLISH a suggestion of counterbalancing plainness or ugliness ⟨will *beautify* the grounds with flower beds⟩. DECK implies the addition of something that contributes to gaiety, splendor, or showiness ⟨a house all *decked* out for Christmas⟩. GARNISH suggests decorating with a small final touch and is used esp. in referring to the serving of food ⟨an entrée *garnished* with parsley⟩.

adorn·ment \-mənt\ *n* (14c) **1** : the action of adorning : the state of being adorned **2** : something that adorns

ADP \ˌā-(ˌ)dē-ˈpē\ *n* [*a*denosine *di*phosphate] (1943) : a nucleotide $C_{10}H_{15}N_5O_{10}P_2$ composed of adenosine and two phosphate groups that is formed in living cells as an intermediate between ATP and AMP and that is reversibly converted to ATP for the storing of energy by the addition of a high-energy phosphate group — called also *adenosine diphosphate*

ad rem \(ˌ)ad-ˈrem\ *adv or adj* [L, to the thing] (1599) : to the point or purpose : RELEVANTLY

adren- *or* **adreno-** *comb form* [*adrenal*] **1** : adrenal glands ⟨*adreno*cortical⟩ **2** : adrenaline ⟨*adren*ergic⟩

[1]**ad·re·nal** \ə-ˈdrē-nᵊl\ *adj* [*ad-* + *renal*] (1875) : of, relating to, or derived from the adrenal glands or their secretions ⟨~ steroids⟩

[2]**adrenal** *n* (1882) : ADRENAL GLAND

ad·re·nal·ec·to·my \ə-ˌdrē-nə-ˈlek-tə-mē\ *n* (ca. 1910) : surgical removal of an adrenal gland — **ad·re·nal·ec·to·mized** \-ˌmīzd\ *adj*

adrenal gland *n* (1875) : either of a pair of complex endocrine organs near the anterior medial border of the kidney consisting of a mesodermal cortex that produces glucocorticoid, mineralocorticoid, and androgenic hormones and an ectodermal medulla that produces epinephrine and norepinephrine — called also *adrenal, suprarenal gland*

Adren·a·lin \ə-ˈdre-nə-lən\ *trademark* — used for a preparation of levorotatory epinephrine

adren·a·line \ə-ˈdre-nə-lən\ *n* (1901) : EPINEPHRINE — often used in nontechnical contexts ⟨the fans were jubilant, raucous, their ~ running high —W. P. Kinsella⟩

adren·al·ized \ə-ˈdre-nə-līzd\ *adj* (1973) : filled with a sudden rush of energy : EXCITED

ad·ren·er·gic \ˌa-drə-ˈnər-jik\ *adj* [*adren-* + *-ergic*] (1934) **1** : liberating, activated by, or involving adrenaline or a substance like adrenaline ⟨an ~ nerve⟩ **2** : resembling adrenaline esp. in physiological action ⟨~ drugs⟩ — **ad·ren·er·gi·cal·ly** \-ji-k(ə-)lē\ *adv*

ad·re·no·chrome \ə-ˈdrē-nō-ˌkrōm\ *n* (ca. 1913) : a red-colored mixture of quinones derived from epinephrine by oxidation

ad·re·no·cor·ti·cal \ə-ˌdrē-nō-ˈkȯr-ti-kəl\ *adj* (1936) : of, relating to, or derived from the cortex of the adrenal glands

\ə\ **abut** \ᵊ\ **kitten, F table** \ər\ **further** \a\ **ash** \ā\ **ace** \ä\ **mop, mar**
\au̇\ **out** \ch\ **chin** \e\ **bet** \ē\ **easy** \g\ **go** \i\ **hit** \ī\ **ice** \j\ **job**
\ŋ\ **sing** \ō\ **go** \ȯ\ **law** \ȯi\ **boy** \th\ **thin** \t͟h\ **the** \ü\ **loot** \u̇\ **foot**
\y\ **yet** \zh\ **vision, beige** \k̲, ⁿ, œ, ue, ʸ\ *see* Guide to Pronunciation

Source: By permission. From *Merriam-Webster's Collegiate® Dictionary, 11th Edition.* © 2011 by Merriam-Webster Incorporated (www.Merriam-Webster.com).

Word Origins

Words have ancestors. Some of the ancestors are words that were borrowed from other languages. *Shampoo,* for example, comes from a Hindi word meaning *to press,* and *moccasin* comes from the Algonquian Indian word for *shoe.* Other word ancestors include mythology, literature, people, places, and customs. The origin of the word *sadist,* which refers to a person who enjoys inflicting pain on others, is attributed to the Marquis de Sade, an eighteenth-century French author who wrote with pleasure about such cruelty.

Etymology.   The study of word origins is called **etymology.** An etymologist traces the development of a word back to its earliest recorded appearance. In dictionaries, the etymology of a word is usually given in brackets. The extent to which the word origin is explained varies from one dictionary to another. Compare the information on the etymology of the word *mentor* given in three dictionaries.

This entry is from the online *Merriam-Webster Dictionary:*

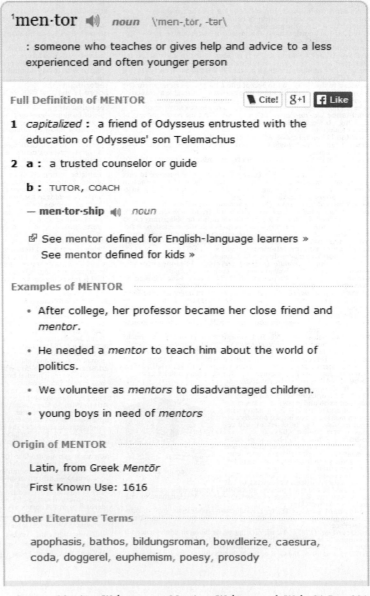

Source: *Merriam-Webster.com.* Merriam-Webster, n.d. Web. 31 Jan. 2014.
http://www.merriam-webster.com/dictionary/mentor

This entry is from the textbook-size edition of *Merriam-Webster's Collegiate® Dictionary*:

¹**men·tor** \'men-ˌtȯr, -tər\ *n* [L, fr. Gk *Mentōr*] (1616)   **1** *cap* : a friend of Odysseus entrusted with the education of Odysseus' son Telemachus   **2 a** : a trusted counselor or guide   **b** : TUTOR, COACH — **men·torship** \-ˌship\ *n*
²**mentor** *vt* (1976) : to serve as a mentor for : TUTOR

Source: By permission. From *Merriam-Webster's Collegiate® Dictionary, 11th Edition.* © 2011 by Merriam-Webster Incorporated (www.Merriam-Webster.com).

In both cases, the entries give information on the origin of the word, but the second explains the mythological background more clearly. Both dictionaries are abridged, which means that information has been condensed. An abridged dictionary is adequate for most college use. In special cases, however, you may desire more information on the origin or the past use of a word. If so, an unabridged, or unshortened, dictionary is necessary, but its large size dictates that you must go to it rather than carry it around with you. Consider the entry for *mentor* in the unabridged *Webster's Third New International® Dictionary:*

men·tor \'men-ˌtȯ(ə)r, -ȯ(ə), -ntə(r)\ *n* -s [after *Mentor*, tutor of Telemachus in the Odyssey of Homer, fr. L, fr. Gk *Mentōr*] **1 :** a close, trusted, and experienced counselor or guide ⟨every one of us needs a ~ who, because he is detached and disinterested, can hold up a mirror to us —P.W.Keve⟩ ⟨was much more than a ~; he supplied decisions —Hilaire Belloc⟩ ⟨has been my ~ since 1946 —Lalia P. Boone⟩ ⟨regarded by patrons . . . as a personal friend as well as fashion ~ —*N.Y. State Legislative Committee on Problems of the Aging*⟩   **2 :** TEACHER, TUTOR, COACH ⟨a writer of monographs, and a ~ of seminars —*Atlantic*⟩ ⟨although he had never accepted a pupil . . . she persuaded him to become her ~ —*Current Biog.*⟩ ⟨one of the game's most successful young ~s —*Official Basketball Guide*⟩

Source: By permission. From *Webster's Third New International® Dictionary, Unabridged.* © 1993 by Merriam-Webster Inc. (www.Merriam-Webster.com).

Your college library probably has several unabridged dictionaries in its reference room. Other excellent choices for etymological research include the *Random House Dictionary of the English Language* and the *American Heritage Dictionary of the English Language.*

Why Study Etymology?   The more you know about a word, the easier it is to remember that word. The etymology gives you the history of a word, which can help you establish new relationships on your "computer chip," or schema, for that word. "Meeting the ancestors" can also help you create a rich visual image of the word by using the background information. For example, the word *trivial* means "of little worth or importance." It comes from the Latin words *tri* for *three* and *via* for *way*, which combine to mean "the crossing of three roads" in Latin. The Romans knew that people would stand and talk at such an intersection. Because many strangers would be listening to the conversations, it was advisable to talk only of small, or trivial, matters. This history of *trivial* can increase your enjoyment of the word while enhancing your ability to remember the definition.

EXERCISE 12

Many English words have their roots in the names of characters in Greek mythology. The words represent a particular characteristic or predicament of the mythological person or creature. Read the entries here to discover their mythological origins and answer the questions that follow.

at·las \'at-ləs\ *n*   **1 a** : a book of maps often including descriptive text   **b** : a book of tables, charts, or illustrations ⟨an *atlas* of anatomy⟩   **2** : the first vertebra of the neck [*Atlas*, a Titan of Greek mythology]

Word History   Atlas was one of the Titans or giants of Greek mythology, whose rule of the world in an early age was overthrown by Zeus in a mighty battle. Atlas was believed to be responsible for holding up the sky, a task which he tried unsuccessfully to have Hercules assume. In his published collection of maps, the 16th century Flemish cartographer Gerhardus Mercator included on the title page a picture of Atlas supporting the heavens, and he gave the book the title *Atlas*. Other early collections of maps subsequently included similar pictures of Atlas, and such books came to be called *atlases*.

Source: By permission. From *Webster's New Explorer College Dictionary* © 2007 by Federal Street Press, a division of Merriam-Webster Inc.

1. *Atlas* means _____

2. Explain the myth. _____

_____

od·ys·sey \'äd-ə-sē\ *n, pl* **-seys** : a long wandering usually marked by many changes of fortune [the *Odyssey*, epic poem attributed to Homer recounting the long wanderings of Odysseus]

Source: By permission. From *Webster's New Explorer College Dictionary* © 2007 by Federal Street Press, a division of Merriam-Webster Inc.

3. *Odyssey* means _____

_____

4. Explain the myth. _____

_____

THESAURUS

Learning Objective 5

Find synonyms and antonyms in a thesaurus

Dr. Peter Mark Roget, an English physician, collected lists of related words as a hobby, and in 1852 the lists were published in a **thesaurus,** or treasury of words. In the book, he related words because they were synonyms, such as *illegal* and *unlawful,* as well as antonyms, such as *peaceful* and *warlike.* This book, still called *Roget's Thesaurus* because of the man who first had the idea, has been revised frequently with the addition of new words and the deletion of obsolete ones.

Roget's Thesaurus is not a dictionary, and you would probably not use it while reading. Instead, it is a valuable source for writers who are stuck on using a particular word again and again and want a substitute. For example, if you are writing a history term paper and have already used the noun *cause* twice in one paragraph and hesitate to use it again, consult *Roget's Thesaurus* for other options. You will find noun alternatives such as *origin, basis, foundation, genesis,* and *root.* If you need a verb for *cause,* you will find synonyms that include *originate, give rise to, bring about, produce, create, evoke,* and many others. Probably over 100 are listed as relating to *cause,* but not all of them are synonymous. Select the one that fits your need in the sentence, adds variety to your writing, and maintains the shade of meaning that you desire.

The words in a thesaurus are ordinarily listed in alphabetical order, and familiar dictionary abbreviations are used for parts of speech. The following example shows an entry for the word *influence.*

> **influence,** *n. & v.* —*n.* influentialness; IMPORTANCE, POWER, mastery, sway, dominance, AUTHORITY, control, ascendancy, persuasiveness, ability to affect; reputation, weight; magnetism, spell; conduciveness; pressure. *Slang,* drag, pull. —*v.t.* affect; move, induce, persuade; sway, control, lead, actuate; modify; arouse, incite; prevail upon, impel; set the pace, pull the strings; tell, weigh. *Ant.,* see IMPOTENCE.

Source: From *The New American Roget's College Thesaurus* by Phillip D. Morehead and Andrew T. Morehead, copyright © 1958, 1962 by Albert H. Morehead. Copyright © 1978, 1985, renewed 1986 by Phillip D. Morehead and Andrew T. Morehead. Used by permission of Dutton Signet, a division of Penguin Group (USA) Inc.

When a word is printed in small capitals, such as IMPORTANCE, POWER, and AUTHORITY, it means that you can find additional synonyms by looking that particular word up in its alphabetical order. Explanations sometimes appear in brackets, and not every word in the dictionary is listed.

Reader's TIP — Using an Electronic Thesaurus

Your word-processing program probably contains a thesaurus. In many versions of Microsoft Word, for example, you can access the thesaurus just as easily as you can access the dictionary. When you want to search for another word to replace one you feel that you have overused, just double left click on the word. When the word is highlighted, right click on it to access the pop-up menu. Scroll down to "Synonyms" and select a word from the list that appears. The selected word will then replace the overused word in your document. In at least one version of Word, the last option on the pop-up menu is "Thesaurus." Choosing that brings up a full thesaurus entry with many more synonyms and some antonyms as well. Other word-processing programs and other versions of Word function differently, but they have in common an easy way to access synonyms as you write.

The example below in this Reader's TIP shows only a few of the synonyms available for the word *right.* In this author's version of Word, 93 synonyms and 10 antonyms appear in the online thesaurus! The example demonstrates that clicking on *just* (one of the synonyms for *right*) brings up a list of synonyms for *just.* Using this handy reference is an excellent way to enhance your writing and expand your vocabulary.

Thesaurus: English (United States)

Looked up:	Replace with Synonyms
right	just

Meanings:	
just (adj.)	just
suitable (adj.)	fair
correct (adj.)	equitable
sane (adj.)	legitimate
front (adj.)	upright
rightful (adj.)	honest
claim (noun)	good
	lawful

Replace   Look Up   Previous   Cancel

EXERCISE 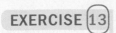 **13** Use the following entry for *right* from a print version of a thesaurus to select an alternative word that fits the meaning of *right* in the sentences below.

1. The first amendment gives Americans the *right* of free speech. _____

2. It was not *right* for the government to force the Indians out of the Southeast in the Trail of Tears. _____

3. Can government payments help *right* some social wrongs of the past? _____

4. Do revolutionaries ignore the difference between *right* and wrong? _____

5. Employers want to make the *right* fit between employee skills and job demands.

RIGHT, RIGHTNESS [922]

Nouns—**1,** rightness, right, what ought to be, what should be, fitness, propriety; JUSTICE, morality, PROBITY, honor, virtue, lawfulness.
2, privilege, prerogative, title, claim, grant, POWER, franchise, license.
3, rightness, correctness, accuracy, precision; exactness; TRUTH.
Verbs—**1,** be right, be just, stand to reason.
3, right, make right, correct, remedy, see justice done, play fair, do justice to, recompense, hold the scales even, give every one his due.
Adjectives—**1,** right, upright, good, just (see JUSTICE); reasonable, suitable, becoming.
2, right, correct, proper, precise, exact, accurate, true.
Adverbs—rightly, justly, fairly, correctly; in justice, in equity, in reason, without distinction of persons, on even terms.
Antonym, see WRONG.

Source: From *The New American Roget's College Thesaurus* by Phillip D. Morehead and Andrew T. Morehead, copyright © 1958, 1962 by Albert H. Morehead. Copyright © 1978, 1985, renewed 1986 by Phillip D. Morehead and Andrew T. Morehead. Used by permission of Dutton Signet, a division of Penguin Group (USA) Inc.

TEXTBOOK GLOSSARY

Learning Objective 6

Consult the glossary to define words used in the textbook

Some technical terms located within a textbook glossary may not be found in an ordinary dictionary. An example might be the term *coupled reactions*. One might locate each word separately within a dictionary, but the words combined (having a particular scientific meaning) might be found only within the glossary of a science textbook. The textbook **glossary** defines words and phrases as they apply to particular fields of study. Consult it before using the dictionary for words that seem to be part of the terminology of the discipline.

EXERCISE  **14** This exercise considers the types of words and the amount of information presented in a glossary. Notice that many of the words take on a special meaning within the particular field of study. Use the biology glossary on page 165 to answer the questions with *T* (true) or *F* (false).

Cumulus One of three basic cloud forms; also the name given one of the clouds of vertical development. Cumulus are billowy individual cloud masses that often have flat bases.

Cup anemometer An instrument used to determine wind speed.

Curie point The temperature above which a material loses its magnetization.

Cutoff A short channel segment created when a river erodes through the narrow neck of land between meanders.

Cyclone A low-pressure center characterized by a counterclockwise flow of air in the Northern Hemisphere.

Dark nebula A cloud of interstellar dust that obscures the light of more distant stars and appears as an opaque curtain.

Deep-ocean basin The portion of the seafloor that lies between the continental margin and the oceanic ridge. This region comprises almost 30 percent of Earth's surface.

Deep-ocean trench A narrow, elongated depression on the floor of the ocean.

Deep-sea fan A cone-shaped deposit at the base of the continental slope. The sediment is transported to the fan by turbidity currents that follow submarine canyons.

Deflation The lifting and removal of loose material by wind.

Deformation General term for the processes of folding, faulting, shearing, compression, or extension of rocks.

Degenerate matter Incomprehensibly dense material formed when stars collapse and form a white dwarf.

Delta An accumulation of sediment formed where a stream enters a lake or ocean.

Dendritic pattern A stream system that resembles the pattern of a branching tree.

Density The weight-per-unit volume of a particular material.

Deposition The process by which water vapor is changed directly to a solid without passing through the liquid state.

Desalination The removal of salts and other chemicals from seawater.

Desert One of the two types of dry climate; the driest of the dry climates.

Desert pavement A layer of coarse pebbles and gravel created when wind removed the finer material.

Detrital sedimentary rock Rock formed from the accumulation of material that originated and was transported in the form of solid particles derived from both mechanical and chemical weathering.

Dew point The temperature to which air has to be cooled in order to reach saturation.

Dike A tabular-shaped intrusive igneous feature that cuts through the surrounding rock.

Dip-slip fault A fault in which the movement is parallel to the dip of the fault.

Discharge The quantity of water in a stream that passes a given point in a period of time.

Disconformity A type of unconformity in which the beds above and below are parallel.

Discordant A term used to describe plutons that cut across existing rock structures, such as bedding planes.

Dissolved load That portion of a stream's load carried in solution.

Distributary A section of a stream that leaves the main flow.

Diurnal tidal pattern A tidal pattern exhibiting one high tide and one low tide during a tidal day; a daily tide.

Diurnal tide Tides characterized by a single high and low water height each tidal day.

Divergence The condition that exists when the distribution of winds within a given area results in a net horizontal outflow of air from the region. In divergence at lower levels the resulting deficit is compensated for by a downward movement of air from aloft; hence, areas of divergent winds are unfavorable to cloud formation and precipitation.

Divergent plate boundary A region where the rigid plates are moving apart, typified by the mid-oceanic ridges.

Divide An imaginary line that separates the drainage of two streams; often found along a ridge.

Dome A roughly circular upfolded structure similar to an anticline.

Doppler effect The apparent change in wavelength of radiation caused by the relative motions of the source and the observer.

Doppler radar In addition to the tasks performed by conventional radar, this new generation of weather radar can detect motion directly and hence greatly improve tornado and severe storm warnings.

Drainage basin The land area that contributes water to a stream.

Drawdown The difference in height between the bottom of a cone of depression and the original height of the water table.

Drift See *Glacial drift*.

Drumlin A streamlined asymmetrical hill composed of glacial till. The steep side of the hill faces the direction from which the ice advanced.

Dry adiabatic rate The rate of adiabatic cooling or warming in unsaturated air. The rate of temperature change is 1°C per 100 meters.

Ductile deformation A type of solid-state flow that produces a change in the size and shape of a rock body without fracturing. Occurs at depths where temperatures and confining pressures are high.

Dune A hill or ridge of wind-deposited sand.

Earthquake The vibration of Earth produced by the rapid release of energy.

Echo sounder An instrument used to determine the depth of water by measuring the time interval between emission of a sound signal and the return of its echo from the bottom.

Elastic rebound The sudden release of stored strain in rocks that results in movement along a fault.

Electron A negatively charged subatomic particle that has a negligible mass and is found outside an atom's nucleus.

Element A substance that cannot be decomposed into simpler substances by ordinary chemical or physical means.

Elements of weather and climate Those quantities or properties of the atmosphere that are measured regularly and that are used to express the nature of weather and climate.

Elliptical galaxy A galaxy that is round or elliptical in outline. It contains little gas and dust, no disk or spiral arms, and few hot, bright stars.

Emergent coast A coast where land that was formerly below sea level has been exposed either because of crustal uplift or a drop in sea level or both.

Emission nebula A gaseous nebula that derives its visible light from the fluorescence of ultraviolet light from a star in or near the nebula.

End moraine A ridge of till marking a former position on the front of a glacier.

Entrenched meander A meander cut into bedrock when uplifting rejuvenated a meandering stream.

Environmental lapse rate The rate of temperature decrease with increasing height in the troposphere.

Eon The largest time unit on the geologic time scale, next in order of magnitude above era.

Ephemeral stream A stream that is usually dry because it carries water only in response to specific episodes of rainfall. Most desert streams are of this type.

Epicenter The location on Earth's surface that lies directly above the forces of an earthquake.

Epoch A unit of the geologic calendar that is a subdivision of a period.

Equatorial low A belt of low pressure lying near the equator and between the subtropical highs.

Equatorial system A method of locating stellar objects much like the coordinate system used on Earth's surface.

Equinox (spring or autumnal) The time when the vertical rays of the Sun are striking the equator. The length of daylight and darkness is equal at all latitudes at equinox.

Source: Lutgens, Frederick K.; Tarbuck, Edward J.; Tasa, Dennis, *Foundations of Earth Science*, 6th edition, © 2011. Printed and electronically reproduced by permission of Pearson Education, Inc., Upper Saddle River, New Jersey.

_____ 1. A *cup anemometer* is used to measure rainfall.

_____ 2. A *dark nebula* consists of dust that masks views of more distant stars.

_____ 3. A *dendritic pattern* refers to the shape of a stream's path.

_____ 4. *Dew point* is the place at which dew collects on the ground.

_____ 5. A *divide* is a deep trench in the Earth's surface.

_____ 6. Information gained from *Doppler radar* is often used to warn of tornados and other severe storms.

_____ 7. A *drumlin* is a hill created by glacial ice.

_____ 8. A new country on a coastline that is created by treaty after a war is called an *emergent coast*.

_____ 9. The *epicenter* of an earthquake refers to the exact location of the fault under the Earth's surface.

_____ 10. An *equinox* occurs twice a year and marks the time when the hours of daylight are greater than the hours of darkness.

ANALOGIES

Learning Objective 7

Refine word knowledge by solving analogies

An **analogy** is a comparison that mimics a previously stated relationship. Solving analogies requires clear thinking about shades of word meaning and about the relationship between the given pair of words. Approach them as brainteasing puzzles that are challenging and fun! Perhaps the best explanation is an example:

EXAMPLE

Apple is to *fruit* as *potato* is to _____.

EXPLANATION The first step in solving an analogy is to pinpoint the initial relationship. What is the relationship between *apple* and *fruit?* Because an apple is a member of the fruit group, you might say that it is one part of a larger whole. To complete the analogy, you must establish a similar relationship for *potato.* In what larger group does a potato belong? *Vegetable* is the answer.

Analogies are challenging and can be very difficult. They test logical thinking as well as vocabulary. Working through analogies is an experience in problem solving.

The Reader's Tip on page 167 explains the many different relationships that can be expressed in an analogy. Study both the list and the examples.

EXERCISE 15

Study the following analogies to establish the relationship of the first two words. Record that relationship, using the categories just outlined. Then choose the word that duplicates that relationship to finish the analogy.

_____ 1. *Leg* is to *table* as *wheel* is to _____.

Relationship? _____

a. chair
b. car
c. motor
d. steer

Reader's TIP **Categories of Relationships for Analogies**

Synonyms: Similar in meaning

   Start is to *begin* as *end* is to *finish.*

Antonyms: Opposite in meaning

   Retreat is to *advance* as *tall* is to *short.*

Function, use, or **purpose:** Identifies what something does. Watch for the object (noun) and then the action (verb).

   Car is to *drive* as *towel* is to *absorb.*

Classification: Identifies the larger group association

   Mosquito is to *insect* as *gasoline* is to *fuel.*

Characteristics and descriptions: Shows qualities or traits

   Sour is to *lemon* as *sweet* is to *sugar.*

Degree: Shows variations of intensity

   Walking is to *running* as *cool* is to *frozen.*

Part to whole: Shows the larger group

   Pupil is to *school* as *sailor* is to *navy.*

Cause and effect: Shows the reason (cause) and the result (effect)

   Work is to *success* as *virus* is to *illness.*

_____ 2. *Soft* is to *firm* as *peaceful* is to _____.

   Relationship? _____

   a. pillow
   b. kind
   c. sleep
   d. aggressive

_____ 3. *Turnip* is to *vegetable* as *oak* is to _____.

   Relationship? _____

   a. wood
   b. fuel
   c. house
   d. glass

_____ 4. *Selling* is to *profit* as *germ* is to _____.

Relationship? _____

a. vaccination
b. carelessness
c. wealth
d. disease

_____ 5. *Kind* is to *considerate* as *courage* is to _____.

Relationship? _____

a. soldier
b. bravery
c. fear
d. fighting

_____ 6. *Towel* is to *absorb* as *oven* is to _____.

Relationship? _____

a. safety
b. speed
c. cook
d. kitchen

_____ 7. *Tiny* is to *small* as *hot* is to _____.

Relationship? _____

a. summer
b. warm
c. cooking
d. temperature

_____ 8. *Soft* is to *pillow* as *humid* is to _____.

Relationship? _____

a. swamp
b. trip
c. camp
d. trees

_____ 9. *Work* is to *success* as *study* is to _____.

Relationship? _____

a. history
b. knowledge
c. professor
d. college

_____ 10. *Needle* is to *sew* as *bulb* is to _____.

Relationship? _____

a. lamp
b. illuminate
c. electricity
d. table

EASILY CONFUSED WORDS

Learning Objective 8

Spell commonly confused words

Correct spelling influences the way in which readers receive the message in your written work. Always check your spelling before calling your work complete. Spelling matters! This section addresses some common words that are often misspelled. Many pairs of words cause confusion because they sound exactly alike or almost alike but are spelled and used differently. *Principal* and *principle* are examples of this confusion. A common error is to write, "The new school principle is Mrs. Thompson." Remember, the *al* word is the person, or "pal," and the *le* word is the rule. To keep most of these words straight, memorize and associate. Study the following words that sound similar and learn their differences.

EXERCISE 16   Circle the correct boldface word to fit the context of each sentence.

1. She exercised on a (**stationary, stationery**) bicycle.

2. Her brother devoured the (**hole, whole**) pizza by himself.

> ### Reader's TIP   Easily Confused Words
>
> | | |
> |---|---|
> | **capital:** city
 capitol: building | **hole:** a depression in the ground
 whole: entire |
> | **to:** in the direction of
 too: also | **stationary:** fixed position
 stationery: paper |
> | **their:** belonging to them
 there: opposite of here
 they're: they are | **its:** belonging to it
 it's: it is |
> | | **your:** belonging to you
 you're: you are |
> | **accept:** receive
 except: all but | |
> | | **threw:** launched
 through: in one side and out the other |
> | **cite:** quote
 sight: vision
 site: place | |

3. The (**capital, capitol**) serves as a meeting place for both senators and representatives.

4. The line for the bookstore begins right (**their, they're, there**).

5. After such a late night, they were much (**to, too**) tired to wake up early.

6. In order to get (**threw, through**) college successfully, studying is necessary.

7. The overhead projector was placed directly in her (**cite, sight, site**) line for the speaker.

8. Sometimes it is difficult to (**accept, except**) the truth.

9. (**Your, you're**) first impression is often a lasting one.

10. (**Vain, vein**) students might spend extra time gazing at themselves in front of the mirror.

11. (**Its, It's**) not the best strategy to watch television while studying for a test.

ENRICHING YOUR VOCABULARY

Many reading selections in this text are followed by practice for vocabulary development called Vocabulary Enrichment (see page 133 for an example). In addition, Vocabulary Lessons using a structural approach appear at the end of most chapters, including this one. In these lessons, prefixes, roots, and suffixes are linked to new words. Plan to make vocabulary enrichment an exciting, lifelong activity.

PERSONAL FEEDBACK 2   Name _____

1. After reading this chapter, what system will you use for remembering new words? _____

   _____

   _____

   _____

2. Why is it not recommended that you look up unknown words as you read? _____

   _____

   _____

   _____

3. List ten adjectives to describe characteristics that you would like in a spouse. Again, stretch your vocabulary beyond easy words. _____

   _____

   _____

   _____

   Share your responses as directed by your instructor.

SUMMARY POINTS

1 What strategies should I use to attack and remember new words? (page 142)

Unlock the meaning of unfamiliar words while reading by using context clues, knowledge of word parts, and, finally, a dictionary or the textbook glossary. Remember words and make them part of your personal vocabulary with the help of the power of association. Make concept cards that include the word, the definition, a sentence, a picture, and the source. Practice and use the new words to make them yours.

2 How can I use context clues to unlock unfamiliar words? (page 145)

Notice various types of clues surrounding the unfamiliar word: definitions, elaborating details, elaborating examples, comparisons, contrasts. Also remember that some words have several meanings. Use the context to know which meaning is intended.

3 How can I use common word parts to unlock meaning? (page 152)

Use familiar prefixes, roots, and suffixes to predict the meaning of an unfamiliar word.

4 What information can a dictionary provide to enrich my word knowledge? (page 156)

Strengthen word knowledge by learning pronunciation, spelling, meaning, parts of speech, word history, and word origin or etymology. All of these details can be found in the dictionary.

5 When is a thesaurus helpful? (page 162)

Use a thesaurus to find alternative words when you are writing.

6 What information can I find in a glossary? (page 164)

Use the glossary at the back of the textbook to find the meanings of words as they are used in that text and in the discipline.

7 What is the value of solving analogies? (page 166)

Analogies require precise thinking about the meanings and functions of words. The key to solving them is to first determine the relationship between the pair of words given and then select a word that repeats that relationship in the second pair.

8 What are some commonly confused words that I should learn to spell correctly? (page 169)

Practice using these words correctly: *stationary/stationery; hole/whole; capital/ capitol; their/they're/there; to/too; threw/through; cite/sight/site; accept/except; your/you're; vain/vein; its/it's.*

COLLABORATIVE   PROBLEM SOLVING

Form a five-member group and select one of the following activities. Brainstorm and then outline your major points. Choose a member to present the group findings to the class.

➤ Make a list of ten words that have multiple meanings.

➤ Create a list of ten words that begin with the prefix *pre.*

➤ Create five analogies, one for each of the following relationships: synonyms, antonyms, function, part to whole, and cause and effect.

➤ Create a list of ten words that end with the suffix *ous.*

➤ Involve the class in a game of Password to challenge your classmates.

VOCABULARY LESSON

Before and After

Study the prefixes, words, and sentences.

Prefixes   *ante*: before   *pre*: before   *post*: after

Words with *ante* = *before*

Can *antenuptial* counseling strengthen marriages? Is an entry an *anteroom*?

- Antebellum: existing before the war

  The *antebellum* home with the white columns was built before the Civil War.

- Antecede: to go before

  Your good name can *antecede* your presence.

- Antecedent: word coming before the pronoun to which the pronoun refers

  The name *Valerie* is the *antecedent* of *her* in the sentence.

- Antediluvian: belonging to the time before the Biblical flood; very old

  She ignored the advice and regarded it as *antediluvian*.

- Antennae: feelers on the head of an insect used as organs of touch

  The insect's *antennae* inspected the food.

- Antescript: a note added before something, such as a prefix to a letter

  The *antescript* indicated why the letter would be late arriving.

Words with *pre* = *before*

Can a *prefix predict* the meaning of a new word?

- Preamble: an introduction

  Schoolchildren learn the *Preamble* to the Constitution.

- Precede: to go before

  Queen Elizabeth should *precede* Prince Philip at state events.

- Predecessor: one who came before another in office

  Her *predecessor* helped orient the new chairperson to the job.

- Preeminent: supreme, before all others

  Our professor is the *preeminent* scholar in contemporary Russian literature.

- Prelude: a musical or dramatic introduction

  As the *prelude* began, the remaining ticket holders were seated in the audience.

- Premonition: a forewarning or omen

  When I heard the dog bark, I had a *premonition* that trouble was near.

- Prejudice: judgment before proof is given

  A lawyer tries to avoid choosing a potential juror who shows signs of *prejudice*.

- Precocious: having early development

  The *precocious* child could read at two years of age.

Words with *post* = *after*

Is the time ante meridian or *post* meridian?

- Posterity: descendants who come after

  Leave a gift for *posterity* and donate money to the college library.

- Posthumous: after death

  The *posthumous* award was given to the widow of the soldier.

- Postnatal: the time immediately after birth

  A *postnatal* examination monitors the health of the new mother.

- Postpone: delay or set the date back

  Let's *postpone* the meeting until tomorrow after lunch.

- Postscript: a note added to a letter after it has been signed

  Karen scribbled an afterthought in the *postscript* to her long letter.

Review

Part I

Choose an appropriate word from the list to complete each of the following sentences.

precocious	premonition	antebellum	prelude	postscript
predecessor	posthumous	preamble	postponed	preeminent

1. The ambassador is a _____ scholar in the history of Nigeria.

2. Shorten the _____ and begin the main point of your speech.

3. As a _____ athlete, the young Tiger Woods golfed on television with adults.

4. The threat of a tornado _____ the game for three hours.

5. A _____ award honors a dead hero.

6. The couple restored the _____ home to its original 1850s appearance.

7. The musical _____ introduced the song to follow.

8. George W. Bush was the immediate _____ of Barack Obama.

9. A superstitious person would see a black cat as a _____ of danger.

10. Sara's letter ended with her quickly remembered thoughts in a _____.

Part II

Answer the following with *T* (true) or *F* (false).

_____11. A prejudiced listener has trouble fairly evaluating both sides.

_____12. An antediluvian outfit is up to date.

_____ 13. A postnatal exam checks the growth of the fetus.

_____ 14. Antemeridian refers to the afternoon.

_____ 15. The antennae of an insect are usually attached to its tail.

_____ 16. The antescript is positioned in the main body of the letter.

_____ 17. An antecedent is a person, place, or thing.

_____ 18. Antenuptial arguments occur after the wedding day.

_____ 19. A presumed appointment needs to be double-checked for certainty.

_____ 20. Environmental regulations consider both the present and posterity.

Getting Information from News Web Sites and Online Communities

If you want up-to-the-minute news and other information (such as gathering material for a research report or searching for medical advice), you can find it instantly on the Internet. Popular Web sites such as CNN.com headline current events both nationally and internationally and also offer spotlight sections on politics, justice, entertainment, technology, health, lifestyles, travel, and finance.

For information on specific groups of interest to you (such as fitness or cooking), you can visit online communities (sometimes known as *forums*). In addition, you can go to medical Web sites when you are searching for medical information or advice.

News and Current Events Web Sites

Searching for news stories is easy, using such popular news-centered Web sites as

CNN—www.cnn.com
Google News—www.news.google.com
Yahoo! News—www.news.yahoo.com
Huffington Post—www.huffingtonpost.com
New York Times—www.newyorktimes.com

If you are searching for local news, your area newspaper probably has its own Web site.

 **EXERCISE 1** Go to either Google News or CNN News and explore news stories that interest you. Record the Web address of two news stories and, on a separate piece of paper, explain what information you found about each.

Online Communities

Online communities provide free, up-to-date information on specific subjects. These communities may be maintained by a company or an individual and are interactive in that a subscriber can post questions and receive timely answers. There are online communities for almost every subject. Here are just a few online communities that can be found on the Internet.

Fitness

www.bodybuilding.com
www.myfitnesspal.com
www.sparkpeople.com

Cooking

www.discusscooking.com
community.cookinglight.com
www.chow.com

To find an online community, use a search engine such as Google. Type in a subject with the words *online community* (e.g., fitness online community). Then, sample the choices offered to find the community that suits you. When visiting, take part in a discussion and remember that these groups are open to all individuals and that some of the information may not have been verified. Keep an open mind as you participate in the community and do not accept every word as fact.

EXERCISE 2 Decide on a topic of interest and find an online community about the topic. Join the community discussion and ask a question related to the topic. Record your question and print any responses that you get.

Medical and Health-Related Web Sites

When you (or a family member or friend) are sick or if you are simply looking for ways to get healthy, you often turn to the Internet for answers. When searching medical and health-related Web sites, be sure to find those sites that are reputable and are continuously reviewed for accuracy and timeliness. For example, a well-known site such as WebMD includes a section called "AboutWebMD" that presents the credentials of medical staff who work for the site as well as policies and awards and recognitions that the site has received. Here are a few popular medical Web sites:

www.webmd.com
www.healthcentral.com
http://www.cdc.gov
www.bettermedicine.com

EXERCISE 3 Go to one of the medical Web sites listed above. Find information on the site that explains who is responsible for the site and who provides the information offered at the site. Write your answer on a separate piece of paper.

A partial page from the Centers for Disease Control and Prevention Web site appears below:

5

Topic, Main Idea, and Supporting Details

Learning Objectives

From this chapter, readers will learn:

1 To define topic, main idea, and major and minor supporting details
2 To identify topics
3 To distinguish topics, main ideas, and details
4 To master main idea and topic questions on comprehension tests
5 To identify stated and unstated main ideas
6 To identify main ideas in longer selections

Everyday Reading Skills: Researching Online

WHAT IS A TOPIC? WHAT IS A MAIN IDEA?

The **topic** of a passage is its general subject. It is the answer to the question, "Who or what is this passage about?" The topic can be described in a single word or in a brief phrase. For example, "*mood disorders*" might be a topic featured in your psychology textbook.

The **main idea** of a passage is the core of the material, the particular point that the author is trying to convey about the topic. The main idea of a passage can be stated in one sentence that condenses specific ideas or details in the passage into a general, all-inclusive statement of the author's message. For instance, if the topic is mood disorders, then the main idea might be, "*Mood disorders can take several forms.*" In classroom discussions, all of the following words are sometimes used to help students understand the meaning of the main idea.

thesis	gist
main point	controlling idea
central focus	central thought

Whether you read a single paragraph, a chapter, or an entire book, many experts agree that your most important single task is to understand the main idea of what you read.

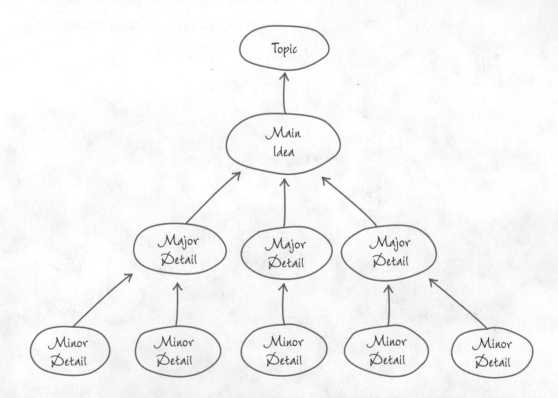

WHAT ARE MAJOR AND MINOR SUPPORTING DETAILS?

Major supporting details provide specific information that explains and elaborates on the main idea. For example, "*major depression*" and "*bipolar disorder*" might be major supporting details that explain the author's point that mood disorders can take several forms. **Minor supporting details** lend even more specific information that further explains the major details. Minor details might take the form of an example or an interesting anecdote. They are often the links that help us remember the more important details. For instance, *"the suicide of comedian and actor Robin Williams,"* might be used to illustrate the effects of severe depression. Likewise, *"periods of abnormally high energy alternating with periods of extreme fatigue"* would describe bipolar disorder.

With the definitions of *topic, main idea,* and *major and minor supporting details* in mind, examine the diagram on the previous page. It illustrates the relationships among these elements of a written selection. Minor details illustrate and explain major details, which in turn support and explain the main idea, and the main idea makes a point about the topic.

Remembering the diagram on page 178 will help you see the relationship of ideas as you read paragraphs, essays, and textbook chapters. In Chapter 6, you will learn to distinguish major and minor details and to identify the pattern in which the details are organized. All that you learn in Chapter 5 and Chapter 6 will combine to enable clear understanding of the author's message.

IDENTIFYING TOPICS

Learning Objective 2
Identify topics

Recognize General and Specific Words

The first step in determining the main idea of a selection is to look at the specific ideas presented in the sentences and try to decide on a general topic or subject under which you can group these ideas. Before tackling sentences, begin with words. Pretend that the sentence ideas in a selection have been reduced to a short list of key words. Pretend also that within the list is a general term that expresses an overall subject for the key words. The general term encompasses or categorizes the key ideas and is considered the topic of the list.

EXAMPLE   The following list contains three specific ideas with a related general topic. Circle the general term that could be considered the subject of the list.

General Topic

Detail   Main Idea   Detail

Detail   Detail

satin

wool

fabric

silk

EXPLANATION   Satin, wool, and silk are different types of fabric. Thus, *fabric* is the general term or classification that could be considered the subject or topic.

EXERCISE 1 Circle the general term or subject for each of the following related groups of ideas.

1. chimpanzees	2. cirrus	3. oats	4. Alps	5. shrimp
orangutans	clouds	wheat	Appalachians	crustacean
apes	cumulus	corn	mountains	crab
gorillas	stratus	grain	Rockies	lobster

Recognize General and Specific Phrases

Topics of passages are more often stated as phrases rather than single words. The following list contains a phrase that is a general topic and three specific ideas related to that topic. Circle the general topic that could be the subject.

EXAMPLE Turn on the ignition.

Press the accelerator.

Insert the key.

Start the car.

EXPLANATION The first three details are involved in starting a car. The last phrase is the general subject or topic.

EXERCISE 2 Circle the phrase that could be the topic for each list.

1. totaling yearly income

   subtracting for dependents

   filing an income tax return

   mailing a 1040 form

2. paying fees

   buying books

   starting college

   going to class

3. picking up seashells

   vacationing at the beach

   walking in the surf

   riding the waves

4. pushing paper under sticks

   piling the logs

   building a fire

   striking a match

EXERCISE 3 Read the lists of specific details and write a general phrase that could be the subject or topic for each group.

1. separate the white and dark clothes

   add one cup of detergent

   insert quarters into the machine

   General topic? _____

2. dribble the ball

   pass the ball down the court

   shoot a basket

   General topic? _____

3. pull up alongside a car

   back into a space

   straighten out

   General topic? _____

4. switch on the power

   select a program

   open a file

   General topic? _____

5. boil water in a large pot

   add salt and oil

   pour noodles into the water

   General topic? _____

Recognize the General Topic for Sentences

Paragraphs are composed of sentences that develop a single general topic. The next practice exercises contain groups in which the sentences of a paragraph are listed numerically. After reading the sentences, circle the phrase that best expresses the topic or general subject of the sentences.

EXAMPLE

1. The law of demand is illustrated in an experiment conducted by the makers of M&M candy.
2. For a twelve-month period, the price of M&Ms remained the same in 150 stores, but the number of M&Ms in a package increased, which dropped the price per ounce.
3. In those stores, sales immediately rose by 20 to 30 percent.

   Candy maker's experiment

   M&Ms drop in price

   M&Ms prove the law of demand

EXPLANATION   The first phrase is too broad. The second phrase relates a detail that is an important part of the experiment. The third phrase links the candy with the purpose of the experiment and thus most accurately states the topic of the sentences.

EXERCISE 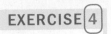 Circle the phrase that best describes the topic or subject for each group of sentences.

Group 1

1. To provide a favorable climate for growing grapes, the winter temperature should not go below 15° F, and the summers should be long.
2. During the growing season, rainfall should be light.
3. A gentle movement of air is required to dry the vines after rains, dispel fog, and protect the vines from fungus disease.

Protecting grapes from disease

Appropriate temperatures for growing grapes

Appropriate climate for growing grapes

Group 2

1. For example, addicted parents may neglect to properly care for their children.
2. Other individuals go from one job to another, never able to hold on to any position for very long.
3. For example, students who are addicted to drugs may repeatedly fail classes because they do not complete assignments.

Drug abuse among college students

Possible symptoms of drug abuse and addiction

Drug abuse in contemporary society

Group 3

1. Aerobic fitness includes maintaining a strong heart, a healthy vascular system, and muscles that effectively use oxygen.
2. The goal of an aerobic workout is to achieve and maintain one's target heart rate for approximately 20 to 30 minutes.
3. One element of aerobic fitness is to engage in an aerobic workout three to five times a week.

Aerobic fitness

Maintaining a healthy heart

The proper aerobic workout

Group 4

1. Salsa, the popular blend of Latin American music, is also the word for *sauce*.
2. According to stories, the expression was contributed to the music world by a Cuban orchestra conductor.
3. While practicing a mambo that needed more life, the orchestra leader told his musicians to "echale salsita" or "throw in the sauce."

Latin American salsa music

The naming of salsa music

Contribution of salsa

Group 5

1. Simply drinking water is the best way to prevent dehydration from sweating.
2. Taking salt tablets before drinking water can dehydrate the body even more by extracting water from body tissue.
3. Plain water is better than beverages containing sugar or electrolytes because it is absorbed faster.

Salt tablets versus water

Value in plain water

Preventing dehydration

EXERCISE 5   Read each group of three sentences, then write a phrase that best states the subject or general topic for the sentences.

Group 1

1. Psychologists conduct research with animals for several reasons.
2. Sometimes they simply want to know more about the behavior of a specific type of animal.
3. In other instances, they want to see whether certain laws of behavior apply to both humans and animals.

General topic? _____

—*Psychology: Themes and Variations*, Sixth Edition,
by Wayne Weiten

Group 2

1. Scientists think that a more reasonably defined danger level means that only 50,000 homes have radon concentrations that pose a danger to occupants.
2. Scientists outside the United States Environmental Protection Agency (EPA) have concluded that the standards the EPA is using are too stringent.
3. The EPA regards 5 million American homes as having unacceptable radon levels in the air.

General topic? _____

_____

—*Physical Geology: Earth Revealed*, Fifth Edition,
by David McGeary, et al.

Group 3

1. They resist accepting a warm pink body as a corpse from which organs can be "harvested."
2. The Japanese do not incorporate a mind–body split into their models of themselves; they locate personhood throughout the body rather than in the brain.
3. In Japan the concept of brain death is hotly contested, and organ transplants are rarely performed.

General topic? _____

—*Cultural Anthropology*, Eleventh Edition,
by William A. Haviland, et al.

IDENTIFYING TOPICS AND MAIN IDEAS

Recognize General and Supporting Sentences

Read the sentences in each of the following groups. The sentences are related to a single subject, with two of the sentences expressing specific support and one sentence expressing the main idea. Circle the number of the sentence that best expresses the main idea. Then read the three phrases and circle the one that best describes the topic of the sentences.

EXAMPLE

1. An accountant who prefers to work alone rather than as a team member may be an important part of the organization but will not become a leader.
2. A CEO who steers a company into increased profits but exhibits poor people skills by yelling at employees and refusing to listen will not keep her job.
3. Companies now demand of their top employees a high level of emotional intelligence (EI), which refers to skills in adaptability, self-control, conflict management, and teamwork.

   IQ no longer matters

   The importance of emotional intelligence

   Polite changes in the workplace

EXPLANATION   The third sentence best expresses the general subject. The other two sentences offer specific supporting ideas. The second phrase, "The Importance of Emotional Intelligence," best describes the general subject of the material. The first phrase is not really suggested, and the last phrase is one of the details mentioned.

EXERCISE 6   Circle the number of the sentence that best expresses the main idea. Then read the three topic phrases and circle the phrase that best describes the subject of the sentences.

Group 1

1. African American and Hispanic teens are not as likely to use tobacco as Caucasian adolescents.
2. Each day approximately 3,000 teens start smoking, and eventually one-third of them will die from smoking.
3. Despite the proven danger, in the past decade tobacco usage among teens has increased.

   Tobacco usage among teens

   Dangers teens face

   Harms of smoking

Group 2

1. Berry Gordy, an ex-boxer and Ford auto worker, borrowed $700 from his family and began to manufacture and sell his own records on the Hitsville USA (later called Motown, for "motor town") label.

2. The next year Smokey Robinson and the Miracles recorded "Shop Around," which was Gordy's first million-copy hit.
3. Gordy signed an 11-year-old boy to record for him under the name of Stevie Wonder.

Gordy's success

Stevie Wonder at Motown

The recording artists at Motown

Group 3

1. The czar's wife believed that the devious and politically corrupt Rasputin, known as the "mad monk," was the only one who could save her son.
2. The son of Nicholas II was afflicted with hemophilia, a condition in which the blood does not clot properly.
3. In Russia during the reign of Nicholas II, hemophilia played an important historical role.

Rasputin's charm

Hemophilia

Influence of hemophilia on Russia

Group 4

1. In the 1990s, however, doctors began advising parents to position babies for sleep on their backs, and now many babies never crawl but still learn to walk at about the same age.
2. What is considered normal infant development can change quickly when new recommendations in infant care are introduced.
3. For example, crawling at six to eight months of age was once an expected milestone when babies were traditionally put to sleep lying on their stomachs.

Developmental effects of changes in infant care

The importance of proper infant care

Infant sleeping positions

Group 5

1. The success of Norman Rockwell's illustrations is based on his simple formula of drawing ordinary people doing ordinary things that make us laugh at ourselves.
2. Rockwell used humor to poke fun at situations but never at people.
3. Rockwell painted adults and children of the neighborhood, first from real life and then, in later years, from photographs

Rockwell's neighborhood

The subjects of Rockwell's paintings

Art from photographs

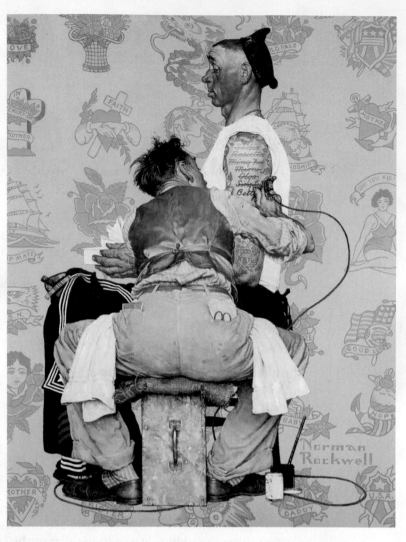

Norman Rockwell, *The Tattoo Artist*, 1944

EXERCISE 7   For each group of sentences, write a phrase that states the topic and then circle the number of the sentence that best expresses the main idea.

Group 1

SD 1. Four hundred Navajos were recruited as marine radio operators, and the codes based on the Navajo language were never broken by the enemy.

MI 2. During World War II, over 25,000 Native Americans served in the armed forces and made amazing contributions toward the war effort.

SD 3. The most famous Indian GI was a Pima Indian, the marine Ira Hayes, who helped plant the American flag on Iwo Jima.

General Topic? _Contributions of Native Americans in WWII_

Group 2

MI 1. Germans view health as having several components.

SD 2. Hard work, cleanliness, and staying warm aid in health maintenance.

SD 3. Stress and germs, as well as drafts, unhappiness, and a sedentary lifestyle, are believed to cause illness.

General topic? _How German view of health?_

—*Culture in Rehabilitation*, edited by Matin Royeen and Jeffrey L. Crabtree

Group 3

SD 1. Logically, the probability of having a "good Samaritan" on the scene would seem to increase as group size increased.

MI 2. When it comes to helping behavior, many studies have uncovered a puzzling situation called the "bystander effect": People are less likely to provide needed help when they are in groups than when they are alone.

SD 3. Evidence that your probability of getting help *declines* as group size increases was first described by John Darley and Bibb Latane, who were conducting research on helping behavior.

General topic? _Bystander effect_

—*Psychology: Themes and Variations*, Sixth Edition, by Wayne Weiten

EXERCISE 8 Each of the following sentence groups contains three specific supporting sentences. Write a general sentence that states the *main idea* for each group. In addition, write a phrase that briefly states the general *topic* of that sentence.

Group 1

1. The battered woman does not want to believe that the man she loves is violent.
2. She doesn't want to face the possibility that he may be violent for the rest of their lives together.
3. She wants to hold on to the hope that someday he will quit drinking and the relationship will change.

—*Marriage and Families in a Diverse Society*, by Robin Wolf

General sentence stating the main idea? _The better woman does not face the truth._

General topic? _Better woman's denial._

Group 2

1. Decades before Jamestown was hailed as the first permanent settlement in America, Pedro Menendez de Aviles founded St. Augustine in Florida.
2. Menendez brought 800 soldiers and colonists to establish this first European settlement in America and to protect the land for Spain.
3. St. Augustine, so named because the landing occurred in the month of August, became a permanent and prosperous Spanish settlement.

General sentence stating the main idea? _St. Augustine was the first permanent settlement of Europeans in America_

General topic? _Spanish settlement in St. Augustine._

Group 3

1. According to a recent report, the average U.S. wedding in 2010 included 200 or more guests and cost $30,166.
2. In 2005, the average wedding hosted fewer than 200 guests and cost $24,168.
3. Among the many expenses included in the overall cost of a wedding are the reception, rings, wedding attire, and photography.

General sentence stating the main idea? _How much money does the wedding cost over the period/time passes.&_

General topic? _Wedding cost average in U.S._ invitations.

—*Business Mathematics*, Twelfth Edition,
by Gary Clendenen, et al.

Differentiate Topic, Main Idea, and Supporting Details

We have said that a topic is a word or a phrase that describes the subject or general category of a group of specific ideas. Frequently, the topic is stated as the title of a passage. The main idea, in contrast, is a complete sentence that states the topic and *adds the writer's position or focus on the topic*. The supporting details are the specifics that develop the topic and main idea.

Read the following example from a textbook paragraph and label the topic, the main idea, and a supporting detail.

EXAMPLE

___T___ Backhanded compliments

___MI___ A backhanded compliment is really not a compliment at all; it's usually an insult masquerading as a compliment.

___SD___ You might give a backhanded compliment as you say, "Looks like you've finally lost a few pounds—am I right?"

—*Interpersonal Communication Book*, Thirteenth Edition,
by Joseph DeVito

EXPLANATION   The first item is general enough to be the topic. The second item is a sentence that expresses the writer's point about the topic, and so it is the main idea. The third item is a specific example, so it is a detail.

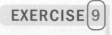

Compare the items within each group and indicate which is the topic (*T*), the main idea (*MI*), and the specific supporting detail (*D*).

Group 1

___SD___ 1. Much in this American document comes from England's Magna Carta, which was signed in 1215.

___T___ 2. British roots in American government

___MI___ 3. The American Constitution has its roots in the power of past documents.

Group 2

___MI___ 1. Children are highly valued in African American families.

_____I_____ 2. Valuing children

_____SD_____ 3. Like Latinos, African Americans view "children as wealth," believing that children are important in adding enjoyment and fulfillment to life.

—*Marriage and Families in a Diverse Society*, by Robin Wolf

Group 3

_____I_____ 1. Effects of population movements in the mid-1800s in the United States

_____SD_____ 2. As European Americans pushed the boundaries of the country west and south, they clashed with Indians and foreign powers that claimed those lands as their own.

_____MI_____ 3. In the 1830s and 1840s, mass population movements affected almost every aspect of American life.

—*Created Equal*, Fourth Edition, by Jacqueline Jones, et al.

Group 4

_____SD_____ 1. Her early research led to an understanding of how viruses infect the plant and destroy its tissues.

_____I_____ 2. Esau's early career with beets

_____MI_____ 3. Sugar beets played a major role in the career of Dr. Katherine Esau, one of this century's most productive plant scientists.

—*Biology*, Fourth Edition, by Neil Campbell, et al.

Group 5

_____I_____ 1. Discrimination against women in higher education

_____SD_____ 2. Harvard, for example, was one of the last colleges to give up sex discrimination and began admitting women to its graduate business program only in 1963.

_____MI_____ 3. In general, the more prestigious the educational institutions, the more strongly they discriminated against women.

—*Sociology: A Brief Introduction*, Third Edition, by Alex Thio

ANSWERING TOPIC AND MAIN IDEA TEST QUESTIONS

Learning Objective 4

Master main idea and topic questions on comprehension tests

To gain insight into recognizing a correctly stated topic or main idea, categorizing incorrect responses to test questions can be helpful. First, remember that the topic is a brief phrase stating who or what the passage is about. The main idea is the point being made about the topic, and it is always in the form of a sentence. When stating the topic or main idea of a passage, it is easy to make the mistake of creating a phrase or a sentence that is either too broad or too narrow. The same mistakes occur when students answer topic and main idea questions on standardized tests. A phrase or sentence that is too broad suggests the inclusion of much more than is stated in the passage. A phrase or sentence that is too narrow is a detail within the passage. It may be an interesting and eye-catching detail, but it is not the subject or point of the passage.

Differentiate Distractors in Test Questions About the Topic

Test questions that require selecting the best title for a passage are really asking you to identify the topic.

EXAMPLE After reading the following passage, decide which of the suggested titles is correct (*C*), too broad (*TB*), or a detail (*D*).

> One interesting research finding shows that listeners can accurately judge the socioeconomic status (whether high, middle, or low) of speakers from 60-second voice samples. In fact, many listeners reported that they made their judgments in fewer than 15 seconds. Speakers judged to be of high status were also rated as being of higher credibility than speakers rated middle and low in status. Listeners can also judge with considerable accuracy the emotional states of speakers from vocal expressions.

> —*Human Communication*, Sixth Edition,
> by Joseph DeVito

_TB_ 1. Importance of voice
_TB_ 2. Speaking
_✓_ 3. Making judgments by voice
_D_ 4. Emotional states of speakers

EXPLANATION The third response most accurately describes the topic of the passage. The first two are too broad and include much more than is in the paragraph. The last response is a detail that is part of one of the experiments with listeners.

EXERCISE 10 Read the passage and label the suggested titles for the passage as correct (*C*), too broad (*TB*), or a detail (*D*).

Passage 1

Immigrants to the United States in the early 1900s often brought traditional courtship patterns to the New World and extended them into the next generation. One Italian man described his thwarted efforts to woo his fiancée in private. When he visited her home, "she sat on one side of the table, and I at the other. They afraid I touch." Finally, less than a month before their wedding, he got permission to take her to the theater. But the family was unwilling to let them go alone. "We came to the aisles of the theater. My mother-in-law go first, my fiancée next, my little sister, my father-in-law. I was the last one. I had two in between. . . . I was next to the old man." He tried to steal a kiss a few days before the wedding, but his fiancée rebuffed him: "No, not yet."

—*Created Equal*, Fourth Edition,
by Jacqueline Jones, et al.

_____B____ 1. The rules of courtship

_____D____ 2. A forbidden kiss

_____D____ 3. Italian immigrants in the early 1900s

_____C____ 4. Old World courtship patterns in the United States

Passage 2

Humpback whales strain their food from seawater. Instead of teeth, these giants have an array of brushlike plates called _baleen_ on each side of their upper jaw. The baleen is used to sift food from the ocean. To start feeding, a humpback whale opens its mouth, expands its throat, and takes a huge gulp of seawater. When its mouth closes, the water squeezes out through spaces in the baleen, and a mass of food is trapped in the mouth. The food is then swallowed whole, passing into the stomach, where digestion begins. The humpback's stomach can hold about half a ton of food at a time, and in a typical day, the animal's digestive system will process as much as 2 tons of krill and fish.

—_Biology_, Fourth Edition,
by Neil Campbell, et al.

_____ 1. Humpback whales

_____ 2. Baleen for teeth

_____ 3. The digestive system of the humpback whale

____C____ 4. How whales filter food

Passage 3

Tar and nicotine are not the only harmful chemicals in cigarettes. In fact, tars account for only 8 percent of tobacco smoke. The remaining 92 percent consists of various gases, the most dangerous of which is carbon monoxide. In tobacco smoke, the concentration of carbon monoxide is 800 times higher than the level considered safe by the U.S. Environmental Protection Agency (EPA). In the human body, carbon monoxide reduces the oxygen-carrying capacity of the red blood cells by binding with the receptor sites for oxygen. This causes oxygen deprivation in many body tissues.

—_Health: the Basics_, Fifth Edition,
by Rebecca J. Donatelle

_____ 1. Carbon monoxide

_____ 2. Harmful tars and nicotine

____C____ 3. Carbon monoxide dangers from smoking

_____ 4. Tobacco and smoking

QUESTIONING FOR THE MAIN IDEA

Learning Objective 5

Identify stated and unstated main ideas

To determine the main idea of a paragraph or selection, ask questions in the following three basic areas. (The order may vary according to how much you already know about the subject.) Usually, you decide on the general topic first, sometimes from the title and sometimes by considering the details. If you are familiar with the material, constructing a main idea may seem almost automatic.

If the material is unfamiliar, however, you may need to connect the key details to formulate a topic and then create your main idea statement.

1. Establish the Topic

Question: Who or what is this about?   What general word or phrase identifies the subject? The topic should be broad enough to include all of the ideas but narrow enough to focus on the direction of the details. For example, identifying the topic of an article, such as "College Costs," "Change in College," or "Changing to Cut College Costs," might all be correct, but the last one may be the most pointed and descriptive for the article.

2. Identify the Key Supporting Details

Question: What are the important details?   Look at the details that seem significant to see if they point in a particular direction. What aspect of the subject do they address? What seems to be the common message? In a passage on college costs, the details might describe benefits of larger classes, telecommunication networks, and video instruction. A common thread is that each idea relates to changes that are targeted at cutting the costs of college instruction.

3. Focus on the Message of the Topic

Question: What main idea is the author trying to convey about the topic?
This statement should be:

- A complete sentence
- Broad enough to include the important details
- Focused enough to describe the author's slant

In the example about cutting college costs, the main idea might be "Several colleges experiment with ways to cut costs."

Stated Main Ideas

Research shows that readers comprehend better when the main idea is directly stated, particularly when it is stated at the beginning of a passage. Such an initial main idea statement, **thesis statement**, or **topic sentence** is a signpost for readers, briefing them on what to expect. This thesis statement or main idea statement provides an overview of the author's message and connects the supporting details. Read the following example and use the three-step method to determine the main idea.

EXAMPLE   MI

Polygraph tests have been viewed as an invasion of privacy and criticized on ethical, legal, and scientific grounds. The physiological changes thought to reveal deception could result from anxiety about being interrogated, anger at being asked to take the test, or fear from pondering the consequences of "failing" the test. You might react in any of these ways if you were "hooked up" to a polygraph.

—*Psychology*, by Stephen F. Davis
and Joseph J. Palladino

1. Who or what is the topic of this passage? _Polygraph tests_
2. Underline the key details.
3. What point is the author trying to make? _____

_____

EXPLANATION   The topic of this passage is "Polygraph Tests." The details give specifics about how physiological changes caused by anxiety, anger, or fear can show up the same way on a polygraph test as a lie response. The author states the main idea in the first sentence.

Textbook authors do not always state the main idea in the first sentence. Stated main ideas may be the beginning, middle, or concluding sentence of a passage. Therefore, do not think of stating the main idea only as a search for a particular sentence. Instead, rely on your own skill in answering the three questions about topic, details, and focus. Connect the details to form your own concept of the main idea, and, if a specific sentence in the paragraph restates it, you will recognize it as the main idea.

EXERCISE 11   Apply the three-question technique to identify the topic, key details, and main idea of the following passages, all of which have stated main ideas.

Passage 1

_MI_

To gain a better idea of what *social structure* is, think of college football. You probably know the various positions on the team: center, guards, tackles, ends, quarterback, running backs, and the like. These positions provide a good example of a social structure. Each is a *status*; that is, each is a social position. For each of these statuses, there is a *role*; that is, each of these positions has certain expectations attached to it. The center is expected to snap the ball, the quarterback to pass it, the guards to block, the tackles to tackle or block, the ends to receive passes, and so on. Those role expectations guide each player's actions; that is, the players try to do what their particular role requires.

—From James M. Henslin, *Sociology: A Down-to-Earth Approach,*
7th ed. © 2007 (excerpt from page 96).
Reproduced by permission of Pearson Education, Inc.

1. Who or what is the topic of this passage? _College football structure_
of social structure
2. Underline the key details.
3. What point is the author trying to make? _____

_____

Passage 2

_MI_

Many of the techniques used by today's police differ quite a bit from those employed in days gone by. Listen to how a policeman, writing in the mid-1800s, describes the way pickpockets were caught in London 200 years ago: "I walked forth the day after my arrival, rigged out as the very model of a gentleman farmer, and with eyes, mouth, and pockets wide open, and a stout gold-headed cane in my hand, strolled leisurely through the fashionable thoroughfares, the pump-rooms, and the assembly rooms, like a fat goose waiting to be plucked. I wore a pair of yellow gloves well wadded, to save me from falling, through a moment's inadvertency, into my own snare, which consisted of about fifty fish-hooks, large black hackles, firmly sewn barb downward, into each of the pockets of my brand new leather breeches. The most blundering 'prig' alive might have easily got his hand to the bottom of my pockets, but to get it out again, without tearing every particle of flesh from the bones, was a sheer impossibility. . . . I took care never to see any of my old customers until the convulsive tug at one or other of the pockets announced the capture of a thief. I then coolly linked my arm in that of the prisoner, [and] told him in a confidential whisper who I was."

—From *Criminal Justice Today: An Introductory Text for the Twenty-First Century,* Tenth Edition, by Frank J. Schmalleger

1. Who or what is the topic of this passage? _Techniques of Police officers to catch the pickpockets in early 200 yrs ago_

2. Underline the key details.

3. What point is the author trying to make? _____

Passage 3

MI

Today, many prosecutors, judges, and even mental health experts believe in the need for a verdict of "guilty but insane." Under this provision, if a person uses the insanity defense but a judge or jury finds the evidence insufficient for legal insanity, they can return a verdict of guilty but mentally ill. This indicates that the defendant is suffering from an emotional disorder severe enough to influence behavior but insufficient to render him or her insane. After such a finding, the court can impose any sentence it could have used on the crime charge. The convicted defendant is sent to prison, where the correctional authorities are required to provide therapeutic treatment. If the mental illness is cured, the offender is returned to the regular prison population to serve out the remainder of the sentence.

—*Introduction to Criminal Justice,* Ninth Edition, by Joseph J. Senna and Larry J. Siegel

1. Who or what is the topic of this passage? _Guilty but insane_
2. Underline the key details.
3. What point is the author trying to make? _____

_____

Passage 4

Different job roles in nursing require different educational preparation from on-the-job training to graduate level degrees. Entry level would be the Nursing Assistant. Most facilities offer on-the-job training for this position through their staff education departments. The Licensed Practical Nurse role requires one year of formal education and board certification. The Registered Nurse will need the minimum of a two-year associate degree or up to a four-year baccalaureate degree. Successful completion of board certification would also be required for practice. Registered Nurses with graduate level degrees such as a master's degree in nursing can practice at a higher level as a nurse practitioner diagnosing, treating, and supporting the patient with simple medical problems or promoting higher standards of care for a specific population of patients, such as the geriatric client.

—Adapted from *Health Science Fundamentals:
Exploring Career Pathways*, by Shirley A. Badasch
and Doreen S. Chesebro

1. Who or what is the topic of this passage? _Nursing education preparation on the job_
2. Underline the key details.
3. What point is the author trying to make? _____

_____

Passage 5

MI

Six Flags is a world-renowned theme park. The company owns and operates thirty-eight different parks spread out over North America, Latin America, and Europe. Locations include Mexico City, Belgium, France, Spain, Germany, and most major metropolitan areas in the United States. In fact, having a park in forty of the fifty major metropolitan areas in the United States has earned Six Flags the title of world's largest regional theme park company. Annually, more than 50 million visitors are reported to entertain themselves at Six Flags theme parks worldwide. The company prides itself in claiming that 98 percent of the U.S. population is within an 8-hour drive to any one of the numerous Six Flags theme parks.

—*Introduction to Hospitality*, Fourth Edition, by John R. Walker

1. Who or what is the topic of this passage? _Six Flags_
2. Underline the key details.
3. What point is the author trying to make? _____

_____

Passage 6

MI

Colleges and universities are denying access to third party credit card marketers in increasing numbers. There were 22 campuses that disallowed the practice in 1988. That number has increased dramatically and is expected to cross 400 in the next couple of years. Private sources that monitor college credit card marketing (*College Marketing Intelligence*) contend that the number is much higher, estimating that 750 to 1,000 college campuses have already banned on-campus credit card marketing.

—*Taking Sides: Clashing Views on Controversial Issues in Marketing,* edited by Barton Macchiette and Abhijit Roy

1. Who or what is the topic of this passage? _Colleges & Univerities are being denied, in the campuses._
2. Underline the key details.
3. What point is the author trying to make? _____

_____

Unstated Main Ideas

Research shows that only about half of the paragraphs in textbooks have directly stated main ideas. This should not be a problem if you understand the three-question technique for locating the main idea. The questions guide you in forming your own statement so that you are not dependent on finding a line in the text.

When the main idea is not directly stated, it is said to be *implied*, which means it is suggested in the thoughts that are revealed. In this case, the author has presented a complete idea but, for reasons of style and impact, has chosen not to express it concisely in one sentence. As a reader, it is your job to systematically connect the details and focus the message.

In the following passage, the main idea is not stated, but it may be determined by answering the three questions that follow.

EXAMPLE   In Australia and Belgium, nonvoters are subject to fines; not only the fine itself but the clear expectation that everyone is legally required to vote helps generate 90+ percent turnout rates. In Italy, nonvoters are not fined, but "Did Not Vote" is stamped on their identification papers, threatening nonvoters with the prospect of unsympathetic treatment at the hands of public officials should they get into trouble or need help with a problem.

—*The New American Democracy*, Election Update Edition,
by Morris Fiorina and Paul Peterson

1. Who or what is the topic of this passage? <u>Penalties for non-voting</u>

   (This gives you the general topic or heading.)

2. What are the key terms or details? <u>In some countries non-voters are penalized in order to encourage voting</u>

3. What idea is the author trying to convey about nonvoting? _____

   _____

(This is the main idea the author is trying to communicate.)

EXPLANATION   The sentence stating the main idea might very well have been the first, middle, or last sentence of the paragraph. Having it stated, however, was not necessary for understanding the passage. In many cases, readers spend time searching for a single sentence that encapsulates the meaning rather than digesting the information and forming ideas. Instead of hunting for a sentence, answer these three questions: "Who or what is this about?" "What are the key terms?" and "What point is the author trying to make?" This passage is about penalties for not voting. The key terms are *"giving fines in Australia and Belgium, and stamping 'Did Not Vote' on identification papers in Italy."* The author's main idea is that in *"some countries nonvoters are penalized to encourage voting."* Apply the three-question technique to determine the main idea.

EXERCISE 12   **Passage 1**

Marilyn, a Southwest Airlines flight attendant, takes the mike as her plane backs away from the Houston terminal. "Could y'all lean in a little toward the center aisle please?" she chirps in an irresistible Southern drawl. "Just a bit, please. That's it. No, the other way, sir. Thanks."

Baffled passengers comply even though they have no idea why.

"You see," says Marilyn at last, "the pilot has to pull out of this space here, and he needs to be able to check the rearview mirrors."

Only when the laughter subsides does Marilyn launch into the standard aircraft safety speech that many passengers usually ignore.

—*Business Essentials,* Third Edition,
by Ronald Ebert and Ricky Griffin

1. Who or what is the topic of this passage? *Using a joke for relaxing the passengers*
2. Underline the key details.
3. What point is the author trying to make? *The air liners uses the joke to tackled down her passengers.*

Passage 2

Children have more taste buds than adults do, which may explain why they are often so picky about eating "grown-up" foods. Even among adults, individuals differ in their sensitivity to taste. Indeed, recent studies have shown that people can be divided into one of three groups: nontasters, medium tasters, and supertasters. Compared to most, supertasters use only half as much sugar or saccharin in their coffee or tea. They also suffer more oral burn from eating the active ingredient in chili peppers. Using videomicroscopy to count the number of taste buds on the tongue, researchers have found that nontasters have an average of 96 taste buds per square centimeter, medium tasters have 184, and supertasters have 425.

—*Psychology,* Second Edition, by Saul Kassin

1. Who or what is the topic of this passage? *Tastebuds*
2. Underline the key details.
3. What point is the author trying to make? *Different sensitivity of taste to adults.*

Passage 3

Most people today can only imagine the housing problems in the early industrial metropolis. In the final decades of the nineteenth century, developers built tenements to house the greatest number of families in the smallest amount of space. Not only were tenement apartments very small, but most had few windows and little ventilation. As many as six families shared a single bathroom. Insulation was poor, and rooms could be stifling in the summer and cold in the winter.

—*Social Problems,* Fifth Edition, by John J. Macionis

1. Who or what is the topic of this passage? *Tenements problems in early industrial metropolis*
2. Underline the key details.
3. What point is the author trying to make? *Living in a tenement in late 1900's were very poor.*

Passage 4

In his book *Bridges, Not Walls*, John Stewart dramatically illustrates the case of the famous "Wild Boy of Aveyron," who spent his early childhood without any apparent human contact. The boy was discovered in January 1800 while digging for vegetables in a French village garden. He showed no behaviors one would expect in a social human. The boy could not speak but uttered only unrecognizable cries. More significant than this absence of social skills was his lack of any identity as a human being. As author Roger Shattuck put it, "The boy had no human sense of being in the world. He had no sense of himself as a person related to other persons." Only after the influence of a loving "mother" did the boy begin to behave—and, we can imagine, think of himself as a human.

In 1970, authorities discovered a twelve-year-old girl (whom they called "Genie") who had spent virtually all her life in an otherwise empty, darkened bedroom with almost no human contact. The child could not speak and had no sense of herself as a person until she was removed from her family and "nourished" by a team of caregivers.

—*Understanding Human Communication*, Eighth Edition,
by Ronald Adler and George Rodman

1. Who or what is the topic of this passage? _____

_____

2. Underline the key details.
3. What point is the author trying to make? _____

_____

Passage 5

A mother had a son who threw temper tantrums: lying on the floor, pounding his fists, kicking his legs, and whining for whatever he wanted. One day while in a supermarket he threw one of his temper tantrums. In a moment of desperation, the mother dropped to the floor, pounded her fists, kicked her feet, and whined, "I wish you'd stop throwing temper tantrums! I can't stand it when you throw temper tantrums!" By this time, the son had stood up. He said in a hushed tone, "Mom, there are people watching! You're embarrassing me!" The mother calmly stood up, brushed off the dust, and said in a clear, calm voice,

"That's what you look like when you're throwing a temper tantrum." Sometimes, traditional approaches such as bribing, threatening, ignoring, or giving in seem so natural that we overlook the possibility that something different, such as embarrassment, might work too.

—*The Creative Problem Solver's Toolbox,* by Richard Fobes

1. Who or what is the topic of this passage? *Stopping a temper tantrum*

2. Underline the key details.

3. What point is the author trying to make? *The mother used the same idea to show her son how it looked when he was temper tantrum.*

EXERCISE 13 In some of the following passages, the main ideas are stated. In others they are implied. Avoid simply searching for a sentence that states the main idea. Instead, apply the three-question strategy that you have learned and practiced throughout this chapter to determine the author's main point.

Passage 1

God's message to Muhammad in the form of the Qur'an (a "reciting") was clear: The Prophet is to warn his people against worshipping false gods and all immorality, especially injustice to the poor, orphans, widows, and women altogether. At the end of time, on Judgment Day, every person will be bodily resurrected to face what they have earned: eternal punishment in hellfire or eternal joy in paradise, according to how he or she has lived. The way to paradise lies in gratitude to God for His bounties, His revelatory guidance, and His readiness to forgive the penitent. It lies in social justice and obedient worship of God, and in recognition of God's transcendence. The proper human response to God is "submission" (*islam*) to His will, becoming *muslim* ("submissive") in one's worship and morality.

—*The Heritage of World Civilizations Combined Edition,*
Ninth Edition, by Albert M. Craig, William A. Graham,
Donald Kagan, Steven Ozment, and Frank M. Turner

1. Who or what is the topic of this paragraph? *God's message to Muhammad*

2. Underline the key details.

D 3. Select the best statement of the main idea of the passage.

   a. The word *Qur'an* means a reciting, and *islam* means submission.
   b. God warned people against worship of false gods.
   c. Muhammad was a prophet who received a message from God that became known as the Qur'an.
   d. God's message to Muhammad was that he must tell people that the way to paradise is to live with concern for justice and submission to God.

Passage 2

Civilization in the Americas before 1492 developed independently of civilization in the Old World. As the pharaohs of Egypt were erecting their pyramid tombs, the people of the desert Pacific coast of Peru were erecting temple platforms. While King Solomon ruled in Jerusalem, the Olmec were creating their monumental stone heads. As Rome reached its height and then declined, so did the great city of Teotihuacan in the Valley of Mexico. As Islam spread from its heartland, the rulers of Tikal brought their city to its greatest splendor before its abrupt collapse. Mayan mathematics and astronomy rivaled those of any other peoples of the ancient world. And as the aggressive nation-states of Europe were emerging from their feudal past, the Aztecs and Incas were consolidating their great empires.

—*The Heritage of World Civilizations Combined Edition,*
Ninth Edition, by Albert M. Craig, William A. Graham,
Donald Kagan, Steven Ozment, and Frank M. Turner

1. Who or what is the topic of this paragraph? *Civilization*
in the Old World.

_____

2. Underline the key details.

A ___ 3. Select the best statement of the main idea of the passage.

    a. Ancient American civilizations developed separately from other world civilizations, but they followed remarkably similar patterns.

    b. The ancient people of Peru were building temples about the same time that ancient Egyptians were building the pyramids.

    c. Ancient American civilizations included the Aztecs, Incas, and Mayans.

    d. The Mayans' understanding of mathematics and astronomy was as advanced as that of any other peoples of the ancient world.

Passage 3

One hallmark of Chinese history is its striking continuity of culture, language, and geography. The Shang and Chou dynasties were centered in north China along the Yellow River or its tributary, the Wei. The capitals of China's first empire were in exactly the same areas, and north China would remain China's political center through history to the present. If Western civilization had experienced similar continuity, it would have progressed from Thebes in the valley of the Nile to Athens on the Nile; Rome on the Nile; and then, in time, to Paris, London, and Berlin on the Nile; and each of these centers of civilization would have spoken Egyptian and written in Egyptian hieroglyphics.

—*The Heritage of World Civilizations Combined Edition,*
Ninth Edition, by Albert M. Craig, William A. Graham,
Donald Kagan, Steven Ozment, and Frank M. Turner

1. Who or what is the topic of this paragraph? *Chinese history striking in one Hallmark. time*

2. Underline the key details.

C 3. Select the best statement of the main idea of the passage.

   a. Western civilization began in Thebes in the valley of the Nile.
   b. China's first imperial capitals were in North China along the Yellow River and the Wei River.
   c. Chinese history has been amazingly consistent in its geography.
   d. Chinese and Western civilizations have developed in much the same way.

Passage 4

One of the most important things to realize about the restaurant industry is that you can't do it alone. Each person in your operation has to work together for you to be successful. The most important ingredient in managing people is to respect them. Many words can be used to describe a manager (coach, supervisor, boss, mentor), but whatever term is used, you have to be in the game to be effective. Managing a kitchen is like coaching a football team—everyone must work together to be effective. The difference between a football team and a kitchen is that chefs/managers cannot supervise from the sidelines; they have to be in the game. One of my favorite examples of excellent people manage-ment skills is that of the general manager of a hotel who had the ware-washing team report directly to him. When asked why, he indicated that they are the people who know what is being thrown in the garbage, they are the people who know what the customers are not eating, and they are the people most responsible for the sanitation and safety of an operation. There are many components to managing people—training, evaluating, nurturing, delegating, and so on—but the most important is respect.

—*Introduction to Hospitality,* Fifth Edition,
by John R. Walker

1. Who or what is the topic of this paragraph? *Managing a restaurant by a successful way / Team work.*

2. Underline the key details.

B 3. Select the best statement of the main idea of the passage.

   a. Managing a kitchen is like coaching a football team.
   b. To be successful, a restaurant manager must develop a team in which respect is the key ingredient.
   c. The people with the least-skilled jobs often know what the cus-tomers like and don't like.
   d. One hotel manager had the ware-washing team report directly to him.

Passage 5

Employability traits are those skills that focus on attitude, passion, initiative, dedication, sense of urgency, and dependability. These traits are not always traits that can be taught, but a good chef can demonstrate them by example. Most of the employers with job opportunities for students consider these skills to be more important than technical skills. The belief is that if you have strong employability traits, your technical skills will be strong.

—*Introduction to Hospitality*, Fifth Edition,
by John R. Walker

1. Who or what is the topic of this paragraph?  _Developing skills_

2. Underline the key details.

_____B_____ 3. Select the best statement of the main idea of the passage.

    a. Attitude is an important employability trait.
    b. Employability traits are often more important than technical skills.
    c. A good chef can teach by example.
    d. Employers like to employ students.

Getting the Main Idea of Longer Selections

Learning Objective 6

Identify the main idea of longer selections

Because of the great quantity of material included in a book, understanding the main idea of longer selections such as chapters and articles seems more difficult than understanding a single paragraph. Longer selections have several major ideas contributing to the main point and many paragraphs of supporting details. To pull the ideas together under one central theme, an additional twist to the three-question strategy is necessary: Simplify the material by organizing paragraphs or sections into manageable categories. These categories represent the major supporting details. Then decide how each subsection contributes to the whole.

1. Establish the topic.
   Ask "Who or what is this about?"
   Consider what the title and first paragraphs suggest about the topic.
2. Identify the key supporting points.
   Ask "What are the major details?"
   Group paragraphs or sections into categories that represent major support.
   Use headings and subheadings as a guide.
3. Focus on the message.
   Ask "What is the point the author is trying to make about the topic?"
   Review the categories you have identified as major supporting details. What point do they make about the topic?

Practice as you read the long selections at the end of most chapters in this textbook.

PERSONAL FEEDBACK 1

Name _____

1. Describe the theme or main idea of a movie that you have seen recently—one that you liked—and give reasons for your positive evaluation.

   Movie Title: _____

   Theme or Main Idea: _____

   Reasons for Positive Evaluation: _____

2. What do you think was the main point of the movie?_____

   _____

   _____

3. Was there anything that you did not understand about the main idea?

   _____

   _____

   Share your responses as directed by your instructor.

EXERCISE 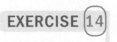 Search the Internet for articles on dreaming. Select an article that interests you, and use the expanded three-question strategy to determine the topic, the major supporting details, and the main idea. Write them on a separate sheet of paper.

SUMMARY POINTS

1 What are topics, main ideas, and major and minor supporting details? (page 178)

A topic is the general subject of a reading selection. It tells who or what the selection is about.

A main idea is the point the author is making about the topic. The main idea might also be called the thesis, main point, central focus, gist, controlling idea, or central thought.

Major supporting details explain and elaborate on the main idea.

Minor supporting details provide further explanation of the major details. They are sometimes the link that helps readers remember the material, but they are not the most important items.

2 How can I identify the topic? (page 179)

Read the passage and ask "Who or what is this about?" Think of a general word or phrase that describes the details in the passage.

3 How can I distinguish topics, main ideas, and details? (page 184)

Keep in mind the relationships among these elements as they are shown visually in the diagram on page 178. Remember that topics are broad labels that describe the general subject of a paragraph or a passage. They are like descriptive titles. Main ideas make a point about the topic. A main idea is a complete sentence that might be stated or implied in the passage. Supporting details give specific information and examples that explain and develop the topic and main idea. Also visualize the umbrella diagram: Details fit under the umbrella of the topic and main idea.

4   How can I master topic and main idea questions on comprehension tests? (page 189)

Incorrect answers to both types of questions usually take two forms: They are either too narrow or too broad. Answers that are too narrow don't cover all of the details in the passage. Answers that are too broad imply information that is not in the passage at all. Occasionally, a test writer will include a distractor that sounds important but is completely unrelated to the passage. Don't let these fool you!

5   How can I identify stated and unstated main ideas? (page 191)

1. Establish the topic. Ask "Who or what is this about?"
2. Identify the key supporting terms. Ask "What are the major details?" Remember that details are more narrow than the topic or main idea. Ask yourself what explanatory information is given.
3. Focus on the message of the topic. Ask "What is the point the author is trying to make about the topic?" Your answer should be a complete sentence of your own that is broad enough to cover the details and focused enough not to imply more than is in the passage.

This strategy should be used whether the main idea is stated in the passage or not.

6   How can I identify the main idea of longer selections? (page 203)

Break the material into subsections and determine how the subsections support the whole. Apply the expanded three-question strategy to the entire selection.

COLLABORATIVE   PROBLEM SOLVING

Form a five-member group and select one of the following questions. Brainstorm and then present the group findings to the class.

➤ Why is prior knowledge the best single predictor of reading comprehension?

➤ Why is comprehension better when the main idea is stated at the beginning of a test passage?

➤ Describe a passage that you might write that would have the main idea stated at the end.

➤ Why should the main idea of a passage be stated in a sentence rather than in a phrase? Give examples.

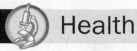

Visit Chapter 5: Topic, Main Idea, and Supporting Details in MyReadingLab to complete the Selection 1 activities.

"Life expectancy would grow by leaps and bounds if green vegetables smelled as good as bacon."

—Doug Larson, Columnist

Do you crave foods that you know are not good for you and struggle to resist them? Scientists have discovered biological reasons for those cravings and so have food manufacturers. New methods of making processed food appeal to us are based on brain chemistry.

The following selection is a magazine feature article that discusses an important health-related topic. The Reader's Tip on page 207 provides additional support for reading news and feature articles.

THINKING BEFORE READING

Preview for clues to the content. Activate your prior knowledge. Anticipate what is coming and think about your purpose for reading. Predict the author's ideas and determine your purpose for reading. Think!

[handwritten: Choclates] What foods are hardest for you to stop eating, no matter how much you've had?

[handwritten: Yes] Have you ever wondered why most people prefer foods that are heavy in salt, fat, or sugar?

[handwritten: Because they want lot of food which has more Calories in it] Why do you think such a large percentage of Americans are overweight?

I want to learn _____.

VOCABULARY PREVIEW

Are you familiar with these words?

palatable	salient	staples	innate	edible
cue	savory	metabolism	curb	deprivation

Which is more *palatable*—ice cream or a celery stick?

What are the *staples* in your family's kitchen?

Does *metabolism* have something to do with digestion?

Your instructor may choose to give a brief vocabulary review before or after reading.

THINKING DURING READING

As you read, use the six thinking strategies of a good reader: predict, picture, relate, monitor, correct, and annotate.

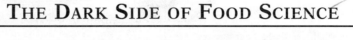

Reader's **TIP**   **Reading and Studying a News or Feature Article**

- Preview the headline and photographs.
- Find the facts: *who, what, where, when, why* and *how*.
- Consider how the angle or focus of a feature story differs from a straight news story.
- Evaluate the credibility of the sources cited.
- When reading a feature story, observe the number of facts compared with the number of opinions.
- Look for bias or judgment on the part of the reporter.

For more suggestions on reading news and feature articles in the newspaper, refer to the Everyday Reading Skills on page 138.

Topic

THE DARK SIDE OF FOOD SCIENCE

Refer also to
Reader's **TIP**
for **Health** on
page 125.

Show me a chicken nugget and I will show you the world. The world, that is, of highly palatable foods engineered by the food industry to go down easily while also stimulating us to crave more.

5 Commercial foods like chicken nuggets, French fries, chips, crackers, cookies and pastries are designed to be virtually *irresistible*. And, for a lot of reasons most of us don't fully understand, they are.

There's a "biological basis for why it's so hard for millions of Americans to resist food," former FDA commissioner David Kessler, MD, explained in a recent National Public Radio (NPR) interview. For many of us, one of the most salient stimuli in our environment is
10 food. And how do you make food even more salient? Fat, sugar and salt."

Of course, fat, sugar and salt have been around as kitchen staples for centuries, but it wasn't until the past few decades that they became as abundant and cheap as they are now. And during the course of those same few decades, food manufacturers have been busily leveraging science and technology to enhance their products—manipulating food
15 in ways that not only play on our innate fondness for sugar, salt and fat, but also dramatically boost their overall taste, texture, aroma and appearance.

Think about the flavor of beef infused into McDonald's signature French fries, the creamy filling injected into a Twinkie or the fake crosshatched grill marks stamped onto a KFC grilled chicken breast, and you begin to get the idea. The stuff regularly served up
20 at every chain restaurant, gas station and food court amounts to an edible—and irresistible—amusement park. And it's all fueled by food science and technology.

"When we were kids," recalls Kessler, "it was enough to put sugar in water, add a little coloring and get a relatively simple sensory experience called Kool-Aid. Since then, food makers have upped the ante." Today we've got Flamin' Hot Cheetos and Double
25 Chocolate Strawberry Cake Krispy Kreme doughnuts.

We need to have a better understanding about what we're up against. That starts with a brief lesson in food technology.

THIS IS YOUR BRAIN ON PROCESSED FOOD

The human brain has many attributes, but resisting Krispy Kreme doughnuts is not one of them. "The most salient foods are those with fat, sugar and salt," Kessler reminds us. "The

30 advantage those foods have is that they are hardwired from our taste receptors directly into our brains."

Being attracted to high-calorie foods worked to our advantage when food was scarce and humans had to hunt and gather for a living, explains Christopher Dehner, PhD, a professor of clinical psychology at Columbia University's Obesity Research Center. "The 35 problem is that, today, the food never runs out." On the contrary, it's dangled in front of us around the clock.

The taste preferences that food-product designers play upon today evolved over many thousands of years as a survival mechanism, notes Dana Small, PhD, a brain researcher at Yale University School of Medicine. They were a means for our ancestors to identify 40 which foods had the dense caloric value their bodies needed to support huge daily energy expenditures. Hardwired as they are, these preferences aren't something from which we can easily free ourselves.

"You may not even like the taste of a sugary treat initially," Small says, "but as long as it has a major caloric impact, the brain will keep you coming back for more." That's why 45 we are more easily triggered to want cake than to want carrots. "Carrots are better for you, but they have fewer calories," Small explains. And from the human body's instinctive, short-term perspective, calories are more essential than nutrients for survival.

In generations past when sugar, fat, and even salt were less available, this instinct was not as hard to resist. But thanks to the growth of fast-food restaurants and processed foods, 50 the cue for a high-calorie treat may now confront us several times a day.

The chemicals in our brains are not designed to help us resist. "For each of us it's going to be different," says Kessler, "but the food industry knows that layering fat on top of sugar on top of salt makes the food that much harder for the brain to resist."

 A SENSORY EXPLOSION

But taste isn't everything. Manufacturers also work hard to develop mouth-watering aro-55 mas and carefully engineered textures. They also invest in ad campaigns that equate their products with happiness and success. "The more multisensory the stimuli," says Kessler, "the greater the reward and the stronger the emotional cues."

Definition—A sensory explosion

Talk about Taste & Texture

Companies are willing to pay big bucks for "sensory science," the kind of in-depth research that tells them exactly how to design a product that appeals to all the senses. No one knows this better than Gail Vance Civille, founder and president of Sensory Spectrum, a New Jersey-based consumer research firm. Civille tests consumer reactions across a range of different sensory areas.

In the all-important area of taste, for example, what used to be a simple question of sweet versus savory has evolved into a complex science that the food industry calls "flavor dynamics."

Take a basic chocolate bar. The expert tasters at Sensory Spectrum identified a wide range of flavors in a basic chocolate bar—everything from winey, woody, nutty, citrusy, floral, alkaline and sourness to flavors of soap, cardboard, casein, cooked milk, spray-dried milk and developed milk. A client can then take this information and tweak its formulas to boost certain flavors and suppress others.

Civille and her colleagues will also evaluate a product's texture. Food manufacturers are always searching for the perfect "mouthfeel," which is why fat is so prevalent in processed food. Fat not only bestows crunch, creaminess and contrast, but it also blends flavors and even acts as a lubricant, allowing people to eat faster.

Another texture trick is to presoften food by mashing it. "Processed food is basically prechewed," notes Kessler. This allows us to eat things like chicken tenders more quickly and easily, which can lead to unconscious eating and overeating.

"We used to have foods that took more work," Civille explained in a recent NPR interview. "We used to have foods that we chewed 15 times and 20 times and 30 times before we swallowed. Now, there's rarely a food out there, outside of a sweet, chewy candy, that you have to chew more than 12 times before it's gone."

III — BREAKING THE CYCLE — *Definition*

With two-thirds of Americans now overweight, it's safe to say that our processed-food addiction is messing with our metabolisms as well as our brains.

A number of health experts, including Kessler, assert that food companies are actively capitalizing on our genetically hardwired impulses. Food scientists like Civille, meanwhile, argue that the food industry is simply giving people what they want. They may both be right.

Civille, for her part, says she does not believe the food industry is consciously trying to "design food to trick, track or coerce consumers." But she does agree with Kessler that government and media both have a role to play in helping to educate consumers about what goes into the processed foods we consume and how some of that pleasure-boosting science and technology can work against us.

Regulations, incentives and information campaigns may all be a long time coming, though. In the meantime, here are some tips that you can use to curb your consumption of processed foods.

A **Create Structure**. The Achilles' heel of a healthy diet, says Kessler, is being caught off-guard—hungry and at the mercy of your environment. Instead, plan what you're going to eat and when. Meals and snacks should be eaten at regular intervals, and they should be appealing enough to keep you satisfied, but predictable enough that your senses don't feel overstimulated.

B **Eat Substantial Foods**. Foods made from ingredients that race willy-nilly through your digestive system, like simple sugars and refined flours, are not as satisfying as foods that digest more gradually. Protein has the best staying power, taking 2.5 times longer to digest than simple sugars. High-fiber foods, like legumes, fruits, veggies and whole grains, also leave the body feeling full longer because they add volume to meals and take longer to digest.

"It's not that you can't ever have another serving of French fries. The goal is to reclaim control over what you eat and when, and to stay conscious of your entire eating experience—before, during and after."

105   **Re-size Portions.** In a culture of supersized portions, it's easy to forget how much it really takes to feel satisfied (vs. stuffed). To regain a sense of portion control, try eating only half your normal amount of food at a single meal. Then pay close attention to how your body feels 30 minutes later. Notice how you feel 90 minutes later. For most people, a just-right meal is one that staves off hunger for about four hours; a just-right snack keeps

110 you satisfied about two hours, says Kessler, who calls this practice "just-right eating."

   Get Comfortable with Eating Real Food. A lot of people opt for easy-to-eat processed foods because "they don't like to be embarrassed when they eat," says Civille. "They don't want to get something stuck in their teeth, and they don't like to be eating complicated foods in public." In the United States, many otherwise-civilized adults

115 aren't confident of proper knife-and-fork techniques, which may incline them toward bite-size, hand-held and nuggetized foods. If you don't yet feel confident eating real foods and enjoying them in all their lovely messiness, make a point of developing that confidence.

   Change Your Relationship with Food. Instead of looking at food as if it's your

120 friend, try and deactivate those emotional connections, says Kessler: "1 look at food that's highly processed and I say, It's only going to make me want more." In much the same way we changed our view of tobacco from a sexy to a decidedly unsexy thing, he adds, we can try to do the same with processed food.

   Don't Bring It into the House. If your pantry is full of processed foods, some part

125 of you will be constantly aware of their presence. Those foods will "call out to you," says Kessler, and just seeing them, or even knowing they are there on the shelf, may be enough to activate your brain and trigger cravings.

   Don't Resort to Deprivation. It's not that you can't ever have another serving of French fries. In fact, Kessler argues, adopting a mindset of deprivation will just trigger

130 more intense cravings. The goal is to reclaim control over what you eat and when, and to stay conscious of your entire eating experience—before, during and after.

   Ultimately, taking back your mind and metabolism means becoming more aware of not only what you eat but also what drives you to eat it. Self-awareness is the greatest tool people can wield against the assault of processed foods, says Kessler.

135   But remember: Self-awareness doesn't mean self-denial. It means learning how to delight in foods that are good for you, and how to enjoy less healthy edible pleasures in moderation, on occasion, when you consciously decide to.

   "By consciously paying attention to the pleasures of taste and the experience of eating, you can deepen the reward value of any food you choose," says Kessler, "so choose well."

(1843 words)

—From *Experience Life Magazine*, October 2010, by Catherine Guthrie

THINKING AND WRITING AFTER READING

RECALL Self-test your understanding.

Your instructor may choose to give you a brief comprehension review.

REACT What is your reaction to the statement that our brains are hardwired to prefer salt, sugar, and fat? _____

_____

REFLECT Have you tried to resist overeating foods that you know are not good for you? If so, what methods have you used? If not, why not? _____

_____

THINK CRITICALLY Considering the serious health consequences of obesity, do you think there should be regulations limiting the processed food industry? Explain your answer. _____

_____

_____

THINK AND WRITE Based on the information in this article, do you have a healthy relationship with food? If you do, provide details that support your claim. If you don't, list changes that you could make to achieve a better diet. _____

_____

_____

EXTENDED WRITING Childhood obesity is a serious problem in the United States, and First Lady Michelle Obama has made fighting it a priority during her husband's presidency. With the information you read in this selection in mind, write a proposal that outlines your suggestions for addressing this health issue.

TOPIC

1. What is the topic of the section "This is Your Brain on Processed Food"?

_____

2. What is the topic of "Breaking the Cycle"? _____

_____

Interpret THE QUOTE

Now that you've finished reading the selection, "The Dark Side of Food Science," go back to the beginning of the selection and read the opening quote again. Its author intended the statement to be humorous while making a point. Why is the quote appropriate for this reading selection?

Name ————————————————————————

Date ————————————————————————

COMPREHENSION QUESTIONS

Answer the following with *a, b, c,* or *d,* or fill in the blank. In order to help you analyze your strengths and weaknesses, the question types are indicated.

Main Idea ———— 1. The best statement of the main idea of this selection is

    a. Consumers should eat substantial foods that are high in protein and fiber and limit their intake of highly processed ingredients.

    b. The processed food industry manipulates flavors, textures, and scents to make foods more appealing, but knowledgeable consumers can control their intake of processed foods.

    c. Humans are genetically drawn to foods that are high in fat, sugar, and salt.

    d. The fact that two-thirds of Americans are overweight is a serious national health problem that must be addressed.

Detail ———— 2. According to the article, humans prefer fat, sugar, and salt because

————————————————————————————————.

    a. these foods were hard to get at times in our history.

    b. they are common ingredients in highly processed foods.

    c. they were especially important to prehistoric people's ability to survive.

    d. they are important to a healthy diet for today's lifestyles.

Detail ———— 3. The article states that manufacturers sometimes include more fat in foods because ——————————————————————————.

    a. it makes food smoother and easier to eat.

    b. it adds needed calories.

    c. consumers demand it.

    d. it creates a pleasing aroma.

Inference ———— 4. The author implies that ——————————————————————.

    a. fat, sugar, and salt are more expensive today than in the past.

    b. exercise is the best way to maintain a healthy weight.

    c. most people prefer eating a healthy diet and avoid processed foods.

    d. most people today expend less energy than our ancient ancestors did.

Main Idea ———— 5. Which statement best expresses the main point of the section, "This Is Your Brain on Processed Food"?

    a. The food industry knows that humans prefer fat, sugar, and salt.

    b. Because human brains have evolved to make us prefer foods high in fat, sugar, and salt, these foods are very hard for us to resist.

    c. Unlike people in times when food was scarce, we are exposed to many high-calorie foods every day.

    d. We are more easily triggered to want cake than to want carrots.

Main Idea _____ 6. Which statement best expresses the main point of the section, "A Sensory Explosion"?

    a. Manufacturers promote their products by linking them with happiness and success.

    b. Expert tasters can recognize many subtle flavors in a plain chocolate bar.

    c. Processed foods require less chewing, so we eat faster and therefore tend to eat more.

    d. Food scientists and manufacturers manipulate texture and aroma as well as taste.

Main Idea _____ 7. Which statement best expresses the main point of the section, "Breaking the Cycle"?

    a. Although we may have to wait a long time for regulations, incentives, and information campaigns, there are ways for us to decrease our intake of processed foods now.

    b. An easy way to reduce our intake of high-calorie foods is to reduce portion size.

    c. We should eat at regular times and plan what we will eat ahead of time.

    d. We should eliminate snacks and avoid all high-calorie and processed foods.

Answer the following with *T* (true) or *F* (false).

Inference _____ 8. The author suggests that to control our impulse to eat unhealthy foods, we must deprive ourselves of them completely.

Detail _____ 9. Gail Vance Civille noted that today's foods require more chewing than the foods of 40 to 50 years ago.

Detail _____ 10. According to the article, some health experts believe that food companies purposely exploit our built-in preferences for fat, sugar, and salt.

VOCABULARY

Answer the following with *a*, *b*, *c*, or *d* for the word or phrase that best defines the boldface word used in the selection. The number in parentheses indicates the line of the passage in which the word appears. In addition to the context clues, use a dictionary to more precisely define the technical terms.

_____ 1. "highly **palatable** foods" (2)

    a. chewable
    b. appetizing
    c. healthful
    d. available

_____ 3. "kitchen **staples** (11)

    a. basic ingredients
    b. fasteners
    c. cooking tools
    d. desserts

_____ 2. "the most **salient** stimuli" (9)

    a. necessary
    b. delicious
    c. expensive
    d. attractive

_____ 4. "our **innate** fondness" (15)

    a. unfortunate
    b. special
    c. inborn
    d. certain

_____ 5. "**edible** amusement park (20)
    a. suitable for eating
    b. attractive
    c. irresistible
    d. especially fun

_____ 6. "**cue** for a high-calorie treat" (50)
    a. advertisement
    b. desire
    c. signal
    d. menu

_____ 7. "sweet versus **savory**" (64)
    a. sugary
    b. fatty
    c. salty
    d. juicy

_____ 8. "with our **metabolisms**" (82)
    a. bodies
    b. hunger
    c. weight
    d. digestion

_____ 9. "**curb** your consumption" (93)
    a. promote
    b. encourage
    c. stop
    d. limit

_____ 10. "mindset of **deprivation**" (129)
    a. healthfulness
    b. denial
    c. support
    d. guilt

Your instructor may choose to give a brief vocabulary review.

VOCABULARY ENRICHMENT

A. The purpose of many invented words is to form shorter expressions that carry the same meaning. **Acronyms** are words made from the initial letters of other words. *Blends* are words formed by combining parts of other words. *Abbreviations* are shortened forms of longer words. Write the definitions and elongated forms of the following words.

> **scu·ba** \ˈskü-bə\ *n, often attrib* [self-contained underwater breathing apparatus] (1952) : an apparatus utilizing a portable supply of compressed gas (as air) supplied at a regulated pressure and used for breathing while swimming underwater
>
> Source: By permission. From Merriam-Webster's *Collegiate® Dictionary, Eleventh Edition*. © 2011 by Merriam Webster Incorporated (www.Merriam-Webster.com)

(acronyms)

1. *Scuba* means _____

2. It comes from _____

> **Medi·care** \ˈme-di-ˌker\ *n* [blend of *medical* and *care*] (1955) : a government program of medical care esp. for the aged
>
> Source: By permission. From Merriam-Webster's *Collegiate® Dictionary, Eleventh Edition*. © 2011 by Merriam Webster Incorporated (www.Merriam-Webster.com)

(blends)

3. *Medi*care means _____

4. It comes from _____

> **¹ad** \ˈad\ *n, often attrib* (1841) **1** : ADVERTISEMENT 2 **2** : ADVERTISING
> **²ad** *n* (1928) : ADVANTAGE 4
>
> Source: By permission. From Merriam-Webster's *Collegiate® Dictionary, Eleventh Edition*. © 2011 by Merriam Webster Incorporated (www.Merriam-Webster.com)

(abbreviations)

5. *Ad* means _____

6. It comes from _____

B. Use an unabridged dictionary in your college library to find the definitions and origins of the following words.

Achilles' heel

7. Definition: _____

8. Origin: _____

maudlin

9. Definition: _____

10. Origin: _____

babel

11. Definition: _____

12. Origin: _____

_____

C. Circle the similar-sounding word that is correct in each sentence.

anecdote: story   **access:** entrance   **moral:** honorable
antidote: medicine   **excess:** more than needed   **morale:** spirit

13. The professor told an amusing (**anecdote, antidote**) about Queen Elizabeth.

14. The new key will give you easy (**access, excess**) to the computer room.

15. After the positive test grades were announced, the class (**moral, morale**) was high.

ASSESS YOUR LEARNING

Review questions that you did not understand, found confusing, or answered incorrectly. Seek clarification. Indicate beside each item the source of your confusion and notice the question type. Make notes beside confusing vocabulary items to help you remember them. Use your textbook as a learning tool.

SELECTION 2 Psychology MyReadingLab™

Visit Chapter 5: Topic, Main Idea, and Supporting Details in MyReadingLab to complete the Selection 2 activities.

"A good laugh and a long sleep are the best cures in the doctor's book."

—Irish Proverb

Over our lifetimes, most of us will have spent about one-third of our time sleeping. What is the purpose of sleep? How much sleep do we really need? What happens during sleep? Although much remains to be learned, sleep researchers have uncovered the answers to these and many former mysteries about this state of consciousness. Scientists believe that all humans and seemingly all animal organisms experience sleep; however, humans are the only species who willingly deprive themselves of sleep.

THINKING BEFORE READING

Preview the selection for clues to the content and activate your schema. Anticipate what is coming and think about your purpose for reading.

How much sleep do you typically get each night? What seems to be the right amount for you?

Have you heard of **REM** and **non-REM** sleep?

How do you feel when you don't get enough sleep?

I want to learn _____.

VOCABULARY PREVIEW

Are you familiar with these words?

deprivation	premise	respiration	trunk	consolidation
motor	longitudinal	erratic	hypothesize	cognitive

Would you rather experience sleep *deprivation* or food *deprivation*?

If I can't accept your *premise*, can I accept your argument?

Does a child who excels at sports have good *motor* skills?

Your instructor may choose to give a brief vocabulary review before or after reading.

THINKING DURING READING

As you read, use the six thinking strategies of a good reader: predict, picture, relate, monitor, correct, and annotate.

SELECTION

2

> ### Reader's TIP   Reading and Studying Psychology
>
> - Seek to understand abstract terms and confusing concepts through the concrete examples that illustrate them.
> - Relate psychological theories to yourself and visualize people you know as examples.
> - Memorize key terms with definitions and examples, especially for multiple-choice tests.
> - Test yourself by turning each boldface heading into a question and recite your answer.
> - Because much of psychology is about theories, connect the names of researchers with their theories. Learn characteristics and examples for each theory.
> - Compare and contrast theories. For example, how do the social learning theorists differ from the behaviorists?
> - Reduce your notes to visual diagrams. For example, to study personality theories, draw charts to list the comparative elements.

SLEEP

What actually happens during our periods of sleep? Before the 1950s, there was little understanding of what goes on during sleep. Then, in the 1950s, several universities set up sleep laboratories where people's brain waves, eye movements, chin-muscle tension, heart rate, and breathing rate were monitored through a night of sleep. From analyses of
5 sleep recordings, researchers discovered the characteristics of two major types of sleep, **REM (rapid eye movement)** and **NREM (non-rapid eye movement)**. Since that time, with advanced brain-imaging instruments, researchers have learned much about the purpose of sleep, individual differences in sleep, and the effects of sleep deprivation.

WHY WE SLEEP

Are you one of those people who regard sleep as a waste of time—especially when you
10 have a term paper due the next day? (Of course, you wouldn't be facing a sleepless night if you hadn't procrastinated about the paper in the first place!) In fact, consistent sleep habits are probably important to getting good grades. Why?

Two theories explain why we need to sleep. Taken together, they provide us with a useful explanation. One, the **restorative theory of sleep**, holds that being awake
15 produces wear and tear on the body and the brain, while sleep serves the function of restoring body and mind. Research on the effects of sleep deprivation that you will read about later in this section supports the restorative theory. The second explanation, the **circadian theory of sleep**, sometimes called the *evolutionary* or *adaptive theory*, is based on the premise that sleep evolved to keep humans out of harm's way during the dark of
20 night, possibly from becoming prey for some nocturnal predator.

Alexander Barely explains how a synthesis of the circadian and restorative theories can be used to explain the function of sleep. That people feel sleepy at certain times of day is consistent with the circadian theory and that sleepiness increases the longer a person is awake is consistent with the restorative theory. In other words, the urge to sleep is partly
25 a function of how long a person has been awake and partly a function of the time of day.

HOW WE SLEEP

Sleep follows a fairly predictable pattern each night. Each sleep cycle lasts about 90 minutes and consists of four stages. The type of sleep we experience in all four stages is known as NREM (non-REM) sleep. It is a type of sleep in which our heart and respiration rates are slow and steady, our movements are minimal, and our blood pressure and brain activity
30   are at their lowest points of the 24-hour period.

When we are fully awake, beta waves predominate. As we become drowsy, alpha waves, which are associated with deep relaxation, begin to appear. When alpha waves outnumber beta waves, which are associated with mental or physical activity, we enter the first of the four NREM sleep stages:

35   • *Stage 1:* Transition from waking to sleeping; irregular waves with occasional alpha waves
   • *Stage 2:* Transition from light to deeper sleep; sleep spindles (waves with alternating periods of calm and flashes of intense activity) appear
   • *Stage 3:* Deeper sleep; slow-wave sleep begins when EEG shows 20% of brain waves
40   are delta waves
   • *Stage 4:* Deepest sleep; Stage 4 sleep begins when 50% of waves are delta waves

About 40 minutes after we enter Stage 4 sleep, delta waves begin to disappear. When that happens, we transition back through Stage 3 and Stage 2 until we reach Stage 1 sleep again. As we reenter Stage 1, our pathway through the night takes a brief side trip
45   into REM sleep. During the REM period, our brains are highly active. Blood pressure rises and heart rate and respiration become faster and less regular. In contrast to this storm of internal activity, there is an external calm during REM sleep. The large muscles of the body—arms, legs, and trunk—become paralyzed.

Observe a sleeper during the REM state and you will see her or his eyes darting
50   around under the eyelids. It is during REM sleep that the most vivid dreams occur. When awakened from REM sleep, most people report that they were dreaming.

Researchers have also found that REM sleep may be critical to the consolidation of memories after learning. Several experiments have shown that participants' performance on existing motor and verbal tasks improves after a period of normal sleep. In one classic
55 study, Karni and others found that research participants who were learning a new perceptual skill showed an improvement in performance 8 to 10 hours later, with no additional practice, if they had a normal night's sleep or if the researchers disturbed only their NREM sleep. Performance did not improve, however, in those who were deprived of REM sleep.

After the first REM period of the night ends, a new sleep cycle begins. Overall, sleep
60 ers average five cycles in a 7- to 8-hour night of sleep, which provides them with a total of 1 to 2 hours of slow-wave sleep and 1 to 2 hours of REM sleep.

VARIATIONS IN SLEEP

The amount of sleep people get varies greatly from one person to another. But how much sleep do we need? Many of us have heard that 8 hours of sleep are required for optimal health. Research suggests that this is not true. In a longitudinal study begun in 1982, more
65 than a million Americans were asked about their sleep habits. Twenty years later, people who reported sleeping 6 or fewer hours per night, along with those who slept more than 8, showed somewhat higher death rates than adults who slept about 7 hours each night.

Sleep varies with age. Infants and young children have the longest sleep time and the highest percentages of REM and slow-wave sleep. However, infants and children also
70 have more erratic sleep patterns than individuals in other age groups. By contrast, children from age 6 to puberty are the most consistent sleepers and sleepwalkers. They fall asleep easily, sleep soundly for 10 to 11 hours at night, and feel awake and alert during the day. Moreover, they tend to fall asleep and wake up at about the same time every day. By contrast, adolescents' sleep patterns are strongly influenced by their schedules.
75 Factors such as part-time employment and early school start times cause many teenagers to sleep little more than 7 hours on a typical week night. When adolescents are free from such scheduling pressures, however, they tend to sleep even longer than elementary-age children. Thus, some sleep researchers think that insufficient sleep may be at least partly responsible for discipline and learning problems in secondary schools.
80 As people age, the quality and quantity of their sleep usually decrease. Some researchers hypothesize that the decline is due to a reduction in the need for sleep that is a part of the natural aging process. Nevertheless, many older adults view the decline as a threat to their quality of life. Large-scale surveys of older adults in North America, Europe, and Japan suggest that up to two-thirds of them experience daytime sleepiness, nighttime awaken
85 ings, and insomnia on a regular basis.

SLEEP DEPRIVATION

What is the longest you have ever stayed awake? Most people have missed no more than a few straight nights of sleep, perhaps studying for final exams. If you have ever missed two or three nights of sleep, you may remember having had difficulty concentrating, lapses in attention, and general irritability. Research indicates that even the rather small amount of
90 sleep deprivation associated with delaying your bedtime on weekends leads to decreases in cognitive performance.

How does a lack of sleep affect the brain? The effects of sleep deprivation go beyond simply feeling tired. In fact, research has shown that failing to get enough sleep affects your ability to learn. So, if you stay up all night to study for a test, you may actually be
95 engaging in a somewhat self-defeating behavior. In a ground-breaking study, Drummond and others (2000) used brain-imaging techniques to map the patterns of brain activity during a verbal learning task in two groups of participants—those in an experimental group who were deprived of sleep for about 35 hours, and those in a control group who slept normally. In the control group, the prefrontal cortex was highly active, as were the
100 temporal lobes. As expected, on average, these rested participants scored significantly higher on the learning task than did their sleep-deprived counterparts.

This study, the first to use brain-imaging techniques to examine the effects of sleep deprivation on verbal learning, indicates that the cognitive functions used in such learning are significantly impaired by sleep deprivation. It also shows that there are mechanisms in 105 the parietal lobes that can reduce this impairment to some degree.

(1,364 words)

—From *Mastering the World of Psychology*, Fifth Edition, by Samuel E. Wood, Ellen Green Wood, and Denise Boyd

THINKING AND WRITING AFTER READING

RECALL Self-test your understanding.

Your instructor may choose to give you a brief comprehension review.

REACT Why is sleep an important research topic for psychologists? _____

_____

_____

REFLECT Do you get the right amount of sleep? How does your average night's sleep compare to the statistics in the article? Do you experience the same effects from lack of sleep as described in the article? Explain. _____

_____

_____

THINK CRITICALLY Recent studies suggest that most American adults get less sleep than is considered best for good health. What effects do you think this might have on the functioning of our society as a whole? _____

_____

_____

THINK AND WRITE Make a list of new information about sleep that you learned from this reading selection. _____

_____

_____

EXTENDED WRITING Use your list of information about sleep to compose a feature article that could be used in your college newspaper. Because your audience would be college students, focus on the aspects of sleep that are most relevant to them and that they would most benefit from knowing.

TOPIC

1. What is the topic of the section, "How We Sleep"? Be more specific regarding the content than just the heading. _____

_____

_____

2. What is the specific topic of the section, "Sleep Deprivation"? _____

_____

_____

Interpret THE QUOTE

Now that you have finished reading the selection, "Sleep," go back to the beginning of the selection and read the opening quote again. Which of the two theories of sleep described early in this reading selection does it represent?

Name —————————————————

Date —————————————————

COMPREHENSION QUESTIONS

Answer the following with *a, b, c,* or *d,* or fill in the blank. In order to help you analyze your strengths and weaknesses, the question types are indicated.

Main Idea ———— 1. The best statement of the main idea of this selection is
    a. Everyone needs sleep for good health.
    b. Humans sleep because of the evolutionary need to provide safety during the dark of night.
    c. Normal sleep cycles include four non-REM stages and one REM stage.
    d. Sleep research has revealed information about the purpose and process of sleep, variety of sleep habits, and effects of lack of sleep.

Detail ———— 2. Times of calm and intense activity alternate during which stage of sleep?
    a. Stage 1
    b. Stage 2
    c. Stage 3
    d. Stage 4

Detail ———— 3. REM sleep occurs first at which time during the sleep cycle?
    a. immediately before the second occurrence of Stage 1
    b. immediately after Stage 2
    c. just before waking
    d. during deepest sleep

Inference ———— 4. Karni's research study involving improvement after learning a new skill demonstrates what conclusion?
    a. that NREM sleep is critical to learning a new skill
    b. that REM sleep is important to learning a new skill
    c. that sleep has little to do with learning a new skill
    d. that practice alone is key to learning a new skill

Main Idea ———— 5. Which statement best expresses the main point of the section, "Why We Sleep"?
    a. The restorative theory says that sleep is needed to replenish body and mind functions that have been depleted during the day.
    b. The circadian theory best explains why we sleep.
    c. A combination of the restorative and circadian theories best explains why we sleep.
    d. Good sleep habits are important to getting good grades.

Main Idea ———— 6. Which statement best expresses the main point of the section, "Variations in Sleep"?
    a. The optimal amount of sleep for most people is seven hours per night.

      b. Age and individual differences affect the normal amount and pattern of sleep.

      c. Adolescents generally need more sleep than elementary school children.

      d. People generally need less sleep in old age.

Inference   _____ 7. A longitudinal study suggests that the healthiest amount of sleep for adults is

      a. 6 hours or less per night.

      b. 8 hours or more per night.

      c. 10-11 hours per night.

      d. about 7 hours per night.

Answer the following with *T* (true) or *F* (false).

Inference   _____ 8. According to the article, having too little sleep reduces the ability to think and learn effectively.

Detail   _____ 9. The most vivid dreams occur during Stage 4 of NREM sleep.

Detail   _____ 10. The first stage of NREM sleep occurs when alpha waves are more numerous than beta waves.

VOCABULARY

Answer the following with *a, b, c,* or *d* for the word or phrase that best defines the boldface word used in the selection. The number in parentheses indicates the line of the passage in which the word appears. In addition to the context clues, use a dictionary to more precisely define the technical terms.

_____ 1. "of sleep **deprivation**" (8)

      a. scarcity

      b. excess

      c. interruption

      d. disorder

_____ 2. "based on the **premise**" (19)

      a. question

      b. guess

      c. idea

      d. statement

_____ 3. "**respiration** rates" (28)

      a. pulse

      b. metabolic

      c. breathing

      d. activity

_____ 4. "arms, legs, and **trunk**" (48)

      a. head

      b. brain

      c. digestive system

      d. torso

_____ 5. "**consolidation** of memories" (52)

      a. preservation

      b. loss

      c. memorization

      d. creation

_____ 6. "**motor** and verbal tasks" (54)

      a. mechanical

      b. involving the muscles

      c. having to do with machines

      d. intellectual

_____ 7. "a **longitudinal**" study
(64)

    a. scientific
    b. short-term
    c. having to do with geography
    d. lasting over a long period of time

_____ 9. "researchers **hypothesize**"
(81)

    a. are certain
    b. fantasize
    c. have a plan
    d. propose an explanation

_____ 8. "**erratic** sleep patterns"
(70)

    a. consistent
    b. unpredictable
    c. calm
    d. comforting

_____ 10. "**cognitive** performance"
(91)

    a. physical
    b. thinking
    c. emotional
    d. singing

Your instructor may choose to give a brief vocabulary review.

VOCABULARY ENRICHMENT

A. An acronym is an invented word formed by the initial letters of a term. **REM**, for example, is pronounced as a word that rhymes with *them,* rather than pronouncing the three letters separately to indicate *rapid eye movement.* Write an *A* beside the following letters that are pronounced as words and thus are acronyms.

_____ 1. HUD   _____ 3. FBI   _____ 5. NAFTA

_____ 2. UNICEF   _____ 4. CIA   _____ 6. radar

B. Study the following easily confused words and circle the one that is correct in each sentence.

conscience: sense of right or wrong
conscious: awareness of self

its: ownership or possessive
it's: contraction of *it is*

to: toward
too: more than enough
two: the number 2

7. Let your (**conscience, conscious**) be your guide when faced with the temptation to oversleep and cut class.

8. Over a lifetime, (**its, it's**) estimated we spend 25 years sleeping.

9. Sleeping for five hours is (**to, too, two**) little for most people.

C. Use the context clues in the following sentences to write the meaning of the boldface psychology terms.

10. Nightmares frequently reflect the frustration and **anxiety** felt in daily life.

_____

11. After years of practice, we **condition** ourselves to get up by the alarm clock.

_____

12. With the birth of the second child, the first child's desire for a bottle at bedtime was a sign of **regression.** _____

   _____

13. Saying that you are too busy to sleep is only **rationalizing.**

   _____

14. Dream therapy offers a **permissive** setting for revealing haunting and embarrassing nightmares. _____

15. Adequate sleep **reinforces** the immune system's ability to fight disease.

   _____

ASSESS YOUR LEARNING

Review questions that you did not understand, found confusing, or answered incorrectly. Seek clarification. Indicate beside each item the source of your confusion and notice the question type. Make notes beside confusing vocabulary items to help you remember them. Use your textbook as a learning tool.

SELECTION 3  History MyReadingLab™

Visit Chapter 5: Topic, Main Idea, and Supporting Details in MyReadingLab to complete the Selection 3 activities and Building Background Knowledge video activity.

"An individual who breaks a law that conscience tells him is unjust, and who willingly accepts the penalty of imprisonment in order to arouse the conscience of the community over its injustice, is in reality expressing the highest respect for the law."

—Martin Luther King, Jr.

A critical event in the struggle for equal rights occurred in Montgomery, Alabama, in 1955. Rosa Parks, a black seamstress who was returning from work and tired, sat down on a bus in a section that was reserved for whites. When asked to get up, she refused. Parks was arrested and ordered to stand trial. Black civil rights officials seized the issue and responded with a boycott of the bus system. Organizational meetings for the boycott were held in a Montgomery Baptist church where the young twenty-seven-year-old minister, Martin Luther King, Jr., took an active role in the protest. Soon the talented and articulate Dr. King emerged as the leading spokesman for the protest and for the civil and economic concerns of black Americans.

THINKING BEFORE READING

Preview the selection for clues to the content. Activate your prior knowledge. Anticipate what is coming and think about your purpose for reading.

In what city is the Martin Luther King, Jr., home place and national memorial?

Where did Dr. King make his "I Have a Dream" speech?

What world leader inspired Dr. King's nonviolent tactics?

I want to learn _____.

BUILDING BACKGROUND KNOWLEDGE — VIDEO

March on Washington 50th Anniversary Celebrated

To prepare for reading Selection 3, answer the questions below. Then, watch this video that recalls the historic march on Washington, D.C. and Martin Luther King, Jr.'s "I Have a Dream" speech.

What do you know about Martin Luther King, Jr.'s "I Have a Dream" speech?

What was the purpose of the March on Washington in 1963?

How do you think race relations in the United States have changed since 1963?

This video helped me: _____.

VOCABULARY PREVIEW

Are you familiar with these words?

| sweltering | centennial | oppressive | podium | resonant |
| galvanized | spurious | dire | recanted | compelled |

Reader's TIP — Reading and Studying History

- Know the *who*, *what*, *when*, *where*, and *why* for people, places, documents, and events.
- Seek to understand the cause-and-effect relationship among events and their causes, results, and consequences.
- Use timelines to familiarize yourself with chronologies to get an overall picture of parallel or overlapping events.
- Learn significant dates to provide a framework for grouping and understanding events.
- Look at maps of the region being studied.
- Distinguish between fact and opinion, and compare your conclusions with the historian's interpretation.

What is a *centenarian*?

At what temperature do you *swelter*?

How do *compel*, *repel*, and *expel* differ?

Your instructor may choose to give a brief vocabulary review before or after reading.

THINKING DURING READING

As you read, use the six thinking strategies of a good reader: predict, picture, relate, monitor, correct, and annotate.

THE DREAM OF NONVIOLENT REFORM

Perspiring in the sweltering heat of a Washington August afternoon, Martin Luther King, Jr., looked down from the steps of the Lincoln Memorial at the largest assembly ever congregated in the United States. Well over 200,000 people, 70 percent of them blacks, jammed the mile-long mall that swept away to the Washington Monument. Angry yet
5 hopeful, they had come to the nation's capital in 1963, the centennial of the Emancipation Proclamation, to personify black demands for equality in society. But the speakers and singers who preceded King had not been particularly effective, the heat and humidity were oppressive, and the great crowd was starting to thin around the edges. As he mounted the podium, King sensed this restlessness and the need for a focus. At first his
10 deep voice was husky, but it soon became resonant with a purpose that quieted and transfixed the multitude and the millions of television viewers. King's eloquence dramatized the anguish of black history. One hundred years after slavery, he pointed out, the black was still "an exile in his own land." It was the future, however, that mattered. "I have a dream," he cried repeatedly, as he sketched his vision of freedom, justice, and harmony.
15 At the end of his speech, King prophesied that one day all people would be able to join together in singing the words of an old Negro spiritual: "Free at last! Free at last! Thank God Almighty, we are free at last." There was an awed silence, then an ear-shattering

roar: The crowd was applauding wildly. King had galvanized the massive assembly. At
that moment he stood at the crest of a mounting wave of African American protest. Yet,
20 as King must have known, his dream would have an agonizing birth. Just five years after
his Washington address, he lay dead on the balcony of a Memphis motel, the victim of the
violence he had devoted his life to overcoming.

. . .

The Poor People's March was set for June 1968, but the whirlwind pace King had kept
since the beginning of the decade allowed him only occasional participation in the planning.
25 One of the detours took him to Memphis, where a garbage strike threatened to evolve into
a racial encounter of crisis proportions. Local black leaders wanted King to organize a peaceful demonstration, but once again he had difficulty working with Black Power militants.
Uncontrollable black looters, arsonists, and street fighters were another source of difficulty.
On March 28, they had transformed a nonviolent march into an orgy of destruction that
30 had provoked an even greater measure of police brutality. As a self-styled "riot preventer,"
King was sick at heart. If Memphis exploded, he feared, the approaching summer of 1968
would be chaos. Already, black leaders like Harlem congressman Adam Clayton Powell were
arousing the urban masses and, as part of their campaign, making references to "Martin
Loser King" and his Uncle Tom tactics. Nonviolence, King felt, was on trial in Memphis.
35 On April 3, 1968, on the eve of the crucial Memphis march, King addressed a capacity crowd at the Masonic Temple located in that city. His mood was strangely somber and
introspective. "Like anybody," he mused, "I would like to live a long life." But longevity,

he added, was not his chief concern; he would rather do God's will. Some of his aides were reminded of the great Washington rally of 1963, where King had expressed his belief
40 that "if a man hasn't discovered something that he will die for, he isn't fit to live!" The following evening, on the way to yet another mass meeting, King walked onto the balcony of his hotel room and leaned over the railing to talk with a colleague. A moment later he crumpled to the ground. An assassin's bullet, fired from a hotel room across the street, had pierced his skull. The killer, arrested two months later and identified as James Earl Ray,
45 was a white drifter with a long criminal record.

Following Ray's confession, investigations of King's murder continued until 1977. Exhaustive reviews of the evidence seemed to prove conclusively that Ray had acted alone in the assassination, and there was no conspiracy. The research did reveal that the Federal Bureau of Investigation, under orders of its director, J. Edgar Hoover, had complicated
50 the last six years of King's life with a program of systematic harassment on the spurious grounds that he was under the influence of the Communist party. The conspiracy theory surrounding King's death reemerged in the 1990's when James Earl Ray, in prison and in dire health, recanted his confession. Talk of Ray being brought to trial—there had been none due to his confession—ended abruptly when Ray died in early 1998.

55 The murder of Martin Luther King, Jr., moved the American people as had few events in recent years. The immediate response in all but the most prejudiced white minds was shame. Millions of whites felt compelled to apologize to black people as a whole and went to their churches for services honoring King. But even among the mourners, white and black eyes did not meet easily. Everyone seemed to recognize that, with King's death, a
60 powerful influence for interracial compassion and understanding had been eliminated— the basis of ordered change and reform.

(878 words)

—In *From These Beginnings*, Sixth Edition, Volume Two,
by Roderick Nash and Gregory Graves

THINKING AND WRITING AFTER READING

RECALL Self-test your understanding.

Your instructor may choose to give you a brief comprehension review.

REACT Aside from their stated reasons, why do you think the FBI would spend six years tracking Dr. King? _____

_____

REFLECT What seemed to be the differences in philosophy among the civil rights leaders? _____

_____

THINK CRITICALLY Why was Martin Luther King, Jr.'s, birthday made a national holiday? _____

_____

THINK AND WRITE Events often call for ordinary men and women to do extraordinary things. How were Rosa Parks and Martin Luther King, Jr., both ordinary and extraordinary? How did events converge to change their destinies and our history?

_____

EXTENDED WRITING Take a moment to think of someone you highly respect. This person might be a historical figure like Dr. King, a living political or human rights leader, or someone you know personally. Write a well-developed paragraph that explains why you respect this person. Give examples of this person's actions, beliefs, or behavior that support your explanations.

TOPIC

1. What is the topic of the first paragraph? _____

2. What is the topic of the last paragraph? _____

   _____

Interpret THE QUOTE

Now that you have finished reading the selection, "The Dream of Nonviolent Reform," go back to the beginning of the selection and read the opening quote again. Under what circumstances does Martin Luther King, Jr. believe it is acceptable to break the law? On a separate piece of paper, explain why you agree or disagree with Dr. King's views on breaking laws.

Name ————————————————

Date ————————————————

COMPREHENSION QUESTIONS

Answer the following with *a, b, c,* or *d,* or fill in the blank. In order to help you analyze your strengths and weaknesses, the question types are indicated.

Main Idea ———— 1. The best statement of the main idea of the selection is
   a. Dr. King started the civil rights movement with his "I Have a Dream" speech in Washington.
   b. Though his life was taken violently, Dr. King was a moving speaker and a major force in the nonviolent movement for civil rights.
   c. Dr. King was killed violently by a drifter.
   d. Dr. King controlled the violence in Memphis but was killed for doing so.

Detail ———— 2. The primary reason that over 200,000 people had congregated in Washington in 1963 was
   a. to hear Dr. King speak.
   b. to urge legislators to pass the Emancipation Proclamation.
   c. to show strength in demanding equal treatment for African Americans in society.
   d. to honor Lincoln for freeing the slaves.

Detail ———— 3. In his "I Have a Dream" speech, Dr. King's major thrust is to
   a. recall the hardships of the past.
   b. blame society for prejudice and hatred.
   c. ask God for forgiveness and strength.
   d. focus on the possibilities of the future.

Inference ———— 4. The author implies that
   a. Black Power militants did not agree with Dr. King's tactics.
   b. Dr. King and Black Power militants shared the same philosophy and strategies.
   c. Adam Clayton Powell supported Dr. King's tactics.
   d. little friction existed among the different leaders supporting civil rights.

Inference ———— 5. Dr. King felt that nonviolence was on trial in Memphis because

————————————————————————————————

————————————————————————————————

————————————————————————————————

Inference ———— 6. The author suggests all of the following *except*
   a. Dr. King was willing to die for his cause.
   b. Dr. King had a premonition that he would not live a long life.
   c. Dr. King knew that fighting for his cause was dangerous.
   d. Dr. King was willing to back off from his nonviolent stand to get the support of other civil rights leaders.

Detail ———— 7. The author states that evidence suggests that
   a. Ray acted alone.
   b. Ray was part of a conspiracy.

c. J. Edgar Hoover was involved in Dr. King's death.

d. Ray was not the man who fired the shots from the hotel room.

Answer the following with *T* (true) or *F* (false).

Inference ———— 8. After Dr. King's death, the American people realized that he was indeed the "riot preventer."

Detail ———— 9. The garbage strike in Memphis was in June 1968.

Detail ———— 10. Ray was brought to trial after he took back his confession.

VOCABULARY

Answer the following with *a, b, c,* or *d* for the word or phrase that best defines the boldface word as used in the selection. The number in parentheses indicates the line of the passage in which the word appears. In addition to the context clues, use a dictionary to more precisely define the technical terms.

———— 1. "**sweltering** heat" (1)

a. never-ending
b. humid and sweaty
c. permanent
d. oncoming

———— 2. "the **centennial** of the Emancipation Proclamation" (5)

a. 10-year celebration
b. 50-year celebration
c. 100-year celebration
d. 200-year celebration

———— 3. "heat and humidity were **oppressive**" (8)

a. overpowering
b. surprising
c. brief
d. energizing

———— 4. "mounted the **podium**" (9)

a. stairway
b. top of the monument
c. steps
d. speaker's stand

———— 5. "**resonant** with a purpose" (10)

a. sensitive
b. hoarse
c. forceful and loud
d. repetitious

———— 6. "**galvanized** the massive assembly" (18)

a. stopped
b. excited
c. frightened
d. shamed

———— 7. "on the **spurious** grounds" (50)

a. false
b. evil
c. criminal
d. socialistic

———— 8. "in **dire** health" (53)

a. fair
b. uncertain
c. questionable
d. terrible

———— 9. "**recanted** his confession" (53)

a. emphasized
b. questioned
c. regretted
d. took back

———— 10. "**compelled** to apologize" (57)

a. nervous
b. obliged
c. angered
d. manipulated

Your instructor may choose to give a brief vocabulary review.

VOCABULARY ENRICHMENT

A. Use the indicated root to form words that complete each sentence.

voc, vok: voice, call

1. Dr. King's message of freedom and love for all mankind _____ a feeling of hope for racial unity in his audience.

2. Dr. King's brave manner of speaking out against injustice has inspired future generations to be more _____ about prejudice.

3. Dr. King's persuasive _____ included simple words like *dream* and *justice*.

gress, grad, gred: step, degree

4. Dr. King's inspiring words are often quoted to _____ in commencement speeches.

5. While Dr. King used peaceful methods of conflict resolution, Black Power militants tended to use more _____ tactics.

6. While many advocates for civil rights wanted instant change, Dr. King recognized that lasting change would be more _____.

spec, spect: see, watch

7. Over 200,000 _____ observed Dr. King's speech on the steps of the Lincoln Memorial.

8. An _____ of the assassination scene indicated that Dr. King had been shot from the window of a neighboring hotel.

9. The Memphis march was intended to be a _____ that would call national attention to the Civil Rights Movement.

B. Use context clues and mark *a, b, c,* or *d* for the meaning that is closest to that of the boldface word.

_____ 10. The fight for racial equality **signifies** a larger struggle for all human rights.
   a. indicates
   b. simplifies
   c. reduces
   d. warns of

_____ 11. Sit-ins by **diligent** believers in racial equality resulted in the desegregation of public facilities in a hundred southern cities.
   a. convincing
   b. hard-working
   c. older
   d. talkative

_____ 12. The Civil Rights Movement accomplished a **tangible** result when the Supreme Court ruled the Alabama segregated bus seating law unconstitutional.

    a. sizable

    b. tremendous

    c. actual

    d. movable

C. Study the following easily confused words and circle the one that is correct in each sentence.

thorough: careful	**straight:** not curving	**loose:** not tight
threw: tossed	**strait:** narrow passage of water	**lose:** misplace
through: by means of		

13. Dr. King's "Letter from a Birmingham City Jail" did a (**thorough, threw, through**) job of explaining his vision to a group of Alabama clergymen.

14. Dr. King's doctrine of passive resistance required followers to stare and walk (**straight, strait**) ahead when confronted by violence.

15. Police often let attack dogs run (**loose, lose**) to menace Civil Rights protesters.

ASSESS YOUR LEARNING

Review confusing questions, seek clarification, and make notes in your text to help you remember new information and vocabulary. Use your textbook as a learning tool.

PERSONAL FEEDBACK 2   Name _____

1. Review your responses to the three longer reading selections. Summarize and comment on your error patterns._____

_____

_____

2. What selection, short or long, has held your attention the best? Why do you think it did so?_____

_____

_____

3. What unforeseen difficulties have you already encountered this term that have interfered with your ability to study?_____

_____

_____

Share your responses as directed by your instructor.

VOCABULARY LESSON

One Too Many

Study the prefixes, words, and sentences.

Prefixes   *mono, mon*: one   *bi, bin, bis*: two   *poly*: many

Words with *mono* or *mon* = one

Can a *monomaniac* be addicted to the Internet? Can a *monotone* put you to sleep?

- Monarchy: a government with only one ruler

  The power of the English *monarchy* has changed since the time of Elizabeth 1.

- Monocle: an eyeglass for only one eye

  An 1800s *monocle* was more difficult to wear than the eyeglasses of today.

- Monogamy: marriage to one person only

  In the United States, *monogamy* is the legally accepted form of marriage.

- Monologue: a discourse by one person

  Jimmy Fallon often starts his late night show with a humorous *monologue*.

- Monochromatic: only one color

  A home decorated in beige has a *monochromatic* color scheme.

- Monotony: sameness

  Talking to customers breaks the *monotony* of working as a cashier.

Words with *bi*, *bin*, or *bis* = two

With cheap concert seats, carry *binoculars*. Are *biweekly* meetings every two weeks?

- Bimonthly: occurs every two months

  Regular *bimonthly* reports are required six times each year.

- Bifocal: having two lenses

  Initial use of *bifocal* lenses can be a difficult adjustment.

- Bigamy: marrying one person while already married to another

  Bigamy is illegal in the United States.

- Bilingual: using two languages

  In the United States, most *bilingual* speakers know Spanish as well as English.

- Bipartisan: representing two parties

  A *bipartisan* committee would include both Democrats and Republicans.

- Biennial: something that occurs at two-year intervals or lasts two years

  Rather than every year, the class decided to have *biennial* reunions.

Words with poly = many

Can a *polytechnic* institute offer classes? Does the city have *polyethnic* districts?

- Polygon: closed figure with many angles

  A square is a *polygon* with four equal sides.

- Polyglot: a linguist who knows many languages

  Having lived abroad extensively, the student returned home a *polyglot*.

- Polygamy: custom of having more than one spouse at the same time

  In cultures with *polygamy*, the additional wives often function as servants.

- Polyandry: custom of having more than one husband at the same time

  Polyandry is the exclusively female version of polygamy.

- Polychromatic: having many colors

  The *polychromatic* fabric emphasized reds and blues on a yellow background.

- Polydactyl: having more than the normal number of fingers or toes

  The *polydactyl* abnormality was evident in three family members.

- Polymorphic: having many forms

  A *polymorphic* cartoon character can change from a cat to a tiger.

Review

Part I

Answer the following with (*T*) true or (*F*) false.

_____ 1. A polyglot is more than bilingual.

_____ 2. Two people talk to each other in a monologue.

_____ 3. A black piano has a monochromatic surface.

_____ 4. Bimonthly meetings occur twice each month.

_____ 5. Bipartisan politics suggests that two parties are willing to negotiate.

_____ 6. The biennial reports were due every January and July.

_____ 7. If white is a color, the U.S. flag is polychromatic.

_____ 8. An exclusively Italian area constitutes a polyethnic neighborhood.

_____ 9. Exciting people tend to enjoy monotony.

_____ 10. Bifocal lenses contain two separate eyeglass prescriptions.

Part II

Choose the best word from the list to fit the following descriptions.

monarch	monocle	monogamy	bilingual	polymorphic
bigamy	monotone	polyandry	polygon	polydactyl

11. More than ten toes _____

12. One tone of voice _____

13. Having two wives _____

14. Having two or more husbands _____

15. One eyeglass _____

16. Many forms _____

17. Speaking two languages _____

18. A queen _____

19. One spouse _____

20. A rectangle _____

Researching Online

The Internet has become as much a part of everyday life for people all over the world as television and the automobile. We use it for social networking, business communication, entertainment, driving directions, and to locate the nearest coffee shop or fast-food restaurant. Many college students are experts at navigating the Internet for these purposes, but very few come to college knowing how to use it for academic research. Academic research on the Internet, such as you will be required to do in college, requires some specialized knowledge and skills.

Definitions

Let's start with a few definitions and the parts that make up a typical Web address, or **URL** (uniform resource locator). This is the URL for the United States Library of Congress: http://www.loc.gov. Add "topics" to the end, and the address takes you directly to the "browse by topic" part of the site.

The following is a key to the numbered components of the sample URL.

1. **Protocol** This is standard for Web addresses and indicates *hypertext transfer protocol,* the type of language computers on the Internet use to communicate with each other. Secure sites are indicated with the "https" protocol.
2. **Server name** This indicates the computer network over which you will "travel" to reach the desired location. In most cases, this will be the World Wide Web.
3. **Domain name** This is a name registered by the Web site owner.
4. **Domain type** This indicates the category to which the site owner belongs.
   "gov" indicates an official government site.
   "edu" indicates a school or educational institution's site.
   "org" indicates an organization or group, such as the American Cancer Society.
   "com" indicates a commercial site whose main purpose is to promote or sell a product.
5. **Directory path** This indicates a particular location within the Web site's host computer.

Navigating a Web site

After you have entered the URL and reached the desired Web site, get an overview of what the site has to offer by scanning headlines, graphics, buttons, animation, category headings, site maps, and tables of contents. Many sites have a "Search" option near the top of the page that will help you find a specific topic.

Library of Congress; www.loc.gov

Notice the section tabs and search box at the top of the page. Many of the photos and topics on this page are **hypertext links**, or simply links. A click of the mouse moves you to another page with more information about that topic. Usually, clicking the "Back" arrow returns you to the original page.

EXERCISE 1

Research the following information about the National Aeronautics and Space Administration (NASA). First, go to the website (www.nasa.gov), click on the home page, and examine the different headings. When you rest the cursor on the major headings, subtopics will appear. Use this navigational tool to answer the following questions.

1. What does NASA do? _____

_____

2. Name two ways that NASA's work impacts earth _____

_____

_____

_____

3. What types of careers are available at NASA? _____

_____

_____

4. Check the latest NASA news items. List two. Write the categories under which you found them. _____

_____

_____

5. Use the "Search" feature to learn what significant event took place on July 20, 1969. _____

_____

Academic Research

College professors often require students to learn about specific topics through scholarly research. The assignment might result in a term paper, a project, or an oral presentation. Your professor will tell you the kinds of information sources that are acceptable, but most professors insist on scholarly sources that reflect the results of solid, reliable research. These materials can be found within the walls of your college library, or they may be accessed through the Internet. In fact, the materials in the most respected libraries in the world can be viewed from your computer or any Internet-capable device. The vast collection in the United States Library of Congress is a good example.

Getting Started

Although Wikipedia and Google are not usually acceptable sources of information for an academic research assignment, they are good places to get a quick overview of a topic. Wikipedia is an online encyclopedia to which users can add and revise entries. The site is monitored, but it does not promise unbiased, factual information. It can, though, provide ideas for narrowing your research topic and search terms. A Google search of your topic is likely to yield a list of many possible sources of information. Scan the list of "hits" for one or two that have promise and skim them. Again, look for general information and for related topics that might help you focus your research.

Scholarly Databases

When you have gained a general knowledge of your topic and have narrowed it to something that can be reasonably covered in the scope of your assignment, begin searching for scholarly, research-based sources of information. Libraries buy subscriptions to databases that contain many publications. Your college library probably offers online access to many such sources either from computers in the library building or through the college Web site. The snapshot below shows the first few databases in a very long list at one college library site. Notice that many of the databases are related to a field of study. When you have decided on a college major and have taken several courses in that field, you will become familiar with the best sources of information in that subject area.

San Jacinto College; www.sanjac.edu

EXERCISE 2 Explore your college library's Web site or find the site for another college library that is available to visitors. Locate the scholarly databases and list three that might be useful to you.

URL of the library Web site _____

1. _____

2. _____

3. _____

Tracking and Recording Your Search

Keep track of all useful sources so that you can find them again easily. There are several ways to do this:

- *Write down* the URL or the steps in the path that you took to find a database or article.
- *Print* the material. If you do this, use both sides of the page if possible to reduce paper usage. Be sure that you also record the URL so that you can find the material again and cite the source in your research report.

- *Save* the material to your computer's hard drive or a portable thumb drive. Be sure to name and organize the various sources so that you can find and identify them later.
- *Bookmark* or save the site to "Favorites" if you are using your own computer. If you are using a public machine, e-mailing a document or a link to yourself is sometimes an option.

No matter how you keep track of your searches, it is extremely important that you have all of the source information for any publication whose information you will use. You must cite the sources when you write your research report so that a reader can find the material you used. Ask your instructor if a particular citation style is required.

Evaluating Sources

Not every article, Web page, or book that you find will be of equal value, so read selectively. Look for titles that contain the focus of your topic. Articles in scholarly journals usually begin with an abstract, which is a brief summary of the article. Read the abstracts quickly to determine the value of the article for your purpose. Don't waste time on materials that are too general or that focus on a different aspect of your subject.

When you find an article that has information you need, read carefully and take notes in your own words. Use what you are learning in your reading course to critically evaluate the material. Pay attention to the tone of the language for clues to the author's purpose in writing. Consider the title, the author, the date it was written, the references cited in it, and the source itself. Scholarly journals are respected for publishing the best research and reporting only factual information. Other sources, however, may seek to persuade readers to accept a particular point of view. For example, an article in the National Rifle Association's magazine can be expected to take a certain position on gun control legislation. Gather information from many sources and draw your own conclusions based on the facts.

Academic Honesty

Colleges and college professors are very serious about academic honesty. Purchasing a paper, cutting and pasting from work that isn't yours, paraphrasing someone else's work, or in any way using someone else's words or ideas as if they were your own constitutes **plagiarism**. The consequences of plagiarism range from a zero grade on the assignment to expulsion from the college.

Sometimes students are unaware that they have plagiarized. Avoid this by "translating" the wording of the original source into your own words when you make notes. Then, when you compose the sentences of your paper, you will not accidentally use the author's phrasing. Remember that your goal is learning. Protect your honorable standing at your institution.

EXERCISE 3

Search a scholarly database for information on distance learning and record your search results here.

1. Name of the database _____

2. For each of three publications that look interesting, list the title, author, and

   source:

- _____
  _____
- _____
  _____
- _____
  _____

3. Open one of the publications. Read the abstract, if there is one, or survey the entire article. Briefly describe the focus of the information.

   _____
   _____
   _____
   _____

4. If you were researching information for a paper or a project, you would need a more narrow, focused topic than simply "distance learning." Write an idea for a narrowed search topic. (Hint: Glance through the list of titles from your search to find focused topics.)

   _____

Reader's TIP Limiting Your Search

- Enter *AND* or a plus (+) sign between each word of your search. For example, using the words *Apple Computer* for your search will turn up thousands of hits that include not only sites about the company but also sites related to apple (the fruit) and sites about computers in general. Using *AND* in your key phrase (*Apple AND Computer*) will return sites that only contain both words in the phrase.
- Enter *OR* to broaden a search. *Apple OR Computer* will return sites that contain information about either apples or computers.
- Enter NOT to exclude items. *Apple AND Computer NOT fruit* will exclude sites that mention fruit.
- Use quotation marks when you want only hits that contain the exact phrase, such as "Apple Computer Financial Report for 2014."

6 Supporting Details and Organizational Patterns

Learning Objectives

From this chapter, readers will learn:

1 To distinguish major and minor details
2 To attend to details in written directions
3 To recognize seven common organizational patterns
4 To use the organizational pattern to annotate the text and make notes

Everyday Reading Skills: Reading and Organizing Research Materials

WHAT ARE SUPPORTING DETAILS?

Learning Objective 1

Distinguish major and minor details

Details develop, explain, and prove a main idea. They are the facts, descriptions, and reasons that convince the reader and make the material interesting. Details answer questions and paint visual images so that the reader has an experience with the author and sees what the author sees and understands. For example, in a passage on the validity of movie reviews, the supporting details might include information on the rating scale, the qualifications of the raters, and the influence of the production companies on the eventual reviews.

Details can be ranked by their levels of importance in supporting a topic. Some details offer major support and elaboration, whereas others merely provide illustrations to relate the material to the reader's prior knowledge and make visualizing easier. All details play a part in our enjoyment of reading, but it is necessary to recognize their varying levels of importance.

Recognize Levels of Importance

To organize related words or ideas into levels of importance, the general topic is stated first, followed by subcategories of details, which may be further subdivided into specific examples. Outlines, diagrams, and **graphic organizers** can help to organize information into levels of importance.

EXAMPLE Notice that by using an outline and a diagram, the following list of words can be unscrambled to show relationships and levels of importance:

horses	grass	botany
zoology	cows	ants
bees	rabbits	entomology
branches of biology	flowers	mosquitoes
trees		

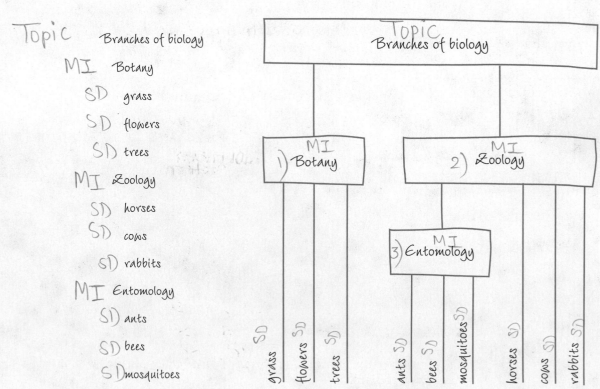

EXERCISE 1   Major ideas and supporting details have been mixed together in the following lists of words. Think about how the ideas should be organized, and insert them in the outline or diagram form provided. The main idea or topic of each list appears either on the line above the outline or in the top box of the diagram.

List 1

radio, television, advertising media, broadcast, direct mail, Internet, print, newspapers, magazines

T ... *MI*

Advertising media *Topic*

  I. *Print* MI
     A. direct mail
     B. newspapers   } SD
     C. magazines
  II. Broadcast MI
     A. Radio
     B. Television   } SD
     C. Internet

List 2

Title

Maine, North Carolina, Southeastern, states in regions of the United States, New Mexico, Southwestern, Arizona, Rhode Island, Georgia, Connecticut, Florida, Northeastern

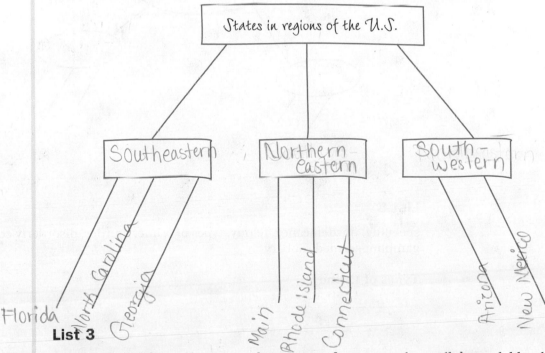

States in regions of the U.S.

Southeastern — Florida, North Carolina, Georgia

Northern-eastern — Main, Rhode Island, Connecticut

South-western — Arizona, New Mexico

List 3

honest, personality, appearance, description of a person, shy, well dressed, blond, straightforward, tall

Description of a person

I. <u>Personality</u> MI
   A. <u>honest</u>
   B. <u>shy</u>   } SD
   C. <u>straightforward</u>

II. <u>Appearance</u> MI
   A. <u>well dressed</u>
   B. <u>tall</u>   } SD
   C. <u>blond</u>

List 4

salsa, pasta, soy sauce, Mexican, ethnic foods, olive oil, fortune cookie, tacos, guacamole, Italian, egg rolls, Chinese

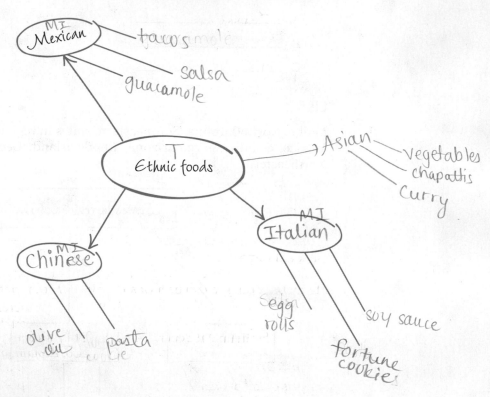

List 5

speeding, misdemeanor, felony, types of crime, murder, disorderly conduct, rape, gambling, armed robbery

Types of Crime

I. <u>Misdemeanor</u>
   A. <u>speeding</u>
   B. <u>disorderly conduct</u>
   C. <u>gambling</u>

II. <u>Felony</u>
  A. <u>armed robbery</u>
  B. <u>murder</u>
  C. <u>rape</u>

List 6

compass, digging tools, hoe, tools, machete, ruler, cutting tools, measuring tools, axe, gauge, jigsaw, spade, shovel

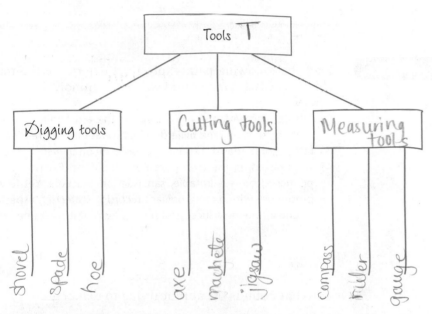

The Roles of Major and Minor Details

The outlines and diagrams on the preceding pages show that all details are not of equal importance. When reading textbooks, you may sometimes feel that you are receiving an overload of details. Not only is it impossible to remember all of them, but doing so can be a waste of time. With practice, you will learn that some details are major and should be remembered, whereas others are of only minor significance in supporting a main idea. How do you determine the importance of a particular detail? It depends on what point the author is making, and it depends on *what information is essential to develop, explain, or prove that point*.

For example, in a passage about communication by sound, the reason a bird sings is of major significance and gives primary support for the main idea, whereas the particular species of bird is a minor detail the author included for secondary support. In a passage on the limitations of acupuncture, the date of origin of the technique is most likely a minor detail, providing a secondary level of support. However, if the focus of the passage is on the history of acupuncture, the date of origin is a major detail, giving primary support to the main idea.

Minor details add interest, help the reader understand by giving examples, create visual images, and generally fill out a passage. Perhaps the author could make the point without them, but minor details tend to enhance the quality of the work. Major details, however, directly support the main idea regardless of whether it is directly or indirectly stated, and they are vital to your understanding the passage.

> **Reader's TIP** **Distinguishing Major and Minor Details**
>
> To determine which details give major or minor support, first identify the author's main point and then ask yourself the following questions.
>
> 1. What details are needed to explain or prove the main idea? (These are major details that give primary support.)
> 2. What details are included just to make the passage more interesting? (These are minor details that provide a secondary level of support.)

EXAMPLE Read the following paragraph. First determine the main point and then decide which details are major and which are minor.

> John Quincy Adams was a chip off the old family glacier. Short (5 feet 7 inches; 1.7 meters), thickset, and billiard-bald, he was even more frigidly austere than his presidential father, John Adams. Shunning people, he often went for early morning swims, sometimes stark naked, in the then pure Potomac River. Essentially a private thinker rather than a politician, he was irritable, sarcastic, and tactless. Yet few men have ever come to the presidency with a more brilliant record in statecraft, especially in foreign affairs. He ranks as one of the most successful secretaries of state, yet one of the least successful presidents.
>
> —*The American Pageant*
> by Thomas Bailey and David Kennedy

1. What point is the author trying to make? *He was a brilliant secretary of the state but he was socially enact*

2. Are the following details major or minor in their support of the author's point?

   _____ a. He was 5 feet 7 inches tall.

   _____ b. He was thickset and bald.

   Major c. He was a private thinker rather than a politician.

   Minor SP d. He swam naked in the Potomac River.

   Major e. He came to the presidency with a brilliant record in statecraft.

EXPLANATION The author's main point is that John Quincy Adams had been a brilliant secretary of state but was a socially inept politician and thus one of the least successful presidents. Items *a* and *b* on appearance are minor details that add interest but lend only secondary support. Item *c* is a major detail because it shows Adams's isolation as a socially inept politician. Swimming naked (*d*) is an interesting minor detail, and the last item (*e*) is a major detail because it develops the main point.

Signal Words to Indicate Levels of Importance. Sometimes the following connecting words signal the importance of details:

Major (primary support):   *first / second   last / in addition*
Minor (secondary support):   *for example / to illustrate*

EXERCISE 2   For each of the following topics, three details are given. Determine which details offer major (primary) support to the topic and which offer minor (secondary) support. Write the appropriate word in the blanks.

1. Reducing the fur trade

   Major a. Through advertising and publicity stunts, PETA, the world's largest animal rights group, has done much to convince the public that wearing fur is cruel.

   Major b. Over the last 15 years, people have come to realize the suffering of animals, and the fur industry has declined dramatically.

   Minor c. For example, Tyra Banks and Cindy Crawford will not model fur.

2. Dorothea Dix's humanitarian reform

   Major a. After visiting a jail to teach a Sunday school class to the female inmates and finding female patients in a mental hospital freezing in unheated, filthy cells, Dix started a lifelong campaign to improve conditions in such institutions.

   Major b. From 1845 to 1885, she was directly responsible for establishing 33 mental hospitals at home and abroad.

   Minor c. Dix was born in Maine but moved to Boston at the age of 12 to live with her grandmother.

3. Diet of an armadillo

   Major a. The armadillo enjoys scorpions, tarantulas, and grasshoppers, but its favorite food is ants, including the eggs and larvae.

   Minor b. If pursued, the armadillo can outrun a human and quickly dig itself into the ground.

   Major c. Sometimes it will eat fungus and wild berries or catch a lazy lizard, but the belief that the armadillo raids henhouses is unfounded.

4. Characteristics of the Millennium Generation (born 1977–2002)

   Minor a. This group is also called "Generation Y" because it followed "Generation X."

   Major b. Members of this group have known digital technology all of their lives and are comfortable with it.

   Major c. Millennials place a high value on making their jobs fit around their families and personal lives.

5. Larceny-theft

   Minor a. Tires, wheels, hubcaps, radar detectors, stereos, CD players, cassette tapes, compact discs, and cellular phones account for many of the items reported stolen.

   Major b. Larceny-theft is the most frequently reported major crime.

   Major c. Larceny-theft may be the most underreported crime category, because small thefts rarely come to the attention of the police.

6. Preterm neonates

Major a. The immature development of preterm neonates makes them unusually sensitive to stimuli in their environment.

Major b. Preterm neonates can easily be overwhelmed by the sights, sounds, and sensations that they experience, and their breathing may be interrupted or their heart rates may slow.

Minor c. Such behavior is quite disconcerting to parents.

EXERCISE 3

Distinguishing between major and minor details is important, whether you are studying a single paragraph, a chapter, or a whole book. After reading each of the following passages, first identify the author's main point. Then determine which of the details listed are major and which are minor in supporting that point. The skills that you will use apply equally to these short readings and to the larger units of text that you will be studying in college textbooks.

Passage 1

PRICE SETTING

The DeBeers Company of South Africa, a syndicate that controls most of the sales of raw diamonds, maximizes profits by determining what quantity of raw diamonds to offer on the world raw-diamond market. DeBeers markets diamonds through an unusual marketing procedure called a sight. About three weeks before each sight, DeBeers sends notices to the 300 largest diamond purchasers, who are asked to send in requests in carats for the amount of diamonds they wish to buy. Two days before the sight (held in London, Luzerne, and Kimberley, South Africa), the buyers are informed how many carats they have been allocated—an amount often below the quantity requested. At the sight each buyer is handed a container of raw diamonds. Buyers who refuse to purchase would run the risk of not being invited back. The market price of diamonds is regulated by the number of diamonds offered in each sight.

—*Essentials of Economics,* Fourth Edition, by Paul Gregory

1. What point is the author trying to make? _DeBeers Company controls the price of diamonds (amount of diamonds they have)._

2. Which details are major and which are minor in supporting the author's point?

Minor a. The sight is held in London, Luzerne, and Kimberley.

Major b. DeBeers invites the 300 largest diamond buyers to the sight.

Major c. The buyers are offered fewer diamonds than the quantity they requested.

Passage 2

HEALTH FOOD?

When 35 million people in the United States gave their loved ones boxes of chocolates last Valentine's Day, they knew they were giving sweet comfort—but health food? Chocolate candy is certainly a significant source of fat and sugar calories, but recent research suggests that chocolate itself—the dark, bitter powder made from the seeds within cacao pods—may also be a significant source of protective molecules. Medical scientists have known for some time that many things that go wrong with our bodies can be traced to destructive molecules called *free radicals*. Many free radicals contain oxygen in a form that reacts strongly with, and damages, various biological molecules and their cellular structures. This process is called *oxidative stress*. So what's a person to do? Well, maybe eat more chocolate!

—*Biology: Life on Earth*, Sixth Edition,
by Teresa Audesirk, Gerald Audesirk, and Bruce Byers

1. What point is the author trying to make? *Sometimes Chocolate is healthy because it contains protective molecules*

2. Which details are major and which are minor in supporting the author's point?

   Major a. Free radicals damage biological molecules and their cellular structure.

   Minor b. About 35 million people in the United States gave chocolates on Valentine's Day.

   Minor c. Chocolate is a source of fat and sugar calories.

Passage 3

GENDER AND COLLEGE PERFORMANCE

I registered for a calculus course my first year at DePauw. Even twenty years ago I was not timid, so on the very first day I raised my hand and asked a question. I still have a vivid memory of the professor rolling his eyes, hitting his head with his hand in frustration, and announcing to everyone, "Why do they expect me to teach calculus to girls?" I never asked another question. Several weeks later I went to a football game, but I had forgotten to bring my ID. My calculus professor was at the gate checking IDs, so I went up to him and said, "I forgot my ID but you know me, I'm in your class." He looked right at me and said, "I don't remember you in my class." I couldn't believe that someone who changed my life and whom I remember to this day didn't even recognize me.

—Patricia Ireland, quoted in *Failing at Fairness:
How America's Schools Cheat Girls*,
by Myra and David Sadker

1. What point is the author trying to make? *Gender discrimination in college - girls*

2. Which details are major and which are minor in supporting the author's point?

   Minor a. The author registered for a calculus course in her first year of college.

   Major b. When the author asked a question in class, her calculus professor responded in frustration, "Why do they expect me to teach calculus to girls?"

   Minor c. The author attended a football game at which her calculus professor worked the gate checking IDs.

Passage 4

ASTEROIDS

MP

(Besides the eight major planets, thousands of smaller planetoids are also part of the solar system). These minor planets are called *asteroids*. There are more than 10,000 known asteroids, but many others are far too small to be seen even through the best telescopes. Most are found between the orbits of Jupiter and Mars, where the gravitational force of Jupiter prevented them from combining to form a single larger planet. The largest asteroid is only about 1,000 km across.

—*Earth's Dynamic Systems*, Ninth Edition,
by W. Kenneth Hamblin and Eric H. Christiansen

1. What point is the author trying to make? _Smaller planetoids in the solar system are not planets._

2. Which details are major and which are minor in supporting the author's point?

   Major a. There are more than 10,000 known asteroids.

   Minor b. There are eight major planets.

   Major c. The minor planets of the solar system are called asteroids.

Passage 5

TECHNOSTRESS

Are you "twittered out"? Is all that texting causing your thumbs to seize up in protest? If so, you're not alone. Like millions of others, you may find that all of the pressure for contact is stressing you out! Known as *technostress*, it is defined as stress created by a dependence on technology and the constant state of connection, which can include a perceived obligation to respond, chat, or tweet. There is much good that comes from all that technological wizardry. For some folks, though, technomania can become obsessive—they would rather hang out online talking to strangers than study, socialize in person, or generally connect in the real world. There are some clear downsides to all of that virtual interaction.

—*Health: The Basics*, Tenth Edition,
by Rebecca J. Donatelle

1. What point is the author trying to make? _Millions of people find pressure for contact & stressing out known as technostress._

2. Which details are major and which are minor in supporting the author's point?

   Minor a. There can be a perceived obligation to respond, chat, or tweet.

   Major b. Technomania can become obsessive.

   Minor c. They would rather hang out online talking to strangers than study.

Passage 6

ORGANIZED CRIME

For many people, the term **organized crime** conjures up images of the Mafia (also called the *Cosa Nostra*) or the hit HBO TV series *The Sopranos*. Although organized criminal activity is decidedly a group phenomenon, the groups involved in the United States today vary greatly. During the past few decades in the United States, the dominance of traditional Sicilian American criminal organizations has fallen to other criminal associations such as the Black Mafia, the Cuban Mafia, the Haitian Mafia, the Colombian cartels, and Asian criminal groups like the Chinese Tongs and street gangs, Japanese yakuza, and Vietnamese gangs. Also included here are inner-city gangs like the Los Angeles Crips and Bloods and the Chicago Vice Lords; international drug rings; outlaw motorcycle gangs like the Hell's Angels and the Pagans; and other looser associations of small-time thugs, prison gangs, and drug dealers.

—*Criminal Justice Today: An Introductory Text for the 21st Century,*
Twelfth Edition, by Frank Schmalleger, PhD.

1. What point is the author trying to make? _Organize a crime_
   in a various groups.

2. Which details are major and which are minor in supporting the author's point?

   Major a. Dominance of the traditional Sicilian American Mafia has fallen to others such as the Black Mafia, the Cuban Mafia, the Haitian Mafia, the Colombian cartels, and Asian criminal groups.

   Minor b. The term "organized crime" conjures up images of the Mafia or the HBO TV series *The Sopranos*.

   Major c. Organized crime also includes inner-city gangs, international drug rings, outlaw motorcycle gangs, prison gangs, and drug dealers.

FOLLOW DETAILED DIRECTIONS

Learning Objective 2

Attend to details in written directions

Some of the normal rules of reading change dramatically when the task is to follow printed directions. Suddenly, all details are of equal importance, and you must switch gears to accomplish this new task. For example, every detail requires attention when you read the directions for a science experiment, a nursing procedure, or a computer program. You cannot read directions as you would a newspaper article.

Readers are not accustomed to attending to every single detail. For most reading, understanding the general idea and important details is adequate. However, this strategy does not work well when you are assembling a bicycle or following travel directions to a party. Confronted with a set of directions, you recognize that the task is different, even tedious, and then commit to reading step by step, sometimes even word by word and phrase by phrase. Consult any diagram that accompanies the directions and read aloud if necessary. Remember that some people are better than others at visualizing graphic designs, so consider finding a partner if you think that you will need help.

EXAMPLE

Select a friend and follow these directions together for calculating pulse rate.

1. Select a pulse point that is comfortable for you and the other person. You can take a pulse rate on the inner surface of the wrist, in the fold of the arm

> ## Reader's TIP   Following Directions
>
> - Change your mindset from normal reading and commit to a different kind of task.
> - Read to get an overview so that you have a general idea of the task and can make a plan.
> - Assemble the necessary equipment, estimate the time, and find a helper if needed.
> - Read each step sequentially and do as directed. Move from word to word and phrase to phrase for a clear understanding. Read aloud if necessary.
> - Use numbers, letters, and guide words such as *first, next, before, after, then,* and *now* to maintain a sequence. Insert your own numbers if steps are not sequenced.
> - Visualize the process. Consult the diagram. Draw your own diagram if none exists.
> - Think logically and keep your goal in mind.

opposite the elbow, on the side of the throat a few inches from the center, or in the bend of the leg behind the knee.

2. Press two or three fingers gently down over the selected pulse point. Do not use the thumb because it has a pulse of its own that could be mistaken for the client's pulse.

3. Once the pulsations are felt, use the second hand on your watch to count the pulsations for 30 seconds.

4. Multiply the number of pulsations by two to calculate the pulse rate per minute. Write down the rate.

5. Wait a few minutes and repeat the procedure to obtain a second pulse rate. Write down the rate.

6. If the difference in the two pulse rates is more than two counts, repeat the procedure using a different pulse point. Write down this rate.

EXPLANATION An overview of these directions indicates that you need a watch with a second hand, paper and a pen, and a willing friend. Find a comfortable pulsation point and calculate the pulse rate. Evaluate your results by considering that a normal resting pulse rate for an adult is 80 pulsations per minute with a range from 60 to 100.

Directions 1

Use the following directions to put numbers and signs on the line below.

_____

1. Put the number 8 in the middle of the line.
2. On the left end of the line, write a 5 and on the right end of the line, put a 7.
3. Equidistant between the 8 and the 7, write down the sum of the two numbers.
4. Equidistant between the number on the far left of the line and the number in the middle, write down the sum of all the numbers on the line.
5. On either side of the number in the middle of the line, insert a minus sign.
6. To the right of the first number on the line and to the left of the last number, insert a plus sign.
7. Put an equals sign after the last number on the line and use the signs to cal-

   culate the total of the numbers listed. What is your total? _____

Directions 2

To get the most cardiac benefit from your workout, the American Heart Association recommends maintaining your heart rate within a certain range during exercise. The range varies for individuals depending on age, general fitness, and heart health. While exercising, check your heart rate periodically. To do this, press your index and middle finger gently against the inside of your wrist or against your neck until you feel your pulse. Count the number of beats in a 10-second time period and multiply that number by six. Maintain, decrease, or increase your exertion level to stay within your optimum exercise range.

When you first begin regular exercise, aim for the lower end of the target range. As you become more fit, gradually increase the intensity of your workout. After six months or so of regular workouts, you might be able to sustain the intensity at the highest level of your target zone. If you have a heart condition, consult your doctor before beginning aerobic exercise.

To calculate your target heart rate range, follow the steps in the following example, which is calculated for a person who is age 20:

	Example
Subtract your age from 220. This is your maximum heart rate.	$220 - 20 = 200$
Multiply your maximum heart rate by 50%. This is the low end of your target range.	$200\,(0.50) = 100$
Multiply your maximum heart rate by 85%. This is the high end of your target range.	$200\,(0.85) = 170$

The target heart rate range for a person who is age 20 is 170–200 beats per minute.

Source: http://www.heart.org/HEARTORG/GettingHealthy/PhysicalActivity/Target-Heart-Rates_UCM_434341_Article.jsp

1. When determining your actual heart rate, why do you count the number of beats for 10 seconds and then multiply by 6? _____

   _____

2. In the example above, what is the target range for a 10-second heart rate check? _____

   _____

3. Calculate your target heart rate, both the low and high end of your range.

   _____

Directions 3

> When in the Course of human Events, it becomes necessary for one People to dissolve the Political Bands which have connected them with another, and to assume, among the Powers of the Earth, the separate and equal Station to which the Laws of Nature and of Nature's God entitle them, a descent Respect to the Opinions of Mankind requires that they should declare the causes which impel them to the Separation.

Printed above is the first paragraph of the U.S. Declaration of Independence. As you can see, the rules for use of capital letters were different in 1776 than they are today.

Select any one of the first 20 words. Count the letters in it and call that number "*n*." Move ahead *n* words, beginning with the word after your selected word. When you reach that *n*th word, count its letters and move ahead as many words as the new letter count. Continue in this manner, counting letters and moving ahead words, until you stop on a word that is beyond the fourth line.

On what word did you stop? _____

—Martin Gardner, "Some Math Magic Tricks with
Numbers," *Games Magazine*, May 1999

Directions 4

Use the compass directions and the grid to complete the following exercise.

1. Begin in the southwest corner of cell X and draw a line that extends north 4 cells.
2. Retrace this line south 2 cells and then draw east 3 cells. Draw north 1 cell.
3. Draw a straight line northeast to the north center of this cell. Draw another straight line to the southeast corner of the cell.
4. Draw due east 1 cell and repeat step 3.
5. Draw due south 3 cells. Draw due west 6 cells.
6. Draw an oval in each of the full cells directly south of those in which you have drawn partial triangles.
7. Draw a line from west to east across the center of the cell directly south of the cell between the ovals.

What have you drawn? _____

Write additional directions to complete the figure? _____

_____

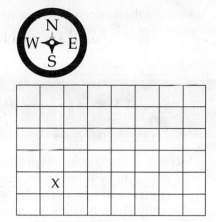

PATTERNS OF ORGANIZATION

The logical presentation of details in textbooks tends to form several identifiable patterns. For example, introductory psychology texts tend to list many definitions and examples, whereas history texts present events in time order with numerous cause-and-effect conclusions. Recognizing these patterns helps you to read more efficiently and take notes for later study. They are blueprints for organizing your thinking.

Each organizational pattern can be predicted by **signal words** (transitions) that indicate the structure. Learn to use the patterns to mark your text and take notes for later study. Your markings and your notes are an organization of main ideas and major supporting details. The following are examples of the organizational patterns that are found most frequently in textbooks.

Simple Listing

To organize and condense material for the reader, introductory texts often enumerate key ideas. The listing technique may be used within one paragraph, or it may be used over three or four pages to pull material together. With a simple listing pattern, the items are of equal value, and thus the order in which they are presented is of no importance.

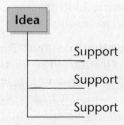

Consider the following addition problems. Does the order of the numbers change the sum?

4	9
7	4
2	5
5	2
+9	+7

Likewise, the order of details in a simple list pattern does not change the main point nor influence the reader's understanding of the passage.

Reader's TIP — Patterns of Organization, Signal Words, and Their Functions

Recognizing the function of a signal word (transition) in a sentence, paragraph, or longer selection offers a clue to the author's pattern of organization. For example, *because* suggests a reason is being given, and the pattern might be cause and effect.

Addition (providing additional information): *furthermore, again, also, further, moreover, besides, likewise*

Cause and Effect (showing one element as producing or causing a result or effect): *because, for this reason, consequently, hence, as a result, thus, due to, therefore*

Classification (dividing items into groups or categories): *groups, categories, elements, classes, parts*

Comparison (listing similarities among items): *in a similar way, similar, parallels, likewise, in a like manner*

Contrast (listing differences among items): *on the other hand, bigger than, but, however, conversely, on the contrary, although, nevertheless*

Definition (initially defining a concept and expanding with examples and restatements): *can be defined, means, for example, like*

Description (listing characteristics or details): *is, as, like, could be described*

Generalization and Example (explaining with examples to illustrate): *to restate, that is, for example, to illustrate, for instance*

Location or Spatial Order (identifying the whereabouts of objects): *next to, near, below, above, close by, within, without, adjacent to, beside, around, to the right or left side, opposite*

Simple Listing (randomly listing items in a series): *also, another, several, for example*

Summary (condensing major points): *in conclusion, briefly, to sum up, in short, in a nutshell*

Time Order, Sequence, or Narration (listing events in order of occurrence): *first, second, finally, after, before, next, later, now, at last, until, thereupon, while, during*

Signal Words to Indicate Listing.   Listed items usually begin with such general phrases as these:

Many of the items included were. . . .

A number of factors were. . . .

Learning Objective 4

Use the organizational pattern to annotate the text and make notes

Signal words used as transitional words to link ideas include:

in addition   also   several   for example   a number of

Also used are numbers such as *one, two, three* (or *first, second, third*) or positions such as *next, last,* or *finally,* where numerical order is not relevant.

Annotate Your Text; Then Take Notes. After reading a listing, circle the topic, that is, the words that best describe what the list contains. Next, underline and number each listed item. Lastly, use your annotations to make brief, organized notes. The example below illustrates the process.

EXAMPLE **INTERVIEWING FOR A JOB** —Topic

There are several tips one should remember when interviewing for a job. [MI] Be sure to ¹arrive on time and remember there is no excuse for being late. ²Attend to appearance and dress to look like a successful company employee. Also, ³do not smoke, chew gum, or accept candy, even if it is offered.

Your notes on "Interviewing for a Job" would be as follows:

Topic: Tips for job interviewing

1. Arrive on time.
2. Attend to appearance.
3. Don't smoke, chew gum, or eat.

EXERCISE 5 For each of the following paragraphs, annotate the text as if you were marking it for later study. After reading each passage, insert a topic onto the blank line at the beginning of the passage. Take notes by first recording the topic and then listing the relevant supporting items. Respond with *T* (true) or *F* (false) to the comprehension items.

Passage 1

Topic: How Cancer treatment works

Cancer treatments vary according to the type of cancer and the stage in which it's detected. [MI] ¹Surgery, in which the tumor and surrounding tissue are removed, is one common treatment. ²Radiotherapy (the use of radiation) or ³chemotherapy (the use of drugs) to kill cancerous cells are also used. Radiation works by destroying malignant cells or stopping cell growth. It is most effective in treating localized cancer masses. When cancer has spread throughout the body, it is necessary to use some form of chemotherapy.

—*Health: The Basics,* Tenth Edition, by Rebecca J. Donatelle

1. Annotate your text; then take notes.

Topic: Cancer Treatments

(1) Surgery

(2) Radiotherapy

(3) Chemotherapy

___F___ 2. Radiotherapy involves the use of drugs to treat cancer.

___F___ 3. Surgery is used when cancer has spread throughout the body.

Passage 2

Topic: Advantages of incumbency

During elections to Congress there are a number of advantages of incumbency (being currently in office). One big one is that incumbents can issue "official" statements or make "official" trips to their district. They can get a lot of free publicity that their opponents would have to pay for. For another advantage, members of the House have office and staff budgets of approximately $350,000 a year; senators are given at least that and often considerably more if their states are large. Both receive 32 government-paid round trips to their districts each year. Also, facilities for making television or radio tapes are available in Washington at a low cost. In addition, there is the *frank,* the privilege of free official mailing enjoyed by Congress. Two hundred million pieces of mail, much of it quite partisan, are sent free under the frank every year.

—*The Basics of American Politics,* by Gary Wasserman

1. Annotate your text; then take notes.

Topic: Advantages of incumbency

(1) free publicity

(2) office & staff budgets

(3) 32 government-paid round trips

(4) television & radio tapes are at low cost

(5) free official mailing (franking)

___F___ 2. A *frank* privilege is a government-paid trip home.

___I___ 3. Incumbents receive publicity that is paid for by taxpayers.

2 Classification

In order to simplify a complex topic, authors frequently begin introductory paragraphs by stating that the information that follows is divided into a certain number of groups or categories. The divisions are then named and the parts are explained.

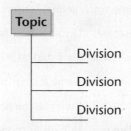

Signal Words to Indicate Classification. Signal words often used for classification are the following:

two divisions   *three groups*   *four elements*   *five classes*

Annotate Your Text; Then Take Notes. After reading, circle the group that will be classified and the number of categories you can expect. Underline any key words that help explain the major details listed. The following is an example of this technique. Lastly, use your annotations to make brief, organized notes.

EXAMPLE   **FIVE KINGDOMS**

Today most scientists believe that living things should be divided into ⟨five kingdoms.⟩ We begin by describing the largest groups, the kingdoms, and then discuss various representatives at lower levels in the taxonomic scheme. The five kingdoms generally accepted by biologists are ① <u>monera</u>, ② <u>protista</u>, ③ <u>fungi</u>, ④ <u>plantae</u>, and ⑤ <u>animalia</u>.

—*Biology: The World of Life*, Seventh Edition,
by Robert Wallace

Your notes on "Five Kingdoms" would be as follows:

Topic: Five kingdoms

1. monera

2. protista

3. fungi

4. plantae

5. animalia

EXERCISE 6   For each of the following paragraphs, annotate the text as if you were marking it for later study. After reading each passage, insert a topic onto the blank line at the beginning of the passage. Take notes by first recording the topic and then listing relevant supporting items. Respond with *T* (true), *F* (false), or *CT* (can't tell) to the comprehension items.

Passage 1

Two main categories of fats

Two types of unsaturated fats

Topic: _____

Fat cells consist of chains of carbon and hydrogen atoms. Those that are unable to hold any more hydrogen in their chemical structure are labeled ⟨saturated fats⟩. They generally come from animal sources, such as meats and dairy products, and are solid at room temperature. ⟨Unsaturated fats⟩, which come from plants and include most vegetable oils, are generally liquid at room temperature and have room for additional hydrogen atoms in their chemical structure. The terms ⟨*monounsaturated fat* (MUFA)⟩ and *polyunsaturated fat* (PUFA) refer to the relative number of hydrogen atoms that are missing. Peanut and olive oils are high in monounsaturated fats, whereas corn, sunflower, and safflower oils are high in polyunsaturated fats.

Which type is healthier?

There is currently a great deal of controversy about which type of unsaturated fat is most beneficial. Although nutritional researchers in the 1980s favored PUFAs, today many believe that they may decrease beneficial HDL levels while reducing LDL levels. PUFAs come in two forms: omega-3 fatty acids and omega-6 fatty acids. MUFAs, such as olive oil, seem to lower LDL levels and increase HDL levels and thus are currently the preferred, or least harmful, fats. Nevertheless, a tablespoon of olive oil gives you a hefty 10 grams of MUFAs.

—*Health: The Basics*, by Rebecca J. Donatelle

1. Annotate your text; then take notes.

   Topic: Categories of Fats
   - (1) Saturated fats come from animals
   - (2) Unsaturated fats (plants)
     - (a) monounsaturated
     - (b) polyunsaturated

   _F_ 2. Butter is an example of an unsaturated fat.

   _F_ 3. Fats are labeled according to the number of carbon atoms in their chemical structure.

Passage 2

Three types

Topic: 3 types of Planets in SS.

Three types of planets formed in our solar system. The ⟨inner planets⟩ are small and made mostly of silicates and iron metal. The ⟨outer planets⟩ are large and made largely of gaseous hydrogen and helium. The ⟨icy planets⟩ also lie in the outer solar system but are small and have surfaces dominated by water ice.

—*Earth's Dynamic Systems*, Ninth Edition, by W. Kenneth Hamblin and Eric H. Christiansen

1. Annotate your text; then take notes.

Topic: 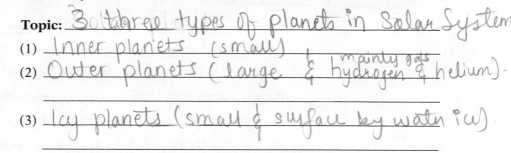 3 or three types of planets in Solar System.
(1) ___Inner planets (small)___
(2) ___Outer planets (large & mainly gas hydrogen & helium).___

(3) ___Icy planets (small & surface by water ice)___

___T___ 2. The icy planets are smaller than the outer planets.

___F___ 3. The outer planets differ from the icy planets only in terms of size.

3) ## Definitions With Examples

In each introductory course, you enter a completely new field with its own unique concepts and ideas. These courses frequently seem to be the hardest because of the overload of information presented. In a single beginning course, you are expected to survey the field from one end to the other. Beyond simply learning vocabulary, you must learn the terminology for major ideas that create a framework for the entire course. You must create a new schema. For example, in an introductory psychology textbook, several paragraphs might be devoted to describing *schizophrenia, paranoia,* or a *manic-depressive cycle.* To remember these terms, you would mark your text and take notes defining the conditions. You would also include examples to help you visualize the terms.

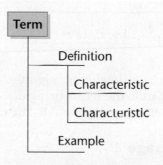

Signal Words to Indicate Definition and Examples. The new terms or concepts may appear as headings, or they may appear in quotation marks, boldface, or italics. Signal words include the following:

for example	*in this case*	*to illustrate*
more specifically	*in more precise terms*	*in one instance*

Annotate Your Text. After reading the definition of a new term, circle the term and then underline the *key defining words.* A word of caution here: Only underline *key* words. Refrain from underlining sentence after sentence, which leaves you with too much highlighted material for later reference. Mark *Ex* by the example that best helps you remember the term. The following paragraph illustrates this technique.

EXAMPLE **DISPLACEMENT**

Father spanks son, who kicks the dog, who chases the cat. Displacement is the shifting of response from one object to another. The boss has yelled at the father. The father is angry at the boss but can't express it safely, so he displaces his anger to his son and spanks him. The son is angry at his father but can't express it safely, so he displaces his anger to the dog and kicks it. The dog is "angry" at the son but can't express it safely, so he displaces his "anger" to the cat and chases it. In the mechanism of displacement, a feeling is displaced to a safer substitute.

—From Morris Holland, *Psychology,* 1E © 1974 Wadsworth,
a part of Cengage Learning, Inc. Reproduced
by permission. www.cengage.com/permissions

Take Notes. For your study notes, jot down the term, define it in your own words, and list an example. Frequently, you will need to condense several sentences into a short phrase for your notes. If you think the text uses a clear and concise definition, it is permissible to use the same words, but don't let yourself fall into the "delayed learning" trap. If you simply copy textbook words that you do not understand, you won't be any better off weeks later when you study your notes for a midterm or final exam. The appropriate time to understand the term is when you first study and take notes on it.

Your notes on displacement might look like this:

Displacement: *Shifting the expression of a feeling from one object to a*

safe substitute

Example: *Son angry at father, so kicks dog*

EXERCISE 7 Read the following paragraphs and write a topic for the beginning of each passage. Circle the terms being defined, underline key phrases, and then write notes for later study. Respond to the comprehension items with *T* (true) or *F* (false).

Passage 1

Topic: _____

Large waves, known as seismic sea waves or by the Japanese term *tsunami*, originate from disturbances on the ocean floor. They are also commonly referred to as *tidal waves*, but they have no relationship with tides at all. **Tsunamis** can be caused by volcanic eruptions, submarine landslides, or even meteorite impact, but most result from earthquakes that displace the ocean floor. It is not surprising then that most tsunamis occur in the Pacific Ocean, which is circled by active volcanoes and intense seismicity, both of which result from a series of subduction zones surrounding the Pacific. For example, in 1999 a magnitude 7.1 earthquake triggered in a subduction zone north of New Guinea created a tsunami that was 15 m high. When it struck the shore, it swept 2,200 people to their deaths.

—*Earth's Dynamic Systems,* Ninth Edition,
by W. Kenneth Hamblin and Eric H. Christiansen

1. Annotate your text; then take notes.

Tsunamis: Caused by volcanic eruptions, submarine landslides, or even meteorite impact.

Example: In 1999, a magnitude 7.1 earthquake triggered in a subduction zone north of New Guinea created tsunami that was 15 m high & 2,200 people died.

___F___ 2. Most tsunamis occur in the Pacific Ocean because of its size, depth, and temperature.

___F___ 3. Tsunamis are also referred to as tidal waves because they are dependent on the ebb and flow of tides.

Passage 2

Topic: _____

Most forget that there is also supposed to be a Type B, defined not by the personality traits its members possess but by the traits they lack. Type B people are the shadowy opposites of Type A people. They are those who are not so very Type A. They do not wear out their fingers punching that elevator button. They do not allow a slow car in the fast lane to drive their hearts to fatal distraction; in fact, they are at the wheel of that slow car.

—"Life as Type A" by James Gleick. From _Faster, the Acceleration of Just About Everything_

1. Annotate your text; then take notes.

Type B people: _____

_____

Example: _____

_____

_____

_____ 2. The author suggests that Type B behavior is defined more by what _isn't_ than by what _is_ (i.e., angry, impolite, rushed).

_____ 3. The author implies that Type A people are unlikely to demonstrate patience.

4) Description

Description is similar to listing; the characteristics that make up a description are no more than a definition or a simple list of details.

Signal Words to Indicate Description. Look for a list of defining details.

Annotate Your Text. Circle the item being described and then underline the _key characteristic_. Only underline _key_ words. The following paragraph illustrates this technique.

```
┌─────────────┐
│ Item or issue │
└─────────────┘
   ├──────── Characteristic
   ├──────── Characteristic
   └──────── Characteristic
```

EXAMPLE **LIZARDS**

(Lizards) are the <u>most successful</u> living group of reptiles. There are <u>3,100 different species</u> of lizards in comparison to snakes, which have 2,000 species. Lizards range in <u>size</u> from a gecko at <u>1.2 inches</u> to monitor lizards at <u>15 feet</u>. The <u>speed</u> of a lizard varies with where it lives. The <u>desert lizard is the fastest</u>.

Take Notes. After marking your text, jot down the topic and underline the key characteristics. Your notes on the previous paragraph would be as follows:

Topic: Lizards

1. Most successful reptiles—3,100 different species

2. Size varies—gecko at 1.2 inches to monitor lizards at 15 feet

3. Speed varies—desert lizard fastest

EXERCISE 8

Read the following paragraphs and write a topic for the beginning of each passage. Circle the item being described, underline key phrases, and then write notes for later study. Respond to the comprehension items with *T* (true) or *F* (false).

Passage 1

Topic: Vertebrates of class Mammalia

Vertebrates of class Mammalia   have hair, a characteristic as diagnostic as the feathers of birds. (Hair) insulates the body, helping the animal maintain a warm and constant body temperature. Mammals are (endothermic,) and their active metabolism is supported by an efficient respiratory system. Mammary glands that (produce milk) are as distinctively mammalian as hair. All mammalian mothers nourish their babies with milk. Most mammals are (born rather than hatched,) and mammals have (larger brains) than other vertebrates of equivalent size.

—*Biology*, Fourth Edition, by Neil Campbell

1. Annotate your text; then take notes.

Topic: Mammalia characteristics
(1) Hair
(2) endothermic
(3) Produce Milk

(4) ___Born rather than hatched___

(5) ___Large brains___

___T___ 2. Apes are mammals.

___F___ 3. According to this information, chickens would be characterized as mammals.

Passage 2

Topic: ___Sharks___

The shark is one of the most fabled, feared, and least understood large animals on earth. They have well-developed jaws and teeth and are reported to be totally humorless. The shark has a very short intestine and a large liver that helps with buoyancy. The body shape itself is quite streamlined, an important adaptation for coping with resistance.

—*Biology: World of Life*, Seventh Edition,
by Robert Wallace

1. Mark your text; then take notes.

Topic: ___Sharks___

(1) ___Jaws & teeth (well developed)___

(2) ___short intestine & a large liver___

(3) ___large liver___

(4) ___streamlined body.___

___T___ 2. The author exhibits a sense of humor in claiming that sharks have none.

___T___ 3. The shark's liver helps it float.

⑤ Time Order, Sequence, or Narration

Items in time order, sequence, or narration are listed in the order in which they occurred or in a specifically planned order in which they must develop. Changing the order would change the results. For example, events in history are typically organized in time order or narration. Novels, biographies, and anecdotes are usually developed chronologically, and instructions and directions are usually developed in sequence.

A diagram or graphic organizer like the one below is a helpful tool for sorting details and especially for future study.

Topic:

When did it happen?	What happened?

Signal Words to Indicate Time Order or Sequence. Signal words often used for time order or sequence include:

first	*second*	*afterward*	*after*	*before*	*when*
until	*at last*	*next*	*most important*	*finally*	*(dates)*

Annotate Your Text. After reading a time-ordered or sequenced section, first circle the topic and time indicators, such as dates or words like *later* or *the next year*. Insert numbers for each important stage and underline key words that explain each one. By its nature, history is full of time-ordered, or chronological, events. Be aware that every event is not of equal significance. History textbooks include many details that help you visualize but that you do not need to remember. Use the subheadings in the text to help you judge the importance of events.

EXAMPLE   **THE LOUISIANA PURCHASE**

The events surrounding the (Louisiana Purchase) occurred as follows: In (1795)[1] Spain granted western farmers the right to ship their produce down the Mississippi River to New Orleans, where their cargoes of corn, whiskey, and pork were loaded aboard ships bound for the East Coast and foreign ports. In (1800,) however, [2] Spain secretly ceded the Louisiana territory to France and closed the port of New Orleans to American farmers, who exploded with anger. The president sent James Monroe to France to purchase the land. Circumstances played into American hands when, also in (1800,) [3] slaves rebelled in Haiti, and France had to send troops to fight. After meeting with a determined resistance and mosquitoes carrying yellow fever, Napoleon exclaimed, "Damn sugar, damn coffee, damn colonies." He was then ready to sell. Finally, in (1803,) [4] the United States officially purchased all of the Louisiana Province, a territory extending from Canada to the Gulf of Mexico and westward as far as the Rocky Mountains. The American negotiators agreed on a price of $15 million, or about 4 cents an acre.

—*America and Its People*, Third Edition,
by James Martin et al.

Take Notes. After marking your text, jot down the topic and number the items that are relevant. Be brief. If these items need explanation, put key words underneath the item or in parentheses beside it. Your notes on the previous paragraph would be as follows:

Topic: Louisiana Purchase

When did it happen?	What happened?
1795	1. Spain allowed shipping
1800	2. Sold to France, which stopped shipping
	3. France failed to win in Haiti
1803	4. U.S. bought all land

EXERCISE 9 Read the following paragraphs and mark your text by writing a topic at the beginning of the passage, circling indicators of time, and underlining what happened. Then write notes for later study. Respond to the comprehension items with *T* (true) or *F* (false).

Passage 1

Topic: _____

She was the twentieth child in a black family of 22 in Clarksville, Tennessee. A weak and sickly infant, she was continually afflicted with childhood diseases, and at four she contracted polio. She was unable to walk without steel braces until she was nine and she continued to wear a supportive device in her shoes until age 11.

Both she and her mother were strong believers that fate was not something you had to resign yourself to, but that people could create their own vision and destiny. Together mother and daughter began a training program for those skinny, wobbly legs. Soon she was running. With renewed energy she began to formulate her own goals with a strategy plan. It did not take long until she was the fastest kid on the block ... and then in the city, in the state, and even the nation.

At age 16 she qualified for the U.S. Olympic team and in 1956 she won a bronze medal in the 100-meter dash. In the 1960 Olympic Games she won three gold medals, for the 100- and 200-meter events and the 400-meter relay. In all three races she broke world records and established herself as the fastest woman on earth.

When asked how she did it, Wilma Rudolph answered, "No one has a life where everything that happened was good. I think the thing that made my life good for me is that I never looked back. I've always been positive no matter what happened."

—*Interpersonal Skills for Leadership,* Second Edition,
by Susan Fritz, et al.

1. Annotate your text; then take notes.

Topic: Goals & Achievements

When did it happen?	What happened?
Childhood	She had polic, unable to walk without stell braces until was nine & wore supportice device in shoes until age 11.
Age 16	started training program & gym. Qualified for U.S. Olympic team.
1956	Won a bronze medal in the 100-meter dash.
1960	Won 3 gold medals in 100-200m & 400m relay. & fastest women on earth.

___F___ 2. Wilma Rudolph began her vigorous training program in the hope of obtaining a college scholarship to Tennessee State University.

___T___ 3. Rudolph views her success as a direct result of optimism in the face of hardship.

Passage 2

Topic: Ebola Virus

Let us consider the deadly Ebola virus as an example of an emerging virus. Ebola outbreaks have occurred several times during the past few decades. The virus was first identified in 1976 in Zaire and Sudan (outbreaks that killed more than 400 people). During the 2000–2001 outbreak in Uganda, several hundred people were infected, with a fatality rate of about 50%. A more serious outbreak occurred in 2014 in Liberia, Sierra Leone and Guinea. Travellers from those regions carried the virus to the United States, and parts of Europe.

Early symptoms to Ebola infection resemble those of influenza or dysentery. Within about three days of infection, victims develop a fever and weakness, followed by a rash and vomiting. The victim hemorrhages internally, and bleeds from the mouth, eyes, ears, and other body openings. Internal organs shut down, and 50% to 90%

of victims die within one to two weeks after infection. The disease is spread by contact with infected body fluids. Like many RNA viruses, Ebola makes frequent mistakes when it duplicates its RNA. The resulting high mutation rate leads to the rapid development of new strains, making it difficult for researchers to develop an effective vaccine.

—Adapted from Solomon, Berg, and Martin,
Biology (with InfoTrac), 6th ed. © 2002 Brooks/Cole,
a part of Cengage Learning, Inc. Reproduced by
permission. www.cengage.com/permissions

1. Annotate your text; then take notes.

Topic: _____

When did it happen?	What happened?
Early	1. Systems like flu & dysentery.
Within 3 days of infection	2. fever & weakness, rash & vo
	3. rash & vomiting
	4. hemorrhages internally internal organs shut down.
	5. Internal organs shut down.
2 weeks	6. 50-90% of victims die.

_____F_____ 2. According to the passage, there has been difficulty creating an effective vaccine to prevent the spread of Ebola because the majority of research funding is committed to finding a cure for HIV.

_____T_____ 3. The passage suggests that, in its early stages, Ebola might be mistaken for the common flu.

⑥ Comparison and Contrast

Another pattern that you will find in introductory texts is one that relates items according to existing comparisons and contrasts. To enrich your understanding of a topic, items are paired and then similarities or differences are listed.

Topic

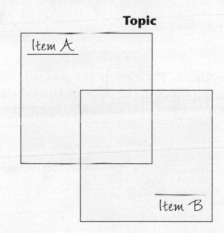

Item A

Item B

Signal Words to Indicate Comparison and Contrast. Signal words often used for comparison or contrast include:

Both

Comparison: *similar*   *like*   *in the same way*   *likewise*

Contrast: *different*   *on the other hand*   *nevertheless*   *however*
           although   *instead*   *conversely*   *but*

Different

Annotate Your Text. After reading the passage, record the topic and then write an abbreviation for similarities or differences in the margin. Circle the items being discussed and underline key words. The following paragraph illustrates the technique.

EXAMPLE   **CHICAGO AND CLEVELAND**

Diff.
Sim.
Sim.

(Chicago), at the southern tip of Lake Michigan, is a port city and an important commercial and industrial center of the Midwest. It is also an important educational, cultural, and recreational center, drawing thousands to its concert halls, art museums, and sports arenas. (Cleveland), on the south shore of Lake Erie, is also a port city and a commercial and industrial center important to its area. Like Chicago, it has several important colleges and universities, a distinguished symphony orchestra, one of the fine art museums of the world, and many recreational centers. The location of the two cities undoubtedly contributed to their growth, but this similarity is not sufficient to explain their wide social diversity.

—*Short Essays*, Seventh Edition, by Gerald Levin

Take Notes. First, write the topics being discussed. Then write the similarities and differences in the appropriate positions in the diagram. Some passages will be mostly comparisons, and some will be mostly contrasts. The following illustration is an example.

Topic: Chicago and Cleveland

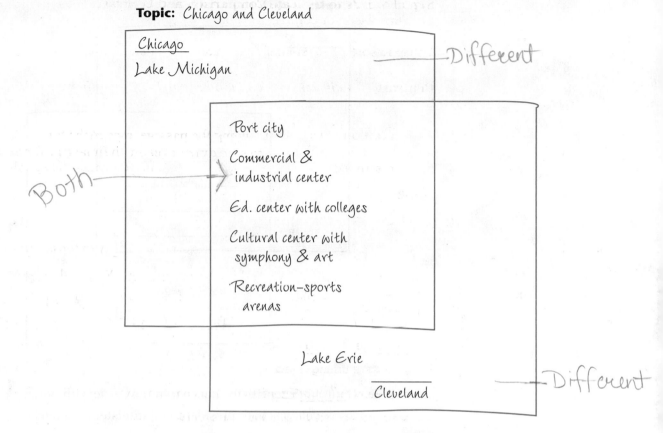

Chicago
Lake Michigan

Port city

Commercial & industrial center

Ed. center with colleges

Cultural center with symphony & art

Recreation–sports arenas

Lake Erie

Cleveland

Different

Both

Different

EXERCISE 10 Read the paragraphs and write the topic at the beginning of the passage. Use an abbreviation to mark similarities or differences, underline key phrases, and then take notes for later study. Respond with *T* (true) or *F* (false) to the comprehension items.

Passage 1

Topic: _____

During World War II, Roosevelt was president of the United States and Churchill was prime minister of England. Both men had similar styles of leadership and were skilled in the uses of power. When in office, Roosevelt asked Congress for broad executive powers to deal with a national emergency even before war was declared. Similarly, Churchill immediately centralized the war in his own hands by becoming both the prime minister and the defense minister. Both leaders had magnetic personalities that drew people to them. Roosevelt was sensitive to people and their dreams, perhaps having learned from his own battle with polio. Churchill was fired with imagination and a love of language. Both were gifted speakers, Roosevelt with his homey illustrations and Churchill with his emotion and vivid imagery.

1. Annotate your text and then take notes. Describe each of the political leaders.

Topic: _WWII_

Roosevelt
    President of U.S.

Style of leardership
magnetic personalities (drew people to them)
gifted speakers
skilled in uses of power
powers to deal with a nation

Prime Minister of England

Churchill

___F___ 2. Churchill's sensitivity came from his battle with polio.
___F___ 3. Roosevelt was both president and minister of defense.

Passage 2

Topic: _Difference b/w new & old economy_

People talk about a new economy—one where the Internet is supposed to change everything. Now some even question whether a "new economy" exists, and if so, how it differs from the old economy.

new — The new economy is less concerned with physical goods. Almost 93 million workers (80 percent of the workforce) do not spend their days making things. Instead they work in jobs that require them to move things, process or generate information, or provide services to peo-

old — ple. In the old economy, information flow was physical: cash, checks, invoices, reports, and face-to-face meetings. But in the new economy, information in all its forms becomes digital.

old — In the old economy, geography played a key role in determining who competed with

new — whom. In the new economy, distance and time differences have vanished. Besides compressing distance, the Internet compresses time. In the new economy, the ability to innovate and get to market faster is a key competitive advantage. Consider this: In less than 18 months after its launch, Hotmail had signed up 12 million subscribers. A few days later its founders sold the company to Microsoft for $400 million in Microsoft stock. Today, with 50 million registered users, Hotmail is the largest Web-based e-mail service in the world.

old

In the old economy, setting up a nursery to sell plants might involve leasing a shed, buying various types of trees and plants, and more. But on the Internet, setting up a nursery can be as simple as registering a domain name, hiring an artist to design some Web pages, and making arrangements with a plant wholesaler. In short, barriers to entry for

new

companies selling over the Internet are virtually nonexistent.

—*Business Today*, Tenth Edition,
by Michael Mescon et al.

1. Annotate your text; then take notes.

Topic: Diff. b/w new & old economics

New economy
less concerned with physical goods
distance & time differences vanished
No geographic boundaries
Things move faster
No barriers

geography played a key role.
cash, checks
Place, store to buy something
Barriers — certain time (open)
Physical goods
old economy

_____F_____ 2. At the time of its purchase by Microsoft, Hotmail had 50 million subscribers.

_____T_____ 3. The author suggests that online nurseries do not need to house their own plants.

7 Cause and Effect

In this pattern, one of several factors, or causes, is shown to lead to or result in certain events or effects. Cause-and-effect patterns can be complex, because a single effect can have multiple causes and one cause can have many effects.

Topic: _____

Cause →	Effect
Why did it happen?	What happened?
→	
→	
→	

Signal Words to Indicate Cause and Effect. Signal words often used to indicate cause and effect include:

for this reason	*consequently*	*on that account*	*thus*
hence	*because*	*made*	*therefore*

Annotate Your Text. Circle the topic and remember that there can be many causes and many effects. Therefore, give both labels and numbers to the causes and effects, as well as underlining key words to explain the items. The following paragraph illustrates the technique.

EXAMPLE **EARLY JOBS**

Cause: (1) summer and (2) after-school jobs

Effects:
1. Money management
2. Skills
3. Belief in work
  a. Anxiety over free time
  b. Guilt over non-work activity

Aside from basic money management, what did I actually learn from all my summer and after-school jobs? Each one may have given me some small skills but the cumulative effect was to deepen my belief that work was the essential aspect of grown-up life. Even now, I am sometimes filled with anxieties at the prospect of stretches of *free time*. When I do not immediately rush to fill that time with work, I have to fight off *guilt*, struggling mentally against a picture of a Real Grown-up shaking a finger at me, someone with the droning voice of our high school career counselor, but with firm overtones of former employers, teachers, even my mother. "This," the voice beats relentlessly into my ear, "is your preparation for life."

—"Blooming: A Small-Town Girlhood,"
by Susan Allen Toth

Take Notes. Write the topic and then write headings to label causes and effects. List and number the causes and effects and add key words that are needed to explain them. Note that an effect may also be the cause of something else. Arrows can indicate these relationships. Here is an example.

Topic: *Effects of early jobs*

Cause → Why did it happen?	Effect What happened?
Summer and after-school jobs →	1. *Money mgt* → 2. *Skills* → 3. *Belief in work as essential* *to adult life* ↓ 4. *Anxiety over fun time;* *guilt over nonwork*

EXERCISE (11) Read the following paragraphs. For each one, write the topic in the answer blank, label the causes and effects, underline key terms, and then take notes for later study. Respond with *T* (True) or *F* (False) to the comprehension items.

Passage 1

Topic: _____

Cause

Have you had your wisdom teeth removed? If you've already suffered through a wisdom tooth extraction, you may have wondered why we even have these extra molars. Biologists think that we have them because our apelike ancestors had them and we inherited them, even though we don't need them. The presence in a living species of structures that have no current essential function, but that are useful in other living species, demonstrates shared ancestry among these species.

The connection between evolutionary ancestry and traits that have no essential function is illustrated by flightless birds such as the ostrich. Ostriches can grow to 8 feet tall and weigh 300 pounds. These massive creatures cannot fly. Nonetheless, they have wings, just as sparrows and ducks do. Why do ostriches have wings? Because the common ancestor of sparrows, ducks, and ostriches had wings, as do all of its descendants, even those that cannot fly. The bodies of today's organisms may contain now-useless hand-me-downs from their ancestors.

—*Biology: Life on Earth*, Tenth Edition, <br> by Teresa Audesirk, Gerald Audesirk, and Bruce E. Byers

1. Annotate your text; then take notes.

Topic: Reasons for the body parts

Cause → Why did it happen?	Effect What happened?
Ancestors have wisdom →	Wisdom Teeth
Common ancestors have wings (birds) →	Ostrich have wings
Ancestors →	Useless body.

<u>T</u> 1. Wisdom teeth in humans have no functional purpose.
<u>F</u> 2. Ostriches have wings and therefore are able to fly.

Passage 2

<u>**Topic:**</u>

Americans are also more conscious of what they are eating. The desire to reduce cholesterol intake has caused a shift away from red meat and dairy products. The trend was substantial enough to cause beef producers to band together and mount an educational campaign to convince consumers that beef is healthful. The trend to healthier foods has primarily affected product rather than promotional strategies. Producers of dairy foods are coming out with lines of low-cholesterol products, cereal companies with high-fiber products, and liquor manufacturers with lower alcohol lines to reflect the trend away from hard liquor.

The combined effects of better medical care and greater health awareness have resulted in increased longevity in the past twenty years. From 1970 to 1990, life expectancy of the average American went from 70 to 76 years, reaching 80 by the turn of the century.

—*Consumer Behavior and Marketing Action,*
Fourth Edition, by Henry Assael

1. Annotate your text; then take notes.

Topic:

Cause → Why did it happen?	Effect What happened?
→	
→	
→	
→	

_____ 2. Americans are eating fewer dairy products.

_____ 3. Eating beef tends to lower cholesterol levels.

Clues to the Organizational Pattern

As shown in the previous explanations, readers have several clues to the organizational pattern of the material that they are reading. Active readers use all of the clues rather than just one because they focus on the meaning.

1. _Transitional words:_ For example, repeated words, such as _because, as a result, therefore, for this reason,_ suggest a cause-and-effect pattern. Be careful, though! Some signal words may be used in several different patterns.
2. _Diagrams or graphic organizers:_ If the details fit into the diagram, the reader has more evidence that the predicted pattern is correct.
3. _Relationship among the details and the main idea:_ This is the most reliable evidence that a reader has to determine the organizational pattern, because it directly reflects the meaning of the material.

Mixed Patterns. In longer reading selections, authors often mix patterns. For example, a simple list pattern may be used in the introductory paragraph, a definition pattern in another paragraph, and a cause-and-effect pattern in yet another paragraph. Rather than be confused by this, readers should keep in mind the overall pattern—the pattern that best develops the author's main point.

EXERCISE 12

Read the following beginning portions of paragraphs. Predict the dominant pattern(s) of organization to be used by the author. Select from the following list:

Simple listing	Classification	Definitions With Examples
Description	Time order, sequence,	Comparison and contrast
Cause and effect	or narration	

1. Many psychologists believe that the basic structure of human personality is represented by five broad factors, known as the Big Five. They are neuroticism, extroversion, openness, agreeableness, and conscientiousness.

—_Human Relations,_ Eighth Edition, by Andrew J. DuBrin

Organizational pattern: _Simple Listing_

2. In some regions, such as Europe and South Asia, it is common for people to cluster in villages and towns; this contrasts with the dispersed settlement pattern of rural North America, where people tend to scatter across the countryside in individual farms and homesteads.

—_Diversity and Globalization,_ Second Edition, by Les Rowntree et al.

Organizational pattern: _Comparision & Contrast_

3. To remain financially sound, Mega Music used the services of _headhunters._ They are paid recruiters who match hiring companies with employees or executives in order

to find a new CEO. The headhunter found a young energetic Yankee named Bill Black. (A *Yankee* is a person from the northeastern region of the United States. The name originated during the Civil War because Yankees were soldiers from the north.)

—*Choices: A Basic Writing Guide with Readings,* Third Edition,
by Kate Mangelsdorf and Evelyn Posey

Organizational pattern: _Definition_____

4. At last all the preparations for my wedding were almost completed and the day was fixed for August 21 of this year 1745. On the eve of the 21st we moved from the Summer to the Winter Palace.

—*Sources of the West: Readings in Western Civilization,*
Sixth Edition, edited by Mark A. Kishlansky

Organizational pattern: _Time Order, sequence, or Narration_

5. Cultivating your spiritual side takes just as much work as becoming physically fit or improving your diet. Here, we discuss how training your body, expanding your mind, tuning in, and reaching out result in spiritual health.

—*Health: The Basics,* Tenth Edition,
by Rebecca J. Donatelle

Organizational pattern: _Cause & effect_____

6. *Comets* are small ice bodies that formed in the outer solar system. Some have elliptical orbits that take them near the Sun.

—*Earth's Dynamic Systems,* Ninth Edition,
by W. Kenneth Hamblin and Eric H. Christiansen

Organizational pattern: _Description/ Definition_____

7. Prison society is strict and often unforgiving. Even so, inmates are able to express some individuality through the choice of a prison lifestyle. John Irwin viewed these lifestyles (like the subcultures of which they are a part) as adaptations to the prison environment.

—*Criminal Justice Today: An Introductory Text for the 21st Century,*
Twelfth Edition, by Frank Schmalleger

Organizational pattern: _Description_____

8. In her classic study of traditional marriage, Jessie Bernard (1982) explained that men experience marriage as the responsibility to provide economic support for the family and the power to make key decisions. In contrast, women experience marriage as providing emotional support to husbands and raising children, sometimes to the point that they have little identity of their own.

—*Social Problems,* Fifth Edition, by John J. Macionis

Organizational pattern: _Contrast & Comparison_____

9. A new cycle began in October when peasants prepared the ground for the planting of winter crops. In November came the slaughter of excess livestock because there was usually insufficient food to keep animals all winter. In February and March, the land was plowed for spring crops—oats, barley, peas, beans, and lentils.

—Western Civilization I: To 1715, Fifth Edition,
by Jackson J. Spielvogel

Organizational pattern: _Time Order experience or Narration_

10. According to crime reports, individuals were the most common target of robbers. Banks, gas stations, convenience stores, and other businesses were the second most common target. Residential robberies accounted for only 13.5% of the total.

—Criminal Justice Today: An Introductory Text for the
Twenty-First Century, Eighth Edition, by Frank Schmalleger

Organizational pattern: _Simple listing_

SUMMARY POINTS

1 How can I distinguish major and minor details? (page 246)

Recognize the varying levels of importance among ideas. Use diagrams and outlines to visualize them.

Major details are essential to support, explain, develop, or prove the main point. Minor details provide interesting and memorable examples of the major details but provide secondary support of the main idea.

2 How can I follow written directions accurately? (page 255)

Attend carefully to all of the details. Every detail is of the same importance in written directions, unlike in typical prose.

3 How can I identify the seven common organizational patterns? (page 259)

Notice the transitional words that typically are used with each pattern. Picture the graphic organizer for the pattern to see if the details fit.

Simple listing: Items of equal value are listed in a passage. Their order does not matter.

Classification: The divisions or categories are named, and the parts are explained.

Definition with examples: A new term is defined, and examples are added for clarification.

Description: This pattern is like a simple list of characteristics that describe something, such as an object or a person.

Time order, sequence, or narration: Events and when they occurred are the focus of the passage.

Comparison and contrast: Items are compared or contrasted to show how they are alike or different.

Cause and effect: Events and their causes are the focus of the passage.

4 How can the pattern help me annotate my text and take notes? (page 261)

Recognizing the pattern requires that the reader look more carefully for the important details. A system of circling, underlining, and numbering makes sense when the pattern is determined. For example, in a time order pattern, it makes sense to circle the time indicators and underline what happened.

Use your annotations and the appropriate graphic organizer to create good study notes.

Form a five-member group and select one of the following activities. Brainstorm and then outline your major points. Present the group findings to the class.

➤ Write step-by-step directions for leaving your classroom and going to a place on campus to eat lunch.

➤ Create a diagram that shows several categories and subcategories for elected state government officials.

➤ Create a list or diagram of ideas that compares and contrasts your college with another college in the state.

➤ Provide two opening sentences stating the main idea for passages with a simple listing pattern of organization and two for a sequence pattern.

PERSONAL FEEDBACK 1   Name _____

1. In this class, who would you feel comfortable calling for assignment information?
   _____
   _____

2. What organizations have you joined?_____
   _____
   _____

3. What campus events or social functions have you attended?_____
   _____
   _____

4. What volunteer work have you recently done on or off campus?_____
   _____
   _____

5. What would make you feel bonded to your college?_____
   _____
   _____

                          Share your responses as directed by your instructor.

SELECTION 1 Communication   MyReadingLab™

Visit Chapter 6: Supporting Details and Organizational Patterns in MyReadingLab to complete the Selection 1 activities.

"He that is good for making excuses is seldom good for anything else."
— Benjamin Franklin

We've all made excuses for our behavior, and sometimes they are true. Sometimes they are lies, and we even convince ourselves that they justify our behavior. Do excuses really excuse what we've done, or would it be better to skip them and go straight to an apology? Sincere apologies have a way of doing what an excuse rarely does—easing a situation that we've created, healing a relationship, and maybe even making us better people. Yet, it is likely that most of us will continue to offer excuses, so here is one by novelist Patricia Briggs that just might work. Try it the next time that you need a good excuse and see what happens. At least it might get a laugh: "A werewolf tossed me against a giant packing crate while I was trying to rescue a frightened young girl who'd been kidnapped by an evil witch and a drug lord."

THINKING BEFORE READING

Preview the selection for clues to the content. Activate your prior knowledge. Anticipate what is coming and think about your purpose for reading.

Is there such a thing as a good excuse?

What constitutes a good apology?

How does it feel when someone accepts your sincere apology?

I want to learn _____.

VOCABULARY PREVIEW

Are you familiar with these words?

counter	typologies	alibi	acknowledge	justification
extenuating	explicitly	legitimacy	minimize	mode

Does *counter* have several meanings?

Is it best to state our thoughts *explicitly*?

What does the word part *typo* contribute to the meaning of *typologies*?

Your instructor may choose to give a brief vocabulary review before or after reading.

THINKING DURING READING

As you read, use the six thinking strategies of a good reader: predict, picture, relate, monitor, correct, and annotate.

Refer to the
Reader's TIP
for **Reading and
Studying Communi-
cation** on page 116

EXCUSES AND APOLOGIES —*Title*

Definitions & examples

Despite your best efforts, there are times when you'll say or do the wrong thing and an excuse and/or an apology may be necessary. **Excuses** are *explanations* designed to reduce the negative effects of your behavior and help to maintain your positive image. **Apologies,** *DEF* on the other hand, are *expressions of regret or sorrow* for having done what you did or for

5   what happened. Often the two are blended—*I didn't realize how fast I was driving* (the excuse); *I'm really sorry* (the apology). Let's separate them and look first at the excuse.

I   THE EXCUSE
Cause & Effect

Excuses seem especially in order when you say or are accused of saying something that runs counter to what is expected or considered "right" by the people with whom you're talking. Ideally, the excuse lessens the negative impact of the message.

10   The major motive for excuse making seems to be to maintain your self-esteem and to project a positive image to yourself and to others. Excuses also represent an effort to reduce stress: You may feel that if you can offer an excuse—especially a good one that is accepted by those around you—it will reduce the negative reaction and the stress that accompanies a poor performance.

15   Excuses also may enable you to maintain effective interpersonal relationships even after some negative behavior. For example, after criticizing a friend's behavior and observing the negative reaction to your criticism, you might offer an excuse such as, "Please forgive me; I'm really exhausted. I'm just not thinking straight." Excuses enable you to place your messages—even your possible failures—in a more favorable light.

A   TYPES OF EXCUSES
Classification

20   Different researchers have classified excuses into varied categories. One of the best typologies classifies excuses into three main types:

1 and • **I didn't do it:** Here you deny that you have done what you're being accused of. You may then bring up an alibi to prove you couldn't have done it or perhaps you may accuse another person of doing what you're being blamed for ("I never said that" or

25   "I wasn't even near the place when it happened"). These "I didn't do it" types are generally the worst excuses (unless they're true), because they fail to acknowledge responsibility and offer no assurance that this failure will not happen again.

2 • **It wasn't so bad:** Here you admit to doing it but claim the offense was not really so bad or perhaps that there was justification for the behavior ("I only padded the

30   expense account by a few bucks").

3 • **Yes, but:** Here you claim that extenuating circumstances accounted for the behavior; for example, that you weren't in control of yourself at the time or that you didn't intend to do what you did ("I never intended to hurt him; I was actually trying to help").

B   GOOD AND BAD EXCUSES

35   The most important question for most people is what makes a good excuse and what makes a bad excuse. How can you make good excuses and thus get out of problems, and how can you avoid bad excuses that only make matters worse?

What makes one excuse effective and another ineffective will vary from one culture to another and will depend on factors already discussed, such as the culture's individualism

40   or collectivism, its power distance, the values it places on assertiveness, and various other cultural tendencies. But, at least in the United States, researchers seem to agree that in the best excuses in interpersonal communication you do the following.

1. Demonstrate that you really understand the problem and that your partner's feelings are legitimate and justified. Avoid minimizing the issue or your partner's feelings ("It

45   was only $100; you're overreacting," "I was only two hours late").

2. Acknowledge your responsibility. If you did something wrong, avoid qualifying your responsibility ("I'm sorry if I did anything wrong") or expressing a lack of sincerity ("Okay, I'm sorry; it's obviously my fault—again"). On the other hand, if you can demonstrate that you had no control over what happened and therefore cannot be
50   held responsible, your excuse is likely to be highly persuasive.

3. Acknowledge your own displeasure at what you did, your unhappiness for having done what you did.

4. Make it clear that your misdeed will never happen again.

II THE APOLOGY (Def)

In its most basic form, an apology is an expression of regret for something you did; it's a
55   statement that you're sorry. And so, the most basic of all apologies is simply: "I'm sorry." In popular usage, the apology includes some admission of wrongdoing on the part of the person making the apology. Sometimes the wrongdoing is acknowledged explicitly ("I'm sorry I lied") and sometimes only by implication ("I'm sorry you're so upset").

    A In many cases the apology also includes a request for forgiveness ("Please forgive my
60   lateness") and some assurance that this won't happen again ("Please forgive my lateness; it won't happen again").

    B According to the Harvard Business School Working Knowledge website, apologies are useful for two main reasons. Apologies (1) help repair your relationships (as you can easily imagine) and, perhaps less obviously, (2) repair your reputation. So, if you do something
65   wrong in your relationship, for example, an apology will help you repair the relationship with your partner and perhaps reduce the level of conflict. At the same time, however, realize that other people know about your behavior and an apology will help improve their image of you.

    C An effective apology, like an effective excuse, must be crafted for the specific situ-
70   ation. An effective apology to a long-time lover, to a parent, or to a new supervisor are likely to be very different because the individuals are different and your relationships are different. And so, the first rule of an effective apology is to take into consideration the uniqueness of the situation—the people, the context, the cultural rules, the relationship,

the specific wrongdoing—for which you might want to apologize. Each situation will call
75 for a somewhat different message of apology. Nevertheless, we can offer some general
recommendations.

1 • **Admit wrongdoing** (if indeed wrongdoing occurred). Accept responsibility. Own
your own actions; don't try to pass them off as the work of someone else. Instead of
Smith drives so slow, it's a wonder I'm only 30 minutes late, say *I should have taken traffic*
80 *into consideration.*

2 • **Be apologetic**. Say (and mean) the words *I'm sorry*. Don't justify your behavior by
mentioning that everyone does it, for example, *Everyone leaves work early on Friday*.
Don't justify your behavior by saying that the other person has done something
equally wrong: *So I play poker; you play the lottery.*

85 3 • **Be specific**. State, in specific rather than general terms, what you've done. Instead of
I'm sorry for what I did, say *I'm sorry for flirting at the party.*

4 • **Express understanding** of how the other person feels and acknowledge the legitimacy of these feelings (for example, *You have every right to be angry; I should have*
called). Express your regret that this has created a problem for the other person (*I'm*
90 *sorry I made you miss your appointment*). Don't minimize the problem that this may
have caused. Avoid such comments as, *So the figures arrived a little late. What's the*
big deal?

5 • **Give assurance that this will not happen again**. Say, quite simply, *It won't happen*
again or better and more specifically, *I won't be late again*. And, whenever possible,
95 offer to correct the problem, *I'm sorry I didn't clean up the mess I made; I'll do it now.*

6 • **Omit the excuses**. Be careful of including excuses with your apology; for example,
I'm sorry the figures are late but I had so much other work to do. An excuse often takes
back the apology and says, in effect, I'm really not sorry because there was good reason for what I did but I'm saying "I'm sorry" to cover all my bases and to make this
100 uncomfortable situation go away.

7 • **Don't take the easy way out** and apologize through e-mail (unless the wrongdoing
was committed in e-mail or if e-mail is your only or main form of communication).
Generally, it's more effective to use a more personal mode of communication—face-
to-face or phone, for example. It's harder but it's more effective.

(1,315 words)

—From *The Interpersonal Communication Book*, Thirteenth Edition,
by Joseph A. DeVito

THINKING AND WRITING AFTER READING

RECALL   Self-test your understanding.

Your instructor may choose to give you a brief comprehension review.

REACT   Is it ever acceptable to offer an excuse? Explain. _____

_____

_____

REFLECT   How do you react when someone sincerely apologizes for behavior that
has hurt you?_____

_____

_____

THINK CRITICALLY   Consider this situation: Your best friend picked you up for
work, and you weren't ready. In fact, you were so late that the boss scolded both
of you and docked your pay. What responsibility do you have in this situation?
What will you do?_____

_____

_____

_____

THINK AND WRITE Describe a situation when you have been at fault for something that upset or hurt a friend, family member, or coworker. _____

_____

_____

EXTENDED WRITING Using the situation that you described above, draft a letter in which you give a sincere apology for your behavior. Check it against the recommendations in the reading selection and revise it, if necessary. Conclude with what you hope the effect of the apology will be.

DETAILS AND ORGANIZATIONAL PATTERNS

Mark the following as major (*M*) or minor (*m*) details in support of the author's main point.

_____ 1. There are several types of excuses.

_____ 2. The qualities of good and bad excuses

_____ 3. Acknowledge your responsibility when you offer an excuse.

_____ 4. An effective apology must be crafted for the situation.

_____ 5. Apologies can repair your relationships.

6. What is the pattern of organization of the first paragraph?

_____

_____

7. What is the pattern of organization of the first three paragraphs in the section, "The Excuse"? _____

8. What is the pattern of organization of the section, "Types of Excuses? _____

_____

Interpret THE QUOTE

Now that you've finished reading the selection, "Excuses and Apologies," go back to the beginning of the selection and read the opening quote again. Do you agree with it? Why or why not?

Name ———————————————————

Date ———————————————————

COMPREHENSION QUESTIONS

Answer the following with *a*, *b*, *c*, or *d*, or fill in the blank. In order to help you analyze your strengths and weaknesses, the question types are indicated.

Main Idea ———— 1. The best statement of the main idea of this selection is

    a. Everyone has times when an excuse and/or an apology is necessary.

    b. An apology is an expression of regret for something you did.

    c. Excuses and apologies can be delivered in ineffective and effective ways.

    d. Several recommendations can make an apology more effective.

Detail ———— 2. According to the article, which is usually the worst kind of excuse— unless it is true?

    a. "Yes, but"

    b. "I didn't do it."

    c. "It wasn't so bad."

    d. A humorous one

Detail ———— 3. The author states that the primary reason for making an excuse is

    a. to maintain self-esteem and project a positive image.

    b. to reduce the stress of a making a mistake.

    c. to reduce the negative reaction of others.

    d. to maintain positive relationships.

Inference ———— 4. Which of the following statements is a logical conclusion from the selection?

    a. Excuses are rarely, perhaps never, effective or appropriate.

    b. The most effective excuses and apologies are honest and sincere.

    c. Apologies always contain a request for forgiveness.

    d. Excuses almost always contain an apology.

Main Idea ———— 5. Which statement best expresses the main point of the section, "The Apology"?

    a. An apology is a statement that you're sorry.

    b. Apologies are useful for two main reasons.

    c. Apologies heal relationships.

    d. Effective apologies have several characteristics and serve several purposes.

Author's purpose ———— 6. Which of the following best describes the purpose of this selection?

    a. to amuse readers with humorous excuses

    b. to give readers ideas about good and poor excuses

    c. to provide information about excuses and apologies

    d. to encourage readers to apologize for wrongdoing

Inference _____ 7. Details in the section, "Good and Bad Excuses," suggest that

    a. some factors about culture were discussed in an earlier part of this textbook.

    b. if you had no control over the situation, the excuse still would not likely be convincing.

    c. it is best to avoid showing that you are not happy with your behavior.

    d. culture has little to do with the effectiveness of an excuse.

Answer the following questions with *T* (true) or *F* (false).

Inference _____ 8. The list of qualities of the best excuses is based on research in all cultures, not just American culture.

Detail _____ 9. According to the article, the first rule for effective apologies is to remember that every situation is different and calls for a different approach.

Detail _____ 10. The author states that it is best to apologize in person.

VOCABULARY

Answer the following with *a, b, c,* or *d* for the word or phrase that best defines the boldface word used in the selection. The number in parentheses indicates the line of the passage in which the word appears. In addition to the context clues, use a dictionary to more precisely define the technical terms.

_____ 1. "**counter** to what's expected" (8)

    a. similarly
    b. like a table
    c. opposed to
    d. exactly

_____ 2. "one of the best **typologies**" (20–21)

    a. proposals
    b. descriptions
    c. classifications
    d. explanations

_____ 3. "bring up an **alibi**" (23)

    a. explanation
    b. scenario
    c. lawyer
    d. story

_____ 4. "fail to **acknowledge**" (26)

    a. refuse
    b. ignore
    c. greet
    d. accept

_____ 5. "there was **justification**" (29)

    a. circumstance
    b. good reason
    c. time
    d. purpose

_____ 6. "**extenuating** circumstances" (31)

    a. apologizing
    b. difficult
    c. truthful
    d. justifying

_____ 7. "is acknowledged **explicitly**" (57)

    a. indirectly
    b. clearly
    c. subtly
    d. partly

_____ 8. "the **legitimacy** of these feelings" (87–88)

    a. shamefulness
    b. harshness
    c. joyfulness
    d. rightfulness

_____ 9. "**minimize** the problem" (90)

    a. maximize
    b. worsen
    c. accept
    d. reduce

_____ 10. "**mode** of communication" (103)

    a. style
    b. language
    c. sign
    d. gesture

Your instructor may choose to give a brief vocabulary review.

VOCABULARY ENRICHMENT

Transitional Words

Transitions are signal words that connect parts of sentences and lead readers to anticipate a continuation or a change in the writer's thoughts. They are the same signal words that suggest patterns of organization and are categorized as follows:

Signal *Addition*: in addition   furthermore   moreover

Signal *Examples*: for example   for instance   to illustrate   such as

Signal *Time*: first   secondly   finally   last   afterward

Signal *Comparison*: similarly   likewise   in the same manner

Signal *Contrast*: however   but   nevertheless   whereas   on the contrary   conversely   in contrast

Signal *Cause and effect*: thus   consequently   therefore   as a result

Choose a signal word from the following words to complete the sentences:

however   consequently   for example   likewise   furthermore

1. Betty Shabazz, the widow of Malcolm X, recognized the value of a college education; _____, she returned to college to earn a doctorate and became a college teacher and administrator.

2. Anthropologists must be persistent. _____, Louis and Mary Leakey initially found primitive tools in Olduvai Gorge, but it was 28 years later that Mary discovered the first skull.

3. His real name was Samuel Langhorne Clemens; _____, millions know him as Mark Twain.

4. Plant hormones that regulate growth include auxins and gibberellins. _____, humans have important growth hormones.

5. People enjoy eating steaks rare. _____, some people use raw steak to cover an open wound, as did the ancient Egyptians.

Choose a signal word from the following words to complete the sentences:

nevertheless	therefore	in this case	similarly	moreover

6. Some vitamins act as antioxidants, which means they neutralize free radicals and _____ reduce the risk of cancer.

7. _____, despite the benefits of antioxidants, new research shows a danger because some minerals in multivitamins cause vitamin C to be released as a free radical.

8. More research on vitamins should be done. _____, doctors should be cautious in recommending vitamins that may not be needed.

9. At least five people were dead from botulism. _____, the poison could be traced to a swollen can of food that should have been discarded.

10. Hornwort is a bryophyta. _____, liverwort is also a bryophyta.

Choose a signal word from the following words to complete the sentences:

on the other hand	for this reason	second
as an illustration	by the same token	

11. A cut in the skin breaks the protective covering around the body and _____ can be dangerous.

12. To give CPR, first lift the neck and tilt the chin upward to open the airway. _____, check for breathing by holding your ear to the victim's mouth.

13. Dogs can be conditioned to respond to smell. _____, humans will sometimes salivate when smelling cookies baking.

14. Abnormal pituitary secretions can cause sudden increases in hormone production. Acromegaly, _____, is a condition known as dwarfism.

15. Plants store glucose in starch granules. Animals, _____, store glucose in glycogen molecules.

ASSESS YOUR LEARNING

Review confusing questions, seek clarification, and make notes in your text to help you remember new information and vocabulary. Use your textbook as a learning tool.

Visit Chapter 6: Supporting Details and Organizational Patterns in MyReadingLab to complete the Selection 2 activities.

> "I now say that the world has the technology that is either available or well advanced in the research pipeline to feed a population of 10 billion people."
> —Norman E. Borlaug, Nobel Prize Laureate for Peace, 1970

Farmers, and agriculture in general, aim to grow as much food as possible and to do it as cheaply as possible. Increasing crop size and quality, improving disease resistance, and controlling insects have always been critical elements. Traditional methods include selecting seed from the strongest plants, creating hybrid plants, and using chemicals to decrease damage from disease and pests. Today, however, biotechnology is able to move at a much faster pace through genetic engineering—changing the genetic structure of plants. Genetically modified organisms (GMOs), plants, in the case of farming, result in good crops that resist disease and pests. Scientists create GMOs by isolating, changing, or combining genes from one organism and inserting them into a host organism. The result is a new version of the host that has the desired traits. Almost all of the corn, cotton, and soybeans grown in the United States is genetically modified. Like many advances in technology, GMOs are controversial. Some people fear they can have negative effects, especially on the environment, but they can also do great good.

THINKING BEFORE READING

Preview the selection for clues to the content. Activate your prior knowledge. Anticipate what is coming and think about your purpose for reading.

Have you heard of genetically modified organisms (GMOs)?

What might be the positive effects of GMOs?

Can you imagine that bioengineering might be a solution to world hunger?

I want to learn _____.

VOCABULARY PREVIEW

Are you familiar with these words?

carbohydrates	deficiency	daffodils	genome	synthesis
transgenic	malnutrition	nutrients	humanitarian	supplementation

Is a steak or a bowl of rice a better source of *carbohydrates*?

Do *daffodils* bloom in the spring?

What do the prefixes *syn*, *trans*, and *mal* mean in *synthesis*, *transgenic*, and *malnutrition*?

Your instructor may choose to give a brief vocabulary review before or after reading.

THINKING DURING READING

As you read, use the six thinking strategies of a good reader: predict, picture, relate, monitor, correct, and annotate.

GOLDEN RICE

Refer to the
Reader's **TIP**
for **Reading and
Studying Science**
on page 66.

Rice is the principal food for about two-thirds of the people on Earth. Rice provides carbohydrates and some protein, but it is a poor source of many vitamins, including vitamin A. Unless people eat enough fruits and vegetables, they often lack sufficient vitamin A and may suffer from poor vision, immune system defects, and damage to their respiratory, digestive, and urinary tracts. According to the World Health Organization, more than 100 million children suffer from vitamin A deficiency. As a result, each year 250,000 to 500,000 children become blind, principally in Asia, Africa, and Latin America; half of those children die. Vitamin A deficiency typically strikes the poor, because rice may be all they can afford to eat. In 1999, biotechnology provided a possible remedy: rice genetically engineered to contain beta-carotene, a pigment that makes daffodils bright yellow and that the human body easily converts into vitamin A.

Creating a rice strain with high levels of beta-carotene wasn't simple. However, funding from the Rockefeller Institute, the European Community Biotech Program, and the Swiss Federal Office for Education and Science enabled molecular biologists Ingo Potrykus and Peter Beyer to tackle the task. They inserted three genes into the rice genome, two from daffodils and one from a bacterium. As a result, "Golden Rice" grains synthesize beta-carotene.

The trouble was, the original Golden Rice didn't make very much beta-carotene, so people would have had to eat enormous amounts to get enough vitamin A. The Golden Rice community didn't give up. It turns out that daffodils aren't the best source for genes that direct beta-carotene synthesis. Golden Rice 2, with genes from corn, produces over 20 times more beta-carotene than the original Golden Rice does, and consequently is bright yellow. About 2 cups of cooked Golden Rice 2 should provide enough beta-carotene to equal the full recommended daily amount of vitamin A. Golden Rice 2 was given, free, to the Humanitarian Rice Board *for* experiments and planting in Southeast Asia.

However, Golden Rice faces other hurdles. Many people strongly resist large-scale planting of Golden Rice (or other transgenic crops). Getting Golden Rice genes into the popular Asian strains required years of traditional genetic crosses. By 2007, the International Rice Research Institute succeeded in incorporating the carotene-synthesizing genes
30 of Golden Rice into Asian rice strains, and the first field trials of these Golden Rice varieties began in the Philippines in April 2008. Locally adapted strains of Golden Rice 2 are expected to be available for farmers in the Philippines to plant in 2013.

Is Golden Rice the best way, or the only way, to solve the problems of malnutrition in poor people? Perhaps not. For one thing, many poor people's diets are deficient
35 in many nutrients, not just vitamin A. To help solve that problem, the Bill and Melinda Gates Foundation is funding research to increase the levels of vitamin E, iron, and zinc in rice. Further, not all poor people eat mostly rice. In parts of Africa, sweet potatoes are the main source of calories. Eating orange, instead of white, sweet potatoes, has dramatically increased vitamin A intake for many of these people. Finally, in many parts of the world,
40 governments and humanitarian organizations have started vitamin A supplementation programs. In some parts of Africa and Asia, as many as 80% of the children receive large doses of vitamin A a few times when they are very young. Someday, the combination of these efforts may result in a world in which no children suffer blindness from the lack of a simple nutrient in their diets.

(590 words)

—From *Biology: Life on Earth*, Tenth Edition, by Teresa Audesirk, Gerald Audesirk, and Bruce E. Byers

THINKING AND WRITING AFTER READING

RECALL   Self-test your understanding.

Your instructor may choose to give you a brief comprehension review.

REACT   Why might people object to genetically modified foods such as Golden Rice? _____

_____

_____

REFLECT   What good might come from genetically modified foods like Golden Rice?_____

_____

_____

THINK CRITICALLY   Does the good of relieving hunger outweigh possible environmental harm that might come from genetically modified foods? Explain your answer. _____

_____

_____

_____

THINK AND WRITE   Make notes in the Cornell style or in outline form to record and organize the details of this selection._____

_____

_____

_____

EXTENDED WRITING Use your notes to write a one-paragraph summary of the selection. Remember that the first sentence should express the main point of the article.

DETAILS AND ORGANIZATIONAL PATTERNS

Mark the following as major (*M*) or minor (*m*) details in support of the author's main point.

_____ 1. Scientists successfully created the first version of Golden Rice using daffodil genes.

_____ 2. Golden Rice 2, the second version, incorporated corn genes.

_____ 3. Lack of vitamin A can cause urinary tract infections.

_____ 4. Funding was provided by the Rockefeller Institute, the European Community Biotech Program, and the Swiss Federal Office for Education and Science.

_____ 5. Carotene-synthesizing genes of Golden Rice were finally incorporated into Asian rice in 2007, and field trials began in 2008.

6. What is the pattern of organization of paragraph 1?

_____

7. What is the pattern of organization of paragraph 4? _____

Interpret THE QUOTE

Now that you've finished reading the selection, "Golden Rice," go back to the beginning of the selection and read the opening quote again and notice its author. Do the author's credentials give the statement more credibility?

Name ——————————————

Date ——————————————

COMPREHENSION QUESTIONS

Answer the following with *a, b, c,* or *d,* or fill in the blank. In order to help you analyze your strengths and weaknesses, the question types are indicated.

Main Idea ———— 1. The best statement of the main idea of this selection is

    a. Every year, 250,000 to 500,000 children in Asia, Africa, and Latin America become blind due to vitamin A deficiency.

    b. Vitamin A deficiency is a terrible health problem in many parts of the world.

    c. Golden Rice was bioengineered to contain enough beta-carotene to prevent vitamin A deficiency in malnourished people.

    d. Golden Rice 2 was due to become available to farmers in the Philippines in 2013.

Detail ———— 2. How much Golden Rice 2 provides enough beta-carotene to make a full day's recommended amount of vitamin A?

    a. 1 cup

    b. 2 cups

    c. 3 cups

    d. 4 cups

Detail ———— 3. What is one reason that Golden Rice 2 isn't the only way to solve world malnutrition?

    a. It doesn't contain as much beta-carotene as it should.

    b. Corn is a better source of beta-carotene than daffodils.

    c. More than 100 million children worldwide suffer from vitamin A deficiency.

    d. Rice is not the main food for people in many parts of the world.

Inference ———— 4. From the details in the selection, we can infer that

    a. private businesses were mainly responsible for the development of Golden Rice.

    b. government and humanitarian organizations provided most of the funding to support the development of Golden Rice.

    c. private companies have no interest in the success of Golden Rice.

    d. Golden Rice will never be successful in Asia.

Main Idea ———— 5. Which statement best expresses the main point of the last paragraph?

    a. Other projects are under way throughout the world to address the problems of malnutrition.

    b. Golden Rice is the best way to solve the problems of malnutrition.

    c. Someday no one will suffer from hunger or malnutrition.

    d. The Gates Foundation is funding research to increase other nutrients in rice.

SELECTION 2

Author's purpose   _____   6. Which of the following best describes the purpose of this selection?

a. to convince readers to support the development of Golden Rice

b. to provide an entertaining reading experience

c. to inform readers of efforts to address malnutrition through development of genetically engineered rice

d. to persuade readers that genetic engineering is a poor way to address world hunger

Inference   _____   7. Details in the last paragraph suggest that

a. the large doses of vitamin A for children in Africa and Asia are not delivered in food.

b. people in Africa no longer eat white sweet potatoes.

c. Golden Rice will not be used in Asia to address vitamin A deficiency.

d. increasing levels of vitamin E, iron, and zinc in rice are a higher priority than increasing vitamin A.

Answer the following questions with *T* (true) or *F* (false).

Inference   _____   8. It was difficult to incorporate Golden Rice genes into popular types of Asian rice.

Detail   _____   9. Eating orange sweet potatoes has increased vitamin A intake for poor people in Africa.

Detail   _____   10. Golden Rice was provided free of charge for planting in Southeast Asia.

VOCABULARY

Answer the following with *a*, *b*, *c*, or *d* for the word or phrase that best defines the boldface word used in the selection. The number in parentheses indicates the line of the passage in which the word appears. In addition to the context clues, use a dictionary to more precisely define the technical terms.

_____   1. "rice provides **carbohydrates**" (1–2)

a. proteins
b. starches
c. vitamin E
d. salt

_____   2. "vitamin A **deficiency**" (6)

a. surplus
b. poisoning
c. shortage
d. cravings

_____   3. "makes **daffodils** bright" (10)

a. roselike flowers
b. popular Christmas flowers
c. unusual blue flowers
d. trumpet-shaped spring flowers

_____   4. "into the rice **genome**" (15)

a. mature grain head
b. full-grown plant
c. chemical fluids
d. chromosomes and genes

SELECTION 2

_____ 5. "beta-carotene **synthesis**"
(21)
a. production
b. loss
c. analysis
d. supply

_____ 6. "other **transgenic**
crops" (27)
a. containing genes
from different species
b. abnormal
c. having a single genetic history
d. highly nutritious

_____ 7. "problems of
malnutrition" (33–34)
a. illness
b. starvation
c. poverty
d. crop failure

_____ 8. "in many **nutrients**"
(35)
a. vitamin A
b. proteins
c. nourishing substances
in food
d. sugars

_____ 9. "**humanitarian**
organizations" (40)
a. profit-making
b. social
c. professional
d. caring

_____ 10. "**supplementation**
programs" (40)
a. feeding
b. additions to make
up for a lack
c. health care
d. pregnancy and
childbirth

Your instructor may choose to give a brief vocabulary review.

VOCABULARY ENRICHMENT

A. Study the similar-sounding words and then circle the one that is correct in each sentence.

alter: change	**coarse:** not smooth	**dual:** two
altar: platform in church	**course:** studies or path	**duel:** fight

1. You must (**alter, altar**) your study habits to make better grades.

2. To change a (**coarse, course**), you must go through a drop/add procedure.

3. The two senators fought a (**dual, duel**) at dawn.

B. Use context clues to mark _a, b, c,_ or _d_ for the meaning closest to that of the boldface word.

_____ 4. From listening to her talk about the trip, I got a **vicarious** pleasure and felt as if I had been there.
a. selfish
b. enormous
c. secret
d. secondhand

_____ 5. The **cardiac** patient was waiting in surgery for a bypass operation.

    a. rested

    b. cancer

    c. emotion

    d. heart

_____ 6. Because of his **phobia**, he did not want to climb to the top of the tower and look down.

    a. rash

    b. fear

    c. disease

    d. mood

C. Use the indicated root to write words to complete each sentence in the groups.
vis, vid: see

7. When she plays tennis, she wears a _____ to keep the sun out of her eyes.

8. From the description you have given me, I cannot _____ the actor's face.

9. The rip was so well mended that the hole is now _____.

tin, ten, tent: hold, hold together

10. We cannot _____ the trip without stopping for gas.

11. The _____ crew cleans the floors at night when no one is in the building.

12. She has been _____ at her present job for a long time and is thus seeking other employment.

clud, clus: shut

13. She gradually became a _____ by staying in the house and not receiving visitors.

14. To _____ the interview, the manager stood up and shook her hand.

15. A correct address should _____ the zip code.

ASSESS YOUR LEARNING

Review confusing questions, seek clarification, and make notes in your text to help you remember new information and vocabulary. Use your textbook as a learning tool.

SELECTION 3   Business   MyReadingLab™

Visit Chapter 6: Supporting Details and Organizational Patterns in MyReadingLab to complete the Selection 3 activities and Building Background Knowledge video activity.

"Hope for the best, but prepare for the worst."

—English Proverb

Preparing for an interview can be challenging. Interviewees often practice answering questions and think about how to present themselves in the best possible light for the jobs they are seeking. Occasionally, a question might be asked that not only borders on the personal but might actually be against the law.

THINKING BEFORE READING

Preview the selection for clues to the content. Activate your prior knowledge. Anticipate what is coming and think about your purpose for reading.

What is your experience with job interviews?

What interview questions are legal, and which questions are not?

How might you respond to an illegal question without ruining your chances of getting a job?

I want to learn _____.

BUILDING BACKGROUND KNOWLEDGE — VIDEO

Interview Tips for College Students

To prepare for reading Selection 3, answer the questions below. Then, watch this video for a few do's and don'ts of interviewing for a job.

Name one thing you should not do when interviewing for a job.

Name one thing that would make you more successful when interviewing for a job.

What particular mistakes is a young college student more likely to make in a job interview?

This video helped me _____.

VOCABULARY PREVIEW

Are you familiar with these words?

intrusion	discrimination	plethora	litigious	plaintiff
severity	prerequisite	haunt	snarlish	naturalization

Is an *intrusion* something that is unwelcome?

If something is *litigious,* does it have something to do with the law?

Was a *naturalized* United States citizen born in this country?

Your instructor may choose to give a brief vocabulary review before or after reading.

THINKING DURING READING

As you read, use the six thinking strategies of a good reader: predict, picture, relate, monitor, correct, and annotate.

WHEN INTERVIEW QUESTIONS TURN ILLEGAL

Refer to the
Reader's **TIP**
for **Reading and Studying Business** on page 107.

You're probably aware that interviewers are not supposed to ask you certain questions. There are five areas of special sensitivity in selection interviewing. Our goal here is twofold: to point out these illegal areas of questions, and to suggest strategic ways to handle them if they occur in your interview.

5   Our aim here is not to turn you into a "legal eagle" on constant alert for any cause to accuse or sue an interviewing company. In truth, many instances of illegal interview questions (such as, "Are you married?") occur in the course of ordinary getting-to-know-you small talk during an interview and aren't intended by the interviewer as an intrusion into your privacy. But innocent or not, illegal interview questions can land a company in court
10   when a job seeker claims discrimination in the interview process.

Learning to avoid illegal questions as an interviewer and handling them well as an interviewee is the focus of what follows.

WHO MAKES THE RULES FOR INTERVIEW QUESTIONS?

No single federal, state, or local agency or court defines for all cases which interview questions are legal or illegal. Instead, a plethora of court rulings, legislative decisions,
15   agency regulations, and constitutional laws combine to produce the often confusing and frequently changing list of what you can and can't ask a job applicant.

HOW TO ANSWER DIFFICULT QUESTIONS

Following are our suggestions for some of the more difficult areas in which the employer must exercise caution when asking questions—and you must be equally careful in how or if you answer them.

MARITAL CIRCUMSTANCES

20   Courts have ruled that it's none of the company's business how many children an applicant has; whether he or she is married, single, divorced, or engaged; whether the applicant plans to become pregnant at any time in the future; how the applicant's spouse or partner feels about overnight travel; or what plans the applicant has made for child care during the workday.

Managers stumble into trouble in this area when making small talk, especially of a
25   disclosing or "sharing" nature with the candidate. *Manager:* "My wife and I have lived here for about 10 years. We love it—especially the school system. Do you have kids?" Innocent? Of course. But if relations turn litigious, the manager will have to admit in court that he inquired about children as part of the selection interview.

What to Do. If you are asked an illegal question in this area, you can give a general
30   response, said graciously: "I would prefer to stick to job-related questions." Or you can

be more pointed: "Are children a requirement for this position?" And, of course, you can always decide simply to play along, but as minimally as possible: "Yes, we have one child. Shall we talk about your requirements for this position?"

AGE

To prevent age discrimination in hiring, courts have disallowed these sorts of questions:
35 "How old are you?" "In what year were you born?" "When did you graduate from high school?" and so forth. You do have the right to ask whether the applicant meets the legal age requirements for work in your city or state.

Managers stray into trouble here when they talk about the average age of their workforce in relation to the candidate: "Our typical employee is probably 8 to 10 years
40 older than you. Do you anticipate problems managing people older than yourself?" You can imagine the later court scene. *Manager:* "But, Your Honor, I never asked her age!" *Candidate/plaintiff:* "My age seemed to be one of his key concerns about my ability to manage." Verdict goes to the plaintiff, with back pay, damages, and court costs.

What to Do. If asked an illegal question having to do with your age, you can respond,
45 with a smile: "Age has never been a consideration for me in my work life." Or you can turn the knife a bit: "Is my age being considered as part of my application?" And, of course, you can simply answer, if you wish: "I'm 27, but my age hasn't been a consideration in past jobs."

DISABILITIES

Companies are forbidden by law from asking an applicant if he or she has mental or physi-
50 cal disabilities. Nor can they inquire about the nature or severity of disabilities, no matter how apparent they seem in the hiring process. Any physical or mental requirements a company establishes as a prerequisite for hiring must be based on "business necessity" and the safe performance of the job.

Managers are misled here by their best intentions: "We have many people with dis
55 abilities working for us and we support their needs in every way possible. For example, we could overcome the problem you have with your hands by giving you an automated speech recognition word processor." If the candidate with disabilities does not get the job, the manager's assumptions about the candidate's typing abilities could come back to haunt in an expensive way.

60   **What to Do.** If you are asked an illegal question having to do with disabilities, you can refer the interviewer to Americans with Disabilities Act (ADA) guidelines: "I believe that under current ADA law you can't make this issue a part of the hiring process." Or you can take the edge off a bit with a general answer: "I know of nothing that will prevent me from fulfilling the job requirements of this position."

SEX AND PHYSICAL APPEARANCE

65   An employer cannot ask questions about the person's gender unless the job specifications strictly require either a male or a female. The burden of proof is on the employer to demonstrate that only a man or a woman can do the job. Employers should beware: Courts and the Equal Employment Opportunity Commission have interpreted very narrowly the notion that only one gender can perform a particular job. In addition, employers
70 should avoid questions about the person's physical appearance, including height, weight, grooming, and dress, unless these bear clearly upon job requirements.

   Again, a manager's small talk in the job interview is the unhappy hunting ground for mistakes in this area of questioning. *Manager to a woman applicant:* "We have a fitness facility here at the plant. But you seem to be pretty fit already." Oops.

75   **What to Do.** If quizzed about matters of gender or physical appearance, you can respond in a general way: "I'm fully prepared to take on these job responsibilities, and I don't think gender or appearance plays a role." Or you can return the question with a question: "Are gender and appearance being considered as part of this hiring process?" These responses need not be said in a snarlish way (though the interviewer may well
80 deserve your anger). You can preserve your chances for the job by handling the questions professionally.

CITIZENSHIP AND NATIONAL ORIGIN

   A company cannot legally inquire into the applicant's place of birth, ancestry, native language, spouse's or parents' birthplace, or residence. Nor can an employer ask directly, "Are you a U.S. citizen?" or "Do you have naturalization papers?" Prior to the decision
85 to hire, these questions may tend to reveal racial or ethnic factors that may bias the employer. Companies should request names or *persons* to notify in case of an emergency rather than specifying *relatives*. Employers should not require that the applicant's photograph be submitted prior to the hiring decision.

   Managers often misstep into this pitfall when inquiring about a candidate's second
90 language capability. *Manager:* "You say on your resume that you speak Spanish fluently. Did you grow up in Mexico?" A person's land of birth cannot be grounds for a hiring decision. Clearly, this question strays into legally hazardous areas.

   What to Do. If asked about your national origin, you can answer "My family history and heritage are getting us off the topic, don't you think? I would rather talk about job
95 requirements." Or you can be more direct: "I assume that where my parents came from isn't one of the requirements for this job."

(1,277 words)

—From *Interviewing for Success,* by Arthur H. Bell and
Dayle M. Smith

THINKING AND WRITING AFTER READING

RECALL Self-test your understanding.

Your instructor may choose to give you a brief comprehension review.

REACT Have you asked or have you been asked questions in any of the categories described in the reading selection? If so, describe the situation. If not, imagine an alternative question or response to one of the situations described in the reading.

_____

_____

_____

REFLECT Why do we have laws that govern interview questions? _____

_____

_____

_____

THINK CRITICALLY Does the legal system serve the needs of employers and potential employees equally? Explain why or why not. _____

_____

_____

_____

THINK AND WRITE Imagine that you are an employer interviewing candidates for a job. Write five questions that would provide information that you will need and that do not violate the rights of the applicant.

_____

_____

_____

EXTENDED WRITING Put yourself in the position of an applicant for a job that you really want and for which you think you are well qualified. Keeping your own situation in mind, write a response to illegal interview questions in each of the five categories discussed in the reading selection.

DETAILS AND ORGANIZATIONAL PATTERNS

Mark the following as major (*M*) or minor (*m*) details in support of the author's main point.

_____ 1. "Do you have kids?" is an inappropriate interview question.

_____ 2. Managers sometimes stumble into trouble when making small talk before the actual interview.

_____ 3. It is illegal to ask about marital circumstances in an interview.

_____ 4. When asked about one's age, an applicant can tactfully respond, "Is my age being considered as part of my application?"

_____ 5. Interview questions about citizenship and national origin are illegal.

6. What is the overall pattern of organization of the selection?

_____

_____

Interpret THE QUOTE

Now that you've finished reading the selection, "When Interview Questions Turn Illegal," go back to the beginning of the selection and read the opening quote again. Does it apply to situations other than job interviews?

Name _____

Date _____

COMPREHENSION QUESTIONS

Answer the following with *a, b, c,* or *d,* or fill in the blank. In order to help you analyze your strengths and weaknesses, the question types are indicated.

Main Idea _____ 1. The best statement of the main idea of this selection is
   a. Job interviewers should be aware of several types of illegal questions, and interviewees should learn how to handle them.
   b. It is illegal to ask an applicant about physical disabilities.
   c. Job interviews are a legal minefield.
   d. Job applicants should learn how to respond to interview questions.

Detail _____ 2. According to the article, what is legal and illegal in interview situations is determined by
   a. the Occupational Safety and Health Administration (OSHA).
   b. courts of law.
   c. the professional standards of each industry or business.
   d. A combination of court rulings, legislative decisions, agency regulations, and constitutional laws.

Detail _____ 3. Under what conditions can an employer specify certain physical or mental requirements as a condition of employment?
   a. An employer can never specify physical or mental requirements.
   b. There are no restrictions for specifying physical or mental requirements.
   c. Only when they are based on business necessity or job safety can an employer specify physical or mental requirements as a condition of employment.
   d. The applicant's mental ability is the only condition that can be specified.

Detail _____ 4. In which situation is it legal to ask about an applicant's age?
   a. It is never legal to ask about an applicant's age.
   b. To determine if the applicant meets legal age requirements set by the city or state.
   c. Only if the employer fears that the applicant's age will negatively affect his or her ability to do the job.
   d. It is always appropriate to consider the applicant's age.

Inference _____ 5. From the selection, a reader can logically infer that
   a. interviewers need to consult a lawyer before conducting an interview.
   b. interviewees should consult a lawyer before undertaking a job search.
   c. the laws most often broken in interview questions involve citizenship.
   d. illegal interview questions often involve personal information.

Author's purpose _____ 6. Which of the following best describes the purpose of this selection?

    a. to alarm employers who fear they might stray into illegal hiring practices

    b. to provide information about illegal interview questions that will help employers and applicants

    c. to arm job applicants with suggestions about responding to interview questions

    d. to persuade employers and job applicants to prepare well before an interview

Inference _____ 7. From the information in the article, the reader can logically conclude that

    a. the best response to an illegal question is to confront the interviewer with the illegality of the question.

    b. an applicant should never reveal personal information in a job interview.

    c. there are ways to respond to illegal questions tactfully without revealing personal information.

    d. it is best for the applicant's hiring prospects to give direct answers to all interview questions, even if it means giving personal information.

Answer the following questions with *T* (true) or *F* (false).

Detail _____ 8. While interviewers cannot directly ask an applicant's age, they can ask when the applicant graduated from high school.

Inference _____ 9. A reader can logically conclude that the legal restrictions on interview questions also apply to application forms.

Inference _____ 10. The reader can conclude that many of the questions determined to be illegal were found to be so because the answers could be used to discriminate against job applicants.

VOCABULARY

Answer the following with *a, b, c,* or *d* for the word or phrase that best defines the boldface word used in the selection. The number in parentheses indicates the line of the passage in which the word appears. In addition to the context clues, use a dictionary to more precisely define the technical terms.

_____ 1. "**intrusion** into your privacy" (8)

    a. invasion
    b. withdrawal
    c. question
    d. interest

_____ 2. "claims **discrimination**" (10)

    a. fairness
    b. careful attention
    c. unfair treatment
    d. poor taste

_____ 3. "**plethora** of court rulings" (14)

    a. shortage
    b. abundance
    c. confusion
    d. list

_____ 4. "relations turn **litigious**" (27)

    a. requiring police action
    b. judgmental
    c. unpleasant
    d. tending to legal action

_____ 5. "goes to the **plaintiff**"
(43)

    a. defendant
    b. judge
    c. guilty party
    d. accuser

_____ 6. "**severity** of disabilities"
(50)

    a. type
    b. details
    c. nature
    d. level

_____ 7. "**prerequisite** for hiring"
(52)

    a. reason
    b. qualification
    c. need
    d. plan

_____ 8. "come back to **haunt**"
(59)

    a. frighten
    b. justify
    c. pay back
    d. worry

_____ 9. "in a **snarlish** way"
(79)

    a. friendly
    b. threatening
    c. funny
    d. violent

_____ 10. "**naturalization** papers"
(84)

    a. citizenship in an
       adopted country
    b. legal birth records
    c. school transcripts
    d. proof of address

Your instructor may choose to give a brief vocabulary review.

VOCABULARY ENRICHMENT

A. Study the following definitions and then circle the similar-sounding word that is correct in each sentence.

conscience: sense of right and wrong   **fair:** just or right
conscious: aware   **fare:** fee for transportation

1. Heroes are often made when people act out of (**conscience**, **conscious**) in spite of the dangers they might face.

2. Interview questions can seem to the employer to be (**fair**, fare) but may actually be illegal.

B. **Analogies:** Supply a word that completes each analogy, then state the relationship that has been established. Refer to page 166 for more help with analogies, including a list of common relationships.

3. _Knife_ is to _cut_ as _gun_ is to _____.

   Relationship? _____

4. _Old_ is to _ancient_ as _new_ is to _____.

   Relationship? _____

5. _Eye_ is to _see_ as _ear_ is to _____.

   Relationship? _____

6. _Go_ is to _come_ as _sell_ is to _____.

   Relationship? _____

7. *State* is to *governor* as *city* is to _____.

   Relationship? _____

8. *Skin* is to *person* as *fur* is to _____.

   Relationship? _____

9. *Smart* is to *intelligent* as *chilly* is to _____.

   Relationship? _____

10. *Razor* is to *sharp* as *cement* is to _____.

    Relationship? _____

11. *Winter* is to *summer* as *wet* is to _____.

    Relationship? _____

C. **Words From Literature:** The names of certain characters in literature have dropped their capital letters and taken on special meaning in the English language. The following are from Spanish and English literature, respectively. Read the entries to determine their definitions and origins.

> **quix·ot·ic** \kwik-'sä-tik\ *adj* [Don *Quixote*] (1718) **1 :** foolishly impractical esp. in the pursuit of ideals; *esp* : marked by rash lofty romantic ideas or extravagantly chivalrous action **2 :** CAPRICIOUS, UNPREDICTABLE *syn* see IMAGINARY — **quix·ot·i·cal** \-ti-kəl\ *adj* — **quix·ot·i·cal·ly** \-ti-k(ə-)lē\ *adv*

> Source: By permission. From *Merriam-Webster's Collegiate® Dictionary, 11th Edition.* © 2011 by Merriam-Webster Incorporated (www.Merriam-Webster.com).

12. *Quixotic* means _____.

13. The origin of the word is _____.

> **Lil·li·put** \'li-li-(,)pət\ *n* (1726) **:** an island in Swift's *Gulliver's Travels* where the inhabitants are six inches tall
> **Lil·li·pu·tian** \,li-lə-'pyü-shən\ *adj* (1726) **1 :** of, relating to, or characteristic of the Lilliputians or the island of Lilliput **2** *often not cap* **a** : SMALL, MINIATURE ⟨a ∼ camera⟩ **b** : PETTY
> **Lilliputian** *n* (1726) **1 :** an inhabitant of Lilliput **2** *often not cap* : one resembling a Lilliputian; *esp* : an undersized individual

> Source: By permission. From *Merriam-Webster's Collegiate® Dictionary, 11th Edition.* © 2011 by Merriam-Webster Incorporated (www.Merriam-Webster.com).

14. *Lilliputian* means _____.

15. The origin of the word is _____.

ASSESS YOUR LEARNING

Review confusing questions, seek clarification, and make notes in your text to help you remember new information and vocabulary. Use your textbook as a learning tool.

SELECTION 3

PERSONAL FEEDBACK 2

Name _____

1. Approximately how much time do you spend each day studying for this class?

   _____

2. Where do you typically study?_____

   _____

3. How do you manage telephone calls and texts during your scheduled study time?

   _____

4. Describe a time this week when you have procrastinated._____

   _____

5. What were the consequences of your procrastination?_____

   _____

Share your responses as directed by your instructor.

VOCABULARY LESSON

See, Hear, and Voice Your Concerns

Study the roots, words, and sentences.

Roots   *Vis, vid*: see   *aud, aus*: hear or listen   *voc, vok*: voice or call

Words with *vis* or *vid* = see

What did Julius Caesar mean by, "Veni, *vidi*, vici"? Can *invisible* ink be seen?

- Visible: can be seen

  On clear nights, stars are more *visible* in the countryside than in cities.

- Visionary: one who sees visions or dreams of the future

  Be both a *visionary* and a good businessperson to create a successful company.

- Visor: a brim to protect the eyes so that you can see better

  Wear a *visor* for tennis so that the sun doesn't interfere with your performance.

- Evident: can easily be seen

  The solution was *evident* to those who had previously encountered the problem.

- Visa: a passport endorsement giving the bearer the right to enter a country

  Prior to visiting certain countries, tourists must apply for a *visa*.

- Vista: a view from a distance

  The *vista* from a mountaintop on an autumn day can be breathtaking.

- Envision: to see in one's mind

  Try to *envision* the furniture in the empty room.

Words with *aud* or *aus* = hear or listen

Does an *audience* sit in an *auditorium*? Can *inaudible* words be heard?

- Audible: can be heard

  Because she speaks so softly, her voice is barely *audible*.

- Audition: a hearing to try out for a role

  The actor nervously began the *audition* for a part in the Broadway musical.

- Audio: sound made by electronic or mechanical reproduction

  The *audio* on my television is not clear.

- Auditory: relating to hearing

  The *auditory* nerves are damaged, and thus hearing is impaired.

- Audit: a formal examination of accounts made by an accountant

  Citizens fear an *audit* by the Internal Revenue Service.

Words with *voc* or *vok* = *voice* or *call*

How can you *voice* your ideas on *vocabulary*? Are *vocal* people heard?

- Evoke: call out from the past

  The ceremony was designed to *evoke* the memory of past heroes.

- Vocation: a call to serve in a particular profession

  Although my plans may change, I am preparing for a *vocation* in nursing.

- Vociferous: making a noisy outcry

  The opponent's remarks drew *vociferous* objections.

- Avocation: a hobby or second calling

  My money comes from banking, but music is my *avocation*.

- Convocation: an assembly or calling together

  The *convocation* celebrated the 75th anniversary of the college.

- Invocation: solemn prayer or divine blessing

  The religious service began with an *invocation*.

- Invoke: to call forth

  The witness *invoked* the Fifth Amendment to avoid answering questions.

Review

Part I

Choose the best word from the list to complete each of the following sentences.

invocation	audience	vocation	vista	visor
vocal	convocation	audit	avocation	visa

1. If customers are __vocal__, they can make their complaints heard.
2. From the cruise ship, the travelers could see a mountain __vista__.
3. Our chorus sang at the __convocation__ honoring our new college president.
4. A company __audit__ indicated funds were incorrectly allocated.
5. The __audience__ clapped after the performance.
6. The priest gave a brief __invocation__ at the beginning of the service.
7. A __visa__ is required to enter Israel.
8. Recreational golfing can become a serious and challenging __avocation__.
9. After 30 years, the electrical engineer retired from his lifelong __vocation__.
10. Wear a __visor__ to protect your eyes from the sun.

Part II

Answer the following with *T* (true) or *F* (false).

_____T_____ 11. Parents invoke their authority to get their children to go to bed.

_____F_____ 12. A vociferous group is quiet and orderly.

_____T_____ 13. A visionary might seek to make a dream become a reality.

_____T_____ 14. The taillights on a motor vehicle should be visible at night.

_____T_____ 15. To promote a cause, activists usually want a vocal spokesperson.

_____T_____ 16. For most people, gardening is an avocation rather than a vocation.

_____T_____ 17. Landing a part in a play usually requires an audition.

_____T_____ 18. Financial records are reviewed in a company audit.

_____T_____ 19. The person who provokes an argument is called a troublemaker.

_____F_____ 20. Teens usually prefer background music to be inaudible.

Reading and Organizing Research Materials

Whether you are researching a topic for a term paper or making a decision about an automobile purchase, you want to find relevant and reliable data to support your final conclusions and recommendations. The material that you use for support will depend on your project, your goals, and the research tools available to you.

The first step is to find the information that you seek. The next step is to record the information in a usable form for your ultimate purpose.

Locating Information

Academic research today is easier than ever. Today, the collections of libraries all over the world are a mouse click or two away. Whether you go to the library building or access the library from a personal or school computer, you will use the Internet to locate its holdings. Review the Everyday Reading Skills feature on page 238 for suggestions about conducting research on the Internet.

Begin with Encyclopedias

Most professors do not accept encyclopedias as legitimate sources for college-level research assignments. However, **encyclopedias** are good starting places that provide background information to help you narrow your topic. They define key words and perhaps mention important researchers that you can then use as search terms for further exploration. The most reliable encyclopedias are those whose entries are written and edited by experts. Remember that Wikipedia, the handy online information source, is an open site. That is, anyone can contribute an entry or change an existing one. Although the site is monitored for accuracy, Wikipedia is best used to get a general sense of a topic and find ideas for further research from other sources. Keep in mind that free, general encyclopedias online are not as comprehensive as subscription-based online encyclopedias or encyclopedias in print. Here are two of several respected encyclopedias that are available online. Some online encyclopedias are free, and others require a subscription fee.

Encyclopaedia Britannica	britannica.com
Grolier	go.grolier.com

In addition to general encyclopedias, specialized volumes provide information on specific topics. *The Encyclopedia of Earth Sciences*, *The Cambridge Encyclopedia of Astronomy*, and *The CIA World Fact Book* are just three examples. Refer to the following Web sites for helpful lists of other general and specialized encyclopedias:

www.freeality.com/encyclop.htm
www.encyclopedia.com

EXERCISE 1 Visit your college library and locate two specialty encyclopedias, excluding general encyclopedias such as the *Encyclopaedia Britannica*. It may be possible to do this remotely from the library link at your college's Web site. Take notes on an interesting entry from each one and share the notes with your classmates.

Use Indexes to Scholarly and Popular Publications

Most research topics can be approached from the viewpoints of several academic disciplines. For example, sexual assault can be addressed from a legal, medical, sociological, psychological, or educational vantage point. Decide on the academic discipline for your research paper and ask a reference librarian to help you select an appropriate index. Then use the index to locate appropriate articles in the *periodical literature*. **Periodical** is a term used to describe all publications that come out on a regular schedule. They include popular magazines and scholarly journals.

> ### Reader's TIP — Defining Your Topic
>
> To define your research topic, consider:
>
> - **Geography:** Pick a specific area.
> - **Time Frame:** Limit the time period under examination.
> - **Interest Groups:** Narrow your research by appropriate descriptors, such as age, gender, or occupation.
> - **Academic Discipline:** What college or department would study this subject?

Articles in **popular sources** (usually newspapers and magazines) are aimed at the general public and written by professional journalists who are usually not specialists in the field. On the other hand, articles in **scholarly journals** contain research results of experts and always include a **bibliography**, a list of the sources consulted by the author of the article. For most college research, you will need to use primarily scholarly journals.

Many articles that you find in indexes will not be relevant to your specific needs. Use the information that appears in the index entries to save time and make decisions. Each entry will display a **citation** to the article that includes the title, author(s), name of the periodical, volume and page numbers, issue date, and descriptive notes or key search terms. Usually the entry will also include an abstract.

If the article title and the date look appropriate to your search, read the abstract. The **abstract** is a short paragraph that summarizes the article, stating the premise that the authors set out to prove, the subjects or location of the project, and the conclusions. If the abstract sounds as if the article will be relevant to your research, print the entry page or record the information so that you can locate a copy of the article. In some cases, the database provides a link to the complete text of the article. However, remember that the best articles for your topic may not be available electronically, but they may be easily accessible in the library collection.

Organizing the Information

When you have located material that fits your purpose, handle it the way you would handle any textbook information. Many students choose to print the articles to read later. If you have a printed copy, annotate it while you read, just as you would if you were reading a textbook, and then take notes. If you read the source material on the computer screen, you must skip the annotations and go directly to the note-taking process.

When taking notes for an academic paper, put the ideas into your own words. By doing this, you will be less likely to use the author's phrasing when you write

U.S. House of Representatives; www.house.gov

your paper. Avoiding plagiarism is extremely important. Record page numbers, URLs, and all other source information. These details will be necessary when you cite the references in your final paper. This habit will also make it much easier for you to find the source again if necessary.

Make it a habit to put your notes in a clear, well-organized form, such as those forms discussed in this chapter. Use the form that best suits the material and your preferences—Cornell, summarizing, outlining, or mapping.

EXERCISE 2

Answer the following questions based on the Internet article, "The U.S. House of Representatives."

1. Would the Internet article be relevant if you were making a class presentation on the U.S. Congress? Yes. _____

_____

2. What kinds of information will you find on this site? _____

_____

_____

_____

3. Is the information reliable? How do you know? (*Hint*: Review the definitions and parts of a Web address in Chapter 5, page 238) _____

_____

_____

4. Use one of the note-taking forms that you learned in this chapter—Cornell, summarizing, outlining, or mapping—to make notes from this article. Remember to cite the complete URL as the source.

7 Inference

Learning Objectives

From this chapter, readers will learn:

1 To define *inference*
2 To explain why authors might imply meaning rather than state it directly
3 To use prior knowledge to make inferences
4 To recognize slanted language as a clue to meaning
5 To draw reasonable conclusions

Everyday Reading Skills: Reading Newspaper Editorials

WHAT IS AN INFERENCE?

Learning Objective 1

Define *inference*

An *inference* is a meaning that is suggested rather than directly stated. Inferences are implied through clues that lead the reader to make assumptions and draw conclusions. For example, instead of making a direct statement, "These people are rich and influential," an author could imply that idea by describing a palatial residence, expensive heirlooms, and prominent friends. Understanding an inference is what we mean by "reading between the lines," because the suggestion, rather than the actual words, carries the meaning.

Inference From Cartoons

Cartoons and jokes require you to read between the lines and make a connection. They are funny because of the unstated rather than the stated meaning. When listeners catch on to a joke, it simply means that they have made the connection and have recognized the unstated inference. For example, what inference makes the following joke funny?

> **Sam:** Do you know how to save a politician from drowning?
> **Joe:** No.
> **Sam:** Good.

Taxpayers like to dislike politicians, and this joke falls into that category. As a rule, when you have to explain the inference in a joke, the fun is lost. You want your audience to make the connection and laugh uproariously.

EXAMPLE   Look at the following cartoon. What is being implied?

EXPLANATION   Betsy has won a billion dollars in the lottery, a dream for many people. However, instead of using the money for new cars, houses, and vacations, she plans to use the money to repay her student loans. Even so, she is not sure that one billion dollars will cover the amount that she owes. The cartoonist used exaggeration to make a point: The cost of going to college is huge!

EXERCISE 1   The following cartoon contains details that imply meaning. Use the details to figure out the meaning of the cartoon and to answer the questions.

© Guy & Rodd/Distributed by Universal Uclick via CartoonStock.com

"SOON YOU WILL START TO NOTICE CHANGES TO YOUR BODY... MASSIVE, HORRIFYING CHANGES."

1. What are the three seated characters in the cartoon? ___Catterpillars___
2. What is the character standing to the left side? ___Butterfly___
3. What is the apparent setting for the cartoon? ___Class (school)___

_____

4. What seems to be the subject of the "lesson"? ___Biology (sex)___

5. What prior knowledge does the reader need to interpret the humor in the cartoon? ___Memories of childhood, changes in your body.___

_____

UNDERSTANDING INFERENCES

To understand inferences requires a higher level of thinking than is needed to recognize details that are stated clearly. Cartoonists, authors, and speakers often ask us to figure out their points for ourselves. They provide the clues, and we provide the prior knowledge and logic that lead us to understanding. The formula below provides a visual reminder of the process of making a reasonable inference:

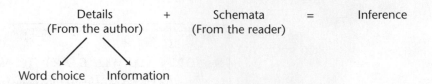

The following sections explain why authors imply meaning instead of stating it and how readers use the author's details and their own schemata to understand inferences.

Recognizing Suggested Meaning

**Learning
Objective 2**

Explain why authors
might imply meaning

In reading, as in everyday life, information may or may not be stated outright. For example, someone's death would seem to be a fact beyond question. An author could simply state, "He is dead," but often it is more complicated than that. In literature and in poetry, such a fact might be divulged in a more dramatic manner, and the reader is left to put the clues together and figure out what happened. Read the following excerpt from a story about a shipwrecked crew's struggle to shore. What clues tell you that the oiler is dead?

> In the shallows, face downward, lay the oiler. His forehead touched sand that was periodically, between each wave, clear of the sea.
>
> —*The Open Boat,* by Stephen Crane

The oiler's head is face down in the shallow water. When the waves rush in to shore, his face is in the water, and when they wash out, his face or forehead touches the sand. He is bobbing at the water's edge like a dead fish and cannot possibly be alive with his face constantly underwater or buried in the sand. The man must be dead, but the author doesn't directly state that.

Two paragraphs later in the story the author writes:

> The welcome of the land to the men from the sea was warm and generous; but a still and dripping shape was carried slowly up the beach, and the land's welcome for it could only be the different and sinister hospitality of the grave.
>
> —*The Open Boat,* by Stephen Crane

The "still and dripping shape" and the "sinister hospitality of the grave" support your interpretation of the clues, even though the author still has not directly stated, "The oiler is dead." Implying the idea is perhaps more forceful than making a direct statement.

Connecting With Prior Knowledge

Learning Objective 3

Use prior knowledge when making inferences

Authors, like cartoonists, use inferences that require linking old knowledge to what is being read at the time. Clues that imply meaning may draw on an assumed knowledge of history, current issues, or social concerns. Just as in making the connection to understand the punch line of a joke, the reader must make a connection in order to understand the inference.

EXAMPLE   **A TURNING POINT**

More than 3,000 people were killed, thousands more were wounded, and the loss of property was unprecedented in the worst terrorist attack in history. The events horrified people around the world who understood that two symbols of American global financial and military dominance had been singled out in a carefully planned and executed mission of destruction. The event was immediately compared to the Japanese attack on Pearl Harbor in 1941.

—*Civilization in the West,* Fifth Edition, by Mark Kishlansky, Patrick Geary, and Patricia O'Brien

1. What was the symbol of financial dominance that is not named here? Where was the attack? *Dominance 911*
2. What is the symbol of military dominance? Where was the destruction? *Towers*
3. When did these terrorist attacks occur? *911, 2001.*
4. Why was the attack compared to the Japanese attack on Pearl Harbor in 1941? *y same attack as NY, Towers.*

PERSONAL FEEDBACK) 1   Name _____

1. Who supplied your references for college admission or for your last job? _____
   _____
   _____

2. What professor would you ask to write you a letter of reference for an award or a
   scholarship? Why would you choose that particular professor? _____
   _____
   _____

3. What preparation have you done for the next term? What courses do you plan to
   take and why? _____
   _____
   _____

Share your responses as directed by your instructor.

EXPLANATION   The symbol of financial dominance was the twin towers of the World Trade Center in New York City. The symbol of military dominance was the Pentagon in Washington, D.C. The attacks occurred on September 11, 2001, when terrorists hijacked passenger planes and used them to bomb buildings. The attacks precipitated a war, just as the Japanese attack on Pearl Harbor brought the United States into World War II. The following exercise illustrates how authors expect readers to make connections using prior knowledge.

EXERCISE 2   Link prior knowledge to answer the questions that follow each passage.

Passage 1

THE BEGINNING OF THE SHOOTING

After seeing the light in the North Church, Paul Revere and William Dawes rode through the countryside alerting the colonists that British troops were moving across the back bay. In Concord and Lexington, trained militiamen were waiting to respond.

Where and approximately when was this? _1775, Boston Massachettius._

_____

_____

Passage 2

FOOT BINDING

Foot binding was a form of violence against women. The woman's tiny feet, which made it difficult for her to walk, were a "marker" of status, indicating that her husband was wealthy and did not need her labor. It also made her dependent on him.

—*Essentials of Sociology: A Down-to-Earth Approach,* Fourth Edition,
by James Henslin

Although not directly stated, foot binding was practiced in what country?

China _____

Passage 3

TELLING THE STORY

The account of that morning some weeks later belongs to history. Three planes take off during the night of 6 August from Tinian in the Mariana Islands. Paul Tibbets is the group's commander. Eatherly opens the formation. There are no bombs in his plane; as for the others, no one suspects what a terrible device is hidden inside the *Enola Gay*. A bigger contrivance, they think, nothing more. Eatherly's job is to pinpoint the target with maximum accuracy. He must establish whether weather conditions allow for the center to be Hiroshima, Kokura or Nagasaki, or whether they should continue towards secondary targets. He tells the story of that morning's events in a voice devoid of emotion which suggests that the recitation is the thousandth one.

—*"The Man from Hiroshima,"* by Maurizio Chierici,
Granta #22, Autumn 1987

1. What is the "bigger contrivance"? _____

_____

2. What was the mission assignment of Tibbets and Eatherly? _____

_____

Recognizing Slanted Language

Writers choose words to manipulate the reader and thus to control the reader's attitude toward a subject. Such words are referred to as having a particular **connotation** or **slant.** The dictionary definition of a word is its **_denotation_**, but the feeling or emotion surrounding a word is its _connotation_. For example, a real estate agent showing a run-down house to a prospective buyer might refer to the house as "neglected" rather than "deteriorated." Both words mean run down. _Neglected_ sounds as if a few things have been forgotten, whereas _deteriorated_ sounds as if the place is rotting away and falling apart.

Some words in our society seem to have an automatic positive or negative slant. Words such as _socialist, cult member,_ and _welfare state_ have a negative emotional effect; words such as _the American worker, democracy,_ and _everyday people_ have a positive effect. The overall result of using slanted language is to shift the reader's attitude toward the point of view, positive or negative, advocated by the author. Recognizing slanted language provides another clue to the author's meaning.

EXERCISE 3   Label the following phrases as either _P_ (slanted positively) or _N_ (slanted negatively).

___P___ 1. warm and winning ways

___P___ 2. an engaging smile

___N___ 3. appearing remote and self-involved

___N___ 4. a cunning salesperson

___P___ 5. candid and open

___P___ 6. the picture of efficiency

___N___ 7. weak and sickly

___N___ 8. words like daggers

___N___ 9. a loose cannon

___N___ 10. spoken without thinking

___N___ 11. not the sharpest knife in the drawer

___N___ 12. a creased brow

___N___ 13. an exasperated look

___P___ 14. wise beyond her years

___P___ 15. a nurturing mother

___N___ 16. an easy mark

___N___ 17. a hostile takeover

___P___ 18. a dream fulfilled

___P___ 19. the promise of tomorrow

___P___ 20. the brotherhood of man

EXERCISE 4 Indicate whether the boldface words in the following passages are *P* (positive) or *N* (negative), and explain your answer.

N 1. Opponents forecast that the increased labor cost from a large minimum-wage hike would jeopardize hundreds of thousands of **unskilled jobs.** *because they can be done by everyone.*

—*Microeconomics for Today*, Fourth Edition, by Irvin B. Tucker

N 2. One of the best *Candid Camera* illustrations of the subtle power of social situations to control behavior is the "elevator caper." A person riding a rigged elevator first obeys the usual silent rule to face the front, but when a group of other passengers all face the rear, the **hapless victim** follows the group and faces the rear as well. *because you are following.*

—*Life-Span Development*, Ninth Edition, by John W. Santrock

P 3. In the United States and other **highly developed** countries, infectious disease accounts for about 4% to 8% of deaths, compared with death rates of 30% to 50% in developing regions. *Fewer death rates*

—*Biology*, Sixth Edition, by Eldra P. Solomon et al.

P 4. Early on in your approach to cooking—or in running a restaurant—you have to determine whether or not you are willing to commit fully and completely to the idea of **the pursuit of excellence**. I have always looked at it this way: if you strive for perfection—an all out assault on total perfection—at the very least you will hit a high level of excellence, and then you might be able to sleep at night. *Do the best*

—*Introduction to Hospitality,* Fourth Edition, by John R. Walker

N 5. Finding Mozart a job was not easy. Most of his prospective employers thought that he was too young and too talented (**"overqualified"** is the word we would use today) for a normal position. Indeed, any music director would

have been threatened by this brash and brilliant youngster. _because_
you are more than capable.

—*Understanding Music*, Fourth Edition,
by Jeremy Yudkin

EXERCISE 5

Write a word or phrase with a positive connotation that could be substituted for each of the following negative words. For example, positive substitutes for the word *criticism* might be *feedback* and *advice*. Answers may vary.

1. strange _extraordinary, unique, special_
2. wild _care free, imaginative_
3. shy _quite_
4. bossy _assertive, ambitious_
5. skinny _slick, tone, slim_
6. nosy _curious_
7. hyperactive _excited, energatic_
8. slow _carefull_
9. old _wisdom, wise, mature_
10. tree hugger _naturalist, environmentalist_

Drawing Conclusions

Learning Objective 5

Draw reasonable conclusions

Readers use both stated and unstated ideas to draw logical conclusions. They use the facts, the hints, and their prior knowledge to piece together meaning. The facts and clues lead to assumptions, which then lead to conclusions. Read the following passage and explain how the conclusion is suggested.

EXAMPLE **MY HOUSE**

My master still went to school every day and, coming home, he'd still bottle himself up in his study. When he had visitors he'd continue to complain about his job.

I still had nothing to eat so I did not become very fat but I was healthy enough. I didn't become sick like Kuro and, always, I took things as they came. I still didn't try to catch rats, and I still hated Osan, the maid. I still didn't have a name but you can't always have what you want. I resigned myself to continue living here at the home of this schoolteacher.

—Excerpt from *I Am a Cat*, by Natsume Soseki

Conclusion: The narrator of the book is a cat.

What clues suggest this conclusion? _Catching rats_

EXPLANATION The term *my master* may lead to an initial suspicion of a pet, and "try to catch rats" clearly suggests a cat. The option of continuing to live in the home supports the idea of a cat. The book, as you might guess, is titled *I Am a Cat*.

EXERCISE 6

In passages 1 through 3, identify the clues that lead to the stated conclusions. In passages 4 and 5, state the conclusion and identify the clues.

Passage 1

CULTS: THE PEOPLE'S TEMPLE — T

Def & examples

A **cult** is usually united by total rejection of society and extreme devotion to the cult's leader. The People's Temple is a dramatic example. In the 1970s their leader, Jim Jones, preached racial harmony, helped the poor, established drug-rehabilitation programs, staged protest demonstrations against social injustices, and helped elect sympathetic politicians. He moved his cult from San Francisco to Jonestown, Guyana, because, he said, evil people in the United States would try to destroy the Temple. He told his flock that to build a just society required a living God—namely, himself. To prove his deity, he "healed parishioners by appearing to draw forth cancers" (which actually were bloody chicken gizzards). He claimed that he had extraordinary sexual gifts, required Temple members to turn over all their possessions to him, and insisted that they call him "Dad" or "Father." Then the People's Temple shocked the world. In November 1978 more than 900 members committed mass suicide at the order of their leader.

—*Sociology*, Third Edition, by Alex Thio

Conclusion: Jim Jones brainwashed cult members into total submission.

What clues suggest this conclusion? *Father (God), evil people would turn over to the temple.*

Passage 2

THE TOBACCO CRAZE

The first European smoker, Rodrigo de Jerez, was with Columbus. Jerez was jailed by the Spanish Inquisition for seven years because of his bad habit, but he was the wave of the future. Slowly, inexorably, the practice of "drinking" tobacco smoke spread throughout Europe. James I, who found smoking "loathsome" and forbade it in his presence, could not stop it. Nor could the Sultan of Turkey, who threatened to execute puffers.

The lure of the exotic—the trendy—has always been potent among the leisured classes, and some European physicians seized on tobacco as a miracle drug—"the holy, healing herb," "a sovereign remedy to all diseases"—prescribing it liberally to their patients. Throughout the 1500s, the Spanish were pleased to meet Europe's demand from their West Indian plantations.

—*The American Past*, Fifth Edition, by Joseph Conlin

Conclusion: Although initially rejected by political leaders, tobacco became an accepted and sought after commodity.

What clues suggest this conclusion? *Smoke as an remedy to exotic, liberal to their parents, Spanish were pleased to meet Europe's demand from their West Indian plantations.*

Passage 3

NICHOLAS II (1894–1917)

Last of the Romanov tsars, Nicholas II was in almost every respect an unfortunate man. Besides having been influenced by a reactionary father and a strong-willed mother, he was dull, weak, stubborn, insensitive, and totally devoid of the qualities required for successfully administering a great empire. The day following his coronation, in conformity with tradition, he scheduled a banquet celebration for the people of the capital. A huge throng, possibly half a million souls, turned out for the great event. At one point the crowd surged forward and more than a thousand people were trampled to death. But Nicholas and the tsarina attended a ball at the French embassy that night and apparently spent a most enjoyable evening.

—*A History of the Western World,* by Solomon Modell

Conclusion: Nicholas and the tsarina had a total lack of concern for the welfare of the people.

What clues suggest this conclusion? _He said it was a most enjoyable evening._

Passage 4

THE FUTURE OF M-COMMERCE

M-commerce has everything to do with speed and location, with short requests for information and prompt, relevant replies. Consider a scenario from the near future. Customers entering a butcher shop are offered a discount for waving their cell phone through an infrared sensor that records the telephone's number. Business at the store is brisk throughout the day. But near closing time, the butcher is anxious to get rid of some prime cuts of Argentine beef.

—*Business Today,* Tenth Edition, by Michael Mescon et al.

What conclusion does the author imply? _He is going to send a text message._

What clues suggest this conclusion? _He can sell all his argentine beef._

Passage 5

LANDMINES

Cheap and easy to deploy, many fighting forces routinely use mines to defend a frontier, deny opponents the use of a road, and many other purposes. Often these landmines remain active long after the fighting has ceased, posing a significant threat to the safety of the civilian population. The magnitude and horror of this problem sparked a grassroots effort to ban landmines.

The campaign received a major boost in 1996 when Diana, Princess of Wales, joined in the effort, going to places most affected by landmines, comforting victims, and bringing the issue to the attention of millions. When Princess Diana died in a car crash in August 1997, sorrow often turned into commitments to support her charitable interests, including the effort to ban mines. Only a few nations remain opposed to the landmine convention.

—*American Government*,
by Karen O'Connor and Larry Sabato

What conclusion does the author imply? _____

_____

_____

What clues suggest this conclusion? _____

_____

_____

EXERCISE 7

Use a combination of inference skills to read the following passages and answer the questions.

Passage 1

TEXAS TOUGH

Lyndon Baines Johnson was a complex man—shrewd, arrogant, intelligent, sensitive, vulgar, vain, and occasionally cruel. He loved power, and he knew where it was, how to get it, and how to use it. "I'm a powerful sonofabitch," he told two Texas congressmen in 1958 when he was the most powerful legislator on Capitol Hill. Everything about Johnson seemed to emphasize or enhance his power. He was physically large, and seemed even bigger than he was, and he used his size to persuade people. The "Johnson Method" involved "pressing the flesh"—a back-slapping, hugging sort of camaraderie. He also used symbols of power adroitly, especially the telephone which had replaced the sword and pen as the symbol of power. "No gunman," remarked one historian, "ever held a Colt.44 so easily" as Johnson handled a telephone.

A legislative genius, Johnson had little experience in foreign affairs. Reared in the poverty of the Texas hill country, educated at a small teachers' college, and concerned politically with domestic issues, before becoming president LBJ had expressed little interest in foreign affairs. "Foreigners are not like the folks I am used to," he often said, and whether it was a joke or not he meant it. He was particularly uncomfortable around foreign dignitaries and ambassadors, often receiving them in groups and scarcely paying attention to them. "Why do I have to see them?" he once asked. "They're [Secretary of State] Dean Rusk's clients, not mine."

—*America and Its People*, Third Edition,
by James Martin et al.

Answer with *T* (true) or *F* (false).

_____ 1. LBJ had an enormous ego.

_____ 2. LBJ used the telephone to influence votes.

_____ 3. LBJ quickly learned to perform in international situations.

_____ 4. LBJ's background is reflected in both his genius and his flaws.

_____ 5. LBJ was the right person to be president during the Vietnam War.

_____ 6. The phrase *replaced the sword* suggests a negative connotation.

Passage 2

THE REIGN OF LOUIS XVI (1774–1793)

A plain, fat, rather stupid young man, who loved to hunt and tinker with locks, Louis XVI succeeded his grandfather (whose one legitimate son, Louis XVI's father, died in 1765) at the age of twenty. His modesty and inherent kindness did not serve him well. He was far too simple, possessed an almost total lack of self-confidence, and could be made to change his mind with relative ease. His wife, Marie Antoinette, an Austrian princess, was pretty, not well educated, shallow, and selfish. Totally unconcerned with the people's welfare, she devoted herself to jewels and costly clothes, gambling and flirtation, masques and balls. Not completely satisfied with court life, she insisted on interfering in governmental affairs and sabotaged, to the extent that she could, whatever chance existed for the reformation of French life. Her liberal emperor-brother, Joseph II of Austria, reprimanded her, but his words went unheeded.

—*A History of the Western World,* by Solomon Modell

Answer with *T* (true) or *F* (false).

_____ 1. Louis XVI and his wife were probably loved and respected by his people.

_____ 2. Despite his wife's influence, Louis XVI had many of the qualities of a great leader.

_____ 3. Louis XVI was firm in his decisions.

_____ 4. Marie Antoinette's extravagance was probably resented by the people.

_____ 5. Joseph II understood the possible repercussions of Marie Antoinette's actions.

_____ 6. The reformation of French life would probably have been a benefit to the people.

_____ 7. The phrase *tinker with locks* suggests hard work.

Passage 3

"LIZZIE BORDEN TOOK AN AX"

Andrew [Borden] was rich, but he didn't live like a wealthy man. Instead of living alongside the other prosperous Fall River citizens in the elite neighborhood known as The Hill, Andrew resided in an area near the business district called the flats. He liked to save time as well as money, and from the flats he could conveniently walk to work. For his daughters Lizzie and Emma, whose eyes and dreams focused on The Hill, life in the flats was an intolerable embarrassment. Their house was a grim, boxlike structure that lacked comfort and privacy. Since Andrew believed that running water on each floor was a wasteful luxury, the only washing facilities were a cold-water faucet in the kitchen and a laundry room water tap in the cellar. Also in the cellar was the toilet in the house. To make matters worse, the house was not connected to the Fall River gas main. Andrew preferred to use kerosene to light his house. Although it did not provide as good light or burn as cleanly as gas, it was less expensive. To save even more money, he and his family frequently sat in the dark.

The Borden home was far from happy. Lizzie and Emma, ages thirty-two and forty-two in 1892, strongly disliked their stepmother Abby and resented Andrew's penny-pinching ways. Lizzie especially felt alienated from the world around her. Although Fall River was the largest cotton-manufacturing town in America, it offered few opportunities for the unmarried daughter of a prosperous man. Society expected a woman of Lizzie's social position to marry, and while she waited for a proper suitor, her only respectable social outlets were church and community service. So Lizzie taught a Sunday School class and was active in the Woman's Christian Temperance Union, the Ladies' Fruit and Flower Mission, and other organizations. She kept herself busy, but she wasn't happy.

In August 1892, strange things started to happen in the Borden home. They began after Lizzie and Emma learned that Andrew had secretly changed his will. Abby became violently ill. Abby told a neighborhood doctor that she had been poisoned, but Andrew refused to listen to her wild ideas. Shortly thereafter, Lizzie went shopping for prussic acid, a deadly poison she said she needed to clean her sealskin cape. When a Fall River druggist refused her request, she left the store in an agitated state. Later in the day, she told a friend that she feared an unknown enemy of her father's was after him. "I'm afraid somebody will do something," she said.

On August 4, 1892, the maid Bridget awoke early and ill, but she still managed to prepare a large breakfast of johnnycakes, fresh-baked bread, ginger and oatmeal cookies with raisins, and some three-day-old mutton and hot mutton soup. After eating a hearty meal, Andrew left for work. Bridget also left to do some work outside. This left Abby and Lizzie in the house alone. Then somebody did something very specific and very grisly. As Abby was bent over making the bed in the guest room, someone moved into the room unobserved and killed her with an ax.

Andrew came home for lunch earlier than usual. He asked Lizzie where Abby was, and she said she didn't know. Unconcerned, Andrew, who was not feeling well, lay down on the parlor sofa for a nap. He never awoke. Like Abby, he was slaughtered by someone with an ax. Lizzie "discovered" his body, still lying on the sofa. She called Bridget, who had taken the back stairs to her attic room: "Come down quick; father's dead; somebody came in and killed him."

Experts have examined and reexamined the crime, and most have reached the same conclusion: Lizzie killed her father and stepmother. In fact, Lizzie was tried for the grue-some murders. However, despite a preponderance of evidence, an all male jury found her not guilty. Their verdict was unanimous and was arrived at without debate or disagree-ment. A woman of Lizzie's social position, they affirmed, simply could not have commit-ted such a terrible crime.

Even before the trial started, newspaper and magazine writers had judged Lizzie inno-cent for much the same reasons. As one expert on the case noted, "Americans were cer-tain that well-brought-up daughters could not commit murder with a hatchet on sunny summer mornings."

Jurors and editorialists alike judged Lizzie according to their preconceived notions of Victorian womanhood. They believed that such a woman was gentle, docile, and physi-cally frail, short on analytical ability but long on nurturing instincts.

Too uncoordinated and weak to accurately swing an ax and too gentle and unintel-ligent to coldly plan a double murder, women of Lizzie's background simply had to be innocent because of their basic innocence.

—*America and Its People*, Third Edition,
by James Martin et al.

Answer with *T* (true) or *F* (false).

_____T_____ 1. Andrew Borden's family suffered from his efforts to save money.

_____T_____ 2. Abby was probably correct in telling the doctor that her illness was due to poison.

_____F_____ 3. Andrew was killed when he discovered his wife dead.

_____T_____ 4. The jury did not carefully consider the evidence against Lizzie.

_____T_____ 5. The Victorian stereotyping of women worked in Lizzie's favor.

_____F_____ 6. The author believes that Lizzie was not guilty.

_____T_____ 7. The quotation marks around the word *discovered* change the connotation of the word.

PERSONAL FEEDBACK   2   Name _____

1. What characteristics do you have that are important for leadership? _____
_____

2. During this term, what have your leadership roles been? _____
_____

3. As the term has progressed, how has your thinking about college changed? _____
_____

4. How are your friends and loved ones affecting your academic success? _____
_____

5. What is most irritating about your roommates or people you live with? _____
_____

6. What will you remember most from this class? _____
_____

Share your responses as directed by your instructor.

SUMMARY POINTS

1 What is an inference? (page 320)
An inference is an implied meaning that is not directly stated but can be deduced from clues in the passage. Inferences require linking old knowledge to what is being read at the time.

2 Why do authors sometimes suggest rather than state meaning? (page 322)
Requiring the reader to infer the author's meaning is often more dramatic and interesting than stating it outright.

3 What is the role of prior knowledge in making inferences? (page 323)

Authors provide clues to their intended meaning but also make assumptions about the reader's prior knowledge of the subject. Therefore, it is important to recognize what you already know and fill in any missing knowledge to understand the clues.

4 How does slanted language relate to understanding the author's meaning? (page 325)

Slanted language manipulates the reader's attitude toward a subject in a positive or negative manner. Recognizing slanted language is another clue the reader has to the author's intended meaning.

5 How can I draw reasonable conclusions? (page 327)

Pay close attention to the details in the passage that provide clues to the author's meaning. Activate prior knowledge that relates to the topic and use logic to connect it to the clues. Making a reasonable inference requires the reader's prior knowledge and recognition of the details that have been provided by the author.

COLLABORATIVE PROBLEM SOLVING

Form a five-member group and select one of the following activities. Brainstorm, complete the activity, and then choose a member to present the group findings to the class.

➤ Use details, dialogue, and characters to create a cartoon about poorly performing public high schools that blames *teachers* for the problems.

➤ Use details, dialogue, and characters to create a cartoon about poorly performing public high schools that blames *students* for the problems.

➤ Use details, dialogue, and characters to create a cartoon about poorly performing public high schools that blames *parents* for the problems.

➤ Use details, dialogue, and characters to create a cartoon about poorly performing public high schools that blames a *lack of money* for the problems.

SELECTION 1 Literature: Short Story MyReadingLab™

Visit Chapter 7: Inference in MyReadingLab to complete the Selection 1 activities.

"Diamonds are nothing more than chunks of coal that stuck to their jobs."

—**Malcolm Forbes**

Diamonds have value because they sparkle and are cherished in the marketplace. That value, or price, is determined by the four Cs of diamonds: cut, clarity, color, and carat weight. If you are searching for specific prices, the range varies. For example, one company lists its one-carat round cut diamonds from $5,000 to $17,000 according to clarity and color. Another company offers one-carat stones with the same round cut for $3,000 to $16,000. For three-carat diamonds with round cuts, the range is $14,000 to $112,000 or $7,000 to $41,000. High prices make diamonds particularly attractive to thieves. Stones are also difficult to trace and easy to sell on the black market. Robbing a jewelry store may be easier than robbing a bank, and some people may think that both produce sure money.

THINKING BEFORE READING

Preview for content and organizational clues. Activate your schema and anticipate the author's opinion. Determine your purpose for reading. Think!

What factors contribute to the appeal and the price of diamonds?

Why are stolen diamonds easy to resell without being traced?

After reading this, I will probably want to _____.

VOCABULARY PREVIEW

Are you familiar with these words?

strolled	fashion plate	reluctantly	commotion	cooler
previous	mingled	dapper	confirmed	wading

Is Beyoncé a *fashion plate*?

Do you *reluctantly* go to the doctor?

When was the last time you *mingled* with people you didn't know?

Your instructor may choose to give a brief vocabulary review before or after reading.

THINKING DURING READING

As you read, use the six thinking strategies of a good reader: predict, picture, relate, monitor, correct, and annotate.

A DEAL IN DIAMONDS

It was seeing a girl toss a penny into the plaza fountain that gave Pete Hopkins the idea. He was always on the lookout for money-making ideas, and they were getting tougher to find all the time. But as he looked up from the fountain to the open window of the Downtown Diamond Exchange, he thought he had found a good one at last.

> ## Reader's **TIP**   Reading and Studying a Short Story
>
> Ask yourself the following questions as you read a short story:
>
> - How would you describe the main character? What other **characters** are well developed? What is the purpose of the "flat" characters? What do the characters learn? How do the characters change?
> - What is the main **conflict** in the story? What are the steps in the development of the **plot**? What is the **climax**? What is the **resolution**?
> - What is the **theme** of the story? What universal truth did you learn from the story?
> - When and where is the story set? How does the **setting** affect the theme?
> - Who is telling the story? How does this **point of view** affect the message?
> - What is the **tone** of the author? What **mood** is the author trying to create?
> - What **symbols** provide vivid images that enrich the theme?
> - What is your evaluation of the author's work?

5   He strolled over to the phone booth at the other side of the plaza and called Johnny Stoop. Johnny was the classiest dude Pete knew—a real fashion-plate who could walk into a store and have the clerks falling over themselves to wait on him. Better yet, he had no record here in the east. And it was doubtful if the cops could link him to the long list of felonies he had committed ten years ago in California.

10   "Johnny? This is Pete. Glad I caught you in."

"I'm always in during the daytime, Pete boy. In fact, I was just getting up."

"I got a job for us, Johnny, if you're interested."

"What sort?"

"Meet me at the Birchbark Bar and we'll talk about it."

15   "How soon?"

"An hour?"

Johnny Stoop groaned. "Make it two. I gotta shower and eat breakfast."

"Okay, two. See you."

The Birchbark Bar was a quiet place in the afternoons—perfect for the sort of meeting Pete wanted. He took a booth near the back and ordered a beer. Johnny was only ten
20   minutes late and he walked into the place as if he were casing it for a robbery or a girl he might pick up. Finally he settled, almost reluctantly, for Pete's booth.

"So what's the story?"

The bartender was on the phone yelling at somebody about a delivery, and the rest
25   of the place was empty. Pete started talking. "The Downtown Diamond Exchange. I think we can rip it off for a quick handful of stones. Might be good for fifty grand."

Johnny Stoop grunted, obviously interested. "How do we do it?"

"*You* do it. I wait outside."

"Great! And I'm the one the cops grab!"

30 "The cops don't grab anyone. You stroll in, just like Dapper Dan, and ask to see a tray of diamonds. You know where the place is, on the fourth floor. Go at noon, when there's always a few customers around. I'll create a commotion in the hall, and you snatch up a handful of stones."

"What do I do—swallow them like the gypsy kids used to do?"

35 "Nothing so crude. The cops are wise to that, anyway. You throw them out the window."

"Like hell I do!"

"I'm serious, Johnny."

"They don't even keep their windows open. They got air conditioning, haven't they?"

"I saw the window open today. You know all this energy-conservation stuff—turn 40 off the air conditioner and open the windows. Well, they're doing it. They probably fig- ure four flights up nobody's goin' to get in that way. But something can get *out*—the diamonds."

"It sounds crazy, Pete."

"Listen, you toss the diamonds through the window from the counter. That's maybe 45 ten feet away." He was making a quick pencil sketch of the office as he talked. "See, the window's behind the counter, and you're in front of it. They never suspect that you threw 'em out the window because you're never near the window. They search you, they question you, but then they gotta let you go. There are other people in the store, other suspects. And nobody saw you take them."

50 "So the diamonds go out the window. But you're not outside to catch them. You're in the hall creating a diversion. So what happens to the stones?"

"This is the clever part. Directly beneath the window, four stories down, is the fountain in the plaza. It's big enough so the diamonds can't miss it. They fall into the fountain and they're as safe as in a bank vault till we decide to get them. Nobody noticed them hit
55 the water because the fountain is splashing. And nobody sees them *in* the water because they're clear. They're like glass."

"Yeah," Johnny agreed. "Unless the sun—"

"The sun don't reach the bottom of the pool. You could look right at 'em and not notice 'em—unless you knew they were there. We'll know, and we'll come back for them
60 tomorrow night, or the next."

Johnny was nodding. "I'm in. When do we pull it off?"

Pete smiled and raised his glass of beer. "Tomorrow."

On the following day, Johnny Stoop entered the fourth floor offices of the Downtown Diamond Exchange at exactly 12:15. The uniformed guard who was always at the
65 door gave him no more than a passing glance. Pete watched it all from the busy hallway outside, getting a clear view through the thick glass doors that ran from floor to ceiling.

As soon as he saw the clerk produce a tray of diamonds for Johnny, he glanced across the office at the window. It was open about halfway, as it had been the previous day. Pete started walking toward the door, touched the thick glass handle, and fell over in an
70 apparent faint. The guard inside the door heard him fall and came out to offer assistance.

"What's the matter, mister? You okay?"

"I—I can't—breathe. . . ."

He raised his head and asked for a glass of water. Already one of the clerks had come around the counter to see what the trouble was.
75 Pete sat up and drank the water, putting on a good act. "I just fainted, I guess."

"Let me get you a chair," one clerk said.

"No, I think I'd better just go home." He brushed off his suit and thanked them. "I'll be back when I'm feeling better." He hadn't dared to look at Johnny, and he hoped the diamonds had gone out the window as planned.
80 He took the elevator downstairs and strolled across the plaza to the fountain. There was always a crowd around it at noon—secretaries eating their lunches out of brown-paper bags, young men casually chatting with them. He mingled unnoticed and worked his way to the edge of the pool. But it was a big area, and through the rippling water he couldn't be certain he saw anything except the scattering of pennies and nickels at the bottom.
85 Well, he hadn't expected to see the diamonds anyway, so he wasn't disappointed.

He waited an hour, then decided the police must still be questioning Johnny. The best thing to do was to head for his apartment and wait for a call.

It came two hours later.

"That was a close one," Johnny said. "They finally let me go, but they still might be
90 following me."

"Did you do it?"

"Sure I did it! What do you think they held me for? They were goin' crazy in there. But I can't talk now. Let's meet at the Birchbark in an hour. I'll make sure I'm not followed."

Pete took the same booth at the rear of the Birchbark and ordered his usual beer.
95 When Johnny arrived the dapper man was smiling. "I think we pulled it off, Pete. Damn if we didn't pull it off!"

"What'd you tell them?"

"That I didn't see a thing. Sure, I'd asked for the tray of stones, but then when there was the commotion in the hall I went to see what it was along with everyone else. There
100 were four customers in the place and they couldn't really pin it on any one of us. But they searched us all, and even took us downtown to be X-rayed, to be certain we hadn't swallowed the stones."

"I was wondering what took you so long."

"I was lucky to be out as soon as I was. A couple of the others acted more suspicious
105 than me, and that was a break. One of them even had an arrest record for a stolen car."

He said it in a superior manner. "The dumb cops figure anyone who stole a car would steal diamonds."

"I hope they didn't get too good a look at me. I'm the one who caused the commotion, and they just gotta figure I'm involved."

110 "Don't worry. We'll pick up the diamonds tonight and get out of town for a while."

"How many stones were there?" Pete asked expectantly.

"Five. And all beauties."

The evening papers confirmed it. They placed the value of the five missing diamonds at $65,000. And the police had no clue.

115 They went back to the plaza around midnight, but Pete didn't like the feel of it. "They might be wise," he told Johnny. "Let's wait a night, in case the cops are still snoopin' around up there. Hell, the stones are safe where they are."

The following night, when the story had already disappeared from the papers, replaced by a bank robbery, they returned to the plaza once more. This time they waited

120 till three A.M., when even the late crowd from the bars had scattered for home. Johnny carried a flashlight and Pete wore wading boots. He'd already considered the possibility that one or two of the diamonds might not be found, but even so they'd be far ahead of the game.

The fountain was turned off at night, and the calmness of the water made the search

125 easier. Wading in the shallow water, Pete found two of the gems almost at once. It took another ten minutes to find the third one, and he was ready to quit then. "Let's take what we got, Johnny."

The flashlight bobbed. "No, no. Keep looking. Find us at least one more."

Suddenly they were pinned in the glare of a spotlight, and a voice shouted, "Hold it

130 right there! We're police officers!"

"Damn!" Johnny dropped the flashlight and started to run, but already the two cops were out of their squad car. One of them pulled his gun and Johnny stopped in his tracks. Pete climbed from the pool and stood with his hands up.

"You got us, officer," he said.

135 "Damn right we got you," the cop with the gun growled.

"The coins in that fountain go to charity every month. Anybody that would steal them has to be pretty low. I hope the judge gives you both ninety days in the cooler. Now up against the car while we search you!"

(1,732 words)

—From *Ellery Queen's Mystery Magazine,*
by Edward D. Hoch

THINKING AND WRITING AFTER READING

RECALL Self-test your understanding.

Your instructor may choose to give you a brief comprehension review.

REACT Greed prompted the robbery, but how did excessive greed figure into the arrest? _____

_____

REFLECT What do you think Pete and Johnny did to escape charges for the diamond robbery when the police caught them? _____

_____

THINK CRITICALLY This story was first published in 1975. What modern changes in building construction and security might make such a heist far less probable today? Write your answer on a separate sheet of paper.

THINK AND WRITE What better or "safer" plan might have been devised for getting diamonds out of the fountain? Explain your ideas. _____

_____

EXTENDED WRITING Search the Internet for information on buying a good-quality diamond. Write a letter to a friend who wants to buy a diamond engagement ring. Provide solid advice based on your research about how to select the best quality diamond. Your letter should include an explanation of the "4 Cs."

INFERENCE QUESTIONS

1. Why does Pete want Johnny rather than himself to steal the diamonds?

   _____

   _____

2. Why does Pete's plan call for retrieving the diamonds a night or two after they are stolen? _____

   _____

   _____

3. What is the meaning of the phrase "Dapper Dan"? _____

   _____

4. Why was Johnny not arrested as a suspect in the crime? _____

   _____

   _____

5. What is suggested by the phrase "Pete didn't like the feel of it"? _____

   _____

   _____

Interpret THE QUOTE

Now that you have finished reading the selection, "A Deal in Diamonds," go back to the beginning of the selection and read the opening quote again. In the story, Pete and Johnny go to great lengths to steal the diamonds, yet what does Malcolm Forbes's quote say about the value of diamonds? On a separate sheet of paper, list three things (other than diamonds) that become valuable over time and explain why.

Name ——————————————————————

Date ——————————————————————

SELECTION 1

COMPREHENSION QUESTIONS

Answer the following *T* (true) or *F* (false).

Inference _____ 1. The diamond heist could have taken place in New York but not in Los Angeles.

Inference _____ 2. Johnny Stoop would have been detained longer by the police if the robbery had been in California.

Inference _____ 3. Pete gambled correctly that office workers having lunch around the fountain would not see the falling diamonds.

Inference _____ 4. The irony of the story is that the police arrested the right men for the wrong reasons.

Inference _____ 5. The reader can conclude that Johnny and Pete will be charged with the diamond robbery.

Inference _____ 6. The security guard was suspicious of Pete's fainting spell.

Inference _____ 7. The reader can conclude that one of the suspected Diamond Exchange customers confessed to a previous arrest.

Inference _____ 8. The two men were worried that the police might find the diamonds in the fountain if they waited longer than a night or two to collect them.

Detail _____ 9. Pete and Johnny found four of the diamonds before they were arrested.

Inference _____10. The police officers suspected that they had apprehended the men who were responsible for the diamond theft.

VOCABULARY

Answer the following with *a, b, c,* or *d* for the word or phrase that best defines the boldface word used in the selection. The number in parentheses indicates the line of the passage in which the word appears. In addition to the context clues, use a dictionary to more precisely define the technical terms.

_____ 1. "**strolled** over" (5)
    a. walked slowly
    b. called
    c. walked quickly
    d. looked

_____ 2. "a real **fashion-plate**" (6)
    a. set of dinner dishes
    b. well-dressed person
    c. jerk
    d. criminal

_____ 3. "almost **reluctantly**" (22)
    a. happily
    b. willingly
    c. quietly
    d. unenthusiastically

_____ 4. "create a **commotion**" (32)
    a. play
    b. job
    c. interest
    d. disturbance

_____ 5. "**previous** day" (68)
    a. subsequent
    b. prior
    c. following
    d. later

_____ 8. "**confirmed** it" (113)
    a. reported
    b. proved
    c. valued
    d. ignored

_____ 6. "He **mingled**" (82)
    a. blended
    b. walked
    c. talked
    d. shopped

_____ 9. "**Wading** in" (125)
    a. walking
    b. looking
    c. finding
    d. hiding

_____ 7. "**dapper** man" (95)
    a. grubby
    b. smelly
    c. elegant
    d. happy

_____ 10. "in the **cooler**" (137)
    a. refrigerator
    b. freezer
    c. drink
    d. jail

Your instructor may choose to give a brief vocabulary review.

VOCABULARY ENRICHMENT

Figurative Language

Writers and speakers use figurative language to spark the imagination and make the message more sensual and visual. The words create images in the mind and activate associations stored in memory. Figurative language is challenging, because figuring out the meaning demands logical and creative thinking.

A. **Simile.** A simile uses the words *like* or *as* to compare two unlike things. The purpose of a simile is to strengthen the message by adding a visual image. Similes usually dramatize the characteristics of nouns. As a reader, you must figure out the unique characteristic that the simile is describing. In the sentence, "The new teacher stood like a statue in front of the class," what does the simile add to the meaning? "Like a statue" describes the teacher as "stiff and unmoving." The simile adds humor and visual interest to the sentence.

Write the meaning of the boldface similes in the following sentences.

1. The boys were **like two peas in a pod** working on their cell phones.

    _____

2. My grandmother claims to be **as old as the hills**. _____

    _____

3. Her face was **as fresh as the morning dew**. _____

    _____

4. When he walked into the arcade, the little boy smiled **like a fox in a hen-house**. _____

5. Looking for the missing check was **like trying to find a needle in a hay-stack**. _____

B. **Metaphor.** Whereas a simile uses the words *like* or *as* to compare two unlike things, a metaphor does not use those words but instead states the comparison directly. For example, "The soccer player was a tiger" is a metaphor that dramatizes the player's aggressive spirit. If the statement had been, "The girl plays soccer like a tiger," the figure of speech would be a simile, but the meaning would remain the same.

Write the meaning of the boldface metaphors in the following sentences.

6. Superman is **made of steel**. _____

7. Her words were **daggers** directed toward his heart. _____

_____

8. She was a **willow** in the winds of time. _____

_____

9. The woman had **built a wall** between herself and others. _____

_____

10. He was her **world**. _____

ASSESS YOUR LEARNING

Review confusing questions, seek clarification, and make notes in your textbook to help you remember the new information and vocabulary. Use your textbook as a learning tool.

SELECTION 2 History MyReadingLab™

SELECTION 2

Visit Chapter 7: Inference in MyReadingLab to complete the Selection 2 activities.

"You can never cross the ocean until you have the courage to lose sight of the shore."
—Christopher Columbus

Each year on the second Monday in October, the United States celebrates Columbus Day. Children learn in elementary school that Christopher Columbus discovered America, but historians disagree about the facts. There is evidence to suggest that sailors from Africa, Scandinavia, Polynesia, China, or Japan might have reached the American mainland before Columbus's documented arrival in 1492. Without doubt, Norse Viking Leif Eriksson arrived on the North American coast in what is now eastern Canada around the year 1000, and his relatives returned later to establish a small, short-lived colony. However, it was Christopher Columbus who established permanent contact between Europe and the "New World." His accidental landing created massive cultural, political, and economic change.

THINKING BEFORE READING

Preview the selection for clues to the content and organizational clues. Activate your schema. Anticipate what is coming and think about your purpose for reading.

What were you taught about the discovery of America?

What motivated Columbus to make his historic voyage?

Why was Columbus's discovery called "America" and not "Columbia"?

I want to learn _____.

VOCABULARY PREVIEW

Are you familiar with these words?

circumference	undaunted	monarchs	rivalry	contemporary
caravels	fabled	falsifier	misconception	leagues

What is meant by the *circumference* of Earth?

Is a queen or king a *monarch*?

Does the word *leagues* have more than one meaning?

Your instructor may choose to give a brief vocabulary review before or after reading.

THINKING DURING READING

As you read, use the six thinking strategies of a good reader: predict, picture, relate, monitor, correct, and annotate.

THE STRANGE CAREER OF CHRISTOPHER COLUMBUS

Refer to the
Reader's **TIP**
for **History** on
page 227.

If it had not been for Christopher Columbus (Cristoforo Colombo), Spain might never have gained an American empire. Columbus was born in Genoa in 1451 of humble parentage, and little is known about his early life. Young Columbus soon devoured the classical learning that had so recently been rediscovered and made available in printed form. He mastered geogra-
5 phy, and—perhaps while sailing the coast of West Africa—he became obsessed with the idea of voyaging west across the Atlantic Ocean to reach Cathay, as China was then known.

In 1484, Columbus presented his plan to the king of Portugal. The Portuguese were just as interested as Columbus in reaching Cathay. However, they elected to voyage around the continent of Africa instead of following the route suggested by Columbus.
10 They suspected that Columbus had underestimated the circumference of the earth and that he would almost certainly starve before reaching Asia. The Portuguese decision eventually paid off quite handsomely. In 1498, one of their captains, Vasco da Gama, returned from the coast of India carrying a fortune in spices and other luxury goods.

Undaunted by rejection, Columbus petitioned Queen Isabella and King Ferdinand
15 of Spain for financial backing. At first, they were no more interested in his grand design than the Portuguese had been. But time was on Columbus's side. Spain's aggressive new monarchs envied the success of their neighbor, Portugal. Columbus boldly played on the rivalry between the countries, talking of wealth and empire. Indeed, for a person with little success or apparent support, he was supremely confident. One contemporary reported
20 that when Columbus "made up his mind, he was as sure he would discover what he did discover, and find what he did find, as if he held it in a chamber under lock and key."

SELECTION 2

Columbus's stubborn lobbying for the "Enterprise of the Indies" gradually wore down opposition in the Spanish court. Finally, Isabella and Ferdinand provided him with a small fleet that contained two of the most famous caravels ever constructed, the *Niña* and the
25   *Pinta*, as well as the square-rigged nao *Santa Maria*. The determined admiral set sail for Cathay in August 1492, the year of Spain's unification.

Educated Europeans of the fifteenth century knew the world was round. No one seriously believed that Columbus and his crew would tumble off the edge of the earth. The concern was with size, not shape. Columbus estimated the distance to the mainland of
30   Asia to be about 3,000 nautical miles, a voyage his small ships would have no difficulty completing. The actual distance is 10,600 nautical miles, however. If the New World had not been in his way, he and his crew would have run out of food and water long before they reached China, as the Portuguese had predicted.

After stopping in the Canary Islands to refit the ships, Columbus continued his west-
35   ward voyage in early September. When the tiny Spanish fleet sighted an island in the Bahamas after only thirty-three days at sea, the admiral concluded he had reached Asia. Since his mathematical calculations had obviously been correct, he assumed he would soon encounter the Chinese. It never occurred to Columbus that he had stumbled upon a new world. He assured his men, his patrons, and perhaps himself that the islands were
40   indeed part of the fabled "Indies." Or if not the Indies themselves, then they were surely an extension of the great Asian landmass. He searched for the splendid cities Marco Polo had described, but instead of meeting wealthy Chinese, Columbus encountered Native Americans, whom he appropriately, if mistakenly, called "Indians."

After his first voyage of discovery, Columbus returned to the New World three more
45   times. But despite his considerable courage and skill, he could never find the treasure his financial supporters in Spain angrily demanded. Columbus died in 1506 a frustrated but wealthy entrepreneur. He was unaware that he had reached a previously unknown continent separating Asia from Europe. The final disgrace came in December 1500 when an ambitious falsifier, Amerigo Vespucci, published a sensational account of his travels across
50   the Atlantic. The story convinced German mapmakers he had proved America was distinct from Asia. Before the misconception could be corrected, the name *America* gained general acceptance throughout Europe.

Only two years after Columbus's first voyage, Spain and Portugal almost went to war over the anticipated treasure of Asia. Pope Alexander VI negotiated a settlement that
55   pleased both kingdoms. Portugal wanted to exclude the Spanish from the west coast of Africa and, more importantly, from Columbus's new route to "India." Spain insisted on maintaining complete control over lands discovered by Columbus, which then still were regarded as extensions of China. The Treaty of Tordesillas (1494) divided the entire world along a line located 270 leagues west of the Azores. Any new lands discovered west of the
60   line belonged to Spain. At the time, no European had ever seen Brazil, which turned out to be on Portugal's side of the line. (To this day, Brazilians speak Portuguese.) The treaty failed to discourage future English, Dutch, and French adventurers from trying their luck in the New World.

(850 words)

—From *American Stories: A History of the United States, Combined Edition,* Third Edition,
by H. W. Brands, T. H. Breen, R. Hal Williams, and Ariela J. Gross

THINKING AND WRITING AFTER READING

RECALL   Self-test your understanding.

Your instructor may choose to give you a brief comprehension review.

REACT   What item of information conflicted or confirmed what you already knew about Columbus? _____

_____

REFLECT   What was the general belief about the shape of the Earth before Columbus's voyage in 1492? _____

_____

THINK CRITICALLY   How would Columbus's plans have changed if he had not believed that the world was round? _____

_____

_____

THINK AND WRITE   Create a timeline to indicate the sequence of events described in this selection.

EXTENDED WRITING   Put yourself in the place of Captain Columbus recording his 1492 voyage in the ship's log. Use the timeline as the basis for the entries, but include your ideas about Columbus's intentions, feelings, and reactions.

INFERENCE QUESTIONS

1. Why do you think there is not much information about Columbus's early life? _____

_____

_____

_____

2. Did the king of Portugal regret his decision not to fund Columbus's voyage? Explain. _____

_____

_____

_____

_____

3. What convinced Ferdinand and Isabella to fund Columbus's voyage?

_____

_____

_____

_____

4. What evidence from the selection supports the idea that Columbus was clever in his proposals to Ferdinand and Isabella? _____

_____

_____

_____

5. Why do you think the author chose the title "The Strange Career of Christopher Columbus"? _____

_____

_____

_____

Interpret THE QUOTE

Now that you've finished reading the selection, "The Strange Career of Christopher Columbus," go back to the beginning of the selection and read the opening quote again. Notice its author. What do you think Columbus meant by the statement?

Name ————————————————

Date ————————————————

COMPREHENSION QUESTIONS

Answer the following with *a, b, c,* or *d,* or fill in the blank. In order to help you analyze your strengths and weaknesses, the question types are indicated.

Main Idea _____ 1. The best statement of the main idea of this selection is

a. Columbus was determined and clever.

b. Columbus's career was highlighted by a discovery whose significance was not understood in his lifetime.

c. Columbus sailed to the New World with the sponsorship of the Spanish king and queen.

d. Columbus arrived in the New World in 1492.

Detail _____ 2. What country was known as Cathay in Columbus's time?

a. China

b. Portugal

c. Spain

d. America

Detail _____ 3. Which of the following is one of the reasons the king of Portugal refused to fund Columbus's voyage?

a. The king had no interest in competing with Spain for an expanded empire and neither did his advisers.

b. The king was not interested in a voyage to Cathay.

c. He thought Columbus was a poor sailor.

d. He thought Columbus had badly underestimated the distance to Cathay and would run out of food before arriving.

Inference _____ 4. From the details in the selection, we can infer that

a. Columbus was hailed as a hero when he returned to Spain with the news that he had landed in Asia.

b. Columbus was not concerned about finding treasure when he landed.

c. Columbus's calculations of distance to land were correct.

d. Columbus nearly gave up finding someone to fund his voyage.

Inference _____ 5. A reasonable inference based on the details in the passage is that at the time of his voyage in 1492, Columbus

a. already had a great deal of experience as a sailor.

b. was still a very young man.

c. had already attempted a voyage across the Atlantic.

d. had already sailed to Asia following the established route to the east around Africa.

Author's purpose _____ 6. Which of the following best describes the purpose of this selection?

    a. to convince readers that Columbus deserves credit for discovering America

    b. to entertain readers with an interesting historical account

    c. to inform readers of the events of Columbus's career, especially those surrounding his first voyage to the New World

    d. to persuade readers that Columbus discovered the New World accidentally

Inference _____ 7. Which of the following details from the selection supports the conclusion that Columbus truly believed that he had landed in a part of Asia?

    a. He knew the world was round.

    b. He still had enough food and water when he landed.

    c. He referred to the Native Americans as "Indians."

    d. He finally found the wealthy cities that Marco Polo described.

Answer the following questions with *T* (true) or *F* (false).

Inference _____ 8. Except for Brazil, which was granted to Portugal, Spain was given control over all of North and South America by the Treaty of Tordesillas.

Inference _____ 9. The English, Dutch, and French disregarded the Treaty of Tordesillas and colonized parts of North and South America.

Inference _____ 10. At least 14 years after his first voyage across the Atlantic, Columbus and most of Europe believed that the New World was an extension of the Asian continent.

VOCABULARY

Answer the following with *a, b, c,* or *d* for the word or phrase that best defines the boldface word used in the selection. The number in parentheses indicates the line of the passage in which the word appears. In addition to the context clues, use a dictionary to more precisely define the technical terms.

_____ 1. "**circumference** of the earth" (10)

    a. length
    b. twice the radius
    c. distance across the Atlantic
    d. distance around

_____ 2. "**Undaunted** by rejection" (14)

    a. not stopped
    b. made fearful
    c. worried
    d. unhappy

_____ 3. "new **monarchs**" (17)

    a. countries
    b. populations
    c. explorers
    d. royals

_____ 4. "**rivalry** between" (18)

    a. friendliness
    b. teasing
    c. competition
    d. warfare

_____ 5. "One **contemporary** reported" (19)

    a. ancestor
    b. person of the same time
    c. expert
    d. person of the next generation

_____ 6. "most famous **caravels**" (24)

    a. light sailing ships
    b. type of steamship
    c. heavy ships
    d. small fishing vessels

SELECTION 2

_____ 7. "of the **fabled** 'Indies'" (40)

    a. mysterious
    b. legendary
    c. wealthy
    d. exotic

_____ 8. "ambitious **falsifier**" (49)

    a. explorer
    b. seafarer
    c. faker
    d. self-promoter

_____ 9. "Before the **misconception**" (51)

    a. lie
    b. idea
    c. truth
    d. error

_____ 10. "270 **leagues**" (59)

    a. sports organizations
    b. about five kilometers or three miles
    c. about one mile
    d. groups

Your instructor may choose to give a brief vocabulary review.

VOCABULARY ENRICHMENT

Idiom

An **idiom** is a phrase used mainly in conversation that has meaning other than the literal meaning of the words themselves. For example, the phrase "My eyes were bigger than my stomach" is an idiom. The exact, literal meaning of the words is anatomically impossible. In our culture, however, the phrase is a creative way of saying, "I took more food on my plate than I could possibly eat." Other languages may not have this exact same expression, but they may have different idioms to express the same idea. Students who learn English as a second language find our idioms confusing when they look for an exact translation.

Idioms are slang phrases, clichés, and regional expressions. Their popularity changes with the times. Grandparents may use idioms that would make a college student shudder. Professional writers try to avoid idioms because they are considered informal.

Write the meaning of the boldface idioms in the following sentences.

1. Thomas's first-born son is **a chip off the old block**. _____

_____

2. It was getting late, and the mother decided to **hit the road** with her children.

_____

3. With that inappropriate comment to his students, the professor really **crossed the line**. _____

_____

4. Many inventors and entrepreneurs are experts at **thinking outside the box**.

_____

_____

5. Her father can be demanding and outspoken, but Suzanne knows that **his bark is worse than his bite**. _____

_____

6. Cynthia's dog has taken obedience class three times yet remains untrained; he is definitely **not the sharpest knife in the drawer**. _____

_____

7. When she learned that her son had made online purchases using her debit card, the mother **raked him over the coals**. _____

_____

8. After seeing the negative effects of his dishonesty, the student vowed to **turn over a new leaf** and turn in only his own work. _____

_____

9. The new coach is in favor of discipline and hard work; he makes his players **toe the line**. _____

10. Students who have jobs and attend college full-time often find themselves **burning the candle at both ends**. _____

_____

ASSESS YOUR LEARNING

Review confusing questions, seek clarification, and make notes in your text to help you remember the new information and vocabulary. Use your textbook as a learning tool.

SELECTION 3   ⚖ Criminal Justice   MyReadingLab™

Visit Chapter 7: Inference in MyReadingLab to complete the Selection 3 activities and Building Background Knowledge video activity.

"Our fight against human trafficking is one of the great human rights causes of our time, and the United States will continue to lead it—in partnership with you. The change we seek will not come easy, but we can draw strength from the movements of the past. For we know that every life saved—in the words of that great Proclamation—is 'an act of justice'; worthy of 'the considerate judgment of mankind, and the gracious favor of Almighty God.'"

—Barack Obama

It is estimated that more than 20 million men, women and children around the world are victims of human trafficking. The United States is a source, transit and destination country for some of these men, women and children—both U.S. citizens and foreign nationals—who are subjected to the injustices of human trafficking, including forced labor, debt bondage, involuntary servitude, and sex trafficking. Trafficking in persons can occur in both lawful and illicit industries or markets, including in brothels, massage parlors, street prostitution, hotel services, hospitality, agriculture, manufacturing, janitorial services, construction, health and elder care, and domestic service, among others.

http://www.whitehouse.gov/issues/foreign-policy/end-human-trafficking

THINKING BEFORE READING

Preview the selection for clues to the content and organizational clues. Activate your schema. Anticipate what is coming and think about your purpose for reading.

What is the difference between human smuggling and human trafficking?

How big is the problem?

What are the challenges for law enforcement?

I want to learn _____.

BUILDING BACKGROUND KNOWLEDGE — VIDEO

Sex Trafficking and the Super Bowl

To prepare for reading Selection 3, answer the questions below. Then, watch this video about what authorities are doing during big events like the Super Bowl to help sex trafficking victims.

Why might efforts to control sex trafficking focus on events like the Super Bowl?

Have you seen billboards or other signs that offer help to trafficking victims? If so, where?

In an airport, for example, what clues might cause authorities to suspect that a person is being trafficked?

This video helped me _____.

VOCABULARY PREVIEW

Are you familiar with these words?

coercion	transnational	distinctions	facilitation	clandestinely
fraudulent	exploitation	notorious	lax	vulnerable

What does the prefix *trans* mean in the word *transnational*?

Does *facilitation* make something easier?

Is a famous person also *notorious*?

Your instructor may choose to give a brief vocabulary review before or after reading.

THINKING DURING READING

As you read, use the six thinking strategies of a good reader: predict, picture, relate, monitor, correct, and annotate.

HUMAN SMUGGLING AND TRAFFICKING

Refer to the
Reader's TIP
for **Criminal Justice**
on page 51.

The global nature of crime requires coordination of law enforcement efforts throughout the world. For American law enforcement it requires activities beyond national borders. In 2000, for example, the U.S. Congress passed the Trafficking Victims Protection Act (TVPA). Trafficking offenses under the law are aimed primarily at international offenders.

5   They include (1) sex trafficking, in which a commercial sex act is induced by force, fraud, or coercion or in which the person induced to perform such act has not attained 18 years of age, and (2) the recruitment, harboring, transportation, provision, or obtaining of a person for labor services, through the use of force, fraud, or coercion, for the purpose of

10   subjection to involuntary servitude, peonage, debt bondage, or slavery. The TVPA also provides funds for training U.S. law enforcement personnel at international police academies.
U.S. police agencies routinely send agents to assist law enforcement officers in other countries who are involved in transnational investigations.

Under the TVPA, human trafficking does not require the crossing of an international
border. It does not even require the transportation of victims from one location to another.
15   That's because victims of severe forms of trafficking are not always illegal aliens. They may
be U.S. citizens, legal residents, or visitors. Victims do not have to be women or children;
they may also be adult males. A revision of the TVPA in 2003 added a new initiative to the
original law. It allows enforcement agencies to collect foreign data on trafficking investigations, prosecutions, convictions, and sentences. The TVPA was authorized again in 2005,
20   2008, and 2013.

According to the United Nations, trafficking in persons and human smuggling are
some of the fastest growing areas of international criminal activity today. There are important distinctions that must be made between these two forms of crime.

HUMAN SMUGGLING

Following federal law, the U.S. State Department defines **human smuggling** as "the facili-
25   tation, transportation, attempted transportation or illegal entry of a person(s) across an
international border, in violation of one or more country's laws, either clandestinely or
through deception, such as the use of fraudulent documents." In other words, human
smuggling refers to illegal immigration in which an agent is paid to help a person cross
a border secretly. The purpose of human smuggling may be to obtain financial or other
30   benefits for the smuggler. However, sometimes people engage in smuggling for other
motives, such as to reunite their families. Human smuggling generally occurs with the
consent of those being smuggled, and they often pay a smuggler for his or her services.
Once in the country they've paid to enter, smuggled individuals rarely remain in contact
with the smuggler. The State Department notes that the vast majority of people who are
35   helped to enter the United States illegally each year are smuggled, rather than trafficked.

Although smuggling might not involve active coercion, it can be deadly. In January
2007, for example, truck driver Tyrone Williams, 36, a Jamaican citizen living in Sche-
nectady, New York, was sentenced to life in prison for causing the deaths of 19 illegal
immigrants in the nation's deadliest known human smuggling attempt. Williams locked
40   more than 70 immigrants in a container truck during a 2003 trip from South Texas to
Houston but abandoned the truck about 100 miles from its destination. The victims died
from dehydration, overheating, and suffocation in the Texas heat before the truck was
discovered and its doors opened.

HUMAN TRAFFICKING

In contrast to smuggling, **trafficking in persons (TIP)** can be compared to a modern-day
45   form of slavery. Former Secretary of State Condoleezza Rice said that "defeating human
trafficking is a great moral calling of our day." Trafficking involves the exploitation of unwilling or unwitting people through force, coercion, threat, or deception. It includes human
rights abuses such as debt bondage, deprivation of liberty, or lack of control over freedom
and labor. Trafficking is often undertaken for purposes of sexual or labor exploitation.
50   U.S. government officials estimate that 800,000 to 900,000 victims are trafficked
globally each year and that 17,500 to 18,500 are trafficked into the United States. Women
and children comprise the largest group of victims, and they are often physically and
emotionally abused. Although TIP is often an international crime that involves the crossing of borders, it is important to note that TIP victims can be trafficked within their own
55   countries and communities. Traffickers can move victims between locations within the
same country and often sell them to other trafficking organizations.

The International Labor Organization, an agency of the United Nations, estimates
that there are 12.3 million people in forced labor, bonded labor, forced child labor, and
sexual servitude throughout the world today. Other estimates range as high as 27 million.

SELECTION 3

TABLE 1 DISTINGUISHING BETWEEN HUMAN TRAFFICKING AND SMUGGLING

Trafficking	Smuggling
Must contain an element of force, fraud, or coercion (actual, perceived, or implied), unless victim under 18 years of age is involved in commercial sex acts.	The person being smuggled is generally cooperating.
Forced labor and/or exploitation.	No forced labor or other exploitation.
Persons trafficked are victims.	Persons smuggled are violating the law. They are not victims.
Victims are enslaved, are subjected to limited movement or isolation, or have had documents confiscated.	Smuggled individuals are free to leave, change jobs, etc.
Need not involve the actual movement of the victim.	Facilitates the illegal entry of people from one country into another.
May or may not cross an international border.	Always crosses an international border.
Victim must be involved in labor/services or commercial sex acts (that is, must be "working").	Person must only be in country or attempting entry illegally.

Note: This table is meant to be conceptual and is not intended to provide precise legal distinctions between struggling and traffcking.

Source: Adapted from U.S. Department of State, Bureau for International Narcotics and Law Enforcement Affairs, Human Smuggling and Trafficking Center, *Distinctions between Human Smuggling and Human Trafficking* (Washington, D.C: January 1, 2005).

60   It is sometimes difficult to distinguish between smuggling and trafficking because trafficking often includes an element of smuggling (that is, the illegal crossing of a national border). Moreover, some trafficking victims may believe they are being smuggled when they are really being trafficked. This happens, for example, when women trafficked for sexual exploitation believe they are agreeing to work in legitimate industries for decent

65   wages. They may even have agreed to pay part of their wages to the trafficker who smuggled them. They didn't know that the traffickers would keep them in bondage, subject them to physical force or sexual violence, force them to work in the sex trade, and take most or all of their income. United Nations literature notes that Chinese syndicates are notorious for continuing to control the lives of migrants at their destination. They disci-

70   pline them by force and demand heavy payment for smuggling services—holding "their clients as virtual hostages until the fees have been paid."

The U.S. Department of State's *Trafficking in Persons* report says that "human trafficking is a multidimensional threat. It deprives people of their human rights and freedoms, it increases global health risks, and it fuels the growth of organized crime." At the individual

75   level, the report notes, "human trafficking has a devastating impact on individual victims, who often suffer physical and emotional abuse, rape, threats against self and family, document theft, and even death."

The distinction between smuggling and trafficking is sometimes very subtle. But fraud,

80   force, or coercion generally distinguishes trafficking from smuggling. However, under U.S. law, if the person is under 18 and induced to perform a commercial sex act, then it is considered trafficking, regardless of whether fraud, force, or coercion is involved. Table 1 provides a guide to distinguishing human trafficking from smuggling.

A WORLDWIDE INDUSTRY

According to the United Nations, human smuggling and trafficking have become a worldwide industry that "employs" millions of people and leads to the annual turnover of bil-

85   lions of dollars. The United Nations also says that many of the routes used by smugglers are well established and widely known. For example, routes from Mexico and Central

America to the United States; from West Asia through Greece and Turkey to Western Europe; and within East and Southeast Asia are regularly traveled. More often than not, the United Nations says, the ongoing existence of flourishing smuggling routes is assisted 90 by weak legislation, lax border controls, corrupt officials, and the power and influence of organized crime.

THE VICTIMS

While there are significant differences between TIP and human smuggling, the underlying conditions that give rise to both of these illegal activities are often similar. Extreme poverty, lack of economic opportunity, civil unrest, and political uncertainty are all fac-95 tors that contribute to social environments in which human smuggling and trafficking in persons occurs.

In addition to targeting people escaping from difficult situations in other countries, traffickers also prey on victims within the United States. Homeless people, runaway and "throw-away" youth, and mistreated and exploited children are most vulnerable. Accord-100 ing to the organization Children at Risk, there are 200,000 American children who are "at risk" to be sex trafficked each year; one out of three runaways is lured into sex trafficking within 48 hours of leaving home.

Traffickers also use social media and Internet sites to entice and entrap victims. Sites such as Craigslist and Backpage.com provide a platform for finding victims as well as for 105 selling them. Because these sites are legitimate businesses protected by the federal Communications Decency Act, policing them is complicated.

NEED FOR AWARENESS

The issue of human trafficking is complex, and there is no one solution. However, citizen awareness is critical. Section 7202 of the Intelligence Reform and Terrorism Prevention Act of 2004 established the Human Smuggling and Trafficking Center within the U.S. 110 State Department. The secretary of state, the secretary of homeland security, the attorney general, and members of the national intelligence community oversee the center. The center was created to achieve greater integration and overall effectiveness in the U.S. government's enforcement of issues related to human smuggling and trafficking in persons.

Visit the Human Smuggling and Trafficking Center via http://www.state.gov/m/ds/ 115 hstcenter. Learn more about the characteristics of suspected human trafficking incidents at http://www.justicestudies.com/pubs/humtraffick.pdf, and about human sex trafficking at http://www.justicestudies.com/pubs/sextraffick.pdf.

To get help or report a tip, call the National Human Trafficking Resource Center at 1-888-3737-888. The National Human Trafficking Resource Center (NHTRC) is a national, 120 toll-free hotline available to answer calls from anywhere in the country, 24 hours a day, 7 days a week, every day of the year. The NHTRC is not a law enforcement or immigration authority and is operated by a nongovernmental organization funded by the federal government.

(1,518 words)

—From *Criminal Justice Today: An Introductory Text for the 21st Century*, Twelfth Edition, by Frank Schmalleger, and *Facts and Issues*, "Human Trafficking in Texas. A Study by the League of Women Voters of Texas Education Fund," Summer 2013

THINKING AND WRITING AFTER READING

RECALL Self-test your understanding.

Your instructor may choose to give you a brief comprehension review.

REACT Was there something in this selection that shocked, surprised, or especially disturbed you? Explain. _____

_____

REFLECT What does the article say about how the United States is addressing the problem of human trafficking? _____

_____

_____

THINK CRITICALLY What additional action might be taken to combat human trafficking?_____

_____

_____

_____

THINK AND WRITE Make Cornell-style notes to record the most important information from the selection. Next, write one paragraph to record your reaction to the reading selection and your thoughts about the topic.

EXTENDED WRITING Write a public service announcement that might be broadcast on television and radio to inform the public of human trafficking. Include actions that individuals can take if they suspect trafficking situations or are victims of human trafficking.

INFERENCE QUESTIONS

Journal #5

6 reasons

1. Why do human smuggling and human trafficking require cooperation among enforcement agencies throughout the world? _____

_____

_____

_____

_____

2. In what ways is trafficking in persons (TIP) similar to the American slave trade of the 1700s and 1800s? _____

_____

_____

3. In what ways is TIP today different than the slave trade of the 1700s and 1800s? _____

_____

_____

_____

_____

4. Why might people unknowingly fall into the hands of a trafficker? _____

_____

_____

_____

_____

_____

5. If some smuggling routes are well known, why aren't border procedures

tightened and corrupt officials arrested? _____

_____

_____

Interpret THE QUOTE

Now that you've finished reading the selection, "Human Smuggling and Trafficking," go back to the beginning of the selection and read the opening quote again. Notice its author. President Barack Obama was speaking in April 2013 to people from all walks of life at the White House Forum on Human Trafficking. What do you think was the "great Proclamation" to which he referred?

SELECTION 3

Name _____

Date _____

SELECTION 3

COMPREHENSION QUESTIONS

Answer the following with *a*, *b*, *c*, or *d*, or fill in the blank. In order to help you analyze your strengths and weaknesses, the question types are indicated.

Main Idea _____ 1. The best statement of the main idea of this selection is

    a. Something must be done to stop human smuggling and trafficking.

    b. The horror of human smuggling and trafficking

    c. Human smuggling and trafficking are serious global problems.

    d. It is often difficult to separate human smuggling from human trafficking.

Detail _____ 2. The Trafficking Victims Protection Act (TVPA) aims especially at

    a. international offenders.

    b. American offenders.

    c. crimes involving human smuggling.

    d. sex trafficking of adults over the age of 18

Detail _____ 3. Human smuggling usually involves

    a. movement of people within the United States from one state to another.

    b. the consent of the people being smuggled.

    c. both smuggling and trafficking.

    d. no harmful or dangerous conditions.

Inference _____ 4. From the details in the selection, we can infer that

    a. human trafficking is a more serious crime than human smuggling.

    b. human trafficking can be punishable with the death penalty.

    c. most trafficking involves forced factory labor.

    d. human smuggling rarely, if ever, results in harm to the smuggled person.

Inference _____ 5. A reasonable inference based on the details in the passage is that the United States began its most serious efforts to combat human trafficking in

    a. 1995.

    b. 2000.

    c. 2005.

    d. 2010.

Author's purpose _____ 6. Which of the following best describes the primary purpose of this selection?

    a. to inform readers about the crimes of human smuggling and trafficking

    b. to frighten readers by describing human smuggling and trafficking

    c. to persuade readers to take action against human smuggling and trafficking

    d. to provide readers with contact information to learn more about human smuggling and trafficking

Detail _____ 7. The selection states that under United States law,

    a. when any person is forced to commit a sex act, it is considered human trafficking.

    b. It is considered human trafficking only if an adult is forced to commit a sex act for commercial purposes.

    c. if a minor commits a sex act for commercial purposes, even if it is voluntary, it is considered human trafficking.

    d. when any person is forced to commit a sex act for commercial purposes, it is considered human trafficking.

Answer the following questions with *T* (true) or *F* (false).

Detail _____ 8. Most people who are assisted to enter the United States illegally are smuggled and then trafficked.

Inference _____ 9. The selection implies that the United Nations is involved in the fight against human smuggling and trafficking.

Inference _____ 10. One of the most important elements in combating human trafficking is public awareness.

VOCABULARY

Answer the following with *a, b, c,* or *d* for the word or phrase that best defines the boldface word used in the selection. The number in parentheses indicates the line of the passage in which the word appears. In addition to the context clues, use a dictionary to more precisely define the technical terms.

_____ 1. "fraud, or **coercion**" (6)

    a. violence
    b. force
    c. weaponry
    d. persuasion

_____ 2. "**transnational** investigations" (13)
    a. national
    b. worldwide
    c. local
    d. secret

_____ 3. "important **distinctions**" (23)

    a. differences
    b. qualities
    c. similarities
    d. decisions

_____ 4. "the **facilitation**" (24–25)

    a. arrangement
    b. planning
    c. destruction
    d. assistance

_____ 5. "either **clandestinely**" or" (26)

    a. secretly
    b. purposely
    c. legally
    d. openly

_____ 6. "**fraudulent** documents" (27)

    a. genuine
    b. damaging
    c. fake
    d. unclear

_____ 7. "labor **exploitation**" (49)

    a. employment
    b. jobs
    c. payment
    d. abuse

_____ 8. "syndicates are **notorious**" (69)

    a. dangerous
    b. honorable
    c. dishonorable
    d. popular

SELECTION 3

_____ 9. "**lax** border controls"
(90)
a. strict
b. sloppy
c. severe
d. careful

_____ 10. "are most **vulnerable**"
(99)
a. in danger
b. frightened
c. injured
d. troubled

Your instructor may choose to give a brief vocabulary review.

VOCABULARY ENRICHMENT

A. Use the context clues in the sentences to write the meaning of the boldface words.

1. **Narratives** never preach but rather deliver a message to our emotions, senses, and imagination through a powerful shared experience.

   _____

   _____

2. The **theme** of a story about a college tennis champion might be that the journey to the top, including the hard work and discipline, was more meaningful than the final victory. _____

   _____

3. Poisoned apples and talking mirrors may not seem realistic in a modern telephone conversation; however, in the context of Snow White, we easily find both **plausible.** _____

   _____

4. E. M. Forster said that "The king died, and the queen died" is a narrative, but changing this to "The king died, and the queen died of grief" creates a **plot.** _____

   _____

5. The **suspense** of a narrative is based on conflict, which perhaps starts out as mild and intensifies as each incident occurs. _____

   _____

   _____

6. Good writers select incidents and details that give **unity** to the story and advance the central theme. _____

   _____

ASSESS YOUR LEARNING

Review confusing questions, seek clarification, and make notes in your text to help you remember new information and vocabulary.

VOCABULARY LESSON

Call Out and Remember to Send

Study the roots, words, and sentences.

Roots *claim, clam*: declare, call out *mem*: remember *mitt, miss*: send

Words with *claim* or *clam* = *declare* or *call out*

Can an *exclamation* point end a sentence? What is *unclaimed* freight?

- Clamor: a racket

  The suitcases made a *clamor* as they fell off the rack.

- Reclaim: regain or demand the return of

  After recovering from an injury, the tennis star *reclaimed* the championship.

- Disclaim: cut off, deny

  If you insult the host, I will *disclaim* ever knowing you.

- Exclaim: cry out

  At the celebration, the patriots *exclaimed* in their joy of victory.

- Irreclaimable: cannot be restored

  The moving company declared that the broken furniture was *irreclaimable*.

- Proclamation: a notice to the public

  A *proclamation* concerning taxation was published in the newspaper.

- Claimant: one who makes a claim

  The *claimant* told the insurance company that a tree hit the car in a hurricane.

Words with *mem* = *remember*

Are most *memos* short? Do holidays jog *unremembered* feelings?

- Memento: something to make one remember

  The small statue is a *memento* of my trip to Italy.

- Memoir: a record to remember

  The soldier's *memoirs* gave a personal perspective to the war.

- Memorandum: a note or reminder

  Because a *memorandum* is a business correspondence, make it short.

- Memorable: worth remembering

  With the family together, Thanksgiving dinner was a *memorable* event.

- Memorabilia: things valued for the memories associated with them.

  Elvis *memorabilia* are sold at Graceland.

- Commemorate: to observe and remember

  Display a flag to *commemorate* Independence Day.

- Memorial: a reminder of a distinguished person or a great event

  The fountain was a *memorial* to the founder of the city.

Words with *mit* or *miss* = *send*

Do you *admit* errors? Will you *permit* me to use you as a reference?

- Missile: something sent through the air

  The *missile* was directed toward enemy territory.

- Emissary: a messenger sent on a mission

  She sent an *emissary* to the French government.

- Remiss: careless

  I would be *remiss* if I did not remind you that the gates close at midnight.

- Remit: pay

  The phone company asked me to *remit* another thirty dollars.

- Submit: surrender

  He had to *submit* to a body search at the airport.

- Emit: to send out

  The car seems to be *emitting* pollution.

Review

Part I

Answer the following with *T* (true) or *F* (false).

___T___ 1. An exhaust emissions check measures automobile pollution.

___T___ 2. Veterans Day commemorates those who served our country.

___T___ 3. To receive an insurance payment, the claimant must suffer a loss.

___F___ 4. Irreclaimable goods are fixed rather than replaced.

___T___ 5. A "We are not responsible for" statement is a company disclaimer.

___T___ 6. To reclaim checked goods, you usually need a ticket.

___T___ 7. To be remiss is to neglect a duty.

___T___ 8. A memoir is nonfiction.

___T___ 9. Olympic memorabilia include collectors' pins for the events.

___F___ 10. If you remit money, you refuse to pay.

Part II

Choose the best word from the list as a synonym for the following.

memorandum	emissary	proclamation	exclamation	memoir
clamor	memorial	remittance	missile	memento

11. book   _memoir_

12. Washington Monument   _memorial_

13. person   _emissary_

14. keepsake   _memento_

15. correspondence   _memorandum_

16. noise   <u>clamor</u>

17. rocket   <u>missile</u>

18. official announcement   <u>proclamation</u>

19. cry   <u>exclamation</u>

20. payment   <u>remittance</u>

Reading Newspaper Editorials

Editorials. Unlike news stories, **editorials** are one of the few types of articles in newspapers that are subjective—that is, they express the opinion of a person or an organization. A newspaper's editorial pages feature the views of its management and editors. Issues discussed in these pieces are usually related to particular local, national, or international news stories.

Although the style of editorials varies as widely as people's opinions, the basic format is usually the same: Two or three brief paragraphs describe a scene or provide historical background leading up to the main theme that the writer intends to discuss. After stating a position, the writer follows up with examples, data, and analysis to support the position. Once the case has been made, alternative ideas and solutions may be provided and may also include the writer's prediction of what will happen if the current situation is not changed. The final paragraphs summarize and restate the main idea of the editorial.

Remember that editorials *always express opinions*, and regardless of how persuasive the writer's argument might be, you are free to reject it. Newspapers encourage readers to express their own opinions—either for or against editorials—in the Letters to the Editor section. Selected letters are published in the newspaper, usually in the same section with the editorials, and they often feature the views of readers who disagree with recent editorials or with the way in which a news story has been reported.

Reader's TIP Reading an Editorial

While reading an editorial, ask yourself the following questions:

- What event prompted the editorial?
- What is the thesis or opinion being promoted by the author?
- Do the details prove the thesis?
- Is the author liberal or conservative?
- What is left out?
- Are the sources, facts, and other support credible?

EXERCISE 1 Read the following editorial to answer the questions.

1. What event does the writer describe to introduce the main idea? _Mayor talking about the City Council taking over the funding._

2. What is the writer's main idea? _People do not choose poverty society is less fortunate._

Tuesday, April 22, 2014

Political Poverty

In a recent speech to the Linville Chamber of Commerce, Mayor Anderson praised the city council for its "new direction" and its efforts to eliminate city programs that "throw money" at social problems. The audience found this statement to their liking and responded enthusiastically.

However, one phrase in the mayor's speech was quite revealing. He believes it is wrong to expect "governments . . . to take over the upbringing of all who choose the low road to poverty."

What sort of misguided thinking is this—not only to blame those who are "grossly neglected" (as the Mayor characterized them) and who have "special needs for their predicaments," but to further stigmatize them by calling theirs "the low road"?

People do not choose poverty. People do not choose the obstacles they must overcome any more than they choose the family into which they are born. The physically challenged, the culturally deprived, and those lacking sufficient education can certainly take the responsibility for changing their circumstances, but cannot be blamed for those circumstances—no matter how convenient it may be for addressing the city's fiscal difficulties.

A moral society bears responsibility for providing aid and education to the less fortunate. We all contribute to this effort by paying our taxes. However, all too often our culture also rushes to blame victims for their own predicaments. This is because we have an unrealistic sense of our own immunity and invulnerability, believing we can avoid or surmount any challenge—in other words, always thinking "that could never happen to me." Perhaps we would feel more humble if we were the ones trying to overcome catastrophic illness without adequate medical care, trying to find a job without the skills provided by a sound public education system, or trying to feed a family on a minimum-wage salary. In such circumstances, the luxury of being as smug and self-assured as the mayor, the city council, and the Chamber members are would certainly be lost.

Proponents of this so-called new direction absolve themselves too easily of moral responsibility when the low road that they have chosen is one of convenience and callous indifference toward those already burdened and less fortunate than themselves.

---

3. What one example does the writer give that would help the mayor better understand this position? *People throws money at social problems*

4. Is the author liberal or conservative? _____

5. Is the main idea supported primarily by facts or opinions? *Opinions* *didn't choose-poverty souely is less fortunate*

EXERCISE 2

Locate an editorial that interests you in a local, city, or national newspaper. Cut out the editorial and answer the following questions:

1. What event prompted the editorial? _____

2. What is the author's opinion on the issue? _____

3. Do the details prove the thesis? Are they credible? _____

4. What has been left out? _____

8 Analytical Reasoning

Learning Objectives
From this chapter, readers will learn:

1 To recognize the characteristics of analytical thinkers
2 To use analytical thinking strategies to solve problems
3 To apply analytical thinking strategies when reading graphic illustrations

Everyday Reading Skills: Reading Credit Card Offers

WHAT IS ANALYTICAL THINKING?

A 2013 survey conducted by the National Association of Colleges and Employers asked hiring managers what qualities and skills they look for when hiring new college graduates. Not surprisingly, "ability to make decisions and solve problems" ranked very high on the list. In fact, it was second, just below "ability to work in a team." Of course, clear thinking is critical to dealing with all of life's challenges, but thinking skills are constantly tested in the workplace and certainly in college.

Solving a problem begins with understanding what the problem is. This process is called *analysis*—careful examination of the details to understand the nature of the whole. What do analytical thinkers do? They work through complex material in a logical, systematic way. They believe that a solution exists and work persistently without giving up. Analytical thinkers also draw on their schemata to comprehend new situations. In other words, they put old and new information together to create solutions.

Developing the habits of analytic thinking offers both immediate and future benefits. For example, after you struggle through and finally understand an introductory biology text, those same new habits of thinking transfer to the next biology course, which then will be easier to understand. You can also apply these thinking skills to different tasks. For instance, the very act of thinking through the complexities of biology will make it easier for you to tackle chemistry and physics. Gradually, you will develop the ability to educate yourself.

Two researchers, Benjamin Bloom and Lois Broder, observed eight key thinking strategies of successful students years ago in a classic study of college students. The list remains pertinent for success in college—and life—today. How many of the following characteristics describe you?

Put a plus sign (+) next to the strategies that you consistently use. Put an asterisk (*) next to those that you want to improve.

_____ Is careful and systematic in attacking the problem

_____ Can read directions and immediately choose a point at which to begin reasoning

_____ Keeps sight of goals while thinking through the problem

_____ Pulls out key terms and tries to simplify the material

_____ Breaks larger problems into smaller subproblems

_____ Is active and aggressive in seeking meaning

_____ Applies relevant old knowledge to the problem

_____ Is persistent and careful in seeking solutions

Successful students aggressively and systematically attack their studying, and they persist to a logical conclusion. As you can see, the strategies of analytical thinking just as easily apply to successful problem solving in everyday life as to success in the academic world. These characteristics contribute not only to success in college but also to the long-lasting personal success that is the ultimate reason for going to college.

The exercises in this chapter provide a chance to practice the strategies of good analytical thinkers, especially as they apply to reading. Approach each activity with a can-do attitude and expect to experience the satisfaction of working out the answers.

PERSONAL FEEDBACK 1   Name _____

1. What does *delayed gratification* mean, and how does it apply to college?_____

   _____

   _____

2. What causes you the most stress? _____

   _____

   _____

3. Describe a problem at home, work, or school that you enjoyed attacking and solving

   systematically. _____

   _____

   _____

4. What do you feel is your greatest problem-solving strength? _____

   _____

   _____

Share your responses as directed by your instructor.

ENGAGE IN PROBLEM SOLVING

Learning Objective 2

Use analytical thinking strategies to solve problems

Analytical thinking can be learned. Like everything else, it requires practice, and the more of it that you do, the better you will become. By increasing your analytical reasoning skills through problem solving, you can also learn the behaviors of good readers. Dividing a complex word problem into steps requires thinking skills that are similar to those used in breaking a paragraph down to get a main idea, draw a conclusion, or trace the details of a process. As you tackle the puzzles in this section, read the setup carefully, break the problems into small parts, and use logic to arrive at the solutions.

EXAMPLE   Read the following word problem and think about how you would figure out the answer.

Mary is shorter than Carol but taller than Kathy. Sue is taller than Mary but shorter than Carol. Which girl is tallest?

Although the problem may seem rather confusing at first reading, when it is broken down in sequential steps, the answer is simple. The best way to solve this problem is to draw a **diagram** so that you can visualize the relative height of each girl. Reread the problem and place each girl in a position on a vertical line.

Mary is shorter than Carol

    ⌈ Carol
    ⌊ Mary

but taller than Kathy.

    ⌈ Carol
    ├ Mary
    ⌊ Kathy

Sue is taller than Mary but shorter than Carol.

    ⌈ Carol
    ├ Sue
    ├ Mary
    ⌊ Kathy

EXPLANATION The diagram indicates that the tallest girl is Carol.

EXERCISE 1 Collaborate with a study buddy to answer the following questions. Share your steps in thinking with each other.

_____ 1. Which set of letters is different from the other three?

    a. GHIF   b. MNOK   c. RSTQ   d. CDEB

_____ 2. Face the south and turn to your right. Make another right turn and then an about-face. In which direction are you now facing?

_____ 3. According to the pattern, which letters should come next in the series?

    KL NO QR T __ __ __

_____ 4. A train arrived at its destination at 7:45, which was 3 hours and 50 minutes after its departure. What time was its departure?

_____ 5. According to the pattern, which numbers should come next in the series?

    1 2 4 5 7 8 10 11 __ __ __

_____ 6. Write the word *manage.* If deleting the first three letters or the last three letters leaves an actual word, circle the second *a* in the original word. If not, circle the first *a*.

_____ 7. According to the pattern, what numbers should come next in the series?

    1 6 11 16 21 __ __ __

8. Sylvia needed dental work in a small town with only two dentists. She met them both. Dr. Drill had beautiful teeth, but Dr. Fill's teeth needed work. Using logic, which dentist should Sylvia choose?

_____

_____

_____

9. Ellen, Carolyn, and Betsy each finished the road race at a different time. Their last names, not in order, are King, Wilson, and Harris. Wilson finished before Harris but after King. Betsy came in before Carolyn, and Ellen was last. What are the last names of Betsy and Ellen?

_____

10. Fran, Sally, and Marsha collect old books from different countries. Together they have a total of eighteen books. Six of the books are from Spain, with one more than that being the total from India and one less being the total from Holland. Sally has two books from Spain, and Fran has an equal number from India. Marsha has twice as many books from India as Fran has. Both Marsha and Fran have only one book each from Holland, and Fran has only one from Spain. How many books does Sally have? How many does Marsha have?

_____

	Holland	Spain	India	**Total**
Fran	1	1	2	4
Sally	3	2	1	6
Marsha	1	3	4	8
Total	5	6	7	18

Do you prefer working alone, or do you benefit more from working with a study buddy? _____

EXERCISE 2   Make notes or diagrams to help you solve the following problems.

1. Which set of letters differs from the other three? _____

_____

     a. ABCD   b. EFGH   c. IJKL   d. MNOP

2. What number would be next in this sequence?

_____

     3   4   6   9   13

—_The Great Book of Math Teasers_, by Robert Muller

3. **The nine-dot problem:** Without lifting your pencil from the paper, draw no more than four straight lines that will cross through all nine dots.

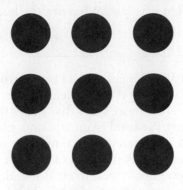

—*Conceptual Blockbusting: A Guide to Better Ideas,* Fourth edition, by James L. Adams

4. **The matchstick problem:** Move two matches to form four squares of equal size.

—*Basic Psychology,* by Howard H. Kendler

5. **Analogy:** What word completes the analogy?

Merchant: Sell : : Customer: _____

Lawyer: Client : : Doctor: _____

—From Richard J. Gerrig and Philip G. Zimbardo, *Psychology & Life,* 17th ed., figure
8.13D (page 266) and figure 18.14D (page 268). ©2005 Pearson Education, Inc.
Reproduced by permission of Pearson Education, Inc.

6. **String problem:** You are in the situation depicted below and are given the
task of tying the two strings together. If you hold one string, the other is out
of reach. Can you do it?

_____

_____

_____

7. **Anagram:** Rearrange the letters to make a common English word.

    KABSET _____

    LCENPI _____

8. **Series completion:** What number or letter would be next in each series?

    2 3 6 4 5 20 6 7 _____

    A B C Z D E F Y G H I _____

ANALYTICAL REASONING IN TEXTBOOKS

**Learning
Objective 3**

Apply analytical
thinking strate-
gies when reading
graphic illustrations

Apply analytical reasoning to every page of every textbook that you read. Reading is problem solving, and reading is thinking. Get in the habit of working
through complex ideas carefully and systematically. Simplify the material and
break it into smaller, more manageable ideas. Draw on what you already know,
and actively and aggressively seek to understand.

To help you visualize complex ideas, textbooks frequently include maps, tables,
diagrams, and graphs. These illustrations condense a lot of information into one
picture. Refer to such graphic illustrations while you read; the material will then
be easier to understand.

> ## Reader's TIP — Thinking About Maps, Charts, Diagrams, and Graphs
>
> 1. Read the title to determine the subject.
> 2. Read any information in italics or boldface.
> 3. Read the footnotes to determine the source of the information.
> 4. Read the labels to determine what each mark, arrow, figure, or design means.
> 5. Figure out the legend, the key, that shows what the markings represent.
> 6. Notice numbers indicating units of measurement, such as percentages, dollars, thousands, millions, or billions.
> 7. Notice trends and extremes. What is the average, and what are the highs and lows?
> 8. Refer back and forth to the text to follow a process or to label parts.
> 9. Draw conclusions based on the information.
> 10. Do not read more into an illustration than is supported by fact. In other words, don't draw conclusions that cannot be proved.

This chapter presents exercises on graphic illustrations and problems that require logical and sequential thinking. Before doing the exercises, read the hints in the Reader's Tip.

EXERCISE 3

Map: Collaborate with a study buddy to answer the following questions.

Earnings of Full-time U.S. Women Workers as a Percentage of Men's Earnings
The gender gap in earnings means that women are more likely to be at the low end of the income scale.

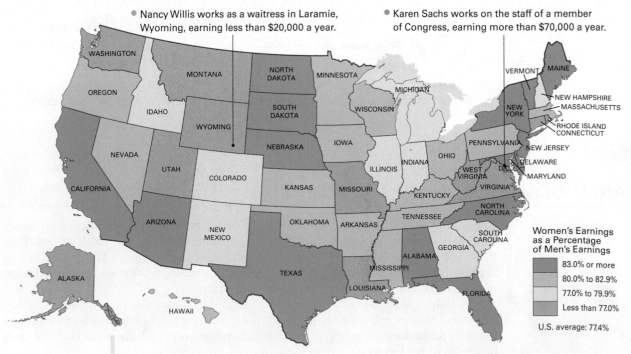

Nancy Willis works as a waitress in Laramie, Wyoming, earning less than $20,000 a year.

Karen Sachs works on the staff of a member of Congress, earning more than $70,000 a year.

Women's Earnings as a Percentage of Men's Earnings

- 83.0% or more
- 80.0% to 82.9%
- 77.0% to 79.9%
- Less than 77.0%

U.S. average: 77.4%

Source: U.S. Department of Labor (2011).

—*Social Problems*, Fifth Edition, by John Macionis

The purpose of the map is to show _____

_____

Use the map to answer the following with *T* (true), *F* (false), or *CT* (can't tell).

_____ 1. Average earnings of women across the United States is 90.0% of average earnings of men.

_____ 2. Women's earnings in Texas compare more favorably to men's than they do in Michigan.

_____ 3. The average salary for women is less than 77.0% of the average for men in only four states.

_____ 4. In more than half the states, the average salary for women is 80.0% of men's or higher.

_____ 5. The average salary for women working full-time in Wyoming is $20,000 a year.

6. Although the map does not show reasons, why do you think women generally make less money than men? _____

_____

_____

_____

_____

EXERCISE 4   **Table:** Collaborate with a study buddy to review the table and answer the questions that follow.

THE TEN LARGEST URBAN AREAS IN THE WORLD, 2010 AND 2025

	2010			2025 (Projected)	
Rank	Urban Area	Population (In millions)	Rank	Urban Area	Population (In millions)
1	Tokyo–Yokohama, Japan	36.7	1	Tokyo–Yokohama, Japan	37.1
2	Delhi, India	22.2	2	Delhi, India	28.6
3	São Paulo, Brazil	20.3	3	Mumbai (Bombay), India	25.8
4	Mumbai (Bombay), India	20.0	4	São Paulo, Brazil	21.7
5	Mexico City, Mexico	19.5	5	Dhaka, Bangladesh	20.9
6	New York–Newark, United States	19.4	6	Mexico City, Mexico	20.7
7	Shanghai, China	16.6	7	New York–Newark, United States	20.6
8	Kolkata (Calcutta), India	15.6	8	Kolkata (Calcutta), India	20.1
9	Dhaka, Bangladesh	14.6	9	Shanghai, China	20.0
10	Karachi, Pakistan	13.1	10	Karachi, Pakistan	18.7

Source: United Nations (2010).

—*Social Problems,* Fifth Edition, by John J. Macionis

The purpose of the table is _____

_____

Use the table to answer the following with *T* (true), *F* (false), or *CT* (can't tell).

_____ 1. The number of U.S. urban areas ranking in the world's ten largest urban areas of population drops from one to zero in the 15-year period projected by the table.

_____ 2. The New York City–Newark metropolitan area is projected to increase in population but fall in the ranking of the world's ten largest urban areas of population over the 15-year period shown.

_____ 3. All of the urban areas listed in the top ten for 2010 are also listed in the world's ten largest urban areas of population in 2025.

_____ 4. In the year 2013, the Shanghai area had over 20 million people.

_____ 5. The smallest amount of growth projected for 2025 is in Tokyo—Yokohama.

6. Why do you think some urban areas are expected to grow dramatically while others are not? Why are there no European cities in the top ten largest urban areas in the world? _____

_____

_____

_____

_____

_____

_____

EXERCISE 5   **Graphs That Spin**

Line graphs are an excellent way to depict trends and illustrate changes over time. Readers can easily see increases and decreases in a graph when the same data presented in a list of numbers are more difficult to absorb. However, graphs also present an opportunity to dramatize or minimize the trends. Readers must pay close attention to the time frame and the scale to interpret the data.

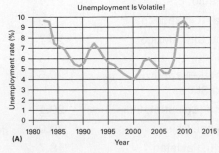

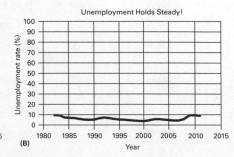

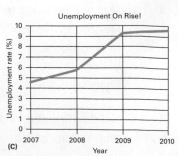

Source: Data from U.S. Department of Labor (2012).

—*Social Problems*, Fifth Edition, by John Macionis

The purpose of the graphs is to _____

_____

_____

Use the graphs to answer the following with *T* (true), *F* (false), or *CT* (can't tell).

_____ 1. Graphs A and B show unemployment rates over the same period of time.

_____ 2. The three graphs report different unemployment rates for 2010.

_____ 3. The high unemployment rates in 2010 were due to cheap labor opportunities overseas.

_____ 4. The time period showing unemployment rates in Graph A covers a smaller range than the scale in Graph C.

_____ 5. From 1980 to 2010, the lowest unemployment rate occurred in 2000.

EXERCISE 6   **Pie graphs:** Collaborate with a study buddy to study the pie graphs and to answer the questions.

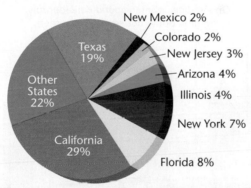

Where U.S. Latinos Live

New Mexico 2%
Colorado 2%
New Jersey 3%
Arizona 4%
Illinois 4%
New York 7%
Florida 8%
California 29%
Other States 22%
Texas 19%

Source: By J. Henslin. Based on *Statistical Abstract of the United States* 2011: Table 19.

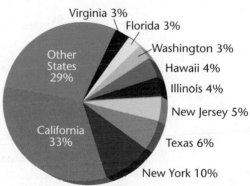

Where U.S. Asians Live

Virginia 3%
Florida 3%
Washington 3%
Hawaii 4%
Illinois 4%
New Jersey 5%
Texas 6%
New York 10%
California 33%
Other States 29%

Source: By L. Morris. Based on *Statistical Abstract of the United States*: 2011, Table 19.

Today, Latinos are the largest minority group in the United States. About 31 to 32 million people trace their origins to Mexico, 4 million to Puerto Rico, 1 to 2 million to Cuba, and about 8 million to Central or South America. As shown, almost two-thirds of Latinos live in just four states: California, Texas, Florida, and New York. Likewise, Asian Americans come to the Unites States from many nations: China, India, the Philippines, Vietnam, Korea, Japan, and other countries. Today, nearly half of this very diverse group lives in three states: California, New York, and Texas.

—Adapted from, *Essentials of Sociology: A Down-to-Earth Approach*,
Tenth Edition, by James M. Henslin

The purpose of the graphs is _____

_____

Use the pie graphs to answer the following with *T* (true), *F* (false), or *CT* (can't tell).

_____ 1. Over 25% of Latino Americans live in Texas and Florida.

_____ 2. The majority of Puerto Rican Americans live in Florida.

_____ 3. Hawaii and Illinois are home to an equal proportion of the Asian American population.

_____ 4. The same number of Latino Americans and Asian Americans live in Illinois.

_____ 5. Arizona is the home state of 4% of the Latino American population but none of the Asian American population.

6. Although the graphs do not reveal this information, why do you think that California has the largest proportion of both Latinos and Asian Americans? _____

_____

_____

_____

EXERCISE 7   **Bar graph:** Collaborate with a study buddy to study the bar graph and to answer the questions.

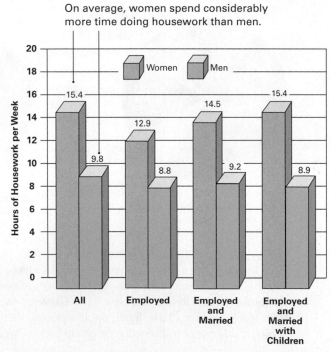

On average, women spend considerably more time doing housework than men.

Source: Bureau of Labor Statistics (2011)

The purpose of the graph is _____

_____

_____

Use the bar graph to answer the following with *T* (true), *F* (false), or *CT* (can't tell).

_____ 1. The graph indicates that employed, married men do less housework if they have children.

_____ 2. Employed married women do more housework if they have children.

_____ 3. The amount of time that men spend on housework varies by less than one hour per week regardless of their employment or household status.

_____ 4. The number of hours that men and women spend on housework has changed significantly over the last 50 years.

_____ 5. According to the data in the graph, women do more housework than men regardless of their employment or family status.

6. How would you explain the greater amount of housework done by women? _____

_____

_____

_____

EXERCISE 8

Diagram: Read the passage and use the drawing to help visualize your thoughts.

Sensory Adaptation

Take three large cereal bowls or small mixing bowls. Fill one with very cold water, another with hot water (*not* boiling or scalding), and the third with lukewarm water. Hold your left hand in the cold water and your right hand in the hot water for at least 1 minute. Then quickly plunge both hands into the lukewarm water at the same time.

Why do you experience the illusion that the lukewarm water feels simultaneously warmer and colder than its actual temperature? The answer is adaptation. You perceive the lukewarm water as warm on your cold-adapted left hand and as cold on your warm-adapted right hand. This illustrates that our perceptions of sensory stimuli are relative and are affected by differences between stimuli we are already adapted to and new stimuli.

The body's sense organs are equipped with highly specialized cells called **sensory receptors** that detect and respond to one type of sensory stimulus—light, sound waves, odors, and so on. Through a process known as **transduction**, the sensory receptors convert the sensory stimulation into neural impulses, the electrochemical language of the brain. The neural impulses are then transmitted to precise locations in the brain. We experience a sensation only when the appropriate part of the brain is stimulated. The sense receptors provide the essential link between the physical sensory world and the brain.

After a time, the sensory receptors grow accustomed to constant, unchanging levels of stimuli—sights, sounds, or smells—so we notice them less and less, or not at all. For example, smokers become accustomed to the smell of cigarette smoke in their homes and on their clothing. This process is known as **sensory adaptation**. Even though it reduces our sensory awareness, sensory adaptation enables us to shift our attention to what is most important at any given moment. However, sensory adaptation is not likely to occur in the presence of a very strong stimulus, such as the smell of ammonia, an earsplitting sound, or the taste of rancid food.

—Mastering the World of Psychology, Fifth Edition,
by Samuel E. Wood, Ellen Green Wood, and Denise G. Boyd

Use the passage and the diagram to answer the following questions with *T* (true) or *F* (false).

_____ 1. The purpose of the experiment is to demonstrate the process of transduction.

_____ 2. The bowl in the center in the experiment contains very hot water.

_____ 3. If you dipped your separate hands in the cold and hot water for only an instant, the lukewarm water would probably just feel lukewarm.

_____ 4. The result would not be as dramatic if the temperatures of the cold and hot water were not so extreme, that is, if they were cool and mildly warm.

_____ 5. Sensory adaptation explains why we become used to some familiar sounds in our environment but are alerted when we are exposed to unusual or extremely loud sounds.

EXERCISE 9

Questionnaire: Answer the following questions from an interpersonal communications textbook and then analyze your responses in order to learn about your listening skills. Compare your results with those of your classmates.

ASSESSING YOUR LISTENING SKILLS

The purpose of this questionnaire is to assess your listening skills. Respond to each statement with a number as follows: 1 for always false, 2 for usually false, 3 for sometimes false, 4 for usually true, and 5 for always true.

_____ 1. I have a difficult time separating important and unimportant ideas when I listen to others.

_____ 2. I check new information against what I already know when I listen to others.

_____ 3. I have an idea what others will say when I listen to them.

_____ 4. I am sensitive to others' feelings when I listen to them.

_____ 5. I think about what I am going to say next when I listen to others.

_____ 6. I focus on the process of communication that is occurring between me and others when I listen to them.

_____ 7. I cannot wait for others to finish talking so that I can take my turn.

_____ 8. I try to understand the meanings that are being created when I communicate with others.

_____ 9. I focus on determining whether others understand what I said when they are talking.

_____ 10. I ask others to elaborate when I am not sure what they mean.

SCORING

To find your score, first reverse your responses for the odd-numbered items. (If you wrote 1, make it 5; if you wrote 2, make it 4; if you wrote 3, leave it as 3; if you wrote 4, make it 2; if you wrote 5, make it 1.) Next, add the numbers next to each statement. Scores range from 10 to 50. The higher your score, the better your listening skill.

—Interpersonal Communication, Third Edition,
by Steven Beebe, Susan Beebe, and Mark Redmond

Write a brief description of the strengths and weaknesses of your listening skills.

I am _____

_____

_____.

EXERCISE 10

Following directions: Experience the specialization of the cerebral hemispheres by performing the following activity. Then respond to the True-False items.

RIGHT AND LEFT HEMISPHERE FUNCTIONS

Get a meter stick or yardstick. Try balancing it vertically on the end of your left index finger, as shown in the drawing. Then try balancing it on your right index finger. Most people are better with their dominant hand—the right for right-handers, for example. Is this true for you?

Now try this: Begin reciting the ABCs out loud as fast as you can while balancing the stick with your left hand. Do you have less trouble this time? Why should that be? The right hemisphere controls the act of balancing with the left hand. However, your left hemisphere, though poor at controlling the left hand, still tries to coordinate your balancing efforts. When you distract the left hemisphere with a steady stream of talk, the right hemisphere can orchestrate more efficient balancing with your left hand without interference.

—From Samuel E. Wood and Ellen R. Wood, *The World of Psychology,* 5th ed. © 2014 (from page 55). Reproduced by permission of Pearson Education, Inc.

———— 1. The right hemisphere controls right-handers' attempts to balance the yardstick with the right hand.

———— 2. To successfully balance the yardstick in the left hand, right-handers use talk to distract the left hemisphere so that the right hemisphere can take control for balance.

SUMMARY POINTS

1 What are the characteristics of analytical thinkers? (page 370)
Good analytical thinkers work persistently in a logical and sequential pattern, drawing on old knowledge to solve new problems while they relate, interpret, and integrate what they know with what they are learning.

2 How do I use analytical thinking to solve problems? (page 371)
Strive first to clearly understand the problem. Then, break it into smaller parts and use logic to arrive at a solution. Sometimes drawing a diagram or jotting down key information helps to organize your thinking. Be persistent in finding an answer. Practice!

3 What analytical thinking strategies should I apply when reading graphic illustrations? (page 375)
Graphic illustrations such as graphs, charts, maps, and diagrams condense complicated information into a graphic representation to highlight differences and allow for quick comparisons. Read the title and legend to understand the topic and study the details carefully. Notice trends and use prior knowledge and logic to interpret the information.

COLLABORATIVE PROBLEM SOLVING

Form a five-member group and select one of the following activities. Brainstorm, complete your activity, and then choose a member to present the group findings to the class.

➤ Record the month in which each class member was born. Create a bar graph showing the number of class birthdays in each month. Put the months on the horizontal line and indicate the number of birthdays in each month on the vertical line.

➤ Record the month in which each class member was born. Create a bar graph showing the number of class birthdays in each month. Indicate the number of birthdays on the horizontal line and put the months on the vertical line.

➤ Record the date of the month on which each class member was born. Create a bar graph showing the number of class birthdays on each date. Put the dates on the horizontal line and indicate the number of birthdays on each date on the vertical line.

➤ Record the date of the month on which each class member was born. Create a bar graph showing the number of class birthdays on each date. Indicate the number of birthdays on the horizontal line and put the dates on the vertical line.

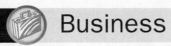

Visit Chapter 8: Analytical Reasoning in MyReadingLab to complete the Selection 1 activities.

"Shoot for the moon. Even if you miss, you'll land among the stars."

—Brian Littrell

What makes workers tick? Surprisingly, money is not the only motivator. Different workers are motivated by different factors. Motivation to work hard can be inspired by the recognition that comes with a simple thank you, an award, or a public acknowledgment for a job well done. For employees who enjoy learning and find repetition dull, new projects and new challenges stimulate enthusiasm for work. Self-starting employees thrive in a flexible environment; they do not like to be micromanaged. To become a successful manager, the trick is to find the appropriate motivator for each employee.

THINKING BEFORE READING

Preview the selection for content and organizational clues. Activate your schema and anticipate what you will learn. Determine your purpose for reading. Think!

Why are you motivated to make good grades in college?

If you were a millionaire, would you get a college degree?

This selection will probably tell me _____.

VOCABULARY PREVIEW

Are you familiar with these words?

stifled	inspire	proponent	premise	pinnacle
crux	deemphasis	hygienic	grievances	verbalizing

How do the prefixes *pre* and *pro* differ?

Are people who get to the *pinnacle* usually inspired?

What committees in your college are set up to hear student *grievances*?

Your instructor may give a brief vocabulary review before or after reading.

THINKING DURING READING

As you read, use the six thinking strategies of a good reader: predict, picture, relate, monitor, correct, and annotate.

MOTIVATING YOURSELF

"It is asking too much to suggest that people motivate themselves in the work environment. Motivation should come from the supervisor, special rewards, or the job itself."

Many people would disagree with the preceding quotation. They would claim that self-motivation is an absolute necessity in many work environments. They would also

Refer to the
Reader's **TIP**
for **Business** on
page 107.

5   claim that the more you can learn about motivation, the more you understand yourself and, as a result, the more you will be in a position to inspire your own efforts.

      Let's assume that you find yourself in a job where things are not going well. You feel stifled and "boxed in." You may, for example, be much more capable than the job demands. Perhaps, too, the pay and benefits are only average, your immediate supervisor is difficult to

10   deal with, and some other factors are not ideal. Even so, you consider the organization a good one, and you recognize that by earning promotions your long-term future can be excellent.

      How can you inspire yourself to do a better-than-average job despite the temporary handicaps? How can you motivate yourself to live close to your potential despite a negative environment? How can you keep your attitude from showing? How can you keep

15   from injuring important human relationships?

      There are many theories or schools of thought on why people are motivated to achieve high productivity on the job. Most of these are studied by managers so that they will be in a better position to motivate the employees who work for them. In this chapter we are going to reverse the procedure. We are going to show you how to motivate your-

20   self. *If your supervisor can be trained to motivate you, why can't you learn to motivate yourself?*

THEORY 1: SELF-IMAGE PSYCHOLOGY

This is frequently called the PsychoCybernetics School. The proponent of this theory is Dr. Maxwell Maltz, a plastic surgeon. The basic idea is that, in order to be properly motivated to achieve certain goals, an individual must recognize the *need* for a good self-image. Dr. Maltz discovered in his work as a plastic surgeon that some patients became much more

25   self-confident and far more motivated after having their faces greatly improved. Why? Maltz came to the conclusion that the image the individual had of himself (or herself) *inside* was more motivating than the changes he had made *outside*. In short, the way an individual *thinks* he or she looks can be more important than the way he or she actually looks to others.

30   **How Can You Use This Theory to Motivate Yourself?** Learn to picture yourself in a more complimentary way. First, research has shown that most people who have poor self-images actually *do* look better to others than they do to themselves. If this is true of you, you might try concentrating on your strong features instead of the weak ones, thus developing a more positive outlook and a better self-image.

35   Second, you might consider improving yourself on the outside as well as on the inside. You may not want to go as far as plastic surgery, but you could change your hairstyle, dress differently, lose or gain weight, exercise, and many other things. According to the theory, however, unless you recognize and accept the improvement, nothing may happen. PsychoCybernetics is, of course, a do-it-yourself project. You do all the work—

40   and you get all the credit, too!

THEORY 2: MASLOW'S HIERARCHY OF NEEDS

This is a very old theory developed by Abraham Maslow in his book *Motivation and Personality*. The premise here is that you have certain needs that must be fulfilled if you are to be properly motivated. These needs are built one on top of the other as in a pyramid.

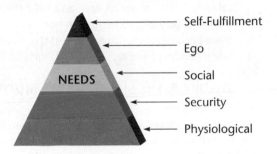

The bottom need is physiological—food, good health. The next is safety and security.
45   The third from the bottom is social needs: One needs to be accepted and enjoy the company of others. Next are ego needs—recognition from others. Finally, at the pinnacle, is one's need for self-fulfillment or self-realization.

The crux of this theory is that the bottom needs must be fulfilled before the others come into play. In other words, you must satisfy your need for food and security
50   *before* social needs become motivating. You must satisfy social and ego needs before self-fulfillment is possible.

How Can You Use This Idea to Motivate Yourself to Reach Goals? If you believe Maslow is right, it would be self-defeating to reverse the pyramid or "skip over" unsatisfied needs to reach others. Chances are good, however, that your first two needs are being
55   adequately satisfied so you could make a greater effort to meet new people and make new friends. This could, in turn, help to satisfy your ego needs. With both your social and ego needs better satisfied, you might be inspired to attempt greater creative efforts which could eventually lead you to greater self-realization.

THEORY 3: PSYCHOLOGICAL ADVANTAGE

This school was founded by Saul W. Gellerman. It contends that people constantly seek
60   to serve their own self-interests, which change as they grow older. People can make their jobs work for them to give them a psychological advantage over other people at the same level. The way to create a psychological advantage in a starting job that is beneath your capacity is to learn all there is about that job. That way, you can use the job as a springboard to something better, a position that will give you more freedom and responsibility.

65   **How Could You Use This to Inspire Yourself?** The best way, perhaps, is to be a little selfish about your job. Work for the organization and yourself at the same time. Instead of letting your job control you, perhaps pulling you and your attitude down, use it as a launching pad. Use it to build human relations that will be important later on. Study the structure of your organization so you will understand the lines of progression better than
70   the other employees. Study the leadership style of your supervisor and others so that you will have a better one when your turn comes.

SELECTION

1

THEORY 4: MOTIVATION-HYGIENIC SCHOOL

This theory was developed by Professor Frederick Herzberg. Basically it claims that undesirable environmental factors (physical working conditions) can be dissatisfiers. Factors of achievement, recognition, and freedom, on the other hand, are satisfiers. All working
75 environments have both negative and positive factors.

How Can You Take Advantage of This Theory? People who maintain positive attitudes under difficult circumstances do so through attitude control. They concentrate *only* on the positive factors in their environment. You can, for instance, refuse to recognize the demotivating factors in your job and concentrate only on those things that will satisfy
80 your needs better.

This could mean a deemphasis on physical factors and more emphasis on psychological factors such as social, ego, and self-fulfillment needs. One individual puts it this way: "I work in a very old building with poor facilities. Even so I have learned that I can be happy there because of the work I do and the great people I work with. One quickly gets used to
85 fancy buildings and facilities and begins to take them for granted anyway."

THEORY 5: THE MAINTENANCE-MOTIVATION THEORY

This school is much like Herzberg's hygienic approach and was developed by M. Scott Myers of Texas Instruments, Inc. His research found that employees usually fall into one of two groups: motivation-seekers and maintenance-seekers. In short, some people look for those factors that are motivating to them and are constantly pushing themselves toward
90 fulfillment. Others are concerned with just staying where they are. Maintenance-seekers spend much time talking about working conditions, wages, recreational programs, grievances, and similar matters and do little or nothing to motivate themselves. Motivation-seekers, on the other hand, look beyond such matters.

How Might You Use This to Improve Your Own Motivation? The obvious answer
95 is, of course, to keep yourself out of the maintenance-seeker classification. To do this you should try not to overassociate with those in the maintenance classification. Without your knowing it, they could pull you into their camp. Try also to talk about positive things instead of being a complainer. Verbalizing negative factors often intensifies the dissatisfaction one feels. Turn your attention to things you can achieve on the job—not to the negative factors.

(1,358 words)

—From *Your Attitude Is Showing,* Ninth Edition,
by Elwood N. Chapman and Sharon Lund O'Neil

THINKING AND WRITING AFTER READING

RECALL Self-test your understanding.

Your instructor may choose to give you a brief comprehension review.

REACT If you could have plastic surgery, what would you have done and what do you think it would do for you?_____

_____

REFLECT For each of Maslow's five levels of needs, name and describe a person you know who fits the level. _____

_____

THINK CRITICALLY Why would a plastic surgeon be the author of a book on self-image and motivation? Write your answer on a separate sheet of paper.

THINK AND WRITE Assuming that your salary is appealing and that you are willing to work, describe what you would consider the perfect work environment for you. What factors would be strong motivators, and what factors would be disincentives? _____

_____

EXTENDED WRITING Review the five motivational theories presented in the selection. Which one best explains what is likely to encourage you to achieve? Write a "message to self" that identifies an important personal goal and lays out specific plans to achieve it using the elements of that theory.

ANALYTICAL REASONING

Use your analytical reasoning skills on the following business problem.

After having worked for the same corporation for over three years, Norman decided that he had made a major mistake. He had been accepted into a formal management training program directly out of college. He had received his first supervisory role before his first year was up, but after that, nothing else happened. He had been on a plateau for over two years. In recent months, he had been feeling extremely frustrated, stifled, and somewhat hostile. He admitted that his attitude was showing. He admitted that his personal productivity had stagnated.

Norman knew the primary reason for his lack of upward progress. His company had been going through a consolidation process and had put a freeze on hiring new employees. Very few middle- and upper-management positions were opening. Nevertheless, Norman finally came to the uncomfortable conclusion that he had to do something about his situation. He had to force some kind of action, even if it was difficult.

He then sat down and listed the advantages and disadvantages of his role with the company.

Advantages	Disadvantages
Good geographical location	Corporation not expanding
Good benefits	Salary only fair
Job security	Limited learning opportunities
Good personnel policies	Overconservative management
Good physical working conditions	Poor supervisor
Little commuting time	Already made some human relations mistakes
Good home neighborhood	Limited opportunities for upward communication with management
Enjoyable type of work	Boring fellow supervisors

After carefully going over the pros and cons of his job—and considering his three-year investment—Norman decided he had the following options:

1. Go to the personnel department and discuss his frustration about being on a plateau with regard to his work.
2. Submit a written request for a transfer involving a promotion.

3. Start a serious search for a new job in a new company.
4. Resign, giving two weeks' notice, and start looking for a new job.
5. Talk to his supervisor and ask for more responsibility.
6. Motivate himself so that management would recognize a change in his attitude and consider him for the next promotion.
7. Relax, continue his present efforts, and wait it out.
8. Motivate himself for three months. Then, if nothing happened, resign.
9. After telling his boss his intentions, go to the president of the company with the problem.
10. Go to the president of the company to discuss his personal progress.

Assume you are Norman. First, on a separate sheet of paper, list which of the listed options you would consider. Second, put them in the order in which you would undertake them. Third, add any steps that you would take that are not on the list. Fourth, justify your decisions.

Interpret THE QUOTE

Now that you have finished reading the selection, "Motivating Yourself," go back to the beginning of the selection and read the opening quote again. How does the quote relate to motivation? On a separate sheet of paper, list three situations in your life when motivation helped you achieve a goal. Also, list three situations in which you could use motivation to reach a goal.

Name ————————————————

Date ————————————————

COMPREHENSION QUESTIONS

Answer the following with *a, b, c,* or *d* or fill in the blank. In order to help you analyze your strengths and weaknesses, the question types are indicated.

Main Idea ———— 1. The best statement of the main idea is

    a. Motivation comes from within and cannot be taught.
    b. People can use different theories of motivation to motivate themselves.
    c. People who are not motivated lose their jobs.
    d. Motivation in an organization is the responsibility of management.

Inference ———— 2. The purpose of this selection is to

    a. improve management.
    b. criticize supervisors.
    c. encourage self-motivation.
    d. analyze mistakes.

Detail ———— 3. According to Maltz's theory, many people make mistakes by

    a. thinking they look worse than others think they do.
    b. trying to look as good as others.
    c. thinking they look better than they do.
    d. trying to hide their weaknesses from others.

Inference ———— 4. In Maslow's hierarchy of needs, winning sales trophies satisfies the

    a. security need.
    b. social need.
    c. ego need.
    d. self-fulfillment need.

Inference ———— 5. Gellerman's theory of psychological advantage is based primarily on

    a. competition.
    b. self-interest.
    c. group cooperation.
    d. the needs of management.

Inference ———— 6. According to the motivation-hygienic theory, a person should

    a. work only in a positive environment.
    b. motivate supervisors to clean up the environment.
    c. ignore the negative factors in the environment and focus on the positive factors.
    d. seek a job with only positive factors.

Inference ———— 7. According to the maintenance-motivation theory, someone who wants to stay in a position for a few more years until retirement is a

Answer the following with *T* (true) or *F* (false).

Inference _____ 8. The author seems to agree with the quotation on lines 1 and 2 at the beginning of the selection.

Inference _____ 9. In Maslow's hierarchy, the need to feel that you are using all of your talents to the best of your ability is the self-fulfillment need.

Inference _____ 10. Maltz's theory is exactly the opposite of Herzberg's theory.

VOCABULARY

Answer the following with *a, b, c,* or *d* for the word or phrase that best defines the boldface word used in the selection. The number in parentheses indicates the line of the passage in which the word appears. In addition to the context clues, use a dictionary to more precisely define the technical terms.

_____ 1. "feel **stifled**" (8)

a. useless
b. smothered
c. angry
d. sick

_____ 2. "**inspire** yourself" (12)

a. motivate
b. force
c. command
d. instruct

_____ 3. "**proponent** of this theory" (21)

a. scholar
b. attacker
c. advocate
d. manager

_____ 4. "The **premise** here" (42)

a. signal
b. mistake
c. meaning
d. supposition

_____ 5. "at the **pinnacle**" (46)

a. bottom
b. crucial time
c. peak
d. most noticeable point

_____ 6. "The **crux** of this theory" (48)

a. crucial point
b. beginning
c. solution
d. reward

_____ 7. "**deemphasis** on physical factors" (81)

a. renewed response
b. less stress
c. complete drop
d. minor stress

_____ 8. "**hygienic** approach" (86)

a. scientific
b. analytical
c. healthful
d. resourceful

_____ 9. "**grievances**, and similar matters" (91–92)

a. successes
b. contests
c. enrichments
d. complaints

_____ 10. "**Verbalizing** negative factors" (98)

a. hiding
b. talking about
c. overlooking
d. remembering

Your instructor may choose to give a brief vocabulary review.

VOCABULARY ENRICHMENT

A. Study these easily confused words and circle the correct one for each sentence.

wares: goods sold   **decent:** morally good   **allusion:** reference
wears: puts on clothes   **descent:** move downward   in literature
where: a place   **dissent:** disagreement   **illusion:** false idea

1. The (**wares, wears**) of the company were posted on the Web site before customers received catalogs.

2. The (**decent, descent, dissent**) between the two employees grew into a major confrontation that hurt company morale.

3. He is operating under the (**allusion, illusion**) that I am going to write the corporate report and then let him take credit for it.

B. Refer to Appendix 3 and use the doubling rule to form the following words.

4. regret + ing = _____

5. swim + ing = _____

6. excel + ent = _____

7. ship + ed = _____

C. Suffixes: Use the boldface suffix to supply an appropriate word for each group of sentences.

ment: act of, state of, result of action

8. Like another _____ to the constitution, theories of motivating can change as researchers document new results with innovative techniques.

9. Just as the mind needs stimulation, an energetic worker needs to eat the right foods so that the body gets the proper _____.

10. My _____ with the manager was postponed until tomorrow at two o'clock.

ence: action, state, quality

11. The therapist showed great _____ in working with the man for hours to achieve a tiny degree of success.

12. While previous authoritarian managers may have valued _____ in following orders, now managers want workers who can problem-solve and share in decision making.

13. A capable and nurturing manager can have a great _____ on your success in a company.

able, ible: can do

14. Highly motivated employees seek extra responsibility and make themselves highly _____ to corporate decision makers.

15. Being a _____ employee means meeting deadlines and getting to meetings on time with the necessary information.

ASSESS YOUR LEARNING

Review confusing questions, seek clarification, and make notes in your text to help you remember new information and vocabulary. Use your textbook as a learning tool.

Science

MyReadingLab™

Visit Chapter 8: Analytical Reasoning in MyReadingLab to complete the Selection 2 activities.

"Like the linkage of the oppositions of continent and ocean in the thermal exchanges of the atmosphere, our linked system of oppositions can generate good harvests and tornadoes, tourist paradises and hurricanes, as well as a global warming and a new Ice Age."

—William I. Thompson

Hurricane specialists can accurately forecast the path of a hurricane with just an 85-mile margin of error when a hurricane is 24 hours away. Forecasting the strength of the storm, however, is more difficult. A Category 5 monster could wallop a community that was expecting a weaker Category 1 tropical storm. Computers cannot accurately show the details of the storm's eye, which changes in shape and intensity as it moves over water and thunderstorms build. The need for accurate forecasting is vital to build the public trust that is necessary for defensive preparations and forced evacuations.

THINKING BEFORE READING

Preview the selection for content and organizational clues. Activate your schema and anticipate what you will learn. Determine your purpose for reading. Think!

What type of natural disaster most threatens your area?

What was the name of last year's most destructive hurricane?

How are hurricanes named?

This selection will probably tell me _____.

VOCABULARY PREVIEW

Are you familiar with these words?

tranquil	rotary	precipitation	deceptive	liberated
aloft	superimpose	debris	torrential	advent

What does the prefix in *advent* mean?

Why is the pronunciation of *debris* unexpected?

What is the opposite of *torrential*?

Your instructor may choose to give a brief vocabulary review before or after reading.

THINKING DURING READING

As you read, use the six thinking strategies of a good reader: predict, picture, relate, monitor, correct, and annotate.

PROFILE OF A HURRICANE

Refer to the
Reader's TIP
for **Science** on
page 66.

Many view the weather in the tropics with favor—and rightfully so. Places such as islands in the South Pacific and the Caribbean are known for their lack of significant day-to-day variations. Warm breezes, steady temperatures, and rains that come as heavy but brief tropical showers are expected. It is ironic that these relatively tranquil regions occasionally
5   produce some of the most violent storms on Earth.

These intense tropical storms are known in various parts of the world by different names. In the northwestern Pacific, they are called *typhoons*, and in the southwestern Pacific and the Indian Ocean, they are called *cyclones*. In the following discussion, these storms will be referred to as hurricanes. The term *hurricane* is derived from Huracan, a
10   Carib god of evil.

Although many tropical disturbances develop each year, only a few reach hurricane status. By international agreement, a hurricane has sustained wind speeds of at least 119 kilometers (74 miles) per hour and a rotary circulation. Mature hurricanes average about 600 kilometers (375 miles) across, although they can range in diameter from 100 kilome-
15   ters (60 miles) up to about 1500 kilometers (930 miles). From the outer edge of a hurricane to the center, the barometric pressure has sometimes dropped 60 millibars, from 1010 to 950 millibars.

At the very center of the storm is the eye of the hurricane. This well-known feature is a zone where precipitation ceases and winds subside. The eye offers a brief but deceptive
20   break from the extreme weather in the enormous curving wall clouds that surround it. The air within the eye gradually descends and heats by compression, making it the warmest part of the storm. Although many people believe that the eye is characterized by clear blue skies, this is usually not the case because the subsidence in the eye is seldom strong enough to produce cloudless conditions. Although the sky appears much brighter in this
25   region, scattered clouds at various levels are common.

HURRICANE FORMATION AND DECAY

A hurricane is a heat engine that is fueled by the heat liberated when huge quantities of water vapor condense. The amount of energy produced by a typical hurricane in just a single day is truly immense. The release of heat warms the air and provides buoyancy for its upward flight. The result is to reduce the pressure near the surface, which in turn
30   encourages a more rapid inflow of air. To get this engine started, a large quantity of warm, moist air is required, and a continuous supply is needed to keep it going.

Hurricanes most often form in late summer and early fall. It is during this span that sea-surface temperatures reach 27°C (80°F) or higher and are thus able to provide the necessary heat and moisture to the air. This ocean-water temperature requirement accounts
35   for the fact that hurricane formation over the relatively cool waters of the South Atlantic and the eastern South Pacific is extremely rare.

Hurricanes diminish in intensity whenever they (1) move over ocean waters that cannot supply warm, moist tropical air; (2) move onto land; or (3) reach a location where the large-scale flow aloft is unfavorable. Whenever a hurricane moves onto land, it loses its
40   punch rapidly. The most important reason for this rapid demise is the fact that the storm's source of warm, moist air is cut off. In addition, the increased surface roughness over land results in a rapid reduction in surface wind speeds.

HURRICANE DESTRUCTION

As shown in the table The "10 Deadliest Hurricanes to Strike the U.S. Mainland 1900–2011," hurricanes can cause devastating loss of life. In addition, the costs of rebuild-
45   ing homes, businesses, public buildings, and infrastructure can be overwhelming. The final accounting from Hurricane Katrina alone is likely to exceed $100 billion. In contrast, Sandy, the catastrophic posttropical storm that made United States landfall in New Jersey in 2012 is blamed for 147 deaths in the United States and damages of $50 billion.

THE 10 DEADLIEST HURRICANES TO STRIKE THE U.S. MAINLAND 1900–2011

Rank	Hurricane	Year	Category	Deaths
1.	Texas (Galveston)	1900	4	8000*
2.	Southeastern Florida (Lake Okeechobee)	1928	4	2500–3000
3.	Katrina (Louisiana/ Mississippi)	2005	4	1833
4.	Audrey (SW Louisiana/Texas)	1957	4	At least 416
5.	Florida Keys	1935	5	408
6.	Florida (Miami/Mississippi/ Alabama/Florida (Pensacola))	1926	4	372
7.	Louisiana (Grande Isle)	1909	4	350
8.	Florida Keys/South Texas	1919	4	287
9. (tie)	Louisiana (New Orleans)	1915	4	275
9. (tie)	Texas (Galveston)	1915	4	275

Source: National Weather Service/National Hurricane Center, *NOAA Technical Memorandum NWS TPC-5*.

*This number may actually have been as high as 10,000–12,000. For a fascinating account of the Galveston storm, read *Isaac's Storm* by Erik Larson (New York: Crown Publishers, 1999).

50 The amount of damage left in the wake of a hurricane depends on several factors, including the size and population density of the area affected and the shape of the ocean floor near the shore. Certainly, though, the most significant factor is the strength of the storm itself as seen in the size of the storm surge, the strength of the wind, and the amount of rain.

Storm Surge Without question, the most devastating damage in the coastal zone
55 is caused by storm surge. It not only accounts for a large share of coastal property losses but is also responsible for 90 percent of all hurricane-caused deaths. A storm surge is a dome of water 65 to 80 kilometers (40 to 50 miles) wide that sweeps across the coast near the point where the eye makes landfall. If all wave activity were smoothed out, the storm surge would be the height of the water above normal tide level. In addition, tremendous
60 wave activity is superimposed on the surge. We can easily imagine the damage that this surge of water could inflict on low-lying coastal areas.

Wind Damage Destruction caused by wind is perhaps the most obvious of the classes of hurricane damage. Debris such as signs, roofing materials, and small items left outside become dangerous flying missiles in hurricanes. For some structures, the force
65 of the wind is sufficient to cause total ruin. Mobile homes are particularly vulnerable. High-rise buildings are also susceptible to hurricane-force winds. Upper floors are most vulnerable because wind speeds usually increase with height. Recent research suggests that people should stay below the tenth floor but remain above any floors at risk for flooding. In regions with good building codes, wind damage is usually not as catastrophic as
70 storm-surge damage. Because hurricanes weaken as they move inland, most wind damage occurs within 200 kilometers (125 miles) of the coast. However, hurricane-force winds affect a much larger area than storm surge and can cause huge economic losses.

Heavy Rains and Inland Flooding The torrential rains that accompany most hurricanes represent a third significant threat—flooding. The 2004 hurricane season was very
75 deadly, with a loss of life that exceeded 3000 people. Nearly all of the deaths occurred in Haiti, as a result of flash floods and mudflows caused by the heavy rains associated with

then Tropical Storm Jeanne. Far from the coast, a weakening storm can produce extensive flooding long after the winds have diminished below hurricane levels. Sometimes the damage from inland flooding exceeds storm-surge destruction.

80   In the United States, early warning systems have greatly reduced the number of deaths caused by hurricanes. At the same time, however, an astronomical rise has occurred in the amount of property damage. The primary reason for this trend is rapid population growth and development in coastal areas.

DETECTING HURRICANES

A location only a few hundred kilometers from a hurricane—just a day's striking distance
85 away—may experience clear skies and virtually no wind. Before the age of weather satellites, such a situation made it difficult to warn people of impending storms. The worst natural disaster in U.S. history came as a result of a hurricane that struck an unprepared Galveston, Texas, on September 8, 1900. The strength of the storm, together with the lack of adequate warning, caught the population by surprise and cost the lives of 6000
90 people in the city and at least 2000 more elsewhere.*

Today many different tools provide data to detect and track hurricanes. The information they provide is used to develop forecasts and to issue watches and warnings. The greatest single advancement in tools used for observing tropical cyclones has been the development of meteorological satellites.

95 The advent of weather satellites has largely solved the problem of detecting tropical storms and has significantly improved monitoring. A combination of observation systems including weather satellites, aircraft reconnaissance, radar and data buoys is necessary to provide data for accurate forecasts and warnings.

(1,291 words)

—From *The Atmosphere: An Introduction to Meteorology*, Twelfth Edition, by Frederick Lutgens and Edward Tarbuck

THINKING AND WRITING AFTER READING

RECALL Self-test your understanding.

Your instructor may choose to give you a brief comprehension review.

REACT Why are mobile homes particularly vulnerable to hurricane damage?

_____

_____

REFLECT Under what conditions might an area benefit from a hurricane?

_____

_____

_____

THINK CRITICALLY Considering the factors involved in the development of a hurricane, why are the coastal states on the Gulf of Mexico so vulnerable to hurricanes? Write your answer on a separate sheet of paper.

THINK AND WRITE   Why is accurate forecasting to build the public trust necessary for defensive preparations and forced evacuations? Describe the possible short-term and long-term results of inaccurate forecasting. _____

_____

_____

EXTENDED WRITING   Create the script for a television or radio segment to be broadcast near the beginning of the hurricane season. Your purpose is to use facts to persuade citizens to evacuate coastal areas ahead of a major storm. In addition to the information in the reading selection, your instructor might require further research to support your paper.

ANALYTICAL REASONING

Use the table on page 397 to answer the following items with *T* (true) or *F* (false).

_____ 1. Most of the deadliest U.S. hurricanes occurred before 1970.

_____ 2. According to the table, Katrina was the deadliest hurricane.

_____ 3. More than four times as many people were killed in the Galveston hurricane of 1900 than were killed by Katrina.

_____ 4. According to the table, Category 5 hurricanes cause more deaths than Category 4 storms.

_____ 5. From the list of the deadliest hurricanes, two have been in the northeastern United States.

Interpret THE QUOTE

Now that you have finished reading the selection, "Profile of a Hurricane," go back to the beginning of the selection and read the opening quote again. What does the quote say about opposites? On a separate sheet of paper, list three situations in which something positive happens as a result of something negative or something negative happens as a result of something positive.

Name ──────────────────────────

Date ──────────────────────────

COMPREHENSION QUESTIONS

Answer the following with *a, b, c,* or *d,* or fill in the blank. In order to help you analyze your strengths and weaknesses, the question types are indicated.

Main Idea ──────── 1. The best statement of the main idea of the selection is

    a. Calm places can produce intense tropical storms.

    b. Hurricanes cause intense damage and leave many people home-less each year.

    c. A hurricane is an intense tropical storm that develops over warm tropical waters and can cause extreme damage from winds and water on land.

    d. A hurricane is a heat engine that produces electricity.

Detail ──────── 2. By international agreement, a hurricane is defined by all of the following *except*

    a. wind speed of 119 kilometers per hour.

    b. rotary circulation.

    c. a drop in barometric pressure.

    d. an eye with a clear blue sky.

Detail ──────── 3. The eye of a hurricane

    a. has the most damaging winds.

    b. produces torrential rains.

    c. is the warmest part of the storm.

    d. signals the end of the storm.

Inference ──────── 4. According to the passage, hurricanes probably begin developing in late summer because

    a. the season will soon be changing to autumn.

    b. the ocean water temperature is highest.

    c. cool winds from the South Atlantic reach the Caribbean.

    d. typhoons and cyclones occur during the winter.

Detail ──────── 5. All of the following will diminish the intensity of a hurricane *except*

    a. cold ocean water.

    b. land.

    c. warm ocean air.

    d. cold land air.

Detail ──────── 6. What is the purpose of the table on page 397? ──────────────

──

──

Detail ──────── 7. The storm surge is characterized by all of the following *except*

    a. it pushes ocean water across coastal property.

    b. it occurs near where the eye of the hurricane hits land.

    c. it always occurs at low tide.

    d. it surges and floods.

Answer the following with *T* (true), *F* (false), or *CT* (can't tell).

Inference   _____   8. The author implies that typhoons, cyclones, and hurricanes are all about the same.

Detail   _____   9. High winds from a hurricane usually kill more people than the storm surges.

Detail   _____ 10. The storm surge can be as much as 80 kilometers high.

VOCABULARY

Answer the following with *a*, *b*, *c*, or *d* for the word or phrase that best defines the boldface word used in the selection. The number in parentheses indicates the line of the passage in which the word appears. In addition to the context clues, use a dictionary to more precisely define the technical terms.

_____ 1. "**tranquil** regions" (4)

    a. warm
    b. calm
    c. breezy
    d. tropical

_____ 2. "**rotary** circulation" (13)

    a. intense
    b. random
    c. rapid
    d. circular

_____ 3. "**precipitation** ceases" (19)

    a. rain
    b. heat
    c. temperature
    d. winds

_____ 4. "**deceptive** break" (19)

    a. fearful
    b. uneventful
    c. turbulent
    d. deceiving

_____ 5. "heat **liberated**" (26)

    a. added
    b. freed
    c. mixed
    d. multiplied

_____ 6. "large-scale flow **aloft**" (39)

    a. below
    b. around
    c. overhead
    d. downhill

_____ 7. "is **superimposed** on" (60)

    a. placed underneath
    b. extremely harsh
    c. overlaid
    d. moved rapidly

_____ 8. "**debris** such as ..." (63)

    a. dirt
    b. insects
    c. water
    d. trash

_____ 9. "**torrential** rains" (73)

    a. sudden
    b. frequent
    c. annoying
    d. fierce

_____ 10. "**advent** of weather satellites" (95)

    a. advertisement
    b. appearance
    c. location
    d. idea

Your instructor may choose to give a brief vocabulary review.

SELECTION 2

VOCABULARY ENRICHMENT

Context Clues

Select the word from the list that best completes each sentence.

tranquil	rotary	precipitation	deceptive	liberated
aloft	barrage	debris	torrential	advent

1. After the storm, the shore was littered with _____.

2. When the summer tourists come to Maine, the small coastal towns are no longer _____.

3. _____ women do not mind speaking out on issues, even when their opinions are unpopular.

4. Five days of _____ rain created flooding in the fields and threatened the livestock.

5. The forecast for the evening is for _____ in the form of snow or sleet.

6. With the _____ of more accurate hurricane forecasting, people are hoping for fewer evacuations.

7. The pickpocket had a _____ way of smiling and asking unsuspecting tourists for directions.

8. The scientists sent a weather balloon _____ to record data for the experiment.

9. Tracie _____ a very thin piece of paper over the drawing to trace it accurately.

10. The _____ fan above the bed moves the air enough to keep the room cool on moderate spring nights.

ASSESS YOUR LEARNING

Review confusing questions, seek clarification, and make notes in your text to help you remember new information and vocabulary. Use your textbook as a learning tool.

Visit Chapter 8: Analytical Reasoning in MyReadingLab to complete the Selection 3 activities and Building Background Knowledge video activity.

"Almost all the ideas we have about being a man or being a woman are so burdened with pain, anxiety, fear and self-doubt. For many of us, the confusion around this question is excruciating."

—Andrew Cohen

The ever-changing issues of gender, and their accompanying status concerns, affect social institutions by solving some problems and usually creating others. For example, in the 1960s, women were underrepresented in the colleges. Advocates for women voiced concerns. In 2005 approximately 213,000 more women than men graduated with bachelor's degrees from colleges in the United States. In 2009, the most recent year for which Census Bureau data were available, the graduation numbers further widened to 231,000 more women than men. Are these numbers a victory for advocacy, or do they define another problem? In another social institution, marriage, the ages are shifting upward. in 1960 the median age for a first marriage was 20 for women and 22 for men. In 2010 the median age was 26 for women and 28 for men. How does this significant shift in age affect the institution, the status of the members, and the culture?

THINKING BEFORE READING

Preview for content and organizational clues. Activate your schema and anticipate what you will learn. Determine your purpose for reading. Think!

How do parents encourage different behaviors for sons and daughters?

How do teachers treat females and males differently?

What jobs tend to be typically male or typically female?

I think this selection will say that _____.

BUILDING BACKGROUND KNOWLEDGE — **VIDEO**

Does Gender Make a Difference in a Job Interview?

To prepare for reading Selection 3, answer the questions below. Then, watch this video about how men and women are perceived in the workplace.

Have you noticed any differences in the way males and females are treated at work? Explain.

What words might you expect to use to describe a female supervisor?

What words might you expect to use to describe a male supervisor?

This video helped me _____.

VOCABULARY PREVIEW

Are you familiar with these words?

humdrum	conventional	stereotypes	bias	banning
spectators	lyrics	competence	pout	rural

Do you live in a *rural* area?

Is there a political *bias* in elections?

Does it take *competence* to fly an airplane?

Your instructor may choose to give a brief vocabulary review before or after reading.

THINKING DURING READING

As you read, use the six thinking strategies of a good reader: predict, picture, relate, monitor, correct, and annotate.

Reader's TIP   Reading and Studying Sociology

- Think broadly about society and social organizations. Search for the historical reasons for human behavior and organizational structures. Make cause-and-effect connections among history, culture, and social organizations.
- Compare and contrast customs and social behaviors across cultures.
- Remain open-minded and be tolerant of cultural differences. Avoid biased value judgments.
- Think objectively and scientifically to evaluate the problems of society.

GENDER AND SOCIAL INSTITUTIONS

At countless bridal showers, women celebrate a friend's upcoming marriage by showering her with gifts to help her keep house. But the scene is very different at bachelor parties, where men give their friend one last fling before he must settle down to the constraints and humdrum routines of married life. We find the same pattern among singles: Contrast
5   the positive image of a carefree bachelor with the negative one of the lonely spinster.[1]

On the face of it, our society constructs marriage as a solution for women but a problem for men. But is this really the case? Research indicates that in general, marriage is good for men and women alike, not only raising levels of personal happiness but also improving health, enhancing sexual satisfaction, and boosting income.

---

[1]The term "spinster" originally referred to a woman who worked spinning thread in a New England textile mill in the early nineteenth century. Most women who worked outside the home at that time were unmarried.

10   But as researcher Jessie Bernard sees it, to the extent that marriages follow the traditional pattern of giving one sex power over the other, tying the knot is a better deal for men and may even be harmful to women. Bernard claims that there is no better prescription for a man to have a long, healthy, happy life than to have a wife devoted to caring for him and keeping an orderly home. Perhaps this is why divorced men are less happy than
15   divorced women and are more eager to remarry.

But when marriage puts women under the control of men, Bernard continues, wives experience less happiness and may even be at risk for depression or other personality disorders. Why? Bernard explains that the problem is not marriage in general but the fact that conventional marriage places men in charge and saddles women with most of the
20   housework.

In the past, most marriages were unequal relationships that put men in charge. So why have women always seemed so eager to marry? Bernard explains that when women were virtually shut out of the labor force, "landing a man" was the only way for a woman to gain economic security. Today, however, women have both more economic opportu-
25   nity and more choices about marriage. This is one reason that more couples are sharing responsibilities, including housework, more equally. As Bernard sees it, moving away from conventional ideas about gender is the key to making both women and men happier and healthier.

Like class, race, and ethnicity, gender shapes just about every part of our lives includ-
30   ing marriage. The importance of gender can be seen in the operation of all the social institutions, as the following survey explains. We begin here with education.

GENDER AND EDUCATION

By the time they begin school, children have learned a great deal about gender from books. Children's books used to be full of gender stereotypes, showing girls and women mostly in the home while boys and men did almost everything else outside the home.
35   Newer children's books present the two sexes in a more balanced way, although some antifemale bias remains.

And what of school itself? Women have made remarkable gains in schooling, especially at the college level. In fact, most college students are women, who earn 62 percent of all associate's degrees and 57 percent of all bachelor's degrees. Even so, gender ste-
40   reotyping still steers women toward college majors in English, education, dance, drama, or sociology while pushing men toward physics, economics, mathematics, computer science, and engineering (U.S. Department of Education, 2011).

Women have also made gains in postgraduate education. In the United States in 2009, women earned 60 percent of all master's degrees and 52 percent of all doctorates
45   (including 60 percent of all Ph.D.s in sociology). Women are now well represented in many graduate fields that used to be almost all male. Back in 1970, for example, hardly any women earned a master's of business administration (M.B.A.) degree; in 2009, more than 76,000 women did so, accounting for 45 percent of all M.B.A. degrees (U.S. Department of Education, 2011).
50   But gender still matters. Men slightly outnumber women in some professional fields, receiving 51 percent of medical (M.D.) degrees, 54 percent of law (LL.B. and J.D.) degrees, and 54 percent of dental (D.D.S. and D.M.D.) degrees (U.S. Department of Education, 2011).

Gender is at work on the playing fields as much as in the classroom. In decades past,
55   extracurricular athletics was a male world, and females were expected to watch instead of play. In 1972, Congress passed Title IX, the Educational Amendment to the Civil Rights Act, banning sex discrimination in any educational program receiving federal funding. In recent years, colleges and universities have also tried to provide an equal number of sports for both women and men. Even so, men benefit from higher-paid coaches and enjoy
60   larger crowds of spectators. In short, despite the federal policy outlawing gender bias, in few athletic programs is gender equality a reality.

GENDER AND THE MASS MEDIA

With some 312 million television sets in the United States and people watching an average of more than four hours of TV each day, who can doubt the importance of the mass media in shaping how we think and act? What messages about gender do we find on TV?

65   When television became popular in the 1950s, almost all the starring roles belonged to men. Only in recent decades have television shows featured women as central characters. But we still find fewer women than men cast as talented athletes, successful executives, brilliant detectives, and skilled surgeons. More often than not, women have supporting roles as wives, assistants, and secretaries. Music videos also come in for criti-
70   cism: Most performing groups are all men, and when women do appear on stage, they are often there for their sex appeal. In addition, many of today's song lyrics reinforce men's power over women.

What about mass media advertising? In the early years of television, advertisers targeted women during the day because so many women were at-home wives. In fact,
75   because most of the commercials advertised laundry and household products, daytime TV dramas became known as "soap operas." On television and in newspaper and magazine advertising, even today, most ads still use female models to sell products such as clothing, cosmetics, cleaning products, and food to women and male models to pitch products such as automobiles, banking services, travel, and alcoholic beverages to men. Ads have
80   always been more likely to show men in offices or in rugged outdoor scenes and women in the home.

Gender bias in advertising is not always so obvious. Look closely at ads and you will see that they often present men as taller than women, and women (but never men) often lie on sofas and beds or sit on the floor like children. In addition, men's facial expres-
85   sions suggest competence and authority, whereas women laugh, pout, or strike childlike poses. Finally, the men featured in advertising focus on the products they are promoting; women, as often as not, pay attention to men.

GENDER AND THE MILITARY

Women have been part of the military since the Revolutionary War. During World War II, when the government officially opened the military to both sexes, women made up just
90   2 percent of the armed forces. By the Gulf War in 1991, that share had risen to almost 7 percent, and 5 of the 148 soldiers killed in that conflict were women. In the fall of 2011, women represented 14 percent of the U.S. military force in Iraq. Between March 2003 and January 2012, the Iraq war claimed the lives of 110 women soldiers; another 34 died in Afghanistan, or about 2.5 percent of all U.S. military (U.S. Department of
95   Defense, 2012).

Today, almost all military assignments are open to women. But there is still resistance to expanding the role of women in the military. The traditional explanation for limiting women's opportunities is the claim that women are not as strong as men, although this argument makes much less sense in a high-technology military that depends less and less
100   on muscle power. The real reason people oppose women in the military has to do with gender itself. Many people have difficulty with the idea of women—whom our culture defines as nurturers—being put in a position to kill and be killed.

GENDER AND WORK

Many people still think of different jobs as either "men's work" or "women's work." A century ago in the United States, in fact, most people did not think women should work
105   at all, at least not for pay. Back then, as the saying used to be, "a woman's place is in the home," and in 1900, just one woman in five worked for income. The most recent data show this share has jumped to three in five (58.6 percent), even as the share of adult men in the labor force declined. Most (67 percent) of women in today's labor force work full time (U.S. Department of Labor, 2011).

In the middle of the last century, the world of paid work was mostly a world of men: More than 80% of men and only one-third of woman were in the labor force.

Working for income is now part of adult life for both men and women.

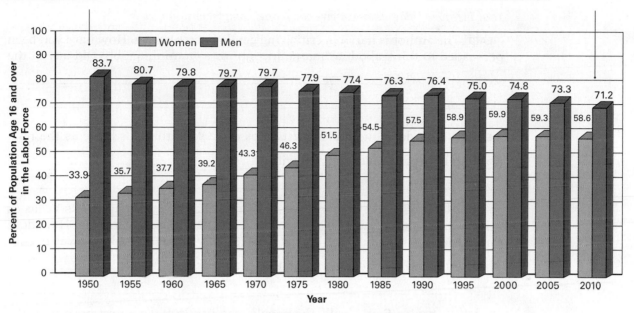

Legend: Women | Men

Y-axis: Percent of Population Age 16 and over in the Labor Force

Year	Women	Men
1950	33.9	83.7
1955	35.7	80.7
1960	37.7	79.8
1965	39.2	79.7
1970	43.3	79.7
1975	46.3	77.9
1980	51.5	77.4
1985	54.5	76.3
1990	57.5	76.4
1995	58.9	75.0
2000	59.9	74.8
2005	59.3	73.3
2010	58.6	71.2

X-axis: Year

Source: U.S. Department of Labor (2011).

110   What accounts for this dramatic rise in the share of working women? Many factors are involved. At the beginning of the twentieth century, most people lived in rural areas where few people had electric power. Back then, women typically spent long hours cooking, cleaning, and raising large families. Today's typical home has a host of appliances, including washers, vacuums, and microwaves, and all this technology has dramatically
115 reduced the time needed for housework so that women and men have more chance to work for income.

In addition, today's average woman has just two children, half the number that was typical a century ago. Nor does having young children prevent today's women from working: 60 percent of married women with children under age six work, as do 71 percent of married
120 women with children six to seventeen years old. From another angle, 53 percent of today's married couples include two partners working for income (U.S. Department of Labor, 2011).

Even though more women now work for pay, the range of jobs open to them is still limited, and our society still labels most jobs as either feminine or masculine. Work that our society has defined as "masculine" involves physical danger (such as firefighting and
125 police work), physical strength and endurance (construction work and truck driving), and leadership roles (clergy, judges, and business executives). Work defined as "feminine" includes support positions (secretarial work or medical assisting) or occupations requiring nurturing skills (child care and teaching young children). A number of jobs that are defined as feminine are performed almost entirely by women even today, such as dental
130 assistant and preschool teacher.

Gender discrimination was outlawed by the federal Equal Pay Act of 1963 and Title VII of the Civil Rights Act of 1964. This means that employers cannot discriminate between men and women in hiring or when setting pay. But gender inequality is deeply rooted in U.S. society; officials investigate thousands of discrimination complaints every year, and
135 few doubt that the real number of cases of discrimination is far higher.

(1,790 words)

— From *Social Problems*, Fifth Edition, by John J. Macionis

SELECTION

3

THINKING AND WRITING AFTER READING

RECALL Self-test your understanding.

Your instructor may choose to give you a brief comprehension review.

REACT The author is harsh in criticizing gender stereotyping. How have you been persuaded to think about a "masculine job" or a "feminine job"? Did any of the stereotyping stick?_____

_____

REFLECT Why do economic opportunities drive something as basic as the relationship between a husband and wife?_____

_____

THINK CRITICALLY In recent years, young brides have been going to Las Vegas or Miami for exciting bachelorette parties with their close girlfriends. How does this mark a change in culture? What does it imply about a breaking away of conventional ideas? Why do you think this change is occurring?_____

_____

THINK AND WRITE Statistically the people who live in the greatest poverty in the United States are single mothers with children. What can be done to empower them? How did they get into their impoverished situation? Are they victims of gender discrimination? How can such situations be prevented? How can they gain financial independence?_____

_____

EXTENDED WRITING A recent news story surfaced about a couple who had made a considered decision to keep their baby's gender a secret from all but a very few trusted relatives. Their purpose was to shield the child from gender discrimination. While this is an extreme solution, it illustrates a concern of many parents. What are your opinions about child-rearing practices that reinforce traditional gender roles? Write a statement of your opinions that takes into account the many aspects of society that shape gender roles—clothing, hair styles, chores, toys, nursery décor, sports activities, behavior expectations—and also considers outcomes mentioned in the selection. Should parents help children embrace the traditional gender roles or help their children reshape them?

Interpret THE QUOTE

Now that you have finished reading the selection, "Gender and Social Institutions," go back to the beginning of the selection and read the opening quote again. Do you agree that how we think of ourselves in terms of our gender is "burdened with pain, anxiety, fear, and self-doubt"? On a separate sheet of paper, write a paragraph on what you think it means to be a man or a woman.

Name ——————————————

Date ——————————————

COMPREHENSION QUESTIONS

Answer the following with *a, b, c,* or *d,* or fill in the blank. In order to help you analyze your strengths and weaknesses, the question types are indicated.

Main Idea   ———   1. The best statement of the main idea of the selection is

    a. Current research indicates that women have nearly achieved social equality with males.

    b. Bias against women continues to be promoted by societal institutions.

    c. The majority of Americans believe that women and men deserve equal pay.

    d. Mothers and fathers in the United States remain unbiased in their parenting duties.

Inference   ———   2. The author's primary objection to bachelor parties in comparison with bridal showers is that

    a. women give gifts to the couple to be used in the marriage.

    b. women are eager to solve problems through marriage.

    c. men "celebrate" a loss rather than a positive gain.

    d. men raise their levels of personal happiness through marriage.

Inference   ———   3. The author would consider a conventional idea about marriage to be all of the following *except*

    a. women doing the laundry.

    b. men washing the dishes.

    c. women cooking breakfast.

    d. men working to provide income.

Detail   ———   4. Despite the passage of Title IX in 1972, the author feels that colleges still discriminate against women by

    a. giving women little chance to play.

    b. banning sex discrimination in any educational program receiving federal funding.

    c. the number of spectators who show up to watch the games.

    d. paying coaches for male sports more than coaches for female sports.

Detail   ———   5. Daytime television dramas are called "soap operas" because

    a. they appeal to at-home wives.

    b. the content is soapy with gossip and sex.

    c. women were targeted during the day.

    d. most began by advertising cleaning products.

Inference   ———   6. The author suggests that women still face limited opportunities in the military primarily because of

    a. the physical demands of military assignments.

    b. the high technology now used by the military.

    c. the public perception of the role of women.

    d. the inability of women to perform many military maneuvers.

Inference _____ 7. The reader can conclude that sociologists consider all of the following social institutions *except*

    a. the family.
    b. the schools.
    c. recreation.
    d. work.

Answer the following with *T* (true) or *F* (false).

Detail _____ 8. According to the passage, 80% of women with children under the age of six work outside the home.

Inference _____ 9. The author suggests that economic opportunity for women is the primary and underlying reason for the weakening of conventional ideas about gender and marriage.

Inference _____ 10. The author implies that a help wanted advertisement cannot legally specify the desire for a male or female applicant.

Answer the following with *T* (true) or *F* (false), referring to the graph on page 407.

_____ 1. In 1955 the percentage of men in the labor force was more than twice the percentage of women.

_____ 2. In the graph, if you were 16 years old in 2000 and without a job, you were considered a nonworker.

_____ 3. From 1950 to 2010, the increase in the number of women in the workforce was more than twice as much as the decline in the number of men working.

_____ 4. From 1950 to 1965, the decrease in men working was 5 percentage points.

_____ 5. For every year indicated on the graph, women showed an increase in their percentage of the workforce.

VOCABULARY

Answer the following with *a*, *b*, *c*, or *d* for the word or phrase that best defines the boldface word used in the selection. The number in parentheses indicates the line of the passage in which the word appears. In addition to the context clues, use a dictionary to more precisely define the technical terms.

_____ 1. "**humdrum** routines" (4)

    a. inspiring
    b. dull
    c. connected
    d. wonderful

_____ 2. "**conventional** ideas" (27)

    a. novel
    b. institutional
    c. strange
    d. traditional

_____ 3. "gender **stereotypes**" (33)

    a. typical representations
    b. caricatures
    c. editorial cartoons
    d. tendencies

_____ 4. "antifemale **bias**" (36)

    a. basis
    b. prejudice
    c. inference
    d. happenings

SELECTION 3

_____ 5. "**banning** sex discrimination"
(57)
    a. highlighting
    b. prohibiting
    c. exposing
    d. hiding

_____ 8. "suggest **competence**"
(85)
    a. completeness
    b. ownership
    c. skill
    d. total helplessness

_____ 6. "crowds of **spectators**" (60)
    a. players
    b. owners
    c. scouts
    d. onlookers

_____ 9. "women laugh, **pout**" (85)
    a. talk
    b. tease
    c. smile
    d. show displeasure

_____ 7. "song **lyrics** reinforce" (71)
    a. melodies
    b. emotions
    c. poetry
    d. words

_____ 10. "**rural** areas" (111)
    a. foreign
    b. elegant
    c. city
    d. country

Your instructor may choose to give a brief vocabulary review.

VOCABULARY ENRICHMENT

Context Clues

Select the word from the list that best completes each sentence.

humdrum	conventional	stereotypes	bias	banning
spectators	lyrics	competence	pout	rural

1. People in _____ India value sons because they can work in the fields.

2. Does a cultural _____ exist regarding women in combat?

3. Advertisers often place males in roles that suggest _____ and authority.

4. It could be said that people following the same routines day after day may be leading a _____ sort of existence.

5. _____ career choices for women were once largely limited to professions such as teaching and nursing.

6. The choir members had so much trouble learning the complicated _____ that the conductor decided to drop the piece from the spring concert.

7. _____ reinforce the myths that all women are good cooks and enjoy housework.

8. Although laws have been passed _____ sex discrimination in the workplace, women continue to be underrepresented in boardrooms across America.

9. In many cases, the number of _____ at men's college sports events greatly exceeds those in attendance at women's games.

10. Television is full of examples of females who _____ to get what they want instead of simply stating their wishes.

Thesaurus

Use a thesaurus, either an online or a book version, to find three alternative words or phrases for each of the following. Answers may vary according to the thesaurus used.

11. primary _____

12. devoted _____

13. restrict _____

14. nurturing _____

15. dramatic _____

ASSESS YOUR LEARNING

Review confusing questions. Seek clarification and make notes in your text to help you remember new information and vocabulary. Use visuals such as symbols, diagrams, and pictures to reinforce your learning. Use your textbook as a learning tool.

VOCABULARY LESSON

Turn and Throw

Study the roots, words, and sentences.

Roots   *vers, vert:* turn   *jac, jec, ject:* throw, lie

Words with *vers* or *vert* = *turn*

Is sex in *advertisements controversial*? Is the coat *reversible*?

- Convert: win over; persuade

  With mind-controlling strategies, the student was *converted* to a cult.

- Revert: turn back to

  Reformed smokers are frequently tempted to *revert* to their old habits.

- Divert: turn away from

  The driver's attention was *diverted* by the accident on the roadside.

- Invert: turn upside down

  If you want to divide a fraction, you need to *invert* and multiply.

- Averse: turned against

  They were divorced, but she was not *averse* to seeing him at parties.

- Introvert: shy and quiet; introspective

  Being an *introvert*, the writer rejected offers to read his poems in public.

- Extrovert: outgoing; gregarious

  An *extrovert* like Oprah Winfrey enjoys the energy of a large studio audience.

- Ambivert: having both introverted and extroverted tendencies

  Most *ambiverts* enjoy both being with people and having some quiet time.

- Pervert: turned to an improper use

  Because of a shoe fetish, the thief was regarded as *perverted*.

- Obverse: facing the opponent; front surface

  The head of the president was depicted on the *obverse* side of the coin.

- Conversant: knowledgeable about a subject

  After another semester of economics, I hope to be more *conversant* on the euro.

- Versatile: having many skills; can turn from one thing to another

  A *versatile* jacket can be worn with several different pants and shirts.

- Subversive: undermining

  The terrorists were engaged in *subversive* activities.

- Vertigo: a dizzy spell when things seem to be turning

  Avoid roller-coasters if you have a tendency toward *vertigo*.

- Version: an adaptation or translation of the original form

  The children's *version* of the Bible had pictures and large print.

- Versus: against

  The next trial was *State of Texas versus John Doe*.

- Vortex: both a whirling and a suction motion, as in a whirlpool

  Watching the whirling water from the cliff, he threw a log into the *vortex*.

Words with *jac, jec, ject* = *throw* or *lie*

Do you have an *objection* to leaving early? Does *rejection* hurt?

- Inject: insert

  Students appreciate professors who *inject* humor into lectures.

- Eject: to throw out

  If the plane is on fire, the fighter pilot can push the *eject* button.

- Dejected: low in spirits

  After failing two tests, the *dejected* student finally sought help in the lab.

- Adjacent: next to

  Consumers save time when a dry cleaner is *adjacent* to a grocery store.

- Conjecture: to form an opinion; guess

  The statement that the new president will step down is merely *conjecture*.

- Interject: throw a word in between others

  Because renters were talking, I could not *interject* a word about a deposit.

- Projection: thrown or caused to appear on a surface or space

  We decided to screen our videos in another classroom where the *projection* equipment was better.

- Abject: degraded

  In the Rio Barrio, the children live in *abject* poverty.

Review

Part I

Answer the following with (*T*) true or (*F*) false.

_____ 1. A conjecture is a fact rather than an opinion.

_____ 2. If a proposal is rejected, it is no longer under consideration.

_____ 3. Subversive activity is clearly evident.

_____ 4. Water in the vortex sprays up like a fountain.

_____ 5. If it is stated as *Wiley versus Rogers*, the two sides are in opposition.

_____ 6. If you are conversant in Spanish history, you know the subject well.

_____ 7. A versatile athlete can play several sports well.

_____ 8. If you invert a cup of coffee, the liquid is likely to spill.

_____ 9. A dejected worker is not a happy employee.

_____ 10. A controversial topic draws little disagreement.

Part II

Select the word from the list that best completes each sentence.

diverted	averse	projections	pervert	extroverted
converted	vertigo	version	adjacent	introverted

1. Inner ear problems can cause loss of balance and _____.

2. The _____ sculptor enjoyed his meditative time alone outdoors.

3. The developer _____ the stream to build on the property.

4. The _____ professor gave lively lectures and enjoyed students.

5. The sex offender's unacceptable behavior labeled him as a _____.

6. By remodeling with glass windows, the porch was _____ to a usable room.

7. Unfortunately I can hear the television in the room _____ to mine.

8. The population _____ for 2025 will influence mass transit decisions.

9. The sign indicates that the home owners are _____ to smoking on the premises.

10. Did you hear the rock singer or the movie star _____ of the story?

Reading Credit Card Offers

Credit card promotions (see the figure on page 417) have become such a problem at colleges that some institutions are banning the advertisers from their campuses. You have probably already received many promotions saying that you are preapproved for a certain credit limit. Some students, enticed by the easy credit and low monthly payments, charge themselves into serious debt, with crippling finance charges that take years to repay. Thus, the misuse of credit cards can be deadly.

Proper use of a credit card, however, can be extremely convenient. Before committing to one, know first that you have the means and the discipline to pay your bill before the due date. If always paid promptly, your only cost for this financial convenience will be the annual fee, which is typically $50 (and for many cards, there is no annual fee).

Reader's TIP Evaluating a Credit Card Offer

- How much is the annual fee for the credit card?
- What is the finance charge rate? Annual rates typically run from 18% to 22%, so finance charges can add up quickly.
- Does the rate start low and change after an initial introductory period? The balance may be subject to a higher interest rate after the initial period when the low rate expires.
- Why do you need the credit card? If you already have one card, why do you need another one?

1. How long will the introductory rate be available on the Hamilton Premier MasterCard advertised on page 419? _____

2. After the introductory period, what is the best annual percentage rate (APR) that you can get if your account balance is less than $2,500? _____

3. If your application is transferred to Hamilton Southwest, what is the highest fixed annual percentage rate (APR) that you might have to pay? _____

3.99%

Introductory APR

THE CARD YOU'VE BEEN WAITING FOR

THE BENEFITS YOU NEED

THE RATE YOU WANT

Dear Stephanie Albert,

This card is not for everyone. It's for people like you who are just starting out and have already demonstrated responsibility with their credit. Because you've shown that kind of special care, Hamilton Bank can make this special offer to you—a Hamilton Premier MasterCard.

The rate shown above is one of the lowest of any major credit card issuer. There's no gimmick here—the fixed rate of 3.99% is yours for nine months and will not increase if the Prime Rate changes.* After nine months, you'll still save with a variable Annual Percentage Rate as low as Prime +5.49%—right now that's only 13.24%.*

This rate saves you money on new purchases and on outstanding balances, too. Move those high rate balances to your Hamilton Premier MasterCard—who knows how much you'll save?

With a Hamilton Premier MasterCard, you'll also enjoy these benefits:
- Credit line up to $100,000
- No annual fee
- Optional Travel Accident Insurance, Lost Luggage Insurance, Auto Rental Insurance, Credit Card Registration and Merchandise Protection

*By filling out the following application, you agree that we reserve the right, based upon your evaluation, to open a Hamilton Standard MasterCard account if you do not qualify for a Hamilton Premier MasterCard account or, if you do not qualify, not to open any account. If we do not open an account, we may submit your application to our subsidiary, Hamilton Southwest, which will consider you for an Excel or Regular MasterCard account with the pricing terms shown below.

HAMILTON BANK SUMMARY OF TERMS

Annual Percentage Rate for Purchases	Variable Rate Information
Preferred Pricing: 3.99% Introductory APR for 9 months. Thereafter, for Hamilton MasterCard: 13.24% if your balances are greater than or equal to $2,500/15.24% if your balances are less than $2,500. For Hamilton MasterCard: 17.24%. *Non-Preferred Pricing:* 22.74%	Annual Percentage Rate is fixed at 3.99% for the first 9 months your account is open. Thereafter, your Annual Percentage Rate may vary. For Hamilton Premier MasterCard, the rate is determined monthly by adding 5.49% if your balances are greater than or equal to $2,500 or 7.49% if balances are less than $2,500 (for Hamilton Standard MasterCard: 9.49% for all balances), to the Prime Rate as published in *The Wall Street Journal.* *Non-Preferred Pricing:* Your Annual Percentage Rate may vary. The rate is determined monthly by adding 14.99% to the Prime Rate. This rate will not be lower than 19.8%.

HAMILTON SOUTHWEST SUMMARY OF TERMS

Annual Percentage Rate for Purchases	Variable Rate Information
Preferred Pricing: For Excel MasterCard: 23.15%. For Regular MasterCard: 27.15%. These rates will not be lower than 21.9% or higher than 29.9% *Non-Preferred Pricing:* Fixed 29.9% APR.	*Preferred Pricing:* Your Annual Percentage Rate may vary. For Excel MasterCard accounts, the rate is determined quarterly by adding 15.4% to the Prime Rate as published in *The Wall Street Journal.* For Regular MasterCard accounts, the rate is determined quarterly by adding 19.4% to the Prime Rate.

9 Critical Reading

Learning Objectives

From this chapter, readers will learn:

1 To use critical reading strategies
2 To recognize an author's purpose or intent
3 To identify an author's point of view or bias
4 To recognize the author's tone
5 To distinguish fact from opinion
6 To recognize valid and invalid support for arguments

Everyday Reading Skills: Evaluating Internet Information

WHAT DO CRITICAL READERS DO?

**Learning
Objective 1**

Use critical reading
strategies

Critical readers do not accept the idea that "If it's in print, it must be true." They do not immediately accept the thinking of others. Rather, they use direct statements, inferences, prior knowledge, and language clues to assess and evaluate. They think for themselves, analyze written material in their search for truth, and then decide how accurate and relevant the printed words are.

This chapter discusses five important strategies that critical readers use to analyze and evaluate reading material. They recognize the author's purpose in writing, identify the author's point of view, recognize the author's tone, distinguish fact from opinion, and recognize valid and invalid support for arguments.

Recognize the Author's Purpose or Intent

**Learning
Objective 2**

Recognize the
author's purpose

Authors write with a particular **purpose** or **intent** in mind. For example, you might be instructed to write a scientific paper on environmental pollution with the ultimate purpose of inspiring classmates to recycle. In writing the paper, you must both educate and persuade, but your overriding goal is persuasion. Therefore, you will choose and use only the facts that support your argument. Your critical reading audience will then carefully evaluate your scientific support, recognizing that your purpose is to persuade and not really to educate, and thus will decide whether to recycle all or some combination of paper, glass, aluminum, and plastic. The author's reason for writing can alert the reader to be accepting or suspicious. These are three common purposes for writing:

- **To inform.** Authors use facts to inform, to explain, to educate, and to enlighten. The purpose of textbooks is usually to inform or explain, but sometimes an author might venture into persuasion, particularly on topics such as smoking or recycling.
- **To persuade.** Authors use a combination of facts and opinions to persuade, to argue, to condemn, and to ridicule. Editorials in newspapers are written to argue a point and to persuade the reader.
- **To entertain.** Authors use fiction and nonfiction to entertain, to narrate, to describe, and to shock. Novels, short stories, and essays are written to entertain. Sometimes an author may adopt a guise of humor in order to entertain and achieve a special result.

EXAMPLE

For each of the following topic sentences, decide whether the author's main purpose is to inform (*I*), to persuade (*P*), or to entertain (*E*).

_____ 1. Telling secrets in the form of public confessions on television talk shows is detrimental to building healthy, satisfying relationships. Such talk shows reveal the worst in human behavior and should be taken off the air.

_____ 2. Self-disclosure in communication means revealing information about yourself, usually in exchange for information about the other person.

_____ 3. Daytime viewers don't seem too surprised to find that Sam has been married to two other women while he has been dating Lucinda, who is carrying his third child and is having an affair with Sam's best friend.

EXPLANATION   The purpose of the first sentence is to persuade the reader to condemn such programs because of the harm that they can cause the participants. The purpose of the second sentence is simply to inform or to educate by giving a definition. The last sentence exaggerates in order to entertain.

EXERCISE 1   Identify the main purpose of each of the following as to inform (*I*), to persuade (*P*), or to entertain (*E*).

_____ 1. Lucy and Rachel were both 11 years old when they met in the textile mill for work. When they were not changing the bobbins on the spinning machines, they would laugh with each other and dream of trips back home.

_____ 2. Samuel Slater opened a new textile mill in Rhode Island in 1790 and employed seven boys and two girls between the ages of 7 and 12. The children were whipped with a leather strap and sprayed with water to keep them awake and alert. By consolidating such a workforce under one roof, Slater could get the children to produce three times as much as entire families working at home.

_____ 3. The textile mills of the late eighteenth century in America were not unlike the sweatshops of Central America today. Children were employed for pennies under the supervision of an adult who was concerned about profits. Today, however, enlightened Americans are buying the product of the labor of foreign children. Perhaps Americans should think before buying.

_____ 4. To be successful in the future, retail companies must embrace e-commerce and establish creative Web sites that are easy for customers to use. Learn to use the Internet for advertising, marketing, and retailing.

_____ 5. In response to a drop in profits, Gap Inc. opened Old Navy stores that were targeted at discount shoppers. This created a three-tiered organization. The company's Banana Republic is designed to appeal to high-end shoppers, The Gap appeals to a middle market that is searching for quality casual clothing, and Old Navy appeals to the bargain hunters.

_____ 6. She quickened her pace as the footsteps behind her became louder. Was he following her, or did he just happen to be turning down Grove Street, too?

EXERCISE 2   Read the passages and identify the author's purpose for each by responding with *a*, *b*, *c*, or *d*.

Passage 1
KEEP YOUR EYES ON FINLAND

Despite its small size and relative isolation in the Arctic Circle, Finland leads the pack in mobile phone technology and its applications. The country is a laboratory of eager users and will soon pioneer the use of so-called third-generation mobile phones that boast lightning-quick access to the Internet. Part of the reason for Finland's advancement is its geography. When telecommunications developed in the 1970s, Finns were more inclined to pursue wireless options because the costs of running cable to isolated pockets of a vast and frozen nation were daunting. Thus wireless technology became a priority for the government and the private sector.

—*Business Today,* Tenth Edition,
by Michael Mescon et al.

_____ 1. The primary purpose of this passage is to

   a. support fast mobile phone access to the Internet.
   b. explain why Finland is the leader in mobile phone technology.
   c. argue against Finland's leadership in mobile phone technology.
   d. compare cable phones with wireless options.

_____ 2. The author describes Finland as a "vast and frozen nation" in order to

   a. compliment the Finns on their struggle with nature.
   b. show that employment is difficult and the industry provides jobs.
   c. explain the cause-and-effect relationship that has motivated excellence in the industry.
   d. show how Finns have reduced spending to increase profits.

Passage 2
JANE ADDAMS

Without knowing why, Jane Addams opened her eyes. It was pitch-black in her bedroom, and at first, she heard nothing more than the muted night noises of the Chicago streets surrounding Hull House. Then she saw what had disturbed her sleep. A burglar had pried open the second-story window and was rifling her bureau drawers. Jane spoke quietly, "Don't make a noise." The man whirled around, then prepared to leap out the window. "You'll be hurt if you go that way," Jane calmly observed. A conversation ensued in the darkness. Addams learned that the intruder was not a professional thief, but simply a desperate man who could find no employment that winter of 1890 and had turned to crime to survive. Hull House had been founded the previous fall as a social "settlement" to serve just such people. It testified to Jane Addams's belief that only unfavorable circumstances stood between the innate dignity and worth of every individual and their realization. Moreover, Addams believed that as a well-to-do, cultivated lady she had a special responsibility for alleviating the social ills accompanying the nation's growth. So she was in earnest when she promised her unexpected visitor that if he would come back the next morning, she would try to help. The burglar agreed, walked down the main stairs, and left by the front door. At 9 A.M. he returned to learn that Jane Addams had found him a job.

—*These Beginnings*, Sixth Edition,
by Roderick Nash and Edward Graves

_____ 1. The primary purpose of this passage is to

   a. explain how Hull House operated on a daily basis.
   b. illustrate Jane Addams's courage and commitment to her cause.
   c. argue the need for social settlements to assist the needy.
   d. educate the public on the reasons for crime.

_____ 2. The author implies that Hull House was designed primarily to serve

   a. drug users.
   b. the mentally ill.
   c. criminals after release from jail.
   d. people down on their luck.

Passage 3

POPULARITY OF PART-TIMERS

Some experts claim that full-time, core employees are paid for eight hours of work but actually work closer to six or seven. This discrepancy is because it may take ten minutes or more for them to get ready to work, two fifteen-minute breaks are required, and often employees start getting ready to leave before the end of their work day. In contrast, part-timers employed for four hours may actually work at top performance for almost the entire period.

Part-time workers can be divided into three classifications: (1) full-time students who seek "peak period" jobs for approximately twenty hours per week to help with educational expenses, (2) housewives who seek part-time work so they can devote more time to children, and (3) retired people who wish to supplement their retirement incomes.

Many supervisors claim that part-timers are a welcome challenge when it comes to weaving them into the general mix of employees. They like the enthusiasm, energy, and flexibility they bring with them. Others claim that the high turnover rate of part-timers negates their advantages. All agree that it takes additional time and energy from the supervisor to convert part-timers into productive members of a work team.

—Supervisor's Survival Kit: Your First Step into Management, Ninth Edition, by Elwood N. Chapman and Cliff Goodwin

_____ 1. The primary purpose of this passage is to

    a. condemn society's reliance on part-time workers.

    b. explain the downside of relying on part-timers in the workforce.

    c. discuss methods that employees can use to increase the productivity of part-time workers.

    d. discuss the pros and cons of part-time work for both employers and employees.

_____ 2. The author implies that

    a. employers are split in their opinions of the advantages of part-time workers.

    b. full-time workers put in fewer hours because part-timers are more committed to getting the job done.

    c. part-time work can be considered to range from twenty to forty hours per week.

    d. the majority of part-time employees are students.

Recognize the Author's Point of View or Bias

Learning Objective 3

Identify the author's point of view

If you were reading an article analyzing Barack Obama's achievements as president, you might ask, "Is this written by a Republican or a Democrat?" The answer would help you understand the point of view or bias from which the author is writing and thus help you evaluate the accuracy and relevance of the message.

Point of view refers to the opinions and beliefs of the author or of the reader, and a critical reader must recognize how those beliefs influence the message. Students sometimes find the term *point of view* confusing because, when discussing literature, point of view refers to the narrative voice that the author is using: first, second, or third person. In this chapter, however, point of view refers to an opinion or position on a subject. For example, if you were reading an article on UFOs, you would ask, "Does the author write from the point of view of a believer or a nonbeliever in aliens?"

Bias is a word that is closely related to point of view. However, the term *bias* tends to be associated with prejudice, and thus it has a negative connotation. A bias, like a point of view, is an opinion or a judgment. Either may be based on solid facts or on incorrect information, but a bias suggests that an author leans to one side, unequally presenting evidence and arguments. All authors write from a certain point of view, but not all authors have the same degree of bias.

Because both writers and readers are people with opinions, their biases interact on the printed page. Thus, critical readers need to recognize an author's bias or point of view as well as their own. For example, a reader might fail to understand an author's position on legalizing prostitution because the reader is totally opposed to the idea. In such a case, the reader's bias or point of view on the subject can interfere with comprehension.

EXAMPLE Respond to the following statement by describing the author's point of view or bias as well as your own.

> African animals are endangered and should not be killed for their fur to make coats. Minks, however, are a different story and should be considered separately. Minks are farmed animals that are produced only for their fur.

Explain the author's point of view or bias. _____

Explain your own position on the topic. _____

EXPLANATION The author implies that minks are not endangered and should be used in making fur coats. Your position may be the same, or you may think that being on the endangered list is not the only issue. You may feel that animals should not be used for clothing.

EXERCISE 3 The following statements adamantly express only one side of an issue. Read each statement and mark whether you agree (*A*) or disagree (*D*). Then describe the point of view or bias of the author and your own position.

_____ 1. Citizens deserve to be protected from pornography on the Internet. Although pictures of child pornography are now prohibited on the Internet, lessons on how to seduce grade school children are perfectly legal in chat rooms and news groups. First Amendment rights should not outweigh our need to protect the population from deviant behaviors.

Explain the author's point of view or bias. _____

_____

Explain your own point of view or bias. _____

_____

_____ 2. Reproductive technology has outpaced the law and is in need of record keeping. In a fertility laboratory, the sperm of one anonymous donor is united with the egg of another anonymous donor. Then the fertilized product is implanted into a hopeful parent who never knows the identity of either donor. Considering that such donors usually make multiple contributions, how can children be sure in future years that they are not marrying brothers or sisters?

Explain the author's point of view or bias. _____

_____

Explain your own point of view or bias. _____

_____

_____ 3. An overwhelming amount of this nation's land is owned by the government in the form of national parks and forests. This is especially true in the West. Much of this land is not needed for public recreation and could be sold to private enterprise, with the proceeds going to pay off part of the national debt.

Explain the author's point of view or bias. _____

_____

Explain your own point of view or bias. _____

_____

_____ 4. Is a parent responsible for a child's actions? Because some parents neglect their parental duties when signs of danger are obvious, public interest in parental duty laws is increasing. Under such laws, parents can no longer look the other way while society suffers the consequences.

Explain the author's point of view or bias. _____

_____

Explain your own point of view or bias. _____

_____

_____ 5. Cities that have teen curfews violate the rights of responsible teens. Those teens who obey are forced to curtail wholesome activities while violators continue as if there were no curfew.

Explain the author's point of view or bias. _____

_____

Explain your own point of view or bias. _____

_____

EXERCISE 4 Read the following description of Napoleon Bonaparte from a freshman history textbook. Keep in mind that Napoleon is generally considered to be one of the great heroes of France and one of the greatest conquerors of the world. Does this passage say exactly what you would expect? Analyze the author's point of view and answer the questions that follow with *T* (true) or *F* (false).

Passage 1

Napoleon was a short, swarthy, handsome man with remarkable, magnetic eyes. Slender as a youth, he exhibited a tendency toward obesity as he grew older. He was high-strung, and his manners were coarse. Militarily, he has been both denigrated and extolled. On the one hand, his success has been attributed to luck and the great skill of his professional lieutenants; on the other, he has been compared with the greatest conquerors of the past. Politically, he combined the shrewdness of a Machiavellian despot with the majesty of a "sun king." It is generally conceded that he was one of the giants of history. He had an exalted belief in his own destiny, but as an utter cynic and misanthrope felt only contempt for the human race. He once exclaimed, "What do a million men matter to such as I?" The world was Napoleon's oyster. He considered himself emancipated from moral scruples. Yet this man, who despised humanity, was worshiped by the millions he held in such contempt. To his soldiers he was the invincible hero, a supreme ruler over men, literally a *demi-god*. He came from nowhere, but was endowed with an extraordinary mind and the charisma required for masterful leadership. He used democracy to destroy democracy. He employed the slogans of revolution to fasten his hold on nations. His great empire collapsed, but his name will never be forgotten.

—A History of the Western World,
by Solomon Modell

_____ 1. The author wants to present Napoleon as a demigod.

_____ 2. The author shows Napoleon as the greatest military leader in history.

_____ 3. The author feels that Napoleon effectively used propaganda for his own benefit.

_____ 4. The author wants to show the differences between the public and the private views of Napoleon.

_____ 5. The author feels that Napoleon adhered to a strict moral code.

_____ 6. The author feels that Napoleon matured into a handsome, well-mannered gentleman.

_____ 7. The author believes that Napoleon's success was due primarily to good luck.

_____ 8. The author feels that Napoleon had little regard for the average person.

_____ 9. The author feels that Napoleon is undeserving of a prominent place in history.

_____ 10. The author feels that Napoleon used ruthless tactics to get what he wanted.

The author gives a cynical description of Napoleon. For example, he relates a quote attributed to Napoleon that shows him in an unfavorable light. The critical reader needs to be aware that other accounts show Napoleon as a great leader who was concerned for his soldiers and wanted the best for France.

Read Passage 2 for a somewhat different view of Napoleon. Then answer the questions that follow.

Passage 2

Few men in Western history have compelled the attention of the world as Napoleon Bonaparte did during the fifteen years of his absolutist rule in France. Schooled in France and at the military academy in Paris, he possessed a mind congenial to the ideas of the Enlightenment—creative, imaginative, and ready to perceive things anew. His primary interests were history, law, and mathematics. His particular strengths as a leader lay in his ability to conceive of financial, legal, or military plans and then to master their every detail; his capacity for inspiring others, even those initially opposed to him; and his belief in himself as the destined savior of the French. That last conviction eventually became the obsession that led to Napoleon's undoing. But supreme self-confidence was just what the French government lacked since the first days of the revolution. Napoleon believed both in himself and in France. That latter belief was the tonic France now needed, and Napoleon proceeded to administer it in liberally revivifying doses.

—*Western Civilizations,*
by Edward McNall Berns et al.

_____ 1. This author has a more positive opinion of Napoleon than did the previous author.

_____ 2. This author believes that Napoleon's initial self-confidence was unwelcome in France.

_____ 3. This author suggests that Napoleon developed a mental obsession about being a destined savior that led to his decline.

_____ 4. This author does not imply that Napoleon hated humanity.

_____ 5. This author believes that Napoleon failed to attend to details and thus lost power.

Recognize the Author's Tone

Learning Objective 4

Recognize the author's tone

The author's **tone** describes the writer's attitude toward the subject. An easy trick to distinguish tone is to think of tone of voice. When someone is speaking, voice sounds usually indicate whether the person is angry, romantic, or joyful. In reading, however, you cannot hear the voice, but you can pick up clues from the choice of words and details.

As a critical reader, tune in to the author's tone and thus let attitude become a part of evaluating the message. For example, an optimistic tone on water pollution might make you suspicious that the author has overlooked information, whereas an extremely pessimistic article on the same subject might overwhelm you, causing you to discount valuable information.

EXAMPLE Identify the tone of the following passage.

Hillary Clinton has shattered glass ceilings and paved the way to better lives for women in the United States and around the world. Her remarkable history is testament to her most heartfelt cause, assuring rights for women and girls. Not only is she a stellar role model—from a stunning speech at a college graduation that landed her on the cover of *Life* magazine in 1974, to strong First Lady, to the nation's first female presidential candidate to be taken seriously, to tough bargaining Secretary of State—but all along she has not wavered from her fight to better the lives of women and girls worldwide.

_____ 1. The author's tone is

    a. critical.
    b. nostalgic.
    c. admiring.

EXPLANATION Details and slanted language such as "shattered glass ceilings," "paved the way to better lives for women," "her remarkable history," and "stellar role model" reveal the author's admiration for Hillary Clinton.

Reader's TIP Recognizing the Author's Tone

The following list of words with explanations can describe an author's tone or attitude:

- **absurd, farcical, ridiculous**: laughable or a joke
- **ambivalent, apathetic, detached**: not caring
- **angry, bitter, hateful**: feeling bad and upset about the topic
- **arrogant, condescending**: acting conceited or above others
- **awestruck, admiring, wondering**: filled with wonder
- **cheerful, joyous, happy**: feeling good about the topic
- **compassionate, sympathetic**: feeling sorrow at the distress of others
- **complex**: intricate, complicated, and entangled with confusing parts
- **congratulatory, celebratory**: honoring an achievement or festive occasion
- **cruel, malicious**: mean-spirited
- **cynical**: expecting the worst from people
- **depressed, melancholy**: sad, dejected, or having low spirits
- **disapproving**: judging unfavorably
- **distressed**: suffering strain, misery, or agony
- **evasive, abstruse**: avoiding or confusing the issue
- **formal**: using an official style
- **frustrated**: blocked from a goal
- **gentle**: kind; of a high social class
- **ghoulish, grim**: robbing graves or feeding on corpses; stern and forbidding
- **hard**: unfeeling, strict, and unrelenting
- **humorous, jovial, comic, playful, amused**: being funny
- **incredulous**: unbelieving
- **indignant**: outraged
- **intense, impassioned**: extremely involved, zealous, or agitated
- **ironic**: the opposite of what is expected; a twist at the end
- **irreverent**: lack of respect for authority
- **mocking, scornful, caustic, condemning**: ridiculing the topic
- **objective, factual, straightforward, critical**: using facts without emotions
- **obsequious**: fawning for attention
- **optimistic**: looking on the bright side
- **outspoken**: speaking one's mind on issues
- **pathetic**: moving one to compassion or pity
- **pessimistic**: looking on the negative side
- **prayerful**: religiously thankful
- **reticent**: shy and not speaking out
- **reverent:** showing respect
- **righteous**: morally correct
- **romantic, intimate, loving**: expressing love or affection
- **sarcastic**: saying one thing and meaning another
- **satiric**: using irony, wit, and sarcasm to discredit or ridicule

- **sensational**: overdramatized or overhyped
- **sentimental, nostalgic**: remembering the good old days
- **serious, sincere, earnest, solemn**: being honest and concerned
- **straightforward**: forthright
- **subjective, opinionated**: expressing opinions and feelings
- **tragic**: regrettable or deplorable mistake
- **uneasy**: restless or uncertain
- **vindictive**: seeking revenge

EXERCISE 5   Mark the letter that identifies the tone for each of the following sentences.

_____ 1. Baseball was invented as an urban game in order for owners to make money, players to become arrogant, and spectators to drink overpriced beer.

    a. objective
    b. nostalgic
    c. cynical

_____ 2. The Puritans came to the new land for religious freedom, yet they allowed their followers little freedom. Anne Hutchinson was banished from the colony for preaching that salvation can come through good works.

    a. optimistic
    b. ironic
    c. sentimental

_____ 3. When I study now, I'm in a lab with 50 noisy computers. What happened to the quiet chair in a corner with a table for your books, papers, and pencils?

    a. objective
    b. cheerful
    c. nostalgic

_____ 4. According to a recent study in a book called *Living Well,* sexually active partners who do not use contraceptives stand an 85% chance of conceiving within a year.

    a. subjective
    b. objective
    c. sarcastic

_____ 5. If given the funding, scientists could trace most aggressive behavior, crime, and violence to either too much testosterone or low blood sugar.

    a. sentimental
    b. subjective
    c. objective

_____ 6. On hot summer days, the health risks increase as automobile exhaust from rush hour traffic pollutes the air, threatens our lungs, and damages the ozone layer.

    a. disapproving
    b. reverent
    c. incredulous

_____ 7. Aging can be isolating and lonely. As mobility becomes more limited, the elderly patiently wait for the excitement of a friend's call or a child's next visit.

    a. evasive
    b. righteous
    c. sympathetic

_____ 8. Is the top of the world as crowded as Times Square? According to official records, the greatest number of people to reach the summit of Mount Everest on a single day is 89. The number of corpses still remaining on Everest is 120.

    a. sarcastic
    b. optimistic
    c. approving

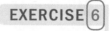 Read the passages and answer the questions that follow by writing in the blanks or answering with *a, b, c,* or *d*.

Passage 1

A CULT FOLLOWING

Happy, motivated employees help to create loyal, satisfied customers. In fact, words like *loyal* and *satisfied* don't do justice to how customers feel about In-N-Out Burger. *Delighted* or even *fanatically loyal* might say it better. The restaurant chain has developed an unparalleled cult following. When a new In-N-Out first opens, the line of cars often stretches out a mile or more, and people stand in line for an hour to get a burger, fries, and a shake. Fans have been known to camp overnight to be first in line. When the first Arizona store opened in Scottsdale, people waited in line for as long as four hours while news helicopters buzzed above the parking lot.

—*Marketing: An Introduction,* Eleventh Edition,
by Gary Armstrong and Philip Kotler

1. What is the tone of the passage? _____

2. What clues reveal the author's tone? _____

_____

_____

Passage 2

BUILD-UP TO DISASTER

Political decisions have consequences. The decision to invade Iraq and the three years of combat there, together with questionable appointments to head the agencies charged with providing federal disaster relief, left the government unprepared in August 2005 to deal with the catastrophic devastation Hurricane Katrina caused. Although Katrina also hit the Mississippi and Alabama coasts hard, New Orleans suffered the worst effects. Federal funding for flood control in New Orleans, which is almost completely surrounded by water and part of which lies below sea level, had been reduced by 44 percent since 2001 when Bush took office. State and federal emergency services were so reduced and disorganized that they offered almost no protection from natural disasters. The plan to evacuate New Orleans if a major hurricane threatened the city ignored the fact that most of its poor residents, who were overwhelmingly black, lacked the means to flee. Moreover, one-third (35 percent) of the Louisiana National Guard, who would be needed to furnish aid and keep order in a disaster, was in Iraq.

—*African Americans: A Concise History, Combined Volume*, Fourth Edition,
by Darlene Clark Hine, William C. Hine, and Stanley Harrold

1. What is the tone of the passage? _____

2. What clues reveal the author's tone? _____

_____

_____

_____

_____

Passage 3

TOXIC WATER

Xiao Sizhu, a farmer in a small Chinese village, died at 55 of esophageal cancer. In an interview shortly before his death, Xiao spoke of swimming and fishing in the tributary of the Yellow River that runs through the village. However, he says, "Now I never go close to the water because it smells awful and has foam on top." One oncologist calls the area "the cancer capital of the world" because of esophageal and stomach cancer rates that are 25 times higher than the national average. The Yellow River itself is being sucked dry by irrigation projects stemming from some 20 dams, and the remaining water is grossly polluted with sewage and industrial wastes. Three chemical spills in 2006 turned the Yellow River red, and another spill turned it white. More than 500 million rural Chinese are forced to use water that is contaminated by human and industrial waste; only 20% of wastewater receives any treatment.

—*Environmental Science: Toward a Sustainable Future*, Twelfth Edition,
by Richard T. Wright and Dorothy F. Boorse

1. What is the tone of the passage? _____

2. What clues reveal the author's tone? _____

_____

_____

_____

_____

Passage 4

ZOO DOO

Sometimes, companies don't realize how valuable their by-products are. For example, most zoos don't realize that one of their by-products—their occupants' manure—can be an excellent source of additional revenue. Sales of the fragrant by-product can be sub-stantial. So far, novelty sales have been the largest, with tiny containers of Zoo Doo (and even "Love, Love Me Doo" valentines) available in 160 zoo stores and 700 additional retail outlets. For the long-term market, Zoo-Doo looks to organic gardeners who buy 15 to 70 pounds of manure at a time. Zoo-Doo is already planning a "Dung of the Month" club to reach this lucrative by-products market.

—Principles of Marketing, Ninth Edition,
by Philip Kotler and Gary Armstrong

_____   1. The authors' tone is

    a. cynical.
    b. disapproving.
    c. incredulous.
    d. playful.

_____   2. The authors' primary purpose is

    a. to argue.
    b. to criticize.
    c. to educate.
    d. to narrate.

Passage 5

COSTCO

But this isn't a story about Wal-Mart. It's about Costco, the red-hot warehouse retailer that competes head-on with Wal-Mart's Sam's Club. Sam's Club is huge. With more than 550 stores and $40 billion in revenues, if Sam's Club were a separate company, it would be the seventh-largest U.S. retailer. But when it comes to warehouse retailing, it's Costco that's the bully, not the other way around.

With about the same number of members but 50 fewer stores, Costco outsells Sam's Club by 50 percent. Its $60 billion in sales makes Costco the nation's third-largest retailer, behind only Wal-Mart and Home Depot and one step ahead of Target. And unlike Wal-Mart and Sam's Club, Costco is growing at a torrid pace. In just the past four years, Costco's sales have surged 55 percent; profits are up 57 percent. Costco's same-store sales are growing at more than twice the rate of Wal-Mart's. How is Costco beating Sam's Club at its own low-price game? The two retailers are very similar in many ways. But inside the store, Costco adds a certain merchandising magic that Sam's Club just can't match.

—Marketing, An Introduction, Ninth Edition,
by Gary Armstrong and Philip Kotler

_____   1. The author's tone is

    a. admiring.
    b. nostalgic.
    c. serious.
    d. amused.

_____ 2. The author's primary purpose is

    a. to entertain.
    b. to criticize.
    c. to narrate.
    d. to convince.

Passage 6

DECIMAL NOTATION

The set of arithmetic numbers, or nonnegative rational numbers, consists of the whole numbers 0, 1, 2, 3, 4, 5, 6, 7, 8, 9, 10, and so on, and fractions like 1/2, 2/3, 7/8, 17/10, and so on. Note that we can write the whole numbers using fraction notation. For example, 3 can be written as 3/1. We studied the use of fraction notation for arithmetic numbers in Chapter 2.

In Chapter 3, we will study the use of *decimal notation*. The word *decimal* comes from the Latin word *decima,* meaning a tenth part. Although we are using different notation, we are still considering the nonnegative rational numbers. Using decimal notation, we can write 0.875 for 7/8, for example, or 48.97 for 48 97/100.

—*Developmental Mathematics: College Mathematics
and Introductory Algebra,* Seventh Edition,
by Marvin L. Bittinger and Judith A. Beecher

_____ 1. The author's tone is

    a. satiric.
    b. objective.
    c. irreverent.
    d. cheerful.

_____ 2. The author's primary purpose is

    a. to narrate.
    b. to argue.
    c. to instruct.
    d. to describe.

Passage 7

O CAPTAIN! MY CAPTAIN!

O Captain! my Captain! our fearful trip is done,
The ship has weather'd every rack, the prize we sought is won,
The port is near, the bells I hear, the people all exulting,
While follow eyes the steady keel, the vessel grim and daring;
  But O heart! heart! heart!
    O the bleeding drops of red,
      Where on the deck my Captain lies,
        Fallen cold and dead.

O Captain! my Captain! rise up and hear the bells;
Rise up–for you the flag is flung–for you the bugle trills,
For you bouquets and ribbon'd wreaths–for you the shores a-crowding,
For you they call, the swaying mass, their eager faces turning;
  Here Captain! dear father!

> This arm beneath your head!
>   It is some dream that on the deck,
>   You've fallen cold and dead.
>
> My Captain does not answer, his lips are pale and still,
> My father does not feel my arm, he has no pulse nor will,
> The ship is anchor'd safe and sound, its voyage closed and done,
> From fearful trip the victor ship comes in with object won;
>   Exult O shores, and ring O bells!
>   But I with mournful tread,
>   Walk the deck my Captain lies,
>   Fallen cold and dead.

—by Walt Whitman

_____ 1. The author's tone is

    a. playful, amused
    b. sarcastic, ridiculing
    c. prayerful, thankful
    d. respectful, mournful

_____ 2. The author's purpose is

    a. to criticize
    b. to honor
    c. to convince
    d. to instruct

Distinguish Fact From Opinion

Learning Objective 5

Distinguish facts from opinions

The reader who cannot distinguish between fact and opinion will always remain gullible. By contrast, the critical reader realizes that most writing contains a combination of facts and opinions and is able to tell one from the other. A **fact** is a statement that can be proven true or false, whereas an **opinion** is a statement of feeling or belief that cannot be proven right or wrong.

EXAMPLE

Mark the following stand-alone statements as _F_ (fact) or _O_ (opinion).

_____ 1. George Washington was the first president of the United States.

_____ 2. George Washington was the best president of the United States.

_____ 3. The author states that George Washington was the best president of the United States.

_____ 4. It is a fact that George Washington was the best president of the United States.

The first and third are statements of fact that can be proven, but the second and fourth are opinions, even though the fourth tries to present itself as a fact. In psychology, for example, it is a fact that Freud believed the personality is divided into three parts; however, it is only an opinion that there are three parts of the human personality. Others may believe the personality should be divided into two parts or ten parts.

Dr. Beatrice Mendez-Egle, a professor at the University of Texas–Pan American, further clarifies the distinction between fact and opinion with the following definitions and table.

A **fact** is an observation that can be supported with incontrovertible evidence. An **opinion,** on the other hand, is a commentary, position, or observation based on fact but that represents a personal judgment or interpretation of these facts.

Fact	Opinion
3/4 of the students in this class are making A's.	This class is really smart.
The temperature in the class is 78°.	This classroom is always hot and stuffy!
Facebook has over 800 million active users.	Many people use Facebook; it is the best way to communicate.

The first two opinions are clearly judgments that would probably be obvious to most readers. The third opinion, however, is mixed with fact; and thus the judgment portion, "it is the best way to communicate," needs the sharp eye of a critical reader to recognize it as an opinion. In order to achieve a certain purpose, a writer can support a particular bias or point of view and attempt to confuse the reader by blending facts and opinions so that both sound like facts.

EXERCISE 7

Mark the following statements from textbooks as *F* (fact) or *O* (opinion).

_____ 1. I maintain it is much safer to be feared than loved, if you have to do without one of the two.

—Machiavelli, quoted in *Western Civilization,* Fifth Edition, by Jackson J. Spielvogel

_____ 2. Everyone complains about federal, state, and local taxes.

—*We the People: An Introduction to American Politics,* Fourth Edition, by Benjamin Ginsberg et al.

_____ 3. Mexican Americans became active as an ethnic group in the 1970s partly due to the leadership of Cesar Chavez and Dolores Huerta to organize poorly paid grape pickers and lettuce workers in California into the National Farm Workers Association.

—*American Stories: A History of the United States,* by H. W. Brands, et al.

_____ 4. At first, young children were barred from the factories, and older ones were allowed to work only a partial adult shift.

—*A Brief History of Western Civilization,* Fourth Edition, by Mark Kishlansky et al.

_____ 5. Taxi drivers have been found to have unusually large hippocampi (a brain structure that plays a special role in spatial memory)—and the longer a driver has worked, the larger they are.

—*Psychology,* Second Edition, by Steven M. Kosslyn and Rogin S. Rosenberg

_____ 6. Leopold Mozart, father of the illustrious Wolfgang Amadeus Mozart, sacrificed his own considerable career to further that of his son.

> —*Understanding Music,* Fourth Edition,
> by Jeremy Yudkin

_____ 7. English, the language of globalization, is both savior and villain in Europe.

> —*Diversity and Globalization: Western World Geography,* Second Edition,
> by Les Rowntree et al.

_____ 8. In the 1920s, Cleveland, Ohio, and Chicago, Illinois, were among the first major cities to perform crime surveys.

> —*Criminal Justice,* by James A. Fagin

_____ 9. Longshoremen, who are on their feet all day and lift, push, and carry heavy cargo, have about half the risk of a fatal heart attack as coworkers like crane drivers and clerks.

> —*Life-Span Development,* Ninth Edition,
> by John W. Santrock

_____ 10. Self-confidence, perhaps more than any other factor, is the secret to success and happiness.

> —*The Career Fitness Program,* Seventh Edition,
> by Diane Sukiennik et al.

EXERCISE 8 The following passage from a history textbook describes Thomas Jefferson. Notice the mixture of facts and opinions that the author uses to develop a view of Thomas Jefferson. Mark the items that follow as (*F*) fact or (*O*) opinion.

> Jefferson hardly seemed cut out for politics. Although in some ways a typical, pleasure-loving southern planter, he had in him something of the Spartan. He grew tobacco, but did not smoke, and he partook only sparingly of meat and alcohol. Unlike most planters he never hunted or gambled, though he was a fine horseman and enjoyed dancing, music, and other social diversions. His practical interests ranged enormously—from architecture and geology to natural history and scientific farming—yet he displayed little interest in managing men. Controversy dismayed him, and he tended to avoid it by assigning to some thicker-skinned associate the task of attacking his enemies. Nevertheless, he wanted to have a say in shaping the future of the country, and once engaged, he fought stubbornly and at times deviously to get and hold power.
>
> —*The American Nation,* Tenth Edition,
> by John Garraty and Mark Carnes

_____ 1. Jefferson hardly seemed cut out for politics.

_____ 2. Jefferson was a typical, pleasure-loving southern planter.

_____ 3. Jefferson grew tobacco but did not smoke.

_____ 4. Controversy dismayed Jefferson.

_____ 5. Jefferson fought deviously to get and hold power.

Recognize Valid and Invalid Support for Arguments

Learning Objective 6

Recognize valid and invalid support for arguments

When evaluating persuasive writing, critical readers realize that support for an argument or a position can be in the form of both facts and opinions. For example, valid reasons for a career change or a vacation destination can include a combination of both facts and feelings. The trick is to recognize which reasons validly support the point and which merely confuse the issue with an illusion of support.

A **fallacy** is an error in reasoning that can give an illusion of support. On the surface, a fallacy can appear to add support, but closer inspection shows it to be unrelated and illogical. For example, valid reasons for buying running shoes might be comfort and price, whereas invalid reasons might be that "everybody has them" and a sports figure said to buy them.

Fallacies are particularly prevalent in **propaganda,** a form of writing that is designed to convince the reader by whatever means possible. Propaganda can be used to support a political cause, advertise a product, or engender enthusiasm for a college event.

Experts have identified and labeled over 200 fallacies or tricks of persuasion. The following list describes some of the most common ones.

Testimonials: Celebrities who are not experts state support.

> *Example:* Maria Sharapova appears in television advertisements endorsing a particular luxury car.

Bandwagon: You will be left out if you do not join the crowd.

> *Example:* All the voters in the district support Henson for senator.

Transfer: A famous person is associated with an argument.

> *Example:* George Washington indicated in a quote that he would have agreed with us on this issue.

Straw Person: A simplistic exaggeration is set up to represent the argument.

> *Example:* The professor replied, "If I delay the exam, you'll expect me to change the due dates of all papers and assignments."

Misleading Analogy: Two things are compared as similar that are actually distinctly different.

> *Example:* Studying is like taking a shower; most of the material goes down the drain.

Circular Reasoning: The conclusion is supported by restating it.

> *Example:* Papers must be turned in on time because papers cannot be turned in late.

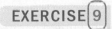

Identify the fallacy in each of the following statements, using (*a*) testimonial, (*b*) bandwagon, (*c*) transfer, (*d*) straw person, (*e*) misleading analogy, (*f*) circular reasoning.

_____ 1. Purchase her new novel, *Growing Up Latino,* which is written in the tradition of outstanding novelist Richard Rodriguez, who wrote *Hunger of Memory: The Education of Richard Rodriguez.*

_____ 2. The first semester of college is like the premiere of a Batman movie because both require the use of imagination.

_____ 3. Customs booklets warn that Cuban cigars are not legally allowed in the United States because the government will not let you bring them into the country.

_____ 4. Pele, the famous soccer player who led Brazil to three World Cup championships, recommends multivitamins by Zip to add energy to your life and strength to your body.

_____ 5. Purchase tickets immediately because everyone in school has signed up for the event and it will soon be sold out.

_____ 6. A student who is late for class would probably be late for a job interview and thus be a failure.

_____ 7. Use the cosmetics advertised by Jennifer Lopez because she says they work for her.

_____ 8. Writing a term paper is like brewing coffee when your crushed beans turn into a flow of ideas.

_____ 9. Join a club to meet new friends because you will meet people that you do not know.

_____ 10. George W. Bush pointed out that the first president of the United States was another George W.

EXERCISE 10

To practice your critical thinking skills, read the passages and answer the questions that follow.

Passage 1

BEETHOVEN'S WORK HABITS

As Beethoven grew older and withdrew more and more from society, he became wholly absorbed in his art. He would habitually miss meals, forget or ignore invitations, and work long into the night. He himself described his "ceaseless occupations." Beethoven felt the strongest urge to produce the music within him, and yet he suffered the same creative anxiety as lesser mortals. "For some time past I have been carrying about with me the idea of three great works. . . . These I must get rid of: two symphonies, each different from the other, and also different from all my other symphonies, and an oratorio. . . . I dread beginning works of such magnitude. Once I have begun, then all goes well."

We are fortunate in possessing many of the sketchbooks in which Beethoven worked out his musical ideas. They present a vivid picture of the composer at work.

—*Understanding Music,* Fourth Edition,
by Jeremy Yudkin

Answer the following with *T* (true) or *F* (false) or with *a, b, c,* or *d.*

_____ 1. The author wishes to show Beethoven as both a preoccupied genius and a person who dreaded a big project.

_____ 2. The author suggests that the sketchbooks reveal some of the thought processes of Beethoven.

_____ 3. The author's tone is condemning.

_____ 4. The author conveys an appreciation for Beethoven as a creative artist.

_____ 5. The author implies that Beethoven did not write down his symphonies until they were completed in his head.

_____ 6. Each of the following words has a negative connotation *except*

a. vivid
b. withdrew
c. anxiety
d. dread

Mark the following statements as *F* (fact) or *O* (opinion).

_____ 7. "He became wholly absorbed in his art."

_____ 8. "He would habitually miss meals … and work long into the night."

_____ 9. "Beethoven felt the strongest urge to produce the music within him, and yet he suffered the same creative anxiety as lesser mortals."

Passage 2

ALEXANDER THE LEADER

The army was crossing a desert of sand. The sun was already blazing down upon them, but they were struggling on under the necessity of reaching water, which was still far away. Alexander, like everyone else, was tormented by thirst, but he was nonetheless marching on foot at the head of his men. It was all he could do to keep going, but he did so, and the result (as always) was that the men were better able to endure their misery when they saw that it was equally shared. As they toiled on, a party of light infantry which had gone off looking for water found some—just a wretched little trickle collected in a shallow gully. They scooped up with difficulty what they could and hurried back, with their priceless treasure, to Alexander. Then, just before they reached him, they tipped the water into a helmet and gave it to him. Alexander, with a word of thanks for the gift, took the helmet and, giving it full view of his troops, poured the water on the ground. So extraordinary was the effect of this action that the water wasted by Alexander was as good as a drink for every man in the army. I cannot praise this act too highly. It was a proof, if anything was, not only of his power of endurance, but also of his genius for leadership.

—*The Campaigns of Alexander* by Arrian,
translated by Aubrey de Sélincourt

Answer the following with *T* (true) or *F* (false).

_____ 1. The author's purpose is to compliment Alexander's troops for giving him the treasured water.

_____ 2. The author implies that part of Alexander's success as a leader was his understanding and endurance of the same hardships as his soldiers.

_____ 3. The author implies that Alexander was willing to die of thirst with his soldiers.

_____ 4. The author's tone is respectful of Alexander.

_____ 5. The reader can conclude that this account could contribute to the positive propaganda about Alexander.

_____ 6. In using the words *extraordinary* and *genius,* the author intends a positive slant.

Mark the following statements as *F* (fact) or *O* (opinion).

_____ 7. "The army was crossing a desert of sand."

_____ 8. "Alexander, with a word of thanks for the gift, took the helmet and, giving it full view of his troops, poured the water on the ground."

_____ 9. "It was a proof, if anything was, not only of his power of endurance, but also of his genius for leadership."

Passage 3

`OPTIMISM`

One measure of how helpless or effective you feel is where you stand on optimism-pessimism. How do you characteristically explain negative and positive events? Perhaps you have known students whose *attributional style* is negative—who attribute poor performance to their lack of ability ("I can't do this") or to situations enduringly beyond their control ("There is nothing I can do about it"). Such students are more likely to persist in getting low grades than are students who adopt the more hopeful attitude that effort, good study habits, and self-discipline can make a difference. Although mere fantasies tend not to fuel motivation and success, genuine positive expectations do.

In their study of professional achievement, psychologists Martin Seligman and Peter Schulman compared sales made by new life insurance representatives who were more or less optimistic in their outlooks. Those who put an optimistic spin on their setbacks—seeing them as flukes or as a means to learning a new approach, rather than viewing them as signs of incompetence—sold more policies during their first year and were half as likely to quit. Seligman's finding came to life for him when Bob Dell, one of the optimistic recruits who began selling for Metropolitan Life after taking Seligman's optimism test, later dialed him up and sold him a policy.

Health, too, benefits from a basic optimism. A depressed hopelessness dampens the body's disease-fighting immune system. In repeated studies, optimists have outlived pessimists or lived with fewer illnesses.

—David G. Myers, *Psychology,* 7th Edition. Copyright 2004 by Worth Publishers Inc. Reproduced with permission of Worth Publishers Inc. in the format Textbook via Copyright Clearance Center

Answer the following with *T* (true) or *F* (false).

_____ 1. The author's purpose is to discuss a positive relationship between optimism and achievement.

_____ 2. The author's tone in telling the Bob Dell story is humorous.

_____ 3. The author indicates that pessimists are likely to receive lower grades than optimists.

_____ 4. According to the passage, optimistic students can achieve better grades even without good study habits and self-discipline.

_____ 5. The author suggests that pessimism affects motivation but does not physically affect the body.

_____ 6. The author implies that an optimist would believe that "It happens when it happens."

Mark the following statements as *F* (fact) or *O* (opinion).

_____ 7. "In their study of professional achievement, psychologists Martin Seligman and Peter Schulman compared sales made by new life insurance representatives. . . ."

_____ 8. "Those who put an optimistic spin on their setbacks ... sold more policies during their first year and were half as likely to quit."

_____ 9. "In repeated studies, optimists have outlived pessimists or lived with fewer illnesses."

Passage 4

A CONTAGION OF WITCHCRAFT

The instability of the Massachusetts government in the early 1690s allowed what ordinarily would have been an isolated, though ugly, local incident to expand into a major colonial crisis. Excessively fearful men and women living in Salem Village, a small, unprosperous farming community, nearly overwhelmed the new rulers of the Massachusetts Bay Colony.

Accusations of witchcraft were not uncommon in seventeenth-century New England. Puritans believed that an individual might make a compact with the devil, but during the first decades of settlement, authorities executed only about fifteen alleged witches. Sometimes villagers simply left suspected witches alone. Never before had fears of witchcraft plunged an entire community into panic.

The terror in Salem Village began in late 1691, when several adolescent girls began to behave in strange ways. They cried out for no apparent reason; they twitched on the ground. When concerned neighbors asked what caused their suffering, the girls announced they were victims of witches, seemingly innocent persons who lived in the community. The arrest of several alleged witches did not relieve the girls' "fits," nor did prayer solve the problem. Additional accusations were made, and at least one person confessed, providing a frightening description of the devil as "a thing all over hairy, all the face hairy, and a long nose." In June 1692, a special court convened and began to send men and women to the gallows. By the end of the summer, the court had hanged nineteen people; another was pressed to death. Several more suspects died in jail awaiting trial.

Then suddenly, the storm was over. Led by Increase Mather, a group of prominent Congregational ministers belatedly urged leniency and restraint. Especially troubling to the clergymen was the court's decision to accept as evidence reports of dreams and visions in which the accused appeared as the devil's agent. Worried about convicting people on such doubtful testimony, Mather declared, "It were better that ten suspected witches should escape, than that one innocent person should be condemned." The colonial government accepted the ministers' advice and convened a new court, which promptly acquitted, pardoned, or released the remaining suspects. After the Salem nightmare, witchcraft ceased to be a capital offense.

No one knows exactly what sparked the terror in Salem Village. The community had a history of religious discord, and during the 1680s, the people split into angry factions over the choice of a minister. Economic tensions played a part as well. Poorer, more traditional farmers accused members of prosperous, commercially oriented families of being witches.

The underlying misogyny of the entire culture meant the victims were more often women than men. Terror of attack by Native Americans may also have played a part in this ugly affair. Indians in league with the French in Canada had recently raided nearby communities, killing people related to the families of the bewitched Salem girls, and significantly, during the trials some victims described the Devil as a "tawny man."

—*American Stories of the United States,* by H. W. Brands, et al.

Answer the following with *T* (true) or *F* (false).

_____ 1. The author's main purpose is to condemn the people of Salem for executing suspected witches.

_____ 2. The author includes the details in the first paragraph to suggest possible reasons for the Salem witchcraft crisis.

_____ 3. Words such as *isolated*, *ugly*, and *unprosperous* in the first paragraph present a negative view of the conditions in Salem.

_____ 4. The author probably believes that the Salem girls were actually victims of witches.

_____ 5. The last paragraph suggests that a generally negative attitude toward women caused women to be accused of witchcraft more often than men.

_____ 6. The details present Increase Mather and the group he led in a positive light.

Mark the following statements as *F* (fact) or *O* (opinion).

_____ 7. "The instability of the Massachusetts government in the early 1690s allowed what ordinarily would have been an isolated, though ugly, local incident to expand into a major colonial crisis."

_____ 8. "After the Salem nightmare, witchcraft ceased to be a capital offense."

_____ 9. "The community had a history of religious discord, and during the 1680s, the people split into angry factions over the choice of a minister."

Passage 5

THEODORE ROOSEVELT AND THE ROUGH RIDERS

Brimming with enthusiasm, perhaps a bit innocent in their naiveté, the Rough Riders viewed Cuba as a land of stars, a place to win great honors or die in the pursuit. Like many of his men, TR believed "that the nearing future held ... many chances of death, of honor and renown." And he was ready. Dressed in a Brooks Brothers uniform made especially for him and with several extra pairs of spectacles sewn in the lining of his Rough Rider hat, Roosevelt prepared to "meet his destiny."

In a land of beauty, death often came swiftly. As the Rough Riders and other soldiers moved inland toward Santiago, snipers fired upon them. The high-speed Mauser bullets seemed to come out of nowhere, making a *z-z-z-z-z-eu* as they moved through the air or a loud *chug* as they hit flesh. Since the Spanish snipers used smokeless gunpowder, no puffs of smoke betrayed their positions.

During the first day in Cuba, the Rough Riders experienced the "blood, sweat and tears" of warfare. Dr. Church looked "like a kid who had gotten his hands and arms into a bucket of thick red paint." Some men died, and others lay where they had been shot, dying. The reality of war strikes different men differently. It horrifies some, terrifies others, and enrages still others. Sheer exhilaration was the best way to describe Roosevelt's response to death and danger. Even sniper fire could not keep TR from jumping up and down with excitement.

On July 1, 1898, the Rough Riders faced their sternest task. Moving from the coast toward Santiago along the Camino Real, the main arm of the United States forces encountered an entrenched enemy. Spread out along the San Juan Heights, Spanish forces commanded a splendid position. As American troops emerged from a stretch of jungle, they found themselves in a dangerous position. Once again the sky seemed to be raining Mauser bullets and shrapnel. Clearly the Heights had to be taken. Each hour of delay meant more American casualties.

The Rough Riders were deployed to the right to prepare to assault Kettle Hill. Once in position, they faced an agonizing wait for orders to charge. Most soldiers hunched behind cover. Bucky O'Neill, however, casually strolled up and down in front of his troops, chain-smoked cigarettes, and shouted encouragement. A sergeant implored him to take cover. "Sergeant," Bucky remarked, "the Spanish bullet isn't made that will kill me." Hardly had he finished the statement when a Mauser bullet ripped into his mouth and burst out of the back of his head. Even before he fell, Roosevelt wrote, Bucky's "wild and gallant soul has gone out into the darkness."

—*America and Its People,* Third Edition,
by James Martin et al.

Answer the following with *T* (true) or *F* (false) or with *a, b, c,* or *d.*

_____ 1. The author's main purpose is to persuade.

_____ 2. The author feels that the Rough Riders had a glorified view of war.

_____ 3. The author shows sarcasm in mentioning the "Brooks Brothers uniform."

_____ 4. In view of his subsequent death, Bucky O'Neill's remark about a Spanish bullet was ironic.

_____ 5. The overall tone of the passage is humorous.

_____ 6. Which of the following phrases is negatively slanted?

    a. sheer exhilaration
    b. jumping up and down
    c. sternest task
    d. casually strolled

Mark the following statements as *F* (fact) or *O* (opinion).

_____ 7. "... the Spanish snipers used smokeless gunpowder. ..."

_____ 8. "Dr. Church looked 'like a kid who had gotten his hands and arms into a bucket of thick red paint.'"

_____ 9. "Some men died, and others lay where they had been shot, dying."

Passage 6

SHYNESS AS A NEW DISEASE

A fast-growing number of people are doing something they would not have thought of doing before: going to their doctors for a prescription drug to cure their shyness.

In the past, many people knew that they were shy, but it never crossed their minds that shyness was a pathology, a disease that requires medical treatment. Recently, though, a number of social forces have converged to turn shyness into a mental disorder. First, in 1980, the psychiatric profession labeled extreme shyness as a *social phobia* or *social anxiety disorder*. At that time, the condition was regarded as a *rare* disorder, as it involved experiencing not only a distracting nervousness at parties or before giving a speech but also a powerful desire to avoid these social situations altogether. Next, some movie stars, big-name athletes, and other celebrities appeared on talk shows, in magazines, and on other media to disclose their struggles with shyness. Finally, the pharmaceutical company Smith Kline Beecham entered the picture by advertising and selling its antidepressant Paxil as a medicine for shyness. And thus, Americans were left with the impression that shyness is far more serious and widespread than they had ever realized.

As a result, many people today regard shyness as a disease, a medical problem serious enough to require treatment with a drug. But shyness is a serious problem only for a very few—those who are extremely bashful or truly incapacitated by fears of others' disapproval and need relief through the use of psychoactive drugs. For the majority, however, shyness is only a mild problem. According to a recent survey, nearly half of all Americans consider themselves shy and still manage to carry on a normal social life. Also consider the fact that many of these Americans may actually not be shy at all. In American culture today, it is difficult *not* to feel shy given the ubiquitous media full of immodest and even brazen talkers, just as it is difficult not to feel fat with the media presentation of extremely thin beauties.

In short, what was once considered a personality trait is now labeled as a disease and treated with drugs.

—*Sociology: A Brief Introduction*, Sixth Edition, by Alex Thio

Answer the following with *T* (true) or *F* (false) or with *a, b, c,* or *d.*

_____ 1. The author's primary purpose is to discuss solutions for shyness.

_____ 2. The author's overall tone is skeptical.

_____ 3. The author writes from the point of view of a shy person who has sought treatment.

_____ 4. The author suggests that Smith Kline Beecham had a role in perception of shyness as a treatable disease.

_____ 5. The words *pathology* and *disorder* convey negative connotations regarding shyness.

_____ 6. All of the following words are positively slanted *except*

     a. movie stars.
     b. big-name athletes.
     c. celebrities.
     d. ubiquitous media.

Mark the following statements as *F* (fact) or *O* (opinion).

_____ 7. "First, in 1980, the psychiatric profession labeled extreme shyness as a *social phobia* or *social anxiety disorder*."

_____ 8. "Americans were left with the impression that shyness is far more serious and widespread than they had ever realized."

_____ 9. "In American culture today, it is difficult *not* to feel shy. . . ."

SUMMARY POINTS

1 What strategies do critical readers use? (page 420)

Critical readers think for themselves, analyze, and evaluate the accuracy of the printed word before accepting it. They recognize the author's purpose, point of view, and tone. They know the difference between facts and opinions, and recognize valid and invalid support for arguments.

2 How do critical readers recognize an author's purpose? (page 420)

Critical readers consider the publication, the words used, and the support given. They know that common goals are to inform, persuade, or entertain. They realize that an author may have more than one purpose but that there is usually one purpose that dominates.

3 How do critical readers recognize the author's point of view or bias? (page 423)

Point of view refers to the author's opinion on the topic. *Bias* is similar but generally has a negative connotation. To determine the author's point of view, critical readers notice the words and supporting evidence given. They also acknowledge that their own opinions might influence their understanding of the author's point of view.

4 How do critical readers recognize the author's tone? (page 427)

Tone refers to the author's attitude toward the subject. Tone is revealed in the words and details that the writer uses to make the point.

5 How do critical readers distinguish between facts and opinions? (page 434)

Facts can be proven true or false, while opinions are statements of belief and cannot be proven true or false. Critical readers evaluate supporting evidence so as not to be taken in by an argument that sounds strong but consists primarily of opinions or limited facts that have been selected to support the point.

6 How do critical readers recognize valid and invalid support for arguments? (page 437)

Critical readers are acquainted with various forms of logical fallacies or errors in reasoning so that they can identify them when reading a persuasive selection. Critical readers use this knowledge and their awareness of facts and opinions to analyze the validity of an argument. Likewise, they use the same strategies to avoid falling prey to propaganda, which is designed to convince in any way possible.

COLLABORATIVE PROBLEM SOLVING

Form a five-member group and select one of the following activities. Brainstorm, complete your activity, and then choose a member to present the group findings to the class.

➤ List five facts and five opinions that could be used to support the argument that people should not smoke.

➤ Write five different statements regarding rap music, each with one of the following tones: humorous, angry, ironic, sarcastic, and nostalgic.

➤ Create a fallacy for each of the six types listed in this chapter: testimonial, bandwagon, transfer, straw person, misleading analogy, and circular reasoning.

➤ List five points that you would make in an argument for capital punishment and five points that you would make in an argument against capital punishment.

SELECTION 1  Essay   MyReadingLab™

Visit Chapter 9: Critical Reading in MyReadingLab **to complete the Selection 1 activities.**

"The end may justify the means as long as there is something that justifies the end."
—Leon Trotsky

Obesity is a serious problem in the United States. Statistics consistently reveal that about one-third of Americans are overweight, and the rate of childhood obesity has tripled in the last 30 years. The effects on well-being are far-reaching— diabetes, heart disease, cancer, high blood pressure, and asthma. In fact, obesity is such a risk to health that First Lady Michelle Obama launched a campaign to focus attention on the problem in children. "This isn't just a policy issue for me. This is a passion. This is my mission. I am determined to work with folks across this country to change the way a generation of kids thinks about food and nutrition," she said about her "Let's Move" initiative. "Let's Move" emphasizes fitness and nutrition education and encourages parents, children, schools, restaurants, youth organizations, and food manufacturers—everyone—to take action to end childhood obesity in one generation. What responsibility should parents shoulder to ensure that children maintain a healthy weight? What methods are effective, and what methods go too far, sometimes causing a lifetime of low self-esteem and even self-hatred?

THINKING BEFORE READING

Preview the selection for clues to the content. Activate your schema and anticipate what you will learn. Determine your purpose for reading. Think!

Have you or someone you know struggled to maintain a healthy weight?

How much importance should parents place on their children's weight?

Is it possible that focusing attention on weight can be harmful?

What methods are acceptable in achieving a goal?

I think this essay will make the following point: _____

_____.

VOCABULARY PREVIEW

Are you familiar with these words?

clambered	obesity	authoritarian	regimen	incarceration
skirmish	tactic	amphetamines	shun	metabolisms

Are *authoritarian* parenting practices the most effective?

Have you ever attempted a weight loss or exercise *regimen*?

How does it feel to be *shun*ned?

Your instructor may choose to give a brief vocabulary review before or after reading.

THINKING DURING READING

As you read, use the six thinking strategies of a good reader: predict, picture, relate, monitor, correct, and annotate.

SHEDDING THE WEIGHT OF MY DAD'S OBSESSION

Refer to the
Reader's TIP
on **Essays** on
page 59.

For years my figure was the target of my father's anger. I've finally come to accept my size and myself.

Instead of selling the fundraiser candy, I ate it. Eight boxes of it. Each Bluebird in our fourth-grade troop was assigned 12 boxes of chocolate candy to sell for a dollar a box. I sold four boxes to my family and then ran out of ideas for selling the rest.

5   As the days passed and the stack of candy remained in a corner of my room, the temptation to eat it overwhelmed my conscience. Two months after we'd been given the goodies, the troop leader announced that the drive was over and we were to bring in our sales money, along with any unsold candy, to the next Tuesday meeting. I rushed home in a panic and counted $4 in my sales-money envelope and 12 boxes of candy gone.

   I thought of the piggy bank filled with silver dollars that my father kept on a shelf in 10 his closet. It was a collection that he added to but never spent. I tried to push this financial resource out of my mind, but Tuesday was approaching, and I still had no money.

   By Monday afternoon I had no choice. I tiptoed into my parents' bedroom, pulled the vanity chair from Mother's dressing table and carried it to the walk-in closet. There was the piggy bank smiling down at me from the high shelf. After stacking boxes on the chair, 15 I reached up and laid hands on the bank. When I had counted out eight silver dollars, I returned the pig to its place and clambered down. For days I felt bad about my theft, but what I felt even guiltier about was eating all those treats.

Throughout my childhood, my parents weighed me every day, and Daddy posted the numbers on my bedroom door. He never called me fat, but I came to learn every syn-
20 onym. He discussed every health aspect of obesity endlessly. The daily tone and timber of our household was affected by Dad's increasingly authoritarian regimens.

I remember one Friday night, months after the candy caper. I heard the garage door rumble shut, and I knew that Daddy was home. He came in the back door, kissed Mother and asked what my weight was for the day. Mother admitted that I was still a pound over
25 the goal he had set. "Get a pillow and a book, Linda," he said.

He firmly ushered me to the bathroom, then shut and locked the door behind me. As the door was closing, I caught a glimpse of Mother and my sister looking on as though they were witnessing an execution. For the next two days, the only time I was allowed out was for meals. It was late Sunday evening when I was finally released from my cell,
30 supposedly taught a lesson by my incarceration.

The bathroom episode was one skirmish in a long war that had begun when, unlike my older sister, I failed to shed the "baby fat" many children are born with. Although I was cheerful, affectionate and good-natured, none of these qualities interested my father. He had one slender child—he meant to have two. It was simply a matter of my self-discipline.

35 My slightly chubby figure had become a target for my physician father's frustration as he struggled to establish his medical practice. Dad told me constantly that if I was a pound overweight, I would be teased at school and nobody would like me. I stayed away from the other kids, fearing harsh words that never came. When I was 16, Daddy came up with the ultimate punishment: Any day that I weighed more than 118 pounds (the weight my
40 father had deemed ideal for my 5-foot, 4-inch frame) I'd have to pay him. In an attempt to shield me from this latest tactic, my exhausted, loving mother secretly took me to an internist friend of the family who prescribed what he described as "diet pills"—amphetamines and diuretics. Although the pills caused unpleasant side effects like lightheadedness, taking them landed me a slim figure and, two years later, an engineer husband.

45 I quit the hated amphetamines at 27 and accepted my divorce as a result of my weight gain. I became a single, working mother devoted to raising my son and daughter. Over time, I realized that people liked my smile and my laugh and, contrary to my father's predictions, didn't shun me because of my size.

Many years ago, at my annual physical, I mentioned to my doctor that I couldn't
50 eat the same quantity of food that normal people eat without getting bigger. He kindly reassured me that people do indeed have different metabolisms, some more efficient than others. This discussion ultimately helped me to accept my size and shed the emotional burden carried over from my childhood.

My sister and her husband have a daughter who was pudgy as a child. They asked me
55 what they should do about her weight "problem." My reply, "Don't make it an issue. Let her find her own weight level." To their great credit, they did.

(842 words)

—From *Newsweek*, November 13, 2000,
by Linda Lee Andujar

THINKING AND WRITING AFTER READING

RECALL Self-test your understanding.

Your instructor may choose to give you a brief comprehension review.

REACT What is your opinion of the methods used by Andujar's father and mother? _____

_____

REFLECT   Do you think that Andujar's father was correct in focusing attention on his daughter's weight? Why? Why not? _____

_____

THINK CRITICALLY   Were the father's actions appropriate? Were the mother's? _____

_____

THINK AND WRITE   In adulthood, Andujar achieved a healthy relationship with her weight, but it came after years of struggle and anxiety. She contrasted her childhood experience with the advice that she gave her sister. List the stated and implied effects of both approaches:

Effects of Andujar's parents' methods	**Effects of Andujar's advice to her sister**
_____	_____
_____	_____
_____	_____

EXTENDED WRITING   What advice would you give parents to help their children maintain healthy, fit bodies while also promoting their emotional well-being? Put your ideas in the form of an essay that could be published in a magazine as Andujar's was in *Newsweek*. Set forth a clear plan and support it with examples, statistics, reasons, personal experiences, and expert opinions. An Internet search on childhood obesity will yield Web sites with reliable information.

CRITICAL READING

1. Describe the author's purpose in writing this essay. Be more specific than simply saying it is to persuade, inform, or entertain. _____

_____

_____

_____

2. What is the author's point of view on the appropriate parental approach to childhood weight issues? _____

_____

_____

3. Select at least three words to describe the tone of the essay. Refer to the list of author's tone words in the Reader's Tip on pages 428–429 for suggestions.

_____

_____

_____

4. What effect might Andujar's father's profession have on the reader's (and the family's) view of his concern about her weight? _____

_____

_____

_____

5. What was the mother's role in the treatment of her daughter? _____

_____

_____

6. List the ways Andujar described her parents. Place a "+" next to those that are positive.

Father	**Mother**
_____	_____
_____	_____
_____	_____
_____	_____
_____	_____
_____	_____
_____	_____
_____	_____
_____	_____
_____	
_____	

Mark the following statements as *F* (fact) or *O* (opinion).

_____ 7. "By Monday afternoon I had no choice."

_____ 8. "Over time, I realized that people liked my smile and my laugh. . . ."

Interpret THE QUOTE

Now that you have finished reading the selection, "Shedding the Weight of My Dad's Obsession," go back to the beginning of the selection and read the opening quote again. Do you agree that a positive, worthwhile result can justify the means used to achieve it? Did the results in Andujar's situation justify the methods used by her parents?

Name ————————————————————

Date ————————————————————

COMPREHENSION QUESTIONS

Answer the following with *a, b, c,* or *d,* or fill in the blank. In order to help you analyze your strengths and weaknesses, the question types are indicated.

Main Idea ——— 1. Which statement best expresses the author's main point?

a. Linda Andujar struggled with her weight as a child and into adulthood.
b. Childhood obesity is a serious problem in the United States.
c. Even when they have good intentions, parents sometimes make serious mistakes in raising their children.
d. The methods Linda Andujar's parents used to control her weight led to poor self-esteem and dependence on diet pills, but she ultimately overcame these problems.

Inference ——— 2. The author was probably _____ years old when the fund-raiser candy incident occurred.

a. 6 or 7
b. 9 or 10
c. 12 or 13
d. 15 or 16

Detail ——— 3. Andujar's father was a

a. scientist.
b. teacher.
c. doctor.
d. salesman.

Inference ——— 4. The language Andujar used to describe her parents suggests that she

a. hated her parents.
b. felt more sympathy toward her mother than toward her father.
c. respected her parents, particularly her father.
d. agreed with their approach to controlling her weight.

Main Idea ——— 5. Which of the following best describes the topic of this article?

a. Linda Andujar's personal experiences with her weight
b. Child-rearing methods
c. Childhood obesity
d. The many ways that parents can damage their children's self-esteem

Detail ——— 6. Andujar's father believed this was the ideal weight for her 5-foot, 4-inch height.

a. 127 pounds
b. 119 pounds
c. 118 pounds
d. 116 pounds

Inference ——— 7. Details in the selection support the following statement:

a. The author resented her sister for being slender.
b. The author no longer speaks to her parents.
c. The author has forgiven her parents for the treatment that she received as a child.
d. The author has a positive, adult relationship with her sister.

Answer the following questions with *T* (true) or *F* (false).

Detail _____ 8. Andujar felt worse about eating the fund-raiser candy than she did about stealing the money.

Detail _____ 9. Andujar believed that her weight was a factor in her wedding and her divorce.

Inference _____ 10. Andujar might have been addicted to amphetamines.

VOCABULARY

Answer the following with *a, b, c,* or *d* for the word or phrase that best defines the boldface word used in the selection. The number in parentheses indicates the line of the passage in which the word appears. In addition to the context clues, use a dictionary to more precisely define the words.

_____ 1. "and **clambered** down" (16)

    a. fell
    b. climbed
    c. ran
    d. skipped

_____ 2. "every health aspect of **obesity**" (20)

    a. a physical disease
    b. the lack muscle tone
    c. a psychological condition
    d. the state of being overweight

_____ 3. "**authoritarian** regimens" (21)

    a. knowledgeable
    b. preferred
    c. overly controlling
    d. reasonable

_____ 4. "authoritarian **regimens**" (21)

    a. cruelty
    b. diet or exercise program
    c. standard
    d. military formation

_____ 5. "a lesson by my **incarceration**" (30)

    a. punishment
    b. imprisonment
    c. torture
    d. teaching

_____ 6. "bathroom episode was one **skirmish**" (31)

    a. small battle
    b. disagreement
    c. war
    d. problem

_____ 7. "from this latest **tactic**" (41)

    a. punishment
    b. sentence
    c. plan
    d. horror

_____ 8. "**amphetamines** and diuretics" (42)

    a. stimulant drug used to control appetite
    b. a drug used to control violent behavior
    c. a drug prescribed for pain
    d. depressant used for violent patients

_____ 9. "didn't **shun** me because of my size" (48)

    a. like
    b. tease
    c. bully
    d. stay away from

_____ 10. "have different **metabolisms**" (51)

    a. physical characteristics
    b. internal organs
    c. processes of converting food in the body
    d. food preferences

Your instructor may choose to give a brief vocabulary review.

VOCABULARY ENRICHMENT

Literary Devices

A. **Personification.** In personification, an inanimate object is given human characteristics. Personification can embellish an image and create a mood. In the sentence, "The wind sang through the trees," the word *sang* gives the wind a human characteristic that adds a soft, gentle mood to the message.

Write the meaning, mood, or feeling that the boldface personification adds to the message in the following sentences.

1. Her skin **crawled** when she saw the face of the man who attacked her best friend. _____

   _____

2. The glowing fireplace was the **heart** of the mountain cabin. _____

   _____

3. The sun **kissed** the window and brightened the dark laboratory. _____

   _____

4. The shelves **stretched** to make room for more new books. _____

   _____

5. As we walked on the beach, the stars **flirted** with the drifting sand. _____

   _____

B. **Irony.** Irony is saying one thing but meaning another. It may be used to show humor or to be sarcastic and ridicule others. The trick in irony is to be able to recognize that the speaker does not really mean what he or she says. The context in which the statement is made gives clues to the speaker's true attitude. Gullible people have trouble picking up irony and are subsequently sometimes fooled and embarrassed. For example, after a basketball game, someone may say to a player who scored only once in seventeen tries, "You're a great shot." Here irony is used to ridicule the poor shooting.

Complete the story in each of the following sentences by choosing the response that best shows irony.

_____ 6. Each time that the professor called on Jason to answer a question, Jason gave the wrong response. After class Frances said to Jason,

   a. "We need to study hard."
   b. "Here's the guy with the brains."
   c. "I hope you weren't embarrassed."

_____ 7. Sue missed only one item on a chemistry exam that almost everyone else failed. When congratulated, Sue retorted,

   a. "Maybe next time I'll study."
   b. "I'm glad I studied."
   c. "My major is chemistry."

_____ 8. As newlyweds, Amanda and Julio moved to a tiny New York apartment. When their parents came to visit, a sign on the door said,

   a. "Welcome to our new place."
   b. "Welcome to the Caribbean Hilton."
   c. "Welcome to our friends and family."

_____ 9. Because George's apartment was so dirty, his friends called him

    a. the Slob.

    b. George the Unclean.

    c. Mother's Helper.

_____ 10. Chris was known to be cheap, so friends started calling him

    a. Mr. Rockefeller.

    b. Mr. Scrooge.

    c. Mr. Chips.

ASSESS YOUR LEARNING

Review confusing questions, seek clarification, and make notes in your text to help you remember the new information and vocabulary. Use your textbook as a learning tool.

Visit Chapter 9: Critical Reading in MyReadingLab to complete the Selection 2 activities.

Experience is a hard teacher because she gives the test first, the lesson afterward.
—Vernon Law

The following selection tells the true story of a high school senior whose future plans were destroyed by his own foolish decision and a police sting operation. The story raised questions that still remain about right and wrong, youthful naiveté and accountability, crime and punishment, justice and mercy. Was justice fairly served in this case and others like it?

THINKING BEFORE READING

Preview for clues to the content and organization. Activate your schema. Anticipate what is coming. Determine your purpose for reading. Think.

What is the most painful lesson that you've learned "the hard way"? What were the results for you personally?

At what age should a person be judged legally as an adult?

Are there situations when the law should bend in favor of mercy?

I want to learn _____.

VOCABULARY PREVIEW

Are you familiar with these words?

undercover	foolhardy	smitten	felony	betrayed
prompting	launched	mandatory	entrapment	callously

Is a person in love *smitten?*

Does *prompting* refer to being on time or being encouraged?

If a fee is *mandatory*, must one pay it?

Your instructor may choose to give a brief vocabulary review before or after reading.

THINKING DURING READING

As you read, use the six thinking strategies of a good reader: predict, picture, relate, monitor, correct, and annotate.

OPERATION D-MINUS

The setting was Park Vista Community High School in Palm Beach County, Florida, in 2011. The main characters were an 18-year-old senior named Justin Laboy and a pretty new girl in school named Naomi. Justin was an honor student planning to join the Air Force after graduation. Naomi was a 25-year-old police recruit posing undercover as a

Refer to the
Reader's TIP
for **Essays** on
page 59.

SELECTION
2

⁵ student. They both came to Florida from New York. He was Puerto Rican; she was Puerto Rican and Dominican. Justin fell for her, even asked her to the prom, but this romance would lead Justin to make a foolhardy decision that would turn his future plans to dust.

No teachers, no parents, and certainly no students knew about Operation D-Minus. Palm Beach County parents and school personnel were concerned about drug deals tak-

¹⁰ ing place in the area high schools. So, with the knowledge of the school principals, no one else, the police department enrolled recent graduates of the police cadet program as students in three high schools. Although he wouldn't have believed so at the time, it was Justin Laboy's bad luck that his school was one of them and that Naomi sat next to him in two of his classes. In the end, newspapers and blogs picked up the story, and Justin gave

¹⁵ his account in an interview broadcast on National Public Radio's "This American Life."

Justin thought it was good luck that brought this great-looking new girl into his life during his last semester of high school. He had no reason to believe Naomi was anything but the high school student she pretended to be. She was very convincing. "The things that she did that I thought made her a real student was that she would sleep in class. She

²⁰ wouldn't do her homework," Justin said. He always did the assignments, so he let her copy his. They spoke a bit in Spanish, joked around, and got into a little trouble once in a while for talking and texting in class.

It wasn't long before Justin was smitten. He sang to her, made up raps for her, and danced for her in front of the class. "And then I would get all blushed up. Be like, oh, man. What am I

²⁵ doing?" He was different with her. He could open up to her and tell her things about himself and his family. She was a good listener, and she shared with him, too. She said she and her mother came to Florida for a better life away from problems in New York. Justin felt they had a special, more mature relationship than he had experienced with previous girlfriends. When he asked her to go to the prom with him, she hesitated and said she would think about

³⁰ it. She was playing hard to get, and he liked that. Justin thought the signs were good.

Being in love can make a person foolish, and it did just that to Justin. When Naomi asked if he could get some marijuana for her, he said he thought he could, but it would take a while. According to the story he told later, he didn't smoke pot or use any drugs, and he certainly didn't sell them. He desperately wanted to please Naomi, though, so he

³⁵ asked around. Days passed, and Naomi kept texting and checking in class to ask if he had the weed. Finally, Justin got a baggie of marijuana, and in class one day he was at last able to tell Naomi he had it. In the radio interview Justin said, "I had never done this in the

school before, so I'm really scared." Naomi told him to slide the baggie into her purse, which she put on his desk. Several times he refused to take the $25 she handed him, but
40 eventually he did, telling her, "so you could just shut up, I'll take the money." It was a devastatingly bad choice that would change his future, one that Justin called the worst decision of his life.

In May of that year, police arrested Justin and 30 others at the three Operation D-Minus high schools. Most were students, and most were charged with selling small
45 amounts of marijuana. In Florida, selling marijuana is a felony offense, and he had sold it on school grounds. That warranted a harsher penalty. Furthermore, Justin was legally an adult. He spent a week in jail, pled guilty, and, in exchange, was sentenced to three years' probation. With a felony on his record, his dreams of joining the Air Force or any of the armed forces were gone. He had plenty of time to think about what had happened while
50 he sat in jail. In fact, he said it took a while for him to remember he sold to Naomi. She was a cop? He said he never would have done this for a guy. If a guy had asked him to get drugs, he would have said, "'Get out of here.' But it's a different feeling when you get it from a girl you like. You're not going to turn down the person you want to be with." He felt hurt and betrayed.

55 "Naomi," on the other hand, told a slightly different story. She acknowledged that she was invited to the prom but said no because it was too expensive and she was new at the school anyway. She said that Justin offered to get her drugs without any prompting from her and did not hesitate to take the $25.

Not surprisingly, Operation D-Minus wasn't the first or last time undercover police
60 posed as high school students to expose drug or other illegal activity. Police in Palm Beach County launched a similar campaign at other high schools and arrested more than 80 people on various drug and weapons charges. Similarly, police in Brooklyn, New York, arrested a student for receiving stolen goods after he bought a cell phone from an undercover police officer. The student said the officer told him he needed the money to feed
65 his daughter. That operation led to 141 arrests for buying and selling stolen electronics. In Angleton, Texas, a police officer posed as a student when the school district requested help controlling a drug problem. Police arrested 10 high school students and 2 former students for selling prescription drugs and marijuana. In Great Barrington, Massachusetts, an undercover officer befriended 18-year-old Mitchell Lawrence and his friends. While hanging out
70 with Lawrence near the school, the officer asked for a marijuana cigarette. Lawrence provided it and accepted a $20 bill at the officer's insistence. Because the "sale" occurred less than 1,000 feet from a school, Mitchell received a mandatory two-year sentence.

Critics of tactics like those used in Operation D-Minus say they trick naïve young people into situations they don't know how to handle. They accuse police and school officials
75 of entrapment in what amount to sting operations. They maintain that playing on students' emotions and then betraying the friendships so callously cultivated violates the officers' duty to protect and serve the community. Worse yet, leveling felony charges against young people for their foolish mistakes ruins students' chances of fulfilling their dreams.

Are such harsh lessons doing more harm than good? What truly dangerous crimes
80 were ignored while spending time and money to keep a little marijuana off the streets? Justin Laboy was an honor student with dreams of joining the Air Force. He had never been in trouble with the law. If he had not fallen for "Naomi," he would now be serving his country in the armed forces. As for "Naomi," she has no regrets about what happened to Justin in Operation D-Minus, she told the radio interviewer. "This gets them to wake
85 up. They need to realize they can't be doing this."

(1,290 words)

—Sources: *This American Life*, Episode 486, 02/08/2013, "Act Two, 21 Chump Street";
Huffington Post, 02/21/2012, "Teen falls in love with undercover cop in marijuana
sting, gets arrested"; *Huffington Post*, 02/14/2012, "Attractive undercover cop poses as
student and entraps teens to 'sell' her marijuana"; *Houston Chronicle*, 01/11/2012,
"12 charged in Angleton High School drug sting"; *AnandTech Forums*, 02/22/2012,
"Teen falls in love with undercover cop in marijuana sting"

THINKING AND WRITING AFTER READING

RECALL Self-test your understanding.

Your instructor may choose to give you a brief comprehension review.

REACT What was your first reaction as you finished reading this selection?

_____

_____

_____

_____

REFLECT Were there any details in this selection that made you question Justin Laboy's story? If so, what were they? _____

_____

_____

THINK CRITICALLY From the few details given in the paragraph about other sting operations, how are they similar and/or different from Justin Laboy's situation?

_____

_____

_____

_____

THINK AND WRITE Make two lists: One list should contain the reasons that Justin Laboy's punishment was appropriate; the other should contain the reasons that it was not appropriate.

Reasons punishment was appropriate	Reasons punishment was not appropriate
_____	_____
_____	_____
_____	_____

EXTENDED WRITING If you were the judge in Justin Laboy's case, what decision would you have made regarding his punishment? Write a statement that you would have read aloud in court. It should include reasons for your decision.

CRITICAL READING

1. What is the purpose of this reading selection? Explain fully. _____

_____

_____

_____

2. What is the tone of the selection? Refer to the list of tone words in the Reader's Tip on page 428–429 if necessary. _____

_____

_____

3. What details in the selection support your answers to items 1 and 2?

_____

_____

_____

_____

_____

_____

_____

_____

4. Do "Naomi's" feelings about her role in the Laboy case have merit? Why or why not? _____

_____

_____

_____

5. What other methods might be used to handle drug dealing in schools and to ensure that schools are drug free? _____

_____

_____

_____

_____

Mark the following statements as *F* (fact) or *O* (opinion).

_____ 6. "Justin was an honor student planning to join the Air Force after graduation."

_____ 7. "No teachers, no parents, and certainly no students, knew about Operation D-Minus."

_____ 8. "It was a devastatingly bad choice. . . ."

_____ 9. "If he had not fallen for "Naomi," he would now be serving his country in the armed forces."

Interpret THE QUOTE

Now that you've finished reading the selection, "Operation D-Minus," go back to the beginning and read the opening quote again. How is its message evident in the story of Justin Laboy?

SELECTION 2

Name ——————————————————

Date ——————————————————

COMPREHENSION QUESTIONS

Answer the following with *a*, *b*, *c*, or *d*, or fill in the blank. In order to help you analyze your strengths and weaknesses, the question types are indicated.

Main Idea ———— 1. Which of the following best states the main idea of this selection?

    a. Police sting operations should be stopped because they unfairly trap innocent victims of any age and ruin their lives.

    b. Justin Laboy's future plans were cruelly changed.

    c. Justin Laboy's case and others raise questions about the fairness of police sting operations involving young people.

    d. Young people should learn to use better judgment and follow the law rather than their emotions.

Detail ———— 2. Other than the police, the only people who knew about Operation D-Minus were

    a. Palm Beach County school board members.

    b. parents of students in three high schools.

    c. the principals of three high schools.

    d. the principals and a few teachers in three high schools.

Inference ———— 3. Which of the following was most likely to make Justin believe he and Naomi had a deeper relationship than "friendly acquaintance"?

    a. They were both Latino and came to Florida from New York.

    b. She said she would think about his invitation to the prom.

    c. He and Naomi talked and texted each other.

    d. They shared their personal situations and problems with each other.

Detail ———— 4. How long did it take for Justin to get the marijuana for Naomi?

    a. a few days

    b. a few weeks

    c. the next day

    d. almost a month

Inference ———— 5. Based on the cases mentioned in the selection, which factor seems to contribute most to heavier sentences?

    a. a record of prior illegal activity

    b. regular drug use

    c. exchange of money for drugs or stolen items in or near a school

    d. delivering drugs or stolen items at school

Author's Purpose ———— 6. Which of the following best explains the purpose of the paragraph that begins with "Not surprisingly. . . ."?

    a. to convince readers that Justin was unfairly treated

    b. to show that Justin's case was one of many high school sting operations

    c. to show that high school sting operations should be stopped

    d. to make readers feel sympathy for the young victims of sting operations

Inference ———— 7. Critics of Operation D-Minus are most likely to object to which of the following?

    a. harsh sentences for young, first-time offenders caught in school sting operations

b. students being punished for engaging in illegal activity at school

c. police involvement in controlling illegal activities in schools

d. using young police officers who pose as students to uncover drug activities in schools

Answer the following with *T* (true) or *F* (false).

Inference _____ 8. If Justin had been 17 years old, he would have received a lighter sentence.

Detail _____ 9. All of the people arrested in the cases described were students.

Inference _____ 10. Justin believes he was trapped because the undercover officer was a female.

VOCABULARY

Answer the following with *a, b, c,* or *d* for the word or phrase that best defines the boldface word used in the selection. The number in parentheses indicates the line of the passage in which the word appears. In addition to the context clues, use a dictionary to more precisely define the technical terms.

_____ 1. "posing **undercover**" (4)

a. disguised
b. with permission
c. safely
d. openly

_____ 2. "a **foolhardy** decision" (7)

a. crazy
b. deliberate
c. reckless
d. drastic

_____ 3. "Justin was **smitten**" (23)

a. stupid
b. happy
c. drunk
d. lovesick

_____ 4. " a **felony** offense" (45)

a. misdemeanor
b. punishable
c. serious crime
d. first-time

_____ 5. "hurt and **betrayed**" (54)

a. deceived
b. injured
c. ruined
d. damaged

_____ 6. "without any **prompting**" (57)

a. ordering
b. encouragement
c. help
d. texting

_____ 7. "**launched** a similar campaign" (61)

a. stopped
b. began
c. finished
d. proposed

_____ 8. "**mandatory** two-year sentence " (72)

a. required
b. optional
c. merciful
d. harsh

_____ 9. "of **entrapment**" (75)

a. a puzzle
b. a raid
c. an attack
d. a trick

_____ 10. "**callously** cultivated" (76)

a. cooly
b. heartlessly
c. freely
d. smoothly

Your instructor may choose to give a brief vocabulary review.

VOCABULARY ENRICHMENT

A. Study the similar-sounding words and circle one for each sentence.

accent: speech pattern	**elicit:** draw out	**eminent:** well-known
ascent: climb upward	**illicit:** improper	**imminent:** about to happen

1. To land a job as a network news anchor on national television, she had to shed her strong Southern (**accent**, **ascent**).

2. Mother's stern look will surely (**elicit**, **illicit**) an apology from my disrespectful younger sister.

3. As tensions built at the border between the two countries, the world feared that war was (**eminent**, **imminent**).

4. Yo Yo Ma, an (**eminent**, **imminent**) French and American cellist, is recognized around the world as a popular classical musician.

5. This was not the first time that the "peeping Tom" had been arrested for his (**elicit**, **illicit**) behavior.

B. **Analogies:** Supply a word that completes each analogy; then state the relationship that has been established. Refer to the Reader's Tip for Analogies on page 167.

6. *Music* is to *piano* as *explosion* is to _____

   Relationship? _____

7. *Whale* is to *mammal* as *ant* is to _____

   Relationship? _____

8. *Bones* are to *leg* as *freckles* are to _____

   Relationship? _____

9. *Attract* is to *repel* as *pretty* is to _____

   Relationship? _____

10. *Tiger* is to *meat* as *cow* is to _____

    Relationship? _____

C. Identify the boldface phrase as simile or metaphor (see pages 342–343), or personification (see page 453) and explain the meaning. For more practice with figurative language, refer to Appendix 4 on page 535.

11. George Washington was the **father of his country**, but he had no children of his own. _____

12. Glaciers are melting **like warm ice cream** because pollution is trapping heat to the earth. _____

13. Some birds migrate over two continents, perhaps **singing their songs** in both English and Spanish. _____

    _____

14. Because of 200 mph winds that strike **like tornadoes,** climbers can ascend Mount Everest only during two months of the year. _____

_____

15. Poetry **speaks to** both the heart and the brain. _____

_____

ASSESS YOUR LEARNING

Review confusing questions, seek clarification, and make notes in your text to help you remember new information and vocabulary. Use your textbook as a learning tool.

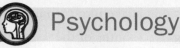

SELECTION 3 Psychology MyReadingLab™

Visit Chapter 9: Critical Reading in MyReadingLab to complete the Selection 3 activities and Building Background Knowledge video activity.

"There are some things one remembers even though they may never have happened."

—Harold Pinter

Introductory college psychology textbooks typically devote an entire chapter to what psychological research has learned about memory, yet many questions remain for further scientific study. For instance, why do we remember certain events vividly but forget others? What factors determine what one person remembers but another person remembers differently about a shared experience? These questions—and their answers—are important in aspects of everyday life. This reading explores what is known about memory in legal settings, specifically in understanding eyewitness testimony.

THINKING BEFORE READING

Notice that references to research articles are included in parentheses throughout this selection. Because psychologists assemble knowledge of their field from research, psychology texts and journal articles always show the sources of information. Each parenthetical citation refers to a research report listed at the end of the chapter from which this selection was adapted. How might the inclusion of these citations influence your reading of the selection?

Preview the selection for clues to the content and for organizational clues. Activate your schema. Anticipate what is coming. Determine your purpose for reading. Think!

Have you ever witnessed an accident or a crime? Did your memory of it match what others remembered? Did your memory change over time?

How convincing is eyewitness testimony in a criminal trial?

Why might witnesses report different observations of the same incident?

I want to learn _____.

BUILDING BACKGROUND KNOWLEDGE — VIDEO

A Memory Champion's Method

To prepare for reading Selection 3, answer the questions below. Then, watch this video about how a man with an average memory can remember the order of an entire deck of cards.

How would you rate your ability to remember?

What tricks do you use to remember things such as people's names or information for a test?

In what ways would improving your memory help you?

This video helped me _____.

VOCABULARY PREVIEW

Are you familiar with these words?

profound	attesting	disrupt	perpetrator	reconstructive
distortion	phenomenon	accosts	hippocampus	simultaneously

Is the word *perp* a shortened, slang version of *perpetrator*?

What do the parts of *reconstructive* say about its meaning?

Is a *hippocampus* part of the human brain?

Your instructor may choose to give a brief vocabulary review before or after reading.

THINKING DURING READING

As you read, use the six thinking strategies of a good reader: predict, picture, relate, monitor, correct, and annotate.

EYEWITNESS TESTIMONY

Refer to the
Reader's TIP
for **Psychology**
on page 217.

In most cases, memory failure is an annoyance. But there are times when it has profound consequences. For example, you have probably heard news reports about people convicted of crimes on the basis of eyewitness testimony who are later cleared by DNA evidence. As you'll see, research on remembering, forgetting, and the biology of memory
5   can help us understand eyewitness testimony.

RELIABILITY

The U.S. Department of Justice issued the first set of national guidelines for the collection of eyewitness evidence in the United States in 1999. Research attesting to the inaccuracy of such testimony and the number of wrongful convictions that occur because of its poor reliability made these guidelines necessary. According to one of the leading researchers in
10   this area, Elizabeth Loftus, studies suggest that eyewitness testimony is highly subject to error and that it should always be viewed with caution (Loftus, 1979).

REASONS FOR DOUBT

Why is the reliability of eyewitness testimony in question? One reason is biological. Witnessing a crime causes physiological stress, and stress hormones disrupt memory functioning (Wolf, 2009). Yet, it is also true that fear can enhance memory. The combined effects
15   of stress and fear on eyewitnesses causes them to remember the central, most frightening details of the event but fail to remember less emotion-provoking details. As a result, eyewitnesses typically experience memory gaps. These gaps may involve just the sort of information investigators need, such as license plate numbers, addresses, the clothing worn by the perpetrator, and so on.
20   As you might suspect, when eyewitnesses experience memory gaps, reconstructive processes fill in the missing information. Consequently, distortions and even false memories sometimes replace such gaps. The longer the delay between witnessing an event and being questioned about it, the more likely a witness is to include reconstructions rather than true memories in descriptions of the perpetrator and the crime itself
25   (Pansky, 2012).
        Moreover, misleading information that is accidentally supplied to an eyewitness during an investigator's interview can result in erroneous recollections of the actual event. This phenomenon is known as **the misinformation effect** (Laney & Loftus, 2009). The

misinformation effect appears to be stronger for emotionally negative events, such as
30 witnessing a crime, than it is for emotionally positive events, such as being a guest at a
party (Porter et al., 2010).

An example will help you see how the misinformation effect works. Suppose you are
walking across campus one day, thinking about an upcoming exam, and a man suddenly
accosts you and steals your backpack. Because of the stress involved in being a crime vic-
35 tim, your hippocampus records only a vague recollection of what the man looked like. Your
memory includes his height, weight, and ethnicity but lacks a clear image of his face. When
you talk to a campus police officer, she shows you a photo of a man who is suspected of committing several such crimes. The officer says, "Is this the man who stole your backpack?" The
photo and question set into motion the process of **retroactive interference** (new information
40 displaces old information). The photo and its verbal label "man who stole your backpack"
fill in the gaps in your own incomplete memory of the man's appearance. Remembering the
source of information isn't something we normally do, so you probably will forget that you
replaced your memory with the officer's question and information in the photo. As a result,
you may mentally superimpose the photo over your own incomplete memory of the perpe-
45 trator's face and believe that it is what you actually saw during the event.

Furthermore, over time, you are likely to repeat your story several times. Your story
may include a verbal description of the perpetrator based on the misinformation that
is now part of your memory of the event. Research shows that, after eyewitnesses have
repeatedly recalled information, whether accurate or inaccurate, they become more con-
50 fident of the information's accuracy (Shaw, 1996). That is, by "practicing" your distorted
memory through repetition, you become even more convinced of its accuracy. You also
become resistant to the suggestion that you might have identified the wrong person.

The confidence eyewitnesses have in their testimony is not necessarily an indication of its
accuracy. In fact, eyewitnesses who perceive themselves to be objective have more confidence
55 in their testimony, regardless of its accuracy, and are more likely to include incorrect information in their verbal descriptions (Geiselman et al., 2000). When witnesses make incorrect
identifications with great certainty, they can be highly persuasive to judges and jurors alike.

REDUCING MISTAKES

Fortunately, eyewitness mistakes can be reduced. Training interviewers to use certain
questioning strategies can lessen the effects of reconstructed memory. For instance,

60 asking witnesses to recall the details of an event before questioning them can prevent the misinformation effect (LaPaglia & Chan, 2012; U.S. Department of Justice, 1999). Such interviewing strategies usually involve asking open-ended questions that prompt the eyewitness to tell his or her own story before being asked specific questions. Investigators typically separate witnesses so their stories are as free as possible from the distorting
65 effects of others' recollections.

Similarly, if eyewitnesses view photographs of a suspect before viewing the lineup, eyewitnesses might mistakenly identify that suspect in the lineup because the person looks familiar. Research suggests that it is better to have an eyewitness first describe the perpetrator and then search for photos matching that description than to have the eyewitness
70 start by looking through photos (Pryke, Lindsay, & Pozzulo, 2000). In addition, asking witnesses to assign a confidence rating (i.e., 90% sure, 80% sure, etc.) to each subject in a lineup is more likely to lead to correct identification of a perpetrator than asking witnesses to make a yes/no decision about each one.

The composition of the lineup is also important. Other subjects in a lineup must resem-
75 ble the suspect in age, body build, and certainly race. Even then, if the lineup does not contain the guilty party, eyewitnesses might identify the person who most closely resembles the perpetrator (Gonzalez, Ellsworth, & Pembroke, 1993). Eyewitnesses are less likely to make errors if a sequential lineup is used—that is, if the members of the lineup are viewed one after the other, rather than simultaneously. Some police officers and researchers prefer
80 a "showup," in which the witness sees only one suspect at a time and indicates whether or not that person is the perpetrator. There are fewer misidentifications with a showup but also more failures to make a positive identification.

(1,060 words)

—From *Mastering the World of Psychology*, Fifth Edition,
by Samuel E. Wood, Ellen Green Wood, and Denise Boyd

THINKING AND WRITING AFTER READING

RECALL Self-test your understanding.

Your instructor may choose to give you a brief comprehension review.

REACT Now that you've read the article, how might you react differently the next time you witness something unusual, whether it is disturbing or not? _____

_____

_____

REFLECT Which of the "Reasons for Doubt" have you experienced? Explain.

_____

_____

THINK CRITICALLY In what ways does this information from psychological research improve criminal justice practices? _____

_____

_____

_____

THINK AND WRITE   Use the headings in the article to create an informal outline of the research on eyewitness testimony.

EXTENDED WRITING   Imagine that you are a psychologist who has been hired by an attorney to evaluate the statements of eyewitnesses in a criminal case. You are expected to provide a written report. Your comments will be used to shape the questioning of witnesses during trial. Based on the information in this article, list the questions that you would raise about the statements. Under each question, explain why the question is appropriate and cite the research that supports it.

CRITICAL READING

1. What is the purpose of this reading selection? Explain fully. _____
   _____
   _____
   _____

2. What is the tone of the selection? _____
   _____

3. How do the research citations contribute to the tone of the article and the
   validity of the information? _____
   _____
   _____
   _____
   _____

4. In what other ways might psychology help to shape police practices?
   _____
   _____
   _____
   _____
   _____
   _____

Mark the following statements as *F* (fact) or *O* (opinion).

_____ 5. In most cases, memory failure is an annoyance.

_____ 6. Witnessing a crime causes physiological stress, and stress hormones
disrupt memory functioning (Wolf, 2009).

_____ 7. An example will help you see how the misinformation effect works.

_____ 8. Research shows that, after eyewitnesses have repeatedly recalled
information, whether it is accurate or inaccurate, they become
more confident of the information's accuracy (Shaw, 1996).

Interpret THE QUOTE

Now that you've finished reading the selection, "Eyewitness Testimony," go back to the beginning of the selection and read the opening quote again. In what ways is it supported by the research cited in the selection?

Name ————————————————

Date ————————————————

SELECTION 3

COMPREHENSION QUESTIONS

Answer the following with *a, b, c,* or *d,* or fill in the blank. In order to help you analyze your strengths and weaknesses, the question types are indicated.

Main Idea _____ 1. The best statement of the main idea of this selection is

    a. Eyewitness testimony is unreliable and, therefore, not useful in court proceedings.

    b. Distorted and false memories sometimes replace memory gaps.

    c. Mistakes in eyewitness reports can be reduced.

    d. Psychological research on memory can help us understand eyewitness testimony.

Detail _____ 2. When an interviewer mistakenly provides inaccurate details that influence an eyewitness's memory of an event, the phenomenon is called

    a. unreliability.

    b. the misinformation effect.

    c. reconstructive processing.

    d. retroactive interference.

Detail _____ 3. Which of the following is *not* a reason cited in the article for doubting eyewitness testimony?

    a. Stress and fear can cause witnesses to remember some details but not others.

    b. Eyewitnesses sometimes erroneously reconstruct information to fill in memory gaps.

    c. At times, witnesses purposely provide wrong information to mislead investigators.

    d. Repeating their recollection of what they saw can cause witnesses to fill memory gaps with information from sources other than their original observation of the event.

Main Idea _____ 4. Which of the following best states the main point of the section, "Reducing Mistakes"?

    a. Psychological research suggests questioning strategies that are more likely to yield accurate information from witnesses.

    b. Police should avoid showing pictures of suspects to eyewitnesses.

    c. Lineups that are done incorrectly often result in wrong identifications.

    d. Interviewers should ask open-ended questions.

Inference _____ 5. Which of the following situations is most likely to provide an accurate report from an eyewitness?

    a. Witnesses discuss their observations at the scene before police arrive.

    b. Police immediately show witnesses pictures of possible suspects.

    c. Police question witnesses separately within minutes of the crime.

    d. A witness who left the crime scene before police arrived is questioned one week later and is able to give a very detailed account.

Inference _____ 6. Which of the following items best explains this situation? A woman is robbed at gunpoint outside a bank while walking to her car. She is able to provide a vague description to police. That night, she sees a security video on television of a man suspected of similar robberies in the area. The next day, she calls police to give a more detailed description of her attacker, and it matches the features of the person in the video.

    a. false memory
    b. misinformation effect
    c. reconstructive memory
    d. retroactive interference

Inference _____ 7. When viewing a lineup, witnesses are most likely to make a correct identification in which circumstances?

    a. All persons in the lineup are of the same race as the witnesses have reported.
    b. The persons in the lineup are of different heights.
    c. The suspects are shown to the witness all at once.
    d. The lineup contains people of different ages.

Answer the following questions with *T* (true) or *F* (false).

Detail _____ 8. Research showing that eyewitness testimony is often unreliable and leads to wrongful convictions caused the establishment of national guidelines.

Detail _____ 9. A "showup" produces fewer positive identifications.

Inference _____ 10. A jury is likely to believe a witness who is very certain about what he or she saw.

VOCABULARY

Answer the following with *a, b, c,* or *d* for the word or phrase that best defines the boldface word used in the selection. The number in parentheses indicates the line of the passage in which the word appears. In addition to the context clues, use a dictionary to more precisely define the technical terms.

_____ 1. "has **profound** consequences" (1–2)

    a. clear
    b. deep
    c. maddening
    d. superficial

_____ 2. "Research **attesting** to" (7)

    a. proving
    b. denying
    c. conducting
    d. relating

_____ 3. "hormones **disrupt** memory" (13)

    a. encourage
    b. enhance
    c. disagree
    d. disturb

_____ 4. "worn by the **perpetrator**" (19)

    a. officer
    b. detective
    c. wrongdoer
    d. victim

_____ 5. "**reconstructive** processes" (20–21)

    a. rebuilding
    b. memory
    c. visual
    d. destructive

_____ 6. "**distortions** and even false memories" (21)

    a. facts
    b. statements
    c. misrepresentations
    d. visual images

_____ 7. "**phenomenon** is known"
as" (28)

    a. mystery
    b. occurrence
    c. miracle
    d. episode

_____ 9. "your **hippocampus**
records" (35)

    a. a large African animal
    b. brain system
      controlling vision
    c. nervous system
    d. area of the brain linked
      with memory

_____ 8. "man suddenly **accosts**
you" (34)

    a. confronts
    b. discredits
    c. accuses
    d. hurts

_____ 10. "rather than
simultaneously" (79)

    a. in a row
    b. at the same time
    c. individually
    d. apart

Your instructor may choose to give a brief vocabulary review.

VOCABULARY ENRICHMENT

A. Create your own analogies for each type of relationship. Think of a second word that establishes the indicated relationship and then finish the analogy with a similar comparison. _____

  1. Degree: _Damp_ is to _____ as _____ is to _____.

  2. Part to whole: _Toes_ are to _____ as _____ is to _____.

  3. Cause and effect: _Careless_ is to _____ as _____ is to _____.

  4. Classification: _Airplane_ is to _____ as _____ is to _____.

  5. Function: _Oven_ is to _____ as _____ is to _____.

B. Choose one of the following transitional words or phrases to complete each sentence.

however   for instance   thus   in addition   in a like manner

  6. Freud was the first to conceptualize a theory of personality; _____, he is considered the father of psychoanalysis.

  7. Freud's theories were considered by many to be too sexual and caused some of his followers to create their own groups; _____, a group of his followers who broke away became known as neo-Freudians.

  8. Karen Horney became a neo-Freudian who, _____, became the first American female psychoanalyst.

  9. Carl Jung began with Freud studying personality; _____, later in life he focused on learning theory.

10. Although the neo-Freudians discarded some of the negativity of Freud, they retained Freud's belief that the subconscious affects the personality and, _____, they popularized their own theories through research and publication.

ASSESS YOUR LEARNING

Review confusing questions, seek clarification, and make notes in your text to help you remember new information and vocabulary. Use your textbook as a learning tool.

PERSONAL FEEDBACK   Name _____

1. List three questions that you have asked in any of your classes during the past two weeks. _____

   _____

   _____

2. What routine do you usually follow at night to get ready for the next day at school?

   _____

   _____

   _____

3. What has pleasantly surprised you about your college experience? _____

   _____

   _____

   _____

4. How did you waste time this past week? _____

   _____

   _____

Share your responses as directed by your instructor.

VOCABULARY LESSON

Bend, Born, and Body

Study the roots, words, and sentences.

Roots   *flex, flect*: bend   *nat, nasc*: born   *corp*: body

Words with *flex* or *flect* = *bend*

Do dancers need to be *flexible*? Can you see your *reflection* in the pond?

- Flex: to bend

  Flex your muscles to show your strength.

- Deflect: bend away from

  The politician was able to *deflect* the vicious questions and move ahead.

- Genuflection: bending the knees, bowing

  My arrogant boss seems to expect total submission and *genuflection*.

- Inflection: the rise and fall of the voice

  The *inflection* in his voice revealed that his feelings had been hurt.

- Reflect: to think back to

  Reflect on literary readings through a discussion with others.

- Reflective: thoughtful

  Quiet, *reflective* moments can give a sense of inner peace.

- Reflector: that which sends back light

  Wear a *reflector* when you walk at night.

Words with *nat* or *nasc* = *born*

Does July 4th create a sense of *nationalism*? Is New York an *international* city?

- Native: belonging to by birth

  Are palm trees *native* to your area?

- Naïve: acting as one born yesterday

  The *naïve* respondent thought she had won a prize.

- Naturalize: to give citizenship to one foreign born

  Gisela has been a *naturalized* citizen of this country for two years.

- Innate: inborn

  Freud believed that mankind had an *innate* fear of spiders and snakes.

- Renaissance: a rebirth or revival

  The inner city is experiencing a *renaissance* with urban pioneers.

- Nationality: country of origin

  Her *nationality* is either Mexican or Costa Rican.

Words with *corp* or *corpor* = body

Are *corporate* headquarters lavish? Is any business *incorporable*?

- Corporal: relating to the body

  The scars indicated *corporal* punishment.

- Corporation: business people united legally

  The president of the *corporation* received stock bonuses.

- Incorporate: to unite legally, add

  You need to *incorporate* a visual display into the oral presentation.

- Corps: group organized for a common cause

  The Peace *Corps* members are sent to remote areas to help people.

- Corpuscle: a cell that flows in the blood

  A *corpuscle* can be a red or white blood cell.

- Corpse: a dead body

  An autopsy was performed on the *corpse* because of questions surrounding the death.

- Corpulent: excessively fat

  Santa Claus is *corpulent* and jolly.

Review

Part I

Answer the following with (*T*) true or (*F*) false.

_____ 1. A reflective thinker seldom recalls the past.

_____ 2. Flexible clay can still be molded.

_____ 3. A corpulent corpse will probably be difficult to move.

_____ 4. Spanking a child is corporal punishment.

_____ 5. Corpuscles are found in many plants.

_____ 6. If you look in a mirror, you can see your reflection.

_____ 7. An innate talent is a genetic gift.

_____ 8. Companies on the New York Stock Exchange are incorporated.

_____ 9. A deflected arrow is repelled from the target.

_____ 10. Immigrants must apply to become naturalized citizens.

Part II

Choose the best word from the list to complete the following sentences.

naïve	corps	reflectors	nationalism	inflection
flex	renaissance	genuflect	native	nationality

11. His final voice —————— indicated that he was asking a question.

12. On Halloween night, parents attach safety —————— to costumes.

13. Some flowers that are —————— to a swamp do not grow in the mountains.

14. The army called on the —————— of engineers to replace the bridge.

15. Freshman are —————— to think that a late paper will not be penalized.

16. When the king entered, servants were to —————— with respect.

17. The music of the military band heightened our feelings of ——————.

18. The —————— of the speaker was Colombian, not Cuban.

19. When you lift weights, you —————— your muscles.

20. New shops herald a —————— of the downtrodden warehouse area.

Evaluating Internet Information

For researching anything from recent movie reviews to Shakespearean interpretations, the Internet offers easy access to up-to-date information. The disadvantage of Internet information, however, is that you must always question its reliability and credibility. Unlike the scholarly periodicals in libraries that are reviewed by experts, there are no gatekeepers on the Internet. Anyone from a Nobel Prize scientist to a paramilitary fanatic can purchase a Web site for approximately $100, self-publish, sound like an expert, and turn up in your search.

Be prepared to use your critical reading skills to evaluate Internet material. Question not only what is said but also who wrote it and who paid for it.

Reader's TIP — Critically Evaluating Electronic Material

Ask the following questions to evaluate:

- What are the author's credentials in the field? Is the author affiliated with a university? Check this by noting professional titles in the preface or introduction, finding a biographical reference in the library, or searching the Internet for additional references to the same author.
- Who paid for the Web page? Check the home page for an address. Does the electronic address end in *edu, gov, org,* or *com*? Depending on the material, this sponsor could lend credibility or raise further questions.
- What is the purpose of the Web page? Is the purpose to educate or to sell a product, a service, or an idea? Check the links to investigate any hidden agendas.
- How do the biases of the author and the sponsor affect the material? Is the reasoning sound? Check the tone, assumptions, and evidence. What opposing views have been left out?

Refer to the Web site on the following page to complete Exercise 1.

EXERCISE 1

1. What is the purpose of this site? _____

2. What are the credentials of the author? _____

3. Who paid for the site? _____

4. Why are you inclined to believe or not believe the information in the letter?
_____

SanRafael.com

San Rafael
Nutrition Company, Inc.

Welcome to the new world of health and fitness, to the incredible benefits of looking great and feeling fantastic! Forget about sweating at the gym, tedious treadmills and crowded aerobic classes. What I have to offer is a no-hassle, easy way to drop unwanted pounds for a healthier, more energetic YOU!!

This is all made possible by the San Rafael Program™, my amazing combination of all natural ingredients, including Translite™ and ZX-12™. Until now, the patented formula in the San Rafael Program™ has been the secret of **Hollywood celebrities** and others whose careers depend on a youthful, healthy appearance. The **three simple steps** of the program have been clinically proven not only to help you lose weight fast and boost your energy level, but also to help rid your body of unhealthy toxins that upset your natural metabolic balance.

To find out more about the astounding results made possible by the San Rafael Program™, click on *Info*. To order samples or to get your own supply of this fantastic product, click on *Shopping*. To find out how you can enjoy the advantages of better health as well as the financial benefits of becoming a distributor of the San Rafael Program™, click on *Network*.

Whatever option you choose, I want to welcome you to a better, healthier life and to becoming a member of the San Rafael family!

Sincerely,

Marilyn Obado

Marilyn Obado
President
San Rafael Nutrition Co., Inc.

Info   **Shopping**   **Network**

EXERCISE 2 Search the Internet for a Web site that sells antiaging products, such as creams that claim to prevent wrinkles or vitamin concoctions that claim to enhance vitality. Print the page and then highlight or make a list of the claims that you feel are exaggerated and are not supported by facts.

10 Survivor Casebook: Apply Your Reading Skills

Learning Objectives

From this chapter, readers will learn:

1 To analyze ideas from multiple sources on a common topic

2 To synthesize ideas from multiple sources

3 To create a new work using multiple sources on a common topic

Everyday Reading Skills: Managing Workplace Reading

SURVIVORS

"We shall draw from the heart of suffering itself the means of inspiration and survival.
—Winston Churchill

Why are some people able to manage difficult situations while others are crushed by them? Perhaps you agree with Winston Churchill that difficulty brings with it the ability to survive. If so, that ability lies within all of us. The strength to fight adversity, no matter how challenging or seemingly hopeless, is regularly celebrated in news stories and personal experiences. The stories cause us to wonder what motivates survivors to overcome difficult situations. Perhaps we question whether we could find the strength of the survivor within ourselves when trouble strikes.

The television show "Survivor" has itself survived in the United States since the year 2000 and has survived longer in other countries. If you are a fan, you know that the program puts willing contestants in unlikely situations in unfriendly physical and social environments. The show thrives on competition within and between ever-changing teams as each player strives to be the lone survivor. Participants often sacrifice trust, loyalty, kindness, and other virtues of normal life as they vie for dominance. They make alliances and break them as quickly as the needs of the game dictate. The popularity of this show points to our natural interest in what it takes to win a game like "Survivor," but do the same qualities support us in real life crises?

A scene from the television show, "Survivor."

**Learning
Objective 1**

Analyze ideas from
multiple sources on
a common topic

Through a collection of readings from multiple sources, this chapter explores the personal stories of individuals who have suffered adversity in real life and have triumphed. Many of their stories are tragic, yet they are all inspirational. Perhaps you will sense that these survivors are stronger because of their challenges. Perhaps, you will find something in these stories that can inspire and strengthen you, too.

This chapter asks you to put all of your reading strategies to work in a way that you are expected to do in many college classes. Remember what you learned and practiced as you honed your ability to fully comprehend and use the ideas you encounter in print. Be an active reader who prepares before reading, actively engages during reading, solidifies memory after reading, and analyzes, evaluates, and then applies what is learned to new situations.

PERSONAL FEEDBACK 1

Name _____

1. Think of a personal difficulty that you struggled to overcome. Describe it briefly here.

_____

_____

_____

2. What personal strengths or other resources helped you to overcome the personal difficulty?

_____

_____

_____

3. Would you do anything differently if faced with a similar situation again? Explain.

_____

_____

_____

Share your responses as directed by your instructor.

What Motivates a Person to Survive?

The stories you will read chronicle the experiences of people who survived sex trafficking, cancer, debt, homelessness, and tragic loss. Prepare to delve into this topic by listing the factors you think motivate people to endure and win against challenging life situations. What keeps you and others going through tough times?

_____   _____

_____   _____

As you read and think about the following selections, look for the motivators that kept these survivors fighting.

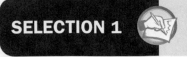

SELECTION 1 | ## Survivor of Sex Trafficking Narrative | MyReadingLab™

Visit Chapter 10: Survivor Casebook in MyReadingLab™ to complete the Selection 1 activities and Building Background Knowledge video activity.

Sex trafficking is a growing and particularly violent form of human slavery. Traffickers recruit their victims in American cities and towns and also bring them into the United States through large international sex trade networks. The Victims of Trafficking and Violence Protection Act of 2000 defines sex trafficking as "the recruitment, harboring, transportation, provision, or obtaining of a person for the purpose of a commercial sex act." While some victims are adults, a large number are children. The law labels as a severe form "sex trafficking in which a commercial sex act is induced by force, fraud, or coercion, or in which the person induced to perform such act has not attained 18 years of age." According to the United States Department of Justice, the average age of children forced into prostitution in the United States is 13–14 years old. The Federal Bureau of Investigation estimates that there are as many as 300,000 child prostitutes in the United States. The National Center for Missing and Exploited Children states that controllers, who average four to six victims each, can make as much as $200,000 per child per year. Fortunately, the United States government and numerous private agencies are working to protect, rescue, and return victims of sex trafficking to free and normal lives.

THINKING BEFORE READING

Activate your schema by recalling what you learned from the reading selection on page 354 about human smuggling and trafficking. Preview the following selection for content and organizational clues. Predict the author's ideas and determine your purpose for reading. Think!

Why do children and teens sometimes run away from home?

What are some circumstances that entrap teens in sex trafficking?

I think this narrative will reveal _____.

BUILDING BACKGROUND KNOWLEDGE — VIDEO

American Girls: Survivors of the Sex Trade

To prepare for reading Selection 1 about sex trafficking, answer the questions below. Then, watch this video about the trafficking of American girls.

How do you think traffickers lure their victims?

Why do you think trafficking victims don't just run away from their keepers?

What challenges do you expect that victims face when they are rescued?

This video helped me _____.

THINKING DURING READING

As you read, use the six thinking strategies of a good reader: predict, picture, relate, monitor, correct, and annotate.

> ### *Reader's* **TIP**   Narratives
>
> "Narrative" is a literary term for a story. Remember that "to narrate" means to tell a story. Authors usually organize narratives in time order. Narratives usually contain a series of events that surround a theme or a main point. An author's purpose in writing a narrative can simply be to tell an engaging story by invoking humor, drama, empathy, or other emotion. On the other hand, the author might also intend to inspire, teach a lesson, or persuade readers of some truth or course of action.
>
> - Notice the signals that mark the timing of events.
> - Pay attention to who is telling the story. If the narrative contains quotes, notice who is speaking.
> - Notice details that add interest to the story.
> - What is the theme or main point of the narrative?
> - What is the author's purpose in writing?

BARBARA AMAYA'S STORY

My name is Barbara Amaya and I am a survivor of trafficking.

I spent the first 12 years of my life in Northern Virginia. When I was only 10 years old, family members abused me. Before the abuse I was a pretty normal little girl: I loved to read, collect stamps, draw, and I was a member of the Barbie fan club. Unfortunately, after
5   I was abused, I became a different little girl. No one helped me or validated the abuse I had suffered, so part of me went into hiding and I became depressed. I didn't want to be around anyone, no longer went to school, and eventually ran away when I was 12.

When I ran away, I was a walking target for traffickers and predators who look for damaged children: I had been abused; I was depressed and was in desperate need of help.
10   It didn't take long for traffickers to find me. Surprisingly it was a couple—a man and a woman—who found me on the streets of Washington, D.C. They took me off of the streets where I was hungry and alone and brought me into their home where they fed me and seemed to care for me. That is, until they initiated me into the world of trafficking. They used me for a few months until they no longer needed me and then sold me to another
15   trafficker. Right in our nation's capital, I was sold into trafficking to a man named Moses. Soon after buying me, Moses took me to New York City where he trafficked me for 8 years.

During my time on the streets of New York I was abused, shot, stabbed, raped, kidnapped, trafficked, beaten, addicted to drugs, jailed, and more—all before I was 18 years old.

To ease my pain, I became addicted to drugs. This habit became very expensive and I
20   was no longer a valuable commodity to my trafficker, so he released me into New York. It was terrible; I was addicted and alone in the city. Thankfully, at a methadone clinic where I had sought treatment, I met a woman named Anita who helped me to find my sister, who had apparently been living in the nearby city of Philadelphia, and that Christmas, she helped me reunite with my family.

25   After a very difficult time detoxing off of methadone, I started to slowly get my life back. I lived in Washington State, Mississippi, and eventually came back to Virginia where

I got married and tried to have a baby. Soon after I started trying to have a baby, I found out that because of all the trauma I had endured on the streets, I was infertile. Somehow, I think it was a miracle; I was able to have treatments and can happily say that I was able to have a daughter.

In all of that moving around and having my daughter, I kept my past a secret. No one knew about the years I had been trafficked or abused but me. Then one night, when my daughter was 15, she decided to run away. My past came rushing back to me, and I was so afraid that the same things that happened to me would happen to my daughter. I couldn't just sit around, so I spent the whole night making phone calls and looking for her. Thankfully, I found her the next morning and, shortly after, told her about my story. After that, she never ran away again, and she is doing well today. I have a wonderful grandson, and I live a contented and quiet life.

I believe I am alive today because God watched over me all those nights on the streets. He kept a part of me untouched inside—despite all the men and all the trauma I endured—a part of me remained clean and whole. I call that part of me my soul.

I choose to believe that I went through all that I did so that today I can help others. If I can educate one person or give hope to one victim of trafficking, then I am doing my job, and everything I went through was worth it. I choose to be a victor, not a victim—not just to survive, but to thrive. Today I tell my story whenever I can so I can help others. I have a book in process called *Girl's Guide to Survival: Life Lessons from the Street* and a Web site at www.barbaraamaya.com.

(731 words)

—From http://richmondjusticeinitiative.com/human-trafficking/survival-stories
by Barbara Amaya

THINKING AND WRITING AFTER READING

1. Why did Barbara Amaya run away from home? _____
_____
_____

2. What clues might have alerted adults who knew Amaya as a 10-, 11-, and 12-year old that something was wrong? _____
_____
_____

3. What did the couple who took in the young Amaya from the streets offer that she was missing in her life? _____
_____

4. In what way did her daughter running away from home change Amaya?
_____
_____

5. To what does Amaya give credit for changing her life? _____
_____
_____
_____

Survivor of Cancer
Narrative

MyReadingLab™

Visit Chapter 10: Survivor Casebook in MyReadingLab™ to complete the Selection 2 activities and Building Background Knowledge video activity.

Although the experience is different for everyone, cancer treatment is tough. In addition to the physical side effects is the great emotional stress, which affects not only the patient but also his or her family and loved ones. Cancer patients often speak of the varied factors that keep them from giving up. Once the treatment is over, cancer survivors also cope with their new lives in different ways. While some prefer to put their experiences behind them, others choose to draw on them and find ways to turn their experiences into something that will help others. Read the inspiring story of Gary Bonacker, who continues to convert his obstacles into something positive.

THINKING BEFORE READING

Preview the selection for content and organizational clues. Activate your schema and anticipate what you will learn. Predict the author's ideas and determine your purpose for reading. Think!

What do you know about cancer treatments?

What have some cancer survivors accomplished after successful treatment?

I will read this to find out _____.

BUILDING BACKGROUND KNOWLEDGE — VIDEO

ON THE RUN
CANCER SURVIVOR'S JOURNEY ACROSS THE U.S.

A Journey of Survival

To prepare for reading Selection 2 written by a cancer survivor, answer the questions below. Then, watch this video featuring Helene Neville, a four-time cancer survivor, who is running the perimeter of the United States to promote cancer awareness and healthy living.

What do you think motivates some cancer survivors to serve as role models for others?

Helen Neville says she is running to "get everyone to think about health and to inspire the next person". What impact do you think she has on the people she meets along her journey?

In what ways can one support a loved one or friend who is battling cancer?

This video helped me: _____.

THINKING DURING READING

As you read, use the six thinking strategies of a good reader: predict, picture, relate, monitor, correct, and annotate.

GARY BONACKER: BIKING FOR LIFE

Refer to the
Reader's **TIP**
for **Narratives** on
page 483.

"I love life and do everything I can to live each day better than the day before. I know I sound like a greeting card," Gary Bonacker says, "but it's a good way to live."

In the spring of 2003, Gary was diagnosed with a Stage 2 brain tumor. But just 10 months after surgery that removed only half of the tumor, Gary rode at the Ride for the
5 Roses cycling event in Austin, Texas.

"It was something I'll remember for the rest of my life," Gary says. It inspired him to go home to Bend, Oregon, and start his own cycling event to raise money for cancer. The Tour des Chutes has grown from 750 riders in 2005 to over 1,100 riders for the 2010 ride. The money raised during the event helps fund the cancer survivorship program at
10 St. Charles Cancer Center, which provides medical care for many of the cancer patients in Bend and other nearby communities.

The years since have not been easy. Gary was diagnosed with his brain tumor in 2003, and he still battles it every day. He requires ongoing treatment to slow the growth of the tumor and is on antiseizure medicines. With fatigue and multiple health problems,
15 he has had to limit his work a great deal.

"There's not a day that I don't go into a dark place, thinking about things I might miss," he says. "But my family, workplace, and friends, and my event help me through it. My other coping strategy is to read about research and learn everything that I can about my disease. I've surprised doctors with information they weren't even aware of. I have
20 heard people with cancer say it is a gift," he jokes. "Well, I would give this gift back, if possible!"

Gary continues to do his best and move on with his life. Besides planning his annual fundraiser, he says that spending time with his family, gardening, and fishing are his best coping strategies. And, of course, cycling.
25 "What's sad is that it took getting cancer to make me look at my life and how I should live it," Gary says. "We take a lot for granted. But I don't any longer."

(369 Words)

—From *Cancer Adventures,*
by Marlys Johnson

THINKING AND WRITING AFTER READING

1. What are the possible reasons that the doctors did not remove all of Bonacker's brain tumor? _____

_____

2. What is the purpose of the Tour des Chutes? _____

_____

3. What are Bonacker's continuing health challenges? _____

_____

_____

4. In what ways has cancer changed Bonacker's life for the better? _____

_____

_____

5. What motivates Bonacker to continue fighting? _____

_____

_____

_____

SELECTION 3   ## Survivors of Serious Debt   MyReadingLab™
Newspaper Feature Article

Visit Chapter 10: Survivor Casebook in MyReadingLab to complete the Selection 3 activities and Building Background Knowledge video activity.

For various reasons, many Americans have accumulated a dangerous amount of debt. According to a University of Michigan study, "one out of five families owes more on credit cards, medical bills, student loans, and other unsecured debt than they have in savings." For people under 35, a major culprit is student loans. The Project on Student Debt by The Institute for College Access and Success reported that seven in ten college graduates in the class of 2012 had student loan debt; they owed an average of $29,400. However, paying for education is not the only problem affecting young people's wallets. Credit card debt, with its high interest rates, and loans from family members also account for a portion of their total debt. The good news is that millennials, people born in the early 1980s to the early 2000s, are more careful about accruing debt than their elders. Still, all should take warning of the harsh burden that debt can place on marriages and on the enjoyment of life. Thoughtful spending, saving, and smart planning can avoid the predicament this couple survived.

THINKING BEFORE READING

Preview the following selection for content and organizational clues. Predict the author's ideas and determine your purpose for reading. Think!

Do you have any financial debts? What kinds?

How do you plan to pay your debts?

In what ways do your debts of any kind, whether heavy or light, influence your life?

BUILDING BACKGROUND KNOWLEDGE — **VIDEO**

Financial Priorities

To prepare for reading Selection 3 about a couple who survived a serious debt crisis, answer the questions below. Then, watch this video that offers one very important step.

What do you think is the reason that many people accumulate large debts?

If you have serious debt, what do you think should be your first step?

What other measures do you think one should take to get out of debt?

This video helped me _____.

THINKING DURING READING

As you read, use the six thinking strategies of a good reader: predict, picture, relate, monitor, correct, and annotate.

THE HARBS: COUPLE ESCAPES CREDIT CARD DEBT AND KEEPS MARRIAGE

Refer to the

Reader's **TIP**

for **News and Feature Articles** on page 207.

On their fifth wedding anniversary, Scott and Jacynta Harb were broke and living off credit cards. Their 10th anniversary proved even worse: They were still broke but by then had racked up $52,000 in credit card debt.

That's right around the time Scott realized that the suburban Atlanta couple had hit
5 rock bottom, debt wise. The Harbs, who have three children, had been using their cards for household expenses while Scott started his own small business, but the debt had spiraled out of control. The only way out was to do something radical: eliminate all spending. So he canceled the couple's only vacation in years.

"I was dev-as-tat-ed," Jacynta, 41, said in a recent phone call, pausing between each
10 syllable for emphasis.

The Harbs' story illustrates how easy it is to let debt involving multiple credit cards—or unsecured high-interest loans—snowball in a short amount of time. And they are not alone. Currently Americans have accrued more than $819 billion in revolving debt, much of that from credit cards.

15 Like many entrepreneurs, Scott had turned to credit cards while launching his business in 2001. He and Jacynta knew they would have to rely on credit to make up for the $600 shortfall in their household's monthly budget. But what they thought would be just months of living without his income stretched into years.

Because they were paying their bills on time, the Harbs were able to obtain even
20 more credit cards over the next five years. They maxed out one card, then another—and another. Finally they had spent to the limit on a total of nine cards, with annual percentage rates between 27% and 29%.

Though the Harbs were never late on a payment, the credit card companies kept raising their interest rates because their debt-to-income ratio was so high. By their tenth
25 anniversary, they were paying $1,500 a month in minimum payments alone.

"We thought it was manageable because we didn't have any creditors calling," Scott, 47, said. "That's the lie you fall into."

The Harbs did finally realize this couldn't continue, and they developed a plan. With a lot of hard work and many sacrifices, they completed a grueling 54-month journey to
30 pay off all their debt. Their austerity plan could serve as an example for anyone who needs to climb out of debt: They worked extra jobs, spent the bare minimum, bought only used cars and furniture, did not take any vacations except camping trips, made no home improvements and cooked all meals at home.

"There were nights when we were both working and kids were with friends," Scott
35 said. "I even worked on Mother's Day to keep paying the bills."

The Harbs also worked out a debt-management plan with CredAbility, a nonprofit credit counseling group in Atlanta. That move helped shave off more than $300 from their total in monthly credit card payments. Every month for the duration of the debt, they made a single payment of $1,132, including a $50 management fee to CredAbility. The
40 credit counselors then paid the couple's nine bills.

Once involved in the debt management program, the Harbs could not open any more credit card accounts and committed to making a set monthly payment for more than four years. "Forced discipline sounds like apple pie compared to that," Scott said. "Each month it was a battle. It was beans and rice."

45 The key to the Harbs' success was asking the banks, with CredAbility's assistance, to lower their interest rates. Chase agreed to lower its rate from 29% to 6%; Discover dropped its rate from 29% to 12.99%; and Bank of America revised its rate from 29% to 14.9%.

But the Harbs' tale is more than a money story; it's also the story of their marriage surviving through perseverance, partnership and sacrifices. "No one gets any credit but
50 me and my wife," said Scott. "It's all about digging in and hard work."

Money problems and marriages are no strangers; many couples call it quits because of differing views on home finances. Research has shown that credit cards can be a powerful negative force in marriages. Couples who paid off debt acquired early in their marriage had a relationship of higher quality over time, said Jeffrey Dew, an assistant professor at
55   Utah State University who studies money and family relationships.

"Consumer debt is stressful," Dew said. "When you are under stress, that will hurt your marriage even though you have a great marriage."

"I have also found in my studies that the more consumer debt couples have, the more often they fight," he said. "Even if you take out fighting about money, they still
60   fight more."

Jacynta, who works as a Weight Watchers leader and is a sales director for a home decor company, said the stress from the debt had affected her marriage. For her, the lowest point came when Scott told her they didn't even have enough money for her to visit her family in Pennsylvania.

65   "I got this awful feeling about it—that [the debt management plan] was not going to work," Jacynta said.

But it did work. When the Harbs marked their 15th anniversary, they traveled to Mexico for a much anticipated family vacation. Being free of credit card debt has been "great" for their marriage, they agreed.

70   "The last six or seven months have been the best of our marriage," said Scott.

(905 Words)

—By Catherine New,
From *Huffington Post*, June 18, 2012

THINKING AND WRITING AFTER READING

1. What were the main causes of the Harbs' debt? _____

_____

_____

_____

2. What strategies could they have used that might have avoided their dangerous total credit card debt and the necessity of their drastic final plan?

_____

_____

_____

_____

_____

_____

3. What specific actions comprised their debt management plan? _____

_____

_____

_____

_____

_____

4. What benefits resulted from the Harbs' ordeal? _____

_____

_____

5. What strengths motivated the Harbs through this debt crisis and helped them maintain their marriage? _____

_____

_____

_____

SELECTION 4

Survivor of Youth Homelessness
Essay

MyReadingLab™

Visit Chapter 10: Survivor Casebook in MyReadingLab to complete the Selection 4 activities and Building Background Knowledge video activity.

Approximately 1,682,900 youth in the United States are without a safe home according to government statistics and the National Coalition for the Homeless. These are young people under the age of 18; the majority are 15 to 17 years old. The causes vary. Unstable family situations, neglect, physical and sexual abuse, financial crises, and discharge from institutional or foster care contribute to the number of young people living without a permanent place to call home. All of them find that life on the streets is hostile, dangerous, and lonely. Many become trafficked for sex or labor, suffer severe depression, anxiety, and physical illness, and have difficulty getting an education.

THINKING BEFORE READING

Preview the following selection for content and organizational clues. Predict the author's ideas and determine your purpose for reading. Think!

Where do youth and teens who run away from home or are pushed out of their homes go?

What services are available to help homeless youth?

I'll read to find out _____.

BUILDING BACKGROUND KNOWLEDGE — VIDEO

Gay Marine's Amazing Journey from Homeless Shelter to Ivy League

To prepare for reading Selection 4 about youth homelessness, answer the questions below. Then, watch this video about why Elegance Bratton became homeless and the surprising way he escaped.

What are some reasons that parents push their kids out of their homes?

What would it be like to be estranged from your family for seven years?

Why is it surprising that a young, gay, homeless man would find a new life by joining the United States Marines and learning to make films?

This video helped me _____.

THINKING DURING READING

As you read, use the six thinking strategies of a good reader: predict, picture, relate, monitor, correct, and annotate.

JESS'S STORY: THE NEW FACE OF HOMELESSNESS

Refer to the
Reader's **TIP**
for **Essays** on
page 59.

The attendant at the drive-through is a teenage schoolgirl with a big smile and a warm welcome. She is impeccably turned out, not a hair out of place. You order a coffee, medium with cream and one sugar, and then decide to go for a bagel with egg and bacon. The young server chats away about the weather as she gets your order ready. She
5   may be thinking about what she is going to buy at the mall when she gets off shift, or perhaps a boyfriend will pick her up and they will go to the movies with friends. This is the early shift, and she shivers as the cold air blows into the serving window. She straightens her back and takes the next order with the same upbeat, energetic manner.

   As you pull out to negotiate the traffic, you are unaware that you have just come face
10 to face with homelessness. The young lady who served you is homeless. The attendant's name is Jess. She is 18 years old and has been homeless since she was 15. Living day to day on the streets, she didn't know where she was going to lay her head at night. "I spent all summer walking around town looking for a place to stay," said Jess. There is a sense of confidence beyond her years that is evident when you spend any time around Jess. There is a
15 determination that has seen her overcome hardships and barriers at which most adults falter. There is also sadness when she tells her story in an emotionless, matter-of-fact monotone. It is a story of a lost childhood; children living on the streets grow up real quickly.

The face of homelessness is changing. Gone are the days when the sight of an old man with unkempt hair, a scraggy beard, and a piece of rope to hold up his pants was the
20 telltale sign of homelessness. These days you are just as likely to come face to face with homelessness as you pick up a coffee at the drive-through window. Homelessness can be seen coming off school buses, wandering around the shopping mall, or hanging out with friends. They are the kids next door.

   Jess is not alone. The statistics across the country are shocking. National organizations
25 like Homeless Youth Among Us quote well over a million children in the United States are living on the streets or couch surfing on any given day.

   Organizations like The Shaw House, a local non-profit homeless shelter in Maine, try to come to terms with this population of homeless children. "We see kids with mental

30 health issues, substance abuse issues, and criminal histories as often as we see kids without any of those problems. Likewise, we see kids whose parents struggle with these issues and kids whose parents who don't have such struggles," said Caseworker Judy Dembowski.

In Jess's case it was the break-up of her parents' marriage that marked the beginning of a personal nightmare full of fear, pain, and a sense of loneliness that never seems to go away. It's tough when your parents split up and you are only 12 years old. It's even harder
35 when they meet other people and you get caught in all the changes, move from state to state, or get left behind with no place to call home.

Jess stayed with an older brother for a while, but he couldn't manage to keep an apartment, so Jess was on her own again. She started couch surfing, a term many homeless people use to describe sleeping on floors, couches or spare cots if they are lucky.
40 Jess tried to maintain her studies and keep up her attendance in school despite her lack of a stable environment. "It's hard enough to live your life day to day, but when you add school to the mix it becomes impossible," she said. To make matters worse, in her sophomore year she was confronted with another hurdle, this one a threat to her physical well-being. The year she ended up on the streets was the same year she discovered she
45 was suffering from rheumatoid arthritis (RA).

Jess started having pains in her wrist, which continued up into her elbow and shoulder. A visit to the doctor revealed arthritis, and she needed shots to relieve the pain. She was unable to do anything about it, though, because she was living on the streets. "Once I was on the streets I lost my MaineCare health insurance, so I couldn't go to the doctor or get medication
50 for my condition. I went without meds for a year, and the pain was terrible but I dealt with it. Sometimes smoking pot would help, or at least I thought it did at the time," she said.

Yet, despite being homeless and having RA, Jess continued her studies at the local high school and kept her grades up and her attendance in class high.

At 16, the need for a pair of shoes got Jess in trouble with the law. She had no money,
55 and the shoes she was wearing were worn out and hurt her feet when she walked. She helped herself to a pair of shoes. She was caught and charged with shoplifting. When the police took her to the station, they also found narcotics in her possession. Jess states the drugs were not hers. "It was a prescription I was holding for someone else," she said.

With theft and narcotics possession charges, Jess could have been in very serious trou-
60 ble. Luckily, a seasoned juvenile corrections officer seemed to understand that the root of Jess's problem was her homelessness. He suggested she get in touch with The Shaw House. Jess remembers the exact date and events. "It was August 25th, 2008. The guy at the Department of Corrections called the Shaw House, and I spoke with a woman called Judy. She told me to come right over and sign in. I haven't been on the streets since."

65 If the streets were daunting, the shelter was another challenging experience for Jess. "I didn't know anybody, so I pretty much stuck to myself," she said. "We had to be in at a certain time; there was a curfew. I couldn't just come and go as I pleased. I wasn't used to rules."

After living in the shelter for a couple of months, Jess moved into the transitional program at Shaw House, a longer-term placement where young people are given the chance
70 to attend school, get a job and prepare for the day they leave to begin their adult lives.

In June 2008 Jess graduated from high school, something she worked very hard to achieve and a personal goal on which she never gave up. She even attended the prom with her boyfriend. After graduation Jess found a job and is currently working. She is still staying at the Shaw House where she has her own room and the support of staff. Jess
75 continues working hard in her transition to becoming an adult and taking her place in the community. She hopes to save some money to get a car and a place of her own. Education is still in her plans with a couple of classes next year.

When asked what she wants to be when she grows up, Jess says she isn't sure but, "Not homeless. That is for sure!"

(1,229 words)

—From www.theshawhouse.org,
by Rick Tardiff

THINKING AND WRITING AFTER READING

1. What external factors helped Jess get off the streets? _____

_____

_____

_____

2. What internal strengths helped Jess survive and eventually escape life on the

   streets? _____

_____

3. Although Jess was happy to go to the Shaw House shelter, she also found it

   difficult to stay there. Why? Comment on Jess's reaction. _____

_____

_____

_____

4. What do you think the future holds for Jess? _____

_____

5. What must Jess do to achieve a successful future? _____

_____

SELECTION 5

Survivor of Personal Tragedy
Newspaper Feature Article

MyReadingLab™

Visit Chapter 10: Survivor Casebook in MyReadingLab to complete the Selection 5 activities and Building Background Knowledge video activity.

When Austin Hatch scored a goal during a high school practice game, the opponents and everyone watching erupted in a five-minute celebration. It was just a practice game, but what might seem like a small success was anything but small. Austin's acrobatic move on the court signaled the beginning of a basketball career that he had counted on and seemingly lost. It was an impressive milestone in a remarkable recovery from a devastating personal tragedy and a serious brain injury.

THINKING BEFORE READING

Preview the following selection for content and organizational clues. Predict the author's ideas and determine your purpose for reading. Think!

What would help you survive the loss of a loved one?

What are some common consequences of a brain injury?

Is it possible to recover fully from a brain injury?

I will read to find out _____.

BUILDING BACKGROUND KNOWLEDGE — VIDEO

Extreme Healing for War Vets

To prepare for reading Selection 5 about personal tragedy, answer the questions below. Then, watch this video about how snowboarding is helping wounded veterans recover.

What stories have you heard or seen about veterans wounded in the Middle East?

What special difficulties do veterans with prosthetic limbs face in their recovery?

How do you think extreme sports might help veterans heal?

This video helped me _____.

THINKING DURING READING

As you read, use the six thinking strategies of a good reader: predict, picture, relate, monitor, correct, and annotate.

AUSTIN HATCH: BASKETBALL DREAMS DEFERRED . . . AND ACHIEVED

Refer to the
Reader's TIP
for **News or Feature
Articles** on page
207.

A California teen who survived two plane crashes—one that killed his mother and siblings and the other that killed his father and stepmother—spoke publicly for first time in the fall of 2013 at a press conference. Two years of grueling pain and physical therapy had passed since he lost the last of his immediate family, and he was finally signing a college
5   basketball deal.

Austin Hatch survived a 2003 Indiana private plane crash that killed his mother, Julie, and his siblings, 11-year-old Lindsey and 5-year-old Ian, and spared only him and his father. The family was returning from their summer home on Walloon Lake when they crashed. Austin, who was 8 years old at the time, only survived the 2003 crash when his
10   father flung him out of the burning plane.

Austin Hatch (left) with his former high school basketball coach.

Together, Austin and his father, Dr. Stephen Hatch, forged a new life. His father remarried and was adamant that he stick with his passion for flying despite the trauma of losing most of his family. Austin showed remarkable skill on the basketball court as a high school player. The standout star of Canterbury High School's team averaged 23 points and
15   9 rebounds per game and shot 45% from behind the 3-point line. As a sophomore, he led his team to a 17-5 record. He hoped to play at the University of Michigan, his father's alma mater.

What became Austin's impossibly tragic tale was national news in 2011. Following the same route as in the 2003 crash, the family's single-engine plane crashed into a
20   garage near the Charlevoix Municipal Airport. Austin lost his father and stepmother and nearly died himself. He was given a small measure of comfort after the crash when his dog, a labradoodle named Brady, was found wandering near the crash site in the days following the accident. Austin's father was the pilot in both accidents. Pilot error was named as the cause of the 2011 crash. Just 10 days prior, the standout Indiana high
25   school basketball player had accepted an offer to play for the University of Michigan after graduation.

Austin sustained severe trauma to his head, a punctured lung, and fractured ribs and collarbone. Doctors put him in a medically induced coma to control swelling in his brain. He awoke eight weeks later to learn that his father and stepmother had died and that his
30   own injuries were serious.

During his arduous 10-month recovery, Austin kept his focus on his dream of playing college basketball. "Basketball has always given me something to shoot for," he said. Doctors warned, however, that he might never recover the basketball skills he had before the accident. With grit and hard work, Austin gradually recovered the ability to walk and talk.

35   A year after the 2011 crash, he took part in drills with his high school team, and just two months later, doctors gave him permission to play at full speed. It is a credit to Austin's character, though, that he chose not to accept game time because he knew he still lacked the speed and strength to be an asset to his team. He didn't want to take playing time from teammates who could contribute more to a winning season.

40   Just before his senior year in high school, Austin decided to leave his home town of Fort Wayne, Indiana, to live with his uncle, Michael Hatch, in Pasadena, California, as part of his recovery. He enrolled at Loyola High School, a Los Angeles-area basketball powerhouse. Despite the emotional torture that has marked most of his childhood, Austin maintained a remarkably upbeat attitude. His coach at Loyola, Jamal Adams, said that Austin's

45   hard work has shown him that 'nothing is impossible'. "I was dealing with the loss of my best friend, my coach, my teacher, my mentor and my No. 1 fan—that same man was also my father, Dr. Stephen Hatch," Austin said.

       Despite all odds, Austin's dream came true. Two years after he was originally offered a spot on the team, Austin announced that he would indeed be fulfilling his dream of joining

50   the University of Michigan's basketball team. Michigan coach John Beilein named Austin as part of the 2014 recruiting class, and he attends on a scholarship. It is unclear in what capacity Austin—who hadn't played basketball even once outside of practices since the crash—will play on the team. But he's still determined to play a role. Austin said, "Coach Beilein told me that he wouldn't offer me a scholarship if he didn't think I had a role on

55   the team that would help them win. He said, 'Austin, whatever you are able to do, whether it be a manager or a practice player or whatever, you're on scholarship no matter what.'"

       Although Austin knows he'll never be the same person or the same basketball player after living through the second crash of his young life, he's pursuing his recovery with his scholarship to the university. "It has been a goal of mine since I can remember," he said at

60   the Los Angeles press conference. "It was kind of surreal to actually sign."

       In addition to his sports-related announcement, Austin touched on his life's tragedies at the news conference. "Aside from the physical trauma that I suffered in the accident," he said, "the emotional pain will never fully subside. I have been put to the ultimate test of resilience, faith, courage, work ethic, things of that nature. I'm not sure there is anyone

65   who has been through and survived two plane crashes. I feel like God has his hand on me," he said." I feel like there's a plan for my life." Friends say that he values life more than ever. After years of arduous recovery, Austin joined the Wolverines in 2014 as he attends the University of Michigan.

(966 words)

—From http://www.dailymail.co.uk,
The Daily Mail

THINKING AND WRITING AFTER READING

1. In what way did the tragedies that Austin experienced change him? _____
   _____
   _____
   _____
   _____

2. What did Austin's decision not to play in a game, even though his doctors and high school coach had approved it, demonstrate about him? _____
   _____
   _____
   _____

3. Why did University of Michigan coach Beilein honor his previous offer of a basketball scholarship, even knowing of Austin's brain damage? _____

_____

_____

_____

_____

4. What factors and qualities made Austin a survivor? _____

_____

_____

_____

_____

_____

5. What do you most admire about Austin Hatch's story? Why? _____

_____

_____

_____

SYNTHESIZE

Learning Objective 2

Synthesize ideas from multiple sources

From the reading selections, you identified the strengths, personality traits, and other factors that enabled these admirable people to survive difficult experiences. Now it is time to pull all of your information together to better isolate their key survival resources. Review your annotations and responses to each of the five selections, and make a list of the internal and external sources of strength shown in the readings. Put an asterisk (*) next to an item each time it is repeated. When you finish, you will see which strategies were most common and which were unique to individuals.

_____   _____

_____   _____

_____   _____

_____   _____

_____   _____

_____   _____

Now examine your list from the beginning of the chapter. Put a checkmark (✓) next to items above that you predicted and list below those that did not appear on your first list but that you have thought of since you started reading the chapter. This exercise might stretch your vocabulary, as different words might have been used to express the same ideas. Focus on isolating ideas rather than on listing every word.

_____   _____

_____   _____

_____   _____

_____   _____

The following is an excerpt from Matthew Stein's book, _When Technology Fails_. Do any of these characteristics appear on your lists? What is missing?

Psychologist Al Siebert's personal fascination with survivors began when he received his military training from a group of veteran paratroopers. His teachers were legendary members of the 503rd Airborne Infantry Regiment. They had lost nine out of ten members in combat in the Korean War. Siebert found that these "survivors" were not the crusty, yelling drill sergeants that he had anticipated. They were tough, yet showed patience. They had a good sense of humor and were likely to laugh at mistakes. They were positive, yet also looked at the downside of things. They didn't act mean or tough, even though they could be as mean and tough as anyone. Siebert noticed that each of these men had a type of personal radar that was always on "scan." He realized it was not dumb luck that had brought these men through their ordeals, but a combination of qualities that tilted the odds in their favor. Siebert believes that we can all benefit in our daily lives by nurturing and developing these positive character traits.

Flexibility. The No. 1 trait to which many survivors attribute their success is the ability to adapt to the situation.

Commitment to survive. When conditions are extremely difficult, it takes a strong will and commitment to survive. Jewish Holocaust and Bataan Death March survivors tell tales of watching their friends lose the will to survive.

Staying cool. Survivors have the ability to stay calm or regain calmness so they can think clearly and intuitively "feel" their way to a correct choice, without being hampered by emotions that have run amok.

Playful curiosity. Survivors usually like to know how things work. They show a playful curiosity that helps them adapt to changing circumstances.

Sense of humor. The ability to laugh helps people manage under the worst conditions.

CREATE

Learning Objective 3

Create a new work using multiple sources

Now that you have immersed yourself in survival stories, use what you have discovered to create a product that represents your knowledge and insights. Use the lists in the previous section as the basis for your content and add your personal insights. Your instructor may give a specific assignment and instructions, but here are some suggestions: Your purpose for each of these projects is to inform and inspire your audience regarding characteristics, tools, and strategies that will help them to survive life's difficulties.

- Write a poem of at least 20 lines that summarizes important survival strategies and characteristics, and encourages listeners to overcome their troubles.

- Find an e-mail partner in your class. Write one, two-page e-mail to your partner in which you refer to the readings and explain your thinking about survival traits. Write a one-page response to your partner's e-mail message. Remember that one of your purposes is to encourage your partner. (Each of you will turn in three pages of your writing plus the partner's e-mails.)

- Outline and write an essay in which you inform and inspire your audience.

- Create a short, original video (3-5 minutes) that illustrates key survival traits and encourages the audience. Include a script to accompany the video.

- Write a rap or song with lyrics and music to inform and inspire your listeners.

- Create a montage of photos or original art that illustrates key survival traits. Include descriptive captions that explain and inspire.

PERSONAL FEEDBACK 2   Name _____

In what ways can you use the insights in this chapter to improve your ability to overcome difficulties that you have now or that might come your way in the future?

_____

_____

_____

_____

_____

_____

_____

Share your response as directed by your instructor.

VOCABULARY LESSON

Come Together, Hold Together, and Shut

Study the roots, words, and sentences.

| **Roots** | *greg*: come together, group | *clud, clus*: shut |
| | *ten, tent, tain, tinu*: hold together, hold | |

Words with *greg* = come together, group

Does a *congregation* sing hymns? Have men's clubs *desegregated*?

- Congregate: to flock together

  Students usually *congregate* in the gym prior to the first class period.

- Gregarious: outgoing; enjoying groups

  Gregarious people enjoy parties.

- Aggregation: a collection or union

  The steering committee was an *aggregation* of members of six sororities.

- Egregious: conspicuous; the worst of the group

  The *egregious* error was easy to detect but costly to fix.

- Segregate: to separate from the group

  Before eating M&Ms, do you *segregate* the red ones?

Words with *ten, tent, tain, tinu* = hold together, hold

Will a lock secure the *contents*? Is daily *maintenance* needed?

- Tenant: one who holds a lease on a house or apartment

  The present *tenant* pays his rent early.

- Tenacity: quality of holding together for a purpose

  Do you have the drive and *tenacity* to run for public office?

- Contented: easy in mind or satisfied

  A *contented* dog is usually one that is well fed.

- Contentment: satisfaction with one's lot

  Money is not essential for *contentment*, but it does help.

- Intent: purpose, concentration, holding one's mind on a single matter

  What is the *intent* of this lengthy proposal?

- Retain: to hold secure

  With a majority in the Senate, the Republicans can *retain* power.

- Continuously: without stopping

  In summer, the Niagara River flows *continuously* over Horseshoe Falls.

- Tenable: able to be held or defended

  Paying for the damage is a *tenable* resolution to the accident.

- Untenable: cannot be held

  Continuing a relationship after being abused is *untenable*.

- Discontented: not content

  I am *discontented* with my grades, because I know I can do better.

Words with *clud* or *clus = shut*

Should *conclusive* evidence result in a conviction? Is your *conclusion* final?

- Recluse: one who shuts himself or herself away from others, a hermit

  The *recluse* left the island only to get provisions.

- Exclude: to shut out

  Do not *exclude* your friends from your joys or sorrows.

- Inclusive: counting everything

  The quoted price is *inclusive* of tax and shipping.

- Seclude: to remove, shut off

  In order to recuperate, he wanted to *seclude* himself from visitors.

- Preclude: to close beforehand or hinder

  Having a mobile phone does not *preclude* the need for an answering machine on your home telephone.

Review

Part I

Answer the following with true (*T*) or false (*F*).

_____ 1. Gregarious students are usually shy.

_____ 2. If you segregate your socks by color, you mix them in one group.

_____ 3. When students congregate in the doorway, entrance can be difficult.

_____ 4. An egregious boor is usually a desirable companion.

_____ 5. Desegregated schools bring together students of different backgrounds.

_____ 6. Contented babies cry excessively.

_____ 7. If you retain your job, you keep your position.

_____ 8. A winning lawyer has a tenable case.

_____ 9. To seclude yourself is to join the group for the celebration.

_____ 10. An inclusive organization welcomes entry to many.

Part II

Choose the word from the list that is a synonym for the following.

intent	tenacity	contents	recluse	conclusion
maintenance	aggregation	tenant	congregation	contentment

11. hermit   _____

12. renter   _____

13. happiness   _____

14. collection   _____

15. purpose   _____

16. final statement _____

17. flock   _____

18. determination   _____

19. upkeep   _____

20. belongings   _____

Managing Workplace Reading

Everyone works at some point. Perhaps you had a full-time job before you entered college, or perhaps you work part time when you are not studying. In any event, all occupations demand some amount of reading. In fact, companies frequently hire expensive consultants to advise employees on efficient methods for meeting workplace reading demands. Typically, these consultants first urge employees to put their reading demands in perspective and set priorities. Memos, for example, may need to be read immediately, but annual reports can probably wait until later. As a next step, the experts strongly suggest handling each item only once. Their advice is "Do not open a letter or e-mail and then set it aside to be handled later. If you open an e-mail, read it and take action." The three action options are: respond to it, put it in the trash, or file it to be used later with other material on the same subject.

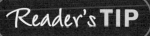 **Reader's TIP** Managing Workplace Reading

- Set priorities before reading.
- Strive to handle each item only once.
- Respond to it, discard it, or file it.

Types of Workplace Reading

Work-related documents usually make points quickly, have a serious tone, and are written to inform rather than to entertain. The importance of a document is determined by the way in which the information it contains can affect your job performance, so only you can set priorities.

E-mail

In many workplaces, communication is done mainly by e-mail. This can be an efficient and convenient way to transmit information, discuss ideas, and issue work orders. Sometimes the number of e-mails that employees must process takes an excessive amount of time. Experienced employees use several time-saving methods to manage their e-mail.

First, they disable the tone that signals an incoming message and read their e-mail only two or three times a day. Second, they read messages once and immediately respond, delete, or file as needed; they try to have no messages in their inboxes at the end of the day. Third, they store important messages in folders with logical names.

For responding to e-mail, experts advise employees to keep their messages brief, polite, and not to "reply to all" unless it is necessary; to re-read outgoing messages before sending them; and to avoid rushing with an e-mail response to an important message by sending a courteous, one-sentence e-mail saying they will reply at a later time.

Specific types of workplace reading, such as those described below, are often sent to employees via e-mail.

Memos

A memo is a brief message used to update coworkers, announce meetings, ask questions, request assistance, or announce decisions. Memos are written in a concise, direct style and can be formal or informal, depending on the sender's level of seniority and the sender's relationship with the recipient. Used correctly, memos are intended for internal messages among company employees and are not generally used for communicating with those outside the organization. They are frequently sent by e-mail.

Memos are usually only a few sentences long but can sometimes continue for several pages. The most important information is given at the beginning (see the illustration below). Notice dates, times, places, and requests for a response or action. Special formatting, such as numbered or bulleted lists, may be applied to other important items to make them stand out.

1. What is the reason for the memo? _____

   _____

2. What is the necessary action? _____

TO: Market Designs Personnel
FROM: Sergio Rodriguez, Director of Personnel Services
DATE: November 1, 2014
CC: Veronica Menser, General Manager
RE: Direct Deposit of Paychecks

Please note that beginning with the second pay period in December, all nonsalaried employees will have the option of direct deposit of their paychecks. In order to take advantage of this option, you must fill out a Direct Deposit Request Form (sample is attached) and return it to the Accounting Department by no later than November 15. Implementation of the direct deposit option will be delayed one month for those employees who submit their requests after that date. If you have any questions, please contact me at extension 225.

Letters

A letter is somewhat more formal than a memo and therefore more appropriate for communication outside a company. Use a letter to give or request information, to congratulate or express appreciation, to register complaints, or to emphasize an action. Like memos, business letters are relatively short and are written in a concise, direct manner.

Newsletters

Newsletters are documents published by businesses, organizations, clubs, or schools that combine news, editorial columns, letters, stories, and graphics on subjects of interest to group members. They look like mini-newspapers or multipage stapled letters. The purpose of a newsletter is to build group spirit, bind members together, recognize member achievement, and chronicle group events. Each member of the particular group usually receives the newsletter.

Newsletters are basically *propaganda* (persuasive public relations information) for the organization. They tend to report on the past and rarely have any critical information that demands action. However, they sometimes contain news of awards, grants, personnel opportunities, and social events that might interest or benefit you. Take note of articles about fellow employees and remember to congratulate them or offer condolences either in person or with a phone call, card, or personal e-mail. Such efforts are not only thoughtful but also build positive relationships that benefit you and the company. If there is a table of contents, use it to guide your reading. If not, read the headings and beginning paragraphs to determine what you care to read.

Reader's TIP Reading Newsletters

- Read selectively. You may want to read all of the newsletter or none of it.
- Read critically. You cannot consider the information in a newsletter to be objective, because it contains information beneficial only to the company or organization. Unflattering information is not included, so the coverage is not balanced.
- Note items that are highlighted; that are set off by numbers, bullets, or capital letters; or that appear in boldface or italic type.

Minutes

Minutes, sometimes called meeting notes, are the official record of business meetings. The minutes include the topics discussed, decisions made, votes tallied, and action taken. Groups rely on the minutes as a reminder and a permanent record, so it is very important that the people present at the meeting review them for accuracy. Any errors should be reported and corrected quickly to avoid future confusion and, perhaps, costly mistakes.

APPENDIX 1 Sample Textbook Chapter

For realistic practice of the strategies learned in Chapter 3, "Textbook Learning," we present Chapter 9 of Joseph A. DeVito's *Interpersonal Messages: Communication and Relationship Skills*, Third Edition. This textbook is widely used in freshman level communication courses. Parenthetical references within the chapter refer to sources that are listed at the end of the book but that are not included here. Approach the chapter as if it were required reading for your communications class. Actively use the three stages of reading: preview, integrate knowledge (predict, picture, relate, monitor, correct, and annotate), and recall (make notes).

CHAPTER

9

Interpersonal Relationships

MESSAGES IN THE MEDIA

On *The Jerry Springer Show* and similar shows like *Maury* and *The Steve Wilkos Show*, you see all sorts of relationship problems, often ineffectively dealt with by the guests. This chapter introduces interpersonal relationships, explains what they are, how and why they develop and perhaps deteriorate, and some of the inappropriate types of relationships.

OBJECTIVES *After reading this chapter, you should be able to:*

1. Describe the advantages and disadvantages of interpersonal relationships and assess your own relationships in light of these.

2. Explain the relationship stages of contact, involvement intimacy, deterioration, repair, and dissolution and give examples of the types of messages that occur at each.

3. Define *jealousy, bullying,* and *relationship violence* and use the suggestions for managing such relationship dark sides.

 Listen to the **Audio Chapter** at **MyCommunicationLab**

195

Interpersonal relationships are among the most important assets you have, and your ability to form meaningful and satisfying relationships rests largely on your interpersonal communication competencies. Here we consider the advantages and disadvantages of interpersonal relationships, the stages relationships go through, and some examples of the "dark side" of relationships.

ADVANTAGES AND DISADVANTAGES OF INTERPERSONAL RELATIONSHIPS

All relationships have advantages and disadvantages, and it is helpful to consider what these may be.

A good way to begin the study of interpersonal relationships is to examine your own relationships (past, present, or those you look forward to) by asking yourself what your relationships do for you. What are the advantages and the disadvantages? Focus on your own relationships in general (friendship, romantic, family, and work), on one particular relationship (say, your life partner or your child or your best friend), or on one type of relationship (say, friendships), and respond to the following statements by indicating the extent to which your relationship(s) serve each of these functions. Visualize a 10-point scale on which 1 indicates that your relationship(s) never serves this function, 10 indicates that your relationship(s) always serves this function, and the numbers in between indicate levels between these extremes. You may wish to do this twice—once for your face-to-face relationships and once for your online relationships.

____ 1. My relationships help to lessen my loneliness.
____ 2. My relationships help me gain in self-knowledge and in self-esteem.
____ 3. My relationships help enhance my physical and emotional health.
____ 4. My relationships maximize my pleasures and minimize my pains.
____ 5. My relationships help me to secure stimulation (intellectual, physical, and emotional).

Let's elaborate just a bit on each of these commonly accepted advantages of interpersonal communication.

VIEWPOINTS Online relationship advantages
Among the advantages of online relationships is that they reduce the importance of physical characteristics and instead emphasize such factors as rapport, similarity, and self-disclosure and in the process promote relationships that are based on emotional intimacy rather than physical attraction (Cooper & Sportolari, 1997). What do you see as the main advantages of online relationships?

1. One of the major benefits of relationships is that they help to lessen loneliness (Rokach, 1998; Rokach & Brock, 1995). They make you feel that someone cares, that someone likes you (the popularity of the "like" button on Facebook and +1 on Google+ attests to the importance of this benefit), that someone will protect you, that someone ultimately will love you.

2. Through contact with others you learn about yourself and see yourself from different perspectives and in different roles, as a child or parent, as a co-worker, as a manager, as a best friend. This function is significantly strengthened by the availability of so many international relationship sites that can expose you to widely varied ways of viewing yourself and relationships. Healthy interpersonal relationships also help enhance self-esteem and self-worth. Simply having a friend or romantic partner (at least most of the time) makes you feel desirable and worthy.

3. Research consistently shows that interpersonal relationships contribute significantly to physical and emotional health (Goleman, 1995; Pennebacker, 1991; Rosen, 1998; Rosengren, 1993) and to personal happiness (Berscheid & Reis, 1998). Without

close interpersonal relationships you're more likely to become depressed—and this depression, in turn, contributes significantly to physical illness. Relationship isolation, in fact, contributes as much to mortality as high blood pressure, high cholesterol, obesity, smoking, or lack of physical exercise (Goleman, 1995).

4. The most general function served by interpersonal relationships, and the function that encompasses all the others, is that of maximizing pleasure and minimizing pain. Your good friends, for example, will make you feel even better about your good fortune and less hurt when you're confronted with hardships.

5. As plants are heliotropic and orient themselves to light, humans are stimulotropic and orient themselves to sources of stimulation (Davis, 1973). Human contact is one of the best ways to secure this stimulation—intellectual, physical, and emotional. Even an imagined relationship seems better than none.

Now respond to these sentences as you did to the above.

____ 6. My relationships put uncomfortable pressure on me to expose my vulnerabilities.
____ 7. My relationships increase my obligations.
____ 8. My relationships prevent me from developing other relationships.
____ 9. My relationships scare me because they may be difficult to dissolve.
____10. My relationships hurt me.

These statements express what most people would consider disadvantages of interpersonal relationships.

6. Close relationships put pressure on you to reveal yourself and to expose your vulnerabilities. While this is generally worthwhile in the context of a supporting and caring relationship, it may backfire if the relationship deteriorates and these weaknesses are used against you.

7. Close relationships increase your obligations to other people, sometimes to a great extent. Your time is no longer entirely your own. And although you enter relationships to spend more time with these special people, you also incur time (and perhaps financial) obligations with which you may not be happy.

8. Close relationships can lead you to abandon other relationships. Sometimes the other relationship involves someone you like but your partner can't stand. More often, however, it's simply a matter of time and energy; relationships take a lot of both, and you have less to give to these other and less intimate relationships.

9. The closer your relationships, the more emotionally difficult they are to dissolve, a feeling which may be uncomfortable for some people. If a relationship is deteriorating, you may feel distress or depression. In some cultures, for example, religious pressures may prevent married couples from separating. And if lots of money is involved, dissolving a relationship can often mean giving up the fortune you've spent your life accumulating.

10. And, of course, your partner may break your heart. Your partner may leave you—against all your pleading and promises. Your hurt will be in proportion to how much you care and need your partner. If you care a great deal, you're likely to experience great hurt; if you care less, the hurt will be less—it's one of life's little ironies.

To complement this discussion of the disadvantages of interpersonal relationships, we'll look also at what has come to be called the "dark side" of interpersonal relationships later in this chapter.

 Can you describe the major advantages and disadvantages of interpersonal relationships? Can you assess and evaluate your own relationships in terms of its advantages and disadvantages?

VIEWPOINTS Parasocial relationships

Parasocial relationships are relationships that audience members perceive themselves to have with media personalities (Giles, 2001; Giles & Maltby, 2004; Rubin & McHugh, 1987). At times, viewers develop these relationships with real media personalities—Wendy Williams, Anderson Cooper, or Ellen DeGeneres, for example—and at other times, the relationship is with a fictional character—an investigator on *CSI*, a scientist on *Bones*, or a doctor on a soap opera. Interestingly enough, Google+ seems to encourage this by suggesting that you "follow public posts from interesting and famous people." You'll even get updates and photos from them—not unlike "real" relationships. What's your view of parasocial relationships? Are there advantages to these relationships? Disadvantages? What's your experience with parasocial relationships?

RELATIONSHIP STAGES

The quality that makes a relationship interpersonal is interdependency: The actions of one person affect the other; one person's actions have consequences for the other person. The actions of a stranger—such as working overtime or flirting with a coworker—will have no impact on you; you and the proverbial stranger are independent, and your actions have no effect on each other. If, however, you were in an interpersonal relationship and your partner worked overtime or flirted with a coworker, these actions would affect you and the relationship in some way.

The six-stage model shown in Figure 9.1 describes the significant stages you may go through as you try to achieve your relationship goals. We'll explain the arrows after describing the stages. As a general description of relationship development (and sometimes dissolution), the stages seem standard: They apply to all relationships, whether friendship or love, whether face to face or online. The six stages are contact, involvement,

Explore the **Concept**
"Relationships" at
MyCommunicationLab

Blog Post
Facial Attraction

For a seldom-discussed view on attraction, see "Facial Attraction" at tcbdevito .blogspot.com. Does this all seem logical?

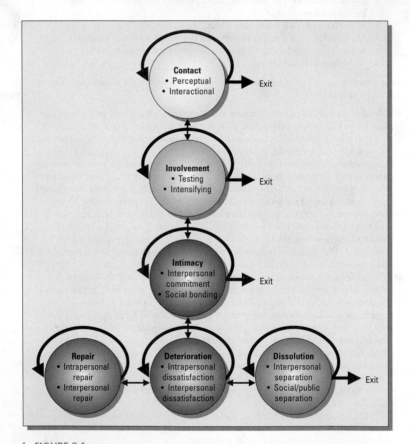

FIGURE 9.1
The Six Stages of Relationships
Because relationships differ so widely, it's best to think of any relationship model as a tool for talking about relationships rather than as a specific map that indicates how you move from one relationship stage to another. The six-stage model is certainly not the only way you can look at relationships. If you want to see an additional model of relationships, go to MyCommunicationLab.

Explore the **Exercise**
"Analyzing Stage Talk" at
MyCommunicationLab

intimacy, deterioration, repair, and dissolution. Each stage can be divided into an initial and a final phase.

Social network sites seem to recognize this stage nature of relationships by enabling you to treat your online "friends" differently. For example, the circles on Google+ and the "friends lists" on Facebook enable you to group people on the basis of the information that you want them to be able to access. This makes it very easy to distinguish acquaintances from intimate friends, for example, as well as family from friends from workplace colleagues.

Contact

At the **contact** stage, there is first perceptual contact—you see what the person looks like, you hear what the person sounds like, you may even smell the person. Or you might browse a group of photos and profiles from an online dating site. From this contact, you get a physical picture: gender, approximate age, height, and so on.

"I can't wait to see what you're like online."

After this perception, there is usually interactional contact. Here the interaction is superficial and impersonal. This is the stage of "Hello, my name is Joe"—the stage at which you exchange basic information that needs to come before any more intense involvement. This interactional contact also may be nonverbal, as in, for example, exchanging smiles, concentrating your focus on one person, or decreasing the physical distance between the two of you. With online relationships, each of you will have read the other's profile and so will know quite a lot about each other before you even begin to talk.

This is the stage at which you initiate interaction ("Hello, I'm Pat") and engage in invitational communication ("May I join you?" "Will you be friends with me?"). The invitational messages in online communication may involve moving to a face-to-face meeting or to phoning each other. According to some researchers, it's at this contact stage—within the first four minutes of initial interaction—that you decide whether you want to pursue the relationship (Zunin & Zunin, 1972).

Physical appearance is especially important in the initial development of attraction because it's the characteristic most readily available to sensory inspection. Yet through both verbal and nonverbal behaviors, qualities such as friendliness, warmth, openness, and dynamism also are revealed at the contact stage. With online relations, people may profile themselves as warm or open or dynamic, and as a result, you may actually see the person's messages confirming this labeling.

The contact stage is also the stage at which you start flirting—messages that signal your romantic interest. Table 9.1 elaborates on the dos and don'ts of flirting.

Involvement

At the **involvement** stage, a sense of mutuality, of being connected, develops. Your ability to empathize with each other increases. During this stage, you experiment and try to learn more about the other person. At the early phase of involvement, a kind of preliminary testing goes on. You want to see if your initial judgment—perhaps at the contact stage, perhaps from reading the person's profile—proves reasonable. So you may ask questions: "Where do you work?" "What are you majoring in?"

200 | **PART 2** Interpersonal Messages in Context

Blog Post

Body Language

For some tips on nonverbal behaviors to avoid during dating and courtship, see "Body Language" at tcbdevito.blogspot.com. What additional suggestions would you add?

TABLE 9.1	

HOW TO FLIRT AND NOT TO FLIRT

Here are a few nonverbal and verbal ways people flirt and some cautions to observe. The most general caution, which applies to all the suggestions, is to recognize that different cultures view flirting very differently and to observe the prevailing cultural norms.

Flirtatious Messages	Cautions
Maintain an open posture; face the person; lean forward; tilt your head to one side (to get a clearer view of the person you're interested in).	Don't move so close that you make it uncomfortable for the other person.
Maintain eye contact for a somewhat longer than normal time; raise your eyebrows to signal interest; wink.	Be careful that your direct eye contact doesn't come off as leering or too invasive; avoid excessive blinking.
Smile and otherwise displace positive emotions with your facial expressions.	Avoid overdoing this; laughing too loud at lame jokes is probably going to appear phony.
Touch the person's hand.	Be careful that the touching is appropriate and not perceived as intrusive.
Mirror the other's behaviors.	Don't overdo it. It will appear as if you're mimicking.
Introduce yourself.	Avoid overly long or overly cute introductions.
Ask a question (most commonly, "Is this seat taken?").	Avoid sarcasm or joking; these are likely to be misunderstood.
Compliment ("great jacket").	Avoid any compliment that might appear too intimate.
Be polite; respect the individual's positive and negative face needs.	But don't be overly polite. It will appear phony.

Here you're committed to getting to know the person even better, and so you might follow the person on Twitter or read the postings, photos, and causes, for example, on Facebook. And at this stage, you continue your involvement by intensifying your interaction; the texting becomes more frequent, the Facebook postings become more complimentary and more frequent, and the photos exchanged become increasingly more personal and revealing.

Here, you not only try to get to know the other person better, but you also begin to reveal yourself. It's at this stage that you begin to share your feelings and your emotions. If this is to be a romantic relationship, you might date. If it's to be a friendship, you might share in activities related to mutual interests—go to the movies or to some sports event together.

Intimacy

At the **intimacy** stage, you feel you can be honest and open when talking about yourself; you can express thoughts and feelings that you don't reveal in other relationships (Mackey, Diemer, & O'Brien, 2000). Because intimacy is essentially an emotional/communication connection, it can occur in face-to-face and in online relationships equally. At the intimacy stage, you commit yourself still further to the other person, establishing

INTERPERSONAL CHOICE POINT

Coming Clean

You're getting ready to meet someone you've only communicated with over the Internet, and you're going to have to admit that you lied about your age and a few other things. What are the things about which you'd have to come clean with most immediately? What are your options for expressing this? What seems the best option?

ETHICAL MESSAGES

Your Obligation to Reveal Yourself

If you're in a close relationship, your influence on your partner is considerable, so you may have an obligation to reveal certain things about yourself. Conversely, you may feel that the other person—because he or she is so close to you—has an ethical obligation to reveal certain information to you.

Ethical Choice Point

Consider: At what point in a relationship—if any—do you feel you would have an ethical obligation to reveal each of the 10 items of information listed here? Visualize a relationship as existing on a continuum from initial contact at 1 to extreme intimacy at 10, and use the numbers from 1 to 10 to indicate at what point you would feel your romantic partner or close friend has a right to know each type of information about you. If you feel you would never have the obligation to reveal this information, use 0. As you respond to these items, ask yourself, what gives one person the right to know personal information about another person? What principle of ethics requires another person to disclose this information in a relationship?

At what point do you have an ethical obligation to reveal:	Romantic Partner	Friend
Age	_____	_____
History of family genetic disorders	_____	_____
HIV status	_____	_____
Past sexual experiences	_____	_____
Marital history	_____	_____
Annual salary and net financial worth	_____	_____
Affectional orientation	_____	_____
Attitudes toward other races and nationalities	_____	_____
Religious beliefs	_____	_____
Past criminal activity or incarceration	_____	_____

a kind of relationship in which this individual becomes your best or closest friend, lover, or companion. Your communication becomes more personalized, more synchronized, and easier (Gudykunst, Nishida, & Chua, 1987). Usually the intimacy stage divides itself quite neatly into two phases: an interpersonal commitment phase, in which you commit yourselves to each other in a kind of private way, and a social bonding phase, in which the commitment is made public—perhaps to family and friends, perhaps to the public at large through formal marriage. Here the two of you become a unit, a pair.

To some people, relational intimacy seems extremely risky. To others, it involves only low risk. Consider your own view of relationship risk by responding to the following questions.

- Is it dangerous to get really close to people?
- Are you afraid to get really close to someone because you might get hurt?

VIDEO CHOICE POINT

Taking the Next Step

Tim and Marisol have been dating for several weeks and things between them have been going well. Tim now realizes that he wants the relationship to be permanent and exclusive, and he wants to express his feelings to Marisol. He isn't sure how to bring this issue up in conversation because he's never felt this strongly about someone before. He considers the topics covered in this chapter as he contemplates his communication choices. See how his choices play out in the video "Taking the Next Step" and respond to the questions posed.

 Watch the **Video** "Taking the Next Step" at **MyCommunicationLab**

202 | **PART 2** Interpersonal Messages in Context

Talking Cherishing

Cherishing behaviors are those small gestures you enjoy receiving from your partner (a smile, a wink, a phone call, an e-mail saying "I'm thinking of you," a kiss). They are (1) specific and positive—nothing overly general or negative; (2) focused on the present and future rather than related to issues about which the partners have argued in the past; (3) capable of being performed daily; and (4) easily executed—nothing you really have to go out of your way to accomplish. Cherishing behaviors are an especially effective way to affirm another person and to increase "favor exchange," a concept that comes from the work of William Lederer (1984).

Prepare a list of 10 cherishing behaviors that you would like to receive from your real or imagined relationship partner. After each partner prepares a list, exchange lists and, ideally, perform the desired cherishing behaviors. At first, these behaviors may seem self-conscious and awkward. In time, however, they'll become a normal part of your interaction, which is exactly what you want.

Lists of cherishing behaviors—yours or your partner's—will also give you insight into your relationship needs and the kind of communicating partner you want.

- Do you find it difficult to trust other people?
- Do you believe that the most important thing to consider in a relationship is whether you might get hurt?

People who answer *yes* to these and similar questions see intimacy as involving considerable risk (Pilkington & Richardson, 1988). Such people have fewer close friends, are less likely to have romantic relationships, have less trust in others, have lower levels of dating assertiveness, have lower self-esteem, are more possessive and jealous, and are generally less sociable and extroverted than those who see intimacy as involving little risk (Pilkington & Woods, 1999). The nature of risk in online relationships is similar to that in face-to-face relationships; for example, in both kinds of relationships you risk losing face and damaging your self-esteem. So there's likely to be considerable similarity in any given individual's attitudes toward risk in both types of relationships.

Deterioration

Explore the **Exercise**
"Learning to Hear
Stage Talk" at
MyCommunicationLab

Although many relationships remain at the intimacy stage, some enter the stage of **deterioration**—the stage that sees the weakening of bonds between the parties and that represents the downside of the relationship progression. Relationships deteriorate for many reasons. When the reasons for coming together are no longer present or change drastically, relationships may deteriorate. Thus, for example, when your relationship no longer lessens your loneliness or when it fails to increase your self-esteem or to maximize pleasures, it may be in the process of deteriorating. Other reasons for deterioration are third-party relationships, sexual dissatisfaction, dissatisfaction with work, or financial difficulties.

The first phase of deterioration is usually intrapersonal dissatisfaction. You begin to feel that this relationship may not be as important as you had previously thought. You may experience personal dissatisfaction with everyday interactions and begin to view the future together negatively. If this dissatisfaction continues or grows, you may pass to the second phase, interpersonal deterioration, in which you discuss these dissatisfactions with your partner.

During the process of deterioration, communication patterns change drastically. These patterns are in part a response to the deterioration; you communicate as you do because of the way you feel your relationship is deteriorating. However, the way you communicate (or fail to communicate) also influences the fate of your relationship. During the deterioration stage, you may, for example, increase withdrawal, communicate less, respond to Facebook pokes and requests for "likes" less often, text infrequently, and have fewer face-to-face meetings. In communication, each person reduces his or her level of self-disclosure.

Repair

The first phase of **repair** is intrapersonal repair, in which you analyze what went wrong and consider ways of solving your relational difficulties. At this phase, you may consider changing your behaviors or perhaps changing your expectations of your partner. You may also weigh the rewards of your relationship as it is now against the rewards you could anticipate if your relationship ended.

If you decide that you want to repair your relationship, you may discuss this with your partner at the interpersonal repair level. Here you may talk about the problems in the relationship, the corrections you would want to see, and perhaps what you would be willing to do and what you would want the other person to do. This is the stage of negotiating new agreements, new behaviors. You and your partner may try to solve your problems yourselves, or you may seek the advice of friends or family or perhaps seek advice from the numerous anonymous websites.

You can look at the strategies for repairing a relationship in terms of the following six suggestions, which conveniently spell out the word REPAIR, a useful reminder that repair is not a one-step but a multistep process: <u>R</u>ecognize the problem, <u>E</u>ngage in productive conflict resolution, <u>P</u>ose possible solutions, <u>A</u>ffirm each other, <u>I</u>ntegrate solutions into normal behavior, and <u>R</u>isk (see Figure 9.2).

Explore the **Exercise** "Giving Repair Advice" at **MyCommunicationLab**

> **INTERPERSONAL CHOICE POINT**
>
> **Strengthening Similarities**
>
> You're dating a person you really like, but you are both so different—in values, politics, religion, and just about everything else. But you enjoy each other more than you do anyone else. What are some of the things you can do to encourage greater similarity while not losing the excitement created by the differences?

- *Recognize the problem.* What is wrong with your present relationship? What specific changes will make it better?
- *Engage in productive conflict resolution.* Conflict is an inevitable part of relationship life, but if it's approached through productive strategies, it may be resolved and the relationship may actually emerge stronger and healthier.
- *Pose possible solutions.* Ideally, each person will ask, "What can we do to resolve the difficulty that will allow both of us to get what we want?"
- *Affirm each other.* Social media sites make this especially easy by providing you with cards, virtual gifts, and the like to help you express your desire to repair the relationship.
- *Integrate solutions into your life.* In other words, make the solutions a part of your normal behavior.
- *Risk.* Risk giving favors without any certainty of reciprocity. Risk rejection by making the first move to make up or say you're sorry. Be willing to change, to adapt.

"When a relationship needs maintenance, it would be great if you could just call a super."

Victoria Roberts/The New Yorker Collection/www.cartoonbank.com

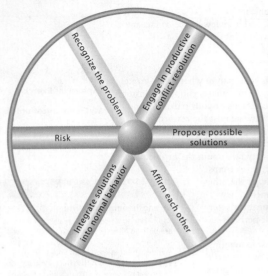

FIGURE 9.2

The Relationship Repair Wheel

The wheel seems an apt metaphor for the repair process; the specific repair strategies—the spokes—all work together in constant process. The wheel is difficult to get moving, but once in motion it becomes easier to turn. Also, it's easier to start when two people are pushing, but it is not impossible for one to move it in the right direction. What metaphor do you find helpful in thinking about relationship repair?

Dissolution

The **dissolution** stage, in both friendship and romance, is the cutting of the bonds that tie you together. Not surprisingly, there are both advantages and disadvantages of relationship dissolution. Often the relationship deserves to be dissolved; it was no longer productive or satisfying. When a "friend" reveals your confidential disclosures on Facebook or otherwise betrays your confidence and this becomes a pattern, it may be time to move from the level of friendship to that of seldom-seen acquaintanceship. Not surprisingly, social networking sites have provided you with easy means for "defriending" and "uncircling." Even in families, certain members or relationships within the family may become toxic and the relationship may be deserving of dissolution. Partners, parents, or children often become enablers, helping a family member to engage in destructive behavior—for example, helping to hide the alcoholism from friends and relatives and thus helping the partner to continue drinking more comfortably and without social criticism. Gay and lesbian children who are rejected by their families after coming out may be better off away from homophobic (and guilt-instilling) parents, siblings, and assorted relatives.

The decision to stay in a relationship that does not fulfill your needs or is destructive or to end the relationship is not an easy one to make because so many factors come into play. Religious beliefs, the attitudes of family members and close friends, and the economic implications of staying together versus separating are just a few of the more obvious factors that would logically influence such decisions.

In most cases, relationship dissolution creates difficulties, most often for both parties. Here are some suggestions for dealing with this often difficult period:

- *Break the loneliness–depression cycle.* Avoid sad passivity, a state in which you feel sorry for yourself, sit alone, and perhaps cry. Instead, engage in active solitude (exercise, write, study, play computer games) and seek distraction (do things to put loneliness out of your mind; for example, take a long drive or shop).
- *Take time out.* Take some time for yourself. Renew your relationship with yourself. Get to know yourself as a unique individual, standing alone now but fully capable of entering a meaningful relationship in the future.
- *Bolster self-esteem.* Positive and successful experiences are most helpful in building self-esteem. As in dealing with loneliness, helping others is one of the best ways to raise your own self-esteem.
- *Seek the support of others.* Avail yourself of your friends and family for support; it's an effective antidote to the discomfort and unhappiness that occur when a relationship ends.
- *Avoid repeating negative patterns.* Ask yourself, at the start of a new relationship, if you're entering a relationship modeled on the previous one. If the answer is yes, be especially careful that you do not repeat the problems. At the same time, avoid becoming a prophet of doom. Do not see in every new relationship vestiges of the old.

INTERPERSONAL CHOICE POINT

Ending the Relationship

You want to break up your eight-month romantic relationship and still remain friends. What are the possible contexts in which you might do this? What types of things can you say that might help you accomplish your dual goal?

Movement among the Stages: Explaining the Arrows

Relationships are not static; we move from one stage to another largely as a result of our interpersonal interactions. It is some of these movements that the arrows in Figure 9.1 depict. Let's look at some relationship processes that revolve around movement.

STAGE MOVEMENT   The six-stage model illustrates the kinds of movement that take place in interpersonal relationships. In the model, you'll note three types of arrows:

- *The exit arrows* show that each stage offers the opportunity to exit the relationship. After saying "Hello" you can say "Goodbye" and exit. And, of course, you can end even the most intimate of relationships.
- *The vertical arrows* between the stages represent the fact that you can move to another stage: either to a stage that is more intense (say, from involvement to intimacy) or to a stage that is less intense (say, from intimacy to deterioration).
- *The self-reflexive arrows*—the arrows that return to the beginning of the same level or stage—signify that any relationship may become stabilized at any point. You may, for example, continue to maintain a relationship at the intimate level without its deteriorating or going back to the less intense stage of involvement. Or you may remain at the "Hello, how are you?" stage—the contact stage—without getting any further involved.

As you can imagine, movement from one stage to another depends largely on your communication skills—for example, your abilities to initiate a relationship, to present yourself as likable, to express affection, to self-disclose appropriately, and, when necessary, to dissolve the relationship with the least possible amount of acrimony (Dindia & Timmerman, 2003).

TURNING POINTS   Movement through the various stages takes place both gradually and in leaps. Sometimes the arrow/movement proceeds slowly from one stage to another, sometimes by leaps and jumps. Most often, you progress from one stage to another gradually. You don't jump from contact to involvement to intimacy; rather, you progress gradually, a few degrees at a time. In addition to this gradual movement, however, there are leaps called **relationship turning points** (Baxter & Bullis, 1986). These are significant relationship events that have important consequences for the individuals and the relationship and may turn its direction or trajectory. For example, a relationship that is progressing slowly might experience a rapid rise after the first date, the first kiss, the first sexual encounter, or the first meeting with the partner's child.

And, not surprisingly, turning points vary with culture. In some cultures, the first sexual experience is a major turning point; in others, it's a minor progression in the normal dating process. What constitutes a turning point will also vary with your relationship stage. For example, an expensive and intimate gift may be a turning point at the involvement or the repair stage, an ordinary event if you're at the intimate stage where such gifts are exchanged regularly, and an inappropriate gift if given too early in the relationship.

VIEWPOINTS   Gender differences in breaking up

Popular myth would have us believe that most heterosexual love affairs break up as a result of the man's outside affair. But the research does not support this (Blumstein & Schwartz, 1983; Janus & Janus, 1993). When surveyed as to the reason for breaking up, only 15 percent of the men indicated that it was their interest in another partner, whereas 32 percent of the women noted this as a cause of the breakup. These findings are surely dated. What do you think we'd find if the same survey were done today? More important, why do you think differences exist at all?

INTERPERSONAL CHOICE POINT

Moving Through Relationship Stages
Your current romantic partner seems to be moving too fast for your liking. You want to take things a lot slower, yet you don't want to turn this person off; this may be The One. What might you say (and where might you say it) to get your partner to proceed more slowly?

Blog Post

From Dating to Mating

For an interesting article on moving from involvement to intimacy, see "From Dating to Mating" at tcbdevito.blogspot.com. Any further suggestions?

VIEWPOINTS Negative turning points

Turning points are often positive, as the examples in the text indicate, but they can also be negative. For example, the first realization that a partner has been unfaithful, lied about past history, or revealed a debilitating condition would likely be significant turning points for many romantic relationships. What have been your experiences with negative relationship turning points?

INTERPERSONAL CHOICE POINT

Meeting the Parents

You're dating someone from a very different culture and have been invited to meet the parents and have a traditional ethnic dinner. What are some of the things you might do to make this potentially difficult situation go smoothly?

INTERPERSONAL CHOICE POINT

Refusing a Gift Positively

A coworker with whom you're becoming friendly gives you a very intimate gift, much too intimate for the relationship as you see it. What are some things you might say to refuse the gift but not close off the possibility of dating?

THE RELATIONSHIP LICENSE   Movement of a somewhat different type can be appreciated by looking at what might be called the **relationship license**—the license or permission to break some relationship rule as a result of your relationship stage. As the relationship develops, so does the relationship license; as you become closer and approach the intimacy stage, you have greater permission to say and do things that you didn't have at the contact or involvement stage. The license becomes broader as the relationship develops and becomes more restrictive as the relationship deteriorates. For example, long-term friends or romantic couples (say, at the intimacy stage) may taste each other's food in a restaurant or may fix each other's clothing or pat each other on the rear. These are violations of rules that normally hold for non-intimates, casual acquaintances, or people in the initial stages of a relationship. In relationships that are deteriorating, the licenses become more limited or may be entirely withdrawn.

In some relationships, the license is reciprocal; each person's license is the same. In other relationships, it's nonreciprocal; one person has greater license than the other. For example, perhaps one person has license to come home at any time but the other is expected to stay on schedule. Or one person has license to spend the couple's money without explanation but the other has no such right. Or one perhaps has the right to be unfaithful but the other doesn't. For example, in some cultures, men are expected to have intimate relationships with many women, whereas women are expected to have relationships only with a legally approved partner. In this case, a nonreciprocal license is built into the culture's rules.

Part of the art of relationship communication—as you move through the various stages—is to negotiate the licenses that you want without giving up the privacy you want to retain. This negotiation is almost never made explicit; most often it is accomplished nonverbally and in small increments. The license to touch intimately, for example, is likely to be arrived at through a series of touches that increase gradually, beginning with touching that is highly impersonal.

RELATIONSHIP COMMITMENT.   An important factor influencing the movement in any relationship is the degree of **relationship commitment** that you and your relationship partner have toward each other and toward the relationship. Not surprisingly, commitment is especially strong when individuals are satisfied with their relationship and grows weaker as individuals become less satisfied (Hirofumi, 2003). Three types of commitment are often distinguished and can be identified from your answers to the following questions (Johnson, 1973, 1982, 1991; Knapp & Taylor, 1994; Knapp & Vangelisti, 2009; Kurdek, 1995):

- Do I have a **desire** to stay in this relationship? Do I have a desire to keep this relationship going?

- Do I have a moral **obligation** to stay in this relationship?
- Do I have to stay in this relationship? Is it a **necessity** for me to stay in this relationship?

All relationships are held together, in part, by commitment based on desire, obligation, or necessity or on some combination of these factors. And the strength of the relationship, including its resistance to possible deterioration, is related to your degree of commitment. When a relationship shows signs of deterioration and yet there's a strong commitment to preserving it, you may well surmount the obstacles and reverse the process. For example, couples with high relationship commitment will avoid arguing about minor grievances and also will demonstrate greater supportiveness toward each other than will those with lower commitment (Roloff & Solomon, 2002). Similarly, those who have great commitment are likely to experience greater jealousy in a variety of situations (Rydell, McConnell, & Bringle, 2004). When commitment is weak and the individuals doubt that there are good reasons for staying together, the relationship deteriorates faster and more intensely.

RELATIONSHIP POLITENESS   Not surprisingly, your level of politeness will vary with your relationship stage. Figure 9.3 depicts a proposed relationship between the levels of politeness and the relationship stages discussed earlier. Politeness, according to this model, is greatest during the contact and involvement stages—you want to put your best foot forward if the relationship is to be established and perhaps moved forward.

During the intimacy stage, you're likely to relax your politeness, at least the rules of politeness that would operate in social settings. As noted earlier, as the relationship becomes more interpersonal, the rules that guide the relationship are not so much the rules of society as they are the rules established by the individuals themselves. With intimates, you know each other so well that you feel you can dispense with the "please" and "excuse me" or with prefacing requests with, for example, "Can I please ask you a favor?" or "Would you mind helping me here?"

Relaxing politeness in intimacy, however, is not necessarily a good thing; in fact, politeness during the intimacy stage helps to maintain the relationship and ensure relationship satisfaction. Relaxing politeness too much may be interpreted as a decrease in

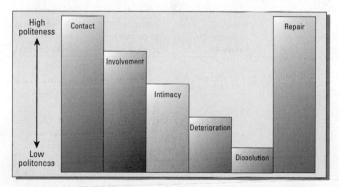

FIGURE 9.3

Politeness and Relationship Stages

Although politeness will not vary in the same way in all relationships, the general pattern depicted here is likely to be representative of many relationships. As you review this figure, analyze your own history of relationship politeness. Did it follow the pattern predicted here? If not, how did it differ?

caring and respect for the other person, which will increase dissatisfaction and perhaps move the relationship away from intimacy.

During the deterioration and dissolution stages, you're not likely to be concerned with politeness. You may even go out of your way to be impolite as an expression of your dislike or even hostility. In some cases, of course, the dissolution of a relationship is an amicable one where politeness would be relatively high with perhaps the idea of remaining friends but at a less intimate level than previously.

If you wish to repair the relationship, then you're likely to be extremely polite, perhaps on the same level as during the contact and involvement stages. Your politeness in starting and growing the relationship is likely to be echoed in your attempts to restart (or repair) your relationship.

 Can you explain the stages of interpersonal relationships (contact, involvement, intimacy, deterioration, repair, and dissolution) and the major movements (stage movement, turning points, relationship license, relationship commitment, and relationship politeness)? Can you give examples of the types of messages that occur at each stage?

SKILL BUILDING EXERCISE

Assessing the End of a Relationship

This exercise is designed to stimulate you to examine the factors that might lead you to dissolve an interpersonal relationship. Here are listed a number of factors that might lead someone to end such a relationship. For each factor, identify the likelihood that you would dissolve relationships of various types, using a 10-point scale with 10 = would definitely dissolve the relationship, 1 = would definitely not dissolve the relationship, and the numbers 2–9 representing intermediate levels. Use 5 for "don't know what I'd do" or "not sure." What factor would lead you to dissolve one or more of your present relationships?

Often the same relationship factors can create mild dissatisfaction or result in the total dissolution of the relationship.

Factor	New friend on Facebook	Budding romance on Facebook	Friend for 10 or more years	Committed co-habitating romantic relationship
1. Person lies frequently about insignificant and significant issues	_____	_____	_____	_____
2. Person lacks ambition and doesn't want to do anything of significance	_____	_____	_____	_____
3. Person is not supportive and rarely compliments or confirms you	_____	_____	_____	_____
4. Person is unwilling to reveal anything significant about past behavior or present feelings	_____	_____	_____	_____
5. Person embarrasses you because of bad manners, poor grammar, inappropriate posts and photos	_____	_____	_____	_____

THE DARK SIDE OF INTERPERSONAL RELATIONSHIPS

Although relationships serve a variety of vital functions and provide enormous advantages, as already noted, not all relationships are equally satisfying and productive. Consequently, it's necessary to explore this "dark" side. Here we consider three such dark sides: jealousy, bullying, and violence in close relationships.

Relationship Jealousy

Jealousy is similar to envy in that in both cases, we experience a negative emotion about our relationship and we often use the terms interchangeably. But they are actually very different. Envy is an emotional feeling that we experience when we desire what someone else has or has more of than we do. And so we might feel envious of a friend who has lots of friends or romantic partners or money when we have significantly less. When we feel **envy**, we may feel that we are inferior to or of lesser importance than someone else. **Jealousy**, on the other hand, is a feeling (most researchers would view it as a type or form of anger) we have when we feel our relationship is in danger due to some rival. Jealousy is a reaction to relationship threat: If you feel that someone is moving in on your relationship partner, you may experience jealousy—especially if you feel that this interloper is succeeding. Usually, the rival is a potential romantic partner, but it could also be a close friend or a job that occupies all our partner's time and thoughts. When we feel jealousy, we may feel angry and anxious.

Watch the **Video**
"Getting Even" at
MyCommunicationLab

THE PARTS OF JEALOUSY   Jealousy has at least three components (Erber & Erber, 2011): a cognitive, an emotional, and a behavioral.

- *Cognitive jealousy.* Cognitive jealousy would involve your suspicious thinking, worrying, and imagining the different scenarios in which your partner may be interested in another person.
- *Emotional jealousy.* Emotional jealousy would involve the feelings you have when you see your partner, say, laughing or talking intimately with or kissing a rival. It includes "emotional infidelity"—feelings of love and arousal.
- *Behavioral jealousy.* Behavioral jealousy refers to what you actually do in response to the jealous feelings and emotions, for example, reading your partner's e-mail, looking on Facebook for incriminating photos, or going through the back seat of the car with the proverbial fine-tooth comb.

**Blog Post
Cyberflirting, Etc.**

For cyberflirting, see "Cyberflirting, Etc." at tcbdevito.blogspot.com. How do you see cyberflirting? What cyberflirting techniques do you find most interesting?

Sometimes we feel jealousy because of some suspicion that a rival is looking to steal our relationship partner. In this case, we may do a variety of things to guard our relationship and our relationship partner, a process called **mate guarding** (Buss, 1988; Erber & Erber, 2011). One popular strategy is concealment. We don't introduce our partner to any potential rival and avoid interaction with any potential rivals. Another strategy is vigilance; we constantly look out for occasions when we might lose our partner to a rival. The least suspicious glance becomes a major problem. Still another strategy is to monopolize the partner, to always be together, and to avoid leaving the partner without anything to do for too long a time. Of course, we also would experience jealousy if our rival actually succeeded.

Much research has reported that heterosexual men and women experience jealousy for different reasons, which are rooted in our evolutionary development (Buller, 2005; Buss, 2000; Buunk & Dijkstra, 2004). Basically, research finds that men experience jealousy from their partner being *physically* intimate with another man whereas women experience jealousy from their partner being *emotionally* intimate with another woman. The evolutionary reason given is that men provided food and shelter for the family and would resent his partner's physical intimacy with another because he would then be providing food and shelter for another man's child. Women, because they depended on men for food and shelter, became especially jealous when their partner was emotionally intimate with another because this might mean he might leave her and she'd thus lose the food and shelter protection.

Not all research supports this finding and not all theory supports this evolutionary explanation (Harris, 2003). For example, among Chinese men, only 25 percent reported physical infidelity was the more distressing while 75 percent reported emotional infidelity to be more distressing.

Another commonly assumed gender difference is that jealous men are more prone to respond with violence. This assumption, however, does not seem to be the case; men and women apparently are equally likely to respond with violence (Harris, 2003).

DEALING WITH JEALOUSY   So what do you do when you experience jealousy (short of violence)? Communication researchers find several popular but generally negative interactive responses (Dindia & Timmerman, 2003; Guerrero, Andersen, Jorgensen, Spitzberg, & Eloy, 1995). You may:

- nonverbally express your displeasure; for example, cry or express hurt.
- threaten to become violent or actually engage in violence.
- be verbally aggressive; for example, be sarcastic or accusatory.
- withdraw affection or be silent, sometimes denying that anything is wrong.

On the more positive side are responses known as "integrative communication": messages that attempt to work things out with your partner, such as self-disclosing your feelings, being honest, practicing effective conflict management, listening actively, and, in short, all the skills we talk about in this text.

Bullying

Bullying, whether in a close relationship, the workplace, or the playground, consists of abusive acts repeatedly committed by one person (or a group) against another. Bullying is behavior that has become a pattern; it's repeated frequently rather than being an isolated instance. On the playground, bullying often involves physical abuse; in the workplace, bullying is generally verbal.

TYPES OF BULLYING   Here are some of the types of bullying found in the workplace:

- gossiping about someone, making others the butt of jokes
- treating others as inferior, for example, frequently interrupting them or otherwise not giving their ideas due attention
- excluding members from social functions
- verbal insults, name calling
- negative facial expressions, sneering, avoiding eye contact
- excessive blaming
- being supervised (watched, monitored) more closely than others
- being unnecessarily criticized, often with shouting and in public

The problem with bullying from the employer's point of view is that it reduces productivity and hurts the bottom line. If one or even a few workers are bullied, they're probably not going to be as productive as

VIEWPOINTS **Bullying**
Sometimes, bullying is a part of the organization's culture, where, for example, first-year interns in a law office are treated unfairly and often abused by their superiors (demonstrated on a variety of lawyer TV shows such as *The Good Wife*). Sometimes it's perpetrated by a group who perhaps bully the newcomers or those who do less creative jobs. What's the status of bullying in organizations with which you're familiar?

they would be if they weren't bullied. It also is likely to lead to workers leaving the company—after the company has trained them but before they have become productive team members—with the added cost of hiring and training new people (and perhaps attendant lawsuits).

A special type of bullying is cyberbullying, which can take place through any electronic communication system—Facebook, Twitter, e-mail, instant messages, blog posts—and can take the form of sending threatening messages or images, posting negative comments, revealing secrets, or lying about another person. In one 2009 survey of 13- to 18-year-olds, 15 percent said they had been cyberbullied, and in another study of 12- to 17-year-olds, one-third said they were threatened or embarrassed by things said about them online. In another study, 88 percent of social media–using teenagers said they witnessed other people being mean or cruel on the sites and 15 percent say they were the targets of such meanness (Lenhart et al., 2011).

Among the reasons why cyberbullying is so important is that it can occur at any time; the messages, photos, and videos can be distributed quickly and widely; and the bully can hide behind false names. Websites, in fact, will do this for you and send messages anonymously. In this way, the person receives a bullying message but without any name attached. Cyberbullying attacks—because they occur electronically—are often more cruel than those made in face-to-face attacks (Hinduja & Patchin, 2008).

According to a Washington State Department of Labor & Industries report, victims of bullying may suffer significant mental and physical problems including high stress, financial problems, reduced self-esteem, and sleep and digestion disturbances. From the point of view of the worker being bullied, it obviously creates an uncomfortable atmosphere, perhaps a desire to avoid going into work, perhaps a preoccupation with the bullying rather than the job. And this is likely to spill over into the person's private life; after all, it would be strange if bullying at work did not create problems with other aspects of life. And although the bullies probably derive some personal satisfaction from wielding power over someone else, they too are likely to fail to be as productive as they might be and may well be personally troubled. From an ethical point of view, bullying destroys a person's right to personal dignity and a workplace free from intimidation and is therefore unethical. And yet bullying is not illegal in the United States, unless it involves harassment based on a person's gender or race, for example.

DEALING WITH BULLYING   Among the actions recommended for combating bullying are these:

1. Workers and organizations need to be clear about their opposition to bullying and that it doesn't profit anyone and will not be tolerated. Accusations of bullying will be investigated promptly and fairly.
2. If possible and there is no danger (physical or institutional), sometimes confronting the bully assertively (not aggressively) will be enough—*I don't like it when you make fun of the way I dress and I want you to stop—it's not funny and it just makes me feel bad.*
3. Taking action when you or someone else is bullied. This suggestion is not always easy to implement, especially if the bullying is part of the corporate culture or is carried out by your boss. But well-kept records of such incidents will often convince even the most reluctant.

Violence

Perhaps the most obvious dark side is seen in the varied forms of relationship violence. Before reading about this important but often neglected topic, take the following self-test.

> **INTERPERSONAL CHOICE POINT**
>
> **Bullying**
> Your colleagues at your new job have been bullying a junior colleague ever since you arrived at the job a few months ago. What are some of your choices for helping your colleague without doing anything that will make you the next victim?

TEST YOURSELF

Is Violence a Part of Your Relationship?

Based on your present relationship or one you know, respond to the following questions with *yes* or *no*.

Do either of you:

_____ 1. get angry to the point of making the other person fearful?

_____ 2. engage in behavior that could be considered humiliating to the other person?

_____ 3. verbally abuse the other?

_____ 4. threaten the other with violence?

_____ 5. engage in slapping, hitting, or pushing the other?

_____ 6. throw things in anger?

_____ 7. make accusations of sexual infidelity?

_____ 8. force the other to have sex?

_____ 9. use abusive sexual terms in reference to the other?

How Did You Do? These nine items are all signs of a violent relationship (it only takes one to make a relationship violent). Items 1–3 are examples of verbal or emotional abuse, 4–6 of physical abuse, and 7–9 of sexual abuse—all of which are explained more fully in the text.

What Will You Do? If any of these questions describes your relationship, you may wish to seek professional help (which is likely available on your campus). Additional suggestions are offered in the text and are readily available online.

Source: These questions were drawn from a variety of websites, including those from SUNY at Buffalo Counseling Services; The American College of Obstetricians and Gynecologists, Women's Heath Care Physicians; and the University of Texas at Austin, Counseling and Mental Health Center.

TYPES OF RELATIONSHIP VIOLENCE   Three types of **relationship violence** may be distinguished: verbal or emotional abuse, physical abuse, and sexual abuse (Rice, 2007).

- *Verbal or emotional abuse* may include humiliating you; engaging in economic abuse such as controlling the finances or preventing you from working; and/or isolating, criticizing, or stalking you. Not surprisingly, some research shows that people who use verbal or emotional abuse are more likely than others to escalate to physical abuse (Rancer & Avtgis, 2006).
- *Physical abuse* includes threats of violence as well as pushing, hitting, slapping, kicking, choking, throwing things at you, and breaking things.
- *Sexual abuse* involves touching that is unwanted, accusations of sexual infidelity without reason, forced sex, and references to you in abusive sexual terms. Table 9.2 offers a brief comparison and summary of violent and nonviolent relationships.

A great deal of research has centered on trying to identify the warning signs of relationship violence. For example, the State University of New York at Buffalo compiled the following list to help you start thinking about your own relationship or those that you know of. It may be a warning sign if your partner:

INTERPERSONAL CHOICE POINT

Verbal Abuse

On your way to work, you witness a father verbally abusing his 3-year-old child. You worry that he might psychologically harm the child, and your first impulse is to speak up and tell this man that verbal abuse can have lasting effects on the child and often leads to physical abuse. At the same time, you don't want to interfere with his right to speak to his child, and you certainly don't want to make him angrier. What are some things you might say or do in this difficult situation?

- belittles, insults, or ignores you.
- controls pieces of your life; for example, the way you dress or who you can be friends with.
- gets jealous without reason.
- can't handle sexual frustration without anger.
- is so angry or threatening that you've changed your life so as not to provoke additional anger.

As you might expect, there are a variety of consequences to relationship violence: physical injuries, psychological injuries, and economic "injuries."

Perhaps the image that comes most quickly to mind with the issue of relationship violence is that of physical violence, and that element

---

TABLE 9.2

VIOLENT AND NONVIOLENT RELATIONSHIPS

Here are some characteristics that distinguish a nonviolent from a violent relationship, drawn largely from the University of Texas website on relationship violence.

Violent Relationships	Nonviolent Relationships
Emotional abuse	Fairness; you look for resolutions to conflict that will be fair to both of you.
Control and isolation	Communication that makes the partner feel safe and comfortable expressing himself or herself.
Intimidation	Mutual respect, mutual affirmation, and valuing of each other's opinions.
Economic abuse	The partners make financial decisions together.
Threats	Accountability—each person accepts responsibility for his or her own behavior.
Power over the other	Fair distribution of responsibilities.
Sexual abuse	Trust and respect for what each person wants and doesn't want.

is certainly a big part of overall relationship violence. Physical injuries may range from scratches and bruises to broken bones, knife wounds, and central nervous system damage. Such injuries can range from minor to life-ending.

Even when physical injuries are relatively minor, however, psychological injuries may be major and may include, for example, depression, anxiety, fear of intimacy, and, of course, low self-esteem. In fact, relationship violence often attacks self-esteem to the point where the victims come to believe that the violence against them was and is justified.

In addition to the obvious physical and psychological injuries, consider the economic impact. It's been estimated that in the United States relationship violence costs approximately $6.2 billion for physical assaults and almost $500 million for rape. Interpersonal violence also results in lost days of work. The Centers for Disease Control and Prevention estimates that in this country interpersonal violence costs the equivalent of 32,000 full-time jobs in lost work each year. Additional economic costs are incurred when interpersonal violence prevents women from maintaining jobs or continuing their education.

DEALING WITH RELATIONSHIP VIOLENCE   Whether you're a victim or a perpetrator of relationship violence, it is important to seek professional help (and, of course, the help of friends and family where appropriate). In addition, here are several further suggestions.

If your partner has been violent:

■ Realize that you're not alone. There are other people who suffer similarly, and there is a mechanism in place to help you.
■ Realize you're not at fault. You did not deserve to be the victim of violence.
■ Plan for your safety. Violence, if it occurred once, is likely to occur again, and part of your thinking needs to be devoted to your own safety.
■ Know your resources—the phone numbers you need to contact help, the locations of money and a spare set of keys.

If you are the violent partner:

- Realize that you too are not alone and that help and support are available.
- Know that you can change. It won't necessarily be easy or quick, but you can change.
- Own your own behaviors; take responsibility. This is an essential step if any change is to occur.

Relationship violence is not an inevitable part of interpersonal relationships; in fact, it occurs in a minority of relationships. Yet it's important to know that there is the potential for violence in all relationships, as there is the potential for friendship, love, support, and all the positive things we look for in relationships. Knowing the difference between productive and destructive relationships seems the best way to make sure that your own relationships are as you want them to be.

 Can you define *jealousy, bullying,* and *relationship violence?* Can you use the suggestions offered here to help you effectively deal with such relationships in your own personal or workplace life?

MESSAGES IN THE MEDIA: WRAP-UP

It's instructive to watch such shows with a view to identifying what went wrong in the relationship. And, Jerry Springer's summary and relationship advice at the end of the show is always logical and well-reasoned.

SUMMARY OF CONCEPTS AND SKILLS

 Listen to the **Audio Chapter Summary** at **MyCommunicationLab**

✓ **Study** and **Review** materials for this chapter are at **MyCommunicationLab**

This chapter explored the nature of interpersonal relationships, including the stages relationships go through, the movements in relationships, the dark side of interpersonal relationships, relationship types and theories, and the role of culture and technology in relationships.

Advantages and Disadvantages of Interpersonal Relationships

1. Interpersonal relationships have both advantages and disadvantages. Among the advantages are that they stimulate you, help you learn about yourself, and generally enhance your self-esteem. Among the disadvantages are that they force you to expose your vulnerabilities, make great demands on your time, and often cause you to abandon other relationships.

Relationship Stages

2. Interpersonal relationships may be viewed as occurring in stages. Recognize at least these: contact, involvement, intimacy, deterioration, repair, and dissolution.
3. In contact, there is first perceptual contact and then interaction.
4. Involvement includes a testing phase (will this be a suitable relationship?) and an intensifying of the interaction; often a sense of mutuality, of connectedness, begins.
5. In intimacy, there is an interpersonal commitment and perhaps a social bonding, in which the commitment is made public.
6. Some relationships deteriorate, proceeding through a period of intrapersonal dissatisfaction to interpersonal deterioration.

7. Along the process, repair may be initiated. Intrapersonal repair generally comes first (should I change my behavior?); it may be followed by interpersonal repair, in which you and your partner discuss your problems and seek remedies.

8. If repair fails, the relationship may dissolve, moving first to interpersonal separation and later, perhaps, to public or social separation.

9. Relationships are fluid, and movement from one stage to another is characteristic of most relationships.

The Dark Side of Interpersonal Relationships

10. Jealousy is a feeling that a relationship is in danger due to some rival and may be cognitive, emotional, and/or behavioral.

11. Bullying consists of abusive acts repeatedly committed by one person or group against another and is especially prevalent n the workplace.

12. Relationship violence may be verbal, physical, and/or sexual.

This chapter also considered a variety of skills. As you review these skills, check those you wish to work on.

_____ 1. *Advantages and disadvantages of relationships.* In evaluating, entering, or dissolving relationships, consider both the advantages and the disadvantages.

_____ 2. *Relationship messages.* Formulate messages that are appropriate to the stage of the relationship. Also, listen to messages from relationship partners that may reveal differences in perceptions about your relationship stage.

_____ 3. *Relationship repair.* Recognize the problem, engage in productive conflict resolution, pose possible solutions, affirm each other, integrate solutions into normal behavior, and take risks as appropriate.

_____ 4. *Managing relationship dissolution.* Break the loneliness–depression cycle, take time out, bolster self-esteem, seek support from others, and avoid repeating negative patterns.

_____ 5. *Jealousy.* Recognize the generally unproductive nature of jealousy.

_____ 6. *Bullying.* Become aware of the tactics of bullies and ways to combat them.

_____ 7. *Violence in relationships.* Become sensitive to the development of violence in a relationship and learn the ways to deal with this problem, should it arise.

VOCABULARY QUIZ: The Language of Interpersonal Relationships

Match the terms dealing with interpersonal relationships with their definitions. Record the number of the definition next to the appropriate term.

_____ turning points (205)
_____ politeness (207)
_____ repair (203)
_____ verbal abuse (212)
_____ jealousy (209)
_____ involvement (199)
_____ intimacy (200)
_____ contact (199)
_____ dissolution (204)
_____ desire, obligation, and necessity (207)

1. Humiliation, criticizing, isolating
2. Testing and intensifying a relationship
3. Types of commitment
4. Perceptual and interactional
5. Commitment and social bonding
6. Separation, the breaking of relationship bonds
7. Significant relationship events
8. Highest in contact and lowest in dissolution
9. Attempts to improve a relationship
10. Reaction to relationship threat

These ten terms and additional terms used in this chapter can be found in the glossary.

 Study and **Review** the **Flashcards** at **MyCommunicationLab**

MyCommunicationLab

Visit MyCommunicationLab for a wealth of additional information on interpersonal communication. Flashcards, videos, skill building exercises, sample test questions, and additional exercises, examples, and discussions will help you continue your study of the fundamentals of interpersonal communication, its theory, and its skills.

APPENDIX 2

Word Parts: Prefixes, Roots, and Suffixes

WORD PART	MEANING	EXAMPLE
Prefixes		
a-, an-	without, not	atypical, anarchy
ab-	away, from	absent, abnormal
ad-	toward	advance, administer
ambi-, amphi-	both, around	ambiguous, amphibious
anna-	year	annual
anti-, contra-, ob-	against	antisocial, contradict
bene-, eu-	well, good	benefactor, eulogy
bi-, du-, di-	two or twice	bicycle, duet, dichotomy
cata-, cath-	down, downward	catacombs
cent-, hecto-	hundred	centipede
con-, com-, syn-	with, together	congregate, synthesis
de-	down, from	depose, detract
dec-, deca-	ten	decade
demi-, hemi-, semi-	half	hemisphere, semicircle
dia-	through	diameter, diagram
dis-, un-	not, opposite of	dislike, unnatural
dys-	ill, hard	dystrophy
ex-	out, from	exhale, expel
extra-	beyond, outside	extralegal
hyper-	above, excessive	hyperactive
hypo-	under	hypodermic
il-, im, in-	not	illogical, impossible
in-	in, into	inside, insert, invade
infra-	lower	infrared
inter-	between	intercede, interrupt
intra-	within	intramural
juxta-	next to	juxtaposition
mal-, mis-	wrong, ill	malformed, mislead
mill-	thousand	milligram
nove-, non-	nine	novena, nonagon
oct-, octo-	eight	octopus
omni-, pan-	all	omnipotent, pantheist
per-	through	perennial, pervade
peri-, circum-	around	perimeter, circumvent
poly-, multi-	many	polygamy, multiply
post-	after	postscript
pre-, ante-	before	prepared, antebellum
pro-	before, for	promoter
proto-	first	prototype
quad-, quatra-, tetra-	four	quadrilateral, tetrad
quint-, penta-	five	quintuplet, pentagon

WORD PART	MEANING	EXAMPLE
re-	back, again	review, reply
retro-	backward	retrogress, retrospect
sequ-	follow	sequence
sex-, hexa-	six	sextet, hexagon
sub-	under	submarine, subway
super-	above, over	supervise
temp-, tempo-, chrono-	time	tempo, chronological
trans-	across	translate, transcontinental
tri-	three	triple, triangle
uni-, mono-	one	unicorn, monocle
vice-	in place of	viceroy

Roots

alter, hap	to change	alteration, mishap
ama, philo	to love	amiable, philosophy
anima	breath, spirit	animate
aqua	water	aquarium, aqualung
aster, astro	star	disaster, astronomy
aud	to hear	audible, auditory
auto, ego	self	autonomy, egotist
bio	life	biology
cap	head	caption, capitulate
cap, capt	to take	capture
card, cor, cord	heart	cardiac, core, cordial
cosmo	order, universe	cosmonaut
cresc	to grow, increase	crescendo
cryp	secret, hidden	cryptogram
dent	teeth	dental
derma	skin	dermatologist
duc, duct	to lead	reduce, conduct
equ, iso	equal	equivocal, isometric
err, errat	to wander	erratic
ethno	race, tribe	ethnic
fac, fact	to do, make	manufacture
fract	to break	fracture
frater	brother	fraternity
gene	race, kind, sex	genetics, gender
grad, gres	to go, take steps	graduation, digress
gyn	woman	gynecologist
hab, habi	to have, hold	inhabit, habitual
helio, photo	sun, light	heliotrope, photograph
homo	man	homo sapiens
lic, list, liqu	to leave behind	derelict, relinquish
lith	stone	monolith
loc	place	location, local
log	speech, science	logic, dialogue
loquor	to speak	loquacious, colloquial
lum	light	illuminate
macro	large	macrocosm
manu	hand	manual, manuscript
mater	mother	maternity
med	middle	mediate
meter	to measure	barometer

WORD PART	MEANING	EXAMPLE
micro	small	microscope
miss, mit	to send, let go	admit, permission
morph	form	morphology
mort	to die	immortalize
mut, mutat	to change	mutation
nat	to be born	natal, native
neg, negat	to say no, deny	negative, renege
nym, nomen	name	synonym, nomenclature
ocul	eye	oculist, monocle
ortho	right, straight	orthodox, orthodontist
osteo	bone	osteopath
pater	father	paternal
path	disease, feeling	pathology, antipathy
phag	to eat	esophagus, phagocyte
phobia	fear	claustrophobia
phon, phono	sound	symphony, phonics
plic	to fold	duplicate, implicate
pneuma	wind, air	pneumatic
pod, ped	foot	tripod, pedestrian
pon, pos	to place	depose, position
port	to carry	porter, portable
pseudo	false	pseudonym
psych	mind	psychology
pyr	fire	pyromaniac
quir	to ask	inquire, acquire
rog	to question	interrogate
scrib, graph	to write	prescribe, autograph
sect, seg	to cut	dissect, segment
sol	alone	solitude
soma	body	somatology, psychosomatic
somnia	sleep	insomnia
soph	wise	sophomore, philosophy
soror	sister	sorority
spect	to look at	inspect, spectacle
spir	to breathe	inspiration, conspire
tact, tang	to touch	tactile, tangible
tele	distant	telephone
ten, tent	to hold	tenant, intent
tend, tens	to stretch	extend, extension
the, theo	god	atheism, theology
therma	heat	thermometer
tort	twist	torture, extort
ven, vent	to go, arrive	convention, advent
verbum	word	verbosity, verbal

Suffixes

-able, -ible	capable of	durable, visible
-acy, -ance, -ency, -ity	quality or state of	privacy, competency, acidity
-age	act of, state of	breakage
-al	pertaining to	rental
-ana	saying, writing	Americana
-ant	quality of, one who	reliant, servant
-ard, -art	person who	wizard, braggart

WORD PART	MEANING	EXAMPLE
-arium, -orium	place for	auditorium
-ate	cause to be	activate
-ation, -ition	action, state of	creation, condition
-chrome	color	verichrome
-cide	killing	homicide
-er, -or	person who, thing which	generator
-esque	like in manner	picturesque
-fic	making, causing	scientific
-form	in the shape of	cuneiform
-ful, -ose, -ous	full of	careful, verbose
-fy, -ify, -ize	to make, cause to be	fortify, magnify, modify
-hood, -osis	condition or state of	childhood, hypnosis
-ics	art, science	mathematics
-ism	quality or doctrine of	conservatism
-itis	inflammation of	appendicitis
-ive	quality of, that which	creative
-latry	worship of	idolatry
-less	without	homeless
-oid	in the form of	tabloid
-tude	quality or degree of	solitude
-ward	in a direction	backward
-wise	way, position	clockwise

APPENDIX 3

Spelling Confusing Words

A president of the United States once said, "Damn a man who can't spell a word but one way." Nevertheless, college professors tend to expect one official spelling for a word. When creating an electronic document, always use the spelling check feature before submitting a final paper. Remember, though, that the spelling check feature doesn't always recognize your intended meaning or context. Use your head or a dictionary before accepting changes. Unfortunately, no "golden rules" of spelling yield perfect results. There are a few spelling rules, but none is without exception. The following four rules may help you get through some rough spots.

RULE 1 Use *i* before *e* except after *c*.

believe	ceiling	receipt
grief	conceited	priest
cashier	yield	piece

Exceptions: height, either, leisure, efficient

RULE 2 Drop the final *e* when adding a suffix that begins with a vowel.

hope + ing = hoping

believe + ing = believing

nice + est = nicest

Keep the final *e* when adding a suffix that begins with a consonant.

use + ful = useful

retire + ment = retirement

lone + some = lonesome

RULE 3 When a word ends in a consonant plus *y*, change the *y* to *i* to add a suffix.

lazy + ness = laziness

penny + less = penniless

marry + age = marriage

RULE 4 Double the final consonant when all of the following apply.

a. The word is one syllable or is accented on the last syllable.
b. The word ends in a consonant preceded by a vowel.
c. The suffix begins with a vowel.

hop + ing = hopping

skip + ing = skipping

repel + ent = repellent

APPENDIX 4

ESL: Making Sense of Figurative Language and Idioms

- What is ESL?
- What is figurative language?
- What are common English idioms?

WHAT IS ESL?

How many languages can you speak? Are you a native English speaker who has learned Spanish, or are you a native Farsi speaker who has learned English? If you have acquired skill in a second or third language, you know it takes many years and plenty of patience to master the intricacies of a language. Not only do you learn new words, but also you must learn new grammatical constructions. For example, the articles habitually used in English—*a, an,* and *the*—do not appear in Russian, Chinese, Japanese, Thai, or Farsi. In Spanish and Arabic, personal pronouns restate the subject, as in *My sister she goes to college.* In Spanish, Greek, French, Vietnamese, and Portuguese, "to" words are used rather than "ing" words, as in *I enjoy to play soccer.* These complexities, which are innately understood by native speakers, make direct translation difficult. The English language has many unusual phrases and grammatical constructions that defy direct translation.

To assist students with these complexities, most colleges offer courses in ESL (English as a Second Language) or ESOL (English for Speakers of Other Languages) that are designed to teach language skills to non-native speakers of English. If you are an ESL or ESOL student, you may have been recruited through an international exchange program with another college, you may be a newly arrived immigrant, or you may be a citizen with a bilingual background. You bring a multicultural perspective to classroom discussions and campus life that will broaden the insights of others. Not only are some of your holidays different from those of others, but also your sense of family life, work, and responsibility may be different. Share your thoughts and ideas with native English speakers as they share the irregularities of the language with you.

WHAT IS FIGURATIVE LANGUAGE?

One aspect of the English language that defies direct translation and confuses non-native speakers, and sometimes even native speakers, is **figurative language**. This is the manipulation of the language to create images, add interest, and draw comparisons by using figures of speech (see Chapter 10, "Inference"). The two most commonly used, *simile* and *metaphor*, are defined as follows:

Simile: a stated comparison using *like* or *as* (*example*: The baby swims like a fish.)

Metaphor: an implied comparison (*example*: The baby is a fish in water.)

Many figurative expressions have become commonplace in the English language. In the previous metaphor, the *baby* is not actually a *fish*, but the meaning is that *the baby swims very well*. However, neither direct translation nor a dictionary will unlock that meaning. When you encounter comparisons that seem out of the ordinary or ill chosen, ask yourself whether a figure of speech is being used, and look within the sentence for clues to help you guess the meaning.

The following practice exercises contain figurative language. Read each dialogue passage for meaning, and then use the context clues to match the number of the boldfaced figure of speech with the letter of the appropriate definition. To narrow your choices, the answers to 1–5 are listed within a–e, and the answers to 6–10 are listed within f–j.

EXERCISE 1

Maria: I am not going to be the one to stand in line for concert tickets this time. It is (1) **a pain in the neck**. Last time Fran left me (2) **holding the bag** on a $40 ticket for about a month.

Lynne: You did (3) **bend over backward** to organize the last outing. I would have (4) **jumped down Fran's throat** when she said she didn't have the cash to pay you. There is no reason (5) **to beat around the bush** with someone who doesn't pay promptly. Some people will (6) **walk all over you** if you let them.

Maria: I (7) **broke my neck** to get in line early. Those tickets were (8) **selling like hotcakes**. I think they (9) **jacked up** the price because they knew the demand would be high.

Lynne: I had to (10) **bite my tongue** not to say something to Fran about your efforts and her lack of gratitude.

_____	1.	a pain in the neck	a.	owed money
_____	2.	holding the bag	b.	avoid a clear answer
_____	3.	bend over backward	c.	criticized angrily
_____	4.	jumped down Fran's throat	d.	bothersome
_____	5.	to beat around the bush	e.	make a great effort
_____	6.	walk all over you	f.	being bought eagerly
_____	7.	broke my neck	g.	raised
_____	8.	selling like hotcakes	h.	keep from speaking
_____	9.	jacked up	i.	take advantage of you
_____	10.	bite my tongue	j.	tried hard

EXERCISE 2

Ron: I've got (1) **to take my hat off to** the group that organized the charity drive for the children's hospital.

Eric: They started out with (2) **two strikes against them** because most people had just made a contribution to the American Red Cross drive.

Ron: The president of the organization is a real (3) **go-getter**. He tried to educate people before asking for a contribution.

Eric: Until he outlined the situation in the Friday meeting, I did not know the hospital was (4) **in a jam**. Purchasing equipment for the cancer unit had put them (5) **in the red**.

Ron: When the 15-year-old boy spoke at the meeting, I was ready to (6) **open my wallet**. He said he had come through the cancer treatment and (7) **passed with flying colors**.

Eric: I gave $5 and was happy to know that my money would help a good cause. Not all charitable solicitations are (8) **on the level**. I like to (9) **double-check** to make sure that the charity is not a (10) **fly-by-night** operation. Now I'm thinking about doing some volunteer work at the hospital.

_____ 1. to take my hat off to	a.	in trouble
_____ 2. two strikes against them	b.	losing money
_____ 3. go-getter	c.	with little chance of success
_____ 4. in a jam	d.	to admire
_____ 5. in the red	e.	ambitious worker
_____ 6. open my wallet	f.	investigate thoroughly
_____ 7. passed with flying colors	g.	give money
_____ 8. on the level	h.	untrustworthy
_____ 9. double-check	i.	honest
_____ 10. fly-by-night	j.	succeeded

EXERCISE 3

Ross: I heard (1) **through the grapevine** that you had a (2) **fender bender** and put a dent in your car.

Howard: Ross, please don't (3) **breathe a word** about that. My parents will not be happy. I was really (4) **out to lunch** at the time and have been (5) **kicking myself** for not being more alert. I want to keep it (6) **hush-hush** for a while.

Ross: Do you have a plan for getting it fixed, or should we (7) **put our heads together** to create one?

Howard: I am waiting for final grades to come out. If I have all A's, I will then (8) **put my cards on the table** with them.

Ross: Man, that is really (9) **using your noodle**.

Howard: If that doesn't work, I'll be (10) **back to the drawing board** and could use your help.

_____ 1. through the grapevine	a.	regretting
_____ 2. fender bender	b.	inattentive
_____ 3. breathe a word	c.	by gossip from other people
_____ 4. out to lunch	d.	tell, talk

_____ 5. kicking myself   e. minor accident

_____ 6. hush-hush   f. thinking

_____ 7. put our heads together   g. ready to start over

_____ 8. put my cards on the table   h. confer

_____ 9. using your noodle   i. secret

_____ 10. back to the drawing board   j. confess all

WHAT ARE COMMON ENGLISH IDIOMS?

An **idiom** is an expression with a special meaning that cannot be understood by directly translating each individual word in the idiom. Because of years of exposure, the meaning is usually understood by native speakers, but it is confusing to those who are learning English as a second language.

Idioms are more common in spoken and informal language than in formal writing. In fact, most idiomatic expressions can usually be replaced by a single formal word. To add to the confusion, some idioms have dual meanings, and many idioms are grammatically irregular.

> ## Reader's TIP   Categorizing Idioms
>
> Idioms are sometimes categorized into the following groups:
>
> - Word families: grouping around a similar individual word
>
>   _Down_ as in _step down, take down, pipe down, narrow down, nail down, run down, tear down, knock down, let down, die down, cut down_
>
> - Verb + Preposition: action word plus a connecting word
>
>   _Hammer away_ means _persist_; _stand for_ means _represent_; and _roll back_ means _reduce_.
>
> - Preposition + Noun: connecting word plus the name of a person, place, or thing
>
>   _On foot_ means _walking_; _by heart_ means _memorized_; and _off guard_ means _surprised_.
>
> - Verb + Adjective: action word plus a descriptive word
>
>   _Think twice_ means _consider carefully_; _hang loose_ means _be calm;_ and _play fair_ means _deal equally_.
>
> - Pairs of Nouns: two words naming a person, place, or thing
>
>   _Flesh and blood_ means _kin_; _part and parcel_ means _total_; and _pins and needles_ means _nervous_.
>
> - Pairs of Adjectives: two descriptive words
>
>   _Cut and dried_ means _obvious_; _fair and square_ means _honest_; _short and sweet_ means _brief_.

EXAMPLE   What does the idiomatic expression *go over* mean in the following sentences?

(a) How did my speech *go over*?

(b) I want to *go over* the exam paper with the professor.

EXPLANATION   In both sentences, the use of the idiom is informal. A more formal version of each would be as follows:

(a) *How was my speech* **received** *by the audience?*

(b) *I want to* **review** *the exam paper with the professor.*

Notice the grammatical irregularity in the first sentence. *Over* is not followed by a noun (name of a person, place, or thing), as a preposition (connecting words like *in*, *out*, and *at*) normally would be according to the rules of grammar; *over* becomes part of the verb phrase (words showing action). Thus, the translation requires a change in wording, whereas the second use of the idiom is grammatically correct and can be directly translated by the single word *review*.

Nobody says that understanding idioms is easy. Books have been written about categorizing, recognizing, and translating thousands of them. To help clear up the confusion, some books group idioms according to families like root words, and others categorize them according to grammatical constructions. Either way, understanding idiomatic expressions depends more on using context clues to deduce meaning and familiarity with the informal, spoken language than with learning rules.

In the following practice exercises, idioms are grouped according to a common word. Use the context clues within each sentence to determine the meaning of the boldfaced idiom.

EXERCISE 4

up	down	around	across	over

1. Let's **nail down** a date for the next meeting before we leave today. _____ _____

2. Close friends should **stand up for** what they know is right. _____ _____

3. Children should not be allowed to **fool around** with matches. _____

4. With a quick example the student was able to **get across** the application of the theory. _____

5. They had a big **blowup** over who was responsible for the telephone bill. _____

6. Yesterday I **ran across** an old friend at the airport. _____

7. Because we are having a party, I asked a few friends in my psychology class to **drop over**. _____

8. The new grocery store is open **around the clock**. _____

9. If the class president would **step down** in March, we could get a more dynamic person for the position. _____

10. After winning the free concert tickets, she was **bubbling over** with excitement. _____

EXERCISE 5   in   about   for   off   out

1. Before school starts, we need to **see about** renting an apartment. _____
_____

2. The manager stayed late at work to **break in** the new employee. _____
_____

3. If you need to shorten the paragraph, **leave out** the last sentence. _____
_____

4. What do the school colors **stand for**? _____

5. Although the designer's name was displayed, the purse was actually a cheap **knockoff**. _____

6. As soon as class is over, we are going to **take off** for a weekend at the beach.
_____

7. Because I have a car this semester, **getting about** is much easier. _____
_____

8. This latest demand **calls for** immediate action from our coalition. _____
_____

9. Let's all **chip in** to buy our professor a gift. _____

10. When cleaning, you do not want to **throw out** something that you may need later. _____

EXERCISE 6
free and easy   part and parcel   give-and-take   null and void
touch and go   spick-and-span   day in and day out
little by little   high and low   sooner or later

1. If you continue to drive with your gas gauge on empty, **sooner or later** you will be stuck on the side of the road. _____

2. By decreasing the medication **little by little**, the body can adjust without a painful reaction. _____

3. Overcooked food and slow service are complaints the restaurant managers hear **day in and day out**. _____

4. The peace negotiations were **touch and go** until the rebels accepted the compromise. _____

5. When I eat in a restaurant, I am more confident about cleanliness if the rest room is **spick-and-span**. _____

6. The opportunity to be with family is **part and parcel** of any holiday celebration. _____

7. After an appeal to a higher court, the previous decision to grant millions in damages could bc declared **null and void**. _____

8. We will never decide which band to book for the party unless club members engage in a little **give-and-take**. _____

9. When she starts making her own money, she won't continue to spend with such a **free and easy** attitude. _____

10. After searching **high and low** for my keys, I found them under the computer. _____

Reader's TIP   Internet Sites to Explore

Dave's ESL Café   www.eslcafe.com
Emphasis in this site is on English as it is spoken in the United States. It includes search tools for ESL books and a general discussion forum for ESL students and teachers.

EF Englishtown   www.englishtown.com
Englishtown offers daily, 5-minute "E-mail English" lessons for no charge. It also provides a 7-day, free trial of classes taught online in the Englishtown school.

English Club   www.EnglishClub.com
This site has a 24-hour ESL Help Desk staffed with teachers to answer questions. Resources are available for both instructors and students in areas such as grammar, speech, and reading at no charge.

Tower of English   www.towerofenglish.com
Tower of English allows students to integrate lots of Web sources into their learning experience. It provides links to online ESL exercises, search engines, reference tools, and news sources. The site also links students to private English tutors in their cities.

APPENDIX 5

Test-Taking Preparation and Practice

- Test Preparation Analysis
- Comprehension Test Practice Exercises

Use the Test Preparation Analysis as a guide to effective studying before a test and as an analysis after the test. Your instructor may ask you to turn in the completed form. You might want to make extra copies for future use.

A practice set of reading comprehension test questions follows the Test Preparation Analysis form. Use the strategies you learned in Chapter 1 as you complete the exercises.

Name _____ **Course#** _____ **Test** ____ **Date** ____

How do you prepare for a major test? Read this as you prepare for the test and complete it after the test. You will be asked to answer the questions when you get the graded test back.

TEST PREPARATION ANALYSIS

How did you prepare for this test? Many college students are unaware that good results on tests require more than studying the night before. Examining the ways you prepared for this test can help you improve your performance on future tests.

Be honest. This is for your benefit!

_____ 1. I read the textbook chapters.

_____ 2. I annotated the chapters as I read them.

_____ 3. I attended class regularly.

_____ 4. I took thorough notes in class.

_____ 5. I read the test review sheet.

_____ 6. I made test review notes using the review sheet as a guide.

_____ 7. I quizzed myself using my notes and/or the review sheet.

_____ 8. I did a partner quiz to complete my studying.

_____ 9. I am following the schedule I constructed for myself and am studying two hours outside of class for every hour in class.

_____ 10. I allowed enough time to prepare well.

List any other methods you used:

Grade on this test _____

Study methods that worked well for me:

_____

_____

_____

What will you do next time? List two to three preparation methods that you will use for the next test.

1. _____

_____

2. _____

_____

3. _____

_____

COMPREHENSION TEST PRACTICE EXERCISES

Main Idea Questions

EXERCISE 1

For further practice on main idea items, read the following passage and answer the two questions. After each possible answer, write why you did or did not choose that response. For main idea distractors, the reasons might be that the incorrect response is *too broad, too narrow, a detail*, or *not in the passage*.

In the United States, every state has laws prohibiting some type of relatives from marrying each other. Today there is universal agreement when it comes to prohibiting mother–son marriage and preventing full siblings from marrying, but the laws vary when it comes to more distant relatives. Thirty states prohibit first cousins from marrying, while twenty do not. Furthermore, the prohibitions are not limited to people related by birth. A dozen states forbid some types of in-laws from intermarrying.

—*Cultural Anthropology: The Human Challenge,*
Eleventh Edition, by William A. Haviland et al.

_____ 1. The best title for this passage is:

a. Marriage Laws _____

b. Marriage Prohibitions Among Relatives in the United States

_____

c. Mother–Son Marriage Prohibitions _____

_____

d. Cultural Taboos Forbidding Intermarrying _____

_____

_____ 2. The best statement of the main idea of this passage is:

a. There is no disagreement with preventing marriage between

brothers and sisters. _____

_____

b. Twenty states allow first cousins to marry. _____

c. There are laws forbidding citizens from marrying relatives in ev-

ery state in the United States. _____

d. Intermarriage results in increased health problems for the chil-

dren of such marriages. _____

Detail Questions

EXERCISE **2**

For further practice on details, read the following passage and answer the detail question. Indicate beside each response why you did or did not choose the item.

> Be quite sure that there isn't a woman who cannot be won, and make up your mind that you will win her. Only you must prepare the ground. Sooner would the birds cease their song in the springtime, or the grasshopper be silent in the summer, . . . than a woman resist the tender wooing of a youthful lover. . . .
>
> In the first place, it's best to send her a letter, just to pave the way. In it you should tell her how you dote on her; pay her pretty compliments and say all the nice things lovers always say. . . . And promise, promise, promise. Promises will cost you nothing. Everyone's a millionaire where promises are concerned. . . .
>
> If she refuses your letter and sends it back unread, don't give up; hope for the best and try again.
>
> *—The Love Books of Ovid,*
> translated by J. Lewis May

_____ 1. The author recommends the following to capture the heart of a young woman:

    a. Playing hard to get. _____

    b. Flattery. _____

    c. Total honesty. _____

    d. Gifts. _____

Inference Questions

EXERCISE **3**

For further practice on inference, read the following passage and answer the inference question. In the blank, indicate the reason for your answer choice.

> [We were invited to a banquet with Attila.] When the hour arrived we went to Attila's palace, along with the embassy from the western Romans, and stood on the threshold of the hall in the presence of Attila. The cup-bearers gave us a cup, according to the national custom, that we might pray before we sat down. Having tasted the cup, we proceeded to take our seats, all the chairs being ranged along the walls of the room on either side. Attila sat in the middle on a couch; a second couch was set behind him, and from it steps led up to his bed, which was covered with linen sheets and coverlets. . . .
>
> [First the king and his guests pledged one another with the wine.] When this ceremony was over the cup-bearers retired and tables, large enough for three or four, or even more, to sit at, were placed next the table of Attila, so that each could take of the food on the dishes without leaving his seat. The attendant of Attila first entered with a dish full of meat, and behind him came the other attendants with bread and other dishes, which they laid on the tables. A luxurious meal, served on a silver plate, had been made ready for us and the other guests, but Attila ate nothing but meat on a wooden platter. In everything else, too, he showed himself temperate; his cup was of wood, while to the guests were given goblets of gold and silver. His dress, too, was quite simple, affecting only to be clean.
>
> *—Priscus, quoted in Western Civilization, Volume 1:*
> *To 1715, Fifth Edition, by Jackson J. Spielvogel*

_____ 1. The author implies that

    a. although luxuries are available to him, Attila chooses a simpler lifestyle.

    b. Attila ordered a victory feast for his leaders before a day of battle.

    c. the Roman peasants were starving while the food and drink flowed at Attila's palace.

    d. while he enjoys the banquet, the author is also fearful of Attila.

    Reason for choice: _____

_____

_____

_____

Author's Purpose Questions

EXERCISE 4   For further practice, read the following passage and answer the purpose question. In the blank, indicate the reason for your answer choice.

> During the Victorian age women were often considered frail and delicate creatures, at least partly because they seemed prone to fainting spells. Did they faint because of their "inner natures" or for some other reason? Consider the fact that many of these women wore extremely tight corsets to give them tiny waists. In fact, the corsets were so tight that women could only take shallow breaths—if they took a deep breath, they ran the risk of being stabbed by the whalebone "stays" in the corset. These stays were thin and very sharp, and not only could they cause a bloody wound, but they could also puncture a lung! One consequence of continued shallow breathing is dizziness—hence the fainting spells common among stylish Victorian women.
>
> —*Psychology: The Brain, the Person, the World,* Second Edition, by Stephen M. Kosslyn and Robin S. Rosenberg

_____ 1. The author's primary purpose in this passage is

    a. to argue.

    b. to condemn.

    c. to entertain.

    d. to explain.

    Reason for response: _____

_____

_____

Vocabulary Questions

EXERCISE 5   For further practice, read the following passage and answer the vocabulary question. In the blank, indicate the reason for your answer choice.

> Chavez's efforts helped spark an outburst of ethnic consciousness among Mexican Americans that swept through the urban barrios of the Southwest. Mexican American leaders campaigned for bilingual programs and improved educational opportunities. Young activists

began to call themselves Chicanos, which had previously been a derogatory term, and to take pride in their cultural heritage; in 1968, they succeeded in establishing the first Mexican American studies program at California State College at Los Angeles. Campus leaders called for reform, urging high school students to insist on improvements. Heeding such appeals, nearly ten thousand students at East Los Angeles high schools walked out of class in March 1968. These walkouts sparked similar movements in San Antonio, Texas, and Phoenix, Arizona, and led to the introduction of bilingual programs in grade schools and the hiring of more Chicano teachers at all levels.

—*American Stories: A History of the United States,*
by H. W. Brands, et al.

_____ 1. As used in the passage, the best definition of *derogatory* is

a. violent

b. appropriate

c. complimentary

d. insulting

Reason for response: _____

_____

_____

APPENDIX 6

Practice for Reading Efficiency

The following exercises will help to increase your awareness of speed and to give you a sense of haste. Time yourself on each exercise and press for improvement. While you are improving your efficiency, remember that comprehension is the primary goal.

EXERCISE 1   In the following lists, the key word is in boldface in the column at the left. It is then repeated in the group of words to the right. As rapidly as possible, locate the identical word, check it, and then move to the next line. Try to do most of this visually rather than saying each word to yourself. When you have finished each list, record your time and compare your performance with that of your fellow classmates.

List 1

1. **lip**	lid	long	left	lip	lap
2. **stand**	start	stand	strong	torn	stop
3. **wander**	willow	wanton	waiting	wander	worry
4. **vain**	vale	vain	vane	vague	value
5. **most**	mort	most	might	host	mast
6. **divide**	divine	devoted	divide	have	doing
7. **someone**	somewhere	someone	sooner	somehow	somebody
8. **week**	weak	meek	week	leak	seek
9. **hazy**	hazy	hazard	hamper	lazy	dizzy
10. **mold**	mole	mound	mold	mind	hold
11. **sight**	height	right	might	sight	light
12. **aide**	aid	aide	add	also	hide
13. **reform**	remake	reclaim	malformed	reform	form
14. **bubble**	raffle	baffle	bubble	rubber	blubber
15. **scarce**	source	sacred	scarce	scorn	serious
16. **fabulous**	famous	fabulous	fashion	false	fasten
17. **reservation**	preservation	occupation	realization	reservation	reserve
18. **reality**	really	reaction	finality	reality	rational
19. **tranquilizer**	transfer	relaxation	tranquilizer	transcribe	transit
20. **phenomena**	pneumonia	phenomena	paralysis	feminine	phrases

Time in seconds = _____

List 2

1. **wing**	wig	wring	wing	with	ring
2. **cram**	crash	carry	ram	ham	cram
3. **like**	mike	like	land	load	hike
4. **sandal**	saddle	sandal	ramble	soften	sweet
5. **prime**	proud	prim	prime	prissy	rime
6. **manage**	mingle	manager	mangle	manner	manage
7. **rash**	rash	rush	race	lush	rich
8. **trace**	trance	trace	trade	train	trail
9. **saline**	saloon	salmon	saline	short	slowly
10. **revenge**	regain	ravenous	rancid	revamp	revenge
11. **tired**	tried	trend	tread	tired	torn
12. **withdrawn**	without	withdraw	within	withdrawn	witness
13. **powerful**	power	potential	powerful	potent	palate

14. **indignant**	indigenous	indigent	distinguish	indignant	indulge
15. **remember**	dismember	remain	reminisce	remission	remember
16. **condescending**	condemning	condense	concise	coherent	condescending
17. **magnanimous**	magnificent	magnanimous	magnetic	malformed	magnify
18. **humorous**	human	hormone	hammock	hammer	humorous
19. **civilization**	civilized	citizenry	civic	civilization	centered
20. **ingenious**	ingenuous	injurious	ingenious	ignoble	engine

Time in seconds = ——————

EXERCISE 2 In the following list, the key word is in boldface. Among the words to the right, locate and mark the one that is most similar in meaning to the key word. In this exercise, you are not just looking at the shapes of words, but you are looking quickly for meaning. This will help you think fast and effectively. When you have finished the list, record your time and check your answers.

List 1

1. **ill**	sin	die	skill	sick	mind
2. **calm**	envy	breeze	peaceful	early	far
3. **nice**	pleasant	needed	new	smooth	plastic
4. **emotion**	drain	feeling	heat	silent	search
5. **close**	cost	tall	mild	flow	near
6. **gun**	knife	rifle	handle	metal	hold
7. **expert**	rule	sort	believer	follower	specialist
8. **obtain**	get	feature	delay	injure	adapt
9. **discuss**	sense	divide	order	talk	find
10. **moisture**	dampness	sample	screen	dark	dirty
11. **village**	mountain	town	river	country	moving
12. **bravery**	origin	voluntary	courage	means	social
13. **loyal**	client	faithful	definite	legal	scale
14. **convert**	swim	chief	movement	policy	change
15. **celebrate**	attain	learn	century	rejoice	statement
16. **argument**	fund	quarrel	meeting	democracy	voice
17. **preserve**	opportunity	solar	system	save	signal
18. **hilarious**	funny	horrible	drama	sensible	even
19. **imitate**	difficult	confer	strike	language	copy
20. **danger**	general	fair	position	risk	army

Time in seconds = ————

EXERCISE 3 In the following list, the key phrase is in boldface. Among the words on the lines below, locate and mark the phrase that is most similar in meaning to the key phrase. Record your time and check your answers. This exercise will help you increase your eye span and grasp meaning quickly from phrases.

List 1

1. **sense a disaster**
   sleep with ease   feel danger near   yearn for adventure   seek your fortune

2. **hurry to leave**
   walk in the rain   spill the coffee   lower the rent   rush out the door

3. **seek legal advice**
   engage an attorney   earn a living   move your address   give to charity

4. **forget to call**
   scream and yell   open an account   send by mail   neglect to phone
5. **offer your services**
   get in the way   offer to help   quit your job   waste your time
6. **listen to music**
   play in a band   buy a piano   hear a tune   turn off the radio
7. **notice a change**
   see a difference   buy a new shirt   work on a project   meet new people
8. **lose money gambling**
   pay for a product   not win a bet   cut expenses   make an offer
9. **clean up a spill**
   go in the kitchen   add more water   wipe away a stain   tear a rag
10. **leap with delight**
    sing a high note   turn the page   ask for help   jump for joy

Time in seconds = _____

EXERCISE 4   Read the following passages (using your pen as a pacer in the *Z* pattern in Passages 1, 2, and 3). Answer the comprehension questions with *T* (true) or *F* (false) and then record your reading time.

Passage 1
NATURAL GAS SAFETY

Natural gas is odorless so, in the early days of using natural gas to heat buildings and cook, someone would occasionally light a match without realizing that a gas leak had filled the air with gas. Poof! Inventors quickly began designing devices that would detect the presence of natural gas in the air and sound an alarm. However, the best solution was not a detection device. Instead, a gas that could be easily smelled was added to the odorless natural gas so that a leak could be detected easily by a human's built-in gas detector, the nose!

(98 words)

—*A Creative Problem Solver's Toolbox,*
by Richard Fobes

Time in seconds = _____

_____ 1. Another gas was mixed with natural gas to create a smell.

_____ 2. Originally, natural gas was odorless.

Passage 2

TYPING KEYBOARD

The earliest typewriters usually jammed when a key
was pressed too soon after the previous key
was released. Most people weren't willing
to tolerate this flaw, so early typewriters
were used mostly by blind people and others
who couldn't write easily by hand. Christopher Sholes
created a clever supporting enhancement that overcame
this jamming tendency. He arranged the letters
on the keys awkwardly! He put the frequently
typed letters E, T, O, N, R, and I on keys
that required finger movement to reach them,
and assigned frequently typed pairs of letters,
such as E and D, to the same finger. His innovation worked!
It successfully slowed down a person's typing speed,
thereby reducing the tendency for his typewriters to jam.
Unfortunately, because Sholes' typewriters became so popular,
this awkward keyboard arrangement is the one
we still use today!

(139 words)

—*The Creative Problem Solver's Toolbox,* by Richard Fobes

Time in seconds = _____

_____ 1. Our present typing keyboard was adopted to enhance speed.

_____ 2. Early typewriters were used by blind people.

Passage 3

DWARF PLANETS

What is a planet? We've been asking that question at least since Greek astronomers came up with the word to describe the bright points of light that seemed to wander among fixed stars. Our solar system's planet count has soared as high as 15 before it was decided that some discoveries were different and should be called asteroids.

Many disagreed in 1930 when Pluto was added as our solar system's ninth planet. The debate flared again in 2005 when Eris—about the same size as Pluto—was found deep in a zone beyond Neptune called the Kuiper Belt. Was it the 10th planet? Or are Eris and Pluto examples of an intriguing, new kind of world?

The International Astronomical Union decided in 2006 that a new system of classification was needed to describe these new worlds, which are more developed than asteroids, but different than the known planets. Pluto, Eris and the asteroid Ceres became the first dwarf planets. Unlike planets, dwarf planets lack the gravitational muscle to sweep up or scatter objects near their orbits. They end up orbiting the sun in zones of similar objects such as the asteroid and Kuiper belts.

Our solar system's planet count now stands at eight. But the lively debate continues as we enter another exciting decade of exploration and discoveries.

(220 words)

—Retrieved 5/15/2011, http://solarsystem.nasa.gov/planets/profile.cfm?Object=Dwarf

Time in seconds = _____

_____ 1. The word *planet* was given to these celestial objects by the Greeks.

_____ 2. Pluto, Eris, and Ceres are now considered dwarf planets.

GLOSSARY

abbreviations Shortened spellings that are useful when taking notes.

abstract Short paragraph that summarizes an article, stating the author's premise, the subject or location of the project, and the conclusions.

acronym Abbreviation pronounced as a word and contrived to simplify a lengthy name and gain quick recognition for an organization or agency. For example, *UNICEF* is the abbreviation for the United Nations International Children's Emergency Fund.

acrostic A sentence in which the first letter of each word corresponds to the first letter of other words; a helpful memory strategy when learning a list of items.

addition pattern Pattern of paragraph organization that includes additional information.

analogy Comparison that measures not only word knowledge but also the ability to see relationships.

annotating Method of highlighting main ideas, significant supporting details, and key terms using a system of symbols and notations, in which the markings indicate pertinent points to review for an exam.

applied level of reading This level calls for reaction, reflection, and critical thinking and involves analyzing, synthesizing, and evaluating.

bar graph Graph comprising a series of horizontal or vertical bars in which the length of each bar represents a particular amount. Often, time is represented by the vertical scale and quantity is measured by the horizontal scale.

bias Author's attitude, opinion, or position on a subject suggesting the facts have been slanted toward the author's personal beliefs. As commonly used, *bias* has a negative connotation suggesting narrow-mindedness and prejudice.

bibliography List of the sources consulted by the author of a scholarly article or paper.

biography The story of a person's life or a portion of it as told by another person.

cause-and-effect pattern Pattern of paragraph and essay organization showing one or more elements as producing or causing a result or effect.

characters The main people in a story; they should be consistent in behavior and should grow and change according to their experiences.

citation In an index entry, a reference to an article that includes the title, author(s), name of the periodical, volume and page numbers, issue date, and descriptive notes or key search terms.

classification pattern Pattern of paragraph and essay organization dividing items into groups or categories.

climax In literature, the turning point near the end of a story in which conflict intensifies to a peak.

comparison and contrast pattern Pattern of paragraph and essay organization listing similarities and/or differences among items.

concept card Vocabulary development aid that contains the new word in a sentence or phrase on one side of a note card and the definition on the other side; a drawing may provide an additional memory link.

conclusion Logical deduction from both stated and unstated ideas, using the hints as well as the facts to interpret motives, actions, and outcomes. Conclusions are drawn on the basis of perceived evidence, and because perceptions differ, conclusions can vary from reader to reader.

conflict Clash of ideas, desires, or actions as incidents in a plot build progressively.

connotation Feeling or emotion associated with a word that goes beyond its dictionary definition.

content test Test that measures knowledge of a particular topic.

context clues The words or phrases surrounding an unfamiliar word that help a reader identify its meaning.

Cornell method System of note taking in which you put questions on one side of a vertical line and you put notes that answer the questions on the other side.

critical thinking Deliberating in a purposeful, organized manner in order to assess the value of old and new information.

critique Review that judges the merits of a work.

databases Computer-based indexes that assist research. A single article may be listed under several topics and may appear in several different indexes.

definition pattern Pattern of paragraph and essay organization initially defining a concept and then expanding with examples and restatements.

denotation Dictionary definition of a word.

description pattern A form or pattern of writing that lists the characteristics of an object, event, person, place, and so on.

details Specifics in a passage that develop, explain, and support the main idea, such as reasons, incidents, facts, examples, steps, and definitions.

diagram Outlined drawing or illustration of an object or a process.

directory path Particular location within a Web site's host computer.

domain name Name registered by a Web site owner.

domain type Category to which the Web site owner belongs.

editorials Subjective articles that express the opinion of a person or organization. A newspaper's editorial pages feature the views of its management and/or editors.

electronic mail (e-mail) Message sent from one person or organization to another person or group of people using the World Wide Web. These messages can be read, printed, saved, forwarded to someone else, and/or discarded.

encyclopedias Reference books that give comprehensive coverage of a subject. Many different encyclopedias, such as the *Encyclopedia of African American Religions*, *Encyclopedia of Earth Sciences*, and *The Cambridge Encyclopedia of Astronomy*, are available for specific topics.

essay Short work of nonfiction that discusses a specific topic. It does not develop as a story does, and it lacks characters and a plot.

etymology Study of word origins, involving the tracing of words back to their earliest recorded appearance.

fact Statement based on actual evidence or personal observation. It can be checked objectively with empirical data and proved to be either true or false.

fallacy Inference that appears to be reasonable at first, but closer inspection proves it to be unrelated, unreliable, or illogical. Tool used in constructing a weak argument.

feature stories In journalism, human interest stories that differ from typical news stories in their timeliness, style, and length.

fiction Writing invented by the imagination.

figurative language Words intentionally used in a different way—out of their literal context—so they take on new meaning.

fixations Stops lasting a fraction of a second that eyes make in order to read. On the average, 5 to 10 percent of reading time is spent on fixations.

forum See *online community*.

generalization and example pattern Pattern of paragraph and essay organization explaining a concept by illustrating with examples.

glossary A brief dictionary of terms relating to a particular field or topic; usually found at the back of a textbook.

graphic organizer A diagram that presents the major and minor details of a text passage in a visual form.

hypertext links In the World Wide Web, phrases that are often distinguished by a different color and are underlined. Clicking on them will not only move you from one page to another within the Web site but also can send you to other related Web sites. The words chosen and underlined as the link describe the information likely to be found at that destination.

idiom An expression that has taken on a generally accepted meaning over many years of use but does not make sense on a literal level. Idioms can be similes and metaphors. For example, *sleeping like a log* is both a simile and also an idiom, because it is an accepted and often used expression that is not literally true.

index Research tool that contains listings of articles organized by the topics within the articles. Most libraries have electronic periodical indexes.

inference Meaning that is not directly stated but suggested through clues that lead one to make assumptions and draw conclusions.

intent Reason or purpose for writing, which is usually to inform, persuade, or entertain.

Internet Global system of interconnected computer networks that serves billions of users; carries information resources, including documents from the World Wide Web (WWW), and supports e-mail.

interpretive level of reading At this level, the reader makes assumptions and draws conclusions by considering the stated message, the implied meaning, the facts, and the author's attitude toward the subject.

inverted pyramid Format of news writing that begins with a summary paragraph and continues with paragraphs that explain details in a descending order of importance.

irony A figure of speech that states the opposite of the intended meaning.

lead In a news story, the first paragraph that catches the reader's attention, establishes a focus, and summarizes the essential points of the story.

letter Formal communication appropriate for outside the company.

line graph Graph incorporating a continuous curve or *frequency distribution*. The horizontal scale (or *axis*) measures one aspect of the data (or *variable*), and the vertical scale measures another aspect, making it easy to see the relationship between the variables at a glance. As the data fluctuate, the line changes direction and, with extreme differences, becomes very jagged.

links See *hypertext links*.

literal level of reading At this level, the reader might be able to answer detail questions asking *who*, *what*, *when*, and *where* but not understand the overall purpose of the passage.

location or spatial order pattern Pattern of paragraph organization identifying the whereabouts of objects.

main idea Central message that the author is trying to convey about the material.

major supporting detail Provides information that explains and elaborates on the main idea.

map Visual representation of a geographic area.

mapping Visual system of condensing ideas or cognitive material through diagramming of major points and significant subpoints to show relationships and importance.

memo Short, informal business note usually for internal business purposes.

metacognition Knowledge of the processes involved in reading and the ability to regulate and direct them.

metaphor Direct comparison of two unlike things that does not use the word *like* or *as*. A metaphor and a simile can communicate the same idea and are differentiated only by the presence or absence of the word *like* or *as*.

minor supporting detail Provides a specific example or other information that explains a major detail.

minutes Official record of the business decisions for a meeting.

mixed pattern Method of organizing writing that includes more than one specific pattern.

mnemonics Technique to help the brain organize and recall information by incorporating the senses through pictures, sounds, rhythms, and other mental tricks to create extrasensory handles or hooks.

mood Overall feeling of the work, often conveyed by the language and symbolism used.

multiple-meaning words Some words are confusing because they have several different meanings. For example, the dictionary lists over 30 meanings for the word *run*.

newsletter Mini-newspaper published within an organization to build group spirit.

news stories Newspaper articles that report the facts of events in descending order of importance.

nonfiction Writing that describes facts and reality.

notetaking Method of jotting down important ideas for future study from a lecture or text.

novel Extended fictional work that has all of the elements of a short story. Because of its length, a novel usually has more character development and more conflicts than a short story.

online community An interactive community or forum centered around a particular subject through which participants post information and ask questions.

opinion Statement of personal feeling or a judgment. It reflects a belief or an interpretation rather than an accumulation of evidence, and it cannot be proved true or false.

outline Method of organizing major points and subordinating items of lesser importance with Roman numerals, letters, numbers, and indentations to show how one idea relates to another and how all aspects relate to the whole.

pattern of organization Organizational structure of a passage that can be a simple listing, time order, definition with examples, comparison-contrast, or cause and effect.

periodicals Publications that come out on a regular schedule, including popular magazines and scholarly journals.

personification Attributing human characteristics to nonhuman things.

pie graph Circle divided into wedge-shaped slices, with each slice representing a percentage of the whole. The complete pie or circle represents 100%.

plagiarism A form of dishonesty in which one uses someone else's words or ideas as if they were one's own; consequences in an academic setting may include failing a course or expulsion from the institution.

plot Action in a story or a play. Sequence of incidents or events linked in a manner that suggests causes for the events.

point of view In writing, point of view is the author's attitude, opinion, or position on a subject. In literature, point of view describes who tells the story and is indicated most commonly by the third person (in which the author is the all-knowing observer). Alternatively, the first person (in which the main character tells the story by using the word *I*) or second person (in which the story is told through the use of the word *you*) may be used.

popular sources Newspapers and magazines aimed at the general public and written by professional journalists who are *reporters* rather than specialists in the field and thus focus on *who, what, where, when, why,* and *how.*

prefix Group of letters with a special meaning added to the beginning of a word.

previewing First stage of reading: a method of reviewing material to guess what it is about, assess what you already know about the topic, decide what you will probably want to know after you read, and make a plan for reading.

previewing a textbook Examining the features and organization of a book before reading any of it in depth.

prior knowledge What is already known about a subject, which is the single best predictor of reading comprehension.

propaganda Information that is widely spread and that is intended to help or harm a person, group, movement, and so on.

protocol Short for *hypertext transfer protocol (http)*, a type of language that computers networked via the Internet use to communicate with each other.

purpose Reason or intent for writing, which is usually to inform, persuade, or entertain.

questionnaire A list of questions submitted for replies which can be collected and analyzed.

recalling Telling oneself what has been learned after reading, relating it to what is already known, and reacting to it to form an opinion.

regression Rereading sentences or paragraphs because one's mind wandered during the initial reading of the material.

resolution A literary term referring to the point in the plot of a novel or story at which the outcome of the conflict is made known.

root Stem or basic part of a word, derived primarily from Latin and Greek.

rubric A checklist by which students' work is graded.

schema Concept of a compartment in the brain, similar to a computer chip that holds all that is known on a subject.

scholarly journals Regularly scheduled publications aimed at scholars, specialists, and students. They contain detailed research results written by specialists in the academic field of study and are frequently theoretical.

server name Indicates the computer network over which the user travels to reach the desired location (in most cases, the World Wide Web).

setting Backdrop for a story and the playground for the characters. Setting may include the place, the time, and the culture.

short story Brief work of narrative fiction with a beginning, a middle, and an end that ranges from 500 to 15,000 words.

signal words Transitional words or phrases that connect parts of sentences, sentences, or paragraphs and lead readers to anticipate a continuation or a change in the writer's thoughts. They can also indicate the organizational pattern.

simile Comparison of two unlike things using the words *like* and *as* (e.g., "His words were like knives to my heart").

simple listing pattern Pattern of paragraph organization that randomly lists items in a series.

slant A bias or point of view.

standardized test Test that measures mastery of a skill such as reading; scores are reported in a form that allows comparison across a large population.

subvocalization Inaudible voice in one's mind that one "hears" while reading.

suffix Group of letters with a special meaning added to the end of a word. Can alter the meaning of a word as well as the way the word can be used.

summary Brief, concise statement of the main idea of a piece of writing and its significant supporting details. The first sentence states the main idea or thesis, and subsequent sentences incorporate the significant details.

summary pattern Pattern of paragraph organization that sums up what has been stated in preceding paragraphs.

symbolism Object, action, person, place, or idea that carries a condensed and recognizable meaning (e.g., an opened window might symbolize an opportunity for a new life).

table Organized listing of facts and figures in columns and rows to compare and classify information for quick and easy reference.

theme Heart, soul, or central insight of—or universal truth expressed by—a work. Message is never preached but revealed to the emotions, senses, and imagination through powerful shared experiences.

thesaurus A list of words and their synonyms.

thesis statement A sentence that states the main point; the topic sentence or main idea statement.

time order, sequence, or narration pattern Pattern of paragraph organization listing events in the order of occurrence.

tone Writer's attitude toward the subject or the audience. For example, an author's word choice may suggest humor, cutting remarks may suggest sarcasm, and ironic remarks may show the gap between the actual and the expected.

topic General rather than specific term that forms an umbrella under which the author can group the specific ideas or details in a passage.

topic sentence Sentence that condenses the thoughts and details of a passage into a general, all-inclusive statement of the author's message.

transitions See *signal words*.

uniform resource locator (URL) On the Web, specific directions for finding your way to a specific site, just as an address and zip code are required to mail a letter. A URL is similar to an e-mail address, except that it routes the user to a source of information called a *Web page* or *Web site* rather than to the mailbox of an individual person.

vocalization moving one's lips as one reads.

ACKNOWLEDGMENTS

Text Credits

3–5: Marelisa Fabrega, 5 Tips for Overcoming Failure. Reprinted with permission.

40: Martin, James; Roberts, J. Randy; Mintz, Steven; McMurry, Linda O.; and Jones, James H., *America and Its Peoples: A Mosaic In the Making*©3rd Ed., © 1996. Reprinted and Electronically reproduced by permission of Pearson Education, Inc., Upper Saddle River.

42: Thomas V. DiBacco, excerpt from "Once Upon a September Day," September 28, 1983, *Los Angeles Times*. Reprinted by permission of the author.

51–53: Pauline Arrillage, "Was Eric Clark Insane or Just Troubled?" April 15, 2006, Associated Press. Reprinted with permission.

59–60: Calvin Mackie, "Run the race . . . it's yours to run," *The Black Collegian*. Reprinted with permission of IMDiversity.

67–68: E. Andrew Boyd, Houston Public Radio's Engines of Our Ingenuity. Reprinted by permission of the author.

89–90: Audesirk, Teresa; Audesirk, Gerald; Byers, Bruce E., *Biology: Life On Earth*, 6th Ed., © 2001. Reprinted and Electronically reproduced by permission of Pearson Education, Inc., Upper Saddle River, New Jersey.

96: Bell, Arthur H.; Smith, Dayle M., *Interviewing For Success*, © 2004. Reprinted and Electronically reproduced by permission of Pearson Education, Inc., Upper Saddle River, New Jersey.

97–98: Donatelle, Rebecca J., *Health: The Basics*, 6th Ed., © 2004. Reprinted and Electronically reproduced by permission of Pearson Education, Inc., Upper Saddle River, New Jersey.

100–101: Reprinted with permission of Dr. Charles Williams.

106: Quote by Timothy Ferriss. Reprinted with permission.

125–129: Donatelle, Rebecca J., *Health: The Basics*, 5th Ed., © 2002. Reprinted and Electronically reproduced by permission of Pearson Education, Inc., Upper Saddle River, New Jersey.

139: "Two weeks after Ike, kids are still not in school," September 26, 2008, Associated Press. Used with permission of The Associated Press Copyright© 2014. All rights reserved.

157: By permission. From *Merriam-Webster's Collegiate*® Dictionary, Eleventh Edition ©2014 by Merriam-Webster, Inc. (www.Merriam-Webster.com).

157: *Longman Advanced American Dictionary*, 3rd Edition, online at: www.longmandictionariesusa.com/laad. Reprinted with permission of Pearson UK.

159: By permission. From *Merriam-Webster's Collegiate*® Dictionary 11th Edition©2014 by Merriam-Webster, Inc. (www.Merriam-Webster.com).

160: By permission. From *Merriam-Webster's Collegiate*® Dictionary 11th Edition©2014 by Merriam-Webster, Inc. (www.Merriam-Webster.com).

161: By permission. From *Webster's Third New International*® Dictionary, Unabridged©1993 by Merriam-Webster, Inc. (www.Merriam-Webster.com).

162: By permission. From *Webster's New Explorer College Dictionary*, 3rd Edition ©2011 by Federal Street Press, a division of Merriam-Webster Inc. (www.Merriam-Webster.com).

162: By permission. From *Webster's New Explorer College Dictionary*, 3rd Edition ©2011 by Federal Street Press, a division of Merriam-Webster Inc.

163: From *The New American Roget's College Thesaurus in Dictionary form* by Philp D. Morehead and Andrew T. Morehead, copyright © 1958, 1962 by Albert H. Morehead. Copyright © 1978, 1985, renewed 1986 by Philp D. Morehead and Andrew T. Morehead. Used by permission of Dutton Signet, a division of Penguin Group (USA) LLC.

164: From *The New American Roget's College Thesaurus in Dictionary form* by Philip D. Morehead and Andrew T. Morehead, copyright © 1958, 1962 by Albert H. Morehead. Copyright © 1978, 1985, renewed 1986 by Philip D. Morehead and Andrew T. Morehead. Used by permission of Dutton Signet, a division of Penguin Group (USA) LLC.

191: Donatelle, Rebecca J., *Health: The Basics*, 5th Ed., © 2002. Reprinted and Electronically reproduced by permission of Pearson Education, Inc., Upper Saddle River, New Jersey.

206: Quote by Doug Larson. Reprinted with permission.

207–210: Catherine Guthrie, "The Dark Side of Food Science," *Experience Life Magazine*, October 2010. Reprinted by permission of the author.

214: By permission. From *Merriam-Webster's Collegiate*® Dictionary, Eleventh Edition ©2014 by Merriam-Webster, Inc. (www.Merriam-Webster.com).

214: By permission. From *Merriam-Webster's Collegiate*® Dictionary, Eleventh Edition ©2014 by Merriam-Webster, Inc. (www.Merriam-Webster.com).

214: By permission. From *Merriam-Webster's Collegiate*® Dictionary, Eleventh Edition ©2014 by Merriam-Webster, Inc. (www.Merriam-Webster.com).

241: Reprinted with permission of the San Jacinto College.

252–253: Audesirk, Teresa; Audesirk, Gerald; Byers, Bruce E., *Biology: Life On Earth*, 6th Ed., © 2001. Reprinted and Electronically reproduced by permission of Pearson Education, Inc., Upper Saddle River, New Jersey.

258: Martin Gardner, "Puzzle from 'Some Math Tricks with Numbers,'" *Games Magazine* © May 1999. Reprinted with permission.

264: Donatelle, Rebecca J., *Health: The Basics*, 6th Ed., © 2004. Reprinted and Electronically reproduced by permission of Pearson Education, Inc., Upper Saddle River, New Jersey.

270: Martin, James; Roberts, J. Randy; Mintz, Steven; McMurry, Linda O.; and Jones, James H., *America and Its Peoples: A Mosaic In the Making*, 3rd Ed., © 1996. Reprinted and Electronically reproduced by permission of Pearson Education, Inc., Upper Saddle River.

303–305: Bell, Arthur H.; Smith, Dayle M., *Interviewing For Success*, © 2004. Reprinted and Electronically reproduced by permission of Pearson Education, Inc., Upper Saddle River, New Jersey.

311: By permission. From *Merriam-Webster's Collegiate*® Dictionary, Eleventh Edition © 2014 by Merriam-Webster, Inc. (www.Merriam-Webster.com).

311: By permission. From *Merriam-Webster's Collegiate*® Dictionary, Eleventh Edition © 2014 by Merriam-Webster, Inc. (www.Merriam-Webster.com).

330: Martin, James; Roberts, J. Randy; Mintz, Steven; McMurry, Linda O.; and Jones, James H., *America and Its Peoples: A Mosaic In the Making*, 3rd Ed., © 1996. Reprinted and Electronically reproduced by permission of Pearson Education, Inc., Upper Saddle River, New Jersey.

331–332: Martin, James; Roberts, J. Randy; Mintz, Steven; McMurry, Linda O.; and Jones, James H., *America and Its Peoples: A Mosaic In the Making*, 3rd Ed., © 1996. Reprinted and Electronically reproduced by permission of Pearson Education, Inc., Upper Saddle River, New Jersey.

336–339: Reprinted by permission of the Hoch Estate and the Sterling & Byrne Literary Agency.

354–357: Schmalleger, Frank J., *Criminal Justice Today: An Introductory Text for the 21st Century*, 12th Ed., ©2013, p. 559. Reprinted and Electronically reproduced by permission of Pearson Education, Inc., Upper Saddle River, New Jersey.

374: Howard H. Kendler, "The matchstick problem and solution to the matchstick problem." Reprinted with permission of Kenneth Kendler.

374: Copyright 2001, James L. Adams, *Conceptual Blockbusting: A Guide to Better Ideas*. Reprinted by permission of Beacon Press, a member of the Perseus Books Group.

375: Gerrig, Richard J.; Zimbardo, Philip G., *Psychology and Life*, 17th Ed., © 2005. Reprinted and Electronically reproduced by permission of Pearson Education, Inc., Upper Saddle River, New Jersey.

376: John J. Macionis, *Social Problems*, 5th Ed., © 2013, pp. 99, 384. Reprinted and electronically reproduced by permission of Pearson Education, Inc., Upper Saddle River, New Jersey.

377: John J. Macionis, *Social Problems*, 5th Ed., © 2013, pp. 99, 384. Reprinted and electronically reproduced by permission of Pearson Education, Inc., Upper Saddle River, New Jersey.

378: Macionis, John J., *Social Problems*, 5th Ed., © 2013, pp. 99, 384. Reprinted and Electronically reproduced by permission of Pearson Education, Inc., Upper Saddle River, New Jersey.

380–381: Macionis, John J., *Social Problems*, 4th Ed., © 2010. Reprinted and Electronically reproduced by permission of Pearson Education, Inc., Upper Saddle River, New Jersey.

396–398: Lutgens, Frederick K.; Tarbuck, Edward J., *The Atmosphere: An Introduction to Meteorology*, 7th Ed., © 1998. Reprinted and Electronically reproduced by permission of Pearson Education, Inc., Upper Saddle River, New Jersey.

404–407: Macionis, John J., *Social Problems*, 3rd Ed., © 2007. Reprinted and Electronically reproduced by permission of Pearson Education, Inc., Upper Saddle River, New Jersey.

442–443: Martin, James; Roberts, J. Randy; Mintz, Steven; McMurry, Linda O.; and Jones, James H., *America and Its Peoples: A Mosaic In the Making*, 3rd Ed., © 1996. Reprinted and Electronically reproduced by permission of Pearson Education, Inc., Upper Saddle River.

447–448: From *Newsweek*, November 13 © 2000 IBT Media. All rights reserved. Used by permission and protected by the Copyright Laws of the United States. The printing, copying, redistribution, or retransmission of this Content without express written permission is prohibited.

483–484: Barbara Amaya, "Barbara Amaya's Story." Reprinted by permission of the author.

486: Reprinted with permission of Cancer Adventures.

489–490: From *The Huffington Post*, June 18 © 2012 AOL Inc.. All rights reserved. Used by permission and protected by the Copyright Laws of the United States. The printing, copying, redistribution, or retransmission of this Content without express written permission is prohibited.

493–494: Rick Tardiff, "Jess's Story," www.theshawhouse.org. Used by permission of Rick Tardiff.

497–498: "Boy who survived two plane crashes—one that killed his mother and siblings and the other that killed his father—speaks out for first time as he signs basketball deal," *Daily Mail*, November 21, 2013. Reprinted by permission of Daily Mail.

509–529: Joseph A. DeVito, *Interpersonal Messages*, 3rd Ed., © 2014, pp. 195–215. Reprinted and electronically reproduced by permission of Pearson Education, Inc., Upper Saddle River, New Jersey.

Photo Credits

Cover: Inmacor/Getty Images. **Page 1:** Shutterstock. **Page 4:** DGP&C/Getty Images. **Page 10:** Shutterstock. **Page 33:** James Woodson/Getty. **Page 52:** Rashadashurov/Fotolia. **Page 59:** Dr. Calvin Mackie. **Page: 68** Jeffrey Hamilton/Getty. **Page 77:** Rebecca Skloot, *The Immortal Life of Henrietta Lacks*, Random House, 2011. **Page 81:** Ammentorp Photography/Shutterstock. **Page: 108** Shutterstock. **Page 116:** Darren Baker/Shutterstock. **Page 128:** Golden Pixels LLC/Alamy. **Page 141:** Paulista/Fotolia. **Page 144:** Vocabulary Cartoons, SAT Word Power, New Monic Books, **Page 151:** New Monic Books Ltd. **Page 177:** Boston Globe/Getty Images. **Page 186:** Brooklyn Museum/Corbis. **Page 196:** John Crowe/Alamy. **Page 208:** Iingles/Shutterstock. **Page 218:** Krimar/Shutterstock. **Page 228:** AP Photo. **Page 245:** Laszlo Halasi/Shutterstock. **Page 256:** MichaelJung/Shutterstock. **Page 271:** AP Photo. **Page 287:** Iofoto/Shutterstock. **Page 295:** Tea Maeklong/Shutterstock. **Page 304:** Adam Gregor/Shutterstock. **Page 319:** Olly/Fotolia. **Page 320:** CartoonStock. **Page 321:** CartoonStock. **Page 337:** FreshPaint/Fotolia. **Page 345:** Georgios Kollidas/Fotolia. **Page 354:** Vladimir Jovanovic/Fotolia. **Page 369:** Nuvolanevicata/Fotolia. **Page 386:** Monkey Business/Fotolia. **Page 419:** AFP/Getty Images. **Page 447:** Elena Elisseeva/Shutterstock. **Page 456:** Andresr/Shutterstock. **Page 466:** Bruce Chambers/ZUMA Press/Corbis. **Page 479:** ChrisDorney/Fotolia. **Page 480:** CBS Photo Archive/Getty Images. **Page 486:** Lsantilli/Fotolia. **Page 490:** Nobeastsofierce/Fotolia. **Page 493:** Vlorzor/Fotolia. **Page 497:** AP Photo/Damian Dovarganes. **Page 509:** AP Photo/Charles Sykes. **Page 510:** allOver images/Alamy. **Page 511:** Angela Hampton Picture Library/Alamy. **Page 513:** Paul Noth/The New Yorker Collection/The Cartoon Bank. **Page 515:** Pearson Education. **Page 517:** Victoria Roberts/The New Yorker Collection/The Cartoon Bank. **Page 519:** Lithian/Fotolia. **Page 520:** Martin Novak/Alamy. **Page 524:** Moviestore Collection Ltd/Alamy. **Page 528:** AP Photos/Charles Sykes.

INDEX